W9-DAX-873

SECOND EDITION

Cultural Anthropology

A Perspective on the Human Condition

SECOND EDITION

Cultural Anthropology

A Perspective on the Human Condition

Emily A. Schultz

Robert H. Lavenda
St. Cloud State University

West Publishing Company
St. Paul   New York   San Francisco   Los Angeles

Library of Congress Cataloging-in-Publication Data

Schultz, Emily A. (Emily Ann), 1949–
    Cultural anthropology : a perspective on the human condition /
Emily A. Schultz, Robert H. Lavenda.—2nd ed.
      p.   cm.
    Includes bibliographical references.
    ISBN 0-314-66571-4
    1. Ethnology.   2. Anthropology.   1. Lavenda, Robert H.
II. Title.
GN316.S38   1990
306—dc20   89-38407
                               CIP

Copyediting: Cheryl Drivdahl
Artwork: Alice Thiede
Interior and Cover Designs: John Edeen
Composition: G & S Typesetters, Inc.
Cover Photo: Forestier/Sygma Photo News

Credits

1 D. E. Cox/TSW Click Chicago; 2 UN Photo 154307; 3 (l. to r.) UN Photo 156237/John Isaac; UN Photo 153444/John Isaac; UN Photo 153938/Margot Granitsas; UN Photo 154321/Gayle Jann; 4 Donald Smetzer/TSW Click Chicago; 7 Irven DeVore/Anthro-Photo; 9 Robert H. Lavenda; 10 Jim Altobell, SCSU Public Relations and Publications; 16 UN Photo 154226/John Isaac; 17 (l. to r.) UN Photo 152625/Kate Bader; UN Photo 156071/John Isaac; UN Photo 154324/John Isaac; UN Photo 156072/John Isaac; 19 Museum of Modern Art Film Still Archives; 22 Art Resource; 23 Historical Pictures Service, Chicago; 29, 31 Robert H. Lavenda; 34 UPI/Bettmann Newsphotos; 44 UN Photo 151746; 45 (l. to r.) UN Photo 151446/John Isaac; UN Photo 149134/Sebastiao Barbosa; UN Photo 152128/John Isaac; UN Photo 154999/ P. S. Sudhakaran; 47 Lawrence Carpenter; 49 Frost Publishing Group/Tony O'Brien; 51 Frost Publishing Group; 63 Borys Malkin/Anthro-Photo; 65, 77 Robert H. Lavenda; 78 UN Photo 152119/John Isaac; 79 (l. to r.) UN Photo 153445/John Isaac; UN Photo 156234/John Isaac; UN Photo 154997/P. S. Sudhakaran; UN Photo 120498; 80 Reprinted with special permission of King Features Syndicate, Inc.; 82 Robert H. Lavenda; 88 Ferster/Anthro-Photo; 96 (l. to r.) Robert H. Lavenda; Robert H. Lavenda; D. J. Chivers/Anthro-Photo; 99 Cathy © 1988 Universal Press Syndicate. Reprinted with permission. All rights reserved; 109 UN Photo 104816; 114 UN Photo 154715/John Isaac; 115 (l. to r.) UN Photo 144059/J. Frank; Gina Marie Macheledt; UNRWA Photo/M. Nasr; UN Photo 153922/Doranne Jacobson; 135 Skaarup/Art Resource; 140 Historical Pictures Service, Chicago; 141 The Bettmann Archive; 142 Alex Kozulin, *Thought and Language,* Lev Vgotsky, The MIT Press; 152 Anthony Andrew Macheledt; 153 (l. to r.) UN Photo 154237/John Isaac; UN Photo 154998/P. S. Sudhakaran; UN Photo 153678/John Isaac; UN Photo 152129/John Isaac; 157 Robert H. Lavenda; 158 The Bettmann Archive, Inc.; 162 Reuters/Bettmann Newsphotos; 168 James W. Fernandez; 169 Springer/Bettmann Film Archive; 171 Robert H. Lavenda: 172 James M. Vaiknoras/Daily News; 178 The Bettmann Archive; 186 UN Photo 153800/Jeffrey Foxx; 187 (l. to r.) Rachel Lavenda; Daniel Lavenda; UN Photo 152749/John Isaac; UN Photo 156461/ John Isaac; 188 Robert H. Lavenda; 192 George Mars Cassidy/ TSW Click Chicago; 193 J. F. E. Bloss/Anthro-Photo; 204 Frost Publishing Group; 205 Rupinder Khullar/TSW Click Chicago; 208 Reprinted from Barbara G. Myerhoff: *Peyote Hunt: The Sacred Journey of the Huichol Indians.* Copyright © 1974 by Cornell University. Used by permission of the publisher, Cornell University Press; 214 James W. & Renate L. Fernandez; 225 Robert H. Lavenda; 226 UN Photo 154231/John Isaac; 227 (l. to r.) UN Photo 153949/Shelley Rotner; UN Photo 156449/John Isaac; UN Photo 141085/John Isaac; UN Photo 156289/John Isaac; 234 Historical Pictures Service, Chicago; 237 Robert H. Lavenda; 240 Historical Pictures Service, Chicago; 242 Reprinted from *A History of Anthropological Thought: Sir Edward Evans-Pritchard,* edited by Andre Singer, introduction by Ernest Gellner. Used by permission of Faber and Faber Limited Publishers; 250 Robert H. Lavenda; 258 American Refugee Committee; 259 (l. to r.) UN Photo 156238/ John Isaac; UN Photo 156438; UN Photo 156318/W. Stone; UN Photo 156683/John Isaac; 260 Opening text is from *Maíra,* by Darcy Ribeiro, translated by E. H. Goodland and Thomas Colchie. Copyright © 1984, Random House, Inc. Reprinted by permission of Random House, Inc.; 260 P. & D. Maybury-Lewis/Anthro-Photo; 264 UN Photo 148578/John Isaac; 266 Lawrence Manning/ TSW Click Chicago; 267 Richard Lee/Anthro-Photo; 271 J. F. E. Bloss/Anthro-Photo; 292 UN Photo 156439/John Isaac; 293 (l. to r.) Robert H. Lavenda; UN Photo 155169/Margot Granitsas; UN Photo 156091/John Isaac; UN Photo 156446/John Isaac; 294 Opening text is from *My Days,* by R. K. Narayan. Copyright © 1973 R. K. Narayan. Reprinted by permission of Wallace and Sheil Agency, Inc.; 299 Robert H. Lavenda; 306 Donald Smetzer/ TSW Click Chicago; 311 Robert H. Lavenda; 314 Lois Moulton/ TSW Click Chicago; 328 American Refugee Committee; 329 (l. to r.) UN Photo 151790; UN Photo 154998/P. S. Sudhakaran; UN Photo 156681/John Isaac; UN Photo 156316/W. Stone; 330 Opening text is from *Lake Wobegon Days,* By Garrison Keillor. Copyright © Garrison Keillor, 1985. Reprinted by permission of Viking Penguin, Inc.; 336 UN Photo 106414; 343 Robert H. Lavenda; 348 James H. Vaughan; 359 Robert H. Lavenda; 360 UN Photo 156436/John Isaac; 361 (l. to r.) UN Photo 156635/John Isaac;

(continued following Index)

For Daniel and Rachel

About the Authors

Photo by R. M. Schmid

Emily A. Schultz grew up in Boise, Idaho, and attended Mount Holyoke College and Indiana University, from which she received her Ph.D. Her dissertation fieldwork was carried out in Guider, northern Cameroon. An independent scholar, Dr. Schultz has just finished a book comparing the work of Benjamin Whorf and Mikhail Bakhtin.

Robert H. Lavenda grew up in Teaneck, New Jersey and attended Dartmouth College. He also earned his Ph.D. at Indiana University. He carried out fieldwork for his dissertation in Caracas, Venezuela, and has spent the last several years studying and writing about community summer festivals in Minnesota. His ethnographic photographs have been exhibited at several university museums and galleries. Dr. Lavenda is Professor of Anthropology at St. Cloud State University, in St. Cloud, Minnesota.

Drs. Schultz and Lavenda have carried out research together since 1974 in Venezuela, Cameroon, Ecuador, and Minnesota. While they organized and directed together a summer student research program in Otavalo, Ecuador, and have consulted with each other on several projects, this is their first co-publication. They are married and have two children, Daniel (nine) and Rachel (four).

Contents in Brief

Contents

EthnoFiles

Preface

Why is a picture of soprano Jessye Norman wrapped in the French flag on the cover of this cultural anthropology text? Here is a Black American woman, whose ancestors came to the New World in European slave ships. She earns her living as an interpreter of an elite, Western European art form that reached its peak of popularity at the end of the late nineteenth and beginning of the twentieth century. She is dressed in the French flag, the symbol of what used to be a great colonial empire which included much of the African continent. She is singing the Marseillaise, one of the great revolutionary hymns of all time. It is the climactic moment of the celebration in Paris of the bicentenninal of the French Revolution, a revolution whose motto was Liberty, Equality, Fraternity.

What kind of world must we live in for the event the photograph captures to have really happened on July 14, 1989, telecast to the world? This image contradicts a range of traditional Western presuppositions about the appropriate relationships among race, language, culture, and geography. Deciphering the image requires calling into question those same presuppositions. Put another way, to interpret this image—indeed, to make sense of the world in which we now live—requires the skills of a cultural anthropologist.

Many tried-and-true beliefs about the way the world works are crumbling daily. At the time we were writing the first edition of this book, well-armed dictators were falling to their unarmed people. As we were writing the second edition, communist parties in Eastern Europe were dissolving themselves and giving up power. Understanding these transformations demands the insights of anthropology no less than does understanding the kinship system of a small tribal community in the Amazon. Indeed, even to understand small tribal communities in the Amazon today requires an awareness of larger global issues (see the beginning of chapter 14). How did these sorts of social transformations take place? Why did they take so many people by surprise? The answers to these questions require understanding the particular histories and cultures, politics and economics, of the societies involved. We believe that our textbook demonstrates that anthropology has a central role to play in providing the concepts and analyses to create such understanding.

Before we began work on the first edition of this textbook, we shared the view of many colleagues concerning textbooks and revisions. Surely it was not because so much changed in cultural anthropology that every three years brought a new edition of a textbook! Nevertheless, here we are, bringing out a second edition. The entire field has *not* been completely transformed over the last three years, although some of the directions we took in the first edition are more firmly established today. But we have still been able to make a significant number of changes. We have found that the opportunity to revise this book has enabled us to make it a better tool for teaching cultural anthropology.

One change is stylistic. The original manuscript was written on the computer, and this has enabled us to revise on a word-by-word basis where necessary. Our major assistance in this task was provided by a remarkable piece of software, Readability Plus, from Scandinavian PC Systems. Among other things, Readability Plus takes text files and analyzes sentences according to the ratio of long words to sentence length. Based on the type of writing it is set to examine, it prepares a list of sentences that are outside the ideal area for that style. We have discovered that it unerringly puts its electronic finger on precisely the sentences we wished we hadn't written. There are, of course, times when complex ideas require complex sentences. Several such sentences in a row, however, do not lead to the comprehension of those complex ideas. So, we have examined all the "deviant sentences," and have rewritten where necessary. We think you will find the results important: we have made the book more readable but have not "dumbed it down."

Several changes have been made to improve the content and presentation for this edition.

- *Chapter 2, Culture and the Human Condition*. This chapter was reorganized and revised after discussion with students. Concepts are now presented in an order those students found easier to follow.

- *Chapter 4, Language*. The most important change concerns the explicitly dialogical orientation of the revised chapter. The section dealing with linguistic relativity has been substantially reworked. It now emphasizes areas of cross-linguistic and cross-cultural intersection that make translation and cross-cultural learning possible, as well as internal stylistic variation within a single language. A new example from Samoa on language learning has been added. The section on semantics has been revised, and a new section on pragmatics includes a discussion of discourse.

- *Chapter 5, Cognition*. This chapter features an expanded discussion of cognition and cognitive style, using work by Jean Lave and her associates to emphasize multiple cognitive styles that are potentially at anyone's command. The chapter has a new emphasis on everyday cognition as a system designed to resolve dilemmas. It contains a more detailed discussion of the work of Lev Vygotsky and the influence his work has had in recent research in cognitive anthropology.

- *Chapter 6, Play, Art, Myth, and Ritual*. The discussion of art has been tightened, and the differentiation of art from play has been clarified.

- *Chapter 7, World View*. The section on religion has been significantly expanded, and includes an ethnographic example from Barbara Myerhoff's *Peyote Hunt*. The material on religion is tightly integrated into the overall discussion of world view.

- *Chapter 8, Forms of Human Society*. The comments of several reviewers led us to revise this chapter (formerly Chapter 11) and move it to the beginning of section 3, "Systems of Relationship." As a result, students can now see more clearly the dialectic between the openness of cognition and the material constraints of practical life.

■ *Chapter 10, Marriage and the Family.* This chapter now contains a discussion of lesbianism as an everyday strategic choice in Mombasa, Kenya. This section contrasts with the discussion of ritual male homosexuality in New Guinea.

■ *Chapter 12, Social Organization and Power.* There is a new discussion of James Scott's work on weapons of the weak. This material strengthens our discussion of responses to oppression by examining everyday forms of peasant resistance.

■ *Chapter 14, The Modern World-System.* This chapter now begins with contrasting excerpts: the first from the tragic situation of the Kréen-Akaróre in the Amazon in 1977, and the second on the unexpected and dramatic Amazonian Indian alliance led by the Kayapo in 1988.

■ *Chapter 15. Conclusions: Why Anthropology?* There are two new extended case studies in applied anthropology.

■ *Glossary.* The glossary is now "on-line." Words are defined in the margin at the point they first appear.

■ *Guest Editorials.* Three essays have been added. They are from Jane Hill, George Marcus, and Marilyn Strathern.

Our two basic assumptions are still the same: (1) human beings bring meaning to their experience and (2) human beings transform the world around them through practical action, rather than passive reaction. We still present anthropology as a discipline that is profoundly concerned with the tension between human creativity and social and historical constraints. The ambiguity of experience and the resolution of that ambiguity through the human capacity to create meaning are still central to this book's vision of anthropology.

Two unique features of the first edition that were well received were the Guest Editorials and the EthnoFiles. These are continued in this edition. The Guest Editorials are designed to acquaint students with the views of some contemporary anthropologists. We asked a number of colleagues to write brief essays about things they would like students to know about anthropology. These guest editorials are now found at the ends of the first fourteen chapters. The contributors are James W. Fernandez, Hoyt Alverson, Ivan Karp, Jane Hill, Michael Herzfeld, Anya Peterson Royce, Emiko Ohnuki-Tierney, George Marcus, David Parkin, Marilyn Strathern, Paul Rabinow, Annette Weiner, Don Handelman, and Stephen Gudeman. Three sections of the book each feature an essay that illustrates a holistic approach to their subject matter, based on the work of a single anthropologist. These include, for section 2, Suzette Heald's work on Gisu initiation; for section 3, Mary Smith's work with Baba of Karo; and for section 4, Michael Gilsenan's work on Islam in the modern world.

The EthnoFiles are short summaries of ethnographic information in a consistent format for the sixty-four societies discussed in some detail in the text. Each EthnoFile identifies the region and the nation in which the society is found. Information is also given on population, environment, modes of livelihood, and political organization. Other useful or appropriate information about each society is also provided. These short and concise descriptions are intended to provide orientation and background. They are not intended to be replacements for ethnographies, nor for details that the instructor might wish to include in class.

As in the first edition, additional study aids include key terms, detailed chapter summaries, and annotated suggested readings.

Adopters of the first edition found the text challenging but not too difficult for introductory students. Our students and the West reviewers were pleased that the text did not condescend to students, and that we recognized that students are able to grasp—and even be excited by—conceptual issues. In addition, we've had good experience with the book in our own classes at St. Cloud State University and elsewhere. Answers on essay exams, for example, now show greater command of the material, and greater sophistication.

So, we think the first edition worked well. We think this edition will work even better. Two students at St. Cloud State University, a freshman and a sophomore, both with no coursework in anthropology, have read this edition. Any time they felt something was not clear, we were able to discuss it with them immediately and make improvements. They like this edition. We hope that other students who read it will like it, too.

As usual, our editor at West, Clark Baxter, has been a pleasure to work with. We want to thank him for his active support. We would also like to thank the reviewers for this edition: E. David Jurji, Bellvue Community College; Jeffrey Ehrenreich, Cornell College; Victoria L. Levine, Colorado College; Lisette Nollner, University of Utah; M. Jean Heriot, University of California, Los Angeles Extension; Peter Knutson, Highline Community College. We have been impressed with the care they have taken in writing detailed critiques of the first edition and making suggestions for the second. We haven't taken all their suggestions, but we have considered each one carefully. Textbook authors, too, are reflexive; even the suggestions we haven't taken moved us to think about the book in new ways. We have listened very carefully to Wendy Cichanski and Deirdra Joyce, the two students who have read this edition. Our great thanks to both, for their help and their willingness to take this on during the quarter.

To Steve Seivert and Deborah Reumann of Dragonfly Software, our thanks for Nota Bene, the finest tool for academics who write with a computer. Thanks also to Mike Green at Pro Data Computers in St. Cloud for the loan of a computer when we really needed a second one to get the manuscript in on time.

Our thanks too to other friends and colleagues who have contributed in various ways to making it possible for us to write and now to revise this book. We owe a special and profound debt to Ivan Karp, who has been our most important source of intellectual stimulation and support throughout this project.

Finally, our children, Daniel and Rachel, have again put up with a great deal as we have worked on the second edition. It's tough when both your mother *and* your father are spending so much time working on revising their book. We hope that when they finally come to read it they will understand why we spent so much time on it, and be pleased.

SECOND EDITION

Cultural Anthropology

A Perspective on the Human Condition

Anthropology Is a Way of Looking at the World

CHAPTER 1

The Anthropological Perspective

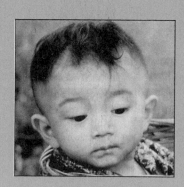

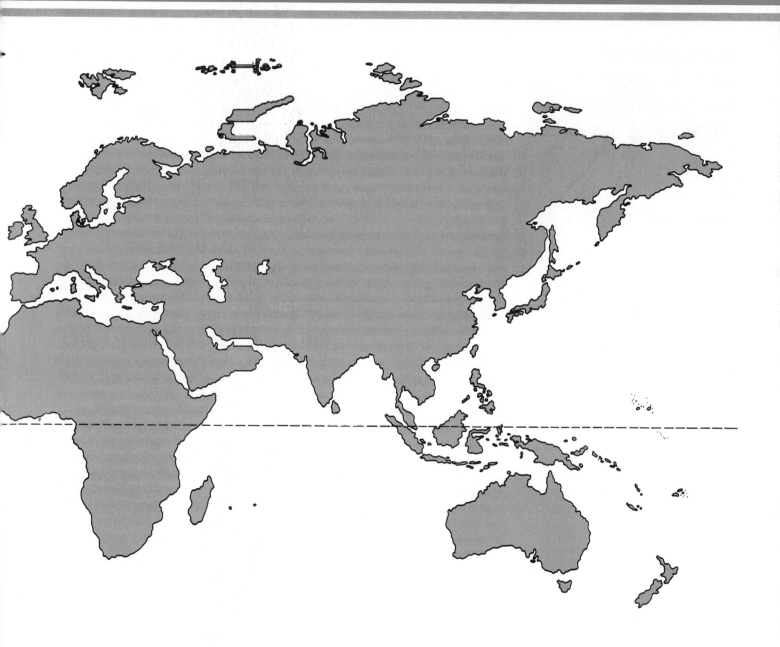

In 1935, the celebrated French anthropologist Claude Lévi-Strauss made his first field trip to visit the indigenous inhabitants of the rain forests of Paraná, one of the southern states of Brazil. In his book Tristes Tropiques, *Lévi-Strauss describes the foods eaten by the Indians he met:*

"Mention must also be made of the *koro*, pale-coloured grubs which are to be found in abundance in certain rotting tree-trunks. Having been jeered at by the whites for eating these creatures, the Indians deny the charge and will not admit to liking them. But you only have to go through the forest to see on the ground traces of some *pinheiro* [pine tree], twenty or thirty metres long, that has been torn down by a storm, then later hacked to pieces and reduced to a mere ghost of its former self. The hunters of *koro* have dealt with it. And if you arrive unexpectedly at an Indian house, you may catch a glimpse of a bowl swarming with the treasured delicacy, before it is hastily whisked out of sight.

"This being so, it is no easy matter arranging to be present at a search for *koro*. Like conspirators, we had to work out a plan at some length. A fever-stricken Indian, the only person left in a deserted village, seemed an easy prey. We put an axe into his hands, shook him and pushed him. But to no purpose; he did not seem to grasp what we wanted of him. Thinking we were about to fail once more, we used our last argument: we would like to eat some *koro*. We succeeded in dragging our victim to a tree-trunk. One blow with the axe revealed thousands of hollow little chambers, deep inside the tree. In each was a fat, cream-coloured creature, rather like a silkworm. I had to keep my word. While the Indian looked on impassively I decapitated my catch; from the body spurted a whitish, fatty substance which I managed to taste after some hesitation; it had the consistency and delicacy of butter, and the flavour of coconut milk." (Lévi-Strauss 1955:160–61)

There are very few organic substances in the world that people somewhere do not eat and even relish! Here a Samoan Island man consumes palolo worms

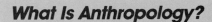

What Is Anthropology?

Some of the central elements of the anthropological experience are to be found in Lévi-Strauss's anecdote. Anthropologists travel far and wide to encounter people whose ways of life are as radically different from their own as possible. As a result, they are sometimes exposed to practices that make them recoil. As they take the risk of getting to know such ways of life better, they are treated to the sweet discovery of familiarity. This shock of the exotic become familiar—as well as its opposite, the familiar become exotic—is something anthropologists come to expect and to anticipate eagerly. In this book, we share aspects of the anthropological experience in the hope that you, too, will come to find pleasure, insight, and self-recognition from an involvement with the unfamiliar.

Anthropology can be defined as the study of human nature, human society, and human history (cf. Greenwood and Stini 1977). It is a scholarly discipline that aims to describe, in the broadest possible sense, what it means to be human. Anything having to do with human beings is of concern to anthropologists.

Anthropologists are not alone in focusing their attention on human beings and their creations. Human biology, literature, art, history, language, society, politics, economics—all these scholarly disciplines have chosen one or another aspect of human life, or the products of human life, on which to concentrate. Anthropology draws upon the findings of these other disciplines and attempts to fit them together with its own data. The subject matter of anthropology is certainly compel-

anthropology
the study of human nature, human society, and human history

ling. What makes anthropology unique, however, is that it tries to integrate all that is known about human beings and their activities at the highest and most inclusive level. That is, anthropology is **holistic**, and holism is a central feature of the anthropological perspective.

Anthropology tries to generalize about human nature, human society, and human history. To do this requires evidence from the widest possible range of human societies and periods of human history. It would not do, for example, to observe only our own social group, discover that we do not eat insects, and conclude that human beings as a species do not eat insects. Thus, in addition to being holistic, anthropology is a **comparative** discipline. Anthropologists want to come up with generalizations about what it means to be human that are valid across space and through time. This means that the field for comparison is vast. It includes any and all human societies, anywhere in the world. It also takes in any and all periods of human history, including periods dating from the emergence of humanlike primates some 5 million years ago.

For this reason, anthropology is interested in the evolution of the human species over time. Indeed, the general public often believes that prehistory is the main focus of the discipline. This perception is probably due to the wide publicity for new fossil discoveries that appears in the newspapers and in magazines like *National Geographic*. Evolutionary theory has contributed not only to the study of human origins but also to the study of genetic variety and inheritance in living human populations. If evolution is understood broadly as change over time, then human societies may also be understood as having evolved, from prehistoric times to the present day. Thus, the anthropological perspective is also **evolutionary** at its core.

The Concept Of Culture

A consequence of human evolution that had the most profound impact on human nature, human society, and human history was the emergence of culture. **Culture** can be defined as sets of learned behavior and ideas that human beings use both to pursue their interests and to identify the interests they ought to pursue. People produce and reproduce cultural forms in their efforts to adapt to and transform the wider world in which they live.

Culture makes us unique among living creatures. Human beings are more dependent on learning for survival than is any other species. We have no instincts that automatically protect us and find us food and shelter, for example. Instead, we have come to use our large and complex brains to learn from other members of society what we need to know to survive. This teaching and learning process is a primary focus of childhood, which is longer for the human species than for any other. In the anthropological perspective, the concept of culture is central to explanations of why human beings are what they are, why they do what they do.

The anthropological perspective is also rooted in *experiencing* other peoples' ways of life. Anthropologists live with a group of people for a year or more in order to learn directly from them about their lives. This experience of being "in the field" is central to modern anthropology and contributes profoundly to the anthropological perspective. All anthropology begins with a group of real people, in a real place, leading lives very different from the anthropologist's own. All anthropology comes back to this intellectual, emotional, and physical experience of a different world.

holistic
the aspect of the anthropological perspective that tries to integrate all that is known about human beings and their activities, at the highest and most inclusive level

comparative
the aspect of the anthropological perspective that seeks evidence for generalization from any and all human societies, anywhere in the world, and any and all periods of human history, including those dating from the emergence of humanlike primates some 5 million years ago

evolutionary
the aspect of the anthropological perspective that holds that if evolution is understood broadly as change over time, then human organisms and human societies may be understood as having evolved, from prehistoric times to the present day

culture
sets of learned behavior and ideas that human beings use both to pursue their interests and to identify the interests they ought to pursue

The Cross-Disciplinary Discipline

The goal of anthropology is to describe what it means to be human. This means that the discipline of anthropology is extraordinarily wide and diverse. For example, at any given yearly meeting of the American Anthropological Association (the professional association to which most anthropologists belong), you will find research papers presented on such topics as infant-feeding practices in other societies, the latest findings concerning the sizes and shapes of the teeth of fossilized primates believed to be ancestral to modern human beings, computer analysis of pot fragments found in an archaeological site, patterns of marriage and divorce in Europe, political struggles in Latin America, traditional food-getting activities in Africa, religious beliefs in Southeast Asia, and mat making in Polynesia. Because of this span of interests, anthropology does not easily fit into any of the usual academic classifications in American universities. The discipline is usually listed as a social science, but it spans the natural sciences, the social sciences, and the humanities.

Figure 1.1 brings some order to the variety of interests found under the anthropological umbrella. At the highest level, we may think of anthropology as the integrated study of human nature, human society, and human history. But traditionally, anthropologists have chosen to approach human nature from two different directions: physical and cultural.

Physical Anthropology

The first, and oldest, specialty within anthropology has been called **physical anthropology** or bioanthropology. Physical anthropologists see human beings first and foremost as biological organisms. Their goal is to discover what makes human

physical anthropology
the branch of anthropology that considers human beings first and foremost as biological organisms; physical anthropologists aim to discover what makes human beings different from other living organisms, as well as what they share with other members of the animal kingdom

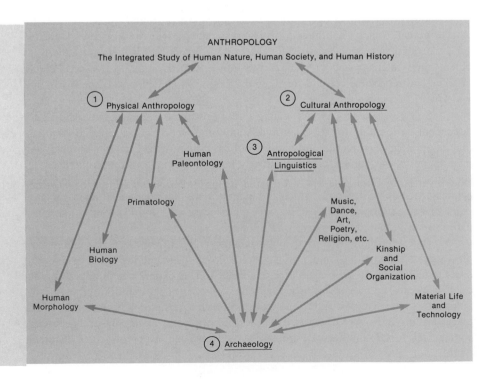

FIGURE 1.1
The Divisions of Anthropology
Anthropology in the United States is traditionally divided into four subfields: (1) physical anthropology, (2) cultural anthropology, (3) anthropological linguistics, and (4) archaeology. Further specialization occurs within each subfield.
Source: From *Anthropology* by E. Adamson Hoebel. Third edition. Copyright 1966 by McGraw-Hill.

ANTHROPOLOGY
The Integrated Study of Human Nature, Human Society, and Human History

① Physical Anthropology
② Cultural Anthropology
③ Anthropological Linguistics
④ Archaeology

Human Paleontology
Primatology
Human Biology
Human Morphology
Music, Dance, Art, Poetry, Religion, etc.
Kinship and Social Organization
Material Life and Technology

Part of physical anthropology involves measuring the physical characteristics —such as height—of human populations in different parts of the world.

beings different from other living organisms, as well as what human beings share with other members of the animal kingdom.

In the nineteenth century, when anthropology was developing as an academic field, physical anthropology flourished. Interest in this field was a by-product of centuries of exploration. Western Europeans had found tremendous variation in the physical appearance of peoples around the world. The question they had long tried to answer was how to make sense of these differences. Physical anthropologists invented a series of elaborate techniques to measure different observable features of human populations, including skin color, hair type, body type, and so forth. Their goal was to find an unambiguous way to assign people to racial categories. They hoped this would at last be possible if careful measurements were made on enough people from many societies around the world.

As time passed and research techniques improved, physical anthropologists also began to measure internal features of populations such as blood types. These measures were added to their calculations. They learned a tremendous amount about physical variation in human beings. They also realized that the biological concept of "race" was worse than useless in describing what they had learned.

The traits traditionally used to identify races are all external and observable, such as skin color, and do not correlate well with other physical or biological traits. The concept of "race," therefore, does not reflect a fact of nature but instead is a label invented by human beings that permits us to sort people into groups. Realizing this, physical anthropologists stopped trying to study race and began paying attention to variation within the human species as a whole.

Modern physical anthropologists often do research on topics of interest to human biologists. Some trace chemical similarities and differences in the immune system, for example—an interest that has recently led them into active work on AIDS (Acquired Immunodeficiency Syndrome). Others investigate the relationship between nutrition and physical development. Modern physical anthropologists take a comparative approach to human biology. Some specialize in the study of the closest living relatives of human beings, the primates, and hence are known as primatologists. Others search the earth for fossilized bones and teeth of our earliest ancestors, and are known as human paleontologists. In both cases, comparison of modern human beings with living and extinct nonhuman populations can throw light on what makes human beings similar to and different from other forms of life.

Whether they study human biology, primates, or human paleontology, physical anthropologists have borrowed methods and theories from the natural sciences—primarily biology, chemistry, and geology. What sets physical anthropologists apart from their nonanthropological colleagues comes from the anthropological perspective that has been part of their training. That perspective reminds them always to consider their work as but part of the overall picture of human nature, human society, and human history.

Cultural Anthropology

cultural anthropology
the branch of anthropology that is concerned with the nature of culture and its connection to human history, human society, and human nature

The second specialty within anthropology is that of **cultural anthropology**. This area is also sometimes called sociocultural anthropology, social anthropology, or ethnology. Cultural anthropology developed as early anthropologists became increasingly aware that human nature, human society, and human history could not be explained with reference to human biology alone. Something else—something called culture—plays an important role in shaping the way human beings live.

Early on, physical anthropologists showed that all people everywhere were too similar to one another to be placed in separate species, or races. As a result, differences in ways of life could no longer be explained by biological differences. Something else must be responsible for the fact that not everyone dresses the same, or speaks the same language, or believes in the same god, or eats insects for dinner. Anthropologists suggested that this "something else" was culture.

If culture consists of learned behavior and ideas that human beings use in adapting to and transforming the wider world in which they live, then the field of cultural anthropology is vast. To understand the human cultural heritage, it would be necessary to know everything, from the way in which human beings find food, to how they find a mate, to how they find meaning in life. Cultural anthropologists tend to specialize in one or another of these domains of culture.

language
the system of arbitrary vocal symbols we use to encode our experiences of the world and of each other

anthropological linguistics
the branch of anthropology that is concerned with the study of human languages

Perhaps the most striking cultural feature of our species is language. **Language** is the system of arbitrary vocal symbols we use to encode our experiences of the world and of each other. People use language to talk about all areas of their lives, from material to spiritual. So an important key to learning about the people whose way of life you are studying is knowing their language. As a result, **anthropological linguistics** has become an important subspecialty of cultural anthropology. Many early anthropologists were the first people to transcribe exotic languages in writing, as well as to produce grammars and dictionaries. Modern anthropological linguists are trained in both linguistics and anthropology. Like physical anthropologists, their commitment to the anthropological perspective sets them apart from their nonanthropological colleagues. For anthropological linguists, language cannot be understood outside the cultural, historical, and physical contexts that make it possible.

Anthropologists have also been interested in other human systems of symbolic representation, such as music, dance, art, poetry, philosophy, religion, and ritual. In these areas, anthropology shares the interests of the disciplines traditionally called the fine arts and humanities.

Other cultural anthropologists are interested primarily in the human social groups who make and use language. They investigate the patterned arrangements that human groups devise for carrying out collective tasks, be these economic, political, or spiritual. This focus within cultural anthropology bears the closest resemblance to the discipline of sociology, and from it has come the identification of anthropology as one of the social sciences. In fact, sociology and anthropology developed during the same period, and many of their interests in social organization are shared. However, historical developments led to sociology's focus on Western capitalist industrialized societies and to anthropology's focus on non-Western, noncapitalist, nonindustrialized societies.

The non-Western, noncapitalist, nonindustrialized societies were thought of as "primitive." For a long time, therefore, anthropology was seen as the study of "primitive" social organization. But anthropology is concerned with all human societies, "primitive" or "civilized". Indeed, anthropological research and comparison have led anthropologists to reject the terms "primitive" and "civilized" in much the same way that physical anthropologists were led to reject the term "race." If early anthropologists spent so much time with "primitive" people, it was because nobody else was interested in gathering the kinds of information needed to make generalizations about the human species as a whole. Today, anthropologists are just as likely to do research in an American city as in a remote African village.

Anthropologists discovered that although primitive societies did not have many forms of Western social organization, such as bureaucracies, churches, and schools, they still managed to carry out a full range of human activity. They did this on the basis of *kinship*, by organizing themselves into groups whose members were all related to one another. As a result, the study of kinship became highly developed in anthropology and remains a focus of interest today. In addition, anthropologists have described a variety of nonkin forms of social organization that can be found outside the Western world. These include secret societies, chiefdoms, and states.

Cultural anthropologists have investigated the patterns of material life found in different human groups. Worldwide variations in clothing, housing, tools, and techniques for getting food and making material goods are among the most striking. Some anthropologists specialize in the study of technologies in different societies, and many are interested in the evolution of technology over time. Anthropologists interested in material life also describe the natural setting for which technologies have been developed and analyze the way technologies and environments shape each other.

Cultural anthropologists normally gather information in all these areas of specialization during an extended period of close involvement with the people in whose way of life they are interested. This period of research is called **fieldwork**. Its central feature is anthropologists' involvement in the daily life of those among whom they live: their **informants**. Fieldworkers gain insight into their informants' ways of life by both participating with informants in social activities and observing those activities as outsiders. This research method is known as participant-observation. The experience of participant-observation is central not only to the enterprise of cultural anthropology but also to human interaction in general.

Following fieldwork, cultural anthropologists write about what they have learned in scholarly articles or in books called ethnographies. An **ethnography** is a description of a single culture. (This is why cultural anthropologists are also sometimes called ethnographers.) Some anthropologists make ethnographic films that document the lives of their research subjects.

Archaeology

Another major specialty within anthropology is **archaeology**. Archaeology involves excavating and studying the remains of extinct human societies. Through archaeology, anthropologists recover much of what they know about human history. This is particularly true for *prehistory*, that long stretch of time before the development

Cultural anthropologists talk to many people, observe their actions, and participate as fully as possible in their way of life.

fieldwork
an extended research period of close involvement with the people in whose way of life an anthropologist is interested

informants
people in a particular culture who work with anthropologists and provide them with insights about their way of life

ethnography
an anthropologist's description of a particular culture

archaeology
the branch of anthropology that involves excavating and studying the remains of human societies

Archaeologists use a wide range of techniques to recover and interpret the remains of past societies.

applied anthropology
the branch of anthropology that uses information gathered from the other subfields in an effort to solve practical cross-cultural problems

of writing. Anthropological archaeologists may be the most versatile of all anthropologists. To do their job properly, they need both physical and cultural anthropology. They need to be able both to identify any human remains they uncover and interpret the nonhuman remains—post holes, garbage heaps, settlement patterns—they find. They need to know enough geology to be able to situate the sites of their digs correctly in time. Depending on the locations and ages of sites they are digging, they may have to be experts on stone-tool manufacture, or metallurgy, or pollen analysis.

The information uncovered by archaeologists is of value to both physical and cultural anthropologists. Archaeologists recover the bones and teeth used to reconstruct human and nonhuman primate evolution. They can lend historical depth to particular cultural traditions, and trace the spread of cultural inventions over time from one site to another. If they are dealing with more recent sites—"recent" meaning within the last few thousand years—they may find evidence of ancient writing systems for anthropological linguists to decode and translate.

Applied Anthropology

In the United States, four major fields within anthropology are recognized: physical anthropology, cultural anthropology, anthropological linguistics, and archaeology. Applied anthropology has in recent years come to be recognized as the fifth major field (see figure 1.1). **Applied anthropology** uses information gathered from the other subfields in an effort to solve practical cross-cultural problems. This field is both so new and so interdisciplinary that it has not yet become a required part of graduate training. American anthropologists are normally trained in the four older fields before choosing an area of concentration. They also choose a region of the world in which to carry out their research.

Uses of Anthropology

Why would a college student take a course in cultural anthropology? An immediate answer might be that an overview of the colorful customs of faraway peoples carries a fascination that is its own reward. But the experience of being dazzled by cultural variety carries with it a risk. As you become increasingly aware of the options that exist for living a satisfying human life, you may find yourself wondering about the life you are living. Contact with the exotic can be liberating, but it can also be threatening if it undermines your confidence in the absolute truth and universal rightness of your own way of life.

The modern world is becoming ever more closely interconnected. As people from different cultural backgrounds come into contact with one another for extended periods, learning to cope with cultural differences becomes more crucial. Anthropologists have had much experience in dealing with both the rewards and the risks of getting to know how other people live. Studying anthropology may help prepare you for some of the shocks you may encounter in dealing with people who do not assume that the world works exactly the way you think it does or should.

Early in 1989, many Europeans and Americans were bewildered and outraged by an outcry from the Islamic world in response to Salman Rushdie's novel *The Satanic Verses.* Many Muslims believe the book to be blasphemous. The leader of Iran, Ayatollah Khomeini, promised a substantial reward to anyone who killed

Rushdie. Western response to the objections of Muslims, and especially to the death threat, showed how ill-prepared we are to understand worlds unlike our own. The *New Yorker* on March 6, 1989, observed that Rushdie was "guilty mainly of unlucky timing in the publication of a book that was written in a tradition different from that of his persecutors, and was not intended for them." Such an observation assumes that the exchange and criticism of ideas within one society has nothing to do with (and should have nothing to do with) the opinions and values of members of other societies. It further assumes that the boundaries between traditions are (and should be) firm and unbridgeable. In the modern world, this is no longer the case. Rushdie's personal history illustrates how fuzzy such boundaries can be. He was born a Muslim in India. Later, he became a British citizen who stopped practicing Islam and married an American who had stopped practicing Christianity. To which tradition does he belong? To which tradition is he accountable?

In the past, Westerners felt secure in their homogeneous isolation from the rest of the world. Their technology and military power seemed to insulate them from everyone else. Today, ignorance of the interconnectedness of the peoples of the world can have tragic consequences. It does not really matter if Salman Rushdie did not intend his book for those offended by it. They can read, they can understand, and they can act. We live in a plural world, and we are only just beginning to figure out how that affects us. In the past we could, perhaps, get by with our ignorance. Today we cannot.

Anthropology involves learning about the various ways people live their lives and make sense of their experiences. With it, you can be better equipped—less threatened, more tolerant—to deal with someone from a different culture. You may never be called on to eat insect grubs. Still, you may one day encounter a situation in which none of the old rules seems to apply. As you struggle to make sense of what is happening, what you learned in anthropology class may help you relax and dare to taste an unfamiliar experience. If you do so, perhaps you too will discover the rewards of an encounter with the exotic that is at the same time unaccountably familiar. We hope you will savor the experience.

Key Terms

anthropology	language
holistic	anthropological linguistics
comparative	fieldwork
evolutionary	informants
culture	ethnography
physical anthropology	archaeology
cultural anthropology	applied anthropology

Chapter Summary

1. *Anthropology* is a scholarly discipline that aims to describe, in the broadest sense, what it means to be human. To achieve this aim, anthropologists have developed a perspective on the human condition that is *holistic*, *comparative*, and *evolutionary*.

2. Because human beings lack instincts that would automatically promote their survival, they must learn from other members of their society what they need to know to survive. For this reason, the concept of *culture* is central to the anthropological perspective.

3. Cultural anthropology is rooted in the experience of *fieldwork*. Information gained during fieldwork in another culture is traditionally written down and published as an *ethnography*.

4. In the United States, anthropology is usually considered to have five major specialties: *physical anthropology*, *cultural anthropology*, *anthropological linguistics*, *archaeology*, and *applied anthropology*.

5. The study of other cultures may be threatening if it undermines your confidence in the truth and rightness of your own way of life. Yet it can also be liberating, enabling you to cope more realistically and tolerantly when you deal with a person from a different culture.

Suggested Readings

Barrett, Richard A. *Culture and Conduct: An Excursion in Anthropology.* Belmont, Calif.: Wadsworth, 1984.

A short, well-written introduction to some of the most interesting questions in contemporary anthropology.

Fagan, Brian M. *Archaeology: A Brief Introduction*, 2d ed. Boston: Little, Brown, 1983.

An up-to-date, engaging introduction to the techniques, assumptions, interests, and findings of modern archaeology.

Freilich, Morris. *The Pleasures of Anthropology.* New York: New American Library, Mentor Book, 1983.

A wide-ranging collection of accessible articles arranged into eight sections. Most of the articles are from the 1960s to the early 1980s, but some enduring classics are also reprinted. All are a pleasure to read and are thought provoking.

Johanson, Donald and Maitland Edey. *Lucy: The Beginnings of Humankind.* New York: Simon and Schuster, 1981.

A well-written, exciting introduction to one aspect of physical anthropology: human origins. This book reads like a good thriller and is highly recommended.

Anthropology as a Vocation: Listening to Voices

James W. Fernandez (Ph.D., Northwestern University) is Professor of Anthropology at the University of Chicago. He has carried out fieldwork in Gabon among the Fang and in Asturias, Spain among mountain cattlekeepers and miners. He has taught at Dartmouth College and Princeton University. Among his many publications, Dr. Fernandez authored Bwiti, *winner of the 1982 Herskovits Prize. His work on metaphor has been signally important in anthropology. He was All-American in soccer at Amherst College from 1950 to 1952.*

Anthropology is a vocation, not a job. It is something we are called to do, not something we are hired to do. I want to consider this in the context of five words: being or being there, listening, negotiating, transcending, and formulating. Contained in these words is a series of obligations that make up the vocation of anthropology. Vocation as a word is subject to diverse definitions, but I do not want to depart much from the etymological sense of the word *vocatio:* a calling, a sense of an urging or an obligation to respond to a situation because of a strong predisposition. And in what does that urging or obligation consist? Only in the obligation to be there, to listen, to negotiate, to transcend, and to formulate.

For me, the anthropological calling has fundamentally to do with the inclination to hear voices. An important part of our vocation is "listening to voices," and our methods are the procedures that best enable us to hear voices, to represent voices, to translate voices. Anthropological work that does not contain voices somehow misses its calling. It is work that misses our opportunity to listen to voices. If it does not contain the authentic voices of the subjects of investigation, throw it aside, because it does not have lasting value. Anthropology is a paying of attention to the voices of those among whom we live and study.

Would it not be true to say that among the disciplines, anthropology most requires a "sense of proportion"? Certainly it is a discipline characterized by a series of paradoxes, of which the most important is the paradoxical method: participant-observation. Such a method surely demands a sense of proportion! How much should be given to participation, and how much to observation? The obligation of the ethnographer to give voice to the voices of others—by his or her own voice—does not escape the paradoxical either. In giving voice to others' voices, what guarantee is there that we do not fall into the temptation of substituting our own voice for theirs? A sense of just proportion in the inevitable mixing of foreign voices and one's own voice must be the guarantee.

Anthropology is a vocation (1) because it permits us to realize in some small part our distinctively human potentialities and (2) because there is a passion implicit in our work and a sense of responsibility that combines the commitments of the scientist and the man or woman of politics.

With respect to this five-phase realization of our vocational potentialities, anthropology enables us to be with others (we are, after all, social animals); to share with them, by listening and negotiating, their preoccupations (we are, after all, animals with a marked capacity for sharing); to transcend a too exclusively ethnocentric involvement (as language-using animals we have unique powers of displacement and self-awareness); and finally by means of transcendence to formulate the general principles that are discovered as we go beyond many particular cases (as language-using animals we have unique powers of concept formation). Please note that the theoretical component in our calling is found at the end of the list of our obligations that together constitute our vocation.

Stubbornly inductive, we resist formulation until we have been there and listened. The deductive approach is weak on being there and weak on listening. It is precociously transcendent and perhaps too powerfully formulative for those who entertain the "politics of listening to voices" as a vocation.

Our pursuit of the formulation of pure structure—our scientific vocation—is stayed by our desire to increase conviviality, that is, by our political vocation. By listening carefully to others' voices and by trying to give voice to these voices, we act to widen the horizons of human conviviality. If we had not achieved some fellow feeling by being there, by listening carefully and by negotiating in good faith, it would be the more difficult to give voice in a way that would widen the horizons of human conviviality. Be that as it may, the calling to widen horizons and increase human conviviality seems a worthy calling—full of a very human optimism and good sense. Who would resist the proposition that more fellow feeling in the world is better than less, and that to extend the interlocutive in the world is better than to diminish it?

At the same time, there is a paradox here, one that demands of us a sense of proportion. Although the anthropologist is called to bring diverse people into intercommunication, he or she is also called to resist the homogenization that lies in mass communication. We are called by our very experience to celebrate the great variety of voices in the human chorus. The paradox is that we at once work to amplify the scale of intercommunication—and in effect contribute to homogenization—while at the same time we work to insist on the great variety of voices in communication. We must maintain here too a sense of proportion. We must recognize the point at which wider and wider cultural intercommunication can lead to dominant voices hidden in the homogenizing process. Human intercommunication has its uses and abuses.

In any case, significant endeavor —endeavor that has the characteristic of a calling and that qualifies as a vocation—is one that responds to human potentials and human evolution as we understand them to be.

There will always be debate about these potentials and this evolution, but the important point is that we continue to amplify the scale of interlocution and grant to other voices their commentary on the subject. The vocation of the anthropologist, therefore, is to feel called beyond himself or herself by other voices—not as in other centuries by divine voices, but by human voices distinctly "other" and characteristically little listened to. We *can* talk about a kind of passion for listening to those voices, and we *must* talk about a responsibility to give voice to those voices.

CHAPTER 2

Culture and the Human Condition

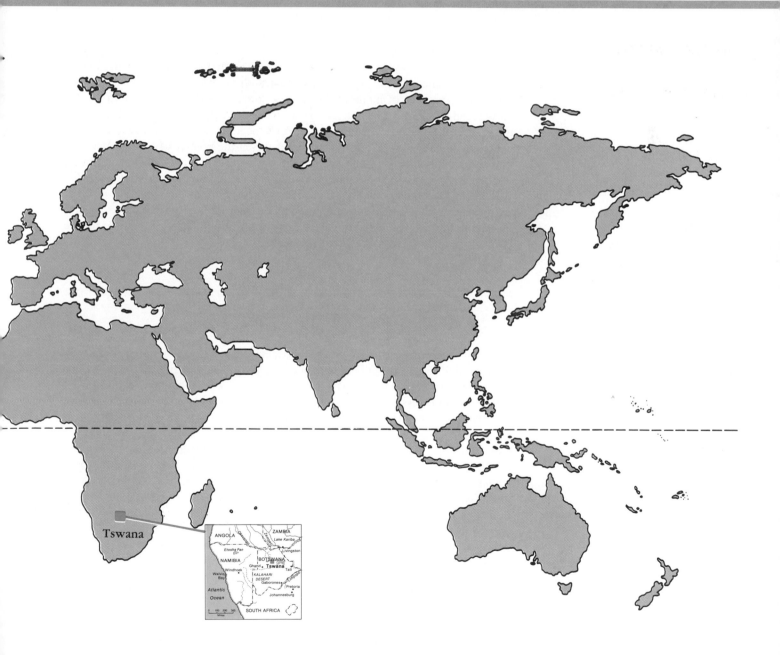

Tswana

The distinguished American anthropologist Clifford Geertz writes:

"There is an Indian story—at least I heard it as an Indian story—about an Englishman who, having been told that the world rested on a platform which rested on the back of an elephant which rested in turn on the back of a turtle, asked (perhaps he was an ethnographer; it is the way they behave), what did the turtle rest on? Another turtle. And that turtle? 'Ah, Sahib, after that it is turtles all the way down.'

"Such, indeed, is the condition of things. . . . Cultural analysis is intrinsically incomplete. And, worse than that, the more deeply it goes the less complete it is. It is a strange science whose most telling assertions are its most tremulously based, in which to get somewhere with the matter at hand is to intensify the suspicion, both your own and that of others, that you are not quite getting it right. But that, along with plaguing subtle people with obtuse questions, is what being an ethnographer is like" (Geertz 1973:28–29).

What is the world like? And what is the human condition within the world? Attempts to answer these questions have taken up an impressive proportion of the intellectual energies of human beings for as long as our species has been on this earth. Anthropologists are not original in trying to supply answers to these questions. And their answers, like those of other theorists in different disciplines, are never exhaustive. This is hardly surprising, given the complexity and richness of human life. However, certain aspects of the way anthropologists go about constructing their answers make anthropology, as a discipline, unique. If we want to ask what it is about the human condition that distinguishes it from the condition of other living species, the short answer proposed by the anthropologist is culture. A longer, more complex answer, which involves exploring the implications of culture for the human condition, makes up the rest of this book.

The Human Condition

What is the *human condition*? When Americans use this expression, they ordinarily have in mind certain features of human existence, which they presume to be identical for all human beings, no matter who they are or where they live. For instance, Americans often assume that all people everywhere possess an identical, unchanging *human nature*. They further assume that this human nature is more basic than differences in language or custom, which are seen as superficial. In addition, Americans usually assume the existence of a *wider world* with certain unchanging attributes of its own. These attributes usually include features of the *natural environment*—rocks, rain, plants, animals—with which human beings must come to terms. Sometimes, certain features of the *social environment*—the state, a distinction between rich and poor—are also thought to be constant. Finally, regularities of change in parts of the wider world—the rhythm of the seasons, the rise and fall of empires, the human life cycle—may also be perceived as constant and therefore inevitable. When we bring together what we believe to be the unchanging features of human nature and the wider world, we begin to draw conclusions and generalize about the human condition.

Anthropology did not develop in an intellectual vacuum. Early anthropologists were seeking to come to terms with peoples and ways of life that challenged their most basic understanding of what "human nature" meant. They naturally turned for help to the most sophisticated ideas of human nature offered by their own culture. As a result, the major theoretical perspectives within anthropology were built upon the philosophical positions that we are about to consider. The following discussion of "isms" in philosophy may seem like a digression from the topic of this chapter, or even of the book, but it is not. Western anthropologists today are more aware than ever before of the degree to which ideas about human nature developed in their own culture have affected their analyses of other cultures. It is important that beginning students in anthropology learn to cultivate a similar awareness.

Dualism

If Americans are asked to reflect on what their society teaches about human nature, many will point to the widespread belief that human nature has two parts. Sometimes these parts are called mind and matter, soul and body, or spirit and flesh. The belief that human nature, or reality as a whole, is made up of two radically different elements, or essences, is called **dualism**.

dualism
the philosophical position that reality consists of two equal and irreducible forces

Mind-matter dualism is as ancient in Western thought as Plato. For Plato, all reality could be divided into mind and matter. Mind was higher and finer and corresponded to the celestial realm of ideal forms. Matter was lower and cruder and corruptible, belonging to the earthly realm. Human nature was dualistic because each person was made up of an earthly material body inhabited by a spirit whose true home was the realm of ideal forms. The drama of human existence consisted in the internal struggle between the body, drawn naturally to base, corruptible matter, and the mind or soul, drawn naturally to pure, unchanging forms.

Mind-matter dualism is also found in Western religious thought. The early church fathers—Augustine, for example—were influenced by Plato's opinions as those opinions had been interpreted and handed down to them by later thinkers. In the Christian version of human nature, human beings are made in the image of God, who is pure spirit. But the God who created us gave us material bodies as well ("temples for the spirit"), and placed us in a material world to live. All was well as long as the first human beings followed the dictates of the spirit and obeyed God. However, being made in God's image, they were endowed with the ability to disobey as well—and eventually they did disobey. The followers of Christ who make up "the elect" can hope to spend eternity rejoined with God in his holy city. But as long as they remain on earth, they must fight the material world and cling to their faith in the face of temptation. Earthly life is thus a struggle between flesh and spirit. For Plato, for Augustine, and for many theologians and philosophers who followed them, this was the only plausible view of human existence. It is sometimes called *conflict dualism*.

The modern form of dualism is widely attributed to the seventeenth-century rationalist philosopher René Descartes. Descartes' most celebrated utterance was "I think; therefore, I am." Descartes was the first Western thinker to advocate systematically a view that likened the body to a machine. What could be more material and less capable of thought than a machine! (Computers would not come along for another three hundred years.) Perhaps it is surprising that Descartes left any room at all for mind in his philosophy, given the persuasiveness of his mechanistic analogy. However, the wider world in which he lived included the Roman Catholic Church, an extremely powerful social and political institution whose dogmas it was not wise to contradict. In any case, people today often speak of *Cartesian dualism* when attempting to describe the view of human nature most widely accepted in modern Western culture.

Dualism has made its way into anthropological theory by means of the so-called "nature-nurture" contrast. When "nature" is opposed to "nurture" in this

Fredric March as *Dr. Jekyll and Mr. Hyde.* This story of an outwardly civilized, cultured man whose inner, brutish self emerges to cause havoc is an example of conflict dualism.

way, "nature" stands for matter, bodily instincts, or genetic programming. "Nurture," by contrast, refers to mind, and especially to learning as the key feature of mind. If a form of human behavior is said to be due to "nature," this means it is rooted in biology or genetics and cannot be altered by learning. If a form of behavior is said to be due to "nurture," this means it is not rooted in biology or genetics, but has been learned and can thus be changed. Many troublesome human behavior patterns (e.g., racial or sexual inequality) seem to involve both "nature" and "nurture." As a result, nature and nurture continue to coexist uneasily with one another, and much anthropological theory sounds dualistic.

Reductionism

Most Western thinkers who have reflected on mind-matter dualism have not been content just to state that human nature consists of two radically different parts. Conflict dualism in particular has caused them anxiety, because it seems so pessimistic. If our nature is composed of two opposed elements, each forever struggling to dominate the other, human life begins to look like an eternal battle whose outcome is always uncertain. Moreover, human nature seems hopelessly contradictory: If we are simultaneously both mind and body, then perhaps we are simultaneously both strong and weak, wise and foolish, good and bad. Our attempt to understand ourselves dissolves in a sea of ambiguity as opposite features of our nature cancel each other out.

To overcome this ambiguity, dualist thinkers have often taken a further step in their analysis of human nature. While admitting that we appear to be equally mind and matter, they insist that appearances are deceptive. They claim that only one of the two essences—mind *or* matter—is our true nature. The other is simply a by-product of that nature, or an unfortunate block preventing its true realization.

The Platonic and Christian theories of human nature have taken this step. Both argue that while human beings are equipped with material bodies, nevertheless their true nature is not material but spiritual. They see the drama of human existence precisely in terms of the struggle of human beings to realize their true spiritual nature in the face of material temptation and corruption. This view is known as **idealism**. Plato, as well as many well-known Christian thinkers, offered classic examples of idealist thought.

It is equally possible to argue that matter, rather than mind, is our true essence. From that perspective, the drama of human existence becomes the struggle to achieve the freedom to exercise our materiality fully in the face of attempts by some elements in society to enslave us with spiritual doctrines. This view is known as **materialism**. Perhaps the most influential materialist thinker in the contemporary world has been Karl Marx.

Both idealists and materialists begin by acknowledging the existence of an apparently dualistic human nature (see figure 2.1). Their next step is to argue that the evidence shows that only one element has independent causal power, while the other element is just a dependent by-product. Each side tries to recast in a new framework the evidence that the other side uses to defend its position. In this way, both idealists and materialists hope to prove that they can explain the opposing evidence better than their rivals can. They can *reduce* their opponents' evidence from the status of independence to one of dependence. Hence, their explanatory schemes are called reductionistic. For example, if human nature resides in reason, then human action is just a by-product of the operation of reason in a being whose physical body is controlled by the mind. Similarly, if human nature resides in matter, the operation of material forces determines human action. Peoples' ideas about what

idealism
the philosophical position that ideas, or the mind that produces such ideas, constitutes the essence of human nature

materialism
the philosophical position that explains the nature of all things, living and nonliving, in terms of the physical substances, forces, or relationships to which they can be reduced

they do are by-products of the operation of material forces in physical bodies that happen to have minds capable of conscious awareness.

Reductionism is the attempt to explain complex phenomena in terms of the simpler or more basic units, or forces, that are held to produce these phenomena: "The units and their properties exist *before* the whole, and there is a chain of causation that runs from the units to the whole" (Lewontin, Rose, and Kamin 1984:5–6). Idealist positions are reductionistic when they claim to reduce human action to the ideas that motivate it; materialist positions are reductionistic when they claim to reduce human ideas to the material forces that generate them.

Reductionism is also *determinism*. To *reduce* the properties of the whole to the properties of its parts is to argue at the same time that the properties of the parts *determine* the properties of the whole. Thus, for idealists, ideas determine action, but not the reverse; for materialists, physical activity determines ideas, but not the reverse.

The following material explores more fully the implications of adopting either an idealist or a materialist position.

The Idealist Position. Idealism claims that ideas, or the mind that produces the ideas, constitutes the essence of human nature. Therefore, to the extent that we are true to the insights of mind, we are true to our nature.

One variety of idealism is known as *rationalism*. Rationalists not only argue that human nature is best defined in terms of mind, they focus on one particular aspect of mind: reason. Understood as the mind's presumed innate logical structures and processes, reason is believed to mirror the wider world and to provide an infallible key to understanding that world. Rationalists argue that ideas that are products of rational thought are necessarily true. That is, such ideas do not need to be confirmed by sight or touch or any of the other physical senses. By strict adherence to logic, which is the language of reason, one can deduce the true nature of reality. The seventeenth-century French mathematician and philosopher René Descartes is perhaps the best known of all rationalist thinkers.

Positions giving primacy to mind are not unique to what the Western world calls philosophy. As noted earlier, the traditional Western religious response to the question of human nature also argues that mind (or spirit), if not reason, constitutes the essence of being human. In one form or another, idealism has been the dominant view of human nature throughout much of Western history. Yet, during the last three hundred years or so, it has been powerfully challenged by the alternative reductionistic claim that matter, not mind, is the true essence of human nature and the wider world.

The Materialist Position. Materialism refers to views of human nature that ascribe primary importance to our physical makeup. Human ideas, beliefs, and values are seen as by-products of material life, reflecting that life but not shaping it. From a materialist perspective, a proper understanding of human nature would reduce the products of our mental life to underlying causes rooted in our material nature.

Although both idealist and materialist positions had their defenders as long ago as the pre-Socratic Greeks, materialism did not come into its own until the seventeenth-century Enlightenment. Descartes' suggestion that human beings were like machines became increasingly persuasive as science, technology, and the Industrial Revolution got underway. As a result, materialist views of the human condition gradually replaced idealist views in learned circles.

A little over two hundred years later, the social philosopher Auguste Comte confidently declared that all idealist (or "metaphysical") views of the human condition had been left behind in the evolutionary march from magic through religion to

reductionism
the philosophical position that explains all evidence in terms of (reduces all evidence to) a single set of principles

FIGURE 2.1
Idealism and Materialism According to Rius
Source: From *Marx for Beginners*, by Rius. English translation copyright © 1976 by Richard Appignanesi. Reprinted by permission of Pantheon Books, a Division of Random House, Inc.

Charles Darwin (1809–1882).

biological determinism

the position that human lives and actions are inevitable consequences of the biochemical properties of the cells that make up the individual, and that these characteristics are in turn uniquely determined by the constituents of the genes possessed by each individual

science. Science measured and mapped the material world. Scientific knowledge of the material world seemed to lead directly to powerful new ways of reshaping that world to serve human needs. Comte and many of his contemporaries were persuaded by their experiences that material progress for humanity was somehow woven into the fabric of history.

The nineteenth century was the great century of evolutionary thought, and Charles Darwin was probably its most famous evolutionary thinker. Darwin is popularly held to have invented evolutionary biology. As noted evolutionary biologist Richard Lewontin (1982) has pointed out, however, Darwin was not the first in arguing that change over time was the rule for biological species. Darwin's innovation was to propose a materialist explanation for such change. His proposal—natural selection—was a random process in which the forces of the material environment interacted with material organisms. Organisms whose material traits helped them to withstand this environmental test survived; other organisms perished. There was no need for mind or God in this process. Paradoxically, Darwin—and many evolutionists after him—believed that random natural selection might still have a purpose. This purpose was to produce the fittest organisms, and to eliminate the unfit. In this way, material progress was built into the process of evolution. The material world, if left to its own devices, would automatically improve the various living species by fitting them ever more perfectly to the environments in which they lived.

Darwin's work was meant to explain the evolution of nonhuman species, but its implications for an understanding of human life were obvious. Long before Darwin wrote about the origin of species through natural selection, other Western thinkers had speculated about the evolution of human society. Indeed, the expression "survival of the fittest," long associated with Darwin, was first used by Herbert Spencer, whose main interest was the evolution of society. Central to Spencer's understanding of society was his belief in progress through order. In this, he shared Comte's perspective. Spencer believed that the material forces of evolution would inevitably produce a better world if they were allowed to do their work without interference (from well-meaning but misguided revolutionaries, for example). Today's society is by definition better than yesterday's, and those who benefit most from it are better than those who suffer from it. It is all a matter of survival of the fittest. For Spencer, the present arrangements of society came about by the necessity of material evolution. Thus, they are the best of all possible arrangements, however cruel they might appear. Attempts to tamper with these arrangements involve going against the grain of evolutionary destiny and are doomed to failure.

Spencer's views have contributed to a perspective called **biological determinism**. Biological determinism is a form of materialist reductionism that has been widely influential in anthropology. Lewontin sums up this modern version of biological determinism as follows:

> *[For the biological determinist], human lives and actions are inevitable consequences of the biochemical properties of the cells that make up the individual; and these characteristics are in turn uniquely determined by the constituents of the genes possessed by each individual. Ultimately, all human behavior—hence all human society—is governed by a chain of determinants that runs from the gene to the individual to the sum of the behavior of all individuals. The determinists would have it, then, that human nature is fixed by our genes. . . . What is more, biology, or "genetic inheritance," is always invoked as an expression of inevitability: what is biological is given by nature and proved by science. (Lewontin, Rose, and Kamin 1984:6)*

Not all materialists have been persuaded that the material forces responsible for the condition of any living species are rooted in biology. Some thinkers are more impressed by the role played by the material environment. These thinkers subscribe to a second form of materialist reductionism, called **environmental determinism**. Environmental determinists argue that the important material forces shaping our lives are to be found outside our material bodies, indeed outside the human species as a whole. Some environmental determinists locate these forces in the nonhuman environment alone. For them, rich soil, or a temperate climate, or too little rainfall, or an absence of domesticable animals might be the environmental forces shaping society, encouraging progressive evolution or arresting it.

environmental determinism
the position that the important material forces responsible for a species' condition in life lie in the environment external to that species

For other thinkers, such as Karl Marx, social forces play a critical role. The collective material actions of people in society, shaped by the interests of the dominant class, are responsible for the human condition at any point in history. Progress is still possible, indeed inevitable, as historical necessity works itself out. Marx and his followers believed that progress was made not through order, which was only the order of some particular ruling class, but through revolution. The old and worse had to be overthrown forcibly to make way for the new and better. This point of view is known as **historical materialism**. To the extent that historical materialism denies a role to ideas, mental activity, or consciousness, it can be considered a third form of materialist reductionism. Some passages in Marx's writings suggest such a reduction: for example, "Hitherto men have constantly made up for themselves false conceptions about themselves. . . . They, the creators, have bowed down before their creation. . . . Let us revolt against the rule of thoughts" (1932:160).

historical materialism
the position that the collective material actions of people in society, shaped by the interests of the dominant class, are responsible for the human condition at any point in history

According to historical materialism, human beings make themselves through the material life process of society. As Marx put it, "the first premiss of all human existence [is] that men must be in a position to live in order to be able to 'make history.' But life involves before everything else eating and drinking. The first historical act is thus the production of the means to satisfy these needs [which] must daily and hourly be fulfilled merely in order to sustain human life" (1932:165).

As living, natural, material organisms, human beings must transform the natural, material world in which they find themselves to meet their natural, material needs. Explanations of human action and human nature must be grounded in the material, physical labor carried out by material, physical beings; human nature is based not in the mind but in the body. For historical materialists, ideas follow from and are caused by the material requirements for collective human survival.

A Dialogue on the Human Condition. Historically, then, our culture has produced two basic positions on human nature and the human condition: the idealist and the materialist. These positions seem to be polar opposites, and indeed each needs the other in order to make its own arguments persuasive. When set forth in everyday or academic discussions, the mutual incompatibility of the two positions is often explicitly recognized. Debate is often heated. Nevertheless, the evidence that one side offers in support of its view is usually not denied outright by the other side. Rather, this evidence is reinterpreted, and an attempt is made to prove that its defenders have misunderstood it.

For example, Marx did not deny that people have ideas. Ideas themselves are not illusory. What is illusory is the notion that ideas by themselves constitute reality, or the belief that ideas by themselves have any power to shape or change human behavior. As Marx said, "Life is not determined by consciousness, but consciousness by life" (1932:164). And life, at its essence, is material life. Thus, for example, it is pointless to appeal to people's ideas about manhood and womanhood to explain a social pattern of male domination. Instead, we must examine the material relationships men have with women as they engage·in everyday practical activities.

Karl Marx (1818–1883).

Marx assumed that these patterns of interaction are determined by the way a society has organized itself to produce food and other material goods. If social organization decrees that men will give orders and women will obey those orders, then the stereotypes of masculinity and femininity will justify this pattern. Beliefs that men are born leaders and women are born to serve do not cause male domination. Rather, these beliefs are understood as by-products of social necessity.

Idealists would never deny that people are living, breathing organisms who act. However, the idealist argues that people are motivated to act by the ideas or beliefs they hold. Endowed with reason, we are able to evaluate the alternatives for action available to us. We are free to select the alternative that best accords with reason (or God's law), and to act on it, thus directing our material bodies to behave in ways that our minds have chosen. For example, an idealist might explain male domination in the following way. If men lead and women follow, this is because both men and women have freely chosen to do so. They have made their respective choices because they (or their ancestors or God) reflected on the natural attributes of men and women. Reflection showed that men seemed to have a natural predisposition to lead, while women were much happier following orders. Male dominance persists over time, therefore, because each generation of men and women continues to see the rationality behind male dominance and freely chooses to act in accord with it.

Because they are free, men and women may to choose to act in ways that violate reason, law, or custom. This is why, the idealist continues, we hold people responsible for their actions in a court of law. If everything people did or said was rigidly determined by material forces beyond the reach of consciousness or reason, we could never hold anybody responsible for anything. Thus, to the extent that we hold people responsible for what they do, we must recognize the power of ideas to shape material behavior.

As mentioned earlier, idealism in one form or another enjoyed wide support for centuries, and met its most serious challenge in the versions of materialism that developed during the Industrial Revolution. The nineteenth century in Europe and America might be seen as the great age of materialism, as it was the great age of science, colonialism, and capitalist expansion. And yet such relentless materialism was not accepted by all students of human nature. Some rejected materialism because they believed it entailed an implausible portrait of human nature. Materialist reductionism suggests that human beings lack creativity, self-consciousness, and an ability to choose. Instead, they are passive, their actions and beliefs shaped by iron historical necessity. As Howard Gardner suggested about a later generation of materialist reductionists, "There is something about their closed systems of exploration—their faith in the limited number of routes the mind can in fact follow—which makes it difficult to envision how one could ever account . . . for the innovative work of an Einstein, a Shakespeare, or a Freud" (1982:39).

In anthropology, the most extreme reaction against the various forms of materialist reductionism has been called **cultural determinism**. In this form of reductionism, the causal arrow points not from body to mind, not from biology to culture, but in the other direction. The ideas, meanings, beliefs, and values that people learn as members of society become the determining agents. In this view, "you are what you learn," rather than "you are what you eat."

It may seem more liberal to allow human beings the freedom to choose what to learn and to create new values and meanings for themselves. Optimistic versions of cultural determinism place no limits on the abilities of human beings to be or do whatever they want. In American cultural anthropology, this perspective reached its

cultural determinism
the position that the ideas, meanings, beliefs, and values people learn as members of society determine human nature

height of popularity in the 1940s and 1950s. Basing their opinion on data collected in many cultures around the world, some anthropologists concluded that it was impossible to argue that there was any universal "right way" of being human. The evidence suggested that the "right way" was always "our way," and that "our way" in one society almost never corresponded to "our way" in any other society.

In these circumstances, the proper attitude of an informed human being could only be that of tolerance. Absolute moral judgments could never be made even about cultural practices that might seem indefensible in *any* culture, such as the systematic murder of members of a minority group carried out by the majority. If the Nazis tried to exterminate the Jews, it was because German culture taught them that this was acceptable. If we find this action unacceptable, then it is simply because our culture teaches us that this is unacceptable. There matters must rest—or so it was believed. As we shall see, much more indeed remains to be said.

Optimistic versions of cultural determinism hold out the hope that if human nature is infinitely malleable, then human beings can choose the ways of life they prefer. In principle, utopia can be realized on earth. Pessimistic versions of cultural determinism rule this out: "You are what you learn" becomes "you are what you are conditioned to be," and this is something over which you have no control. Human beings are once again viewed as passive creatures who are conditioned to think, believe, and do whatever their culture tells them to do.

The school of thought known as behaviorism offers an example of pessimistic cultural determinism. Based on the work of psychologist B. F. Skinner, behaviorism views all organisms as passive entities whose behavior is shaped by countless forces in the wider world, most of which are beyond their awareness, and all of which they are powerless to control. Skinner also recognizes, though, that much of the human environment is a human, cultural creation. This is presumably a way of allowing human beings a kind of collective control over their destiny, particularly once they have come to understand the laws according to which conditioning occurs. However, even if people come to understand how they are conditioned, understanding will be achieved only if it rewards them in some way (or, as the behaviorists put it, brings them positive reinforcement). This theory locates the causes of human behavior in a realm that is wholly beyond human control.

Interactionism

One popular way to avoid the struggle between idealism and materialism is to argue that both positions have a certain persuasive power. Perhaps it would be more worthwhile to end the arguments by recognizing that both mind and matter are real and important. It may be true that an open commitment to dualism breeds uncertainty about our ultimate nature. Nevertheless, a frank recognition that both nature and nurture contribute to make us what we are might allow us to escape from the seemingly endless battle between opposed reductionisms.

This approach is more complex than either reductionist account considered earlier. It accepts the materialist claim that the body is the source of natural, material causation, but it also accepts the idealist claim that the mind (soul, spirit) can be modified, is capable of learning, and somehow escapes the material constraints of the body. As human beings live their lives, body and mind both exert their own deterministic pressures. Ultimately, for any given form of behavior, body and mind must *interact* with one another to produce the actions that themselves appear whole and unitary. This form of dualism is called **interactionism**.

In interactionist approaches to human nature, "it is neither the genes nor the environment that determines an organism but a unique interaction between them"

interactionism
the position that neither genes nor environment alone, but rather their interaction, determine the nature of an organism

(Lewontin, Rose, and Kamin 1984:268). If dualism describes human nature's two parts, interactionism explains the ways in which those two parts affect each other.

For interactionism to appear plausible, two assumptions must be made. First, we must assume that natural entities (body, mind, human individuals, separate societies) are isolated from one another and from the environment. Second, we must assume that these isolated individual entities are the only entities with genuine independent existence. Our scientific task then becomes observing the ways these isolated objects bounce off one another (like billiard balls), and off the environment. The behavior of any individual human being can thus be explained as a vector of the interacting forces of the individual's own body and mind, nonhuman physical objects, other human bodies, other minds, and so forth.

Interactionism relies heavily on metaphors borrowed from Newtonian physics. The great achievements that followed acceptance of Sir Isaac Newton's method of describing the material world inspired students of human nature to try to describe human thought and action in similar terms. Compared with the embattled positions of idealism and materialism, interactionism seems most reasonable. "It has the seductive appeal of a middle way that does not sacrifice a basic commitment to cause-and-effect determinism, nor even to reductionism" (Lewontin, Rose, and Kamin 1984:270), but seeks instead to discover how much of what we think or do can be attributed to biology, and how much to culture.

How helpful is this view? Is the boundary between one person's body and mind, or between one body and another body, as clear-cut as interactionism makes it out to be? Are the boundaries between societies equally clear-cut? Are people never in any doubt as to which traditions are theirs and which are ours? How does interactionism explain the fact that all members of any society do not agree perfectly with one another on all matters? Disagreement should not be possible if individuals are all conditioned to accept only the values of their closed societies and are incapable of conceiving of alternatives.

Holism

Interactionism's ability to explain human nature depends upon the plausibility of its assumptions. If we cannot draw clear-cut boundaries between the entities that are supposed to be interacting with one another (say, mind and body, or individual and society), we have no way to measure scientifically the separate contribution of each entity to the human behavior we are trying to explain. In fact, it has proved notoriously difficult for interactionists to show where mind ends and brain (i.e., matter) begins, or where precisely one society ends and a second society begins. Investigators have been known to disagree violently over whether some particular cultural item is or is not a genuine part of one or another tradition. For instance, are oriental rugs part of Western culture, or do they belong only to the Asian societies that began selling them to Western merchants several hundred years ago (Spooner 1986)? Many observers have concluded that the interactionist portrait of human nature is, in its own way, as implausible as the reductionist portraits. Individual human beings often appear as passive in interactionist accounts as they do in reductionist accounts. The main difference seems to be that they are pummeled, body and mind, by a wider range of deterministic forces than any reductionist account would allow. The margin of choice, creativity, or responsibility for such creatures seems equally slim.

Many anthropologists have long argued that there is yet another point of view that is less distorting than interactionism, materialism, or idealism. This is the anthropological point of view called **holism**. Holism does not assume that sharp boundaries separate objects from one another, or from their environments. Rather, it assumes that objects and environment interpenetrate each other and even define each other. Holism denies that isolated objects are the only independent reality. Instead, it claims that everything that exists is mutually determined by everything else that exists. From a holistic perspective, attempts to divide reality into mind and matter, or to ascribe a certain percentage of all human behavior to genes and the remaining percentage to culture, are misguided. These efforts are able at most to isolate and pin down certain aspects of a process that, by its very nature, resists isolation and dissection.

A contribution of unique and lasting value has been made by anthropologists who have struggled to develop a holistic perspective on the human condition. The effort has been present throughout the history of the discipline. Holism continues to hold great appeal for those who seek a theory of human nature that is as rich and complex as its subject matter.

One traditional way of expressing the holistic insight has been to state that the whole (i.e., a human being, a society) is more than the sum of its parts. That is, individual human organisms are not just *x* percent genes and *y* percent culture added together. Rather, human beings are what they are because the interpenetration of genes and culture has produced something new, something whose attributes cannot be reduced to the materials that were used to construct it. Similarly, a society or a culture is not just the sum of the behaviors of its individual members. Instead, human beings living in groups become different kinds of creatures. They are so deeply affected by shared cultural experiences that they become different from what they would have been had they matured in isolation from other people. Indeed, we have discovered that human beings subjected to tragic isolation do not behave in ways that appear recognizably human. Anthropologist Clifford Geertz noted that human beings raised this way would be neither failed apes, nor "natural" people stripped of their veneer of culture; they would be "mental basket cases" (1973:40).

These observations suggest also that social living and cultural sharing are necessary for human beings to develop what we recognize as a *human* nature. Human beings, and human societies, are open systems, able to learn, develop, embrace alternatives, and change, shaped by internal attributes as well as by external influences. Human beings and human societies are open to a variety of environmental influences and products, even as the environment itself is open to the influences and products of our varied activities.

Our understanding of the relationships between aspects of a whole is enriched if we approach those relationships in a dialectical manner. For us, **dialectical** means two principal and related things. First, it refers to a network of cause and effect, in which the various causes and effects affect each other: "It is impossible to partition out the 'causes' [of events] . . . into *x* percent social . . . and *y* percent biological." Second, the biological and the social are neither separable, nor antithetical, nor alternatives, but complementary: "All causes of the behavior of organisms . . . are simultaneously social and biological . . . chemical and physical" (Lewontin, Rose, and Kamin 1984:282). Put another way, the parts of a whole take shape because of the associations they have with other parts and with the whole itself. The properties of parts and wholes *codetermine* one another. It follows that anthropology is itself part of a whole. This leads to the further realization that all our understandings of what it means to be a human being—anthropological, biological, scientific, or commonsensical—are located in a wider social and historical context.

holism
the position that objects and the environment interpenetrate and even define each other

dialectical
refers to a network of cause and effect, in which the various causes and effects affect each other

We are proposing a holistic and dialectical view of human nature, a view that rejects reductionism and interactionism, as well as the dualism that both presuppose. Dialectical holism is based on the insight that human beings are open systems. It also offers the claim that the wider world, the environment, is also open to modification by the objects (including people) that inhabit it. For human beings, part of the wider world is human society, so human society too must be considered an open system. A comparison of this holistic perspective with the other alternatives discussed so far is found in figure 2.2.

As you compare the holistic and dialectical perspective on human nature with the other perspectives, you may be troubled. Surely nothing is more certain than the reality of objects, their clear-cut identifiability! Here I am, you may say, together with the book I am reading and the chair I am sitting in. These are three objects. If they were not clearly isolated from one another, my fingers would press through the pages and my seat would be on the floor! Furthermore, if I put my book down in frustration and walk out of the room, the book and chair will remain behind, unchanged, until I return. So how can you tell me that the properties of book and chair, and of myself, mutually shape one another?

The perspective proposed here may seem unlikely to someone who has been raised in Western culture and who accepts as common sense the assumptions that lead to dualism or reductionism. Yet a holistic, dialectical view of the human condition is richly supported by observation and experience. Holism becomes plausible as soon as we begin to suspect that objects and the environment are not isolated from one another, or to question the notion that isolated objects are the only entities that have an independent existence.

Why doubt these assumptions? Is there any evidence that the isolation of object from environment is not absolute? The evidence is everywhere. Consider human beings as living organisms. To continue to exist, they need food and water on a regular basis. Food and water come from the environment. Whenever we eat or drink, the environment is penetrating us as objects and being transformed by processes inside our bodies into forms that renew our bodies and keep them in working

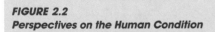

FIGURE 2.2
Perspectives on the Human Condition

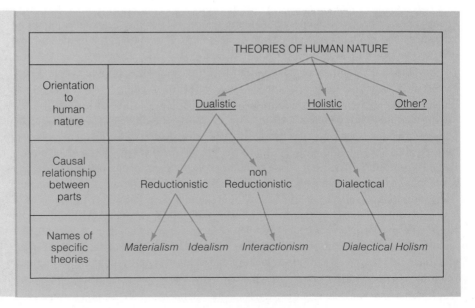

order. Moreover, the act of supplying food and water is one way we penetrate the environment, shape it, take from it and thereby alter it in some small way. Sometimes the environment is easily able to replace what we take from it. But as our experiences with soil erosion from agriculture and pollution from industry remind us, the human transformation of the environment can be far-reaching, devastating, sometimes irreversible.

It is not merely human beings who are open systems, whose natures are co-determined by the interpenetration of internal and external forces. All living organisms are open systems. They have had a massive influence on the environments of this planet throughout its history, even as the environments of the planet have influenced them. For example, the oxygen atmosphere on which humans and other animals depend is the result of the accumulation over millennia of a gas that was a waste product to the plants that expelled it. Plants drawing sustenance from the earth eventually, over time, had an enormous and irreversible effect on that earth.

For a moment, examine more closely just what is meant by an *environment*. Ordinary use of the word implies the existence of something—a group of organisms, perhaps—for which the natural world forms an environment. Every environment is thus an environment for something. Remove the something and we no longer have an environment; we have simply the physical world in all its complexity and diversity.

Now consider the claim that organisms define their environments. Think of any living organism you like, even a human being. Organisms make only limited use of the physical world in which they find themselves, and that use is guided by their internal characteristics. An organism that is capable of synthesizing its own food supply will be related to the physical world in a way very different from an organism that lacks this ability.

Biologist Stephen Jay Gould (1983) asks us to imagine what human society would be like if human beings possessed chlorophyll in their cells and, like plants, had no need to seek other plants or animals for food. Human history would clearly have been very different. There would have been no need to invent agriculture or animal husbandry, for example; indeed, no need to gather or hunt for a living. Or, as Richard Lewontin, Steven Rose, and Leon J. Kamen suggest, "If humans were the size of ants, . . . if we had eyes that were sensitive, like those of some insects, to ultraviolet wavelengths, or if, like some fishes, we had organs sensitive to electrical fields, the range of our interactions with each other and with other organisms would doubtless be very different" (1983:13–14).

These changes would not isolate human beings from the wider world, any more than plants or insects or fish are isolated. But they would mean that we would relate to the wider physical world differently than we do now. That is, we would define our environment for ourselves in a different way. Aspects of the physical world that are crucial parts of our current environment would either change their meaning for us or go unnoticed. We might, for example, remain alert to the presence of plants like poison ivy or animals like rattlesnakes, with whom contact might still be problematic. But the presence of plants like wheat or animals like chickens would be largely irrelevant to us.

The second assumption underlying reductionism and dualism is that isolated objects are the only things that are independently real. If objects are not isolated, either from one another or from their environment, it makes no sense to speak of anything existing independently, let alone being independently real. We might even say that the illusion of objects existing independently of one another and the environment can be sustained only by ignoring history, for the changes that objects

This hill has been transformed by the work of peasant farmers in northern Cameroon who grow sorghum on the terraces they have laboriously constructed.

and the environment work on each other often reveal themselves only with the passage of time.

Now return to the frustrated student sitting in a chair reading this book. If the mutual shaping of organism and environment can only be detected with the passage of time, the effect of your fingers on the book's pages (and vice versa), or the effect of your bottom on the chair's seat (and vice versa), will not likely be noticed after a few minutes. The effect becomes more noticeable, however, if you are seated in the same chair all day, reading chapter after chapter, cramming for a final exam. Constant contact with the book's pages will leave the tips of your fingers with an odd sensation, and your entire body will feel cramped from sitting in the same position hour after hour. A day's hard study and sweaty palms may distort the shape of the book's pages or smear its print. Highlighter pen marks and marginal notes in pencil or ink may further modify the original state of the book. And if you are reading a copy of the book that has already passed through the hands of several students, the binding may be falling apart by the time you are finished. If the chair in which you were sitting is a sturdy wooden one in your dormitory room, it may withstand well the bottoms of many students before its joints have loosened beyond repair and its legs collapse.

So far, this description has examined the way in which different objects mutually shape one another materially. But this is not the only way in which they can shape each other. Particularly in this century, scientists have become increasingly aware that the codetermination of organisms and environment involves not just matter but information as well. Recent work in particle physics has reminded us how mysterious matter is, and work in information theory and computer intelligence suggests that information is no less mysterious. The transformation of signals from the wider world into information that an organism can process, and the exchange of information between organisms, is usually what we are referring to when we talk about an organism learning.

Of all living organisms, human beings are the most dependent upon learning for their survival, and what they learn concerns both the physical and social environments in which they live. We tend to think of learning as primarily a mental process, a capacity of mind. However, a holistic, dialectical view of the human condition would describe human beings as creatures whose bodies and brains, actions and thoughts are equally involved in the learning process, codetermining one another. The result of their constant association would be the production of a human nature embedded in a wider world that also helps to define the human condition. A most important aspect of that wider world, which shapes us and is shaped by us, is culture.

Culture as Unique to the Human Species

The human condition is distinguished from the condition of other living species by culture. Other living species are open systems, as we are, and other living species learn. But the openness of the human condition, and the extent to which we depend upon learning to survive, is something unique in the animal kingdom. Because human beings have brains capable of open symbolic thought, and organs such as hands capable of manipulating matter powerfully or delicately, we interpenetrate the wider world more deeply than does any other species. This characteristic human relationship with the wider world makes cultural creation not only possible but necessary for our very survival. Apart from sucking, grasping, and crying, humans have no instincts or innate responses that would ensure their survival without their learning the culture of the group into which they are born. Even those elementary responses of newborns fade after a few weeks, and must by that time have been replaced by learned responses if an infant is to survive. Our dependence on culture is total. Without it, we cannot survive as biological organisms.

Culture is learned. We begin learning as infants, from other members of the group to which we belong. Culture is therefore also shared. Human beings do not reinvent culture for themselves each generation. They acquire massive chunks of it from older members of their society, although they may later modify this heritage in some way. The transmission and enriching of cultural traditions depend on culture being shared, just as human survival depends on social living. Biologically and culturally, human nature is therefore a social nature.

Human beings are social by nature. How does a dialectical view of the human condition shape our view of human society? To begin with, it emphasizes that ideas and action, labor and language, are social, shared phenomena. None of these most human attributes appears in a vacuum, or is the creation of an isolated individual. Our survival depends on the labor and the wisdom of others, and yet we can contribute our own labor and wisdom to the collective tradition, enriching it and changing it. There can be no society without individuals, but society is more than just the sum of the individuals that make it up. According to the dialectical perspective, society and individual create each other. There can be no society without individual human beings, and without society we can never come to have a sense of self, as distinct from other. To know the self, we need to know the other, the not-self, which other members of society become. We would not be able to survive physically or to communicate or think or create were it not for the shared tradition that we learn from other members of society, and the shared labor on which our existence depends. Nor could there be society without the individual members who make it up and carry out collective activities.

Culture is learned. Culture is shared. Culture also tends to hang together, to be coherent—in part because culture is a social product. People working and talking together shape their collective experience. Some ground rules that everyone accepts must be negotiated if communication and cooperation are to take place at all. Among people who have grown up together, speaking the same language, engaging in joint activities, these ground rules usually need not ever be spelled out. And because of all this, members of a society who share a common culture assume that the way they interpret the world is the way the world truly is. Of course the world appears to be as their culture says it should be.

Culture is learned, beginning when we are infants and continuing throughout our lives. From a young age, girls in northern Cameroon learn to carry heavy loads on their heads.

Cultural Differences

The power of culture to sustain this assumption is remarkable. That power is never more evident than when a person from one culture meets a person from a different culture. The same objects or events frequently mean different things to people in different cultures. In fact, what is an object or event in one tradition may not be so recognized in another. This powerful lesson of anthropology was illustrated by the experience of some Peace Corps volunteers working in southern Africa.

In the early 1970s, the Peace Corps office in Botswana was increasingly concerned by the number of volunteers who seemed to be "burned out," failing in their

---

EthnoFile 2.1
TSWANA

Region: Southern Africa

Nation: Botswana

Population: 1,200,000 (also 1,500,000 in South Africa)

Environment: Savannah to dessert (Kalahari)

Livelihood: Cattle raising, farming

Political organization: Chiefs and headmen

Other: Labor migration by men to South African mines is now an important part of Tswana life

---

assignments, and increasingly hostile to their Tswana hosts. It asked American anthropologist Hoyt Alverson, who was familiar with Tswana culture and society, for advice. (*See EthnoFile 2.1: Tswana.*) Alverson (1977) discovered that one major problem the Peace Corps volunteers were having involved exactly this issue of similar actions having very different meanings.

In one instance, the volunteers complained that the Tswana would never leave them alone. They stated that whenever they tried to "get away" and sit by themselves for a few minutes to have some "private time," one or more Tswana would quickly join them. This made the Americans angry. From their perspective, everyone is entitled to a certain amount of privacy and time alone. To the Tswana, however, human life is social life; the only people who want to be alone are witches and the insane. But these young Americans did not seem to be either witches or lunatics. The Tswana who saw them sitting alone therefore "naturally" assumed that there had been a breakdown in hospitality, and that the volunteers would welcome some company. Here the same strip of behavior—an American walking out into a field and sitting by himself or herself—had very different meanings.

Even within a single culture, the meaning of an object or an action may differ depending on context. Anthropologist Clifford Geertz quotes philosopher Gilbert Ryle, who pointed out many years ago that there is a world of difference between a wink and a blink, as anyone who has ever mistaken one for the other has undoubtedly learned.

Thus, human experience is inherently ambiguous. To resolve the ambiguity, experience must be interpreted. Human beings turn to their own cultural traditions in search of an interpretation that makes sense, hangs together, is coherent. They do this daily as they go about life among others with whom they share traditions. But their interpretive activity does not cease at the boundary of the culture, because there are no clear-cut boundaries. Self and other need not belong to the same society or share the same traditions, and yet the attempt to communicate and the interpretive activity continue. Serious misunderstandings may arise when two individuals are unaware that their ground rules differ. At this point, the concepts of ethnocentrism and cultural relativism become relevant.

Ethnocentrism

ethnocentrism
the opinion that one's own way of life is natural or correct, in fact the only true way of being fully human

Ethnocentrism is the term anthropologists use to describe the opinion that one's own way of life is natural or correct, indeed the only true way of being fully human. Ethnocentrism cannot arise unless the ethnocentric person has already encountered an alien way of life that, compared with his or her own, appears unnatural, incorrect, nonhuman.

Ethnocentrism is one solution to the inevitable tension between cultural self and cultural other. It is a form of reductionism; it reduces the other way of life to a distorted version of one's own. If our way is the right way, then their way can only be a wrong way. At best, their truth is a distorted truth; at worst, it is an outright falsehood. (Of course, from their perspective, our way of life may seem equally to be a distortion of theirs.)

The members of one tradition may go beyond merely interpreting another way of life in ethnocentric terms. They may decide to try to do something about the discrepancies they observe. They may, for example, assume that the other way of life is wrong, but not fundamentally evil. This usually means that they see the members of the other group as needing conversion to their own point of view. If the others are unwilling to change their ways, the failed attempt at reduction may enlarge into an active dualism: we versus they, civilization versus savagery, good versus evil.

Both reductionistic and dualistic ethnocentrism have shaped the way members of Western culture have traditionally dealt with non-Western ways of life. While ethnocentrism is characteristic of all societies, Western industrialized countries have far more power to impose their vision of the world on other, weaker societies. In a world where some nations have the power to end human life as we know it, ethnocentrism becomes hideously dangerous.

The Cross-Cultural Relationship

Is it possible to avoid ethnocentric bias? A holistic approach to the relationship of self and other, across as well as within cultural traditions, holds promise. This approach views cross-cultural relationships as being not fundamentally different from intracultural relationships. Although cross-cultural relationships are often much more difficult to negotiate because the people involved can take much less about each other for granted, they are possible. Like all human relationships, they affect all parties involved in the encounter, changing them as they learn about each other.

This sort of interwoven learning experience is common to all human relationships, but it is potentially much more radical when the parties come from different cultural backgrounds. The other may help you see possibilities for belief and action that are drastically at odds with everything your tradition considered possible. By becoming aware of these unsuspected possibilities, you become a different person. Knowledge changes people, and change (learning) is only possible as a result of contact with the other. The other is affected in the same way. Neither will be the same again.

The possibility of cross-cultural learning—and transformation of self as a result—is at once an enormously hopeful and an immensely threatening possibility. For once it occurs, we can no longer claim that any single cultural tradition has an exclusive monopoly on truth. This does not mean that the traditions in question must therefore be based entirely on illusion or falsehood. It does mean that the truth embodied in any cultural tradition is bound to be partial, approximate, open to further insight and growth.

One way truth is enriched is by challenges to previous formulations that arise from new experiences in the natural or social world. The outcome of these challenges may be to confirm a previous formulation. But it may also involve modification of our earlier understanding as we confirm new insights pointed out to us by other observers from different traditions.

Cultural Relativism

cultural relativism
understanding another culture in its own terms sympathetically enough so that the culture appears to be a coherent and meaningful design for living (Greenwood and Stini 1977:182)

Anthropologists must come to terms with the consequences of this phenomenon as they do their fieldwork. One result has been the formulation of the concept of **cultural relativism**. Definitions of cultural relativism have varied as different anthropologists have tried to draw conclusions from their cross-cultural experience. One definition that attempts a holistic approach is the following: "[Cultural relativism involves] understanding another culture in its own terms sympathetically enough so that the culture appears to be a coherent and meaningful design for living" (Greenwood and Stini 1977:182).

According to this definition, the goal of relativism is understanding. If the Nazis tried to exterminate the Jews, cultural relativism demands that we attempt to understand how this undertaking was conceived and implemented as a meaningful course of action in German society in the early part of the twentieth century. Knowledge about German culture in particular (including its history) and European culture in general (including the rise of fascism outside Germany) can help us understand these events. An explanation based on this knowledge implies that the Holocaust was not a momentary aberration brought on by a handful of madmen who managed to seize power in Germany for a few years and implement policies totally at odds with German culture and history. Rather, nazism was intimately related to certain cultural patterns and historical processes that are deeply rooted in German, and European, society.

Therefore, to understand nazism from a relativistic point of view, we must ask why the Nazis were able to achieve power and why Jews were the chosen scapegoats. Answering these questions involves investigating the historical roots of anti-Semitism and nationalism in Germany. Moreover, the success of the Nazis in achieving their program, insofar as they did accomplish what they set out to do, is

Was nazism due to the perversion of German morality by a charismatic madman who wished to rule the world, or was its appeal rooted in long-standing social, historical, and cultural patterns?

not explained in terms of German culture and society alone. Such boundaries are never clear, and it is unlikely that so many Jews would have died without the overt and covert assistance rendered Germany by the other countries of Europe. Even the United States is implicated, since the American government refused to accept Jews as political refugees and, as a result, helped deliver them into the hands of their enemies.

This relativistic understanding accomplishes several things. It makes Nazi Germany comprehensible and even coherent. It reveals to us, to our horror, how the persecution and murder of human beings can appear perfectly acceptable when placed in a particular context of meaning. One thing this relativistic understanding does not do, however, is allow us to easily either excuse or condemn the Nazis for what they did on the grounds that "it was all due to their culture." For many people, the deterministic interpretation would be preferable. For some, it would absolve the Germans of any blame since it would mean they had no choice but to do what their culture dictated. For others, this view absolves non-Germans of blame: after all, if German culture led to the Holocaust, then responsibility lies squarely on the German people.

These attempts to contain the evil of the Holocaust by making one or another group of people exclusively responsible for it are understandable. After all, the active, leading roles were played by Germans, and in particular by members of the Nazi party. But to leave matters here is to give an incomplete account of a complex historical phenomenon. And to call the incomplete account "relativistic", as some have done, is to vulgarize the holistic understanding of cultural relativism that makes a complex historical explanation possible.

To accept the argument that "their culture made them do it," we are required to accept three familiar assumptions about human nature and human society. First, we are asked to assume that cultures have neat boundaries between them and are sealed off from one another, neither overlapping nor interpenetrating. Second, we are asked to assume that every culture, within its closed world, offers people only one way to interpret any given phenomenon. That is, we are asked to accept the notion that cultures are monolithic and permit no variety, harbor no contradictions, and allow no dissent. Third, we are asked to assume that human beings living in these closed cultural worlds are passively molded by culture, helpless to resist indoctrination into a single world view, and incapable of inventing alternatives to that view.

But as we saw in our discussion of cultural determinism, all these assumptions are belied by human experience. Cultures are not sealed off from one another. Their boundaries are fuzzy, their members exchange ideas and practices. Cultures are not monolithic. Even without the alternatives introduced from the outside, *every cultural tradition offers a variety of ways to interpret experience*, although official sanction may be accorded to only one. Finally, human beings are not passive lumps shaped unresistingly to fit a single cultural mold. There is no such thing as a single cultural mold in a society acquainted with variety, be that variety internally or externally generated. Furthermore, in a society where options exist, choices must be made. Like it or not, an individual must deliberate and decide, for example, whether to plant cotton and peanuts the way his father and his father's father did, or to run away from home, convert to Islam, marry the daughter of a cattle herder, and raise cattle. As Emily Schultz's field research in northern Cameroon revealed, some young men made the first choice and some made the second choice. But both were socioculturally recognized options, even if the first met with official approval and the second was officially deplored.

Abundant evidence exists to suggest that German society in the early twentieth century did not conform to the sealed-off, monolithic model. Germany was not closed to the rest of the world. Moreover, German cultural tradition had more than one strand. Some Germans supported fascism, some laid low, others resisted actively—but all were Germans and drew on German tradition to justify their choices. This suggests that there was (and is) more to German culture than those aspects that the Nazis made use of. It suggests that nazism could have been (and was) denounced by Germans as well as non-Germans. And this suggests that the recognition of evil is not simply a matter of condemning what your culture teaches you to condemn. Some Germans clearly understood why the Nazi program appealed to many of their fellow citizens, and still condemned it, in terms of traditional German values.

Understanding something is not the same as approving of it. Often we are repelled by alien cultural practices when we first encounter them. Sometimes when we understand these practices better, we are led to change our minds. We may conclude that the alien practices are more suitable for the people who employ them than our own practices would be. We might even recommend that the alien practice be adopted in our own society. But the opposite may also be the case. We may understand perfectly the cultural rationale behind such practices as slavery, infanticide, head-hunting, or genocide—and still refuse our approval. We may not be persuaded by the reasons offered to justify these practices, or we may be aware of alternative arrangements that could achieve the desired outcome using less drastic methods. Moreover, it is likely that any cultural practice with far-reaching consequences for human life will have critics as well as supporters *within* the society where it is practiced. This is certainly the case in American society, which is far from achieving moral consensus on such sensitive topics as abortion or capital punishment or nuclear warfare.

Cultural relativism makes moral reasoning more complex. It does not, however, require us to abandon every value our own society has taught us. Our culture, like every other culture, offers us more than one plausible way of evaluating our experiences. Exposure to the traditional interpretations of an alien culture forces us to reconsider the possibilities our culture recognizes in light of new alternatives, and to search for areas of intersection as well as areas of disagreement. What cultural relativism does discourage is the easy solution of refusing to consider alternatives from the outset. It also does not free us from sometimes facing difficult choices between alternatives whose "rightness" or "wrongness" is less than clear-cut. In this sense, "cultural relativism is a 'tough-minded' philosophy" (Herskovits [1951] 1978:37).

The Human Factor in Culture

Human life requires us to choose among alternatives, to act, even when the "correct" choice is unclear and the consequences of our action are uncertain. This alone suggests that the human condition is not totally controlled by forces that remain unaffected by the meaningful activity initiated by human beings.

Human History

The human condition is rooted in time and shaped by the passage of time. As part of the human condition, culture is also historical, being worked out and passed on from one generation to the next. As palaeoanthropologists have shown, the human species is itself a product of evolution over millions of years. Hence, human history is an essential aspect of the human story.

Anthropologists have sometimes disagreed about how to approach human history. Nineteenth-century thinkers like Herbert Spencer argued that the evolution of social structures over time was central to the study of the human condition. Other anthropologists, often sensitive to the excesses of people like Spencer, were not interested in change over time. Some, like A. R. Radcliffe-Brown in the 1930s, could justify this lack of interest by pointing out that in societies without written records, knowledge about past life was nonexistent. Any attempt to reconstruct such past life would be an unfounded attempt at "conjectural history."

Most often, one gets the sense that for some anthropologists history was simply without interest. Western capitalist culture, with its eye on the future and its faith in progress, has had little use for the past. In this view, the past is always a bad old past that will necessarily be superseded by a better, glorious future. If a society has moved beyond the bad old past and reached an improved stage of development, it becomes important to discover how that improvement can be sustained indefinitely. It is therefore no wonder that some earlier anthropologists built clockwork models of social structures that could be trusted to run reliably, without "losing time." In these models, human beings and societies are both likened to machines. If a living organism is used as the model of society, and if organisms are nothing but machines, then a machine model of society, with individuals as robotlike moving parts, is not at all farfetched.

A holistic and dialectical approach to human history rejects these clockwork models. Human history is biocultural. Culture is part of our biological heritage. Our biocultural heritage has produced a living species that uses culture to surmount biological and individual limitations. The result has been the emergence of creatures who are capable of studying themselves and their own biocultural evolution.

Human Agency and Interaction

Human history is a dialectic between biology and culture. It is also a dialectic between individual and group, self and other. One result of a dialectical approach is the renewed attention it pays to the actions of individual human beings. Once we abandon reductionistic schemes, the human agent reappears. The agent is not isolated; he or she is not divorced from cultural and historical context. But the human being who must deliberate and choose to act cannot be ignored in our consideration of the human condition. This is so because we cannot assume that human interaction or human communication is guaranteed to unfold without a hitch. Reductionist schemes assume that nothing can resist—or even tries to resist—whatever force is seen to be the prime mover, whether that force is the environment, biology, ideas, or history. Yet anthropological research, as well as reflection on our own personal experience, reminds us that human life rarely moves along without friction.

Human interaction is problematic: its outcome is never guaranteed, its terms must often be negotiated anew, and unresolved ambiguity can always disrupt the best-laid plans. Some scholars even liken human existence to a mine field, which we must painstakingly try to cross without blowing ourselves up. As a result, human agents play a vital role as they work to interpret the actions of others or to construct their own, as they attempt to forge relationships with others or to break them off.

Human Experience

A holistic and dialectical approach to the human condition also requires that we examine closely the nature of human *experience*. It is in light of experience, with its ragged edges and ambiguities, that human beings make their interpretations and construct their actions. Experience for human beings is both mental and physical. It is also individual and social, involving the human group as well as its wider environment. By attending to experience, we might be able to avoid the pitfalls of reductionism. We expend much energy attempting to make sense of our experience. But we also create, with the help of one another and our culture, the very experiences of which we are trying to make sense!

The Promise of the Anthropological Perspective

The anthropological perspective on the human condition is not easy to maintain. It denies that our common sense can be taken for granted, an assumption with which we are all most comfortable. It only increases the difficulty we encounter when faced with moral and political decisions. It does not allow us an easy retreat back to ethnocentrism when the going gets rough. For once we are exposed to the kinds of experience that the anthropological undertaking makes possible, we are changed—for better or worse. We cannot easily pretend that these new experiences never happened to us. Once we have had a genuine glimpse of the other, seen him or her in his or her humanity, there is no going back, except in bad faith.

So, anthropology is guaranteed to complicate your life. At the same time, the anthropological perspective can give you a broader understanding of human nature and the wider world, of society, culture, and history. It therefore also promises to lay groundwork that can help you construct more realistic and authentic ways of coping with the complications.

Key Terms

dualism
idealism
materialism
reductionism
biological determinism
environmental determinism
historical materialism

cultural determinism
interactionism
holism
dialectical
culture
ethnocentrism
cultural relativism

Chapter Summary

1. The belief that human nature has two parts is known as *dualism*. Mind-matter dualism is ancient in Western thought, associated with such figures as Plato, St. Augustine, and Descartes. It has made its way into anthropological theory by means of the "nature-nurture" controversy.

2. *Reductionism* is the attempt to explain complex phenomena in terms of the simpler or more basic units that are believed to produce them. Many dualist thinkers have tried to reduce mind to matter, or matter to mind. In either case, the attempt is made to show that only one of the two elements has independent causal power. The other element is just a dependent by-product. Reductionism is the same as *determinism*.

3. *Idealism* claims that ideas, or the mind that produces them, is the essence of human nature. It is therefore a reductionist position. It claims that human behavior ultimately depends on what human beings think or believe. Rationalism is a form of idealism.

4. *Materialism* refers to views of human nature that ascribe primary importance to our physical makeup. As a result, human ideas, beliefs, and values are seen as by-products of material life, reflecting it but not shaping it.

5. In the nineteenth century, the work of Herbert Spencer formed the foundation of a kind of materialist reductionism called *biological determinism*. This view claims that all human behavior can be explained with reference to a series of biological causes, beginning with the genes.

6. *Environmental determinism* is a form of materialist reductionism that claims that human life is shaped not by biology but by natural or social forces in the environment. Some environmental determinists locate these forces in the non-human environment alone. But others argue that the collective material actions of people in society over time shape human life. The latter position is known as *historical materialism*, and is associated with Karl Marx.

7. The most extreme reaction against the various forms of materialist reductionism has been called *cultural determinism*. This idealist position argues that the ideas, meanings, beliefs, and values that people learn in society determine their behavior. Optimistic versions of cultural determinism hold out the hope that we can change these determining agents and make ourselves whatever we want to be. Pessimistic versions conclude that "you are what you are conditioned to be," and that this is something over which you have no control.

8. If both mind and matter are seen to be responsible for certain behaviors, it can be said that their interaction determines the nature of an organism. *Interactionism* only makes sense, however, if we assume (1) that natural objects are isolated from one another, and (2) that these isolated objects are the only objects with genuine existence. If we apply interactionism to the analysis of human behavior, we must treat individual human beings (or individual societies) as if they were isolated objects. We must then observe the way these objects bounce off one another, or off the environment.

9. In preference to dualism, anthropologists have suggested *holism*. Holism assumes that objects and environments interpenetrate and even define each other. Thus, the whole is more than the sum of its parts. Human beings and human societies are open systems that cannot be reduced to the parts that make them up. Holism is *dialectical*, rather than deterministic. That is, it holds that parts and wholes mutually define, or codetermine, each other. This book adopts a holistic and dialectical approach to human nature, human society, and human history.

10. *Culture* distinguishes the human condition from the condition of other living species. Culture is learned, shared, and adaptive. It also tends to be coherent. Because human experience is often ambiguous, adaptation requires cultural interpretation. Cultural interpretation is a constant, necessary process, whether it is carried on among members of a single cultural tradition or between members of very different cultural traditions.

11. *Ethnocentrism* is a form of reductionism. It can be countered by a holistic, dialectical approach to the relationship of self and other. Such an approach makes it possible to understand another culture as a coherent and meaningful design for living. This is *cultural relativism*. Cultural relativism makes moral decisions more difficult because it requires us to take into account many things before we make up our minds. Cultural relativism does not require us to abandon every value our society has taught us. However, it does discourage the easy solution of refusing to consider alternatives from the outset.

12. Human history is an essential aspect of the human story, a dialectic between biology and culture. Culture is worked out over time and passed on from one generation to the next. Since human beings must interpret their experience in order to act, the story of our species also involves human agency. Because interpretations may differ from actor to actor, the outcome of human interaction is open.

Suggested Readings

Gamst, Frederick, and Edward Norbeck. *Ideas of Culture: Sources and Uses.* New York: Holt, Rinehart and Winston, 1976.
A useful collection of important articles about culture. The articles are arranged according to different basic approaches to culture.

Garbarino, Merwyn S. *Sociocultural Theory in Anthropology: A Short History.* New York: Holt, Rinehart and Winston, 1977.
A short (114-page) chronological consideration of the development of anthropological thought. Evenhanded and clear.

Geertz, Clifford. "Thick Description: Towards an Interpretive Theory of Culture" and "The Impact of the Concept of Culture on the Concept of Man." In *The Interpretation of Cultures.* New York: Basic Books, 1973.
Two classic discussions of culture from a major figure in American anthropology. These works have done much to shape the discourse about culture in anthropology.

Lewontin, Richard. *Human Diversity.* New York: Scientific American Publishing Company, 1982.
Although Lewontin is an evolutionary biologist, not an anthropologist, this work is of great value to the student of anthropology. It is highly anthropological in outlook, particularly in terms of the dialectical holism discussed in this chapter.

Voget, Fred. *A History of Ethnology.* New York: Holt, Rinehart and Winston, 1975.
A massive, thorough, and detailed work. For the student seeking a challenge.

Is a Science of Culture Possible

Hoyt Alverson (Ph.D., Yale University) is Professor of Anthropology at Dartmouth College. His field work has been among the Tswana of Botswana. He is a the author of Mind in the Heart of Darkness *which won both the Herskovits Prize and the University of Chicago Folklore Prize in 1978. Dr. Alverson is presently working on issues in the study of metaphor.*

"Science" as typically understood is based on three assumptions: (1) there is a "real" world with an order that is separate from human interpretations of that order: (2) both the "real" world and human interpretations of the real world independently affect human experience, and (3) the effects of the real world can be represented by logically rigorous but otherwise relatively simple symbolic languages known as *truth conditional* languages.

These assumptions are just that—assumptions: they cannot be proven. They have guided scientific inquiry, and their use has led to models of reality that have been very successful in accounting for human experience. But the success of scientific models is not the same thing as absolute truth, which would depend on proving the assumptions themselves true. Scientists are willing to accept that some models successfully account for experience in the long run because they represent what is real, and, conversely, that other models fail because they misrepresent reality. This is what is meant by "proof" in science.

We can now ask the crucial question: is a science of culture—a science of anthropological nature—a possibility? If we answer yes, we are committed to setting severe limits on what culture—that is, on what being human—may be conceived to be. Regarding the first assumption, culture in general, including its changes, evolution, and particular geographical or historical manifestations, would have to exhibit a determinate structure. With regard to the second assumption, the effects of this "structure of culture" upon human experience would have to be separable from any effects resulting from the biological and cultural processes of perception and cognition. With regard to the third assumption, this structure of culture would have to be represented by a scientific model using a logically rigorous yet simple symbolic language.

For several reasons, many anthropologists argue that the assumptions of science concerning the conditions that reality must meet to be suitable for scientific explanation make a science of culture impossible and paradoxical. (1) The world's cultures are simply too varied and too dependent on environmental and historical contingencies to be reduced to a single structure. (2) It is practically and logically impossible to separate the structure of culture from the biological and cultural processes of perception and cognition, by means of which human beings know anything at all (that is, a species that is defined by culture cannot pry itself away from culture in order to behold it as a spectator). (3) Many anthropologists, and others, claim with good evidence that because of the species-specific endowment of rational thought and language, human beings are genuinely "free," that is, their actions are not determined by specific processes and forces. (Structure, by contrast, is understood to determine acts or events, even if only probabilistically). If the actions of human beings are potentially or actually not determined by outside phenomena, there is no sense in which culture could be reduced simply to structure. Freedom (not to be confused with randomness, chaos, or uncertainty) means simply that other phenomena do not necessarily have even a probabilistic effect on people's actions.

If these objections are well-founded, the most one can hope for in the study of culture, or of any human behavior, is a *phenomenology*—a continuous description or interpretation of what observed culture means to its participants and to its observers, anthropological or otherwise. Any study of what something means presupposes and requires the culture-bound, indeed person-bound, experience of a human subject. Meaning only exists relative to people and experience. The structure that science presupposes is presumed to exist independently of all people and any experience. Those who seek a science of culture are appropriately called "universalists" or "antirelativists." Those who seek a phenomenology of culture are often known as "relativists." A third point of view is that some aspects of culture exhibit structure in the sense set forth here, while other aspects are considered undetermined, free. This "dualist" position will often assert that what people do is structured—determined—but that their thoughts and their ideas about right and wrong are free, or that "the economy obeys laws, but individuals have free will." Such dualism is essentially a confession of ignorance about the limits of determinism and freedom.

Intellectual honesty and the practical demands of research encourage people to choose sides—to be either a relativist, committed to the interpretive view of culture, or a universalist, committed to belief in the existence of structure and the explanation of it. The common-sense, dualist position is not commended by serious thinkers. Its value is largely therapeutic, masking the dissonance that comes from not knowing what to believe.

It should by now be apparent that one's assumptions concerning the existence of structure in culture, or the existence of freedom in human action, determine whether one believes that there can be a science of culture or not. Note that the possibility of developing a science of culture has nothing to do with the use of mathematics, the precision of one's assertions, or the elegance of one's models. If a phenomenon actually has structure, then a science of that phenomenon is at least conceivable. If a phenomenon exhibits freedom and is not ordered, then a science of that phenomenon is inconceivable. The human sciences, including anthropology, have been debating the issue of structure versus freedom in human cultural behavior for the past two hundred years, and no resolution or even consensus has emerged.

Some persuasive models of culture, and of particular cultures, have been proposed, both by those working with scientific, universalist assumptions, and by those working with phenomenological, relativistic assumptions.

To decide which of these approaches is to be preferred, we must have a specific set of criteria for evaluation. Faced with good evidence for the existence of both structure and freedom in human culture, no coherent set of criteria for comparing the success of these alternative models is conceivable. The prediction of future action, for example, is a good criterion for measuring the success of a model that purports to represent structure: it must be irrelevant to measuring the success or failure of a model that purports to describe freedom. For the foreseeable future, and maybe for the rest of time, we may have to be content with models that simply permit us to muddle through.

Hoyt Alverson

CHAPTER 3
Fieldwork

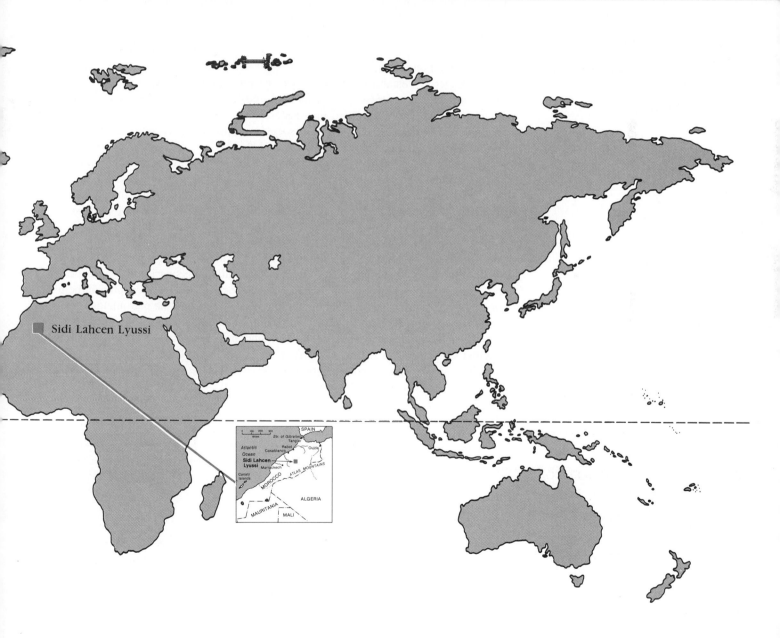

Sidi Lahcen Lyussi

*Lawrence Carpenter is a linguistic anthropologist who has worked for a number of years among the Quichua-speaking indigenous people who live in and around the town of Otavalo, in highland Ecuador. (**See EthnoFile 3.1: Otavalo.**) He has established close ties with a number of the people with whom he has worked, becoming a ritual coparent to their children, participating in weddings and wakes, and in many other ways becoming a semipermanent member of the village to which he returns for a visit nearly every year. But his participation in the life of that village was not originally a foregone conclusion.*

The first time Carpenter was invited to attend a feast in the village itself was early in his first field trip. Traditional feasting among the Indians of highland Ecuador involves heavy consumption of alcoholic beverages. Sometimes the drink is *chicha*, a locally brewed corn beer; other times it is a powerful sugarcane alcohol approaching 100 proof, called *trago* or *aguardiente*. In either case, the object of alcohol consumption is to achieve a state of communion with the spirit world; traditional celebrations cannot be successfully carried out in any other state.

Eager to "establish rapport" with the people whose way of life interested him, Carpenter was pleased to accept the invitation. He ate, drank, and smoked cigarettes with them. Afterward they accompanied him down the mountain to his apartment. His introduction into their society seemed to have gone off smoothly, and he was pleased that he had been accepted so easily.

Some weeks later, when research was well under way, one of the villagers mentioned that first party, reminding Carpenter of everything that had gone on and the way the Indians had accompanied him home. "You know," the Indian added casually, "we had decided ahead of time that if you had not drunk with us, we were going to beat you up. You would have ended up at the bottom of the mountain."

Carpenter was shocked. What he had originally taken as a gesture of acceptance by the Indians had been, for them, nothing of the kind. They had been testing his honesty. They knew that most outsiders, especially missionaries and tax collectors, were always seeking acceptance into Indian society, and would approach them much the way Carpenter had. They resented missionizing and the patronizing interference that seemed to come with it. And so they had devised their test. They knew that missionaries frowned on drinking and smoking cigarettes, so they would see whether Carpenter was willing to drink. If not, they would know that he was really just a missionary or a tax collector in disguise, and they would show him what they thought of his hypocrisy by beating him up.

EthnoFile 3.1
OTAVALO

Region: South America (Andes)

Nation: Ecuador

Population: 45,000 (late 1970s)

Environment: Mountain valleys and uplands, 9,000 feet and above

Livelihood: Agriculture, weaving

Political organization: Villages within national political system

Other: The people are famous as weavers and as textile entrepreneurs; some Otavaleños travel throughout the world selling textiles

Anthropological linguist Lawrence Carpenter drinking *trago* with his Otavalan Indian informants and friends.

Carpenter experienced the kind of delayed shock one often feels after narrowly escaping a serious automobile accident. He had come close not only to losing the opportunity to do research in that community, but also to possibly serious injury. How fortunate that he had not been prevented from drinking alcohol with his hosts for medical reasons, or because he was a recovering alcoholic, or even for personal reasons having nothing to do with religion. None of those reasons for sobriety might have made any difference to his hosts, and he would still have ended up at the foot of the mountain.

A Meeting of Cultural Traditions

In fieldwork—the classical method of anthropological research—shocks of the kind just described are to be expected. Anthropologists use the expression **culture shock** to refer to the jolt that often accompanies an encounter with cultural practices that are unexpected and strange to us. Culture shock is unsettling because it calls into question our previous understanding of the way the world works. At the same time, culture shock creates a new context for learning and discovery. Fieldwork institutionalizes culture shock (Karp and Kendall 1982:262). It deliberately brings together people from different cultural traditions. From their confrontation, fieldwork generates much of what anthropologists can claim to know about people in other societies.

Gathering data by going to live for an extended period in close contact with members of another society is called **participant-observation**. Anthropologists gather data in other ways too. They consult archives and previously published literature relevant to their research topics. Sometimes they even administer questionnaires and psychological tests as part of their fieldwork. But participant-observation, which relies primarily on face-to-face contact with people as they go about their daily lives, was pioneered by anthropologists and remains characteristic

culture shock
the feeling, akin to panic, that develops in people living in an alien society when they realize they cannot understand what is happening around them

participant-observation
the anthropological research method in which researchers live among the people whose culture they are studying, observing them at close range and participating in their lives as much as possible

of anthropology as a discipline. The fieldwork experience of participant-observation is perhaps the best method available to scientists who seek fully to appreciate the nature of culture and the human condition.

The Mechanics of Fieldwork

Fieldwork is the final phase of formal anthropological training. It is also the experience that characterizes and defines the discipline. Most anthropologists hope to be able to return frequently to the field throughout their careers.

During graduate school, beginning anthropologists usually make a final decision about where they wish to do their research and on what topic. This decision may be influenced by where their professors have done research, where they can find societies with particular features of interest to them, their fluency in particular languages, and the current international political climate.

Once the decision has been made, students prepare for their research by learning all they can about the place and people they intend to visit. This means reading history, government documents, ethnographies by other anthropologists who worked among the people in question or their neighbors, and so forth. Preparation may also include specialized language study, although for languages that are not widely spoken, this is sometimes difficult or impossible. The goal is to learn as much as possible about the culture students will enter before they actually arrive in the field. In this way, culture shock can be minimized and time in the field can be put to more efficient use.

Then anthropologists must obtain funding for their research. In the United States, this generally requires submitting grant proposals to private foundations or government agencies. Research proposals are evaluated competitively. They are written for an audience of other anthropologists, and they must address issues of concern to the discipline.

If funding is granted, the anthropologist must then get permission to carry out research in the geographical region chosen. For research outside the United States, this means contacting the government of the country where the research site is located, or a research center or local university, or both. If the research project is approved, the researcher will establish professional ties with local scholars and institutions while the project is under way. In many countries, such professional affiliation is required by law. Anthropologists view this affiliation as a significant part of their fieldwork. Colleagues at the appropriate institution can provide useful contacts, information, and shoptalk. Anthropologists are also concerned about what they can give to the people and the nation hosting them. The least they can do is share their work with host colleagues. Once affiliation is granted, the appropriate visa must be obtained. This accomplished, the anthropologist is ready to leave for the field.

Living conditions in the field depend on the nature of the host society. The method of participant-observation requires living as closely as possible to the people whose culture you are studying. Anthropologists who work among remote peoples in jungles, deserts, or tundra need to bring along their own living quarters: tents, bedding, cooking equipment, food supplies. Research funding is not designed to support luxurious living. But many anthropologists are surprised to discover how many amenities they can happily live without.

EthnoFile 3.2
BLACKSTON

Region: North America

Nation: United States

Population: 100,000

Environment: Urban ghetto

Livelihood: Low-paying full-time and temporary jobs, welfare

Political organization: Lowest level in a modern nation-state

Other: This is an anonymous northern city; Blackston is not its real name

---

Living conditions in the field can themselves provide major insights into the culture under study. This is powerfully illustrated by the experiences of Charles and Bettylou Valentine, whose field site was a poor neighborhood they called Blackston, located in a large city in the northern United States (C. Valentine 1978:5). *(See EthnoFile 3.2: Blackston.)* The Valentines lived for the last field year on one-quarter of their regular income; during the final six months, they matched their income to that of welfare families.

> *For five years we inhabited the same decrepit rat- and roach-infested buildings as everyone else, lived on the same poor quality food at inflated prices, trusted our health and our son's schooling to the same inferior institutions, suffered the same brutality and intimidation from the police, and like others made the best of it by some combination of endurance, escapism, and fighting back. Like the dwellings of our neighbors, our home went up in flames several times, including one disaster caused by the carelessness or ill will of the city's "firefighters." For several cold months we lived and worked in one room without heat other than what a cooking stove could provide, without hot water or windows, and with only one light bulb (1978:5).*

Not all field sites offer such a stark contrast to the middle-class backgrounds of many fieldworkers, and indeed some can be almost luxurious. But physical and mental dislocation and stress can be expected anywhere. People from temperate climates who find themselves in the tropics have to adjust to the heat; workers in the Arctic have to adjust to the cold. In hot climates especially, European or American anthropologists encounter plants, animals, insects and diseases (e.g., malaria) with which they have had no previous experience. In any climate, fieldworkers need to adjust to local water and food.

In addition, there are the cultural differences—which is why they came. Yet the immensity of what they are getting into by coming is difficult for them to anticipate. Initially, just getting through the day, finding a place to stay and food to eat, may seem an enormous accomplishment—but there is also supposed to be data to gather, research to do!

Early in their stay, it is not uncommon for fieldworkers to feel that the adjustments required may be too great. With time, however, they discover that the great process of human survival begins to assert itself: they begin to adapt. The

Anthropologists carry out their research in all kinds of environments. Bettylou and Charles Valentine lived for five years in the ghetto of a large city in the northern United States.

rhythms of daily activity become familiar. Their use of the local language improves. Faces of the local inhabitants become faces of neighbors who greet them on the village paths. And, incredibly, the time comes when they find they are able to turn their attention to the research questions that motivated the undertaking in the first place.

Scientific Fieldwork?

When anthropology began to take on its own identity as an intellectual discipline during the nineteenth century, it aspired to be "scientific." Anthropology still aims to be scientific in its study of human nature, human society, and human history, but we have learned that there is more than one way of understanding "being scientific." In the twentieth century, scientists and philosophers have grown increasingly aware that the traditional "scientific method," based on the success of the physical sciences, is only one way of doing science. Many have begun to question the assumptions on which that traditional scientific method is based. This is true for physics, chemistry, and biology, as well as for the social sciences. It means that attempts to do anthropology based on the traditional way of doing physical science must also be questioned.

The Positivist Approach

The traditional way of doing physical science, which early social scientists tried to imitate, is now often called *positivistic science*. Its proponents based their view of science on a set of principles most fully set out in the writings of a group of influential thinkers known as positivists. One such thinker was Auguste Comte, a nineteenth-century sociologist, who coined the term positive philosophy. The others were a group of philosophers and mathematicians known as the Vienna Circle, who were active in the second and third decades of the twentieth century. They called themselves logical positivists (Giddens 1978:237).

The terms positivist and positivism have come to be used more widely in Western scientific and philosophical circles. Today, **positivism** is a label for a particular way of looking at the world, and a particular set of proposals for studying the world scientifically. Positivists hold that reality can be known through the five senses. For them, that reality is material, and scientific explanations concerning that reality must be testable against sensory experience.

Positivists also believe that a single scientific method can be used to investigate any domain of reality, whether it be planetary motion or chemical reactions or human life. Their hope is that all scientific knowledge will ultimately be unified.

In addition, positivists believe that facts and values are separate from each other. Facts relate to the nature of physical, material reality: what *is*. Values, by contrast, are nothing more than speculation about what *ought to be*. Thus, scientific research into subatomic structure, genetic engineering, in vitro fertilization, or human sexual response must be viewed equally as a disinterested quest for knowledge. This quest cannot be compromised because it offends some people's moral or political sensibilities. Truth remains the truth, whether people like it or not, whether it conforms to their idea of what is good and proper or not.

The goal of the positivist program was to produce **objective knowledge**, knowledge about reality that is true for all people in all times and places. Positivist

positivism
the position that reality is material and that scientific explanations of reality must be testable against sensory experience. Positivism claims that a single scientific method can be used to investigate all domains of reality, including human life. Positivism distinguishes facts from values, focuses on facts alone, and aims to produce objective knowledge about reality that is true for all people in all times and places

objective knowledge
knowledge about reality that is true for all people in all times and places

science was viewed as the route to that objective knowledge, providing theories that are true because they describe the way the world is, independent of its meaning for human groups. For the positivist, there is a reality, and science can lay it bare. As you may have deduced, based on the discussion in chapter 2, positivism is one kind of materialist reductionism.

Applying Positivist Methods to Anthropology

What happens when positivist principles are used to guide scientific investigation in anthropology? Since anthropological research is carried out in fieldwork, a positivist approach will affect the way field research is done. For the positivist, the prototypical research scenario involves a physical scientist in a laboratory. This prototype creates obstacles for those who would study human life as it is lived in a natural setting.

Early anthropologists were aware of these obstacles, and they tried to devise ways to get around them. Their first step was to try to approximate lab conditions by testing their hypotheses in a series of different cultural settings. These settings were carefully selected to exhibit naturally the same range of variation that a laboratory scientist could create artificially. As a result, the field could be seen as a "living laboratory." Each research setting would correspond to a separate experimental situation. This is called the method of *controlled comparison*. Margaret Mead used this method in the 1930s, when she studied four societies in an attempt to discover the range and causes of gender roles.

The next step was to record the data. For positivists, the only reality is material reality perceived through the senses. Therefore, the anthropologist's observations had to be of material behavior or the material products of such behavior, which can be seen or heard, smelled, tasted, or touched. Observations would include how people move their bodies in space and the actions they perform, what they say (verbal behavior), the objects they make and use, the smell and taste of their food, and

Margaret Mead, shown here with one of her informants, carried out comparative research in several different societies.

so on. All the information thus received through the senses had to be recorded objectively and dispassionately.

The final step was to formulate an explanation for the behavior that had been so carefully observed and recorded. To be faithful to positivistic principles, this explanation had to avoid any references to God or fate or mind. Material explanations had to be sought to account for material behavior.

Positivistically inclined anthropologists were encouraged by the enormous successes that the physical sciences had attained by following these principles. They were convinced that a similar commitment on their part would help them unlock the secrets of human social life. In fact, a great deal was learned by fieldworkers committed to the positivistic view of science in anthropology. Research carried out from the middle of the nineteenth century through the middle of the twentieth century was clearly superior to much of the slipshod, impressionistic writing on other cultures that preceded it. For decades, anthropologists following this research program traveled into the remote corners of the world. They recorded as accurately as they could the ways of life of peoples their contemporaries had neither heard of nor cared to know. Their research was systematic, accurate, and sometimes insensitive.

How could scientists be accused of insensitivity? Recall that positivist scientists regard the behavior of human beings as no different from the behavior of rocks or molecules, which have no thoughts or feelings, no freedom or dignity. Anthropologists can be charged with being insensitive to the humanity of their research subjects when their positivistic reports treat human beings as if they, too, lacked thoughts, feelings, dignity, the freedom to choose. We must emphasize that anthropologists often developed close personal ties to the people whose lives they studied. And anthropologists often became advocates for these people, intervening on their behalf with the government, for example. But in their books and articles, those same anthropologists felt compelled to write as though they had been invisible in the village, recording and analyzing data objectively, like machines, with no human connection to the "subjects."

To the positivist, human consciousness is simply an illusion. It is a concept invented to stand for material processes that are internal to human beings and that nonscientists cannot understand. Rocks and molecules might have minds and consciousness and as a result thoughts and feelings, but their inner lives are not accessible to scientific measurement. Why should scientists assume that it is any easier to measure the inner life of human organisms? This response has been offered by positivistic social scientists to the charge of insensitivity. It is perfectly in keeping with positivistic principles, specifically the separation of fact and value. Thoughts and especially feelings, particularly hurt feelings, have to do with values, such as human freedom and human dignity, which have presumably been violated. Positivistic science has nothing to do with values, apart from discovering what a people's values are. Its findings carry no value implications.

The suggestion of insensitivity is nevertheless troubling, for the subject matter of the social sciences differs in one major respect from the subject matter of all the physical sciences: It involves human beings who belong to the same species (and possibly to the same society) as the scientists themselves. Scientists experience their own inner consciousness, have their own thoughts and feelings, and are often more concerned than most people with their own freedom and dignity. If the subjects of their study are also human beings, how can they justify denying to those human subjects the same "inner life" they claim for themselves?

Many anthropologists have striven mightily to think of their informants as objects rather than as human beings. They have placed primary emphasis on behavior, regarding even people's own theories and explanations of their actions as simply more verbal behavior to be analyzed later. They have proceeded on the assumption that complete objectivity is possible. In the context of fieldwork, such objectivity requires attempting "to negate or lose all traces of [their] culture so that someone else's culture can be studied" (Myerhoff and Ruby 1982:25). They have done their research assuming that their presence in the community, while perhaps a novelty at first, will go unnoticed as soon as they immerse themselves in the local culture and become part of the local community. Perhaps above all, they have been confident that the behaviors they observe and record are objective samples of reality, each carrying its own meaning within it. Patient scientific analysis will reveal that each behavior speaks for itself.

Generations of anthropologists have claimed to have carried out fieldwork in this spirit. They have revealed a great deal that was unknown and have added profoundly to our knowledge of the range of human possibilities. But we can ask two questions of them. First, is this knowledge based on a pure sample of reality? And second, did they obtain this knowledge through objective observation and dispassionate analysis? Increasing numbers of anthropologists are coming to answer no to both questions.

The Reliability of Positivist Fieldwork

Let us examine each of these questions in turn.

Is the knowledge gained through positivistic fieldwork based on a pure sample of reality? In answer to this first question, positivists argue that we can trust the evidence of our senses. Sight, touch, sound, smell, and taste put us into direct contact with reality. The information conveyed to our brains by our senses therefore constitutes a direct sample of reality. To the extent that observations through our senses are objective, undistorted by bias, the evidence of our senses will constitute pure samples of reality. For positivist observers, the world is as it appears to be. Yet if the sensory impressions conveyed to our brains are complex or ambiguous, our decision about the world's true state of affairs will depend on the assumptions we make about the way the world works.

Mental activity completely divorced from any contact with sensory experience can lead one astray, but the same is true for sensory experience completely divorced from mental reflection. Neither mental activity nor sensory experience takes place in isolation from the other. Each shapes the other. Positivists have seen this mutual shaping as contamination and have tried to devise ways of purifying experience to eliminate it. But in attempting to escape distortion, this approach distorts human experience to a far greater degree. To the extent that it misunderstands the nature of human experience, it will produce knowledge that is defective. In neither case can it be claimed that sensory knowledge is based on a "pure sample of reality."

Have positivist fieldworkers obtained their knowledge through objective observation and dispassionate analysis? On the basis of the preceding discussion, the answer to this second question must be no. This is particularly the case if the sensory signals observed and analyzed are ambiguous. Interpretations of ambiguous signals are inevitably influenced by assumptions about the way the world works. Thus, the particular assumptions of positivist science must have contributed to the creation of the knowledge that positivist fieldworkers offer as a result of their labors. Different observers, working from different assumptions, would have produced different knowledge.

It is absurd to conclude that all knowledge is therefore contaminated or distorted and thus not knowledge at all. Clearly, much of what we call knowledge serves us well, and is not based on total falsehood. But this is not the same as saying that all knowledge is therefore completely true, objectively true, for everyone in all times and places. There are many ways of understanding the world, and each embodies some truth but none is immune to correction. Put another way, all knowledge is a product of the dialectic between observation and reflection. Our understanding of reality is based on the aspects of the wider world that we pay attention to. On the one hand, what we pay attention to is guided by the assumptions we make about the world, and no observation can be made without some set of assumptions that frame the observation. On the other hand, we are open creatures. We may detect (or someone else may point out to us) signals in the wider world that call into question our traditional assumptions.

Science was born when some members of our society decided to pay systematic attention to material signals that tended to be downplayed or ignored by the dominant religious outlook. As scientists increased their experience with these previously unknown phenomena, they began to develop a new set of assumptions about the way the world worked. The history of science in our own culture, particularly its struggle with religion, shows vividly that cultures offer alternatives. Neither science nor religion is more truly Western than the other. Historically, each has codetermined the other. It is this codetermination—the dialogue between Athens and Jerusalem—that has made Western culture distinctive.

Thus, positivism encourages us to pay attention to certain kinds of material behavior. This emphasis has without question brought much truth to light. But only dialogue with alternative points of view can put positivistic truth in proper perspective. The dialogue may be internal to our own culture, but the potential for enrichment increases enormously when we enter into dialogue with members of another culture.

The Reflexive Approach

All this means that we must carefully reexamine exactly what anthropologists have been up to. If they cannot be and never were objective, dispassionate observers, what have they been doing? Barbara Myerhoff and Jay Ruby suggest that

> *the more the ethnographer attempts to fulfill a scientific obligation to report on methods, the more he or she must acknowledge that his or her own behavior and persona in the field are data. Statements on method then begin to appear to be more personal, subjective, biased, involved and culture bound; in other words,* the more scientific anthropologists try to be, by revealing their methods, the less scientific they appear to be. *(1982:26)*

Things are not always what they appear to be. Paradoxically, from the positivist point of view, doing good science about human beings seems to require more than just becoming involved, in human terms, with our informants. It also requires viewing this involvement not as a necessary evil, but as central to our method. If the "objects" of anthropological investigation are actually "subjects" (i.e., human beings like ourselves), then scientific accuracy demands that we treat these objects of study as if they really were human beings. "The subject matter of social studies are persons who use language, construct meanings, follow rules, give accounts of their action—beings, in short, who have considerable insight into their own nature. Such powers cannot justifiably be excluded from any adequate science of social life" (Crick 1976:90).

Field methods and knowledge are thus intimately connected. The data that the fieldworker brings back from the field cannot be separated from the fieldwork experience itself. But what is the fieldwork experience? Anthropology involves a person studying other persons, subjects studying other subjects. If this is the case, is fieldwork just one person's subjective impressions of other people? No, because the fieldwork experience is a *dialogue*, not a solitary activity. A human chemist is alone with nonhuman chemicals, but the human anthropologist in the field is surrounded by other human beings. Moreover, not only are anthropologists trying to figure out the natives, the natives are also trying to figure out the anthropologists. So, fieldwork is a series of very human encounters between human beings. In addition, anthropologists must remember that they are people, too. Understanding the way of life of another human society "requires interpretation, imagination, insight, perceptivity, human sympathy, humility, and a whole series of qualities—human qualities. It requires, fundamentally, that the student be himself or herself a human person" (Smith 1982:68).

To gather data about a culture, anthropologists are obliged to interact closely with the sources of that data: their informants. As a result, field data are not subjective, but *intersubjective*. That is, they are the product of long dialogues between researcher and informant. These dialogues are often patient and painstaking collaborative attempts to sort things out, to piece things together. When successful, the outcome is a new understanding of the world that both anthropologist and informant can share.

Recognizing the humanity of one's informants in this way has nothing to do with trying, through sheer imagination, to reproduce the inner psychological states of those informants—which is what positivists have often accused their critics of trying to do. Such an imaginative effort, assuming it is possible, is solitary, whereas fieldwork is a dialogue. The focus of fieldwork is the range of **intersubjective meanings** that informants share. Fieldworkers can come to understand these meanings by entering into dialogue and practical activity with their informants. The intersubjective meanings that guide informants are public, not private; they create "the social matrix in which individuals find themselves and act" (Dallmayr and McCarthy 1977:80). To make these meanings explicit, however, anthropologist and informant together must occasionally step back from the ordinary flow of daily life and examine it critically. They must think about the way members of the culture normally think about their lives. This "thinking about thinking" is known as **reflexivity**, and the anthropological fieldwork experience can thus be considered a reflexive experience.

intersubjective meanings
the shared, public symbolic systems of a culture

reflexivity
critical thinking about the way one thinks; reflection on one's own experience

Both anthropologists and their informants have important reflexive roles to play in the fieldwork that generates anthropological knowledge. Anthropological theory has come to acknowledge this reflexivity, recognizing it as the least distorting path to knowledge about human social life. The best ethnography has always been reflexive, whether it was done in 1935 or 1985 and whether the ethnographers realized this explicitly. To put it another way, "being reflexive is virtually synonymous with being scientific" (Myerhoff and Ruby 1982:28).

Anthropology's Commitment to Reflexivity

Reflexivity has been defined as thinking about thinking. It can also be defined as self-consciousness—that is, consciousness of one's own consciousness, awareness of one's own awareness. A capacity for reflexivity seems to be part of human nature. Nevertheless, it appears that reflexive consciousness requires cultivation. After all, most people in most societies at most times take the world they know for granted. We call this uncritical acceptance of the rightness of one's own tradition ethnocentrism. However, the anthropological concept of ethnocentrism is a reflexive concept, a product of anthropological thinking (theorizing) about the way people ordinarily think. Anthropologists cultivate reflexivity when they refuse to take their own customary, commonsense opinions at face value. This is especially the case when they subject customary scientific thought to close critical analysis.

The commitment to reflexivity has had far-reaching implications for the ways anthropologists carry out their research. It makes anthropologists scientifically obligated to make public the way in which they gather data. Fieldworkers do not merely participate and observe and let it go at that. They must also reflect on the nature and extent of that participation and observation and reveal to others (notably those who read what anthropologists write) the results of this reflection.

Some anthropologists have argued that they must also share their conclusions with their informants, and even include their informants' reflections on those conclusions in their published ethnographies. Some have even published with informants as coauthors. This may appear to be reflexivity with a vengeance: anthropologists thinking about how their informants think, thinking about the way they think about the way their informants think, asking their informants to think about the way a particular anthropologist thinks about the way anthropologists in general think about how their informants think. But this kind of mutual reflexivity is at the heart of anthropological knowledge.

Let us look at one anthropological attempt to maximize reflexivity in a published ethnography. Charles Valentine (1978:7–8) notes that his wife, Bettylou Valentine, persuaded several of her informants to comment on her manuscript before publication. She visited them for lengthy discussions and found that, in general, they agreed with her conclusions. Some were worried that readers of her book might recognize who they were, however, so she made an effort to further disguise their identities. In the published volume, Bettylou Valentine states her own conclusions, based on her own research and analysis. She also allows her informants a voice, permitting them, in a final chapter, to state where and why they disagree with her. Any reader of this book is not left with some finished, absolute version of the truth. Valentine's ethnography presents a vivid experience of the open-endedness of the dialogue between anthropologist and informant. It makes clear the inability to finalize any single interpretation of human experience.

The Human Experience of Fieldwork

Fieldwork is human experience. It involves entering the intersubjective world of one's informants and making that world, in part, one's own. The radical consequence of this is that one's own world is both enlarged and changed. Reflecting on these changes, in turn, alters one's images of oneself and one's society. And there is no going back.

Fieldwork requires anthropologists to open themselves to new experiences and to the possibility of change. This may well be a thrilling, joyful experience, but it can also be troubling and depressing—in fact, it will be all these things. "Human learning [is] an exploration of what man as such is, what he and she have been, what they may be. . . . The persons (or groups) who enter on it are therefore exposing their actual selves to their potential selves" (Smith 1982:77). Scientists who believe they know the path to objective truth find experiences that might weaken their faith to be troubling. For positivists, "in principle, it is possible to learn techniques without ceasing to be basically the kind of person that one was before; to come out of the learning process at heart as one went in" (ibid.: 76). Yet anthropological fieldwork institutionalizes vulnerability to self-reflection as it institutionalizes culture shock. If anthropologists leave the field unchanged, they may well have missed the fieldwork experience itself.

The recognition that our informants are our potential selves can be unnerving. But if we steady our nerves and face this possibility, we may discover that our appreciation of the human condition has deepened. Veteran anthropologist Robert Murphy says, "To the extent that we capitalize on this merger of subject and object, we can say that our fieldwork is 'reflexive.' Today's graduate students have assimilated this lesson well, and they are doing ethnographic research far superior to that done by their mentors" (1986:228). This achievement is humbling. Particularly for anthropologists steeped in Western ethnocentrism, it may seem humiliating to admit that a hunter or gatherer can teach them something new and important about life, something of which their own civilization was ignorant. But facing this possibility, and acknowledging it, can free us to grow.

The Dialectic of Fieldwork: Interpretation and Translation

Fieldwork is a risky business. Fieldworkers not only risk offending their informants by misunderstanding their way of life. They also must face the shock of the unfamiliar and their own vulnerability. Indeed, they must embrace this shock and cultivate this vulnerability if they are to achieve any kind of meaningful understanding of their informants' culture.

In the beginning, fieldworkers can be reassured by some of the insights that anthropological training has provided. Basic to these is the working assumption of *panhuman rationality*. Over one hundred years of research in physical anthropology have demonstrated that all human beings are members of the same biological species. This means that with regard to such human potentialities as intelligence, we should expect to find the same range of variation in all human groups. We can therefore resist ethnocentric impulses by recalling "that if what we observe appears to be odd or irrational, it is probably because we do not understand it and not because it is a product of a 'savage' culture in which such nonsense is to be expected" (Greenwood and Stini 1977:185).

Interpreting Actions and Ideas

The problem becomes how to make sense of what we observe. We must interpret our observations. But what exactly does **interpretation** involve? Jean Paul Dumont offers the following suggestion:

> *Interpretation . . . can refer to three rather different matters: an oral recitation, a reasonable explanation, and a translation from another language. . . . In all three cases, something foreign, strange, separated in time, space or experience is made familiar, present, comprehensible: something requiring representation, explanation or translation is somehow*

interpretation
the process by which something foreign, strange, separated in time, space, or experience is made familiar, present, comprehensible

"brought to understanding"—is interpreted. (1978:4, quoting Palmer 1969:14)

How does one go about interpreting the actions and ideas of other human beings? We cannot treat human subjects as if they were no different from molecules in a test tube. We need a form of interpretation that does not turn our informants into objects. That is, we need a form of interpretation based on reflexivity rather than objectivity. Paul Rabinow suggested that what we require has already been set forth in the philosophy of the French thinker Paul Ricoeur:

> *Following Ricoeur, I define the problem of hermeneutics (which is simply Greek for "interpretation") as "the comprehension of self by the detour of the comprehension of the other." It is vital to stress that this is not psychology of any sort. . . . The self being discussed is perfectly public. . . . [It is] the culturally mediated and historically situated self which finds itself in a continuously changing world of meaning. (1977:5–6)*

For the anthropologist in the field, then, interpretation becomes a task of coming to comprehend the *cultural self* by the detour of comprehending the *cultural other*. The self being discussed is public because it is intersubjectively constructed, using elements drawn from the cultural systems of anthropologist and informant alike. As we come to grasp the meaning of the other's cultural self, we simultaneously learn something of the meaning of our own cultural identity.

Learning to understand what makes other people tick may seem plausible, as long as we can claim to be from the same culture. After all, members of the same culture can be presumed to share at least some of the same intersubjective symbolic language. They have therefore at least a small foundation on which to build. But the anthropologist in the field and his or her informants cannot be assumed to share such a language. On what can they build their intersubjective understanding? The gulf between self and other may seem unbridgeable. Yet anthropologist and informant engaged in participant-observation do share something: the fieldwork situation itself.

Anthropologist and informant find themselves in physical proximity, observing and discussing the same material activities. At first, they may talk past one another, as each describes these activities from a different perspective, using a different language. Recall, however, that all cultures and languages are open enough to entertain a variety of points of view and a variety of ways of talking about them. Continued discussion allows anthropologist and informant to search for areas of intersection in possible ways of understanding and describing the same strip of behavior. Any intersection, however small, can form the foundation on which anthropologist and informant may then build a *new* intersubjective symbolic language. This process of building a bridge of understanding between self and other is what Rabinow referred to as "the dialectic of fieldwork" (1977:39).

The Dialectical Process ▬▬▬▬

Both fieldworker and informant begin with little or nothing in the way of shared experience that could allow them to "figure one another out" with any accuracy. But if they are motivated to make sense of one another and willing to work together, steps toward understanding and valid interpretation—toward recognition—can be made.

For example, traditional fieldwork often begins with collecting data on kinship relations in the host society. A trained anthropologist comes to the field with certain ideas about kinship in mind. These ideas derive in part from the anthropologist's own experience of kinship in his or her own culture. They are also based on ideas about kinship that the anthropologist has taken from professional research into the subject. As the fieldworker begins to ask kinship questions of informants, he or she may discover that the informants have no word in their language that accurately conveys the range of meaning carried by the anthropological term *kinship*. This does not mean that all is lost. At this point, successful fieldwork seems to involve entry into the dialectic process of interpretation and translation.

The dialectic process works something like this. The anthropologist poses a question about kinship, using whatever term in the informants' language comes closest to it in meaning. The informants do their best to interpret the anthropologist's question in a way that makes sense to them. That is, each informant is required to exercise reflexivity, thinking about the way members of his or her society think about a certain domain of experience. Having formulated an answer, the informant responds to the anthropologist's question in terms that he or she thinks the anthropologist will understand. Now it is the anthropologist's turn to interpret this response, to decide whether it carries the kind of information the anthropologist was looking for.

Translating

In the dialectic of fieldwork, both anthropologist and informant are active agents. Each is engaged in trying to decipher the other's intent. If there is goodwill on the part of both, each is also trying to provide responses to the other that the other can make sense of. As more than one anthropologist has remarked (e.g., Rabinow 1977; Crick 1976:104), anthropological fieldwork is **translation**. Moreover, the informant is just as actively engaged in translation as is the anthropologist. As time passes and the partners in this effort learn from their mistakes and successes, their ability to communicate increases. Each learns more about the other; the anthropologist gains skill at asking questions that make sense to the informant, and the informant becomes more skilled at answering those questions in terms that are relevant to the anthropologist. The validity of this ongoing translation is anchored in the ongoing cultural activities in which both anthropologist and informant are participant-observers.

translation
in anthropological fieldwork, learning to talk about one culture using the terms that will make it comprehensible to members of another culture

The Dialectic between Self and Other

Out of this mutual translational activity comes knowledge about the informant's culture that is meaningful to both anthropologist and informant. This is new knowledge. And this is what dialectical holism is all about: the whole (i.e., knowledge about the culture) is more than the sum of its parts (i.e., the anthropologist's knowledge and the informant's knowledge). Knowledge of the culture arises out of the collaboration of anthropologist and informant. They create a world, usually thin and fragile, of common understandings and experiences.

It is possible to argue that all learning about another human being is the result of a dialogue between self and other. We have suggested that informants are equally involved in this dialogue and may end up learning as much or more about anthropologists as anthropologists learn about them. But it is important to emphasize that in field situations, the dialogue is initiated by anthropologists. Anthropologists come to the field with their own sets of questions, which are determined not by the field situation but by the discipline of anthropology itself (see Karp and Kendall 1982:254). Furthermore, when anthropologists are finished, they are free to break off dialogue with informants and resume discussions with fellow professionals. The only links between the first and second dialogues are the anthropologists themselves. Professional colleagues will rely on fieldworkers to speak for their informants in a dialogue from which informants traditionally have been excluded. Fieldwork therefore involves differences of power, and places a heavy burden of responsibility upon researchers.

Communication in Fieldwork: Constructing Meaning

Meaning in culture is never fully given ahead of time. Rather it is constructed by those who use it, negotiated between them, sometimes with great difficulty. Cultural meaning is never self-evident. Put another way, human experience is ambiguous. This is often true even for the highly patterned experience that human beings have as a result of culture. Events may be seen as patterned and coherent by one observer, chaotic and pointless by another, even if they are recognized as the same events by both observers. Even if both observers see a pattern to their experiences, they may not see the same pattern. Sometimes both observers see the same pattern, but disagree on its significance. Human beings must make an effort not only to make sense of their ambiguous experiences for themselves, but also to communicate about them with other people whose perspective may be vastly different.

Nowhere is the problematic nature of human communication more obvious than in anthropological fieldwork. Establishing rapport with informants has always been seen as an indispensable first step. Publicly, however, anthropologists have come to recognize that there are no foolproof formulas that will automatically get your potential informants to accept you. The appearance of a fieldworker in their midst is a disruptive event that changes the world of informants. How this disruption is managed may determine whether or not fieldwork will continue. It can also lead to deepened insight into the ways in which the cultures of both anthropologist and informant are put together.

In most non-Western societies, the arrival of a fieldworking anthropologist has no precedent. Yet most groups are able to cope with this event in one way or another. For example, the foreign stranger may be adopted into the local kinship network. Once this has happened, the context for all future events in the community has been altered. The stranger's status has been changed. It will never again be true that there is no tradition among the informants for handling anthropologists, no context in which anthropologists make sense. A makeshift attempt at coping with out-of-the-ordinary events becomes a precedent. And the precedent becomes a point of reference, a contextual rule—if only a rule of thumb—to be applied again when events bring other foreign strangers into their midst.

Jean Briggs is an anthropologist who was "adopted" by a family of informants. Briggs worked among the Utkuhikhalingmiut (Utku, for short), an Inuit (Eskimo) group in Alaska. *(See EthnoFile 3.3: Utkuhikhalingmiut)*. She sets out

EthnoFile 3.3
UTKUHIKHALINGMIUT
(Utku Inuit)

Region: North America

Nation: Canada (Northwest Territories)

Population: 35

Environment: Tundra

Livelihood: Nomadic fishing, hunting, gathering

Political organization: Communal

Other: The number of visits to this area by North American sportsmen is increasing; the people prefer to be called Inuit rather than Eskimo

the series of steps her informants took in their attempts to figure her out, once she took on the role of "daughter" in the home of her new "father," Inuttiaq, and "mother," Allaq: "From the moment that the adoption was settled, I was 'Inuttiaq's daughter' in the camp. [They] drilled me in the use of kin terms appropriate to my position, just as they drilled [Inuttiaq's] three-year-old daughter, who was learning to speak" (Briggs 1980:46). The context of their interactions had clearly changed as a result of the adoption, and Briggs's family had new expectations both of Briggs and of themselves: "Allaq, and especially Inuttiaq . . . more and more attempted to assimilate me into a proper adult parent-daughter relationship. I was expected to help with the household work . . . and I was expected to obey unquestioningly when Inuttiaq told me to do something. . . . Inevitably, conflicts, covert but pervasive, developed" (ibid.: 47).

Here is one of the "ruptures in communication" discussed earlier. Briggs began to sense that all was not as it should be, and she found herself taking on a reflexive stance. She began to realize that part of the problem had to do with differences between her ideas of how parents ought to relate to their daughters and Utku beliefs on these matters. Another part of the problem related to contradictions she experienced between her role as daughter and her role as anthropologist. The dialectic of fieldwork brought sharply to awareness—aided in the construction of—her understanding of the meanings of "daughter" and "anthropologist" in her own culture. Perhaps only in a context like that of fieldwork would any of us be forced, by the necessities of everyday life, to spell out for ourselves exactly what our own cultural background consists of.

Briggs was not the only person who had to be reflexive. Her Utku informants were forced to think again about the way they had been dealing with her since her arrival. As she was able to reconstruct it, their understanding of her went through three stages. At first, her informants thought she was strange, anomalous. After her adoption, they saw her as educable. But when the communication breakdown occurred, they concluded that she was "uneducable in important ways . . . a defective person" (Briggs 1980:60–61). Either her informants could find no further way of making clear what was expected of her, or else it became obvious to them that she was unwilling to do what she knew they expected of her. This conclusion on their part might have meant the end of Briggs's fieldwork, were it not for the timely intervention of a third party. An Utku woman who knew both Briggs and her adoptive family was able successfully to explain to Briggs's informants the aspects of her behavior that had been most distressing.

The Effect of Fieldwork on Informants

Because informants play active roles in the fieldwork enterprise, it is appropriate to discuss the role of informant in more detail. Many fieldworkers have long considered *informant* to be a term of respect for those who agree to try to explain their way of life to an anthropologist. Unfortunately, the term has come to have a sinister connotation in recent years, as law enforcement professionals have used it to describe those who betray their partners in crime. Rabinow observes: "The present somewhat nasty connotations of the word do apply at times, but so does its older root sense 'to give form to, to be the formative principle of, to animate.'. . . The informant gives external form to his own experiences, by presenting them to meet the anthropologist's questions, to the extent that he can interpret them" (1977:153).

Strictly speaking, any member of the culture with whom the anthropologist speaks or interacts can be considered an informant. But most fieldworkers soon discover that some informants seem more interested in the anthropologist's work and better able to understand what he or she is trying to accomplish than do others. According to Rabinow, these "key informants" have "the ability to explain even the simplest and [to them] most obvious things in a variety of ways." The best informants not only are patient and intelligent, but also have "an imaginative ability to objectify [their] own culture for a foreigner, so as to present it in a number of ways" (Rabinow 1977:95).

Informants tend to be somewhat marginal to their own communities. They are likely to be as curious about the anthropologist's way of life as he or she is about their way of life. This is the unsettling part of informant-anthropologist interactions: the feeling that one's informants are shrewder than oneself, more aware, and in greater control of what is going on. Again, it is only ethnocentrism that prevents us from expecting this, even among people with primitive technology. After all, our informants are human beings, and as Malcolm Crick reminds us, "to be a person requires the exercise of considerable anthropological skills. It requires self-understanding, communicative ability, and other-understanding. Thus it is that in all the social sciences those being investigated possess exactly the same powers as those doing the investigating" (1976:104).

Fieldwork changes both the anthropologist and the informants. What kinds of effects can the fieldwork experience have on informants? Anthropologists have not always been able to report on this. In some cases, the effects of fieldwork on informants cannot be assessed until long after the anthropologist has returned home. In other cases, it becomes clear in the course of fieldwork that the anthropologist's presence and questions have made the informants aware of their own cultural selves in new ways that are both surprising and uncomfortable.

As he reflected on his own fieldwork in Morocco, Rabinow recalled some cases in which his informants' new reflexivity led to unanticipated consequences. One key informant, Malik, among other tasks, helped Rabinow compile a list of landholdings and other possessions of the villagers of Sidi Lahcen Lyussi. *(See EthnoFile 3.4: Sidi Lahcen Lyussi.)* As a first step in tracing the economic status of the middle stratum in society, Rabinow suggested that Malik list his own possessions, since Malik appeared to be neither rich nor poor. "As we began to make a detailed list of his possessions, he became touchy and defensive. . . . It was clear that he was not as impoverished as he had portrayed himself. . . . This was confusing and troubling for him. . . . Malik began to see that there was a disparity be-

EthnoFile 3.4
Sidi Lahcen Lyussi

Region: North Africa

Nation: Morocco

Population: 900

Environment: Village in
Middle Atlas Mountains

Livelihood: Farming, some
stock raising

Political Organization:
Village in modern nation-state

Other: This village serves as a
religious center associated with
the saint after whom it is named

tween his self-image and my classification system. The emergence of this 'hard' data before his eyes and through his own efforts was highly disconcerting for him." (Rabinow 1977:117–18).

Malik's easy understanding of himself and his world had been disrupted, and he could not ignore the disruption. He would either have to change his self-image or find some way to assimilate this new information about himself into the old self-image. The objectification of experience that had been easy for him when others were concerned now became much more difficult. In the end Malik concluded that he was not well-off. He was able to do this by arguing that wealth lay not in material possessions alone. Although he might be rich in material goods, his son's health was bad, his own father was dead, he was responsible for his mother and unmarried brothers, and he had to be constantly vigilant in order to prevent his uncle from stealing his land. He was indeed not well-to-do, as he had always known, but his experiences with Rabinow had forced him to define his situation in a new way in order to maintain his old self-image (ibid.: 117–19).

Bettylou Valentine's determination to acknowledge the point of view of her informants in Blackston was made clear from the outset. *(See EthnoFile 3.2. Blackston.)* Yet before the publication of her ethnography, she discovered that some

A Moroccan village.

informants were not pleased with what she said about them. One woman read in the manuscript about her own illegal attempts to combine work and welfare to better her family's standard of living. Angry, she denied to Valentine that she had ever done such a thing. Valentine talked to her informant at some length about this matter, which was well documented in field notes. It gradually became clear that the woman was concerned that if the data about her illegal activities were published, her friends and neighbors on the block would learn about it. In particular, she was afraid that the book would be sold on corner newsstands. Once Valentine explained how unlikely this was, her informant relaxed considerably.

> *The exchange made clear how different interests affect one's view. From my point of view, corner newsstand distribution would be excellent because it would mean the possibility of reaching the audience I feel needs to read and ponder the implications of the book. Yet Bernice and Velma [the informant and her friend] specified that they wouldn't mind where else it was distributed, even in Blackston more generally, if it could be kept from people on Paul Street and the surrounding blocks. (B. Valentine 1978:122)*

The Effect of Fieldwork on the Researcher

What does it feel like to be in the field, trying to figure out the workings of an alien way of life? What are the consequences of this experience for the fieldworker? Graduate students in anthropology who have not yet been to the field often develop an idealized image of the field experience of good fieldworkers. In this ideal situation, fieldworkers are a bit disoriented at first, and their potential informants are suspicious. But uncertainty soon gives way to understanding and trust as the anthropologist's good intentions are made known and accepted. The fieldworker succeeds in establishing rapport. In fact, the fieldworker becomes so well loved and trusted, so thoroughly accepted by the locals, that he or she is adopted into their family, treated as one of them, and allowed access to the tribal secrets. Presumably, all this happens as a result of the personal attributes of the fieldworker. If you have what it takes, you will be taken in and treated like one of the family. If this doesn't happen, you were obviously cut out for some other kind of work.

But much more than the anthropologist's personality is responsible for successful fieldwork. Establishing rapport with the people being studied is an achievement of anthropologist and informants together. Acceptance is problematic, rather than assured, even for the most gifted fieldworkers. After all, fieldworkers are outsiders, usually with no former ties to the community in which they will do their research. It is therefore not just naive to think that the locals have accepted you as one of them without any difficulty. It is also bad science (Karp and Kendall 1982).

It is remarkable that anthropologists can still be seduced by the idealized image, even though they are trained by experienced fieldworkers and should be expected to know better. Rabinow recalled the relationship he formed with his first Moroccan informant, a man called Ibrahim, whom he hired to teach him Arabic. Rabinow and Ibrahim seemed to get along well together, and, because of the language lessons, they saw each other a great deal. This led Rabinow to think of Ibrahim as a friend. When Rabinow planned a trip to another city, Ibrahim offered to go along as a guide and stay with relatives. This only confirmed Ibrahim's friendliness in Rabinow's eyes.

But things changed once they arrived at their destination. Ibrahim told Rabinow that the relatives with whom he was to stay did not exist, that he had no money, and that he expected Rabinow to pay for his hotel room. When Rabinow was unable to pay for Ibrahim's room, Ibrahim pulled out his wallet and paid for it himself. Rabinow was shocked and hurt by this experience, and his relationship with Ibrahim was forever altered. Rabinow remarks: "Basically I had been conceiving of him as a friend because of the seeming personal relationship we had established. But Ibrahim, a lot less confusedly, had basically conceptualized me as a resource. He was not unjustly situating me with the other Europeans with whom he had dealings" (1977:29).

Rabinow's experience illustrates what he called the "shock of otherness." Fieldwork institutionalizes this shock. Having to anticipate culture shock at any and every turn, anthropologists sometimes find that fieldwork takes on a tone that is anything but pleasant and sunny. For many anthropologists, the mood that characterizes fieldwork, at least in its early stages, is one of anxiety—the anxiety of an isolated individual with nothing familiar to turn to, no common sense on which to rely, no relationships that can be taken for granted. There is a reason anthropologists have reported holing up for weeks at a time reading paperback novels and eating peanut butter sandwiches. Emily Schultz recalls how difficult it was every morning to leave her compound in Guider, Cameroon. Despite the accomplishments of the previous day, she was always convinced that no one would want to talk to her *today. (See EthnoFile 7.1: Guider.)*

View of Guider, northern Cameroon.

Seeing one's informants as fully human requires anthropologists to allow their own humanity to express itself. But expressing their humanity is exceedingly difficult, for most anthropologists do not wish to offend their informants. The situation is complicated, particularly at the beginning, by the fieldworker's imperfect awareness of the sorts of behavior that are likely to offend informants, or even what constitutes an offense in the culture being studied. As a result, the unwritten rule of thumb for fieldworkers has long been summed up in the motto "The informant is always right." Many fieldworkers therefore forbid themselves to express anger or disgust or disagreement. But this behavior is likely to cause problems for both them and their informants. After all, what sort of human being is always smiling, never angry, without opinions?

Jean Briggs felt a conflict between duty to this unwritten code and participation in the culture of the Utku: "Hostility [among them] is ignored or turned into a joke; at worst it becomes the subject of gossip behind the offender's back. . . . My training in self-control was less perfect than theirs, and at the same time the strains were greater. . . . [Nevertheless] gossip was not open to me as an anthropologist" (1980:49). Briggs could only have entered into the gossip network by agreeing to share with some informants her hostility toward other informants, a move which she believed could easily sabotage her fieldwork. Ultimately, however, avoiding gossip did not prevent the development of serious misunderstanding and bad feeling.

Rabinow came face to face with the consequences of the fieldworkers' motto in his relations with his informant Ali. Ali had agreed to take Rabinow to a wedding at some distance from town; they were to go in Rabinow's car. Unfortunately, Rabinow was ill the day of the wedding. He did not want to break his promise to attend, and thus risk offending Ali and ruining any future chances to attend weddings, but he felt terrible. Ali agreed to stay only a short time at the wedding and then leave.

Once they arrived, however, Ali would not leave. He would disappear for long stretches, returning to announce that they would definitely be leaving soon, only to wander off again leaving Rabinow to his own devices. Rabinow found himself feeling worse, trying to smile at members of the wedding party, and growing angrier and angrier with Ali. At last, many hours after their arrival, Rabinow managed to get Ali into the car and they headed for home.

Things did not improve. Rabinow was certain that his annoyance must be obvious to Ali as they drove along. Yet Ali kept asking him if he was happy, looking for the sign of a pleased guest and a good host. When Rabinow steadfastly refused to answer him, Ali then declared that if Rabinow was unhappy, he, Ali, was insulted, and would get out of the car and walk back to town. Rabinow had had enough. He stopped the car to let his companion out and then drove on without him.

Rabinow was sure that he had sabotaged his fieldwork completely. In retrospect, he acknowledges that this event led him to question seriously whether or not the informant is always right. He says, "If the informant was always right, then by implication the anthropologist had to become a sort of non-person. . . . He had to be willing to enter into any situation as a smiling observer. . . . One had to completely subordinate one's own code of ethics, conduct, and world view, to 'suspend disbelief' . . . and sympathetically and accurately record events" (Rabinow 1977:46). The quarrel with Ali forced him to shuck the anthropologist's all-accepting persona and allow the full force of his personality through. Rabinow chose to be true to himself on this occasion, regardless of the consequences for his fieldwork.

The results could have been disastrous, but Rabinow was lucky. This rupture of communication with Ali was the prelude to Rabinow's experiencing one of his most significant insights into Moroccan culture. After his anger had cooled, he attempted to make up with Ali. To his great surprise, after only a few hours of warm apologies, his relationship with Ali was not only restored, but even closer than before! How was this possible? Rabinow had unwittingly behaved toward Ali in the only manner that would impress him in Moroccan terms. Rabinow learned that Moroccan men test each other all the time, to see how far they can assert dominance before their assertions are challenged. In this world, anyone who is all-accepting, such as an anthropologist, is not respected or admired but viewed as weak. "There was a fortuitous congruence between my breaking point and Moroccan cultural style. Perhaps in another situation my behavior might have proved irreparable. . . . By standing up to Ali I had communicated to him" (ibid.: 49).

The experience of Jean Briggs among the Utku is another illustration of the way in which the same behavior in different cultural circumstances is interpreted differently. Briggs seemed constantly to be receiving from her informants the message that anger was dangerous and must never be shown. She also became aware of the various ways her informants diverted or diffused angry feelings. Nevertheless, she remained ignorant of the full power of this value in Utku interpretations of behavior until she found herself in the position of having violated it seriously.

Beginning a few years before her fieldwork, Briggs relates, sportsmen from the United States and Canada had begun to charter planes to fly into the inlet where her informants lived during July and August. Once there, these sportsmen borrowed canoes belonging to the Utku. Although there had at one time been several usable canoes in the community, only two remained during the summer she was there. Some sportsmen borrowed one canoe, but ran it onto a rock. They then asked the Utkus if they could borrow the one remaining canoe, which happened to belong to Briggs's "father," Inuttiaq.

Briggs translated the request to Inuttiaq. She was annoyed that the sportsmen's carelessness had led to the ruin of one of the two good canoes in the community. Since canoes are used for practical subsistence activities and are not pleasure craft, the loss of one canoe spelled serious economic consequences for her informants. So when the white men asked to use the last canoe afloat, Briggs said, "I exploded." She lectured the sportsmen about their carelessness and insensitivity, explaining how important canoes were to the Utku. Then, remembering Inuttiaq's often-repeated admonition never to lend his canoe, she told the sportsmen that the owner of the one remaining canoe did not want to lend it. You may imagine her shock and surprise, then, when Inuttiaq insisted that the canoe be lent.

But this was only the beginning. Briggs discovered that, following her outburst, her informants seemed to turn against *her*, rather than the sportsmen. "I had spoken unbidden and in anger. . . . Punishment was a subtle form of ostracism. . . . I was isolated. It was as though I were not there. . . . But . . . I was still treated with the most impeccable semblance of solicitude" (Briggs 1980:56–57).

Unlike Rabinow, Briggs discovered gradually just how much at odds her breaking point was with Utku cultural style. This breach might well have ended her fieldwork, had not by chance a Westernized Utku friend, Ikayuqtuq, come to her rescue. "I had written my version of the story to Ikayuqtuq, had told her about my attempt to protect the Utku from the impositions of the kaplunas [white men] and asked her if she could help to explain my behavior to the Eskimos" (ibid.: 58). Ikayuqtuq did write to Allaq and Inuttiaq, although the letter did not arrive until three months later. During that time, Briggs seemed to be frozen out of Utku society.

Once the letter arrived, everything changed. Briggs's friend had found a way to translate the intentions behind her behavior into terms that Allaq and Inuttiaq could understand. As Briggs recalls, "the effect was magical." Inuttiaq began to tell the others what a dangerous task Briggs had taken on, to defend the Utkus against the white men. The ice melted. And Briggs knew that things had truly been restored (and perhaps deepened) when Inuttiaq called her "daughter" once again.

In these examples, ruptures of communication between anthropologists and their informants ultimately led to a deepening of insight and a broadening of intersubjective understanding. This is what all fieldworkers hope for—and dread, since negotiating the rupture can be dangerous and no happy outcome is assured. The risks may seem greater when the informants' culture is very different from the anthropologist's, and, consequently, it might seem that the resulting insights must also be more startling. Yet Bettylou Valentine discovered that fieldwork in a black ghetto, in the United States, among Americans, also held surprises: "At the start of fieldwork I assumed at a subconscious level that my college education . . . would enable me, unlike many ghetto residents, to handle successfully any problem resulting from the impact of the larger society on my family, myself, or any less-skilled ghetto resident I chose to help. This assumption was proved totally wrong many, many times" (1978:132).

The Humanizing Effect of Fieldwork

Anthropological knowledge is the fruit of reflexivity, produced by the mutual attempts of anthropologist and informant to understand one another. As a result, anthropological knowledge ought be able to provide answers to questions about human nature, human society, and human history. Somehow, good ethnography should not only be able to persuade its readers, on intellectual grounds, that the ethnographer's informants were human beings. It should also allow readers to experience the informants' humanity.

Charles Valentine explicitly states this as the ultimate aim of his wife's ethnography about life in Blackston: "This book . . . reports how those who are both Black and poor persist in being human despite inhumane conditions" (1978:2). One important element in retaining their humanity was institutionalized celebrating. By middle-class standards, Blackstonians had little money to spend. Bettylou Valentine was initially surprised at how much of their cash was used on food, drink, and such items as stereos, all used in entertaining friends and relatives.

> *Some people might characterize such lavish entertainment in the face of limited resources as improvident and likely to keep people from saving enough to escape from the slum. Yet the amounts of money spent could not really make a difference in the basic circumstances of inadequate housing, racial discrimination, limited job opportunities, poor city services, and all the other things that Blackstonians escape from, at least temporarily, through dancing and partying. The social life of Blackston, willingness to share, free and easy access to whatever liquor and food there was among friends, neighbors, and kin are the features that those who moved away commented on most often and said they missed. (B. Valentine 1978:122)*

The "practical ethic"—bourgeois or marxian—that many Western ethnographers bring with them into the field often leads to frustration. Researchers are discouraged by the sight of their informants "wasting" resources that ought to be invested either in individual self-betterment (the bourgeois option) or in the collective overthrow of the oppressing classes (the marxian option). In either case, there seems to be the unspoken judgment that people who are poor, powerless, and rational ought to have more self-control. They should live frugally, devoting what energy and resources they do have either to prudently accumulating capital or to furthering the revolution. This judgment would seem to deny the poor and powerless the right to celebrate, the right to escape from their lot. It seems to be based on the questionable premise that, "rationally" and "objectively" speaking, the poor and powerless have nothing to celebrate and no right to attempt, irresponsibly, to escape from their condition. The poor and powerless who do celebrate or escape thus run the risk of being considered irrational, or unworthy of sympathy or support.

Could it be, however, that celebration and escape involve something central to human nature? Could it be that to deny the appropriateness of these activities for the poor and powerless is also to deny the humanity of the poor and powerless? Celebration and escape are not objectionable among the well-to-do and powerful. Disapproval of these activities for the less privileged seems to presume that the less privileged are either superhuman or subhuman. These people are expected to endure privation without succumbing to the ordinary human need for sociability. If they should succumb, they appear irrational, and thus less than fully human. After all, who in his right mind could find a reason, let alone the means, to celebrate in the midst of squalor?

Judgments such as these, conscious or unconscious, reveal the gulf that separates the observer from the observed. The gulf is only widened by language referring to "them" and "us," particularly when the use of such terms reveals no reflexive awareness. Perhaps the most powerful lesson fieldwork teaches is the realization, in the mind and in the gut, that "there is no primitive. There are other men living other lives" (Rabinow 1977:151).

Fieldworkers find themselves in a privileged position, enjoying as they do the opportunity to experience "the other" as human beings. This experience comes neither easily nor automatically. It must be cultivated, and it requires the cooperation and effort of one's informants as well as oneself. Those who have achieved a measure of cross-cultural understanding find themselves—or should find themselves—less and less willing to talk about "us" and "them." Indeed, the appropriate language should be "not 'they,' not 'we,' not 'you,' but 'some of us' are thus and so" (Smith 1982:70).

Coming Up with the Facts of Anthropology

If anthropological knowledge is the intersubjective creation of fieldworker and informant together, so too are the facts that anthropologists collect. The **facts** of anthropology are not ready-made, existing out there in the real world only waiting for someone to come along and pick them up. The facts of anthropology are first created in the field. They are created anew whenever the fieldworker, back home, reexamines field notes and is transported back into the field experience. And they are created yet again when fieldworkers discuss their experiences with other anthropologists.

Given this perspective on the facts of anthropology, there is no way for the facts to speak for themselves. Facts "speak" only when they are interpreted, placed in a context of meaning that makes them intelligible. What constitutes a cultural fact is ambiguous. Anthropologists and informants can disagree; anthropologists can disagree among themselves; informants can disagree among themselves. The facts of anthropology exist neither in the culture of the anthropologist nor in the culture of the informant. "Anthropological facts are cross-cultural, because they are made across cultural boundaries" (Rabinow 1977:152). Different anthropologists from different cultures interacting with Rabinow's informants most probably would have made a different collection of cultural facts. Informants from a different culture interacting with Rabinow would have made different collections of cultural facts than they might have made interacting with a different anthropologist.

facts
building blocks of anthropological knowledge that are created in the field, are created anew whenever a fieldworker who is back home reexamines field notes and is transported back into the field experience, and are created yet again when fieldworkers discuss their experiences with other anthropologists

Anthropological Knowledge as Open-ended

The idea that anthropological knowledge is grounded in the experience of fieldwork is disconcerting. We have suggested that there is no such thing as purely objective knowledge and that when human beings are both subject and object of study, one must speak in terms of reflexivity rather than objectivity. The cultivation of reflexivity allows us to produce less-distorted views of human nature and the human condition, and yet we remain human beings interpreting the lives of other human beings. We can never escape from our humanity to some point of view that would allow us to see human existence and human experience from the outside. We must instead rely on our common humanity and our interpretive powers to show us the parts of our nature that can be made visible.

If there truly is no primitive, no subsection of humanity that is radically different in nature or in capacity from the anthropologists who study it, then the ethnographic record of anthropological knowledge is perhaps best understood as a vast commentary on human possibility. As with all commentaries, it depends on an original "text"—in this case, lived human experience. But that experience is ambiguous, speaking with many voices, capable of supporting more than one commentary and more than one interpretation. Growth of anthropological knowledge is no different, then, from growth of human self-understanding in general. It ought to contribute to the domain of human wisdom that concerns who we are as a species, where we have come from, and where we may be going.

Like all commentaries, the ethnographic record is and must be unfinished. Human beings are open systems, human history continues, and problems and their possible solutions change. There is no true version of human life. For anthropologists and for others, the true version of human life, from the narrowest to the broadest senses, consists of all versions of human life.

This is a sobering possibility. It makes it appear that "the anthropologist is condemned to a greater or lesser degree of failure" in even trying to understand another culture (Basham 1978:299). Informants would equally be condemned to never know fully even their own way of life. And the scientific attitude, cultivated in the Western world, resists any admission that ultimately the exhaustive understanding of anything is impossible.

But total pessimism does not seem warranted. We may never know everything, but it does not follow that we can learn nothing for our efforts. "Two of the fundamental qualities of humanity are the capacity to understand one another and the capacity to be understood. Not fully certainly. Yet not negligibly, certainly. . . . There is no person on earth that I can fully understand. There is and has been no person on earth that I cannot understand at all" (Smith 1982:68–69).

Moreover, as our contact with the other is prolonged and as our efforts to communicate are rewarded by the construction of intersubjective understanding, we can always learn more. Human beings are open creatures, and our ability to learn new things is vast. This is significant, for even if we can never know everything, it does not seem that our capacities for understanding ourselves and others is likely to be exhausted soon. This is not only because we are open to change, but also because our culture can change, our wider environment can change, and all will continue to do so as long as human history continues. The ethnographic enterprise will never be finished, even if all nonindustrial ways of life disappear forever, if all human beings move into cities, if everyone ends up speaking English. Such superficial homogeneity masks vast heterogeneity beneath its bland surface. In any case, given the dynamics of human existence, nothing in human affairs can remain homogeneous for long.

Key Terms

culture shock
field work
participant-observation
positivism

objective knowledge
intersubjective meanings
reflexivity
interpretation

translation
informant
facts

Chapter Summary

1. Anthropological *fieldwork* traditionally involves extended periods of close contact with members of another society. This form of research, called *participant-observation*, institutionalizes *culture shock*. Anthropological knowledge is a product of reflection on the experiences of culture shock generated by fieldwork.

2. The nineteenth century saw the birth of positivistic science in Western intellectual circles. *Positivism* is based on the assumption that reality can be known through the five senses. Positivists believe that a single scientific method can be used to investigate any domain of reality, and they expect that all scientific knowledge will eventually be unified. They argue that facts have nothing to do with values. Their aim is to produce knowledge about reality that is true for all people in all times and places.

3. Early anthropologists who wanted to be scientific attempted to adapt positivism to their needs. Doing so involved adopting a view of controlled laboratory research as the prototype of scientific investigation and attempting to apply the prototype to the field situation. It also meant trying to record objectively only observable behavior of the people under study, and attempting to explain that behavior in material terms. In this way, highly accurate data were systematically collected in many parts of the world.

4. Anthropologists with a positivistic outlook have been charged with insensitivity to the humanity of their research subjects. The positivist program in anthropology attempts, metaphorically, to turn human beings into objects, similar to the rocks and molecules that physical scientists study. This attempt has dehumanized both the informants (who are reduced to objects) and the fieldworkers (who are reduced to intelligent recording machines).

5. In a situation where human beings are studying other human beings, research is inevitably colored by the context and cultural presuppositions of both the anthropologists and the people they study. Positivism views this as contamination of the data. However, if the objects of anthropology are human beings like ourselves, then scientific accuracy requires that we relate to them as human beings.

6. We suggest that a concern with objectivity be replaced with a concern for *reflexivity*: that anthropologists must think about the way they think about other cultures. Successful fieldwork involves informants who also must think about the way they think, and try to convey their insights to the anthropologist.

7. The *dialectic of fieldwork* is a reflexive interchange between anthropologist and informant. It is a collaborative undertaking involving dialogue about the meaning of experience in the informant's culture. The outcome of this dialogue is an intersubjective understanding (i.e., an understanding between two subjects, anthropologist and informant) of the informant's culture.

8. Fieldwork is human experience. Knowledge of informants and their culture is gained in the same way as human beings gain knowledge about other human beings in any circumstances, even in their own cultures. Meaning must always be negotiated. There is no such thing as a final set of meanings, a final interpretation, that cannot be renegotiated at some future date.

9. Fieldwork forces fieldworkers to face the shock of the unfamiliar and their own vulnerability. As a result, fieldwork can be a profoundly alienating experience for the fieldworker. The only remedy for this alienation is to construct, with the aid of one's informants, an intersubjective world of meaning.

10. Because cultural meanings are intersubjectively constructed during fieldwork, cultural facts do not speak for themselves. The facts of anthropology are made and remade every time they are subjected to a fresh analysis and interpretation.

11. Learning about another culture is often greatest following a rupture of communication between anthropologist and informant. Ruptures occur when current intersubjective understandings prove themselves inadequate to account for experience. A rupture always carries the possibility of bringing research to an end. But when the reasons for the rupture are explored and explanations for it are constructed, great insights are possible.

12. Fieldwork has the potential to change both fieldworkers and informants, since their experiences of human possibility have been widened. This growth in self-awareness is not always comfortable. Nevertheless, the deepening of insight that it makes possible, the opportunity to experience the humanity of one's informants (or one's interviewer!) can be immensely satisfying.

13. The ethnographic record of anthropological knowledge is perhaps best understood as a vast commentary on human possibility. Like all commentaries, it is—and must be—unfinished. We may never learn all there is to know, but we can always learn more.

Suggested Readings

Agar, Michael. *The Professional Stranger: An Informal Introduction to Ethnography*. New York: Academic Press, 1980.

Just what it says it is: an informal, breezy introduction to anthropological fieldwork. Agar draws heavily on his own fieldwork in South India, in Austria, and among drug addicts in Houston and New York. Some of his conclusions (the goal of ethnography for him is accurate paraphrase) are quite similar to ours. Includes useful material on writing research proposals.

Belmonte, Thomas. *The Broken Fountain*. New York: Columbia University Press, 1981.

A powerful work about both the author's fieldwork in a slum in Naples and the slum itself.

Briggs, Jean. *Never in Anger: Portrait of an Eskimo Family*. Cambridge: Harvard University Press, 1970.

A moving, insightful study of fieldwork, as well as of an Utku family.

Lévi-Strauss, Claude. *Tristes Tropiques*. New York: Pocket Books, 1974.

Originally published in French in 1955, this book with the untranslatable title is considered by some to be the greatest book ever written by an anthropologist (although not necessarily a great anthropology book). This is a multifaceted work about voyaging, fieldwork, self-knowledge, philosophy, and much more. It well repays the effort required in some places.

Rabinow, Paul. *Reflection on Fieldwork in Morocco*. Berkeley: University of California Press, 1977.

An important, brief, powerfully written reflection on the nature of fieldwork. Very accessible and highly recommended.

Read, Kenneth. *The High Valley*. New York: Columbia University Press, 1964.

A sometimes poetic, often moving memoir of the author's fieldwork in New Guinea in the 1950s.

Valentine, Bettylou. *Hustling and Other Hard Work*. New York: Free Press, 1978.

An innovative, provocative study of ghetto life. Reads like a good novel.

Why Read Ethnographies

Ivan Karp (Ph.D., University of Virginia) is Curator of African Ethnology at the Smithsonian Institution in Washington, D.C. He has carried out fieldwork among the Iteso in Kenya and has taught at both Colgate University and Indiana University. Dr. Karp has written and edited several books and is currently doing research on culture and concepts of personhood in African society.

What is an ethnography? An ethnography is a study by an anthropologist of a society, an institution, a belief system, a people, or a segment of a population. An ethnography might examine trance among hunter-gatherers of the Kalahari, how American truckers manage to maintain their enterprises, playing the xylophone in southern Africa, or the political organization of an Islamic state in Pakistan. Ethnographies can be so broad as to describe the cultural assumptions underlying social relations in modern Japan or the principles of rank and stratification found in all the different societies living on the Indian sub-

continent. More often, ethnographies are more specific, situated in communities or segments of communities. Anthropologists have described the nature of space in suburban America, the changing social organization of neighborhoods in rural Kenya, and street corner behavior in Washington, D.C. Even such seemingly minute elements of a people's life and culture as the different meanings that Quakers and American Indians give to silence have been subjected to anthropological study.

While anthropologists have taken the total range of human behavior and productions as their field of inquiry, they have not been so successful at describing and explaining the power centers of our own society. Even though anthropology is the child of colonial domination, other peoples of the world have been more willing to have their lives subjected to scrutiny than have the power brokers of our own society. Nevertheless, anthropologists try to set what they study in comparative perspective. They always strive to demonstrate how the exotic forms they describe are both similar to and different from what we ourselves know. None of the situations they describe are taken by them to be natural. Even anthropologists working in our own society adhere to this principle: people's assumption that their way of doing things is natural simply is not true from a cross-cultural perspective.

This book describes an attitude called ethnocentrism. Anthropologists usually argue that ethnocentrism is both wrong and harmful, especially when it is tied to racial, cultural, and social prejudices. Ideas and feelings about the inferiority of blacks, the cupidity of Jews, or the

lack of cultural sophistication of farmers are surely to be condemned. But can we do without ethnocentrism? If we stopped to examine every custom and practice in our cultural repertoire, how would we get on? For example, if we always regarded marriage as something that can vary from society to society, would we be concerned about filling out the proper marriage documents, or would we even get married at all? Most of the time we suspend a quizzical stance toward our own customs and simply live life.

Yet many of our own practices are peculiar when viewed through the lenses of other cultures. Periodically, for over fifteen years, I have worked with and lived among an African people. They are as amazed at our marriage customs as my students are at theirs. Both American students and the Iteso of Kenya find it difficult to imagine how the other culture survives with the bizarre, exotic practices that are part of their respective marriage customs. Ethnocentrism works both ways. It can be practiced as much by other cultures as by our own.

Paradoxically, ethnographic literature combats ethnocentrism by showing that the practices of cultures (including our own) are "natural" in their own setting. What appears natural in one setting appears so because it was constructed in that setting—made and produced by human beings who could have done it some other way. Ethnography is a means of recording the range of human creativity and of demonstrating how universally shared capacities can produce cultural and social differences.

This anthropological way of looking at other cultures—and, by implication, at ourselves—constitutes a major reason for reading ethnography. The anthropological lens teaches us to question what we assume to be unquestionable. Ethnography teaches us that human potentiality provides alternative means of organizing our lives and alternative modes of experiencing the world. Reading ethnographies trains us to question the received wisdom of our society and makes us receptive to change. In this sense, anthropology might be called the subversive science. We read ethnographies in order to learn about how other peoples produce their world and about how we might change our own patterns of production.

CHAPTER 4
LANGUAGE

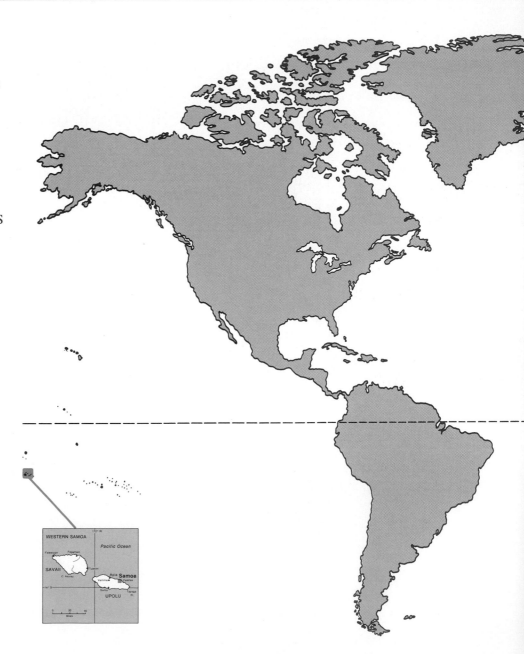

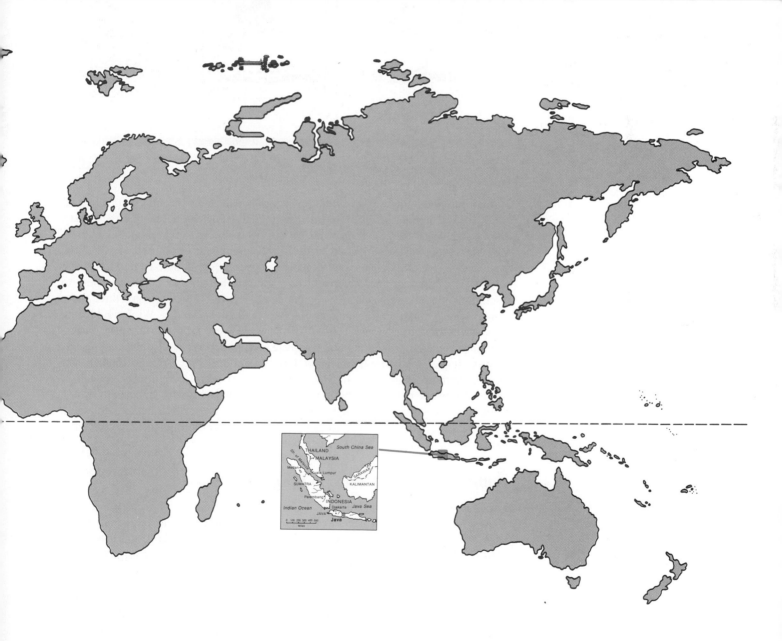

by George Herriman

Language and Culture

Human **language** has impressed and puzzled human beings in all cultures and all times. It is a unique faculty, possessed by human beings alone, setting them apart from other living species. It provides basic tools for human creativity, making possible the cultural achievements that we view as monuments to our species' genius. And yet, despite all language makes possible, its tools are double-edged. Language allows people to communicate with one another, but it also creates barriers to communication. A major barrier is linguistic diversity. There are some three thousand mutually unintelligible languages spoken in the world today. Why should there be such barriers to communication? If the world were rational, linguistic understanding would be immediate and complete, for all people in all times and places. In this chapter we will explore ambiguity, limitations, and power of human language. Anthropologists usually regard language as a part of culture. As such, it shares common features with the rest of culture. It is learned, not innate; it is a social phenomenon, an attribute of the group; it is historically transmitted through teaching and learning; it tends to hang together coherently, thus making communication possible; and it is coded in symbols.

Anthropological Interest in Language

Language has been a central focus of anthropological interest for at least three reasons. First, fieldworkers need to be able to communicate with their informants, whose languages are often unwritten. This means that a certain level of linguistic skill is needed by all anthropologists, especially those who must learn their informants' languages without formal instruction.

Second, speech can be written down or tape-recorded, and so lifted out of its cultural context to be analyzed on its own. This offers the possibility of examining closely one domain of culture and uncovering its secrets. The knowledge gained about language can then be applied to the analysis of other domains of culture. The motto seems to be this: "What is true about language is true about (the rest of) culture." Some schools of anthropological theory have taken this motto especially seriously, basing their analyses of culture explicitly on ideas taken from **linguistics**, the scientific study of language.

linguistics
the scientific study of language

Third, and most important, all people use language to code their experience and to structure their understanding of the world and of themselves. Learning the language used by members of another culture thus involves learning something about one's own culture as well. In fact, learning another language inevitably provides unsuspected insights into the nature of one's own language and culture. This experience often makes it impossible to take language of any kind for granted ever again.

Studying another language forces us to become aware of certain things about language that we might otherwise never notice. It quickly becomes apparent, for example, that successful linguistic communication depends on numerous prior assumptions that native speakers are expected to share. These same assumptions may not be shared by speakers of a different language. Language learners first discover that word-for-word translation from one language to another does not work. Sometimes this is because there are no equivalent words in the second language. But even when there appear to be such words, the word-for-word translation may not mean in language B what it meant in language A: it may have a very different meaning, or it may sound like gibberish.

Here are two examples. (1) When we have eaten enough, we say in English "I'm full." This may be translated directly into French as *Je suis plein*. To a native speaker of French, this sentence (especially when uttered at the end of a meal) has the nonsensical meaning "I am a pregnant [male] animal." (2) In Spanish, a common expression that means "She gave birth" is *Ella dio a luz*. Translating this word-for-word into English gives the sentence "She gave to light." Attempts at translation are thus often frustrating and even unsettling. The world that formerly seemed simple to talk about suddenly loses its intelligibility. Speakers who are competent in their own native language turn into babbling fools.

Studying a second language, then, is less a matter of learning new labels for old objects than it is a matter of learning how to identify new objects that go with new labels. It also involves learning new relations linking these objects to one another and to oneself. Mastering grammar and vocabulary is still not sufficient for successful linguistic communication, however. We must also master knowledge of the appropriate contexts in which different linguistic forms may be used. Knowledge about context is cultural knowledge. The linguistic system abstracted from its cultural context must be returned to that context if a holistic understanding of language is to be achieved.

Talking about Experience

Language, like the rest of culture, is a product of human attempts to come to terms with experience. Languages and cultures that have persisted over time have made it possible for their users to make enough sense of the world to survive, even to thrive. Therefore, just as there is no such thing as a primitive culture, there is no such thing as a primitive language.

Traditionally, languages are identified with reference to concrete groups of people called *speech communities*. Members of particular speech communities do not all possess identical knowledge about the language they share, and do not all speak the same way. This is possible because all languages are full of alternative ways of speaking. Individuals and subgroups within a speech community make use of these linguistic resources in different ways. As a result, there is a tension in language between diversity and commonality. Individuals and subgroups attempt to use the varied resources of a language to create unique, personal voices. These efforts are countered by the pressure to negotiate a common code for communication within the larger social group. Consensus is never guaranteed or given ahead of time; members of social groups must actively work to create whatever agreement is achieved. At the same time, individual persons and groups must actively work to impart their own stylistic shape to language they share with others in the speech community. In this way, language is produced and reproduced through the activity of its speakers. Any particular language that we may identify at a given moment is a snapshot of a continuing process.

The resources of language stretch to accommodate the experiences with which speakers deal. There are many ways to communicate our experiences, and there is no absolute standard favoring one way over another. Some things that are easy to say in language A may be difficult to say in language B. Yet other aspects of language B may appear much simpler than equivalent aspects of language A. For example, English ordinarily requires the use of determiners (e.g., *a, an, the*) before nouns, but this rule is not found in all languages. Likewise, the verb *to be*, called the copula by linguists, is not found in all languages, although the relationships we convey when we use *to be* in English may still be communicated. In Fulfulde, the language of the Fulbe of northern Cameroon, the phrase *Him'be boi 'don nder luumo* can be translated "There are many people in the market," although no single Fulfulde word corresponds to the English *are* or *the*.

Him'be boi 'don nder luumo.

English speakers learning Fulfulde find that certain things are easier to say in Fulfulde than in English, since there is no need to worry about determiners or the verb *to be*. This may give the impression that the entire language is simple. However, languages that are simple in one area may be quite complex in another, and Fulfulde is no exception. Fulfulde nouns consist of stems that can be assigned to different classes. Each class represents a particular noun category: human and singular, human and plural, animal, plant, and so on. Each noun class provides the noun stem with a characteristic ending and, in addition, may affect the form of the initial consonant of the stem, if there is one. For example, the stem *pul-* refers to the Fulbe people. When the *pul-* stem is put into the human singular class, it receives the ending *-o*, the *l* is lengthened (doubled, when written in the Roman alphabet), and the result—*pullo*—refers to a member of the Fulbe ethnic group. When the same stem is put into the human plural class, it receives the ending *'be*, the initial *p* changes to *f*, and the result is *Ful'be*. These types of grammatical rules are quite alien to English speakers. Perhaps the closest rule in the English language is the use of *an* rather than *a* before nouns beginning with a vowel (e.g., an apple).

Differences across languages are not absolute. In Chinese, for example, verbs never change to indicate tense; instead, separate expressions referring to time are used. English speakers learning Chinese are often struck by the simplicity of this structure. They may even conclude that Chinese as a whole must be simple, or that those who speak it cannot distinguish between past, present, and future. This structure seems completely different from English structure. But consider such English sentences as "Have a hard day at the office today?" and "Your interview go well?" These "abbreviated questions" used in informal English are very similar to the formal patterns in languages such as Chinese and other languages of Southeast Asia (Akmajian, Demers, and Harnish 1984:194–95).

This kind of intersection between two very different languages demonstrates at least three important things. First, it shows the kind of cross-linguistic commonality that forms the foundation both for learning new languages and for translation. Second, it highlights the variety of expressive resources to be found in any single language. We learn that English allows us to use either tense markers on verbs or unmarked verbs with adverbs of time. In addition, we learn that the former grammatical pattern is associated with formal usage, whereas the latter is associated with informal usage. Finally, it shows that the same structures can have different functions in different languages.

As anthropological linguist Elinor Ochs observed, most cross-cultural differences in language use "turn out to be differences in *context* and/or *frequency of occurrence*" (1986:10). In the preceding example, the verbal pattern associated with formal contexts of use in Chinese is associated with informal usage in English. This discovery leads us to suspect that Chinese must have informal usage as well, and to wonder how the grammatical patterns of informal usage differ from those of formal usage. These are the kinds of questions anthropological linguists are continually asking about the languages they study.

Design Features of Human Language

One anthropological linguist who has spent many years thinking about language is Charles Hockett. Hockett was curious about how human language was different from the communication systems of other animals. In 1966, he listed sixteen differ-

design features
characteristics of human language that, when taken together, differentiate language from other known animal communication systems

ent **design features** of human language that in his estimation set human language apart from other forms of animal communication. Those design features are as follows:

1. *Vocal-auditory channel*. Language is produced by the vocal tract and received by the ears. Hockett does not consider written languages or channels that are not vocal-auditory, such as signing and drum signals.

2. *Broadcast transmission and directional reception*. Linguistic signals are transmitted in all directions but are heard as coming from a particular direction.

3. *Rapid fading*. The sounds of spoken linguistic signals cannot be heard for very long.

4. *Interchangeability*. Adult members of any speech community can be both transmitters and receivers of linguistic signals.

5. *Complete feedback*. The person who sends a linguistic message also receives the message he or she sends.

6. *Specialization*. Linguistic signals themselves have little direct physical effect; only the triggering effects are important. Hockett observed that "even the sound of a heated conversation does not raise the temperature of a room enough to benefit those in it." On the other hand, linguistic signals can trigger a great expenditure of energy: "Go to New York and get me a bagel."

7. *Semanticity*. Linguistic signals are associated with features in the physical, social, and cultural worlds of speakers. That is, some linguistic forms refer to things, or have denotations.

8. *Arbitrariness*. There is no necessary connection between a particular sound cluster in a language and its meaning. For example, nothing inherent about a large quadruped that is well-suited for long-distance running forces people to call the animal a horse, rather than *cheval* or *pferd*.

9. *Discreteness*. The possible messages in any language can be broken up into separate units.

10. *Displacement*. Linguistic messages may refer to things remote in time or space, or both, from the site of the communication.

11. *Openness*. New linguistic messages are coined freely and easily, either by blending, analogizing from, or transforming old messages, or by assigning new meanings to old forms on the basis of context.

12. *Tradition*. The conventions of a language are passed down by teaching and learning. They are not inherited genetically.

13. *Duality of patterning*. Every language has both a phonological subsystem and a grammatical subsystem. As a result, a conveniently small number of meaningless sounds can generate an infinite number of meaningful messages.

14. *Prevarication*. Linguistic messages can be false. This feature seems to be based on semanticity, displacement, and openness. Because of this feature, it is possible to formulate hypotheses, and to lie.

15. *Reflexiveness*. In a human language, we can talk about the way people talk.

16. *Learnability*. A speaker of one language can learn another language.

Openness and Arbitrariness

Certain design features that Hockett lists seem especially helpful in defining what makes human language distinctive. These include openness, displacement, arbitrariness, duality of patterning, semanticity, and prevarication. Of these, openness is probably most important. It emphasizes the same point that the celebrated linguist Noam Chomsky emphasized (1965:6): human language is creative. Speakers are constantly creating new messages that hearers understand. Someone may never before have said to you, "Put this Babel fish in your ear," but if you know English, you can understand the message.

Openness is absent in the vocal communication systems of apes such as chimpanzees and gorillas. The number of calls in such systems are few, and any particular call is produced only when the animal finds itself in a particular situation. Specific situations commonly include the presence of food or danger, friendly interest and the desire for company, and the desire to mark the animal's location, to indicate sexual interest, to indicate need for maternal care, or to signal pain. If the animal is not in the appropriate situation, it does not produce the call. In addition it cannot emit a signal that has some features of one call and some of another. For example, if it encounters food and danger at the same time, one of the calls will take precedence.

Openness is not the only feature of human language missing in the call system of apes. Displacement, which can be understood as an extension of openness, is also absent. Human beings can talk about absent or nonexistent objects and past or future events as easily as they discuss their immediate situations; nonhuman primates cannot. Closed call systems lack displacement: for apes, out of sight is, if not out of mind, at least out of speech.

Closed call systems also lack the feature of arbitrariness. Arbitrariness too is connected with openness. It refers to the open nature of the link between sound and meaning: there is no necessary link between any particular sound and any particular meaning. For example, the sound sequence /boi/ refers to a "small male human" in English, but means "more" or "many" in Fulfulde. One aspect of linguistic creativity is the free, creative production of new links between sounds and meanings. In this way, arbitrariness can be seen as the flip side of openness. If all links between sound and meaning are open, then the particular link between particular sounds and particular meanings in a particular language must be arbitrary. In closed call systems, by contrast, links between the sounds of calls and their meanings appear to be fixed and under considerable direct biological control.

Arbitrariness is evident in another design feature of language, duality of patterning. Human language is patterned on two different levels: sound and meaning. On the first level, the significant sounds (or phonemes) that characterize any particular language are not random. Rather, they are systematically patterned. This pattern, in turn, is a function of the way the vocal possibilities of our speech organs can be combined to produce distinguishable sounds. The pattern of sounds in any language is a small subset of all the possible sounds human speech organs can make. In addition, the sound patterns of all languages are not identical, although they may overlap to a greater or lesser degree. On the second level of patterning, grammar puts the sound units together according to its own, separate rules. The resulting sound clusters are the smallest meaning-bearing units of the language, called morphemes.

Since Hockett first wrote, many linguists have suggested that there are more than just two levels of patterning in language. Some additional levels are considered later in this chapter in the section entitled "The Components of Language." In all cases, the principle relating levels to each other is the same: Units on one level of analysis, patterned in one way, can be put to work on a different level according to a different pattern. Human language is thus seen to have many levels, and the patterns that characterize one level cannot be reduced to the pattern of any other level. Ape call systems, by contrast, lack multilevel patterning.

Arbitrariness shows up again in the design feature of semanticity, which reminds us that linguistic signals are associated with aspects of the social, cultural, and physical world of a speech community. Language refers to objects and processes in the world, and people use it to help them make sense of those objects and processes. Nevertheless, any linguistic description of reality, however accurate, is always somewhat arbitrary. This is because all linguistic descriptions are selective, highlighting some features of the world and downplaying others.

Perhaps the most striking consequence of the open, arbitrary nature of human language is captured in the design feature of prevarication. Hockett's remarks about this design feature deserve particular attention: "Linguistic messages can be false, and they can be meaningless in the logician's sense." In other words, not only can people use language to lie, but utterances that seem perfectly well-formed grammatically may yield semantic nonsense. As an example, Chomsky offered the following sentence: "Colorless green ideas sleep furiously" (1957:15). This is a grammatical sentence on one level—the right kinds of words are used in the right places—but on another level it is completely illogical. Openness makes this possible. It also makes the formation of scientific hypotheses possible. The ability of language users to prevaricate—to make statements or ask questions that violate convention—is a major consequence of open symbolic systems. Apes using their closed call systems can neither lie nor formulate theories.

Opening Closed Call Systems

Charles Hockett and Robert Ascher (1964) suggest that the major switch in human evolution occurred when the closed call systems of our ape ancestors opened up. Once this happened, different sounds would be freely associated with the same meaning, or the same meaning might be freely associated with different sounds. Multilevel patterning became possible. Sounds could be produced according to one set of principles, and then organized into words and sentences and stretches of discourse according to different sets of principles. As a result, semanticity widened and became more complex and ambiguous. In addition, sounds and meanings became further detached, and detachable, from the immediate context in which they were being used. This made it possible to discuss things and events that were distant or nonexistent, giving birth to displacement. Language itself became detachable from context and could be commented on. This is the design feature of reflexiveness.

Language and Cognition

cognition
the mental process by which human beings gain knowledge

Cognition refers to the mental processes by which human beings gain knowledge. The study of human language and the study of human cognition have long gone hand in hand. In particular, as more has been learned about language, psychologists and other social scientists have applied that knowledge to other areas of human mental functioning. Unfortunately, some have attempted to reduce human knowledge to the structures of language. Today, experts are able to document a variety of ways that the nonlinguistic cognitive activity of human beings can affect the language development of human beings, particularly when both are studied in the context of use. The study of language in isolation—an approach never endorsed by anthropologists—is no longer in favor even outside anthropology.

The result has been a growing awareness of the influence of context on what people choose to say. The results of this change in focus have been dramatic and are potentially quite radical. Intensive studies of language use in context have led to significant increases in understanding. Alison Elliot reports, for example, that studies of child language no longer amount to a list of errors that children make when attempting to master the adult grammar, or to acquire what Chomsky called **linguistic competence**. Instead, linguists are studying children's verbal interactions in social and cultural context and are drawing attention to what children can do very well. "From an early age they appear to communicate very fluently, producing utterances which are not just remarkably well-formed according to the linguist's standards but also appropriate to the social context in which the speakers find themselves. Children are thus learning far more about language than rules of grammar. [They are] acquiring communicative competence" (Elliot 1981:13).

Communicative competence is a term coined by American anthropological linguist Dell Hymes (1972). As an anthropologist, Hymes was sensitive to the role of context in shaping successful language use. He therefore objected to Chomsky's notion that linguistic competence consisted only of being able to make correct judgments of sentence grammaticality (Chomsky 1965:4). Hymes observed that the meaning of the words and sentences that adult speakers utter cannot be exhaustively described by referring to grammar alone. Competent adult speech must be socially and culturally appropriate.

For example, children as well as adults need to know how to use personal pronouns appropriately when talking to others. This is particularly important in languages in which a speaker's choice of pronouns of address depends on his or her own status and the status of the person being addressed. For native speakers of English, the problem almost never arises with regard to pronoun choice, since we address all people to whom we are talking as "you." But any English speaker who has ever tried to learn a European language—French, for example—has struggled with the rules about when to address an individual using the second-person plural (*vous*, or "you"), and when to use the second-person singular (*tu*, or "thou"). To be safe, most students use *vous* for all individuals, since it is the more formal term and they want to avoid appearing too familiar with native speakers whom they do not know well. But if you are dating a French person, at which point in the relationship does the change from *vous* to *tu* occur, and who decides? Moreover, sometimes—for example, among university students—the normal term of address is *tu*, even for people whom the speaker does not know well; it indicates social solidarity. American students of French who find themselves in a French-speaking community wrestle with these and other dilemmas about how to address people. These things seem to have nothing to do with grammar, yet the choices a person makes can mark that person as someone who knows how to speak French or who does not.

The French case is quite simple, compared with other cases. Clifford Geertz has written about Javanese, for example, in which all the words in a sentence must be carefully selected to correspond to the status of the person addressed. *(See Ethno-File 4.1: Java.)* Even a simple request like "Are you going to eat rice and cassava

linguistic competence
the ability of native speakers of a language to distinguish correctly between grammatical and ungrammatical sentences

communicative competence
the ability of native speakers of a language to use words in ways that are socially and culturally appropriate

EthnoFile 4.1
JAVA

Region: Southeast Asia

Nation: Indonesia

Population: 85,000,000

Environment: Tropical island

Livelihood: Intensive rice cultivation

Political organization: Highly stratified state

Other: This densely populated island was made up of several great highly stratified noble courts before the Dutch conquest

now?'' requires that speakers know at least five different varieties of the language in order to communicate socially as well as to make the request (see figure 4.1). It is impossible to say anything in Javanese without also communicating your social position relative to the person to whom you are speaking. This example illustrates the range of diversity present in a single language. It also shows the way in which different varieties of a language are related to different subgroups within the speech community.

In summary, the design feature of openness is central to linguistic creativity. In fact, human cognition in general may operate on a design feature of openness. Openness would seem to be a necessary precondition for any creative use of symbols. What would the concept of *cognitive openness* refer to? One suggestion is that it would stand for the ''central aspect of human thought and cognition, namely, *the ability to understand the same thing from different points of view*'' (Ortony 1979:14; emphasis added). In language, this means being able to talk about the same experiences from different perspectives, to paraphrase using different words and various grammatical constructions. At its most radical, it would go beyond this to mean that the experiences being talked about can themselves be differently conceived, labeled, and discussed. In this view, no single perspective would necessarily emerge as more correct in every respect than all the others.

Even when talking about their rice paddies, speakers of Javanese must consider their status and the status of the person to whom they are speaking.

The Sapir-Whorf Hypothesis

During the first half of the twentieth century, two American anthropological linguists became intrigued by the fact that the grammars of different languages often described the same situation in different ways. Edward Sapir and Benjamin Whorf were impressed enough to conclude that language had the power to shape the way people saw the world. This claim has been called the linguistic relativity principle, or the **Sapir-Whorf hypothesis**. This hypothesis has been highly controversial, since ways of testing it have proved difficult and the results of testing have been ambiguous.

Researchers devised two versions of the hypothesis. The so-called strong version is known as *linguistic determinism*. It implies that the grammars of people's native languages determine the way people think about the world around them. It reduces patterns of thought and culture to the patterns of the grammar that sup-

Sapir-Whorf hypothesis

the position, associated with Edward Sapir and Benjamin Whorf, that language has the power to shape the way in which people see the world

Speaking to persons of:	Level	"Are	you	going	to eat	rice	and	cassava	now?"	Complete sentence
Very high position	3a	menapa	pandje-nengan	baḍé	ḍahar	sekul	kalijan	kaspé	samenika	Menapa pandjenengan baḍé ḍahar sekul kalijan kaspé samenika?
High position	3									Menapa sampéjan baḍé neḍa sekul kalijan kaspé samenika?
Same position, not close	2	napa	sampéjan	adjéng	neḍa				saniki	Napa sampéjan adjéng neḍa sekul lan kaspé saniki?
Same position, casual acquaintance	1a	apa		arep		sega	lan		saiki	Apa sampéjan arep neḍa sega lan kaspé saiki?
Close friends of any rank; also to lower status (basic language)	1		kowé		mangan					Apa kowé arep mangan sega lan kaspé saiki?

FIGURE 4.1
Dialect of Nonnoble, Urbanized, Somewhat Educated People in Central Java
Source: Reprinted with permission of The Free Press, a Division of Macmillan, Inc., from *The Religion of Java,* by Clifford Geertz. Copyright © 1960 by the Free Press.

posedly caused them. If language determined thought in this way, it would be impossible to translate from one language to another, or even to learn another language whose grammar is very different from the grammar of one's native tongue.

Since human beings do learn alien languages and translate from one language to another, the strong version of the Sapir-Whorf hypothesis cannot be correct. Indeed, it is based on some of the same faulty assumptions discussed in chapter 2, when we considered other forms of reductionism. Linguistic determinism would make sense only if we could assume three things: first, that speech communities are totally isolated from one another; second, that members of those isolated speech communities are exposed to only one version of their native language; and third, that language learning is a passive, rather than active, undertaking. Only passive creatures living under conditions of strict uniformity and isolation could become so thoroughly conditioned by the way their native language cuts up the world that they would be unable to imagine alternatives.

But it is impossible to draw firm boundaries around any speech community. Even if it were possible, every language possesses a range of ways of speaking that would provide its native speakers with alternative ways of describing the world. In any case, linguists have data showing that in most of the world's societies, monolingualism is the exception rather than the rule. Moreover, people who grow up bilingual do not also grow up schizophrenic, as if trying to reconcile in a single mind two contradictory views of reality. Indeed, bilingual children ordinarily benefit from knowing two languages, do not confuse them, can switch readily from one to another, and even appear to demonstrate greater cognitive flexibility on psychological tests than monolinguals (Elliot 1981:56).

In the face of these objections, other researchers have offered a weak version of the Sapir-Whorf hypothesis. This version rejects linguistic determinism for the preceding reasons, but continues to claim that language shapes thought and culture. If the shaping power of language can be countered by cultural practice or rational argument, however, many scholars conclude that this weak version is without scientific interest.

Neither Sapir nor Whorf favored linguistic determinism. Sapir argued that language's importance lies in the way it directs attention to some aspects of experience rather than to others. He was impressed that human beings could not experience reality except as it was mediated by cognitive processes. Language was only one manifestation, although an important one, of these processes. As a result, he observed that "it is generally difficult to make a complete divorce between objective reality and our linguistic symbols of reference to it" (Sapir [1933]1966:9, 15).

Whorf's views have been more sharply criticized by later scholars. His discussions of the linguistic relativity principle are complex and ambiguous. At least part of the problem arises from Whorf's attempt to view grammar as the linguistic pattern that shaped culture and thought. His fellow linguists understood grammar to refer to rules for combining sounds into words, and words into sentences. Whorf did not reject this definition of grammar, but he believed that linguistic investigation showed that grammar needed to be conceived more broadly. Some of Whorf's texts suggest that he was working to extend grammar to include a new level of patterning that went beyond words and sentences. Whorf died before being able to work out the theoretical language with which to describe such a level.

Components of Language

Anthropologists have been much concerned with the way human languages are put together, both because of their general interest in human symbolic processes and for practical reasons associated with language learning in the field. Originally they hoped that coming to understand the sound patterns of language would be sufficient. But it soon became apparent that patterns in other areas of language could not be reduced to patterns governing speech sounds. This led to the recognition that languages had different levels, or components, each with its own particular rules. The duality-of-patterning design feature acknowledges the discovery that the patterning of speech sounds follows different principles than the patterning of word formation or sentence structure.

At first, the study of speech sounds, called phonology, was distinguished from the study of word formation and sentence structure, called grammar. Eventually, this two-component theory of language proved inadequate. In the late 1950s and early 1960s, linguist Noam Chomsky demonstrated that sentences had certain properties that could not be explained by rules governing word structure. And so grammar was subdivided into morphology, the study of word structure, and syntax, the study of sentence structure. This theory soon expanded to include a fourth component, semantics, the study of meaning.

Formal semantics, however, defines meaning as "reference." It has traditionally been concerned with defining the meanings of words and phrases in terms of the objects, or ideas, or concepts they refer to in the wider world. It has also been interested in showing the ways in which the meanings of words and phrases relate to one another within the language itself (e.g., whether they mean the same thing, whether they are opposite in meaning, etc.).

This approach to meaning was of only limited help to anthropologists who were learning a new language in the field. Often, formal semantic studies of the language they were learning did not exist. They found themselves building their understanding of what words and phrases meant from the contexts in which those words and phrases were used. Many began to urge that the study of meaning as "use" receive more attention, especially since meanings derived from the way people used words were not always the same as meanings determined by formal semantic analysis. A number of linguists shared these concerns. And so a fifth component of grammar, pragmatics, was proposed to study the way speakers of a language use that language to communicate with one another.

A focus on language in use is simultaneously a focus on the context in which language is used. Sometimes the context is provided by other words or sentences in the language. This means that the linguist must often study stretches of speech longer than sentences to explain certain problems of language use. Linguists use the term *discourse* to refer to stretches of speech that are longer that a single sentence and that are linked together by a shared theme. Discourse analysis can explain patterns of linguistic use by relating it to the larger *linguistic context* in which individual sentences are embedded. Moreover, by paying attention to the broader *non-linguistic context* of language use, discourse analysis can explain certain features of meaning that would otherwise remain beyond the reach of formal linguistics altogether.

Edward Sapir once commented that "all grammars leak." One way of understanding the growth over time of the number of components of language recognized by linguists is to see each new component as an attempt to plug the leaks in an earlier theory. Problems in phonology that seemed to escape phonological explanation leaked out of that component, and morphology was developed to contain the leak, to explain what had previously resisted explanation. So it goes with all the remaining components of grammar. By the time the component of pragmatics is reached, however, the linguistic phenomena that resist explanation begin to spill over into the domain of culture. Let us examine each component of language in turn. The following discussions pinpoint the various leaks linguists have recognized, as well as linguists' attempts to plug the leaks. They also demonstrate the way in which culture and language codetermine each other.

Phonology: Sounds

The study of the sounds of language, **phonology**, is a biocultural study from the outset. The sounds of human language are special because they are produced by a set of organs, the speech organs, that belong only to the human species. These organs are primarily for ingestion and breathing and secondarily for the production of speech. Air expelled from the lungs passes through the throat, mouth, or nasal passages, or some combination of these, on its way out of the body. The various

phonology
the study of the sounds of language

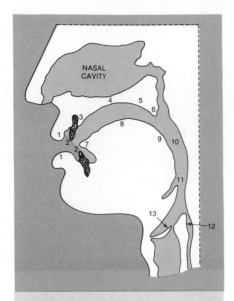

FIGURE 4.2
The Speech Organs
1. Lips, 2. teeth, 3. teethridge (alveolar ridge), 4. hard palate, 5. Soft palate (velum), 6. uvula, 7. tip of tongue, 8. blade of tongue, 9. back of tongue, 10. pharynx, 11. epiglottis, 12. food passage, 13. vocal cords.

sounds of language are made when the air passage changes shape or is obstructed by the tongue or teeth as a stream of air is expelled (See figure 4.2). Part of the phonologist's job is to map out possible arrangements of speech organs that human beings may use to create the sounds of language. Another part is to examine individual languages to discover the particular sound combinations they contain, as well as the patterns into which those sound combinations are organized.

The sounds of language can be studied from the perspective of speakers, hearers, or the sound medium itself. Most work in phonology has been done from the perspective of speakers who produce, or articulate, the sounds of language using their speech organs. No language makes use of all the many sounds that the human speech organs can produce. Most languages recognize (and require) relatively few sounds, which may then be combined in a patterned way to form all the utterances in the language. For example, American English uses only thirty-eight sounds, traditionally referred to as consonants and vowels.

Although all languages rely on only a handful of sounds, no two languages have selected exactly the same set of sounds. Furthermore, different speakers of the same language often differ from one another in the way their speech sounds are patterned. This results in the production of "accents," which make up one kind of variety within a language. This variety is not random; the speech sounds characteristic of any particular accent are patterned. Speakers with different accents are usually able to understand one another in most circumstances, but their distinctive speech sounds are clues to their ethnic, regional or social-class origins.

Traditionally, the characteristic speech sounds of a language are called *phonemes*. Linguists are interested in discovering not only how phonemes are patterned in any particular variety of a language, but also how different phonemic systems (accents) are related to one another. They have discovered that related phonemic systems vary from each other in an orderly manner. The sound changes that occur over time within any particular phonemic system are equally orderly.

Phonemes were originally conceived of as the building blocks of language, little atoms that could not be further broken down and analyzed. But phonologists discovered that it was possible to analyze the elements that constituted phonemes, just as atomic physicists discovered that atoms could be smashed to reveal subatomic particles. These smaller, subphonemic elements were called *distinctive features* of phonemes. Each phoneme of a language can be conceived of as a bundle of distinctive features.

Morphology: Word Structure

morphology
the study of word structure

Morphology is the study of the way words are put together. It developed as a subfield of linguistics as soon as linguists realized that the rules they had devised to explain sound patterns in language could not account for meaning patterns as well. This was immediately obvious when they began to study the structure of words.

What is a word? For speakers of a language such as English, a word might be defined as a short, meaning-bearing stretch of speech, clearly separable from other similar stretches of speech, and capable of being moved around in sentences or reappearing in different sentences. English speakers tend to think of words as the building blocks of sentences, while sentences are thought of as strings of words. But words are not all alike. Some words, like *book*, cannot be broken down into smaller elements. Other words, like *bookworm*, can be broken down.

The puzzle deepens when we try to translate words from one language into another. Sometimes expressions that require only one word in one language (e.g., *préciser* in French) require more than one word when translated into another language (e.g., "to make precise" in English). Other times, we must deal with languages whose utterances cannot easily be broken down into words at all. Consider the utterance *nikookitepeena,* from Shawnee, an American Indian language, which can be represented in English as "I dipped his head in the water" (Whorf 1956:172). Although this utterance is composed of parts, the parts do not correspond to words possessing the characteristics we attribute to words in English or French.

To make sense of the structure of languages such as Shawnee, anthropological linguists needed a concept that could be used to refer to both the words in English sentences and the parts of Shawnee utterances. This led to the development of the concept of *morphemes*, which have traditionally been defined as "the minimal units of meaning in a language." The various parts of a Shawnee utterance can be identified as morphemes, and so can many of the words of English. Describing minimal units of meaning as morphemes, and not as words, allows us to compare the morphology of English with the morphology of other languages.

In a language like Shawnee, the rules for putting morphemes together will be different from the rules used in English. A morphological analysis of the preceding Shawnee utterance would subdivide it into five morphemes: *ni-kooki-tepe-en-a.* Each morpheme can be described as belonging to a separate class of morphemes defined in terms of its function in the whole utterance. In other words, *ni* not only means "I," it also belongs to the class of morphemes that occur at the beginning of utterances and refer to the subject of a sentence (See table 4.1). Since the morphemes of Shawnee cannot stand alone, as English words can, their position in the utterance determines the function they will play, and the meaning they will bear, in the utterance.

The words of English utterances are more independent than the parts of Shawnee utterances. Yet even English words must be ordered in a particular sequence to convey particular meanings. Consider, for example, the differences among the following: "The dog is on the rug," "The rug is on the dog," and "Rug the the on is dog." Only certain ways of ordering morphemes are possible in English. Certain English words (known as complex words because they are made up of more than one morpheme) often contain morphemes that can never stand alone. Consider, for example, *walked* and *unhappy*. English morphemes such as the past tense marker *-ed* and the negative prefix *un-* both carry meaning and affect the meaning of the words to which they are joined. They cannot be joined to just any words, and they cannot stand alone; their use is patterned.

There are languages in which individual words carry so much meaning that their order in a sentence becomes almost irrelevant. In Latin, for example, each word indicates its function in the sentence. The sentence "Catullus loved Clodia" can be expressed in Latin in six different ways: (1) *Catullus Clodiam amabat*, (2) *Catullus amabat Clodiam*, (3) *Clodiam Catullus amabat*, (4) *Clodiam amabat*

Table 4.1
Morphemes of Shawnee Utterance and Their Glosses

ni	kooki	tepe	en	a
I	immersed in water	point of action at head	by hand action	cause to him

Catullus, (5) *Amabat Clodiam Catullus*, and (6) *Amabat Catullus Clodiam* (Lyons 1969). To change the sentence so that Clodia loved Catullus would require not a shift in word order but a change in the function markers: *Clodia Catullum amabat* and so on.

The study of morphemic patterning in a language such as Shawnee seems hopelessly complicated to native speakers of English. Yet the patterning of morphemes in English itself is not simple. Why is it that some morphemes can stand alone as words (e.g., *sing*, *red*) and others cannot? What determines a word boundary in the first place? Words, or the morphemes they contain, are the minimal units of meaning. Thus, they represent the fundamental point at which the arbitrary pairing of sound and meaning occurs.

Syntax: Sentence Structure

syntax
the study of sentence structure

A third component of language is **syntax**, or sentence structure. Linguists began to study syntax when they discovered that certain patterns of word use could not be explained by morphological rules alone. In languages like English, words in sentences cannot occur in just any order (recall the preceding examples about rugs and dogs). But rules governing word order cannot explain everything puzzling about English sentences. For example, one thing we usually know about a word is the part of speech (noun, verb, adjective, etc.) to which it belongs. In many cases, we cannot know to which part of speech a word belongs unless we know the structure of the sentence in which the word appears.

Suppose we find that the following sentence is perfectly acceptable in English: "Smoking grass means trouble." For native speakers of American English who came of age in the 1960s, this sentence exhibits what linguists call *structural ambiguity*. That is, we must ask ourselves what means trouble: the act of smoking grass (i.e., marijuana), or the act of noticing grass (i.e., the grass that grows on the prairie) that is giving off smoke? Either reading of the sentence is possible. To distinguish them from each other, we need to invent a way of distinguishing the use of *smoking* as a noun (and "smoking grass" as a noun phrase) and *smoking* as an adjective modifying the noun *grass* (producing again the noun phrase "smoking grass").

We can explain the different meanings carried by structurally ambiguous sentences if we assume that the role a word plays in a sentence is not determined by the structure of the word itself. Rather, it depends on the overall structure of the sentence in which the word is found. We conclude that sentences are ordered strings of words and that those words must be classified as parts of speech in terms of the function they fulfill in the sentence.

Even these two assumptions are not sufficient to account for other acceptable English sentences like "The father of the girl and the boy fell into the lake." This sentence also exhibits structural ambiguity, but the ambiguity cannot be explained once we classify the words as parts of speech. How many people fell into the lake? Just the father, or the father and the boy? This ambiguity can be resolved only if we assume that each reading of the sentence depends on how the words of the sentence are grouped together. That is, should we group the words "of the girl and the boy" together, understand it to modify the word *father*, and conclude that one person fell into the lake? Or should we conclude that "of the girl" modifies *father*, group together "the father (of the girl) and the boy," and conclude that two people fell into the lake?

This sort of grouping is called *structural grouping*. It classifies the various parts of speech that occur in a sentence into categories that represent the building blocks of the sentence itself. In the previous example, we had to decide which noun phrase was the subject of the sentence, since there were two noun phrases that might have filled that role.

We are now able to define sentences as ordered strings of words that belong to different classes and that may be assigned various structural roles in the string where they occur. But these three features do not account for the structure of all well-formed English sentences. Chomsky (1965) noted that native speakers of English believe that sentences like "The boy watered the garden" and "The garden was watered by the boy" are related to one another. He argued that this perceived connection could be explained if we could show that these two sentences had something in common even though they appeared to be structured differently.

Chomsky called the visible (or audible) appearance of a sentence its *surface structure*. But he argued that all sentences also possess a *deep structure,* which cannot be seen (or heard). He claimed that native speakers sense that two sentences are related because the sentences share the same deep structure. In the preceding example, the surface structure of the first sentence accurately reflects its deep structure. The second sentence, however, has been derived from the first by applying a *transformational rule*. In this case, the rule is called the passive transformation. That is, it transforms an active sentence (The boy watered the garden) into a passive one (The garden was watered by the boy).

By assuming both the existence of a deep structural level to syntax and the existence of transformational rules that can derive one grammatical sentence from another, Chomsky could account for the native speaker's intuitions about related sentences. Chomsky's transformational linguistics has inspired many years of active research into the structure of sentences in English and other languages.

Semantics: Meaning ▬▬▬

Semantics, the study of meaning, was avoided by linguists for many years. The reason for this is not difficult to find. *Meaning* is a highly ambiguous term. What do we mean, for example, when we say that a sentence means something? We may be talking about what each individual word in the sentence means, or what the sentence as a whole means, or what I mean when I utter the sentence.

We sometimes talk about words meaning what they refer to in the "real world." That is, we think of meaning as *reference*. Understanding meaning as reference leads to the creation, for example, of *operational definitions*. In these, a term is defined by describing the operations one would have to perform in order to experience whatever the term refers to. For example, the term *monkeys* might be defined operationally as "the animals you will observe if you drive to the zoo and look inside the first cage from the entrance."

One problem with thinking of meaning as reference is that it is difficult to indicate unambiguously exactly what a particular term refers to. To take the monkey example again, the operational definition given is adequate only until we ask what the word *animal* means. Perhaps we then define animal as "any living creature capable of growth and locomotion." We go to the zoo and discover that within the first cage from the entrance are several animals so defined. Some are crawling on the ground between the blades of grass, others are flying from their perches on the bars of the cage to the trees growing within the cage. Yet others are scampering up the

semantics
the study of meaning in language

tree or sitting in the branches, are covered with fur, and occasionally approach the bars and reach out toward their human observers.

If this were not enough, in a second cage are much larger animals that resemble the ones in the first cage in many ways, except that they have no tails. And in a third cage are yet other animals, far smaller than the animals in the first two cages. They resemble the other animals, except that they use their long tails to swing from the branches of a tree. Which of these animals are monkeys?

To answer this question, the observer must decide which features of similarity or difference are important, and which are not. Having made this decision, it is easier to decide which animals in cage 1 are monkeys, and whether the animals in cages 2 and 3 are monkeys as well. But such decisions are not easily come by. Biologists have spent the last three hundred years or so attempting to classify all living things on the planet into mutually exclusive categories. To do so, they have had to decide, of all the traits that living things exhibit, which ones matter.

To a large degree, this mania to classify has also been a central focus of formal semantics. Formal semantics began with the goal of linking words to the world by specifying unambiguously what each word referred to. It soon became apparent that this effort could not succeed until linguistic classification systems themselves were better understood. Better understanding led many thinkers to the conclusion that these classification systems needed considerable refinement before they could carry out their task. As a result, attention shifted away from the way words are linked to the world, and was instead focused on the ways words are linked to each other. Analysts had to specify the way in which the words of a language were meaningful. Then they traced the meaning relations that linked words to one another within in the language. Typical meaning relations include synonymy (same meaning), homophony (same sound, different meaning), antonymy (opposite meaning), meaning inclusion, meaning overlap, and so forth.

The history of formal semantics is thus paradoxical. While it began with an interest in relating words to the world, it ended up ignoring the world entirely.

Determining which of these animals belongs to the category monkey requires deciding which of the animals' physical characteristics are most significant.

Formal semantics has taught us much that we might never have learned without abstracting language from the hurly-burly conditions of its everyday use. But abstract analyses of language cannot tell us all there is to know about language as a cultural creation of human societies.

For instance, formal semantics has traditionally been preoccupied with a form of meaning called *denotation*. This refers to what a word means "in itself," how it is different from all other words in the language. To find a word's denotation, we might consult a dictionary. According to *The American Heritage Dictionary*, for example, a pig is "any of several mammals of the family Suidae, having short legs, cloven hoofs, bristly hair, and a cartilaginous snout used for digging." A formal definition of this sort is useful if you are relating the word *pig* to other words in English, such as *cow* or *chicken*. Each word can be related to the others in terms of semantic features they share, or semantic features they do not share. Moreover, these meaning relations hold even if all real pigs, cows, and chickens have been wiped off the face of the earth. But difficulty arises as soon as we recognize that words never just mean what they denote. Words also have *connotations*, additional meanings that derive from the typical contexts in which they are used in everyday speech. In the context of student antiwar demonstrations in the 1960s, for example, a pig was a police officer.

Formal semantics avoided having to reconcile the frequent lack of harmony between denotations and connotations of the same word. Denotations were said to be language based and rule-like, independent of the ways speakers chose to use them. Connotation was an idiosyncratic and unpredictable by-product of speaker use. Put in terms used earlier, formal semantics tried to reduce meaning to denotation. Reduction seemed unproblematic, since denotational definitions were supposedly based on clear-cut features of the objects to which they referred. It was assumed, for instance, that acquaintance with real pigs would make it obvious that the traits listed in the dictionary definition of pig were the traits that mattered.

However, knowing which traits matter and which do not is never self-evident. Formal semantics is based on the conviction that one primary classification can be discovered that is better or truer than any alternative. The job of the formal semanticist is to discover this single classification. Yet, everyday experience teaches us that no single classification is adequate for all our needs. As our purposes for classifying change, so too will the objects that are grouped together as similar or different. For example, bats and birds both have wings, and in this respect they might be put together in the same category. But bats give birth to live young, and birds lay eggs. In this respect they differ, and so they might be assigned to different categories.

The ability to classify and reclassify our experiences is the hallmark of openness. And a focus on purpose is at the same time a focus on the context for which such a purpose is appropriate. This suggests that much of the referential meaning of language escapes us if we neglect the context of language use.

Pragmatics: Language in Contexts of Use

Pragmatics can be defined as the study of language in contexts of use. This definition has a double focus. On the one hand, it emphasizes the purposes of users, the different functions to which users put language in the various contexts of daily life. On the other hand, pragmatics emphasizes that every attempt we make to do things with words occurs in a context. This context offers limitations and opportunities concerning what we may say and how we may say it. Everyday language use is thus

pragmatics
the study of the way speakers of a language actually use the language to communicate with one another

often characterized by a struggle between speakers and listeners over definitions of context and appropriate word use.

Traditional formal semantics had only the narrowest view of context: that provided by the formal definitions of other words and phrases in the language. However, anthropological linguists such as Michael Silverstein (1976, 1985) have shown that the referential meaning of certain expressions in language cannot be determined without going beyond this narrow context. Two kinds of context are involved: linguistic and nonlinguistic.

Linguistic contexts are of three types. The first is the narrow referential context recognized by traditional semantics. The second is created by speech that comes before the word or phrase whose meaning is in question. For example, consider the following two sentences: "I read a great book last week. It was a birthday present from my aunt." The meaning of the word *it* in the second sentence cannot be specified with reference to the other words and phrases in that sentence. Instead, we must consult the preceding sentence to learn that *it* refers to the book. The first sentence provides a linguistic context determining the meaning of *it* in the following sentence.

The third kind of linguistic context is related to the linguistic design feature of reflexiveness. Recall that this design feature is based on our ability to talk about the way we talk. We do this when we report what someone else said. Consider the following sentences: "I read a book today." "John said, 'I read a book today.'" The second sentence is meaningful only if we assume the existence of a prior situation in which John said, "I read a book today."

Here we have to go beyond the traditional bounds of formal semantics to make sense of a particular word or phrase. We also have to go beyond the boundaries of a single sentence. Put another way, the rules of syntax and semantics are not able to explain the kinds of reference illustrated in these examples.

Pragmatics forces us to look outside individual sentences to determine the referential meanings of words. Pragmatics therefore requires us to pay attention to discourse. *Discourse* refers to a stretch of speech longer than a sentence, united by a common theme. One example of discourse would be a series of sentences uttered one after another in the speech of a single individual. But discourse may also be defined to include a series of rejoinders in a conversation among two or more speakers. In fact, if we accept the persuasive arguments of such theorists of discourse as M. M. Bakhtin and V. N. Voloshinov (e.g., Voloshinov 1929), the series of rejoinders in conversation would be the primary form of discourse. In their view, the speech of any single individual, whether a simple yes or a book-length dissertation, is but one rejoinder in an ongoing dialogue with others on a particular theme.

Pragmatics may also mean looking outside language as a whole to the nonlinguistic context in which speech is embedded. *Nonlinguistic context* consists of objects and activities that are present in the situation of speech at the same time we are speaking. We cannot provide the referential meaning of certain expressions in language without considering this nonlinguistic context. Consider the English sentence "Who is that standing by the door?" We need to inspect the actual physical context at the moment this sentence is uttered to find the door and the person standing by the door, and thus give a referential meaning to the words *who* and *that*. Furthermore, even if we know what a door is in a formal sense, we need the nonlinguistic context to specify for us what counts as a door in this instance (e.g., a rough opening in the wall that cannot be closed off).

Once we begin to study the nonlinguistic context, we begin to notice other things, especially if we compare the way two different speakers, or speakers of two

cathy® by Cathy Guisewite

Panel 1: "WHEW! I'M BEAT. WANT TO STOP SOMEWHERE FOR A DRINK, CATHY?" "A DRINK?"

Panel 2: "DOES HE MEAN "DRINK," AS IN "POTENTIAL DATE"...OR "DRINK," AS IN "FRIENDLY CO-WORKER DRINK"?"

Panel 3: ""DRINK," AS IN "START A SERIES OF PERSONAL COMPLICATIONS THAT WILL DESTROY MY CAREER"....OR "DRINK," AS IN "DEVELOP THE KIND OF GREAT BUSINESS FRIENDSHIP THAT COULD HELP SHOOT ME TO THE TOP"??"

Panel 4: "WHAT DO YOU SAY?" "I DIDN'T UNDERSTAND THE QUESTION."

different languages, choose to represent the objects and activities that are before them as they are speaking. The same situation can be represented differently by different speakers of the same language, by different speakers of different languages, by the same speaker to different audiences, and so forth. Consider the monkey example referred to earlier in the chapter. A person who knew little about nonhuman primates might be inclined to group the creatures in all three cages together and call them monkeys. Primatologists, by contrast, would distinguish apes from monkeys, and New World monkeys from Old World monkeys. They would be able to supply a separate label and a formal definition for the creatures in each cage: snow monkey (an Old World monkey), gorilla (an ape), spider monkey (a New World monkey).

Or consider a famous cross-linguistic example described by anthropologist Harry Hoijer (1953:559), who discusses the Chiricahua Apache place name

> "tonoogah, *for which the English equivalent (not the translation) is 'Dripping Springs.' Dripping Springs, a noun phrase, names a spot in New Mexico where the water from a spring flows over a rocky bluff and drips into a small pool below; the English name, it is evident, is descriptive of one part of this scene, the movement of the water. The Apache term is, in contrast, a verbal phrase and accentuates quite a different aspect of the scene. The element* to, *which means "water," precedes the verb* noogah, *which means, roughly, "whiteness extends downward."* tonoogah, *as a whole, then, may be translated "water-whiteness extends downward," a reference to the fact that a broad streak of white limestone deposit, laid down by the running water, extends downward on the rock."*

Each of these examples shows how different speakers may represent elements of the same nonlinguistic context differently in their speech. That is, each speaker takes up a different *referential perspective* with regard to the nonlinguistic context of speech (Wertsch 1985:168). Sometimes different referential perspectives may seem to have so little in common with each other that we might conclude the speakers were talking about completely different matters. Much confusion is eliminated if we can establish that all speakers were attending to the same context. Once we know that this is the case, we can inspect that context for clues that would make sense of each speaker's description.

Further dialogue about a common context often allows speakers to make their alternative referential perspectives comprehensible to one another. Thus, a primatologist understands why nonprofessionals might think all nonhuman primates look alike. However, some conversation between primatologist and naive observer, replete with much pointing and comparison, might be enough to lead the observer to recognize differences separating the creatures in the three cages mentioned earlier, and to remember the linguistic expressions that mark those differences. Similarly, if Apache speakers and English speakers know enough of one another's languages to interpret their respective names for the same place, they should have no difficulty appreciating the alternative referential perspectives represented in each place name. Moreover, with a little creativity, both referential perspectives might be represented in a single language; for example, *tonoogah* might be translated into the English place name Limestone Streak.

In the course of anthropological fieldwork, individuals equipped with different languages and different cultural backgrounds work collaboratively to arrive at an understanding of shared nonlinguistic events. The more they learn, the more proficient each becomes in adopting the referential perspective of the other. When successful, the fieldwork experience teaches informant and anthropologist alike how to describe the same event from more than one referential perspective. However, such understanding is not limited to cross-cultural and cross-linguistic situations. All languages contain a variety of resources upon which their speakers may draw to articulate different referential perspectives on the same nonlinguistic events.

The choice of perspective can have far-reaching consequences. Whether one chooses, for example, to describe the guerrilla army fighting the Sandinista government in Nicaragua as "freedom fighters," "right-wing thugs," or "the guerrilla army fighting the Sandinista government in Nicaragua" is a powerful clue to one's political affiliation. And this shows us that referential perspectives are at the same time *ideological perspectives*. As Wertsch comments, "Just as one must use some referential perspective when speaking of objects and events, one must also use some ideological perspective. The fact that certain voices seem to be ideologically neutral to a particular audience . . . stems from a particular sociohistorical setting" (1985:229).

Thus, Nicaraguans who have suffered at the hands of the Sandinistas might well find the freedom fighter label to be an obvious, ideologically neutral description, and might object to any supposedly value-free referential perspective (such as "guerrilla army fighting the Sandinista government") that does not take their suffering into account. Nicaraguans who have suffered at the hands of the guerrilla army might be equally likely to deny the accuracy of a value-free perspective, but they will certainly reject the description of the guerrillas as freedom fighters. The only way to resolve these seemingly irresolvable referential (and ideological) perspectives would seem to involve intense collaborative negotiation, not unlike what goes on between informant and anthropologist in the field. But such negotiation is extremely difficult to bring about, as recent Central American history has shown.

And so we begin to see, in outline, the complex dialectic between language and culture. We cannot use language without in some way needing to consider the context of use. But taking context into consideration means adopting a referential perspective with respect to that context. And adopting a referential perspective means adopting an ideological perspective as well. But ideological perspectives are cultural creations, selectively drawing upon the varied resources available in any language to construct a coherent point of view on lived experience. This means, as Wertsch concludes, that anyone's characteristic way of speaking "carries with itself a great deal of sociohistorically specific ideological baggage" (1985:229).

This might be seen as an argument for linguistic or cultural determinism, but it is not. Every language and culture can support a variety of points of view and ways of talking about them. Members of every culture, speakers of every language, must come to terms with these alternatives in the societies to which they belong. As a result, all people have the potential to master a variety of referential and ideological perspectives, to develop a *multilingual consciousness*. Here, the insights of Whorf, for example, become suggestive. Much of Whorf's writing on linguistic relativity can be seen as an attempt not only to describe, but to create in the minds of his readers, the experience of multilingual consciousness (Schultz 1989).

Linguistic Inequality

Languages are not monolithic, but rather contain a multiplicity of resources that speakers may draw upon in order to articulate particular referential perspectives. These individual referential perspectives are also ideological perspectives, as is shown by people who make value judgments about the different language varieties used by individuals or groups in their society. We might call such judgments a kind of linguistic ethnocentrism, in which one variety is taken as the standard against which all other varieties are measured.

The linguistic features that distinguish one variety of a language from another are rarely viewed neutrally. Emily Schultz recalls vividly an event she witnessed as a college undergraduate during the turbulent 1960s. She was attending a political address given by a militant black from a northern urban ghetto. After his speech was over, the speaker accepted questions from the audience. One questioner, a young woman, asked respectfully what whites such as herself ought to do to help the black cause. Unfortunately, she spoke with a very definite southern white accent, which was lost on no one, least of all the speaker. The atmosphere in the room was electric with danger even before the speaker opened his mouth to reply, and his response, the contents of which are now forgotten, bristled with hostility and anger. The young woman's words were relatively innocuous, but her accent was not. The questioner's accent that that of the oppressors; the speaker's accent was that of the oppressed. In the context of his speech, which urged that oppression be overthrown, the questioner's accent made her the enemy, no matter what she said.

This example illustrates one way the term "linguistic inequality" tends to be used by linguists: in reference to value judgments about other people's speech. Northern black ghetto speech and southern white speech were each evaluated with reference to a context of dominance and subordination. When blacks were slaves, and for a long time after, their speech was considered by whites and even some blacks to be unquestionably inferior, just as white speech was considered superior. With the civil rights movement of the 1960s this evaluation was reversed for militant blacks. Their accents, legacies of oppression, were viewed positively, whereas their oppressors' accent was devalued. In neither case, however, was anything being claimed about what the linguist would label strictly linguistic or communicative matters. Both the black militant and the white woman in the audience spoke standard English, and there was nothing ungrammatical about the sentences they used for question and response. Indeed, the audience understood both speakers without difficulty, in addition to being able to understand the black man's hostile reaction to the white woman's accent.

Speech in the Inner City

Strictly linguistic inequality is normally measured in different ways. Studies in the 1960s by William Labov and his colleagues dealt with such strictly linguistic matters in the speech of inner-city black children. Previous researchers had claimed that inner-city black children suffered from *linguistic deprivation*. The researchers had said that these children started school with few words and no grammar, and that this was the reason they could not perform as well as white children in the classroom. Labov's response to this series of assertions was to demonstrate two things. First, he proved that the form of English spoken in the inner city was not a defective pseudolanguage. Second, he showed how a change in research context permitted inner-city black children to display a level of linguistic sophistication that previous white researchers had never dreamed they possessed.

When black children were in the classroom, a white-dominated context, being interrogated by white adults about topics of no interest to them, they said little. This did not necessarily mean, Labov argued, that they had no language. Rather, their minimal responses were better understood as defensive attempts to keep threatening white questioners from learning anything about them. For the black children, the classroom was only one part of a broader racist culture existing beyond the classroom. The previous white investigators had been ethnocentrically oblivious of the effect this context might have on the results of their research.

Labov reasoned that reliable samples of black speech had to be collected in contexts where the racist threat was lessened. This meant doing fieldwork in the homes and on the streets of the inner city. He and his colleagues recorded enormous amounts of speech in Black English produced by the same children who had nothing to say when questioned in the classroom. Labov's analysis demonstrated that Black English was a variety of English that had certain rules not found in Standard English. This can be seen as a kind of strictly linguistic difference, in that most middle-class white speakers of Standard English would not use these rules, whereas most black speakers would. This kind of linguistic difference shows up when speakers of the two varieties must talk with one another. It thus becomes a marker of the speaker's membership in a particular speech community. Such differences can exist in phonology, morphology, syntax, semantics, or pragmatics.

Speech of Women and Men

Strictly linguistic differences in language knowledge or language use are not the sole preserve of ethnic groups. They also exist in the speech of men and women. In American society, women and men are expected to behave differently in many of the same situations. Carole Edelsky (1977) hypothesized that these different expectations might include different speech norms as well. She suggested that adult communicative competence might include rules for "talking like a lady" as well as for "talking like a man."

Edelsky set out to discover what these rules were and when they appeared in the speech of growing children. She tested first graders, third graders, sixth graders, and adults to measure their knowledge of the norms. The test involved presenting the research subjects with such sentences as "Won't you pretty please hand me that hammer" or "Damn it, get me that perfume!" She discovered that by the sixth grade, children were aware that linguistic usages displaying weakness or elaborateness are marked for females, whereas casual profanity is marked for males.

Adults in Edelsky's sample applied these rules as a formula and persisted in defending them as literally descriptive of their own or other people's actual speech, even when faced with direct evidence to the contrary. "One subject, male, said men would not use *Oh dear* 'because it's a protected word, more passive, that men don't use.' This statement was separated by an interval of about 10 minutes from the following one, made by the same subject, 'I can't come up with anything. Oh dear, I'm just going to run the tape down'" (Edelsky 1977:237).

Edelsky calls the rigidity of the formula in adults and older children *over-generalization*. In the terms used in this text, it would conform to an ideologically rigid referential perspective.

The Dialectic between Language and Culture

If different groups in society have characteristically different histories and experiences, they are likely to develop characteristically unique referential perspectives to talk about those histories and experiences. These referential perspectives may be evaluated positively or negatively by other groups in the society. Evaluation often has more to do with who is speaking than with that person's referential perspective itself. A point of view that may be unobjectionable when uttered by a high-status member of society may sound subversive when spoken by a low-status person. In any society with even minimal social variety, the use of particular words, grammatical structures, or pronunciations will carry different messages to different audiences. Only in a linguistic laboratory, where context has been deliberately stripped away, can strictly linguistic equality or inequality reveal itself. In all other contexts, the statuses of speakers confer status on their speech.

By what processes, then, do linguistic expressions become so heavily laden with cultural meanings? Through learning processes that depend on schemas, prototypes, and metaphors.

Schemas

In any human society, experience itself tends to be patterned. For example, we repeatedly experience the change of seasons or the transformation of water into ice and ice into water. We repeatedly experience other people around us; watch them perform similar activities' watch them grow, one after another, from childhood to adulthood to old age.

A patterned, repetitive experience has been called a **schema**, or an experiential gestalt. A gestalt is a holistic, unified pattern whose identity cannot be reduced to the parts that make it up. Schemas might also be understood as chunks of experience that appear to hang together as wholes, exhibiting the same properties in the same configuration whenever they recur. One reason it is difficult to describe fully and adequately certain aspects of experience—a close friend, spring, college, baseball—is that we experience them as unities. As human beings grow up in any society, they gradually become aware of the chunks of experience that their culture (or subculture) recognizes. Language provides both labels for these culturally relevant experiential chunks, and a variety of grammatical means for describing how these chunks relate to one another.

Language is thus embedded in experience, and the experiences that shape language are culturally patterned schemas. A schema important for many Western children is *Christmas*. This term refers to a chunk of experience with recognizable characteristics recurring regularly once every year. The Christmas schema might involve the nature of the weather at Christmastime (cold, snowy) and particular events (baking cookies, singing carols, attending church, putting up a Christmas tree, buying and wrapping gifts, etc.). In the experience of a child, all these attributes may be equally relevant parts of a larger whole. It takes time and conditioning for parents to persuade children what the "true meaning of Christmas" really is. Sometimes mature members of the society who celebrate Christmas may disagree

schema
a patterned, repetitive experience that appears to hang together as a whole, exhibiting the same properties in the same configuration whenever it recurs

about the true meaning of the event, depending, for example, on whether they are or are not religious Christians. Non-Christian members of Western societies are likely to experience Christmas in a very different way.

A child's first words are deeply embedded in the schemas to which they refer. How do language and meaning become further refined so that children learn, for example, to talk not only about Christmas but also about trees and carols and church services and presents? This awareness seems to grow as schematic chunks of experience become more familiar and subdivided into subschemas.

We may refer to schemas as *domains of experience*. Cultural learning involves exploring the different domains of experience that one's culture recognizes. When we apply words to domains of experience, or to the elements and relationships that constitute them, we can call them *semantic domains*.

Domains of experience that are culturally organized tend to have an organized vocabulary associated with them. Ordinarily, the more central a domain of experience is to the cultural life of the group, the more elaborate is this vocabulary. For example, the Aymara of South America depend on potatoes for subsistence, and raise many different varieties. Not surprisingly, the Aymara vocabulary for referring to potatoes is highly elaborated.

But it is not just objects and events, like potatoes or holidays, that are organized and categorized linguistically. Children learn that people, too, can be categorized in terms of status, and that certain linguistic forms may be used by some people, but not others. Martha Platt (1986) expected that Samoan children would actively use the verb *sau* (to come) before they used the verb *aumai* (to bring/give,) because *sau* is semantically simpler than *aumai*. Yet she discovered that Samoan children actively used the verb *aumai* before they used *sau*! *(See EthnoFile 4.2: Samoa.)*

Why would children apparently master a more difficult word before a simpler one? This question was easily answered once Platt noted that Samoan children frequently encounter both words in everyday speech in the form of commands (e.g., "Come here!" "Bring me this!" "Give her that!"). They also quickly learn that high-status persons may use *sau* to summon a person of equal or lower status. *Aumai*, in contrast, may be used to address low-status and high-status persons alike. Status is closely related to age in Samoa. Thus, children ordinarily use *sau* only when summoning children even younger than they are, or when conveying the request of a high-status person (e.g., a parent) to a third party.

EthnoFile 4.2
SAMOA

Region: Oceania

Nation: Western Samoa

Population: 182,000

Environment: Tropical island

Livelihood: Horticulture, fishing, wage labor in capital

Political organization:
Ranked, with linguistic markers for high- and low- status people; now part of modern nation-state

Other: Margaret Mead did fieldwork in this famous anthropological site in the 1920s; her work was challenged after her death by Derek Freeman in a dispute over the explanation of human nature

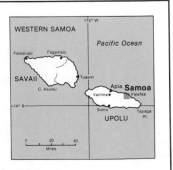

Contexts may also be categorized. Children learn how to distinguish formal from informal contexts and to master the speech forms appropriate to each. In America, they must learn, for example, that linguistic forms that can be used with impunity on the playground are not permitted in the classroom, where other forms are expected. Difficulties in the classroom may occur when the formal and informal speech styles of children from different subgroups of society do not coincide with the formal and informal speech styles that are enforced as the standard.

The orderly knowledge of familiar semantic domains is used to help us make sense of new experiences. This is the familiar process that psychologists call *generalization*. Much of a child's early language-learning activity involves coming to understand which generalizations are culturally acceptable and which are not. This, in turn, involves a child's ability to identify similarities and differences in accordance with cultural prescriptions.

Prototypes

Human beings accept without question most of the domains of experience that their culture recognizes. In other words, we take the experiences that our culture pays attention to as **prototypes** of human experiences. We use them as a baseline for judging other experiences as typical or not, human or not. This is the ground out of which ethnocentrism sprouts.

prototypes
examples of typical instances, elements, relations, or experiences within a particular culturally relevant semantic domain

Prototypes of various sorts appear to be central to the way meaning is organized in human language. The words of our language refer to typical instances, typical elements or relations, typical experiences within one or another culturally relevant domain.

If the prototype we are using is well established in our culture and our language, ordinarily we should be able to use it, and have other people understand our use of it, without trouble. The term *idiom* is often used to refer to these well-worn ways of talking about our daily experiences. When we organize experience and assign meaning on the basis of prototypes, however, the categories we use have fuzzy boundaries. And since our experiences do not always neatly fit our prototypes, often we will not be sure which prototype applies. Is a tossed salad a prototypical tossed salad if in addition to lettuce and tomatoes and onions it also contains raisins and apple slices? Is a library still a prototypical library when it contains fewer books than microfilms and videotapes and computer diskettes? In cases like this, suggested linguist R. A. Hudson, a speaker must simply recognize the openness of language and apply linguistic labels creatively.

Prototypes are a dialectical product of human culture and the wider world. Furthermore, just as experience escapes the attempt of language to confine it, so too does it escape the net of culture. Culture and language therefore direct our attention to some aspects of experience rather than to others. They often create new experiences for us that would not exist without their intervention. But human cognition is open, and this means that we are always potentially able to view our experiences from more than one perspective. It therefore always remains possible for us to discover aspects of our experience that our particular culture or language have downplayed or ignored. Thus we all have the potential to restructure our understanding of the world.

Metaphor

A central aim of linguistic theory is to account for ambiguity. The traditional approach has been to handle ambiguity by eliminating it, by "disambiguating" ambiguous utterances. However, an analysis of meaning based on prototypes accepts ambiguity from the outset as part of human experience and therefore as part of language as well.

Linguistic ambiguity is most clearly illustrated by various forms of figurative or nonliteral language, of which **metaphor** is the most striking example. A metaphor proclaims the existence of a meaningful link between two expressions from different semantic domains. For example, human beings and birds ordinarily are thought to belong to separate semantic domains, but the metaphor "Arnold is a turkey" asserts that at least one person and one species of bird belong in the same semantic domain. This assertion creates ambiguity: are people and birds (or Arnold and a turkey) alike or different? We cannot know until we place the statement "Arnold is a turkey" into some kind of context. If we know, for example, that Arnold is characteristically inept, ignorant, and annoying, and that turkeys are prototypically stupid and clumsy, the metaphor "Arnold is a turkey" becomes intelligible and apt.

When ambiguous linguistic utterances are placed in a particular context, their apparent ambiguity is often resolved, relative to the context in question. But this resolution does not reveal the literal meaning of a sentence. The same sentence can literally and unambiguously mean different things in different contexts.

Consider the following sentence: "The woman who just left is my mother." This statement is straightforward enough, apparently unproblematic. But if we are Americans, this is so only as long as we believe that the speaker is the biological offspring of the woman who just left. What if the speaker had been adopted by the woman who just left? We might still consider the statement unproblematic, if we could be sure the speaker did not know that she had been adopted. But what if the speaker's very next utterance was "She and Dad adopted me when I was just a baby."

Is it literally true that the woman who just left was the speaker's mother? Or is she speaking metaphorically? Suppose we say to her, "But that woman and her husband aren't your *real* parents. You really mean that they are your *adoptive* parents. The woman who gave birth to you is your real mother." Perhaps the speaker will become annoyed and insist, "No, she and my dad are my real parents. They are the ones who raised me. They did everything that parents do for their children." "Aha," we reply. "You are speaking metaphorically. What you really mean is that they are *like* parents to you." "No, I don't," the speaker retorts, genuinely angry now. "They are not *like* parents to me, they *are* my parents!"

This scene raises virtually all the problems raised by linguistic openness. How are we to assess the speaker's statements about the woman who just left? Is the speaker merely ignorant of her parentage? No. Is she then uninformed about what mothers really are? Not really. Her account of what her parents did for her is pretty close to parental prototype in American culture, but she seems to have missed a central attribute of that prototype, namely that in American kinship only biological parents are considered "real" parents. We point this out to her. Her angry response indicates that she is well aware that this is conventionally part of the parent prototype and that she rejects the conventional prototype. This is made clear by her denial of the simile "*like* parents to you."

Do we conclude that the speaker is crazy? Does she think she can challenge the prototypes of parenthood that are part of her cultural tradition and get away with it? Is human perversity once again rearing its ugly head, making a shambles of the carefully constructed cultural prototypes that our ancestors labored so long and hard to establish?

metaphor
a form of thought and language that asserts a meaningful link between two expressions from different semantic domains; "Arnold is a turkey" is a metaphor

Dear Abby: Thanks for pointing out the stupid statements some well-meaning people make concerning adopted children. One of the most stupid is to say—in front of the child—"And this is Alice, John and Jane's daughter. They adopted her, you know." Then all the information about the adoption comes flowing out like water from a fountain. Why can't they leave it at that? But the worst by far is, "I'll bet you love her like she was your own child." How dare they? She *is* our own child.

—Had It with Dummies

FIGURE 4.3
Source: Taken from the "Dear Abby" column by Abigail Van Buren. Copyright 1986.

Yes. At least the challenge to received truth is genuine. Whether such challenges are made only by crazy people is another question. But there is definitely a tendency—one might almost say a tradition—in the Western world to regard those who fail to adopt prototypical referential perspectives as either ignorant, mad, or perverse. If they assert that black is white, are they not going against the grain of the universe? Perhaps we can forgive them if they make this assertion out of ignorance, and even madness we can cope with. But if we suspect that a person making this scandalous assertion is otherwise quite sane, then what other explanation can there be but that he or she is consciously bent on unraveling the fabric of the cosmos, allowing chaos to rush in?

This is the radical threat posed by metaphor. But it is at the same time a radical promise. If we take metaphors seriously, then we must also seriously question our previous prototypes about the world and ourselves. Unlike similes, unlike unconventional statements surrounded by expressions like "for the sake of argument," metaphors give no clues that would allow us safely to relegate them to the domain of the nonliteral. When we use metaphor, we are suggesting that the world as we understand it might be otherwise understood. This is what learning is all about.

We can recognize utterances as metaphorical only if we have non-metaphorical utterances with which to compare them. But nonmetaphorical utterances are based on culturally constructed prototypes. When we use metaphor, we are suggesting that the conventionally accepted prototypes are not the only possible prototypes, or even the most illuminating prototypes, that we might construct to help us account for particular experiences. Conventionally accepted prototypes are therefore not absolutely, literally true. We agree to accept them as literally true in order to get on with life. And we may decide to challenge them for the same reason.

Literal language is, in other words, a language of conventionalized metaphors. Once the members of a society agree to live by certain metaphors, once they "ratify" those metaphors, the metaphors become accepted as literally true. Thus *literal* is better understood to mean "conventionally accepted."

Ambiguous and metaphorical utterances shock our ears because they violate convention in a manner similar to the way profanity in the speech of small children violates convention. Thus, reality is reality under a certain description; literal language is literal under a certain convention. Apt metaphors, particularly when they are linked to one another systematically, have the power to reshape our view of the wider world.

Pidgin Languages: Negotiating Meaning

Up to this point, we have been looking at contexts of language use in which speakers and listeners are able, for the most part, to draw upon overlapping ranges of linguistic variety in order to communicate, however imperfectly. In some situations, however, potential parties to a verbal exchange find themselves sharing little more than physical proximity to one another. Such situations arise when members of communities with radically different language traditions, and no history of previous contact with one another, come face to face and are forced to communicate with each other. Nothing can be presumed as given for members of both speech communities involved, other than the new shared experiences growing out of enforced contact. From these new experiences develop new schemas as well as a new form of language: **pidgin**.

pidgin
a reduced language that has no native speakers; pidgins are said to develop in a single generation between members of communities that possess their own native languages

"When the chips are down, meaning is negotiated" (Lakoff and Johnson 1980:231). The study of pidgin languages is the study of the radical negotiation of new meaning, the dialectical production of a new whole (the pidgin language) that is different from and reducible to neither of the languages that gave birth to it. The shape of a pidgin reflects the context in which it arises—generally one of colonial conquest or commercial domination. Vocabulary is usually taken from the language of the dominant group, making it easy for the dominant group to learn. Syntax and phonology may be similar to the subordinate language (or languages), however, making it easier for subordinated speakers to learn. Morphological complexity tends to disappear (Holm 1988).

Pidgins are considered to be reduced languages that have no native speakers. They develop, in a single generation, between groups of speakers who do have native languages. When speakers of a pidgin language pass that language on to a new generation, linguists refer to the language as a creole. The creolization of pidgins normally involves growing complexity in phonology, morphology, syntax, semantics, and pragmatics, such that the pidgin comes to resemble conventional languages.

The distinction seems straightforward: pidgins are not real languages, but creoles, which develop out of pidgins, are real languages. In fact, this distinction is far from clear-cut. "There is no moment at which a particular pidgin suddenly comes into existence, but rather a process of variety-creation called pidginization, by which *a pidgin is gradually built up out of nothing*. We might well ask whether this process is essentially different from what happens in everyday interaction between people who think they speak the same language, but who are in fact constantly accommodating their speech and language to each other's needs" (Hudson 1980:70; emphasis added).

Language and Truth

For Thomas Kuhn, a philosopher of science, metaphor lies at the heart of science. Changes in scientific theories are "accompanied by a change in some of the relevant metaphors and in corresponding parts of the network of similarities through which terms attach to nature" (Kuhn 1979:416). Kuhn argued that these changes in the way scientific terms link up to nature are not reducible to logic or grammar. "They come about in response to pressures generated by observation or experiment"—that is, by *experience*, by *context*. And there is no neutral language into which rival theories can be translated and subsequently evaluated as unambiguously right or wrong (Kuhn 1979:416). Kuhn asks the question "Is what we refer to as 'the world' perhaps a product of mutual accommodation between experience and language?"

If our understanding of reality is the product of a dialectic between experience and language (or, more broadly, culture), then ambiguity will never be permanently removed from any of the symbolic systems that human beings invent. Ambiguity is part of the human experience from the outset, and human beings must work to limit it within cultural boundaries. Reflexive consciousness makes human beings aware of ambiguity, of alternatives. The experience of doubt, of not being sure what to believe, is never far behind.

This is not merely the experience of women and men in Western societies. E. E. Evans-Pritchard (1963) describes the same sort of vertigo among the Azande of central Africa. *(See EthnoFile 7.3: Azande.)* The Azande people are well aware of the ambiguity inherent in language, and they exploit it by using metaphor (what they call *sanza*) to disguise speech that might be received badly if uttered directly. For example, "A man says in the presence of his wife to his friend, 'Friend, those swallows, how they flit about in there.' He is speaking about the flightiness of his wife and in case she should understand the allusion, he covers himself by looking up at the swallows as he makes his seemingly innocent remark" (Evans-Pritchard 1963:211). Evans-Pritchard later observes that *sanza* "adds greatly to the difficulties of anthropological inquiry. Eventually the anthropologist's sense of security is undermined and his confidence shaken. He learns the language, can say what he wants to say in it, and can understand what he hears, but then he begins to wonder whether he has really understood . . . he cannot be sure, and even they [the Azande] cannot be sure, whether the words do have a nuance or someone imagines that they do" (1963:228).

However much we learn about language, we will never be able to exhaust its meanings or circumscribe its rules once and for all. Historian of religions Wilfred Cantwell Smith (1982:65) speaks of the temple of Madurai, which he came to know during his years of research in India. He asks what it means to refer to this particular structure as a temple. The first Europeans who saw it apparently assigned the term because it was, from their perspective, a pagan religious structure not to be confused with a Christian church building. This first labeling of Hindu temples was rather slipshod, impressionistic, and ethnocentric. It was followed in later periods by intensive research carried out by Western scholars who were scientifically trained and who were therefore able to provide a much fuller definition for the expression "Hindu temple." These scholars systematically and accurately recorded and analyzed the temple's architectural configuration and the artwork with which it was decorated, compared it with other similar structures, and so on. Later scholars noticed that the temple could not be fully understood unless some attention were also paid to the people who performed rituals there, the markets set up around it, and so on. Eventually, some Western scholars even developed reflexive consciousness and began to incorporate into their understanding of this temple, and others like it, the opinions of Hindu informants. Never has so much been known about Hindu temples as is known today, and presumably this knowledge will increase in the future. Nevertheless, "it is still the case today that *no one on earth, neither Hindu nor outsider, yet fully knows what a temple is*" (Smith 1982:65). Human language and human cognition are open systems, and as long as human history continues, new forms will be created and old forms will continue to be put to new uses.

The Meenakshi Temple at Madurai.

Key Terms

language
linguistics
design features
cognition
linguistic competence
communicative competence

Sapir-Whorf hypothesis
phonology
morphology
syntax
semantics

pragmatics
schema
prototypes
metaphor
pidgin

Chapter Summary

1. *Language* is a unique faculty of human beings, permitting them to communicate, but also setting up barriers to communication. It is a part of culture, and therefore is learned, social, transmitted through teaching and learning, more or less coherent, and symbolic.

2. People use language to code their experience and structure their understanding of the world and of themselves. Learning different languages brings into relief the shared nature of language and culture, and the prior assumptions that speakers make and share.

3. Of the sixteen *design features* of language, six are particularly important: openness, arbitrariness, duality of patterning, displacement, semanticity, and prevarication.

4. The suggestion that language has the power to shape the way in which people see the world is often referred to as the *Sapir-Whorf hypothesis*. The strong version of this hypothesis amounts to linguistic determinism, the weak version makes the shaping force of language too weak to be of scientific interest. Neither Sapir nor Whorf favored linguistic determinism.

5. Today, the study of language is usually subdivided into five specialties: *phonology*, *morphology*, *syntax*, *semantics*, and *pragmatics*.

6. Pragmatics is the most recent specialty within linguistics. It breaks new theoretical ground because it considers the way contexts of use affect what words mean. Pragmatics requires us to pay attention to discourse. It also requires us to pay attention to nonlinguistic contexts. Different speakers may take up different referential perspectives with regard to the same nonlinguistic context. Referential perspectives are ideological perspectives that carry heavy burdens of cultural and historical meaning. At this point, the cultural shaping of linguistic meaning is clearest. Successful communication occurs when speaker and listener are able to understand the same event from each other's referential perspectives.

7. The study of *linguistic inequality* highlights the study of language in context, and the negotiation of meaning.

8. Language is embedded in experience, and we usually generalize on the basis of experiences we know well. The domains of experience that our culture recognizes become unquestionably true and appropriate for us, and we tend to take those experiences as prototypical human experiences. These *prototypes* are central to the way in which meaning is organized in language.

9. Linguistic ambiguity can only be resolved in context, which means that there is no one literal meaning of a word or sentence. As a result, *metaphor* is a particularly important domain of linguistic inquiry. Metaphor poses a radical threat to our conventional understanding, since it calls into question the prototypes by which we live.

10. The study of *pidgin* languages is the study of the radical negotiation of new meaning. In pidgins, two groups of language speakers who come in contact (often as a result of colonization or commercial domination), invent a new language that is different from either of its parents.

Suggested Readings

Akmajian, A., R. Demers, and R. Harnish. *Linguistics*, 2d ed. Cambridge: MIT Press, 1984.
> A clear, direct introduction to the study of language as a formal system. This text is particularly good on phonology, morphology, and syntax.

Hickerson, Nancy. *Anthropological Linguistics*. New York: Holt, Rinehart and Winston, 1981.
> A good, brief introduction to the different ways in which anthropologists study language.

Lakoff, George and Mark Johnson. *Metaphors We Live By*. Berkeley: University of California Press, 1980.
> An important, clear, very accessible book that presents a radical and persuasive view of metaphor.

Trudgill, Peter. *Sociolinguistics*, 2d ed. Baltimore: Penguin Books, 1982.
> An excellent, thorough, very readable introduction to language in its social context.

Listening in on the Struggle for the New World

Jane H. Hill (Ph.D., University of California, Los Angeles) is professor of Anthropology at the University of Arizona. She has done fieldwork in southern California, Arizona, and central Mexico, among speakers of languages of the Uto-Aztecan family of American Indian languages. Before coming to Arizona she taught at Wayne State University. She is the author (with Kenneth C. Hill) of Speaking Mexicano. *Her work has emphasized "speaking"—the ongoing construction of possible human languages, in contexts ranging from everyday talk to epic poetry. Such languages can be used as a set of tactics in the struggle for symbolic and material resources, and as a set of tools for the building of satisfying human identities.*

For five hundred years, American Indian, European, African, and Asian peoples have battled for the right to define the New World. Battle, indeed, for people are dying today, and the benign domestic image of the stewpot and all of us "melting" into homogeneity hardly fits the violence and terror of the struggle. The symbolic battle is fought partly with the voices of ordinary people. Listening in on the quiet talk of American Indian people is one clue to the mighty processes by which human beings forge new ways of being, processes that have been thrown into high relief by the epic of conquest and resistence, colonization and revolution, that is the living history of the Americas.

On the territory they've staked out on the great post-Columbian battlefield, American Indians remain diverse, full of surprises, yet continually and undeniably distinct from what their intellectuals call "occidental." Their self-making is often conducted in extraordinary material poverty and confusion. The big Tohonno O'odham reservation where I've been working has all the usual reservation problems: hot sun and dust, not enough money, too much liquor, and political scandals that might bring a blush to the cheek of an old-time Chicago alderman. Dr. Ofelia Zepeda (an O'odham poet and linguist) and I have been doing a dialect survey of the reservation. From the survey I remember most an old man who lives in a fly-blown village maybe one hundred miles west of Tucson. Inside his little adobe house, a wardrobe of well-worn flowered cowboy shirts hung from the ceiling, an old coffee pot on a battered TV tray and a hanging light bulb were hooked up to the main house by a very long orange utility extension cord, the furniture was mainly old car seats, and the dirt floor was made cozy with about two dozen carpet samples in a variety of weaves and colors. I perched on the old man's little cot, and Ofelia found a place on an old sofa that didn't have too many springs coming up or cowboy shirts hanging down. We then taped our interview, along with a lot of winter wind and a couple of memorable sonic booms. The tone of the place was what the postmodern theoreticians call *pastiche*. You'd think there was no proper culture there at all, just a sort of random accumulation of the debris of civilization that got caught going down the drain with the Indians.

But you'd be wrong. The old man was a great shaman. It's a mystery why he gave us two hours, because for a consultation on a serious matter, he commanded a fee that would not disgrace a good neurosurgeon. At night, with clients sitting on the car seats under the cowboy shirts, he can sing his way along the flowery paths that Elder Brother Shaman marked between the cracks of time, soothing the animal spirits that, disturbed by human foolishness, make O'odham people ill, and doing battle with black sorcerors who might sicken a baby for a taste of its innocence. He lives out back in a little house partly to avoid distractions, so he can focus his power, but partly so his family won't be harmed in case some evil force gets loose as he works.

The old man doesn't speak much English; he doesn't need to, because the animal spirits and the sorcerors speak O'odham, in exquisite poetry. So curing and blessing, the tasks of the wise and elderly, are centers of creation in the language. But life isn't all being sick, so good announcers kid around in O'odham over the public address system at the powwow and the rodeo, and grandparents lecture kids when they get out of line, and old ladies get on the new telephone system to round up hot dishes for potlucks. They use English too, to put a citified spin on a joke, or give a little bureaucratic solidity to a meeting, and they're afraid that young people speak English too much. But O'odham English has a special quietness and courtesy to it, and O'odham itself is showing up in new places and shapes. The hardworking staff of the bilingual education program is producing alphabet books, and counting books, and cookbooks, and nature stories, and biographies about O'odham people who had especially worthwhile lives. Children, and young men and women (and even the odd white enthusiast) are composing new kinds of O'odham poetry, and writing it down, claiming their desert—the noble nurturing saguaros, and the Old Woman Sitting Mountain, and the toe-tapping dance music— with "O'odham thoughts."

In Mexico, for ten years, I've listened in on the continuing creation, through a synthesis of Spanish and what linguists call "Nahuat", of a way of speaking called Mexicano. Speakers claim thereby a unique and privileged citizenship in a modern state, Mexico, which through its very name claims their heritage yet denies that they are proper exemplars of the national identity. Here one sees a picturesque sort of material ruin that gives little clue to the stubborn indigenous presence indexed in the kitchen talk of women, despised and beneath the notice of the national myth makers. Listening to it, catching the proportion of this kind of root and that, one learns who people think they are, and there they lie along the battle lines.

The study of American Indian languages is done these days more and more by linguists who are native speakers; their unique intuitions cannot be duplicated. However, I've had the privilege of listening to the murmur of the voices that, even when the clash of arms is briefly quiet, constitutes the soft background radiation of the creation of the history of human beings.

CHAPTER 5
COGNITION

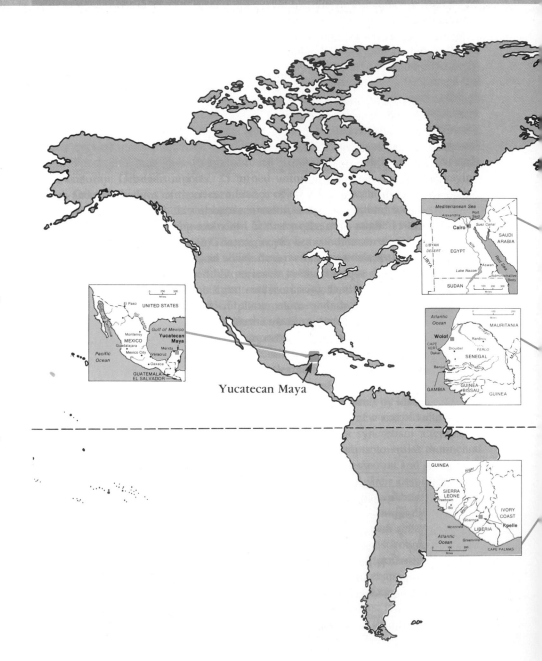

Yucatecan Maya

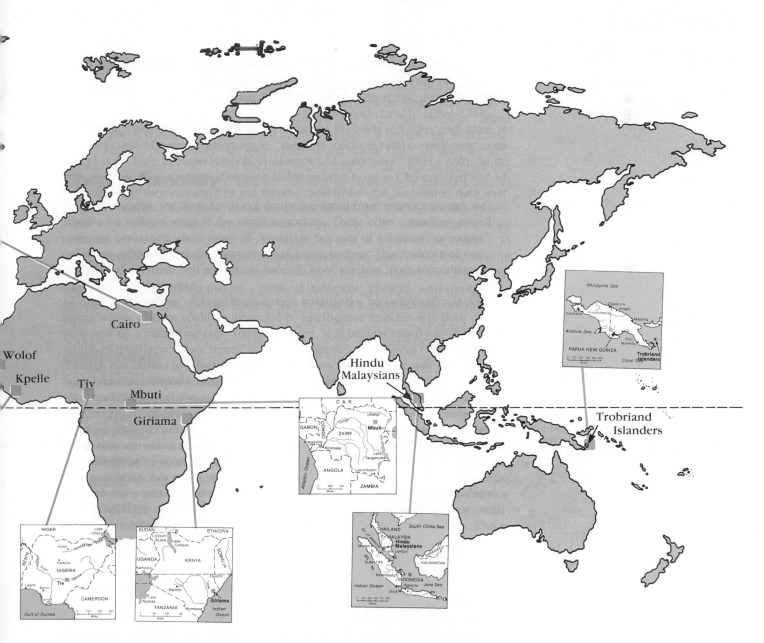

Wolof

Kpelle

Tiv

Cairo

Mbuti

Giriama

Hindu
Malaysians

Trobriand
Islanders

FIGURE 5.1 *Source:* From *States of Mind,* by Jonathan Miller. Copyright ©1983 by the Contributors. In the United States: Reprinted by permission of Pantheon Books, a Division of Random House, Inc. In Canada: Reproduced by permission of BBC Enterprises, Ltd.

We have just seen that our capacity for language is not easily separated from other capacities that we possess for making sense of the world around us. These other capacities are generally referred to as cognitive capacities. This chapter is devoted to exploring the nature of human cognition and its relationship to culture.

If you examine figure 5.1, you will see that marks on a piece of paper can be ambiguous. The signals we receive from the outside world tend to be open to more than one interpretation, be they words, patterns of light and dark striking the retinas of our eyes, smells, tastes, or shapes we feel with our hands.

Culture groups different kinds of signals together for us and directs our attention to the resulting bundle, or schema, to which a linguistic label is often applied. When we learn from this culturally shaped experience, we are able to assign new experiences to preexisting categories, thus interpreting these new experiences. The signals to which we pay attention, plus our interpretation of them, together build our picture of the world.

Cognition as an Open System

In chapter 4, cognition was defined as the mental processes by which human beings gain knowledge. Like language, cognition is an open system. Human beings not only may talk about the world in a variety of ways, they may also perceive the world in a variety of ways. If no one set of perceptions is obligatory, then any particular way of perceiving must be arbitrary. What we perceive depends greatly on what we have learned to perceive in the past. Thus, our perception in any new situation depends on an entire collection of experiences from prior situations, which we use to help us make sense of what we perceive at the present moment. This is called displacement. Not only our eyes, but also all our senses, can play tricks on us. If they are artful enough, people can trick other people into perceiving something that "does not exist." Prevarication is thus a built-in possibility of cognition, just as it is of language. In short, our understanding of language can be applied metaphorically to other cognitive processes that are not linguistic. Both linguistics and cognitive psychology have recently begun to focus on the same problem: the problem of meaning.

If we take language as a model of cognition in general, cognition is likely to be viewed as an essentially symbolic process. Language and perception both require human beings to construct symbolic representations of their experiences in order to make sense of them. As a result, the evidence of our senses is never self-evident. The meaning of what we see, touch, smell, taste, or hear depends on context. In fact, two contexts are normally invoked: the immediate context of the perception itself and the displaced context stored in memory and shaped by culture. As with sentences, so too with the objects of perception. The "same" object can mean different things in different contexts. Consider what seeing a butcher knife means (1) lying on a chopping block in your kitchen next to a pile of mushrooms or (2) in the hand of a burglar who has cornered you in your kitchen at midnight.

Cognition is often thought to have three aspects: perceptual, intellectual, and emotional. Perception as a cognitive process has been thought to link people to the world around them or within them: we perceive size, shape, color, pain. Intellect and emotion have referred to the two principal ways in which perceptions might be dealt with: rationally and logically on the one hand, passionately and intuitively on the other. Anthropologists and psychologists are beginning to suggest, however, that this approach to cognition is highly problematic. Particularly troubling is the traditional overvaluing of reason and logic, to the neglect of other cognitive capacities. Human nature presents itself to us as a whole that is not reducible to the parts that make it up. We are coming to see that the value of emotion is no more and no less than the value of metaphor. Just as there cannot be metaphor without literal conventions, there cannot be feeling separated from thought.

Cognitive Capacities and Intelligence

What is going on inside us that makes it possible for us to receive signals from the outside world (or from within our own bodies) and then interpret those signals in a way that makes appropriate action possible? One traditional answer has been that every person either possesses at birth or develops over time certain basic cognitive capacities. These hypothetical capacities were thought of as substances or properties, and the goal of psychological testing was to measure how much of each cognitive capacity an individual had. Intelligence has most often been "measured" in this way. Using an "instrument" called the intelligence test, the "amount" of intelligence measured is assigned a number, the intelligence quotient, or IQ. In the past, some researchers were quick to equate differences in performance on intelligence tests with differences in intelligence, no further questions asked. Today, such a reductionist approach is being subjected to intense scrutiny.

It is difficult enough to identify and measure cognitive capacities in individuals. The difficulty only increases when different groups of human subjects perform differently on the same psychological test. How should these disparate results be interpreted? Recall how Labov was able to determine that the same test meant one thing to white schoolchildren and something quite different to black schoolchildren. Researchers who were unaware of this drew faulty conclusions from their test results. Perhaps all such group differences in performance are similarly contaminated.

Michael Cole and Sylvia Scribner (from whose work much of what follows derives) are two psychological anthropologists who have extensive experience in cross-cultural psychological testing. In their fieldwork, they repeatedly encountered situations in which the same psychological test produced results in non-Western societies that differed from results obtained in Western societies. They rejected the classical interpretation of these differences, which was that non-Western subjects were just less intelligent. Their knowledge of their informants was not limited to the narrow laboratory setting in which the psychological tests were administered. In the broader social and cultural context of everyday life, their informants' intelligence and full humanity were obvious.

So why do intelligent informants often perform poorly on psychological tests? In the work of the Russian psychologist Lev Vygotsky, Cole and Scribner (1974) found an approach that pointed toward an answer. Vygotsky distinguished between **elementary cognitive processes** and the higher **functional cognitive systems** into which these processes are organized. Elementary cognitive processes include the ability to make abstractions, to categorize, to reason inferentially, and so forth. All normal human beings everywhere are equipped with these abilities. Different cultures, however, organize these elementary processes into different functional systems. Culture also assigns different functional systems to different tasks in different contexts.

Consider once again the inner-city black children whose "speech capacity" was being measured by white psychologists. The same test was used, the same instructions were given, the same controlled testing situation was employed for

elementary cognitive processes
basic human mental abilities such as abstraction, inferential reasoning, and categorization

functional cognitive systems
culturally linked sets of elementary cognitive processes that guide perception, conception, reason, and emotion

black children and for white children. White middle-class children responded easily and fluently, whereas black children of the same age produced only monosyllables or silence. The meaning children assigned to the test situation seemed to influence the cognitive processes they decided to use in coping with the demands of the test. White children interpreted the test and the testing situation as a nonthreatening opportunity to display their verbal ability, which they did. Black children interpreted the same test and situation as a threatening personal and social attack, and they responded by refusing to respond. When interviewed in a nonthreatening context, those same children displayed considerable verbal ability.

If we accept this analysis, the concept of schema introduced in chapter 4 takes on a greater complexity. Culture not only identifies and labels recurring schemas for us. It also guides us in deciding how to cope cognitively with different categories of schemas. In other words, there are different ways of defining tasks, and once tasks are defined there are different strategies for dealing with them. Administering an adequate psychological test is as difficult as doing good anthropological fieldwork, with the same rewards and pitfalls.

Perception

perception
processes by which people organize and experience information that is primarily of sensory origin

Perception can be defined as "processes by which people organize and experience information that is primarily of sensory origin" (Cole and Scribner 1974:61). The nature of perception has long been central to an understanding of human cognition. After all, positivist science is based on the premise that we can trust the evidence of our senses. In this view, a suitably objective observer should be able to describe the world as it truly is. If other people describe the world differently from the scientific observer, then those others must have perceptions that are in some way distorted. Either they are not being objective, or their ability to discriminate is impaired, or perhaps they are attempting to trick and mislead. In any case, it is assumed that there is a reality out there and that human beings, by discipline and training, can attain the objectivity needed to encounter reality directly and to describe it in undistorted form.

Most modern researchers are far less certain about what we perceive when we perceive something. True, our perception is sometimes impaired, either for physical reasons (we are not wearing our glasses) or because our observations are not disinterested (our child's forehead feels "cool" because we are terrified he or she might have a fever). And people do sometimes play jokes on one another, insisting that they have seen things they really have not seen. But what about people whose physiological equipment is functioning properly, who have no stake in the outcome, and who are not trying to deceive? Many investigators have begun to ask questions that attempt to relate people's descriptions of their experiences, or their performances on psychological tests, to their understandings of context.

Cross cultural research on perception has produced some interesting results. For example, nonliterate South African mine workers were tested using two-dimensional line drawings of three-dimensional objects (see figure 5.2). Results of these tests indicated that the mine workers persistently tended to interpret the drawings in two dimensions. When asked at which animal the man was pointing his spear on card 1, subjects would usually respond, "the elephant." The elephant is, in fact, directly in line with and closest to the spear point in the drawing. However, the elephant ought to be seen as standing on top of the distant hill, if the subjects interpret

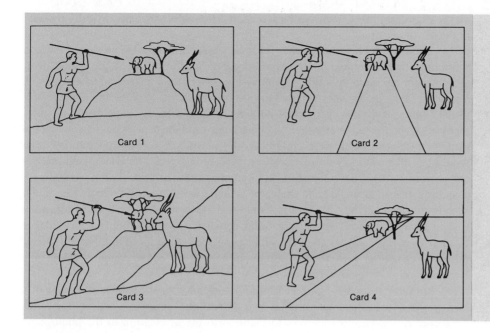

FIGURE 5.2
Pictures for Study of Depth Perception in Africa Source: From *Culture and Thought: A Psychological Introduction,* by Michael Cole and Sylvia Scribner. Copyright ©1974 John Wiley & Sons, Inc. Reprinted by permission of John Wiley & Sons, Inc.

the drawings three-dimensionally. Did their responses mean that these Africans could not perceive in three dimensions?

J. B. Deregowski devised the following test. He presented different African subjects with the same drawings, asked them to describe what they saw, and got two-dimensional verbal reports. Next, he presented the same subjects with the line drawings in figure 5.3. This time, he asked his subjects to construct models based

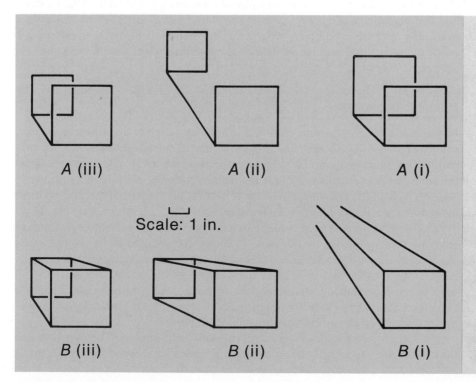

FIGURE 5.3
Drawings Used for Construction Models in Depth Perception Test
Source: From *Culture and Thought: A Psychological Introduction,* by Michael Cole and Sylvia Scribner. Copyright ©1974 John Wiley & Sons, Inc. Reprinted by permission of John Wiley & Sons, Inc.

on the drawings, using materials he provided. His subjects had no difficulty producing three-dimensional models.

Deregowski devised another test of visual perception. He presented African schoolgirls with a photograph of several objects on a flat surface: a toy Land Rover, a toy hunter, and two toy buffalo. The subjects were then instructed to arrange the actual toys with the same orientation toward one another as represented in the photograph. Deregowski discovered that his subjects consistently made errors of judgment in orientation whenever their viewing angles and the camera angle were not the same. Did this mean that the children could not perceive orientational clues that would be obvious to any normal observer? Deregowski said no. He argued that the errors could easily be explained if one hypothesized that the children were simply assuming that their angles and the camera angle were the same. Given this initial assumption, the children's task, as they understood it, would have been to adjust the toys in a way that would have reconciled the evidence of the picture and the evidence of their own eyes. Above all, "the subjects seemed to be more influenced by their desire to render a *meaningful* reproduction than by camera angle" (Cole and Scribner 1974:74; emphasis added).

In these tests, the "correct" solution depended on the subject's mastery of a Western convention for interpreting two-dimensional drawings and photographs. This convention requires viewers to distinguish the orientation in the photograph from their own orientation in space. Once this has been done, other cognitive processes involving the estimation of distance, and so on, are brought into play.

The Western rule seems to be as follows: When in doubt, consider the drawing or the photograph as it is, in and of itself, outside any particular context. This seems to be what we mean by objectivity. But people who have not learned this particular Western perceptual convention will not find it obvious that context must be eliminated. Indeed, the most interesting result of tests like these was the discovery that Western ways of interpreting photographs are conventional. That is, drawings and photographs do not necessarily speak for themselves. They can make sense to us only once we accept certain rules for interpreting them. In the West, a major rule involves clearly separating what one sees from what one knows (Cole and Scribner 1974:74).

Illusion

Just as studies of metaphor provide insight into the nature of literal language, so do studies of visual illusions provide insight into the nature of the visual perception of reality. Indeed, the contrast between literal and metaphorical language is not unlike the contrast between reality and illusion that is often made in discussions of perception. In both cases, knowledge of context permits the literal and the metaphorical, the real and the illusory, to be distinguished.

Richard Gregory is a cognitive psychologist who has spent over two decades studying visual illusions. In his view, illusions are produced by *misplaced procedures*: perfectly normal, ordinary cognitive processes that have somehow been inappropriately selected and applied to a particular set of visual signals. For him, perceptions are symbolic representations of reality, not direct samples of reality. Perceivers must often work very hard to make sense of the visual signals they receive. When they are wrong, they are subject to illusion.

Gregory (1983) describes four types of visual illusion. The first is **distortion**: what you see appears larger or smaller, longer or shorter, and so on, than it

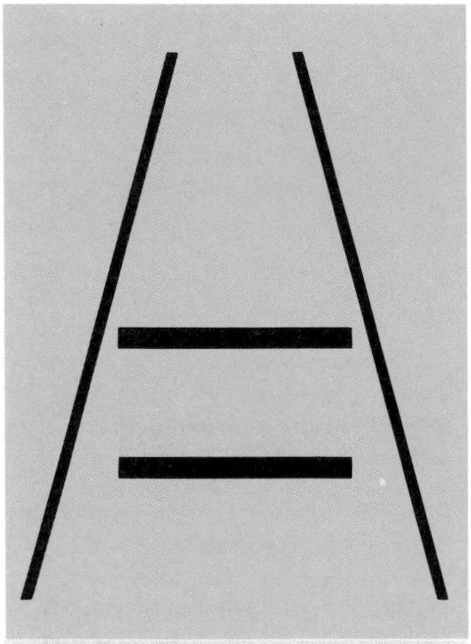

FIGURE 5.4
Distortion: The Ponzo Illusion *Source:* From *States of Mind,* by Jonathan Miller, Copyright ©1983 by the Contributors. In the United States: Reprinted by permission of Pantheon Books, a Division of Random House, Inc. In Canada: Reproduced by permission of BBC Enterprises, Ltd.

distortion
the illusion that occurs when what you see appears larger or smaller, longer or shorter, and so on, than it really is

really is. Consider the Ponzo illusion, illustrated in figure 5.4. Typically, the upper parallel line appears to be longer than the lower parallel line. The standard explanation of this illusion is that we are looking at a two-dimensional drawing but interpreting it as if it were in three dimensions. In other words, the Ponzo illusion plays on our ability to see three-dimensional space in a two-dimensional drawing.

This helps to explain the responses that Africans gave to the drawing of the man, the elephant, and the antelope, in figure 5.2. Western observers interpret that drawing as a two-dimensional representation of three dimensional reality. In the Ponzo illusion, the shapes trick us because they are very similar to what we perceive when we stand on a railroad track and look toward its vanishing point on the horizon. Africans are also familiar with railroad tracks. But they did not attempt to interpret the Ponzo-like lines on card 2 as representations of three-dimensional reality. On the contrary, they seemed to work very hard to keep the relationships between objects in two dimensions, even if this meant that the sizes of the objects themselves appeared distorted. When we compare the Western interpretation of the Ponzo illusion with the African interpretation of the man, elephant, and antelope drawing, an important discovery emerges. Both sets of drawings are ambiguous, both are potentially open to distortion. How people interpret them depends on pre-existing cultural conventions.

The second type of visual illusion is **ambiguity**. This occurs when the set of visual signals is constant but the perceiver's awareness of it flips from one image to another. Consider the Necker cube and the face/vase drawing in figure 5.5. As you stare at these patterns, they seem to move. First one face of the Necker cube is in front, a second later it pops to the back. At one moment you are admiring the contours of a beautifully symmetrical vase; the next moment, you see two human profiles facing one another. Experiments have demonstrated that this flipping back and forth of the image has nothing to do with the visual signals themselves; the pattern of lines on the retina remains fixed. What seems to be happening is that the mind is confronting a pattern that can be interpreted in at least two equally probable ways. It keeps hopping between each probable interpretation, testing various interpretive hypotheses, in an attempt to resolve the ambiguity. But because the signals are so perfectly ambiguous, no resolution is possible. The image appears to flip endlessly from one possibility to the other.

Gregory's third type of illusion is **paradox**: a contradiction in terms, or at least an image that appears to be visually contradictory. Consider figure 5.6. Here we are tripped up again and again as we apply a given set of cognitive procedures to make sense of the visual signals we are receiving. We seem to have made sense of the image only to encounter some other part of it that upsets our previous theory.

Gregory's fourth type of illusion is **fiction**: seeing things that are not there. Consider the Kanizsa illusions in figure 5.7. The actual visual signals consist of three acute angles and three dots. And yet when asked, most observers unhesitatingly declare that they see a white triangle overlapping a triangle with a black border. The effect is even more dramatic in the second Kanizsa illusion, where the white triangle's sides appear to curve inward and its points block out portions of three black circles beneath them. These illusions are fictions because nothing—no change in brightness across the edges of the "overlapping triangles," for example— signals to us that we are dealing with overlapping triangles rather than six separate black shapes arranged in a ring on a white background.

Gregory argues that we respond as we do to illusions of this kind because our experience in the world has made us familiar with certain patterns that we come to

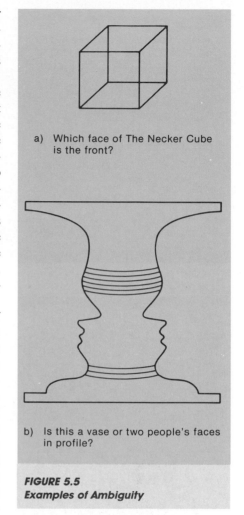

a) Which face of The Necker Cube is the front?

b) Is this a vase or two people's faces in profile?

FIGURE 5.5
Examples of Ambiguity

ambiguity
the illusion that occurs when the set of visual signals is constant but the perceiver's awareness of it flips from one image to another

paradox
a perceptual illusion in which an image appears to be visually contradictory

fiction
a perceptual illusion in which the viewer sees things that are not there

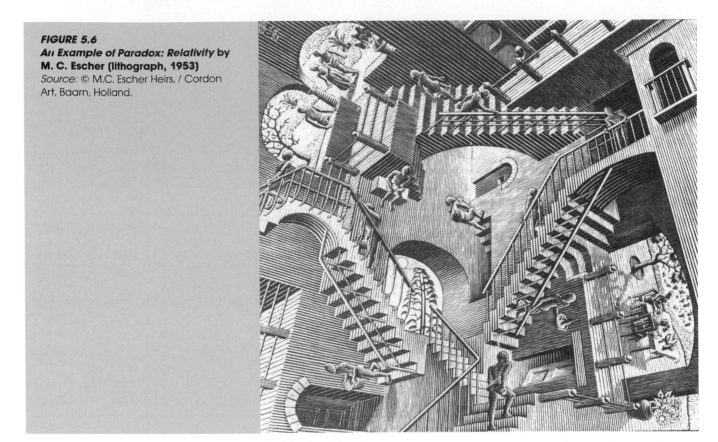

FIGURE 5.6
An Example of Paradox: Relativity by
M. C. Escher (lithograph, 1953)
Source: © M.C. Escher Heirs, / Cordon
Art, Baarn, Holland.

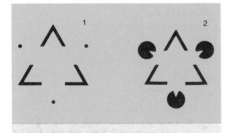

FIGURE 5.7
Example of Fiction: The Kanizsa Illu-
sions *Source:* From *States of Mind*, by
Jonathan Miller. Copyright ©1983 by
the Contributors. In the United States:
Reprinted by permission of Pantheon
Books, a Division of Random House, Inc.
In Canada: Reproduced by permission
of BBC Enterprises, Ltd.

cognitive style
a recurring pattern of perceptual and intellectual activity. Cultures provide people
with a range of cognitive styles

expect. For example, when we encounter surprising gaps where we would normally
expect to encounter continuous edges, we tend to assume that something is getting
in the way of those continuous edges.

Perceptions are shaped by our habitual experience, by the schemas in terms
of which we order our lives. We all encounter visual illusions from time to time in
the everyday world. Unlike the drawings used for psychological tests, the sources of
these illusions are not often abstract patterns devoid of context. And unlike subjects
in a laboratory, we usually are free to use our other senses, to move our bodies in
space, to manipulate the source of the puzzling signals until we resolve the ambiguity to our satisfaction. As with figurative language, however, we resolve the ambiguity only with respect to that particular context. Technically, according to Gregory,
we are making hypotheses about what those visual signals most probably represent
in the world we know. That world is a culturally shaped world.

Cognitive Style

The term **cognitive style** refers to a recurring pattern of perceptual and intellectual
activity. Cultures provide people with a range of cognitive styles that are appropriate
for different cognitive tasks in different contexts. Perhaps one important cultural
difference between Africans and Americans concerns precisely whether or not the
test-taking situation is a special context to which a special cognitive style should
apply.

Psychological anthropologists have attempted to compare cognitive styles cross-culturally. Some have argued that the styles of individuals and of groups can be located on a continuum between a global style and an articulated style. People with a **global style** tend to view the world holistically; they see first a bundle of relationships and only later the bits and pieces that are related. They are said to be field dependent. In contrast, people with an **articulated style** tend to break up the world into smaller and smaller pieces, which can then be organized. They also tend to see a sharp boundary between their own bodies and the outside world. People using an articulated style are able to consider whatever they happen to be paying attention to apart from its context, and so are said to be field independent (Cole and Scribner 1974:82).

On this scale, people in Western societies appear to be field independent, whereas most people in most non-Western cultures appear to be field dependent. More detailed research shows that generalizations like these can be highly misleading. For instance, the preferred cognitive style of an individual often varies from task to task, and from context to context. People who use articulated styles for some tasks also use global styles for other tasks. In fact, they may bring a range of different styles to bear on a single task.

Research by Jean Lave and her colleagues (1988) demonstrated that middle-class Americans are not field independent in every task in all contexts. This is the case even when the task they are performing involves mathematics, which would seem to be the most abstract of cognitive activities. Lave and her associates wanted to test the widespread assumption that cognitive style does not vary across contexts. In particular, they wanted to find out whether ordinary people used the same mathematical skills in the supermarket and the kitchen that they displayed in the classroom. As part of the research, subjects were given a pencil-and-paper math test to determine how well they could solve certain problems in a schoolroomlike context. The same subjects were also observed as they shopped for groceries, and the way they used mathematics in making buying decisions was noted. Finally, they were presented with paired grocery items and asked to calculate the best buy.

The results of this research were surprising. First, the subjects averaged only 59 percent correct on the pencil-and-paper test, but achieved averages of 98 percent correct on the supermarket experiment and and 93 percent on the best-buy experiment. Second, the researchers found that the high scores on the last two experiments were achieved with very little reliance on the formal mathematical strategies taught in school. Many observers would have expected subjects trained in formal mathematics to rely on its infallible methods to help them make wise economic decisions. On the contrary, the test results suggested that shoppers were better able to make wise economic decisions using informal calculation strategies. The three most common informal strategies were *inspection* (recognizing that one item was both lower in price and larger in volume), *best-buy calculations* (comparing two quantities and two prices first, and choosing the better value), and a *difference strategy* (deciding whether a marginal difference in quantity is worth the marginal difference in price) (Lave 1988:107ff.).

Lave notes that some psychologists would conclude from these results that there was something "primitive" or "illogical" about the informal strategies—and, by extension, about the people who used them (e.g., Lave 1988:79ff., 107ff.). In the terms we used earlier, these strategies are all closer to the global, field-dependent end of the cognitive-style continuum. Should we conclude, therefore, that ordinary middle-class Americans fail to think rationally when they shop for groceries? This conclusion is contradicted by the experimental evidence showing

global style
a way of viewing the world that is holistic; people with this style first see a bundle of relationships and only later the bits and pieces that are related, and so they are said to be field dependent

articulated style
a way of viewing the world that breaks it up into smaller and smaller pieces, which can then be organized; people with this style consider whatever they happen to be paying attention to apart from its context, and so are said to be field independent

that the shoppers' informal strategies were exceptionally accurate. In addition, shoppers did occasionally use formal mathematics as an alternative to the other informal strategies. But they did so only when the numbers for quantity and price were easy to transform into unit/price ratios. This did not happen very often, however, because units and prices in supermarkets are often given in prime numbers, making rapid mental calculation tedious and complicated. Rather than waste time and effort, shoppers chose to rely on other calculation strategies.

This last observation points to a major difference between math use in the school and math use in the grocery store. In the school, the only purpose of a mathematical exercise is to obtain a single correct answer. "The puzzles or problems are assumed to be objective and factual. . . . Problem solvers have no choice but to try to solve problems, and if they choose not to, or do not find the correct answer, they 'fail'" (Lave 1988:35). Matters are otherwise outside the classroom. Shoppers do not visit supermarkets as an excuse to practice formal mathematics. They go to purchase food for their families. As a result, the choices they make are influenced not merely by unit/price ratios, but by the food preferences of the other family members, the amount of storage space at home, the amount of time they can spend shopping. In the supermarket, as Lave puts it, "'problems' are dilemmas to be resolved, rarely problems to be solved" (1988:20). Formal mathematics may help resolve some dilemmas, but in other cases it can be more trouble than it is worth. Shoppers, unlike students in the classroom, are free to decide to abandon calculation, to use means other than formal mathematics to resolve a dilemma (Lave 1988:58).

One feature all Lave's subjects shared was the knowledge that pencil-and-paper tests in schoollike settings required an articulated, field-independent style. In non-Western societies, attending a European- or American-style school seems to impart the same knowledge to non-Western people. But even Western subjects may reserve that cognitive style for the classroom, preferring a variety of more global strategies to resolve the dilemmas of everyday life. We have seen how some of these dilemmas can be generated by a lack of fit between the background information we take for granted and sensory signals that are ambiguous. This lack of fit may be between knowledge of our family's food preferences and confusing price ratio information on two products we are comparing. It may be between our expectation that straight edges are normally continuous and surprising gaps in our visual field. In any case, our awareness of the cognitive dilemmas we face should make us more sympathetic to cognitive "errors" we see being made in cultures different from our own, by people who may be employing different cognitive styles.

Colin Turnbull is an anthropologist who worked for many years among the Mbuti pygmies of central Zaire. *(See EthnoFile 5.1. Mbuti.)* He discovered that

---

EthnoFile 5.1
MBUTI

Region: Central Africa

Nation: Zaire (northeastern)

Population: 40,000

Environment: Dense tropical forest (Ituri Forest)

Livelihood: Nomadic hunting and gathering

Political organization: Communal bands of 7 to 30 families (average 17 families)

Other: Subjects of a classic ethnography by Colin Turnbull, *The Forest People* (1962), the Mbuti are a well-known example of a peaceful people

EthnoFile 5.2
TROBRIAND
ISLANDERS

Region: Oceania

Nation: Papua New Guinea

Population: 8,500 (1970s)

Environment: Tropical island

Livelihood: yam growing

Political organization: Chiefs and others of rank

Other: A famous matrilineal people and superlative navigators, the Trobrianders are the subjects of classic ethnographies by Bronislaw Malinowski, especially *Argonauts of the Western Pacific* (1927)

people who live all their lives in a dense forest have no experience of distance greater than a few feet and are therefore not accustomed to taking distance into consideration when estimating the size of an object in the visual field. Turnbull took one of his informants, Kenge, on a trip that brought them out of the forest and into a game park. For the first time in his life, Kenge found himself facing vast, rolling grasslands nearly empty of trees, backed by a huge inland lake. Kenge's response to this experience was dramatic: "When Kenge topped the rise, he stopped dead. Every smallest sign of mirth suddenly left his face. He opened his mouth but could say nothing. He moved his head and eyes slowly and unbelievingly" (Turnbull 1961:251).

When Kenge finally saw the animals grazing on the plain, he asked Turnbull what insects they were. When told that the "insects" were buffalo, Kenge laughed and accused Turnbull of lying. Then he strained to see better and inquired what kind of buffalo could be so small. Later, when Turnbull pointed out a fishing boat on the lake, Kenge scoffed at him and insisted it was a floating piece of wood (Turnbull 1961:252).

Cole and Scribner had a similar experience with one of their informants, a young Liberian who had lived his entire life inland. He had never seen the ocean until they took him with them to Monrovia, the Liberian capital, which is also a large port city. On seeing specks in the distance that the anthropologists insisted were boats, he observed that men who put out to sea in such small boats must be very brave (Cole and Scribner 1974:97).

Other interesting perceptual anomalies have been recorded in the anthropological literature. Bronislaw Malinowski reported that the Trobriand islanders of the South Pacific claim that a child never resembles its mother, brothers, sisters, or any relatives on the mother's side of the family. *(See EthnoFile 5.2: Trobriand Islanders.)* Indeed, as he discovered, "it is extremely bad form and a great offence to hint at any such similarity. To resemble one's father, on the other hand, is the natural, right, and proper thing" (Malinowski 1929:204).

In one of his books, Malinowski reproduced a photograph of two brothers from the island of Kiriwina who, from a Western point of view, appear to be virtually identical. When he pointed out again and again the bases for this judgment, his informants continued to deny it. The informants were willing to agree that both men resembled their father a great deal. But they were unwilling to draw what seemed to Malinowski to be an unavoidable, logical conclusion: if A resembles B, and C resembles B, then A resembles C.

The vehemence of the Trobrianders' defense of their dogma on family resemblance becomes less amazing when we consider that their theory about conception relates the physical resemblance of children to their fathers but not to their mothers. They believe that the semen of the father molds the shape of the child's face while it is still in the womb. These two facts together go a long way in explaining why no Trobriander would want to suggest that people resemble their matrilineal kin. Such an observation, given the Trobriand theory of conception, would amount to an assertion that one's mother had had sexual intercourse with her brothers or other male relatives, an accusation of incest.

It therefore appears that these cultural assumptions shape the cognitive style of Trobrianders who are searching for family resemblance. Malinowski discovered that when he asked his informants to tell him the ways in which people resembled relatives on their fathers' side, he and they agreed as to which features were involved. Malinowski was also impressed with the genuineness of his informants' assertions; they did not seem to be trying to deceive him. He concluded that they did indeed perceive family resemblance differently from the way he did.

When people in another culture fail to see similarities between objects that we think ought to be obvious to any observer, we are apt to become impatient. Yet many Americans are subject to similar kinds of "blindness." Consider what usually happens when Americans are asked to classify the offspring of mixed marriages between whites and people of color. In the United States, Americans have tended to classify anyone with the slightest black ancestry as "black;" they would also probably tend to classify as black anyone who showed any prototypically "black" facial features, ignoring any features that were prototypically "white." This is just the opposite of the tendency in Latin American countries. In Brazil, for example, the slightest physical evidence of white ancestry is enough for people to claim classification with whites rather than with people of color. When Malinowski asked who the offspring of Trobriand women and white men resembled, his informants insisted that those children had white men's faces, and cited this finding as proof for their theory of conception (Malinowski 1929:208).

An American—particularly a white middle-class American—would most likely insist that prototypically black facial features are too obvious to ignore. Yet which traits are more obvious: blue eyes, fair skin, thick lips, curly hair? Some people in Venezuela exhibit all these traits at once. Do they look more white or more black? In northern Cameroon, in a town like Guider, we find people whose skin is extremely dark yet whose facial features are very "Caucasian" (e.g., thin lips, long noses). *(See EthnoFile 7.1. Guider.)* As Schultz went about her fieldwork in Guider, she found herself meeting many people who reminded her physically of white people she knew in the United States. When she reflected on this, she realized that she was no longer paying attention to skin color when she looked at people in Guider.

This very ambiguity in visual perceptions of similarity and difference eventually undermined attempts by early anthropologists to classify humanity into mutually exclusive "races." The closer anthropologists looked, and the more features they measured, the clearer it became that there was no neat way to separate human beings into such categories. There was too much overlap; the classifications set up inevitably had fuzzy boundaries. Eventually, the concept of race was seen by physical anthropologists to be useless as a scientific concept. It was incapable of clarifying the kinds of variation they had observed. Worse, it was tainted by social and political connotations of biological superiority and inferiority that had no scientific justification.

People's continued insistence that they do not see what is obvious to others (or, conversely, their persistence in seeing things that others say are not there) might be explained in terms of the different, habitual referential perspectives that people of different cultural backgrounds take toward the same experience. Notice that one need not be unaware of some features in order to reject them. For example, Schultz would not have insisted that her informants in Guider had white skin; rather, skin color simply stopped being relevant for her in the fieldwork context. This is similar to the way Americans do not usually pay attention to eye color, although if asked to state the color of someone's eyes, they could do so. The physiology of perception has nothing to do with the kinds of distinctions we are noting here. It is a question of habitually paying selective attention to some visible traits, and downplaying or ignoring the others that are not culturally relevant.

The study of illusion thus raises all kinds of questions about the nature of reality, just as the study of metaphor raises questions about the nature of literal language. It demonstrates that there can be a gulf between what we see and what we know, what we perceive and what we conceive. At the same time, in the ordinary contexts of everyday life, these discrepancies seem to be manageable: there is coherence between what we perceive and what we conceive. Moreover, because our link with the world is a dialectical one, what we conceive shapes our perceptions. There is no sharp boundary between what we perceive and what we conceive. New perceptions can lead us to modify our conceptions (i.e., we learn). But new conceptions can lead us to perceive aspects of the world around us that we used not to pay attention to. As a result, **cognition** is perhaps best understood as "a nexus of relations between the mind at work and the world in which it works" (Lave 1988:1).

cognition
the nexus of relations between the mind at work and the world in which it works (see also definition of cognition, chapter 4, p. 86)

Conception

One way to illustrate the link between perception and conception, between what we see and what we know, is to compare the way people in different societies classify various phenomena in the world. Patricia Greenfield carried out a study among the Wolof of Senegal, West Africa, using sets of pictures mounted on cards (see figure 5.8). *(See EthnoFile 5.3: Wolof.)* Each subject was asked to pick out the two pictures in a set that were most alike, and then to explain why they were most alike. This test was administered to three different groups: traditional rural Wolof

EthnoFile 5.3
WOLOF

Region: West Africa

Nation: Senegal

Population: 2,700,000

Environment: Savannah

Livelihood: Farming

Political organization: Highly stratified kingdom

Other: The Wolof are a major ethnic group in Senegal

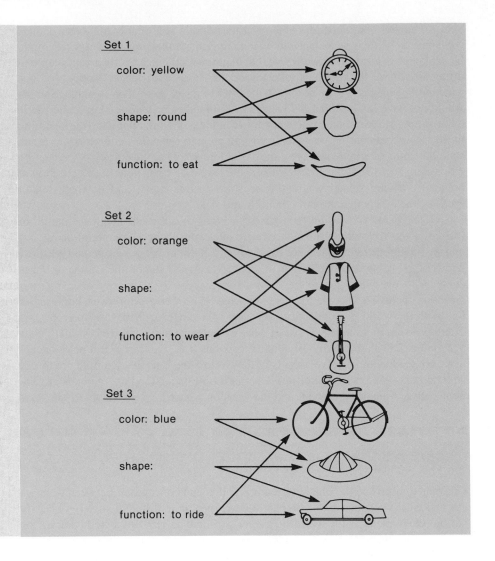

FIGURE 5.8
Three Picture Displays in Wolof Classification Study, with Their Attributes
Set 1: clock, orange, and banana; *Set 2:* sandal, *bubu* (Wolof robe), and guitar; *Set 3:* bicycle, helmet, and car.
Source: From *Culture and Thought: A Psychological Introduction,* by Michael Cole and Sylvia Scribner. Copyright ©1974 John Wiley & Sons, Inc. Reprinted by permission of John Wiley & Sons, Inc.

people who had never been to school, ranging from six years of age to adulthood; schoolchildren from the same rural town from which the first group was taken; and schoolchildren from Dakar, the capital city of Senegal.

The most striking result of Greenfield's experiments was the discovery of a high correlation between the amount of schooling a subject had received and the kinds of classifications made. All the schoolchildren, whether urban or rural, performed much the way American schoolchildren did. That is, the greater the number of years in school, the greater the children's preference to classify the objects in terms of form or function, and the lesser their preference to classify in terms of color. In addition, children with more schooling tended to explain their classifications in terms of conceptual categories (e.g., "round ones"). Those who had never been to school, no matter what their ages, preferred to classify in terms of color. They also were unlikely to explain their classifications in terms of feature-based conceptual categories. Greenfield concluded that this difference could be attributed to the experience of Western schooling, in which people with normal perceptual abilities were trained in "European habits of perceptual *analysis.*" Such training requires children to learn to pay attention to a variety of features beyond color. Presumably Wolof who do not receive such training have little need (at least in the testing situation, as they understood it) to pay attention to more than color to create a classification (Cole and Scribner 1974:103–5).

The probable influence of Western-style education on ways of classifying appeared in another study carried out by D. W. Sharp and Michael Cole in Yucatán, Mexico. *(See EthnoFile 5.4: Yucatecan Maya.)* Using the cards pictured in figure 5.9, they tested four groups of rural children and young adults: first graders, third graders, sixth graders, and teenagers who had attended no more than three years of school during their lives. They discovered that not all subjects were able to sort all the cards successfully according to a single rule (color, form, or number). However, the third graders were more successful than the first graders, and the sixth graders were more successful than the third graders. Given these data alone, it might seem that age is the important variable. But the teenagers with three years of school or less performed successfully at a level between that of the first graders and the third graders. Sharp and Cole concluded: "It seems quite possible that one consequence of educational experience is to instill the notion that any set of objects can be treated (classified) in a variety of ways—there is no 'one correct way,' regardless of the task at hand." That would explain the teenagers' level of performance (Cole and Scribner 1974:106–8).

Douglas Price-Williams (cited in Cole and Scribner 1974:116–17) suspected that the performance of African children on classification tests had been negatively affected because the children had been asked to sort unfamiliar abstract shapes. In his research among the Tiv of Nigeria, he decided to choose as test items ten different kinds of animals (represented mostly by plastic toys) and ten different kinds of plants familiar to Tiv children. *(See EthnoFile 5.5: Tiv.)* With each set of objects, he asked the children to pick out the ones that belonged together and to tell him why they had chosen as they did. Each child was then asked to regroup the objects again and again until the child stated that there were no other groupings possible.

The results were impressive. The youngest children (six years old) could classify and reclassify all the objects three or four different ways, whereas the oldest children (eleven years old) found five or six ways to do so, and it made no difference whether they had attended school or not. A second result had to do with the ways the children had gone about constructing their classifications. Although they grouped the animals primarily in terms of concrete attributes, such as size, color, or place

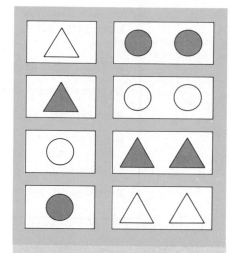

FIGURE 5.9
Cards Used in Mexican Reclassification Study
Objects portrayed vary in color (gray and white), form (circle and triangle), and number (one and two).
Source: From *Culture and Thought: A Psychological Introduction,* by Michael Cole and Sylvia Scribner. Copyright ©1974 John Wiley & Sons, Inc. Reprinted by permission of John Wiley & Sons, Inc.

EthnoFile 5.4
YUCATECAN MAYA

Region: Middle America

Nation: Mexico and Guatemala

Population: 2,000,000 (all Maya) (1960s)

Environment: Arid semidesert

Livelihood: corn farming

Political organization:
Peasant society in modern state

Other: These descendents of the great precolonial civilization are now corn-farming peasants who maintain a strong sense of cultural viability

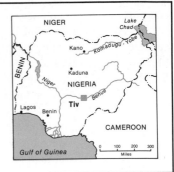

EthnoFile 5.5
TIV

Region: West Africa

Nation: Nigeria (northern)

Population: 800,000

Environment: Undulating plain—wooded foothills to sandbanks

Livelihood: Farming

Political organization: No rulers traditionally; part of nation-state today

Other: It has been suggested that Tiv art helps to prevent the emergence of classes in Tiv society

where they are found, they grouped the plants primarily in terms of the abstract attribute of edibility.

These studies, taken together, reinforce the conclusion that competent members of all societies employ a range of cognitive styles. We cannot speak of abstract thinking and concrete thinking as mutually exclusive. Many of the non-Western peoples with whom anthropologists work are unfamiliar, however, with the context-free cognitive style required in the schoolroom. Members of those societies can learn this cognitive style if they attend school. But, as the Tiv research illustrates, this does not mean that they never use abstract categories outside the classroom. Paradoxically, the Tiv children were able to display sophisticated classifying skills when the experimental task was made more, rather than less, context dependent. But perhaps the paradox is not so great after all. In Lave's research, the full range of her shoppers' calculating skills were displayed only when she studied mathematics in the supermarket, rather than the classroom.

Cross-cultural research in cognition is a delicate business. For the researcher, the trick is first, to devise a test that will give people who use different cognitive styles an opportunity to show what they know and what they can do. The researcher must also discover whether different groups of subjects being tested understand the tasks they are being asked to perform in the same way. Ways must be found to assess cognition that are not bound to the traditional psychological testing laboratory or to the classroom. In recent years, a number of researchers have been moving in this direction.

Reason and the Reasoning Process

As we have just seen, one great Western dualism is between what we see and what we know. Another, at least equally great, is between what we think and what we feel.

From the earliest days of the West's discovery of other societies, there has been a debate about the extent to which nonliterate non-Western peoples might be said to possess reason. How might one go about determining whether or not the members of a particular society are "rational" or "irrational"? To begin, we need to explore what we mean by **rational thinking**.

Most cognitive psychologists have adopted Jerome Bruner's famous definition of thinking as "going beyond the information given." This means that thinking is different from remembering (which refers to information already given) and also from learning (which involves acquiring information that was not given beforehand).

rational thinking
an active cognitive process that involves going beyond the information given

Going beyond the information given thus implies a dialectic between some information already at hand and the cognitive processes of the person who is attempting to cope with that information. This definition highlights the "nexus of relations between the mind at work and the world in which it works." Thinking is open and active, and it has no predetermined outcome.

Many psychologists and anthropologists have tried to assess the levels of rational thinking present in non-Western populations. One measure that has been used several times is the test of *conservation*. Swiss psychologist Jean Piaget devised this test as a way of measuring children's cognitive development. Children who "conserve" are able to recognize that the quantity of some substance remains constant even when its shape changes. According to Piaget, attaining this ability is an important step on the way to mature rational thought.

A classic conservation experiment would proceed in the following way. Children are shown a short, squat beaker of water. The experimenter pours the water from this beaker into another beaker, which is tall and thin. Naturally the water level rises much higher in the tall, thin beaker. Each child is then asked whether the amount of water has changed. It seems that not until Western children reach the age of six or seven do they become aware that the amount of water remains the same, or is "conserved." Before this time, they tend to argue that the tall, thin beaker has more water in it. The results of this experiment can be used to demonstrate concept formation (i.e., the concept of volume). But they have often been used to demonstrate the presence or absence of rational thought. This is presumably because to conclude that the same volume changes in amount as it is poured from one beaker into another is "irrational" in any normal adult (Cole and Scribner 1974:146ff.).

Conservation tests have been tried in several different societies, always with ambiguous results. Some people are able to "pass" the test, others are not, and there is no clear way to predict who will be successful and who will not be. "Until we have some better idea of what induces some members of traditional societies to solve conservation problems while their neighbors do not, we cannot be certain about the significance of conservation tests as a tool for understanding the relation between culture and cognitive development" (Cole and Scribner 1974:156).

Culture and Logic

Another set of cognitive tests has to do with verbal reasoning ability. These tests present subjects with three statements in the form of a syllogism—for example, "All men are mortal, Socrates is a man, therefore Socrates is mortal." The first two propositions are called the *premises*, and the third statement is the conclusion. For a syllogism to be sound, the conclusion must follow from the premises.

Syllogistic reasoning is enshrined in Western culture as the quintessence of rational thought. It has therefore been suggested that the rational capacities of non-Western peoples could be tested by presenting those people with logical problems in syllogistic form. Presumably their rationality would be confirmed if they could deduce correctly when the conclusion followed logically from the premises, and when it did not.

Cole and Scribner devised logical problems involving syllogistic reasoning and presented them to their Kpelle subjects. Typically, the logical problem was embedded in a folktale-like story. The experimenter read the story to the subjects and then asked them a series of follow-up questions designed to reveal whether the subjects could draw a correct conclusion from the premises given.

syllogistic reasoning
a form of reasoning based on the syllogism, a series of three statements in which the first two statements are the premises, and the last is the conclusion, which must follow from the premises

EthnoFile 5.6
KPELLE

Region: West Africa

Nation: Liberia (central and western)

Population: 86,000

Environment: Tropical forest

Livelihood: Rice farming

Political organization: Chiefdoms

Other: Poro and Sande secret societies are found among the Kpelle, who have been the subjects of several studies in cross-cultural cognition.

Here is one story they prepared: "At one time Spider went to a feast. He was told to answer this question before he could eat any of the food. The question is: Spider and Black Deer always eat together. Spider is eating. Is Black Deer eating?" (Cole and Scribner 1974:162). The syllogism is contained in the question at the end of the story. Given the two premises, the conclusion should be that Black Deer is eating.

Now consider a typical Kpelle response to hearing this story (Cole and Scribner 1974:162):

Subject: *Were they in the bush?*

Experimenter: *Yes.*

Subject: *Were they eating together?*

Experimenter: *Spider and Black Deer always eat together. Spider is eating. Is Black Deer eating?*

Subject: *But I was not there. How can I answer such a question?*

Experimenter: *Can't you answer it? Even if you were not there, you can answer it. (Repeats the question.)*

Object: *Oh, oh, Black Deer is eating.*

Experimenter: *What is your reason for saying that Black Deer was eating?*

Subject: *The reason is that Black Deer always walks about all day eating green leaves in the bush. Then he rests for a while and gets up again to eat.*

The subject's answer to the question and subsequent justification for that answer seem to have nothing whatever to do with the logical problem the subject is being asked to solve. One simplistic way to interpret this response would be to call it "irrational," but reread the original story. The story itself contains an element of paradox: Spider will not be allowed to eat until he answers a question, yet the question he is to answer presumes that he is already eating! Of course, the paradox exists only if the subjects assume that the contextual material about the feast is relevant to the logical problem they are being asked to solve. Yet it is precisely this that we cannot assume. As we have seen, people have to be trained to exclude context from their judgments of truth or falsity, literality or figurativeness.

The experimenters devised this story the same way schoolteachers devise word problems for students of mathematics. That is, the contextual material is nothing more than a kind of window dressing. Smart students quickly learn to disregard the window dressing and seek out the mathematical problem it hides. In the same way, the Kpelle subjects hearing the story about Spider and Black Deer are supposed to demonstrate "logic" by disregarding the contextual material about the feast, and seeking out the syllogism embedded within it. However, Kpelle subjects did not understand that they were being read this story in a testing situation for which considerations of context or meaningfulness were irrelevant. In the preceding example, the subject seemed to have difficulty separating the logical problem both from the introductory material about the feast and from the rest of his experiential knowledge.

Cole and Scribner interpreted their subject's response to this problem as being due not to irrationality but to a "failure to accept the logical task" (Cole and Scribner 1974:162). In a follow-up study, Cole and Scribner discovered that Kpelle high school children responded "correctly" to the logical problems 90 percent of the time. This suggests a strong correlation between Western-style schooling and willingness to accept context-free analytic tasks in testing situations (Cole and Scribner 1974:164).

But this is not all. David Lancy, one of Cole and Scribner's colleagues, discovered that Western-style syllogisms are very similar to certain forms of Kpelle riddles. Unlike syllogisms, however, those riddles have no single, "logically correct" answer. "Rather, as the riddle is posed to a group, the right answer is the one among many offered that seems most illuminating, resourceful, and convincing as determined by consensus and circumstance. This emphasis on edification as a criterion for 'rightness' is found in Kpelle jurisprudence as well" (Lancy cited in Fernandez 1980:47–48).

Cole and Scribner conclude: "We cannot draw conclusions about reasoning processes from the *answers* people give to logic problems. We have first to ask: 'What is their understanding of the task? How do they encode the information presented to them? What transformations does the information undergo, and what factors control these?'" (Cole and Scribner 1974:166). From their perspective, the functional **reasoning styles** of nonschooled non-Western people remain a mystery. But there is no evidence that the reasoning processes of these people are different from those of educated Western people, or of Western-educated people from their own societies.

This suggests that what we call **logic** is a functional reasoning style characteristic of Western culture. If so, then it would seem that the ability to reason "logically" is a cultural matter that must be learned. People equipped with the same basic rational cognitive processes, but reared in a different cultural system, might develop different logics of their own. Perhaps most such "logics" have in common that they do not allow their users to divorce the reasoning process from a wider context.

This suggestion is not as farfetched as it may sound. Cole and Scribner (1974:145) point out that modern cognitive psychologists do not identify rational thinking with "logic." The reasoning styles of ordinary people do not necessarily conform to any of the models of logic formalized by philosophers. If they did, there would be no need to take college courses in logic. Traditionally, logicians have scorned the "illogical, irrational" thought processes of ordinary people in everyday life. But everyday reasoning is not so chaotic, as Lave's grocery shoppers illustrated. Nor is formal Western logic as consistent as logicians would like laypeople to believe.

reasoning styles
the ways in which people understand a cognitive task, encode the information presented to them, and transform that information. Reasoning styles are culturally shaped

logic
a symbolic system used to represent objects and relationships between objects in the world; formal logic is a reasoning style characteristic of Western culture.

Logical systems are symbolic systems. They are used to represent objects and relationships between objects in the world. But the objects and relationships we experience in our lives can always be represented in more than one way. As a result, logical systems require that their creators choose which attributes of experience to represent and which to ignore. As Barry Barnes and David Bloor put it, "Just as our experience of a shared material world does not itself guarantee shared verbal descriptions of it, so our shared rationality does not guarantee a unique logical system" (1982:44). Barnes and Bloor prefer to see traditional Western logic as "a learned body of scholarly lore, growing and varying over time" (1982:45). The rules of logic that this body of lore is supposed to represent are a set of conventionally accepted rules governing styles of reasoning. These conventions and traditions have grown out of some of the preoccupations of Western culture.

Beyond that, formal logic itself is not perfect. This is not because of any supposed rational limits of human beings. Rather, as the mathematician Kurt Gödel demonstrated, no logical system is entirely self-consistent. At some point, each system must come to rest on axioms that are assumed, not proved. Logicians themselves often set out the points where they allow "intuition" to decide for them which of different arguments they will accept.

This is not to deny that the rules of Western logic may be very useful. Since they are in part engendered by careful attention to human experience of the world, they are hardly random in origin. But other logics, particularly other logics that do not require the elimination of context for their application, may be equally useful to people in other ways. Most of us, for example, would question the rationality of shoppers who spent hours at the supermarket calculating unit/price ratios while their hungry families were waiting for dinner. Indeed, if we in the West continue to exclude context from our logic, we may threaten our own existence as the consequences of our logic erode our lands and pollute the air and water. We too might benefit from a style of reasoning that does not allow context to be forgotten. Western logic, like literal language, does not offer us the only plausible, meaningful, or useful perspective on the human condition.

Emotion

emotion
the product of a dialectic between bodily arousal and cognitive interpretation; emotion is constituted of states, values, and arousals

Cognitive psychologists who try to define **emotion** in cross-cultural terms run into a familiar problem. They discover not just that different cultures talk about emotion in different languages, but that not all languages even possess a term that might be translated as "emotion." One way out of this tangle is to try to develop a theory of cognitive functioning that would account for the experiences that some cultures recognize as emotional. This is the path scholars such as George Mandler have chosen.

In traditional Western dualism, reason or thought have been associated with the mind, and emotion with the body. Mandler (1975) agrees that any attempt to explain emotion must deal with the nature of the bodily arousal we associate with it. But there is more to emotion, as commonly understood, than mere bodily arousal. Recall the butcher knife referred to earlier in this chapter. What do we feel when we see a butcher knife sitting beside mushrooms on a cutting board in our kitchen? What do we feel when we see that same knife in the hands of a burgler who is bent on attacking us? The knife alone does not trigger our feeling. The *context* in which we encounter the knife is equally important.

The context itself is often ambiguous, and our emotional experience changes as our interpretation of the context changes. Imagine you are walking along a sidewalk on a moonlit night when suddenly a black shadow looms over you. Fear enfolds you: someone is leaping out of the bushes to attack you! But then you see that the black shadow was cast by tree branches being tossed in the wind, and your fear melts away. The signals taken in by your nervous system have not changed. But your analysis of the *meaning* of the signals has changed, and this has altered your emotional response.

Thus, emotion can be understood as the product of a dialectic between bodily arousal and cognitive interpretation. Mandler (1975:97) suggests that bodily arousal can trigger an emotional experience by attracting our attention and prompting us to seek the source of arousal. Conversely, a particular *interpretation* of our experience can trigger bodily arousal. Arousal may heighten or diminish, depending on the way we interpret what is happening around us. In the case of the looming shadow, an interpretation of the visual signals as representing danger led to heightened visceral arousal. But all these gut responses rapidly diminished as soon as the same signals were reinterpreted as being harmless.

Approaching emotion from this perspective accomplishes three things: (1) it integrates mind and body in a holistic fashion; (2) it acknowledges ambiguity as a central feature of emotional experience, in the same way that we have argued it to be central to linguistic, perceptual, and conceptual experience; and (3) it suggests the ways different cultural interpretive frameworks might have a role in shaping not only what we think but also what we feel.

The nature of the dialectic involved is complex, as we might expect it to be in a creature as physically and cognitively complex as a human being. Some external signals automatically trigger bodily arousal without meaning analysis: for example, bodily injury, loud noises, interruption of ongoing plans, sudden loss of support. In addition, some signals may originally be without meaning to us but may acquire meaning on the basis of past experience: for example, dogs, hot stoves, classrooms on exam day. When we encounter these at a later time, therefore, they may trigger bodily arousal.

Consider, however, that a fear of dogs that has developed out of unpleasant experiences with dogs in childhood may persist when we are in the presence of dogs that make no move to attack or even come near us. In this situation, our interpretation is based on displaced experiences having nothing to do with our current context. In this way, meaning analysis continues to trigger visceral arousal in the absence of a real threat. This is not all. Loss of support—feeling the floor give way beneath us, for example—is an apparently innate triggering mechanism for visceral arousal, and ordinarily we feel fear when the ground unexpectedly gives way beneath us. Yet loss of support leads to pleasure for many people who experience it as sky divers, on hang gliders, or on a roller coaster.

Consider examples from other cultures. Hindu participants in the religious festival of Thaipusam, in Kuala Lumpur, Malaysia, ritually pierce their tongues, cheeks, or other parts of their bodies, and march in a long procession to demonstrate their devotion to the god Murngin. *(See EthnoFile 5.7: Hindu Malaysians.)* They do this while in a trance, and report the experience to be euphoric, "like floating on the air, followed by the wind" (a phrase from an ethnographic film of the same name). Initiation rituals in many non-Western societies often involve circumcision or bodily scarification without the use of anesthetic. Why would anybody actively seek out pain in these contexts, as the initiates do? These people ordinarily request to undergo initiation, and they are not physically restrained during the rites.

Although sudden loss of support is normally frightening, in some contexts it can be pleasurable and may be eagerly sought.

EthnoFile 5.7
HINDU
MALAYSIANS

Region: Southeast Asia

Nation: Malaysia

Population: 1,360,000

Environment: Tropical

Livelihood: Varies; farming,
industry, commerce, civil service

Political organization:
Modern nation-state

Other: Many people observe a
ritual to the Hindu god Murngin,
during which their bodies are
pierced while they are in a
trance state, with no serious
aftereffects

What are we to make of such experiences and such reports? Are sky divers, piercers of their own flesh, and tribal initiates mentally ill? Are they masochists who find pleasure where any normal person would find just the opposite? Sky divers usually seem able to fit into the routines of daily life without difficulty once they are on the ground. Thaipusam participants experience little bleeding and rapid healing of their self-inflicted wounds; indeed, many repeat the ritual on a yearly basis. If anything, they often seem better adjusted to everyday life after the experience than before it. They are usually motivated to participate in the first place because of problems they have experienced. Their sacrifice is understood to be a request to their god for assistance or thanks for help he has already given. Tribal initiates are proud of passing through the ordeal successfully and go on to become responsible adults in their communities.

On the other hand, sky divers would probably feel fear if they were riding in an elevator whose cables suddenly snapped, leading them to experience a sudden loss of support. Thaipusam participants and tribal initiates are not known to enjoy repeatedly injuring themselves with knives or fishhooks in everyday contexts. But we do not need to go outside our own society to find examples of the same experience having different meanings. Some people in our society die a thousand deaths if they are required to speak publicly before a crowd of strangers; others find the same experience exhilarating; still others find the experience neither pleasurable nor anxiety producing, merely routine. In the first case, bodily arousal is triggered and, together with the negative meaning analysis, produces fear. In the second case, bodily arousal together with a positive meaning analysis produces pleasure. In the third case, no bodily arousal is triggered, perhaps because the meaning analysis indicates nothing out of the ordinary, that is, no reason for fear or pleasure.

Why should we experience emotion at all? The role of emotion in human life may be rooted in the evolutionary history of a species of high intelligence capable of thinking before acting. Visceral arousal alerts us to something new and unexpected in our environment, something that does not easily fit into any of the conventional schemas with which we have been operating. Once our attention is caught in this way, the rest of our cognitive processes are brought to bear on the interrupting phenomenon. We engage in the characteristic human activity of attempting to make sense of this new experience by viewing it from as many perspectives as we can muster, until we find a way to make it meaningful.

Mandler's discussion of emotion has much in common with Cole and Scribner's discussion of other areas of cognition. Like Cole and Scribner, Mandler argues that what we refer to as emotions are *functional systems*. Each links elementary processes that involve the body's arousal system to other elementary processes that are involved in the construction of perception, conception, and reasoning. The result is a holistic emotional experience that depends simultaneously on mind, body, and the wider world.

Our emotions, then, just as our thoughts, are complex constructions. "Emotions are not something that people 'have,' they are constituted of people's states, values and arousals" (Mandler 1983:151). They are wholes greater than, and irreducible to, the sum of their parts. They are built up out of material sensations and interpretations of those sensations. But just because our feelings are in part created by us, there is always ambiguity about their appropriateness, just as there is always ambiguity at the heart of perceptions, conceptions, and reasoning.

Human knowledge is erected on a base of sensory experience and interpretation of sensory experience, each shaping the other dialectically. Emotion is no less important to this endeavor than reason. Emotional arousal alerts us to those unconventional, unexpected, interrupting phenomena to which the rest of our cognitive processes can then be applied. Viewed in this way, it would be a foolish person who ignored his or her guts when trying to sort out a confusing experience. Indeed, the guts are usually what alert us to confusion in the first place. Viewed in this way, the need of "whole-body" experience for understanding also becomes more comprehensible. Mandler reminds us, "Just telling people what a situation is going to be like isn't enough, and it isn't good enough training when you encounter the real situation" (Mandler 1983:152). Generations of new spouses, new parents, and anthropological fieldworkers can testify to the overwhelming truth of this statement.

Thus, emotion is shaped in an important way by experience. We experience visceral arousal when our familiar world is somehow interrupted. That arousal may either dissipate or develop into an emotional experience, depending on the meaning we assign to it. Possible meanings arise out of cultural interpretations of recurring experiential schemas. We should not be surprised to find some overlap in the categories of feeling recognized by different cultures. After all, certain experiential schemas that interrupt the familiar world—birth and death, for example—are human universals. At the same time, we should expect that the wider cultural context will in each case modify the angle from which such experiences are understood. Categories of feeling will therefore be modified as well.

Emotion in the United States

Let us consider the emotion of jealousy. What prototypical situation evokes this emotion in us? We feel jealousy when an established close relationship with one person is interrupted by the appearance of a third person who threatens to replace us in the first person's affections.

Imagine two different occasions on which a person might feel jealousy. In the first case, Jennifer is nine years old and has a best friend, Skip, with whom she is very close. A new child moves into the neighborhood. Jennifer introduces the newcomer to Skip, and then discovers that Skip and the newcomer seem to be seeing more of one another than either sees of Jennifer. We would probably describe the responses to *threat*, *betrayal*, and *loss* that Jennifer is feeling as jealousy.

In the second case, Jennifer has grown up. She is in love with Skip, but for various reasons she has hidden this affection, perhaps out of propriety. It is highly unlikely that Skip is even aware of Jennifer's affection. Lola enters the scene. From Jennifer's perspective, Lola is no more suitable for Skip than she is, and therefore ought properly to hide any affection for Skip that might develop. But, to Jennifer's surprise, Lola not only falls in love with Skip but openly makes this affection known! What is more, Skip returns Lola's affection, and they become a couple.

Jennifer is jealous. What are the components of jealousy here? Jennifer is *outraged* that Lola should break rules of propriety that Jennifer chose to observe. Jennifer also sees that breaking the rules of propriety did not prevent Skip from falling in love with Lola, and so Jennifer *regrets* not having taken the risk Lola took, for had Jennifer done so, perhaps Skip would have responded to Jennifer instead. Perhaps, further, Jennifer feels *cheated* that Lola is more attractive than she and therefore had an unfair advantage in attracting Skip's attention. Jennifer may also be *annoyed* at Skip for being so easily swayed by Lola's good looks, as opposed to Jennifer's sound character. Perhaps all these responses are reinforced by Jennifer's *past history* of romantic rejections. One could go on—indeed, soap operas and romance novels usually do go on to detail every element that contributes to the construction of a character's feelings, and jealousy is a common emotion in such fiction.

Here, in an adult, we have a far more complex configuration of elements that together construct Jennifer's jealousy. Even though we are discussing two experiences of jealousy in the life of the same individual, no one, not even Jennifer, would argue that the jealousy experienced as a nine year old feels the same way this current adult jealousy feels. Some of the elements in both experiences seem the same; they give Jennifer reason to group them together as experiences of jealousy. But other elements are far different. In the adult, sexuality has entered the picture, as have all Jennifer's intervening personal experiences, including experiences of jealousy, since the age of nine. Both experiences bear a family resemblance to the prototypical cultural experience of jealousy, but neither can be reduced to it, or to each other.

Emotion in an East African Culture

Now consider the construction of emotion in a culture different from our own. The culture of the Giriama of coastal Kenya, in East Africa, has been studied by David Parkin (1984). (*See EthnoFile 5.8: Giriama.*) Several features of Giriama thinking must be explained before their understanding of what we call emotion can be considered. First, the Giriama theory of human nature does not recognize a mind-body dualism of the Western sort. This coincides with their unwillingness to set up sharp, mutually exclusive oppositions of any kind when discussing human nature. Parkin

EthnoFile 5.8
GIRIAMA

Region: East Africa

Nation: Kenya

Population: 150,000

Environment: Varies; coastal to desert, lush, hilly, flat

Livelihood: Farming and herding

Political organization: Men of influence but no coercive power

Other: Giriama healing rituals presuppose the union of mind, body, and emotion

tells us that such behavior as spirit possession, madness, hysteria, witchcraft, persistent violence, drunkenness, and thieving are explained "as the result of what we might call imbalances in human nature."

> *I call them imbalances because the Giriama do not believe that a person can be intrinsically or irredeemably evil: at some stage, usually remarkably quickly, he will be brought back into the fold, even if he subsequently leaves it again. A large number of terms, roughly translatable as greed, lust, envy, jealousy, malice, resentment, anger, are used to refer to these imbalances of character and the accompanying behavior. (Parkin 1984:14)*

As with us, the Giriama associate different feelings with different parts of the body. In the West, we conventionally connect the brain with reason and the heart with emotion, and we usually do not confuse the two unless we are deliberately attempting to contradict convention. For the Giriama, however, the heart, liver, kidney, and eye are the seat of both reason and emotion. Although the Giriama may distinguish thinking from feeling in discussing the actual behavior of real people, they nevertheless presume a common origin for both (ibid.:17). Indeed, the Giriama seem to have a folk theory of human cognition that in its basic framework is not unlike the perspective described throughout this chapter.

What about particular emotions? Although the categories of feeling recognized by Giriama overlap in some respects with the experiences labeled by English terms for emotions, Parkin suggests that there are important differences. These differences stem from the nature of the prototypical domains of experience that Giriama culture conventionally recognizes, and from the prototypical thoughts and feelings that are appropriate to those domains. Consider what the term *utsungu* means as a label for a category of feeling:

> Utsungu *means poison, bitterness, resentment, and anger, on the one hand, but also grief on the other. It is the feeling experienced at a funeral of a loved or respected relative or friend. A man or woman is grieved at the loss but also bitter that it has happened at all, and angry with the witch who caused the death. Since the witch will be made to pay, the sentiment carried with it both the consequences of the loss of a dear one and the intention to avenge his or her death." (Ibid.: 118)*

We too feel "grief" at the death of a loved one. But the prototypical Western experience of grief does not contain the additional meaning analysis involving anger at witchcraft and the desire for vengeance! One would have to be a Giriama—or have lived in another culture in which witchcraft was understood as the usual cause of death and in which such wrongful death could be avenged—for one to begin to feel the complex emotional configuration that Parkin describes for the Giriama.

The Process of Socialization and Enculturation

We have discussed the various cognitive processes that all normal human beings seem to possess. We have also described some of the ways that different cultures link these processes together into functional cognitive systems guiding perception, conception, reason, and emotion. The cognitive systems of different members of a society need not be identical for those different members to get on with their lives. All that seems necessary is a minimal negotiated agreement.

Acquiring the functional cognitive systems characteristic of a culture takes time. We can think of cognitive learning as similar to language learning. It involves a dialectical interaction between organism and environment, and an important part of that environment is other people. Children use their own bodies and brains to explore the world around them. But from their earliest days, other people are actively working to steer their activity and attention in a particular direction. As a result, their exploration of the world is not merely trial and error. The path is cleared for them by others who shape their experiences—and their interpretations of their experiences—for them.

Two terms in the social sciences refer to this process of culturally and socially mediated cognitive development. The first term, **socialization**, originated in sociology. It focuses on the organizational problems facing human beings as material organisms who must live with each other. Creatures with material bodies must learn to pattern their physical behavior and adapt it to the ways of acting that are considered appropriate in the society in which they are living. The second term, **enculturation**, originated in anthropology. It focuses on the cognitive problems facing human beings as intelligent, reflexive creatures who must live with each other. These creatures must learn to pattern their ways of thinking and feeling and adapt them to the ways of thinking and feeling considered appropriate in the culture into which they were born. The process of becoming human requires both these processes. After all, children learn ways of acting, thinking, feeling, and speaking at the same time, as they participate in the characteristic activities of their group. We will use the term *socialization/enculturation* to represent this holistic experience.

Socialization/enculturation is a process whose product is a socially and culturally constructed **self**, capable of functioning successfully in the society in which the person lives. Anthropologists do not have any global theory of socialization/enculturation. Important thinkers have addressed the issues involved, however, and have come up with theories that attempt to account for at least some of the processes through which mature human selves are produced. Three major theorists have had a significant influence on anthropological approaches to cognitive development and socialization/enculturation: Sigmund Freud (1856–1939), Jean Piaget (1896–1980), and Lev Vygotsky (1896–1934).

Freud and Emotional Development

Freud's theory of personality development emphasizes in particular the patterning of the emotions in early childhood. Freud argued that all human children passed through a universal sequence of experiences within the family. How they negotiated those experiences would have a lifelong impact on their emotional health.

According to Freud, human beings are, first and foremost, physical organisms. Their action in the world is guided by an innate predisposition to seek pleasure and avoid pain. This instinctive desire takes the form of drives for food and for sex. The drives exist in the unconscious, in a domain of the personality that Freud called the *id*. If the drives go unsatisfied for too long, the pressure will cause psychological damage. In this way, Freud, who was far from optimistic about human destiny, saw murder and rape as natural responses of human beings (he was thinking primarily of male human beings) whose natural drives were frustrated.

Initially, newborn children are at the mercy of the id; Freud sees them as demanding and egocentric. Gradually, however, children discover that their de-

socialization
the process by which human beings as material organisms, living together with other similar organisms, must learn to pattern their behavior and adapt it to the ways of acting that are considered appropriate in the society in which they are living

enculturation
the process by which human beings as intelligent, reflexive creatures, living together with other similar organisms, must learn to pattern their ways of thinking and feeling and adapt them to the ways of thinking and feeling considered appropriate in the culture into which they were born

self
the result of the process of socialization/enculturation within an individual

Sigmund Freud (1856–1939).

mands will not all be met instantly and that their caretaker's will is not under their control. With the emergence of this awareness there develops a child's *ego*, the domain of the personality that embodies reason and common sense. As children grow older and learn more about the wider social world, they develop within their personalities a third domain, that of the *superego*.

The superego is an internalized representation of the rules of the social group. It corresponds to what we refer to as a person's conscience, and can redirect drives into socially acceptable channels. But society's rules may be very demanding, and offer little satisfaction. Freud argued that people unable to withstand the social forces that channel or repress their innate drives may suffer psychological disturbances. They will seek pleasure in bizarre or unconventional ways in an attempt to satisfy *repressed* drives whose demands their egos are too weak to control.

Piaget and Rational Development

In contrast to Freud, the Swiss psychologist Jean Piaget placed primary emphasis on the development of reason in children. He proposed four stages of development in children's reasoning powers.

The earliest stage is the *sensorimotor stage* (birth to age two). Children in this stage learn about the environment through their senses, by exploring and manipulating the physical world around them. They cannot yet speak, and thus cannot rely on language to teach them about the world. As a result of their explorations in this stage, children begin to develop schemas, or recognizable, recurring configurations of experience.

As soon as children begin to learn language, they embark on the *preoperational stage* (about age two to age seven). Children at this stage have developed schemas about the world, but their schemas are not yet mature. For example, during the preoperational stage children are consistently misled by the illusions of greater volume, length, or weight in tests of conservation.

The third stage is that of *concrete operations* (age seven to age eleven). Children who reach this stage have mastered the illusions that misled them at their previous level of development. During this stage they construct an increasingly sophisticated understanding of the structure and operation of the material world around them. They have difficulty, however, in abstracting from concrete experience.

Piaget's fourth stage is that of *formal operations*. It usually appears about the time children enter their teens. Children at this stage become able to manipulate abstract concepts. They can understand the symbolism of mathematics, for example, and carry out calculations using the symbols themselves without direct reference to the concrete world that the symbols represent. Eventually, they become able to discuss concepts for which there is no concrete reference in the world of experience—concepts such as negative numbers. The stage of formal operations is the highest level of rational development. Piaget believed that not everyone would necessarily achieve this stage.

The theories of Freud and Piaget are stimulating and suggestive. Yet they pose problems for anthropologists who attempt to use them in sociocultural research. Both Freud and Piaget take a highly individualistic approach to socialization/enculturation. For both, children come into the world as independent individuals, able to begin making sense of the world around them without the guidance of others.

In the case of Freud, the id is an autonomous natural force, given in material human nature, propelling each individual toward egotism. Left on their own, human beings aim only to satisfy themselves, and they relate to other people only as means

Jean Piaget (1896–1980).

to this end. Thus, cooperation and sharing, mutual dependency, are seen by Freud as foreign to human nature. When human beings curb their biologically rooted impulses in order to live together in society, they are therefore violating their own natures and cannot but suffer. For Freud, a child's coming to terms with his or her parents and other people is a traumatic event that, if not successfully negotiated, produces scars that can last a lifetime. And there is no remedy, since we can neither eliminate our natural selfishness nor survive without other human beings.

For Piaget, too, human beings are naturally egoistic, and for the same "biological" reasons. For him, early childhood is a time when young, independent human animals develop, on their own, the inborn capacity for rational thought given to them in the genes. Socialization/enculturation is needed if a child is to learn to get along with other members of the group. But language, culture, and the company of other people cannot help children learn how the world works, and may even interfere with such learning. For Piaget, children's knowledge of the world must come through their own self-generated operations.

Vygotsky and Sociohistorical Development

The theories of Freud and Piaget assume that the important factors influencing development are rooted in the biological characteristics of individual organisms. As a result, both theories are intended to explain social and cultural patterns as by-products of the efforts of self-contained individuals to come to terms with the wider world. Both theories are therefore reductionistic.

Anthropologists need a theory of cognitive development that is holistic. Many psychologists and anthropologists believe they have found one in the work of Soviet psychologist Lev Vygotsky. Vygotsky did his path-breaking work in the early decades of the twentieth century and died before the age of forty. Yet he helped found a major school of Soviet psychology that continues to thrive. The writings of this *sociohistorical school* have become widely available in the West only in the past few years. They have already inspired some of the most interesting recent research in cognitive anthropology.

For Vygotsky, human life is social from the outset. As he put it, "The social dimension of consciousness is primary in time and in fact. The individual dimension of consciousness is derivative and secondary" (Vygotsky 1978:30). In this respect, Vygotsky took the same theoretical point of departure as George Herbert Mead (1863–1931), who also argued that individuality and identity can be acquired only in a social context.

In the years before Vygotsky's work was well-known, Mead was an influential figure among psychological anthropologists who were dissatisfied with individualistic reductionism. Like Vygotsky, Mead believed that human nature is completed and enhanced, not curtailed or damaged, by socialization and enculturation. Indeed, the successful humanization of human beings lies in people's mastery of symbols, which begins when children start to learn language. As children come to control the symbol systems of their cultures, they gain the ability to distinguish objects and relationships in the world. Most important, they come to see themselves as objects as well as subjects.

For Mead, this ability is acquired through the process of *role playing*. Very young children are at first unaware that they and the world around them are not continuous with one another. Gradually, however, they come to recognize, for example, that their parent's point of view is different from their own. Children then enter a stage of development in which they imitate the roles of those few people—

Lev Vygotsky (1896–1934)

the *particular others*—with whom they are well acquainted. This imitative play is especially obvious when children begin to talk and can be observed scolding their toys the same way they were recently scolded.

As children grow older, they move into the *game* stage, wherein they have become expert enough at taking the roles of other people to be able to enter into complex interactions with others. They can keep in mind not only their own role in the game, but also the roles of all the other participants. At the same time, their experience of other people is widening beyond the immediate family, and they develop the ability to take the role of the *generalized other*, or society at large. Being able to play games and take the role of the generalized other successfully requires a mastery of symbolism, since the games' rules and society's point of view are both highly abstract and mediated by language.

Mead points out the role of society and culture in enabling human beings to pursue their projects. The birth of reflexivity and its role in the formation of self-identity is significant in Mead's thought, as is the related emphasis on role playing as the central activity of socialization/enculturation. Put another way, metaphor appears squarely at the center of children's growing awareness of the world around them—after all, what is role playing? When a child pretends to be a daddy or a mommy or the person driving the big tractor-trailer or the person wearing glasses in the television program, that child is saying "I am the daddy," "I am the mommy," "I am the truck driver," "I am the one with glasses," even though all these statements are literally false. Role playing is a holistic metaphorical activity by means of which children take on the roles of other people in society, roles that one day they may have literally to assume.

Mead's analysis focused primarily on face-to-face interaction among people. Anthropologists needed a theoretical framework that would go beyond face-to-face interactions and account for the social, cultural, and historical contexts in which those interactions unfold. Here Vygotsky's work becomes important. Vygotsky wanted to create a psychology that was compatible with a marxian analysis of society. His formulations are far from doctrinaire; indeed, during the Stalin years in Russia, his work was censored. At the same time, his marxian orientation ensured that he would have to pay attention to the social, cultural, and historical context in which individual action is embedded.

At the beginning of the chapter, we introduced one of Vygotsky's theoretical contributions, the distinction between elementary cognitive processes and functional cognitive systems. This distinction is useful to anthropology because it provides a way of describing the similarities and differences we observe when we compare the way people from different cultures think and feel. These differences have implications for cognitive development as well. The functional systems employed by adult members of the society must be acquired by children as they mature. For Vygotsky, acquisition takes place in a context of face-to-face interaction between, typically, a child and an adult. When children learn about the world in a context such as this, they are not only—or even primarily—working on their own. On the contrary, they are learning about the world as they learn the symbolic forms (usually language) that others use to represent the world.

This learning process creates in the child a new plane of consciousness based on the dialogical, question-and-answer format of social interaction. From this Vygotsky inferred that our internal thought processes would also have a dialogical format. Mead suggested something similar when he spoke of every person being able to carry on internal conversations between the *I* (the unsocialized self) and the *me* (the socially conditioned self). Only on this basis can an individual's sense of identity develop as the self comes to distinguish itself from the conversational other.

One interesting Vygotskian concept is the *zone of proximal development*. This zone is the distance between a child's "actual development level as determined by independent problem solving" and the level of "potential development as determined through problem solving under adult guidance or in collaboration with more capable peers" (Vygotsky 1978:86). Psychologists everywhere have long been aware that children can often achieve more when they are coached than when they work alone. Western psychologists, with their individualist bias, have viewed this difference in achievement as contamination of the testing situation, or as the result of cheating. Vygotsky and his followers, however, have seen it as an indispensable measure of potential developmental growth that simultaneously demonstrates the way that growth is rooted in social interaction.

The concept of the zone of proximal development provides us with a way of describing the inadequacies of traditional IQ tests. For anthropologists and comparative psychologists, it also provides a way of linking cognitive development to society, culture, and history. This conclusion is based on Vygotsky's explicit association of coaching or formal instruction with, as he put it, the "historical characteristics of humans" (Wertsch 1985:71). That is, interaction in the zone of proximal development is shaped by social, cultural, and historical factors. To the extent that these factors vary from society to society, we can expect cognitive development to vary as well.

Is Cognitive Development the Same for Everyone?

The theories of development reviewed here picture the development process as progression through a series of stages. Vygotsky excepted, these theories also tend to assume that the stages are the same for all human beings, or at least all human beings in a particular society. We have seen some of the problems that are raised when anthropologists try to account for cross-cultural differences with reference to a universal scheme of development. But we must not forget that each culture harbors variation within itself. A Vygotskian perspective can help us explain not only cross-cultural differences in development, but also differences in the cognitive development of different subgroups in a single society.

Carol Gilligan (1982) carried out a comparative study on the moral development of women and men in American society. She argues that middle-class American boys and girls begin their moral development in different sociocultural contexts. Boys are encouraged from an early age to break away from their mothers and families and make it on their own. In this context, they learn that independence is good, that dependency is weakness, and that their first duty is to themselves and what they stand for. By contrast, girls mature in a sociocultural context in which their bond to their mothers and families is never sharply ruptured. They learn that connection to others is good, that the destruction of relationships is damaging, and that their first responsibility in any difficult situation is to ensure that nobody gets hurt.

Gilligan did not adopt a Vygotskian perspective in this study, although she was influenced by Mead. But the Vygotskian concept of the zone of proximal development provides a useful tool for describing how the differential moral development of boys and girls is accomplished. In Vygotskian terms, the moral development of boys and girls proceeds in different directions as a result of the coaching each receives by adults and other more mature members of society. When faced with the same dilemmas, and unsure how to act, boys are encouraged to make one set of choices, girls another. In this way, each gender category builds up a different set of assumptions as to what constitutes the "good." As a result, American men and women consistently see one another acting immorally. For example, attempts made by men and boys to be true to themselves and strike out on their own may be condemned by women and girls because such action can be highly destructive to personal relationships. Attempts made by women and girls to encourage intimacy and closeness may be condemned by men and boys because men and boys see such ties as confining and repressive.

As Gilligan reminds us, men as a group hold power over women as a group in American society. Men have therefore been able to insist that their moral perspective is the correct one. This observation is very much in keeping with Vygotsky's insistence that explanations of cognitive development be situated in a wider social and historical setting. Changes in that wider setting, moreover, may be expected to affect the developmental paths embedded within it. As American women gain power and begin to articulate their own position, Gilligan suggests, women's "different voice" will increasingly make itself heard to challenge the male definition of morality.

Cognition and Context

Human cognition is a holistic phenomenon that involves perceiving, thinking, feeling, and acting in the world. Each cognitive domain shapes the others. What we perceive triggers thoughts and feelings and suggests possible actions. At the same time, how we think and feel and act shapes our perceptions. This is so, it appears, because "any fact, or small set of facts, is open to a wide variety of interpretations" (Cole and Scribner 1974 : 172). The question then becomes one of trying to explain the different interpretations.

There are no clear-cut answers to this question. Cross-cultural research by anthropologists does, however, rule out any explanation that relies on innate differences in mental or emotional capacity from one society to another. Such a naive conclusion can appear plausible only if ethnographically unsophisticated people consider test results apart from the context in which they were produced. The researcher's task thus becomes one of trying to explain coherently why normal, intelligent people from different cultures do not all score the same on psychological tests. The sociohistorical approach pioneered by Vygotsky and his colleagues holds much promise in making this task feasible, especially if that approach is enriched by ethnographic research on cognitive practices occurring outside the testing laboratory, as illustrated by the work of Lave and her associates.

Attempts to understand human cognition cross-culturally have taught anthropologists some unexpected lessons. As Cole and Scribner put it, we have learned "a long list of how-not-tos" with regard to psychological testing. We have learned less about the intelligence of people in other cultures than about our own ethnocentric presuppositions about meaning and rationality.

Cross-cultural studies of cognition make us increasingly aware of the importance of context, not just the immediate context of the laboratory situation, but also the displaced context of culture (that of the subjects and that of the experimenters), which may be invisible in the lab but is present in people's minds. We must also take into consideration historical context. When administering a psychological test on visual illusions to the Fang, James Fernandez (1980) discovered that one's informants-subjects may question the "real" reason behind such a bizarre activity as psychological testing. *(See EthnoFile 6.4: Fang.)* Years of colonial domination and exploitation at the hands of white outsiders make Africans' suspicions of the anthropologist's motives far from irrational.

A further conclusion can be drawn. If human understanding of the world is holistic, so too must be the anthropologist's understanding of another culture, whether the anthropologist is explicitly aware of it or not. That is, anthropological understanding is achieved holistically. It involves not just perception, not just rational analysis, but the entire range of interacting human cognitive processes, including those we label emotional.

An excellent description of a holistic experience is given by anthropologist Michael Gilsenan (1982), who worked for a time among urban Muslims in Cairo, Egypt. Gilsenan spent many hours with his informants in the local mosque observing their prayers. During these sessions, he himself attempted to assume a properly reverential attitude. Along the inside wall of the mosque were verses from the Qur'an. These were not painted, but were formed of bright green neon tubing. Green is the color of the prophet Muhammad, so finding that color used prominently in mosque decoration is not surprising. However, Gilsenan's experiences in Western culture did not include schemas in which neon light and serious worship went together. For several months he struggled to rid himself of his traditional associations. Then one day, Gilsenan reports, "I turned unthinkingly away from the swaying bodies and the rhythms of the remembrance of God and saw, not neon, but simply greenness. . . . No gaps existed between color, shape, light, and form. From that unreflecting and unsuspecting moment I ceased to see neon at all" (1982:266).

Nothing had happened to Gilsenan's eyes or his other senses. They were still receiving the same signals they had always received in this context. But the *meaning* of the signals had been altered. Experience in the mosque had established for Gilsenan a new context for neon light, and increasing familiarity with that context made it seem less and less out of place, more and more natural. Eventually, Gilsenan's attention was attracted not by the medium, but by what it represented: the color green. Gilsenan remained able to report that the green light he saw had been produced by green neon tubing. That fact seemed irrelevant, however, given the new context he had come to make use of in interpreting his experience. The experience of greenness in the context of a mosque filled with praying men could not be reduced to the neon tubing. That experience was shaped as well by history, and the

---

EthnoFile 5.9
CAIRO

Region: Middle East

Nation: Egypt

Population: 11,000,000

Environment: Capital city; Mediterranean and desert

Livelihood: Modern stratified society

Political organization: Modern nation-state

Other: Cairo is a great center for Islamic learning

faith of the worshipers, and numerous displaced cultural associations invisible to an ignorant, inexperienced outsider.

These transformations of perception and understanding remain mysterious, but they seem to occur whenever we have an insight of any kind. Insights, like apt metaphors, reshape the world for us, throwing new aspects of it into sharp focus, casting other aspects of it into the background. And our ability to achieve insights, like our ability to create apt metaphors, remains the most central and most mysterious aspect of human cognition.

Key Terms

elementary cognitive processes
functional cognitive systems
perception
distortion
ambiguity
paradox
fiction
cognitive style
global style

articulated style
rational thinking
syllogistic reasoning
reasoning styles
logic
emotion
socialization
enculturation

Chapter Summary

1. Our capacity for language is not easily separated from other capacities we possess for making sense of the world around us. These other capacities, called cognitive capacities, share many of the design features of language, including openness, arbitrariness, displacement, and prevarication. The evidence of our senses is, thus, never self-evident. It depends upon context, both immediate context and cultural context.

2. Researchers have often pictured human intelligence metaphorically as a substance whose amount could be measured by intelligence tests the way flour can be measured by a measuring cup. Today, however, it is unclear exactly what the results of intelligence tests represent. In consequence, the current emphasis in research has shifted to a focus upon *cognitive processes* and the way these are organized into culturally shaped *functional systems*.

3. Psychological anthropologists have tried to explain why intelligent informants perform poorly on Western intelligence tests. These tests often require subjects to interpret drawings and photographs. Western subjects know they must separate the object they are asked to interpret from any particular context. This seems to be what we mean by objectivity. But the elimination of context is a Western perceptual convention that may not be shared by non-Western people. The confusion only increases when the test drawings or photographs are ambiguous. Drawings and photographs do not speak for themselves, but can only make sense to us once we have mastered the group's conventions for interpreting them.

4. The contrast between literal and metaphorical language is not unlike the contrast between reality and illusion that is often made in discussions of perception. Illusions may be understood as the result of normal cognitive processes that have somehow been inappropriately selected and applied to a particular set of visual signals. Four important types of visual illusion are *distortion*, *ambiguity*, *paradox*, and *fiction*.

5. Some anthropologists argue that people in different cultures have different *cognitive styles* that can be located on a continuum ranging from *global style* at one end to *articulated style* at the other. Research suggests that a single individual may use a global style for some tasks and an articulated style for other tasks. Indeed, one culture may prescribe that an articulated style be used for a task that another culture would approach with a global style. Most information on cognitive styles has come from laboratory testing. But Jean Lave has shown that cognitive activity outside the laboratory often involves the use of a variety of cognitive strategies. In these everyday situations, the goal of cognition is not to solve a problem by finding the single correct answer. Instead, people try to resolve dilemmas in a way that allows them to get on with life. Cognition is thus best understood as the relations that link the mind at work to the world in which it works.

6. We may become impatient with people from a different culture if they fail to see similarities between objects that we think ought to be obvious to any observer. Yet the obviousness of particular features depends upon what any given culture chooses to emphasize, and what it chooses to ignore. People may be perfectly aware of certain features if asked about them, and simply ignore those features in ordinary circumstances because they carry no cultural relevance. Western schooling trains people to pay attention to a wider variety of perceptual features than would ordinarily be relevant culturally.

7. Most cognitive psychologists define thinking as "going beyond the information given." Several attempts have been made to measure the levels of *rational thinking* present in non-Western populations. The results are mixed. There seems to be no way to predict who will perform well or poorly on Piaget's conservation test, and tests of *syllogistic reasoning* assume background knowledge that non-Western subjects cannot be assumed to have. In addition, informants may interpret syllogisms as riddles with no single correct answer.

8. *Rational thinking* is not the same as logic. Western logic is better understood as a reasoning style that is characteristic of Western culture and must be learned. The rules of logic are thus conventionally accepted rules, part of an elaborate tradition. Rules of Western logic can be very useful in reasoning, but other logics may be equally valid in other ways to people in other societies, particularly if they do not require the elimination of context for their application.

9. Our *emotions*, like our thoughts, are not just something we have; they are constructed of our state of mind, our cultural interpretations, and our levels of bodily arousal. Different cultures recognize different domains of experience and different categories of feeling as appropriate to these domains. For this reason, it is difficult to translate what emotions mean from one culture to another.

10. Human beings must learn to pattern their behavior, their ways of thinking, and their ways of feeling and adapt them to the standards considered appropriate in their cultures. The result of this process is the formation of a socially and culturally constructed *self*. Freud emphasized the patterning of emotions in the development of the self. Piaget emphasized the development of reasoning. Mead and Vygotsky argued that society and culture enhance and complete the development of the self, which occurs as language is mastered. Mead's emphasis upon role playing in *socialization* and *enculturation* places metaphor at the center of children's growing awareness of themselves and others. Vygotsky's concept of the zone of proximal development stresses that cognitive development is a dialogic process. Children progress through that process at different rates and in different directions, depending on the amount and kind of coaching they receive by others. This concept makes it possible to explain why people in different cultural subgroups are socialized and enculturated in different ways. This is illustrated by Gilligan's work on the moral enculturation of girls and boys in American society.

Suggested Readings

Barnouw, Victor. *Culture and Personality*, 4th ed. Homewood, Ill.: Dorsey Press, 1985.
> An enduring classic, this book is an encyclopedia of psychological anthropology.

Cole, Michael, and Sylvia Scribner. *Culture and Thought: A Psychological Introduction*. New York: Wiley, 1974.
> A clear, readable survey of the literature and case studies on the cultural shaping of cognition.

LeVine, Robert. *Culture, Behavior, and Personality*. Chicago: Aldine, 1973.
> A more psychoanalytic approach to the field of psychological anthropology. Readable and provocative.

Miller, Jonathan. *States of Mind*. New York: Pantheon Books, 1983.
> A series of interviews in which Jonathan Miller (English actor, writer, physician, director) talks to several of the most interesting scholars on the mind, including George Mandler, Richard Gregory, and Clifford Geertz. The results are witty and enjoyable reading.

For a Poetics of Social Life

Michael Herzfeld (D.Phil., Oxford University) is Professor of Anthropology at Indiana University. He has done fieldwork in Greece, especially Crete. Dr. Herzfeld has written three books, two of which have received important awards. His research interests focus on symbolism and rhetoric, especially as these link the local community to the nation-state.

One burning issue in modern anthropology concerns the relationship between the individual and the larger society. Is society a kind of metallic grid that we all have to move through in lockstep? How many of us feel that it is? And yet how many of us have *not* felt that there were not simply limitations on what we may or may not do, but also outer edges that we could explore, tease, distort (rules that we could bend)? Just as a poem takes the language of ordinary discourse and makes it the object of its own attention, so can a socially creative person make something interesting out of ordinary conventions by pushing them to the very edge of violation, but no further.

This is what a *poetics* of social interaction must imply. The celebrated linguist Roman Jakobson defined the *poetic function*—the quality that we all recognize in poetry and in highly expressive prose—as an orientation toward the message as such. A poem is a poem because it draws the reader's attention to its own form, which often exploits the peculiarities of everyday language and makes them the object of its linguistic play—puns, metaphors, rhymes, odd word orders, and so on—all of them suggesting a multiplicity of messages, none of them ultimately reducible to a single, clear-cut meaning.

That kind of play on form is also crucial to social life. Social life is marked by a high degree of *indeterminacy* and by a set of conventions, which seem both to set limits to that fluid quality and also themselves to shift shape and content all the time. People who play with social form are seeking a special position for themselves, and at the same time helping to fashion—or refashion—the norms and values that the society lives by.

In the Cretan village where I worked, men steal sheep "to make friends"—in other words, to impress others with their prowess so much that the latter would seek them as allies in the tough, competitive world of the highland pastures. But just stealing a sheep is not enough. You must do it in an original way, just within the bounds of the normal: stealing from a much older and tougher shepherd, getting your rival or a policeman to eat the meat of an animal you have just stolen, capturing the animals by some trick (such as setting fire to the brushwood around the sheepfold). And when you tell the story, you add "pepper" to it, making the tale as tasty as stolen meat. If you are a dull narrator, you are probably a dull thief, and if you are a dull thief, you are not worth the trouble of turning into an ally. Think of the exaggerations of normalcy required of someone who wants to be a "regular" person, especially popular—two phrases that imply being so conventional that you really are not literally conventional (or regular!) at all. One must be a poet of one's own social self to stand out in society, but one should not stand out so far as to become unacceptable. Social skill consists in negotiating this delicate balance.

Thus, there are rules, but they become "visible" when skilled social actors bend them. Not everyone can do this well enough, of course, and most societies have misfits whose major misfortune lies in their inability to know when to stop. A man in the Cretan village who came from a poor, weak patrigroup but who liked to shout loudly in arguments over cards and politics simply attracted more and more scorn. But those who do know what they are doing use their social comportment as a kind of *rhetoric*—not, that is, just in the form of elegant words, but as a means of persuasion that includes gestures, social manners, generosity, and a great deal more in addition to the verbal skills that make a person persuasive.

All social life has this rhetorical quality. Some anthropologists, following both their colleague the late Victor Turner and the philosopher Kenneth Burke, have also suggested that social life be seen as a kind of drama. These approaches do not necessarily mean that we should avoid talking about *social structure,* which has long been a staple concept in the discipline. They do imply that social structure exists by virtue of its being constantly reproduced, and this then gives rise to a whole set, infinitely extendable in theory, of parallel structures in art, poetry, music, and architecture.

Architecture is an interesting case in point; after all, we do talk about social *structure*. In many cultures, houses and divided into male and female zones, each with its distinctive equipment, and each invested with a meaning that depends on the other part (what in symbolic studies is called *complementary opposition*). In some cultures, the outside of the house is regarded as male, public, and expressive of the culture of the official polity or state, while the inside of the house is female, private, and full of familiar items that have little historical significance in the larger society. But we should not assume that people passively accept these divisions; the very threat that one *might* violate them is a source of real power, though not of official power. Once again, we see that the certainties of social and cultural life turn out, on closer inspection, to be manipulable elements in a larger social rhetoric, one that uses cultural forms to lay claim to legitimacy and authority.

Nowadays, it is often a nation-state government that makes these claims on the most inclusive level. But at all levels of social life the possibility that a social *performance* will somehow undermine a collective *representation* is always a threat. To manage one's social life well means knowing just how far to let the performance go in subverting the generally accepted order—or it may (to borrow a term from linguistic philosophy) *constitute* that order. Just as a jury, in pronouncing the suspect guilty, establishes guilt in a social frame regardless of who actually committed the deed, so every social action *constitutes* new links, new perceptions, and new possibilities. When a poor male villager on the island of Rhodes, Greece, "makes good" by dint of hard work, he may feel he now has the right to treat the powerful members of the community as his equals. He tests this by clowning a little more than they, to see whether he gets their amused admiration—in which case he has successfully constituted his new status—or their covert but poisonous jeers.

Scholars have a poetics of social life too. Watch them vying with one another as each tries to achieve more impressive forms of pomposity, more honorable status, more titles and "respect." Some play it well, others play it less well. The more they try to formalize their actions, the more likely they are to find their bluff called, and the more they make modest disclaimers and tell one another how provisional their work is, the more they may be hoping to score a hit. Watch yourself and your friends do the same things too. This is a good exercise in *reflexivity,* the analysis of one's own role in what one studies. We are all in it together, because we are all participants in a social world.

CHAPTER 6
Play, Art, Myth, and Ritual

CHAPTER OUTLINE

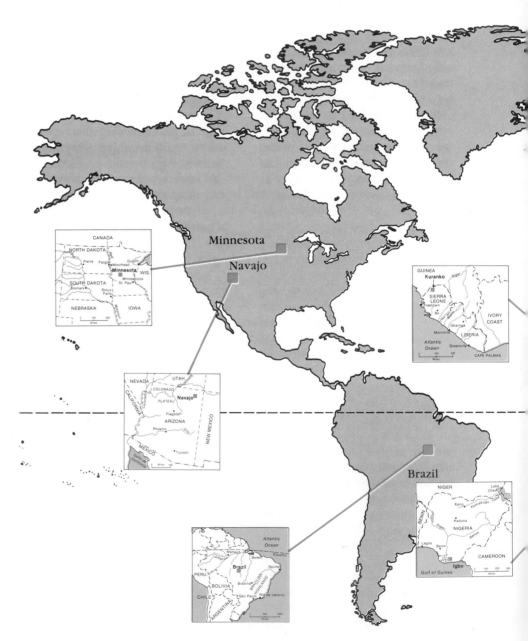

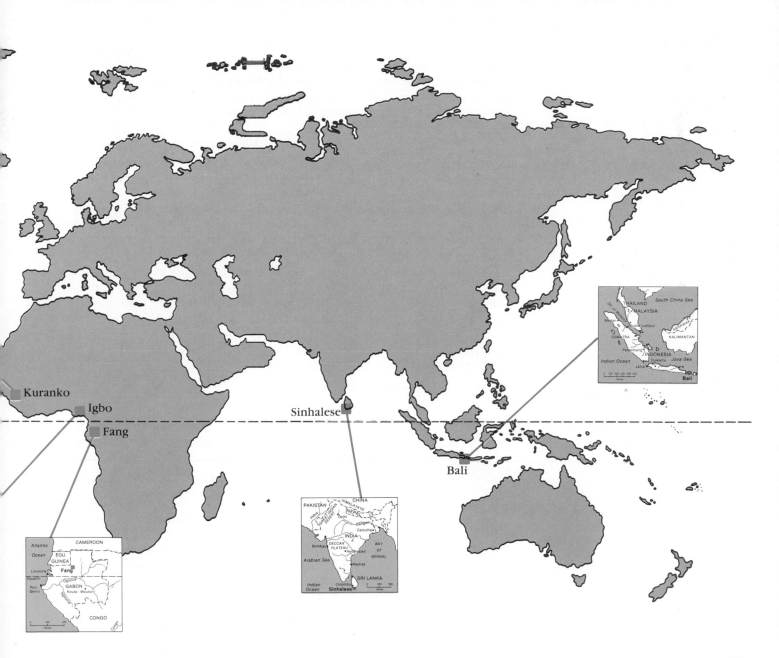

Kuranko

Igbo

Fang

Sinhalese

Bali

One of the authors of this book, Robert Lavenda, carried out fieldwork in Caracas, Venezuela. He writes:

"In October 1974, I was in the early stages of fieldwork in Caracas, Venezuela. Toward the end of the month, excitement about the heavyweight boxing championship featuring George Foreman and Muhammad Ali began to build. Boxing is extremely popular in Venezuela, and the Caracas newspapers devoted a great deal of attention to this bout. They gave Ali little chance of winning. It was late in his career, and he had already lost once to Foreman. Too old, they said, too out of shape, too big a mouth, too strong an opponent.

"I managed to resist interest in the fight until the last moment. I had other work to do and didn't care for boxing. Besides, I didn't have a television in my apartment. On the night the fight was to be telecast on the national network, I went out to dinner alone. On my way home, I was surprised to see the city almost deserted. Then I remembered that the fight was about to start. I was feeling lonely, and my curiosity got the better of me. I passed a bar that had a television, so I stopped in. The preliminaries, native dancing from Zaire, were just ending. The bar gradually filled up. A couple of people seemed to know each other, but the rest were strangers.

"As the fight began, I became aware that we were all Ali fans. As he did better and better, we became increasingly excited, and communication among the patrons increased. When finally, miraculously, Ali won, pandemonium broke loose. The crowd seemed to explode into a paroxysm of *abrazos* ("embraces," appropriate to men in Latin America), tears, cries of joy, and calls for rounds of beer. Strangers before, all were now united in a feeling of oneness and joy. None of us had any idea who the others were or what they did, but it didn't matter—we had witnessed something wonderful, and felt a comradeship that transcended our strangerness."

What had Lavenda been involved in? Was he a spectator at a sporting event? Had he witnessed a myth come to life? Perhaps there was a ritualistic quality to everyone's response in the bar. Was there something aesthetically satisfying about the way Ali had triumphed over all odds?

In this chapter, we consider how anthropologists go about trying to make sense of events like that in the bar. To do this, we will examine play, art, myth, and ritual. These four elements of human experience are not unrelated. Indeed, their interrelationships are the focus of some of the most exciting work being done in anthropology today.

Play

All mammals play, and human beings play the most and the longest. Yet play is troubling to Western science. Play seems senseless in its contempt for everyday reality, admitting the very chaos and misrule that reason tries so hard to subdue. Because of the Western attitude toward play, relatively little attention has been paid to it. The traditional Western definition of play has been a negative one: play is not work, not real, not serious, not productive, and so on (see Schwartzman 1978:4). Contrary to the pleasures of their own experiences, anthropologists and other social scientists sometimes write about life as though it were a grim-faced pursuit of food, shelter, sex, and the like. But enjoyment of life is as much a part of being human—

and must be as much a part of our definition of culture—as kinship, food production, and politics. Play is central to the human condition.

What Is play?

There have been many definitions of **play**. One generally accepted by anthropologists was offered by Edward Norbeck, who said that play is a

> *characteristic behavior of mankind at all ages of life that arises from a genetically inherited stimulus or proclivity and is distinguished by the combination of traits of being voluntary, somehow pleasurable, distinct [in time] from other behavior, and distinctive in having a make-believe or psychically transcendental quality. (1974:270)*

Human play differs from animal play in that it is culturally molded. The ways people play, when they play, what they play, with whom they play, and what particular kinds of play mean all vary from culture to culture. Play "includes sports and games of all kinds, dancing, singing, wit and humor, dramas, comedies, theatrical performances and other forms of mimicry, art, music, and other branches of aesthetics, induced states of psychological transcendence such as those resulting from drinking alcohol and using drugs that alter the sensibilities, and religious ecstasy, however induced" (Norbeck 1974:270). These actions range from the highly organized and strictly bounded in time and space, to brief forays into the realm of play.

What kind of action is play? Don Handelman (1977) suggests that we should think of play as a way of *organizing* activities, rather than as a particular set of activities. This means that play may occur as we carry out tasks that are generally characterized as "work." For example, a secretary typing letters may begin to "play" as she starts to focus her attention on creating a scallop pattern in the right margin by varying the length of each line she types. This illustrates another attribute of play: the relationships of means to ends are altered so that the ends no longer determine the means.

The consequences of this reversal can be dramatic. For example, in a nonplay context, saying "You bastard" to someone can lead to an invitation to step outside. If said in play, however, the same words imply something different—perhaps admiration for someone who is clever. By delivering an insult in play, a closeness between two people may be established or enhanced. Because means and ends are separated in play, players are permitted a high degree of freedom. Indeed, play activity involves a reduction in the types of roles available to participants. Instead of being a college student, a Unitarian, a Jaycee, a son, a fraternity brother, or a factory worker, you and the other players are simply "players." This establishes the social limits of the play activity.

For play does have limits. When friends insult one another in play, they may end up feeling even closer than they were before. But since play is usually not wholly divorced from everyday reality, there may still be an undertone of ambiguity. There may still be a note of insult. If someone chooses to take offense, play is threatened. When the everyday roles reassert themselves, play ends.

Play and Reality

Play also differs from everyday, nonplay reality in regard to time. In play, the perception of ordinary time ceases; it is "timeless experience" (Fagen 1981:495).

play
a "characteristic behavior of mankind at all ages of life that arises from a genetically inherited stimulus or proclivity and is distinguished by the combination of traits of being voluntary, somehow pleasurable, distinct [in time] from other behavior, and distinctive in having a make-believe or psychically transcendental quality" (Norbeck 1974:270)

meta-communication
communication about the process of communication itself

framing
the placement of a cognitive boundary around certain behaviors, which marks them as play or as ordinary life

Moving from everyday reality to play requires a radical transformation of referential perspective. According to Gregory Bateson (1972), it requires moving to a level of communication that is more abstract than either everyday reality or play. This level of communication, called **meta-communication**, is communication about communication. It is communication about the relationship between those who are communicating. Think for a moment about the phrase "Open the window." This is on one level a simple request, but what can it communicate about the relationship between the speakers? One possibility is that it is an order, that the meta-communication is "I have the right to compel you to open the window." Another is that it is a plea: "You are able to open this window. I am not." Yet another is that it is an admission of equality: "You are now at the point of doing something that I too can do."

In play there are two kinds of meta-communication. The first, called **framing**, places a cognitive boundary around certain behaviors and says that they are "play" or that they are "ordinary life." Dogs, for example, have the *play face*, a signal understood by other dogs (and recognizable by humans beings too) indicating a willingness to play. If dogs agree to play, their fangs are bared, and one animal attacks the other. But the bite is not consummated; it becomes a nip. Both dogs have agreed to enter the *play frame*, an imaginary world in which bites don't mean bites. To put it another way, a basic elements of Western logic—that A = A—does not apply in play. Human beings have many ways of marking the play frame. A few markers that may be familiar to you are the smile, the phrase "Just joking," a particular tone of voice, the referee's whistle, the words "Let's play" or "Let's pretend" or "You can be the king." The marker serves to say that "everything from now until we end this activity is set apart from everyday life."

The second kind of meta-communication arises inside the play frame itself and is a commentary on the nature of ordinary life (Handelman 1977:186). Because play sets up a separate reality in which the world is organized differently, it suggests that the perspective of ordinary life is only one way to make sense of experience. We often say, for example, that jokes keep us from taking ourselves too seriously. What does this mean? Through jokes we are able to see that there are alternative, even ridiculous, explanations for our experience. A Johnny Carson, George Carlin, or Eddie Murphy monologue forces us to stand back from the events being commented on. We take these events out of their usual context and realize that they can be understood in other ways. Play is therefore *reflexive*. Beyond that, when comics start talking about the president, or the military budget, or football, or accountants, we begin to feel that perhaps they are not taking anything seriously. *Anything* can be understood differently. They are not telling us about the way things should be but rather about the way things might be. This too is a characteristic of all play. It communicates about "what can be" rather than about "what should be" or about "what is" (ibid.).

Play as a Source of Creativity

If this is correct, then perhaps play becomes the central source of creativity in human life. This does not mean, however, that play is unambiguously good or bad. Since play is about possibilities, it cuts both ways. It can be a force for positive creativity or a force for the negative. It can just as easily lead to degradation as to uplift, to humiliation as to creative triumph. It can distract from the critical problems of life as well as solve them. It can as easily destroy the social structure as creatively construct it.

Play is not always "good." To idealize it is to lose sight of its meta-communicative elements and to become blind to the folly of the world that it parodies (Sutton-Smith 1984:4–13). Because play has the potential for "randomized creativity," it is dangerous to the ordinary social order. Its meta-communications, if valid, would threaten that order and therefore must be weak. To remove the threat of an alternate reality, we define play as "unserious," "untrue," "pretend," "make-believe," "unreal," and so forth (Handelman 1977:189). This danger to the established political order is one that many political figures recognize, and attempts to control play and humor are not uncommon.

Consequences of Play

Another paradox of play is that it is "supposed to be divorced from reality, yet it is also supposed to be rife with real-life consequences" (Csikszentmihalyi 1981:14). What are some of the other real-life consequences of play? Particularly according to people who study animal play behavior, play provides exercise. Through play, the young animal (which can include the young human being) gets the exercise it needs to build up its body for the rigors of adulthood. Play is also important for the emergence of cognitive skills involving the development of the brain. In addition, it aids learning through exploration of the environment (see Fagen 1981:350–55).

Play is seen as practice or rehearsal for the "real world." Animals play at fighting so they will know how to fight for their lives when their survival is at stake. Similarly, children are said to play house as a way of learning the appropriate sex roles and skills needed for adulthood. This approach in anthropology has commonly seen children's play as an imitation of adult activities and therefore as a way of learning culture (see Schwartzman 1978:100, 101). Others have suggested that play (especially make-believe play) increases children's creativity and originality. It is said to accomplish this by allowing children to overcome their limitations of age, experience, and maturity and by permitting a richer reproduction of adult life (Sarah Smilansky, cited in Schwartzman 1978:116).

Psychologist Brian Sutton-Smith has examined children's play and games in which reversal of the regular world occurs. He suggests that these "games of order and disorder" (for example, ring-around-a-rosy, in which an orderly circle is formed and then destroyed) are not always enculturative; they may seek to challenge and reverse the social order. In these games, the social order is created only to be destroyed as everyone first acts together and then collapses. In his research (summarized in Schwartzman 1978:124ff.), Sutton-Smith suggests that these activities are important not because they provide a socializing force for society, but because they allow for innovation.

Play as Commentary on the Real World

The idea that play is a source for changing ordinary life is a long way from the idea that play teaches adult roles. Helen Schwartzman (1978:232–45) has demonstrated the way play, through satire and clowning, may serve to comment upon and criticize the world of adults with which children must contend.

In the process of playing, children learn that behavior is "contexted" (e.g., there is a difference between play and nonplay), that contexts influence the authority structure of relationships (e.g., there are differences between symmetrical and asymmetrical relationships), and that these relationships can be commented on. At another level, it is possible to suggest that these play texts are a commentary on the whole notion of hierarchical ranking as children experience it in families, at school, and so on. By providing children with an opportunity for commentary or

Child's play sometimes provides the opportunity for children to take on metaphorically roles they may one day have to assume literally.

interpretation, play suggests the possibility of reinterpretation, challenge, and even change in relationships. Make-believe play creates these possibilities because it is both a text and a context. This, then, is the beginning of humor, art, and all forms of social satire and critique and is perhaps the most significant feature of this play form. (Schwartzman 1978:245)

Certain adult play forms, such as the pre-Lenten Carnival, discussed later in this chapter, also act as a commentary on the "real world." They sanction insults and derision of authority figures, inversions of social status, clowning, parody, satire, and the like (see ibid.: 124).

Play as Preparation for Life?

If we accept that play allows the player to practice behaviors without dreading their consequences, it follows that there is a reality external to play, toward which life is directed. That is, play serves to prepare a person for life and is therefore less serious than "real life." This is a well-known justification for play in Western society, illustrated by the famous claim that "the Battle of Waterloo was won on the playing fields of Eton." Another example was the appointment of a former marine officer as head coach of the Minnesota Vikings. The assumption was that since football is like war, someone experienced in the latter would do well coaching in the former. (The experiment didn't work; the coach lasted one season.) Other examples are claims that the game Monopoly prepares players for capitalism, or that video games prepare players for the next generation of fighting aircraft.

Play and Alternative Views of Reality

Rock climbing is play that nonetheless may have serious real-world consequences.

What about rock climbing? "Is climbing a vertical face of rock at the risk of one's life play, or is it done in earnest?" (Csikszentmihalyi 1981:16). The activity certainly carries with it serious consequences if one is not successful. Is rock climbing, then, not play? It fits the rest of any other definition of play, and yet "the climber is as immersed in reality as anyone can be in this world." But this suggests that there is no uniform reality "out there." Each person's view of reality "is relative to the goals that cultures and individuals create" (ibid.: 17). Reality is defined in terms of the goals toward which each player directs attention at any given time. In other words, people do not always submit to the rules of the "paramount reality" of ordinary life, which is their basic referential perspective.

Play allows us to recognize that any particular referential perspective is relative. It exists when there is an awareness of alternatives, "of two sets of goals and rules, one operating here and now, one that applies outside the given activity" (ibid.: 19). Unless we are aware that we can act according to a set of rules that are different from those of our paramount reality, we cannot play. More important, without play there is no awareness of alternatives. Play demonstrates the openness in human experience. But openness in play is like openness in any other aspect of human life: it is ambiguous. Because of this ambiguity, those with power in any society will attempt to shape play to fit their ends.

Sport

One form of play that interests many people is **sport.** "Sport belongs in the world of play and leisure, yet business elites, mass media, and government and political leaders recognize its potential for making profits, disseminating propaganda, and eliciting pride" (Lever 1983:1).

A Definition of Sport

The most comprehensive anthropological definition of game and sport comes from Kendall Blanchard and Alyce Cheska.

> *[A game is] a competitive activity that involves physical skills, strategy, and chance, or any combination of these elements. . . .*
>
> *Sport . . . is a physically exertive activity that is aggressively competitive within constraints imposed by definitions and rules. A component of culture, it is ritually patterned, gamelike, and of varying amounts of play, work and leisure. In addition, sport can be viewed as having both athletic and nonathletic variations,* athletic *referring to those activities requiring the greater amount of physical exertion. (Blanchard and Cheska 1985:60)*

From this definition, play is only one component of sport. It can be work for the players and an investment for the owners of professional teams. Through the play element in sport, a frame is drawn around the activity. Conflict in games and sports is different from conflict in ordinary life. Competitors agree "to strive for an incompatible goal—only one opponent can win—within the constraints of understood rules" (Lever 1983:3). Conflict becomes the whole point of the activity, rather than the means of settling a disagreement. As said earlier, in play, the relationships of means and ends are altered. Sport is struggle for the sake of struggle. "Athletes and teams exist only to be rivals; that is the point of their relationship. In the world of sport, there should be no purpose beyond playing and winning. Unlike rivals in the real world, who have opposing political, economic, or social aims, sports competitors must be protected, not persuaded or eliminated" (ibid.: 4).

Sport is play, but it is embedded to a far greater degree than open play in the prevailing social order. Sport reflects the basic values of the cultural setting in which it is performed. "Even a sport that has been introduced from a foreign source is very quickly redefined and adjusted to fit the norms and values of tradition" (Blanchard and Cheska 1985:55).

Effect of Culture on Sport

Sports are transformed when they are translated from one culture to another. For example Navajo basketball is a different game from that played by the Mormon Anglos who introduced it to the Navajo. *(See EthnoFile 6.1: Navajo.)* "Behaviorally, [Navajo basketball] is less aggressive, structured, outwardly enthusiastic, and morally educative; while at the same time it is more individualistic, kin-oriented, and pure good times than that of the town's Anglo-Mormon population" (Blanchard 1974, cited in Blanchard and Cheska 1985:55).

An even more striking example of how translating a sport from one culture to another can transform that sport is found in the Trobriand Islands. *(See Ethno–File 5.2: Trobriand Islanders.)* The English sport of cricket was introduced to the Trobriands in the very early years of the twentieth century by an English missionary. By the 1970s, in the more rural parts of the islands, it had become a different game. Played between two villages, it became a substitute for warfare and a way of establishing political alliances. No matter how many men decked out in full war regalia came from the visiting village, they all played if there were as many players from the host village. If the hosts had forty men ready to play and the visitors had thirty-six, then there were thirty-six to a side instead of the "correct" eleven. The game was always won by the home team—but not by too many runs because that would shame the visitors. War magic was employed to aid batsmen and bowlers.

sport
"a physically exertive activity that is aggressively competitive within constraints imposed by definitions and rules. . . . [a] component of culture, [sport] is ritually patterned, gamelike, and of varying amounts of play, work and leisure" (Blanchard and Cheska 1985)

EthnoFile 6.1
NAVAJO

Region: North America

Nation: Southwestern United States (northwestern New Mexico, northeastern Arizona, southeastern Utah)

Population: 100,000

Environment: Rugged landscape

Livelihood: Farming, sheep herding, silver work and other arts

Political organization: Clans, public consensus; now a tribal council

Other: The Navajo are a matrilineal people, recently involved in a bitter land dispute with the Hopi

Teams had dances and chants for taking the field, leaving it, and celebrating outs. These dances and chants were used to comment on current events and became fertile ground for additional competition beyond that of the sporting event itself. The bat was redesigned for greater accuracy, and the entire activity was associated with the ceremonial exchange of food and other goods. Cricket, the sport of empire, was radically transformed.

Play need not reflect the basic values of the cultural setting. It also comments on those values and is a way of transcending them, of opening up a window to novelty and change. In games and sport, by contrast, the meta-message within the play frame is used to *reflect* ordinary life, rather than to *comment on* it. Institutionalized games and sport *present* the social order (Handelman 1983).

Football and American Life

A provocative example of this is offered by W. Arens (1981) in his analysis of football in the United States. Arens tries to account for the centrality of football in American life and the virtual absence of football anywhere else in the world. He argues that there are similarities between important features of the game and important features of American society. "The sport combines the qualities of group coordination through a division of labor unmatched in any other sport and minute specialization." For example, there are even separate kickers, one for place-kicking and another for punting. Football is highly mechanized and highly technological. Coaches use elaborate headsets. There are spotters in the press box. Players wear elaborate protective equipment made of space-age materials. Computers and video equipment are used for analyzing other teams. The game involves variation in play: running, passing, and kicking. Through all these means, sanctioned violence is expressed (Arens 1981:4–5). This violence is a coordinated, technologized, impersonal violence; it is different from the violence of boxing, for example. Through these qualities of group coordination, division of labor, minute specialization, mechanization, and controlled violence, football "epitomizes the spirit and form of contemporary American society" (ibid.: 4).

Sport and Play

Does this mean that sport is never play? Not necessarily. Sport can be play in at least two ways. Sport that is not institutionalized seems to fit the definition of play used here, because the players have set aside their previous paramount reality for another. This type of sport would include sandlot baseball; pickup basketball, football, volleyball, or soccer games; stickball; and the like. It is also true that in societies where it has never been institutionalized, sport is play.

Within the world of institutionalized sport, even if the players are working and not playing, the spectators are playing. A sporting event is more than the players, coaches, referees, trainers, and so forth. It includes the spectators. For them, the contest allows the opportunity to play. They are able to enter a different world, a world in which they are invited to make-believe—to identify with their heroes, to rage at the opponents, to imagine coaching the team or starring; to suffer, to rejoice.

The Function of Sport in the Nation-State

The full institutionalization of sport seems to have taken place in the nation-state, and only fairly recently. The most important and universal consequence of sport in the nation-state is that it helps complex modern societies cohere (Lever 1983:3). In her study of soccer in Brazil, aptly titled *Soccer Madness*, Janet Lever argues that large-scale organized sport presents a mechanism for building political unity and allegiance to the nation. "Sport's paradoxical ability to reinforce societal cleavages while transcending them makes soccer, Brazil's most popular sport, the perfect means of achieving a more perfect union between multiple groups . . . [by giving] dramatic expression to the strain between groups while affirming the solidarity of the whole" (Lever 1983:5, 9).

In Brazil, there is at least one professional soccer team in every city. The larger cities have several teams, representing different fundamental social groups. In Rio de Janeiro, for example, separate teams tend to be supported by the old rich, the modern middle class, the poor, the blacks, the Portuguese, and a number of neighborhood communities. The teams come to stand for these different groups in a concrete, visible fashion. Through these teams, separate group identities are maintained. At the same time, the teams bring their opposing fans together through a shared enthusiasm for soccer. City and national championships work similarly to unify what had been diverse. Unless a fan's team is in the national finals, that fan must transfer his or her loyalty to another team that represents the entire city or region.

For many Brazilians—indeed, for many people around the world—the experience of supporting a soccer team may be their first and perhaps only experience of a loyalty beyond the local community. Unity is achieved by demonstrating that different local teams, and the groups they represent, are in conflict only at one level.

EthnoFile 6.2
BRAZIL

Region: South America

Nation: Brazil

Population: 157,000,000

Environment: Varied, from Atlantic coast to tropical rain forest of Amazon basin

Livelihood: Industry, farming, mining, manufacturing, and so on

Political organization: Modern nation-state

Other: This is the largest and most populous country in Latin America

In Brazil, soccer provides a mechanism for creating national unity, or a sense of "Brazilianness," among fans.

At a higher level, the fans of those teams are really united; for example, fans of all Rio teams support the team that goes on to represent Rio in the national championships. This process reaches a climax in international competition, as the supporters of many local soccer teams back the national team. At this highest level of significant integration, soccer provides a way of affirming one's "Brazilianness." Americans felt similar emotion at the 1980 Winter Olympics. The unheralded U.S. hockey team first defeated a Soviet team that was generally regarded as the best in the world, and then went on to win the Olympic Gold Medal. This event became a focus for national feelings and allowed for the expression of those feelings in a concrete way.

There is one important exception to the global mass culture of sport: it regularly separates women from men. Soccer is incredibly important to Brazilian men, and to many other men in the rest of the world, but it is much less important to women. The sex segregation of the sport has significant consequences for the experience of growing up male or female. It also affects relationships later in life between men and women who do not share the same fundamental experiences. This is beginning to change in Brazil. More teenage girls are joining fan clubs and accompanying boys, without chaperones, to professional games (ibid.: 154). But there seems to be a long way to go. Here too there is a fundamental ambiguity: as sports join together in one domain, they separate in another. Sports can maintain and sharpen distinctions that are already significant in many other areas of a culture.

Deep Play

Clifford Geertz (1972) discusses a particularly gripping form of play, the Balinese cockfight. *(See EthnoFile 6.3: Bali.)* He sees this "popular obsession of consuming power" as a story that the Balinese tell themselves about themselves. The cockfight is so deeply embedded in Balinese culture that, at least for men, the language

EthnoFile 6.3
BALI

Region: Southeast Asia

Nation: Indonesia

Population: 3,000,000

Environment: Large tropical island: mountains, ridges, slopes, plains

Livelihood: Intensive rice cultivation (irrigation); animal raising

Political organization: Highly stratified state; now an Indonesian province

Other: This is one society that has thoroughly integrated play, art, and ritual

of everyday moralism is filled with imagery of the fighting cock, the masculine symbol par excellence. But the cocks are not just symbolic expressions of the owner's self. They are also expressions of what for the Balinese is, on every level, the direct inverse of the human: the animal.

Geertz tells us that this opposition between human beings and animals on Bali cannot be overemphasized. In identifying with his cock (a pun that Geertz intends), the Balinese man is also identifying with what he most fears, hates, and is fascinated by: The Powers of Darkness. The connection of cocks and cockfighting with these powers is explicit. The cockfight is understood as a blood sacrifice to the demons, and the appropriate rituals and chants are carried out before each fight. When Geertz was in Bali in the early 1960s, public responses to natural evils—illness, crop failure, volcanic eruptions—almost always involved cockfights (Geertz 1972:7).

The fight itself is held in a ring about fifty feet square. It begins in the late afternoon, runs until sunset, and is usually made up of nine or ten separate matches. After cocks have been matched, a steel spur, four to five inches long and razor sharp, is attached to the leg of each animal. At a signal, the two animals usually fly at each other in "a wing-beating, head-thrusting, leg-kicking explosion of animal fury so pure, so absolute, and in its own way so beautiful, as to be almost abstract, a Platonic concept of hate" (ibid.: 8–9). The round is usually over in less than thirty seconds, as one cock lands a solid blow with the spur. The action then stops for about two minutes. The handler of the injured bird works on it, trying to keep it alive for the second and final round. The fight is over when one of the animals dies. No matter how badly wounded, a bird has won if it is still standing at the death of its opponent. Fights usually last between fifteen seconds and five minutes.

Cockfighting involves gambling. There are two major kinds of wagers. The first kind is a central bet between the owners of the cocks. The second kind involves many separate bets by spectators. The Balinese try to create an interesting, or *deep*, match by making the central bet as large as possible. This is not because someone expects to win a great deal of money; rather, it ensures that the cocks will be as equal and as fine as possible, which in turn ensures that the outcome will be as unpredictable as possible (ibid.: 15).

Why is such a match interesting to the Balinese? To answer this question, Geertz borrows the concept of deep play from the philosopher Jeremy Bentham. **Deep play** is play in which the stakes are so high that, from a practical perspective,

deep play
play in which the stakes are so high that, from a utilitarian perspective, it is irrational for anyone to engage in it at all

it is irrational for anyone to engage in it at all. In deep play, both players are in over their heads; together they stand to lose more than either might gain. The alternative reality, which was assumed for pleasure, has overtaken them. It will inevitably lead to pain when the paramount reality, which is their regular state, is resumed.

Why do they do it? For the Balinese, betting can be very costly. But not only money is at stake in a cockfight. Equally at stake in deep matches are esteem, honor, dignity, and respect, which the money represents. These are at stake "playfully," for no one's status actually changes because of the outcome of a cockfight. But the cockfight is a meta-communication about how things might be. "What the cockfight talks about is status relationships, and what it says about them is that they are matters of life and death" (ibid.: 25).

The cockfight is a Balinese reflection on violence and the aspects of Balinese culture associated with violence: "animal savagery, male narcissism, opponent gambling, status rivalry, mass excitement, blood sacrifice. . . . Balinese go to cockfights to find out what a man, usually composed, aloof, almost obsessively self-absorbed . . . feels like when, attacked, tormented, challenged, insulted, and driven in result to the extremes of fury, he has totally triumphed or been brought totally low" (ibid.: 27).

Deep play is not unknown in American society. Sutton-Smith (1984:3; 1980:5) suggests that sexual activity without the use of contraceptives among college students is deep play. Here, where images of manhood, chastity, competition, spontaneity, and lust rage, a play frame is created in which the potential for loss is far higher than that of the Balinese in their cockfights. Since the appearance of Acquired Immunodeficiency Syndrome, the stakes for unprotected sex have escalated. To a potential loss of esteem, honor, dignity, and economic opportunity must now be added the loss of life. Nevertheless, for some of those most at risk, for complex reasons, the play continues.

Art

One kind of play that has traditionally interested anthropologists is art. Prototypically, art includes sculpture, drawing, painting, dance, theater, music, and literature. It also often encompasses processes and products with a family resemblance to these, such as film, photography, mime, oral narrative, festivals, and national celebrations.

A Definition of Art

art
"play with form producing some aesthetically successful transformation-representation" (Alland 1977:39)

Anthropologist Alexander Alland defines **art** as "play with form producing some aesthetically successful transformation-representation" (1977:39). For Alland, "form" refers to the rules of the art game: the culturally appropriate limitations or restrictions on the way this kind of play may be organized in time and space. Another way to think about this is in terms of style. A style is a schema, a distinctive patterning of elements, that is recognized within a culture as appropriate to a given medium. For example, certain things make a painting a portrait: it is of a person, it resembles the person in some appropriate way, it is done with paint, it can be displayed, and more. By "aesthetic," Alland means appreciative of, or responsive to, form in art or nature (1977:xii). "Aesthetically successful" means that the creator of the piece of art (and possibly its audience as well) experiences an emotional response. To be sure, emotional response is important, but to speak of an emotional response alone is too narrow. Alland probably emphasized this aspect of aesthetic appreciation because emotion is so often ignored or scorned in our dualistic, reason-worshiping culture. It would be more accurate to characterize aesthetic response as holistic, as involving all our faculties, especially as these are shaped by our social and cultural experience.

V. N. Voloshinov argued that our aesthetic response to form in a work of art is based in no small part on our culturally shaped evaluation of the appropriateness of form to content. "Through the agency of artistic form the creator takes up *an active position with respect to content.* The form in and of itself need not necessarily be pleasurable . . . ; what it must be is a *convincing evaluation* of the content. So, for instance, while the form of 'the enemy' might even be repulsive, the positive state, the pleasure that the contemplator derives in the end, is a consequence of the fact that the form is *appropriate to the enemy* and that it is *technically perfect* in its realization"(Voloshinov 1926:108). Evaluations of appropriateness and of technical perfection clearly involve a broad range of intellectual, emotional, and moral judgments on the part of the person responding to a work of art.

Aesthetic value judgments guide the artist's choice of form and material. They also guide the evaluations that observers make as they contemplate the artist's work. It is therefore a mistake to think of art in terms of works, of objects, alone. Voloshinov argues that art is a creative "event of living communication" involving the work, the artist, and the artist's audience (1926:107). Artists create their works with an audience in mind, and audiences respond to works as if they were addressed to them. Sometimes the response is enthusiastic, sometimes it is highly critical. In either case, the aesthetic event does not leave its participants indifferent.

This view suggests that aesthetic creation involves more than an artistic product, like a painting or a poem. Art also includes the *process* through which some product is made. James Vaughan (1973:186) points out, for example, that the Marghi of northeastern Nigeria do not appreciate a folktale as a story per se, but rather enjoy the *performance* of it. Closer to home, a photographer may feel that the art is in the taking of a picture—"seeing" it, setting it up in the viewfinder, taking it, and perhaps printing it—and not the final print. *(See EthnoFile 11.7: Marghi.)*

Transformation-Representation ▪▪▪▪▪▪

To understand the term **transformation-representation** in Alland's definition of art, we must recall that symbols represent something other than themselves. They are arbitrary in that they have no necessary connection with what they represent. This means that they can be cut away from the object or idea represented and can be appreciated for their own sake. They may also be used to represent a totally different meaning. Consider the tone poem "Also Sprach Zarathustra," by Richard Strauss. This orchestral work originally represented themes from a philosophical book of the same name by nineteenth-century German philosopher Friedrich Wilhelm Nietzsche. The musical interpretation came to be appreciated by classical music lovers on its own terms, quite apart from the book. Since 1967, however, this piece of music has been known almost universally as the theme from the film *2001: A Space Odyssey.*

Because transformation and representation depend on each other, Alland (1977:35) suggests that they be referred to together as transformation-representation. This idea may be familiar, since transformation-representation is another way of talking about metaphor. A drawing, for example, is a metaphoric transformation

transformation-representation
the process in which experience is transformed as it is represented symbolically in a different medium

of experience into visible marks on a two-dimensional surface. Similarly, a poem metaphorically transforms experience into concentrated and tightened language. This process is one place where the technical skill of the artist is involved.

Reflecting and Affecting Culture

Alland's definition of art attempts to capture something universal about human beings and the cultures within which they live. This is different from a definition that describes art narrowly as aesthetic objects produced by refined minds in high civilizations.

In the Western prototype of art, for example, there is a distinction between art and nonart. Some paintings, songs, stories, carvings, dances, and the like are art, and some are not. From this perspective, the *Mona Lisa* is art, but a painting of Elvis Presley on black velvet is not. Why? Part of the answer involves the high degree of specialization in Western societies. This has led to the emergence of an "art establishment" that includes critics, art historians, art teachers, journalists, schools, museums, and the like—as well as artists. These people define what is art and what is not, sometimes by invoking universal standards. In doing so, they are responding to the stratification and divisions of the culture in which they are embedded.

This division into categories of art and nonart is not universal. In many cultures, there is no category of art distinct from other human activities. Only in a few societies are there people who earn a living telling other people what is art and what is not. This is not to say that aesthetic judgments are not made in other societies, for they are. The categories that people employ, however, are culture-specific.

All art is embedded in culture. It "will reflect or be controlled by culture to a greater or lesser degree, depending on the nature of the relationships between art and other cultural areas" (Alland 1977:120). Artists in nonliterate societies produce and use symbols that are of central importance to their societies. Art becomes a means for presenting and representing the basic metaphors of a culture. For this reason, art works to maintain the social order in many societies. In Western society, however, "art is strongly affected by those market factors which pervade every other aspect of our daily life" (ibid.: 120). It has become increasingly rare to find art-establishment art involved with the central symbols of the wider culture. Rather, this art is involved with symbols meaningful to others within the art establishment itself, or to particular elites in society, who have appropriated the power of art for their own purposes.

Is Art a Universal Language?

A common claim in Western society is that art is a universal language. The preceding discussion discussion implies that if that claim is true, it is true only at a remote level. Although it is possible to respond only to the way a given culture manipulates form in space or time, to *understand* requires more. To understand art in American society, for example, we can examine the works of art themselves and how they were made. But we must also look at who the artists are, at their positions in society, at the social groups they form, and at the relationship of their social groups to other groups in American society. We must look at the consumers of art: how they understand art, what they use art for, the extent of their influence on artists, and more. This same process of investigation is required to understand the art world of any culture, for art is embedded in culture and can be understood only in context.

Consider how music loses meaning when divorced from the culture that produces it. All we hear are sounds and rhythms arranged in time. But like all symbolic products, music gains strength from its associations. Certain pieces of music remind us of places, of people, of times in our lives, and as well fit into our understanding of form and structure. The Javanese gamelan is a percussion orchestra made up of various-sized gongs and xylophones. To Western listeners, the sounds of the gamelan are recognizable as music because of their family resemblance to the Western prototype of music. But we may not perhaps *like* the sounds. The host of associations that the Javanese have with the music is missing on our part, as is any sense of how the music is put together. When we listen to Mozart or Bach, the Beatles, John Coltrane, Duke Ellington, Rogers and Hammerstein, the Talking Heads, King Creole, AC/DC, Whoopee John, or any other music from our own tradition, we are aware that these are different styles of music. Each style has characteristic arrangements of sound and rhythm in time that we have learned to expect. A composer's ability to play with those expectations and thus to introduce a certain amount of acceptable novelty makes us respond to a piece. When the composer goes beyond those expectations, we usually recognize the result as music but say we don't like the piece—that is, the piece is at the margins of our prototype of music. The response of many people to atonal music, to the twelve-tone compositions by Schoenberg, Webern, or Berg, or the response of your parents to some of the music you listen to, are examples of this. When a composer goes too far beyond our expectations, we claim that the result is not music at all. Even for us, music is embedded in a set of cultural expectations.

Talking about art as a kind of play has several implications. Like play, art presents its creators and participants with alternative realities, a separation of means from ends, and the possibility of commenting on and transforming the everyday world. However, art is play subject to limitations of form and content. That is, art must conform to culturally appropriate rules if it is to be considered art. This means that art enjoys a different position in the social system than does play. Most significantly, art is taken more seriously than pure play, with the result that challenges to its rules are culturally far more threatening.

Fang Sculpture and the Social Structure ▬▬▬

In studying the aesthetics of the Fang of central Africa, James Fernandez discovered that they had very definite ideas about what was pleasing to them in their own sculpture. *(See EthnoFile 6.4: Fang.)* Fernandez arranged a set of statues in a row and asked the Fang which figures they liked the most and why. The Fang commented on the finished or unfinished quality of each object—whether it was smooth or rough.

EthnoFile 6.4
FANG

Region: Central Africa

Nation: Gabon

Population: 400,000 (1978)

Environment: Tropical forest with intense rainfall

Livelihood: Farming, hunting

Political organization: Village councils, headmen

Other: Many Fang practice the Bwiti religion, which was detailed in a remarkable ethnography by James Fernandez: *Bwiti* (1982)

A Fang sculpture. This mask by Eye Meugeh represents a forest spirit.

They talked about the balance of the object, especially whether its quadrants were balanced with one another. If one leg or one arm or one shoulder was different in its proportions from the opposite, this was always mentioned and criticized (Fernandez 1971:363). People said there should be balance in the figure, or else it would not be real—it would have no life or vitality in it. They sometimes preferred statues that were, to Western eyes, stolid, formal, even suppressed.

The Fang are well aware that the proportions of these statues are not those of living men. For them, "what the statue represents is not necessarily the truth, physically speaking, of a human body but a vital truth about human beings, that they keep opposites in balance. Both the statues and men have this in common and therefore the statues in this sense are accurate portrayals—accurate representations of living beings" (ibid.).

Fernandez goes on to demonstrate that both Fang social structure and aesthetic life elaborate on two basic sets of oppositions—one spatial (right and left; northeast and southwest) and one qualitative (male and female)—and create vitality in so doing. He further suggests that in this, the social structure is the expression of aesthetic principles at work. In other words, art provides a way of understanding social structure. Instead of being a mere reflection of it, art can be seen as playing a significant role in people's creation of and commentary about social structure.

Shaping Attitudes through Javanese Theater

In his study of *ludruk*, a Javanese theater form, James Peacock demonstrates how such plays give life to a system of classification that is shared by actors and audience (Peacock 1968; Avery and Peacock 1980). *(See EthnoFile 4.1: Java.)* In the early 1960s, ludruk were created, performed, and viewed by the working class of the port city of Surabaya. They interwove comedy, melodrama, songs, and dances into performances that lasted from several hours to all night (Avery and Peacock 1980:190).

The ludruk is performed by an all-male cast in modern dress. The plot involves the interactions of members of different classes. The songs are performed by transvestite singers, who, dressed in aristocratic style, sing of mythical loves and modernizing the country. The comedy comes from clowns.

Dressed in working-class clothes, the clowns take the parts of servants, workers, peasants, thieves, and the like and deliver humorous monologues about everyday problems. They are structurally opposed to the transvestite singers. This image of the clown in ludruk is also connected to a more ancient image. The traditional Javanese clown combined the highest and the lowest of power, position, physical type, and wisdom. In traditional Javanese thought, the wisest and most powerful of the gods, Semar, is portrayed as a fat, ugly servant and clown.

By studying more than eighty performances, Peacock was able to determine two basic plot types. Traditional plots used themes from mythology and the social and cultural organization of the Javanese past. Modern plots employed themes associated with the modernizing Republic of Indonesia and were gaining in popularity. Peacock also noticed in both forms of plot certain basic structures that represented a shared system of classification.

[One dominant structure] is built up of opposites: high is contrasted to low, male to female, spiritual to material. Overriding the oppositions, however, is a fundamental unity, and this is demonstrated in the plays by myriad mixtures, reversals, and other relationships. Thus the clown shows that low is really high; the transvestite, that male can be female. Extending

the system off-stage, the audience and actors are both opposed and united: one pays and the other is paid, one expresses and the other responds, and, to take the last scene of the melodrama as an example, an on-stage couple reverses the heterosexual, same-class features of the audience by being homosexual, and of mixed class. One function of the ludruk, then, is to vitalise for actors and audience a shared system of categories, a cosmology, in which they jointly participate and which bestows meaning on existence by joining opposites in unity. (Ibid.: 196–97)

Peacock shows that the experience of ludruk shapes the values, attitudes, and emotions of the audience and actors outside the theater. This is especially the case of the modern-plot plays, which encourage the audience to adopt modern attitudes. Peacock argues that the members of the audience begin to feel, act, and think differently in everyday life, because of their experience of ludruk (ibid.:238).

A Marx Brothers Film as Commentary on Society

Similarly, Ivan Karp (1981) has argued that the Marx Brothers film *Duck Soup* may be read as a transforming commentary on the etiquette of public occasions and on hierarchy. In the film, each brother approaches reality differently. Groucho inverts the norms and values of ordinary reality. Chico approaches reality from a completely different direction. Harpo obliterates it. Karp notes that all three characters "say *NO* to the application of constraints on behavior to which the rest of their world unthinkingly acquiesces." In scene after scene, Groucho and Chico "break the frame" by taking their dialogue scenes together completely out of the story line of the film. Alone, each is rude, impolite, and very funny to us, but not to the people around them. They seem to be able to get away with anything. Harpo is a complete mystery: he never speaks, is not clearly male or female, and is not clearly child or adult. He seems almost outside culture. The constraints that make social action possible are violated by all three.

The significant point here, contends Karp, has to do with structure. In the film, the Marx Brothers launch an assault on structure through laughter. By viewing the film, moviegoers may identify with the Marx Brothers in that assault. If they do, their own private and formless experience of the structure they live in is given form, legitimated, and transformed. The experience of viewing *Duck Soup* means laughing at the pompous stuffed shirts, the pretensions, the conventions of society, and all the rest that the Marx Brothers laugh at. Having done so, who can take as seriously the kinds of events, persons, and institutions—the structures—that are the core of that film?

A Balinese Painting: Mediating Oppositions

Art also has the potential to move participants and viewers in the direction of unification of mind, emotion, and body. In an analysis of a Balinese painting (see figure 6.1), Gregory Bateson (1972) argues that the total mind is an integrated network of which consciousness is but a part. We can never consciously get a sense of the entire network, of its *integration*—how its parts are connected—because much of it is not and cannot by definition be conscious. This integrated network makes up what Bateson calls the *systemic* nature of mind (1972: 145). "Wisdom," then, consists in recognizing this, and in living life accordingly. Art has the potential to bring about a correction in understanding in the direction of wisdom (Bateson 1972: 147).

Harpo Marx in the film *Duck Soup*.

FIGURE 6.1
The Start of a Cremation Process **by Ida Bagus Djati Sura from Batuan, 1937**
According to Gregory Bateson (1972), the contrast between the turbulence of the lower part and the serenity of the upper part of this Balinese painting provides a visual metaphor for understanding human life.
Source: Courtesy of The Institute for Intercultural Studies.

In the Balinese painting that he discusses, Bateson points to a contrast between the serene and the turbulent.

> *In the final analysis, the picture can be seen as an affirmation that to choose either turbulence or serenity as a human purpose would be a vulgar error. The conceiving and creating of the picture must have provided an experience which exposed this error. This unity and integration of the picture assert that neither of these contrasting poles can be chosen to the exclusion of the other, because the poles are mutually dependent. This profound and general truth is simultaneously asserted for the fields of sex, social organization, and death. (Ibid.: 151–52)*

EthnoFile 6.5
IGBO

Region: West Africa

Nation: Southeastern Nigeria

Population: 19,720,000

Environment: Tropical, coast to highlands

Livelihood: Farming, trading

Political organization: Councils of elders

Other: The Igbo are one of the three major ethnic groups of Nigeria; they are renowned as entrepreneurs

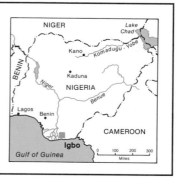

Here too we find the mediation of oppositions within Balinese culture, oppositions that are at the heart of the cockfight as well. *(See EthnoFile 6.3: Bali.)*

Communicating Through Igbo Dance

Judith Lynne Hanna (1979:162ff.) discusses the way dance-plays performed by the Ubakala Igbo introduce innovation and mediate paradoxes. *(See EthnoFile 6.5: Igbo.)* She points out that these dance-plays also "generate pleasure, reaffirm social bonds, and assist in dissipating tension" (Hanna 1979:162). These last experiences are not unique to dance, but are characteristic of most communal art forms. For the Ubakala Igbo, they are strongly expressed through dance. Because men and women, as well as old and young, participate in different ways, the dance-play makes plain the roles available to the Ubakala Igbo, especially those of age and sex. Similar messages are communicated through the correlation of social roles with movement style, structure, music, and costume. Dance also permits emotional communication that is prohibited in everyday life: "Women and youth can speak publicly, venting strong emotions without breaking those norms of etiquette related to interactions with males and seniors" (ibid.: 172–73).

These dance-plays can also affect the wider society of which they are a part. They do so by mediating or commenting on paradoxes that appear both in the dance and in the wider social world. Some of these paradoxes involve the same social roles that the dance-play underlines: in-group versus out-group, and male versus female. Other paradoxes are more directly involved with the structure of the dance itself. These include desire for individual competitive achievement through solos versus pressures toward cooperation and interdependence in dance movements; desire to change the style of the dance versus respect for the authority of elders who are responsible for the current style; and obedience to the dance leaders versus defiance of their authority. In the dance, comments, both verbal and in movement, are made about overbearing authorities and the conceited. At the same time, the cooperation of the dancers engaged in that commentary serves to counteract the divisive potential of those who engage in it.

Guidar dancers.

Community Festivals

Summer community festivals in Minnesota may also be seen as art and play, because they too can be aesthetically successful transformation-representations

EthnoFile 6.6
MINNESOTA

Region: North America

Nation: United States

Population: 4,100,000 (1980)

Environment: Temperate (barely) plains, hills, forests

Livelihood: Industry (farming, mining, manufacturing)

Political organization: Modern state

Other: Home of the mythical Lake Wobegon, as well as a tremendous number of community festivals

(see, for example, Lavenda 1983, 1984; Lavenda et al. 1984). *(See EthnoFile 6.6: Minnesota.)* They may comment about social organization and even transform it. These festivals are organized along a continuum ranging from a highly corporate model on one end to a highly familial one on the other.

The prototypical case of corporate organization is the Glenwood Waterama. This festival has two levels of organization: a controlling triumvirate of three men, and a number of three-couple committees in charge of fund raising, publicity, the parade, the queen pageant, and various other festival events. In each case, the organizers are from the business and professional community of the town. People recruit friends or newcomers to the organization, and no one has ever been in the controlling triumvirate twice.

For nearly thirty years, this style of organization has continued, forming chains of friends and business acquaintances, linking together people who have no other links. While the membership of Glenwood's business and professional communities has changed greatly over the years, the organization of Waterama has provided stability. Working on Waterama gives newcomers three major advantages. First, it provides an opportunity to meet other like-minded residents quickly. Second, it allows newcomers to make a contribution to the community in a highly visible and positively valued fashion. Third, it provides the opportunity for newcomers to form ties with other people in the community that are based on neither kinship nor long-term residence. In a sense, Waterama becomes a metaphor for the city: it *is* Glenwood.

Oral Narrative and Moral Perception: The Kuranko

Folktales have often been studied as examples of verbal art. Anthropologist Michael Jackson (1982) observed how the Kuranko of West Africa use the art of folktales to help them resolve some of the ethical problems they encounter in everyday life. *(See EthnoFile 6.7: Kuranko.)* Tellers of folktales encourage ethical discussion by performing in ways that dramatize uncertainty, promote ambivalence, and exploit ambiguity. This stimulates listeners to resolve problems of choice by thinking them through and reaching judgments that everyone can agree on. Through the play element of these narratives, individual narrators may vary the content as seems appropriate. In addition, because of the play element, the narratives "break free of the constraints and organizations of everyday life and entertain new possibilities of thought and action" (Jackson 1982:51). The child listening to the folktales learns

Queen pageants are an important part of many community festivals.

EthnoFile 6.7
KURANKO

Region: West Africa

Nation: Northeastern Sierra Leone

Population: 125,000; 45,000 in Guinea (1970s)

Environment: Foothills and margins of Guinea highlands; savannah

Livelihood: Shifting cultivation of upland rice

Political organization: Chiefs and councils of elders

Other: The folktale is a particularly important way of developing moral insight for the Kuranko

that the social world is contingent, that it is not something external and preexisting but is rather the product of human activity.

The Revolutionary Potential of Art

Art has a revolutionary potential, as well. The potential for overthrowing existing social systems is inherent in public celebrations such as Carnival (the three days of riotous celebration before Ash Wednesday, including Mardi Gras). This potential has long been recognized by authorities in the countries where Carnival is celebrated. They have frequently tried to control it or to use it for their own ends.

One intriguing study of the revolutionary potential of art was done by Charles Kiel (1979) on song among the Tiv of West Africa. *(See EthnoFile 5.5: Tiv.)* In an extended and passionate discussion, Kiel tries to explain Tiv song in terms that are not bound to Western art. He argues that Tiv composers act as the "conscience of the kinship group" to attack the exploiters—those who have caused pain, poverty, alienation, anxiety, "in short, oppression" (Kiel 1979:7). For the Tiv, song becomes a counterforce to evil, disease, and death. Through its structure, its words, and the friction and tension that it creates are generated energy, dynamism, and life.

Myth

Precisely because human creativity is open, people may be likely to ignore the boundaries of paramount reality unless they are repeatedly reminded of them. The process of *sanctification* marks the objects and relationships that constitute paramount reality. To sanctify statements is to certify their absolute, literal truth. This means that sanctity is a way of talking about objects, not a property of objects. There are certain assumptions in myths that cannot be verified but that are accepted as unquestionably true by those who believe in the system of which the myth is a part. Those assumptions are sanctified. *Myths* are generally defined as sanctified or sacred narratives about past events (frequently at the beginning of time) or about events in the future (usually the end of time).

Myths have implications for action. They may justify past action, or explain action in the present, or generate future action. For people who believe in them, they are true. To be persuasive, they must offer plausible explanations for people's experience of human nature, human society, and human history. But this "truth" of myth is not the same thing as the empirical truth of positive science. The power of myths comes from their ability to make life meaningful for those who accept them. Myths therefore possess an intersubjective truth, rooted in metaphor.

In Western society, myths were long thought to be flawed attempts at science or history. Sometimes they were considered delusions. In general, they were of interest to antiquarians, folklorists, psychoanalysts, or editors of collections of fairy tales for children. In fact, it is as children that most of us in the Western world first come in contact with myths. Starting in primary school, we read myths and legends from different countries and different societies. They are cleaned up to some degree, and are presented as isolated tales, divorced from the social context in which they normally occur. At best, they are taken to be indicative of the imaginative potential of the human mind. At worst, they are seen as expressions of ignorance or as the expression of forbidden desires of the individual or collective unconscious.

Myth as a Charter for Social Action

Early in the twentieth century, Anglo-Polish anthropologist Bronislaw Malinowski introduced a new approach to myth. He believed that to understand myths it is necessary to understand the social context in which they are embedded. Malinowski argued that myths serve as "charters" or "justifications" for present-day social arrangements. In other words, a given myth reinforces some aspect of social life that needs sanctification.

Malinowski's famous example is of the origin myths of the Trobriand Islanders ([1926] 1948). *(See EthnoFile 5.2: Trobriand Islanders.)* Members of every significant kinship grouping know, mark, and retell the history of the place from which their group's ancestress and her brother emerged from the depths of the earth. These origin myths are set in the time before history began. When it emerged from the earth, each ancestress-and-brother pair brought a distinct set of characteristics that included special objects and knowledge, various skills, crafts, spells, and the like. On reaching the surface, the pair took possession of the land. That is why today the people on a given piece of land have rights to it. It is also why they possess a particular set of spells, skills, and crafts. Since the original sacred beings were a woman and her brother, the origin myth can also be used to endorse present-day social arrangements. Membership in a Trobriand clan depends on a person's ability to trace kinship links through women to that clan's original ancestress. A brother and a sister represent the prototypical members of a clan because they are both descended from the ancestress through female links. Should anyone question the wisdom of organizing society in this way, the myth can be cited as proof that this is indeed the correct way to live.

In Trobriand society, clans are ranked relative to one another in terms of prestige. To account for this ranking, Trobrianders refer to another myth that explains how ranking came about. To believe in this myth, Malinowski asserts, is to accept a transcendent justification for the ranking of clans. Malinowski made it clear, however, that if social arrangements change, the myth changes too—in order to justify the new arrangements. In the Trobriand myth that explains rank, one clan's ancestor, the dog, emerges from the earth before another clan's ancestor, the pig. In the past, this was the justification for ranking the dog clan highest in prestige. At some point, however, the dog clan was replaced in prominence by the pig clan. This change was translated into mythic terms by having the dog eat food that was taboo.

In so doing, the dog gave up its claim to higher rank. Thus, to understand a myth and its transformations, one must understand the social organization of the society that makes use of it.

For some years, anthropological studies of myth did not go beyond Malinowski's level of analysis. But things began to change in the mid-1950s following the appearance of a series of books and articles by the French anthropologist Claude Lévi-Strauss. Lévi-Strauss transformed the study of myth. He argues that myths have meaningful *structures* that are worth studying in their own right, quite apart from the uses to which the myths may be put. He suggested that myths should be interpreted the way we interpret musical scores. In a piece of music, the "meaning" emerges not just from the melody (reading across), but also from the harmony (reading up and down) (Lévi-Strauss 1967). In other words, the structure of the piece of music, the way in which each line of the music contributes to the overall sound and is related to other lines, carries the meaning.

Myth as a Conceptual Tool

For Lévi-Strauss, myths are tools for overcoming logical contradictions that cannot otherwise be overcome. They are put together in an attempt to deal with the oppositions of particular concern to a particular society at a particular moment in time. Using a linguistic metaphor, Lévi-Strauss argues that myths are composed of smaller units: phrases, sentences, words, relationships. The units are arranged in ways that give both narrative (or "melodic") coherence and structural (or "harmonic") coherence. These arrangements represent and comment upon aspects of social life that are thought to be opposed to each other. Examples include the opposition of men to women; opposing rules of residence after marriage (for example, with the groom's father or the bride's mother); the opposition of the natural world to the cultural world, of life to death, of spirit to body, of high to low, and so on.

Lévi-Strauss also makes a stronger claim. He argues that the oppositional structure of myth represents the way the human mind itself operates in dealing with experience. The human mind processes information about the world in opposed pairs. The complex syntax of myth works to relate those opposed pairs to one another, in an attempt to overcome their contradictions. However, these contradictions can never be overcome; for example, the opposition of death to life is incapable of any earthly resolution. But myth can transform an insoluble problem into a more accessible concrete form. Mythic narrative can then provide the concrete problem with a solution. The solution may be the traditionally accepted, "sanctified" solution, or it may be a solution that is totally unacceptable. In either case, the concrete problem is resolved. By analogy, believers in the myth may conclude that the more abstract contradiction has been resolved as well.

Thus, a culture hero may bridge the opposition between death and life by traveling from the land of the living to the land of the dead and back. Alternatively, a myth might propose that the beings who transcend death are so horrific that death is clearly preferable to eternal life. Perhaps a myth describes the journey of a bird that travels from the earth, the home of the living, to the sky, the home of the dead. This is similar to Christian thought, where the death and resurrection of Jesus may be understood to resolve the opposition between death and life by transcending death.

From this point of view, myths do not just talk about the world as it *is*, they describe the world as it *might be*. To paraphrase Lévi-Strauss, myths are good to think with. Through mythic thinking, other ways to live our lives might be proposed. Lévi-Strauss insists, however, that the alternatives myths propose are ordinarily rejected as impossible. Thus, even though myths allow for play with sanctified metaphors, this play is under strict control.

Is Lévi-Strauss correct? There has been a great deal of debate on this issue since the publication in 1955 of his article "The Structural Study of Myth" (see Lévi-Strauss 1962). But even those who are most critical of his analyses of particular myths agree that the structures of myths are meaningful. Mythic structures display the ability of human beings to play with possibilities as they attempt to deal with basic contradictions at the heart of human experience in the world.

For Malinowski, Lévi-Strauss, and their followers, those who believe in myths are not conscious of the way their myths are structured, or of the functions their myths perform for them. More recent anthropological thinking (such as the work of Michael Jackson, cited earlier) takes a more reflexive approach This research recognizes that ordinary members of a society are often aware of the way their myths structure meaning. This knowledge allows them to manipulate the way myths are told or interpreted, in order to make an effect, to prove a point, or to buttress a particular referential perspective on human nature, society, or history.

Ritual

Play allows unlimited consideration of alternative referential perspectives on reality. Art permits consideration of alternative perspectives, but certain limitations restricting form and content are imposed. Myth aims to narrow down radically the possible referential perspectives, and is often used to promote a single perspective presumed to be valid for everyone. It thus offers a kind of intellectual indoctrination. But societies aim to shape action as well as thought, to orient all human faculties in the approved direction. This is why art, myth, and ritual are often closely associated with one another.

A Definition of Ritual

ritual
a repetitive social practice composed of a sequence of symbolic activities that are set off from the social routines of everyday life, that adhere to a culturally-defined ritual schema, and that are closely connected to a specific set of ideas often encoded in myth

Our definition of **ritual** has four elements. First, ritual is a repetitive social *practice* composed of a sequence of symbolic activities, in the form of dance, song, speech, bodily actions, the manipulation of certain objects, and so forth. Second, it is set off from the social routines of everyday life. Third, rituals in any culture adhere to a characteristic, culturally-defined ritual schema. This means that members of a culture can tell that a certain sequence of activities is a ritual even if they have never seen that particular ritual before. Finally, ritual action is closely connected to a specific set of ideas that are often encoded in myth. These ideas might concern the nature of evil, the relationship of human beings to the spirit world, and so forth. The purpose for which a ritual is performed will guide the way these ideas are selected and symbolically enacted in any given ritual.

The Western prototype of ritual includes the notion that it is "religious." In anthropological terms, ritual includes a much broader range of activities. According to the definition given in the preceding paragraph, a birthday party for children, a scientific experiment, a college graduation ceremony, and the procedure in a court of law are all rituals in American society. So are the preparations a baseball player goes through before stepping into the batter's box, pledge night in a fraternity, a bridal shower, a wedding, a bar mitzvah, and the Catholic Mass. All of these practices fit the definition, and all Americans recognize them as, at the very least, "ritualistic." Beyond that, these events all involve ways of embodying in action certain ideas that are important in American society. Through that action, the ideas are reflected or transformed. Some of these ideas are sanctified.

Ritual as Action

A ritual has a particular sequential ordering of acts, utterance, and events: a *text*. Because ritual is action, we must pay attention to the way the ritual text is performed. The *performance* of a ritual cannot be separated from its text; text and performance shape each other dialectically. Through ritual performance, the ideas of a culture become concrete, take on a form, or, as Bruce Kapferer (1983) puts it, give direction to the gaze of participants. At the same time, ritual performance can serve as a commentary on the text, to the extent of transforming it. Recall that this possibility is at the heart of play and art; it is also at the heart of ritual. Our understanding of the world does not come merely from mind, but rather from a coming together of mind, emotion, and body. By performing our ideas, our ideas become real.

Rites of Passage

Let us examine this process by looking at one kind of ritual performance, **rites of passage**. At the beginning of the twentieth century, the Belgian anthropologist Arnold Van Gennep noticed that certain kinds of rituals around the world had similar structures. These were rituals associated with the movement (or passage) of people from one position in the social structure to another. They included births, initiations, confirmations, weddings, funerals, and the like.

rites of passage
rituals that mark the movement and transformation of individuals from one social position to another

Van Gennep found that all these rituals began with a period of *separation* from the old position and from normal time. During this period, the ritual passenger left behind the symbols and practices of his or her previous position. For example, in induction into military service, recruits leave their families behind and are moved to a new place. They are forced to leave behind the clothing, activities, and even the hair that marked who they were in civilian life.

The second stage in rites of passage involves a period of *transition*, in which the ritual passenger is neither in the old life nor yet in the new one. This period is marked by rolelessness, ambiguity, and perceived danger. It is often a period in which the person or persons involved are subjected to ordeal by those who have already passed through. In the military service, this is the period of basic training, in which the recruits, not yet soldiers but no longer civilians, are forced to dress alike and act alike. They are subjected to a grinding-down process, after which they are rebuilt into something new.

The final stage is that of *reaggregation*, in which the ritual passenger is reintroduced into society, but in his or her new position. Here, for example, is the graduation from basic training, and the visit home, but this time in uniform, on leave, as a member of the armed forces, a new person.

Our understanding of rites of passage was greatly increased through the work of Victor Turner (1969). Turner concentrated on the period of transition, which he saw as important both for the rite of passage and for social life in general. Van Gennep referred to this part of a rite of passage as the liminal period, from the Latin *limen*, "threshold." It is characteristic of being on the threshold that one is betwixt and between, neither here nor there, neither in nor out. Turner notes that the symbolism accompanying the rite of passage often expresses this ambiguous state.

In a rite of passage, people leave their old identities behind. Young men becoming Buddhist monks mark their transformation by shaving their heads and wearing distinctive garments.

liminality
the ambiguous transitional state in a rite of passage, in which the person or persons undergoing the ritual are outside their ordinary social positions

communitas
an unstructured or minimally structured community of equal individuals, frequently found in rites of passage

Liminality, he tells us, "is frequently likened to death, to being in the womb, to invisibility, to darkness, to bisexuality, to the wilderness, and to an eclipse of the sun or moon" (Turner 1969:95). People in the liminal state tend to develop an intense comradeship in which their nonliminal distinctions disappear or become irrelevant. Turner calls this modality of social relationship **communitas**. Communitas is best understood as an unstructured or minimally structured community of equal individuals.

Turner goes on to suggest that liminality and communitas are not just characteristic of rites of passage. The same sense of communitas seems to hold in other kinds of positions within a society. It also occurs in positions of marginality (at the edges of structure) and inferiority (beneath structure). Prostitutes and slaves are, respectively, marginals and inferiors who are located outside the structure. They both challenge and maintain structure. College students seem to fit the definition of a communitas of the marginal, and slaves seem to fit that of a communitas of the inferior.

Turner contends that all societies need some kind of communitas as much as they need structure. Communitas gives "recognition to an essential and generic human bond, without which there could be no society" (ibid.:97). That bond is the common humanity that underlies all culture and society. Periods of communitas are always brief, however. Communitas is dangerous, not just because it threatens structure but because it threatens survival itself. Lost in a world of communitas, the things structure ensures—production of food and physical and social reproduction of the society—cannot be provided. Someone always has to take out the garbage and clean up after the party. Communitas gives way to structure, which in turn generates a need for the release of communitas. The feeling of oneness reported in the earlier anecdote about the Ali-Foreman fight is communitas, and communitas is also possible in play.

Play and Ritual as Complementary

How does ritual differ from play? Play and ritual (like metaphorical and literal language) are complementary forms of meta-communication (Handelman 1977). If the movement to play is based on the premise of metaphor ("Let's make-believe"), the movement to ritual is based on the premise of literalness ("Let's believe"). From the perspective of the ordinary social order, the result of these contrasting premises is the "inauthenticity" of play and the "truth" of ritual.

Because of the connection of ritual with sanctity, the meta-communication of the ritual frame ("This is ritual") is associated with two additional meta-communications: "All messages within this frame are sanctified" and "All messages within this frame are true." Both the frame and the messages within the frame become imbued with morality, and so contrast with the amoral meta-communication of play. It is ritual that asserts *what should be* to play's *what can be*. Consider, however, the medieval European Feast of Fools, a ritual in which the younger and lower-ranking Catholic clergy annually parodied the sacred rites and customs of the Church. Even there, the messages of sanctity and morality are still transmitted, since they are coming through the ritual frame.

The ritual frame is far more rigid than the play frame. One result of this is that ritual is the most stable liminal domain, while play is the most flexible. Players can move with relative ease into and out of play, but such is not the case with ritual.

Finally, play usually has little effect on the social order of ordinary life. Handelman suggests (1977:189) that this permits play a wide range of commentary on the social order. Ritual is different: its role is explicitly to maintain and to transform.

Combining Play, Art, Myth and Ritual

Many anthropologists have suggested that play, art, and ritual may be, and often are, experienced together. Bruce Kapferer (1983) has made these connections clear in a masterful study of demon exorcism in Sri Lanka. *(See EthnoFile 6.8: Sinhalese.)* The demon exorcism ceremonies of the Sinhalese Buddhist working class and peasantry last an entire night and are designed to cure disease. The performance combines in "a marvelous spectacle" ritual, comedy, music, and dance. Its

EthnoFile 6.8
SINHALESE

Region: South Asia

Nation: Sri Lanka (city: Galle)

Population: 12,580,000 (population of Galle: 115,000)

Environment: Tropical island

Livelihood: Farming, urban life

Political organization: Highly stratified state

Other: Demon exorcism is a highly developed aesthetic performance; in the 1980s, the Sinhalese engaged in bloody strife with the Tamil ethnic group

goal is "to change the experiential condition of [the] patients and to bring patients back into a normal conception of the world" (Kapferer 1983:177, 236). In other words, the entire performance is transformative. During the course of the ceremony, a demonic reality is created and then destroyed.

At the beginning of the exorcism, the patient and the audience are in different realities. The audience is in the paramount reality of everyday life, the patient is in the alternative reality of his or her illness. In that reality, demons are central and powerful actors. During the Evening Watch, through music, song, and eventually dance, the audience becomes increasingly engaged in this alternative reality. In this part of the ceremony, the demons are portrayed as figures of horror.

At midnight, the process is complete: the audience has joined the patient's reality. The demons, played by actors, appear. At this point, the Midnight Watch begins. This part of the ceremony is a comic drama that will last until nearly 3:00 a.m. The eruption of comedy into what had been an intensely serious ceremony transforms the demons into figures of ridicule. Through the comedy, the demonic reality begins to dissolve and fragment as the gods appear and reassert their dominance. As this occurs, the sick person begins to stand outside himself or herself and to see that the demons are really subordinate to the gods, not superior to them.

The last part of the exorcism is the Morning Watch, which continues until 6:00 a.m. During the Morning Watch and the end of the ceremony, the patient and audience become reengaged in the reality of ordinary life. The final comic drama of the performance "confirms the demonic absurdity, and destroys the demonic as powerful and relevant to normal experience in daily life" (ibid.: 220). Having played on the mind, body, and emotions of the patient and the audience, the performance ends.

To understand the performance as a whole, the interactions of all aspects of the performance must be grasped. Kapferer calls this the ceremony's aesthetics. He argues that the ceremony succeeds because it is composed of many different parts that fit together in a way that is satisfying to the Sinhalese. Only in the aesthetic are ideas, symbolic objects, and actions brought into the relationship from which their meaning comes.

Here then, is the overriding logic for this chapter: play, art, myth, and ritual have a great deal in common. All are part of the elemental human capacity to create and to see the world from a variety of perspectives. The human capacity to play works itself out in individual cultures in specific ways, but it is always present. It is in the combination of these elements that the satisfactions of human creativity, and its dangers, arise.

Key Terms

play	transformation-representation
meta-communication	myth
framing	ritual
sport	rites of passage
deep play	liminality
art	communitas

Chapter Summary

1. *Play* is common to all mammals, but it reaches its greatest development in human beings, who play throughout their lives. Play is a way of organizing activities, not merely a set of activities. This means that play can occur in what we call work.

2. Bateson argues that play is *framed* differently from the activities of ordinary life. We put a frame that consists of the message "this is play" around certain activities, thereby transforming them into play. This is a kind of *meta-communication*.

3. Play permits the creation of alternative realities, and allows us to recognize that different referential perspectives on reality are relative.

4. By setting up a separate reality, play enables us to comment on the everyday world, and suggests that the perspective of ordinary life is only one way to make sense of experience.

5. Play can be seen as having certain functions: exercise, practice for the real world, increase of creativity in children, challenge of the social order, learning by children that behavior occurs in context, commentary on the real world.

6. When *sports* are translated from one culture to another, they are frequently transformed to fit the patterns appropriate to the new culture.

7. *Deep play* is a variety of play in which the stakes are so high that it appears irrational for anyone to engage in it at all; the alternative reality that was assumed for play becomes all-consuming.

8. *Art* is a kind of play that is subject to certain culturally appropriate restrictions on form and content. It aims to evoke a holistic aesthetic response from those who make it or contemplate it. It succeeds when the form is culturally appropriate for the content and is technically perfect in its realization. Aesthetic evaluations are culturally shaped value judgments. We recognize art in other cultures because of its family resemblance to what we call art in our own culture.

9. Some of the *transformation-representations* of art include such abstract phenomena as social structure, systems of classification, cosmologies, basic metaphors, and the like. Art gives form to these abstractions.

10. *Myths* are sanctified or sacred narratives about events at the beginning of time or about events to come at the end of time. They aim to narrow down the possible referential perspectives on reality that are permitted within a society. To understand myths, considerable ethnographic background is required. Malinowski viewed myths as social charters. Levi-Strauss argued that myths are tools people use to overcome logical contradictions that cannot otherwise be overcome. Myths can serve both purposes.

11. *Ritual* is a repetitive social practice composed of sequences of symbolic activities such as speech, singing, dancing, bodily actions, and the manipulation of certain objects. In studying ritual, we pay attention not just to the symbols but to how the ritual is performed. As with art, the ideas of a culture become concrete through ritual action.

12. *Rites of passage* are rituals in which members of a culture move from one position in the social structure to another. These rites are marked by periods of separation, transition, and reaggregation.

13. During the period of transition, people who are going through a rite of passage are without role or status, in a threshold or *liminal* position. People in the transitional period develop an intense comradeship and a oneness of feeling known as *communitas*.

14. Ritual and play are complementary, not identical. Play is based on the premise "Let us make-believe," while ritual is based on the premise "Let us believe." As a result, the ritual frame is far more rigid than the play frame.

Suggested Readings

Alland, Alexander. *The Artistic Animal*. New York: Doubleday Anchor Books, 1977.

> An introductory look at the biocultural bases for art. This work is very well written, very clear, fascinating

Blanchard, Kendall, and Alyce Cheska. *The Anthropology of Sport*. South Hadley, Mass: Bergin and Garvey, 1985.

> An excellent introduction to the field.

Fagen, Robert. *Animal Play Behavior*. New York: Oxford University Press, 1981.

> The definitive work.

Kapferer, Bruce. *A Celebration of Demons*. Bloomington, Ind.: Indiana University Press, 1983.

> Neither introductory nor easy, but for the more advanced (or more interested) student, well worth the work.

Lever, Janet. *Soccer Madness*. Chicago: University of Chicago Press, 1983.

> A fascinating study of soccer in Brazil.

Schwartzman, Helen. *Transformations: The Anthropology of Children's Play*. New York: Plenum, 1978.

> A superlative work that considers the ways in which anthropologists have studied children's play, with some insightful suggestions about how they might do this in the future.

Turner, Victor. *The Ritual Process*. Chicago: Aldine, 1969.

> An important work in the anthropological study of ritual, this text repays the reading in its eloquent analysis of rites of passage.

The Anthropology of Performance and the Performance of Anthropology

Anya Peterson Royce (Ph.D., University of California, Berkeley) is Professor of Anthropology and Music and Dean of the Faculties at Indiana University. Her principal fieldwork was carried out in Juchitán, Mexico among Isthmus Zapotec. She has also conducted research in Europe. Dr. Royce has published numerous books and articles on dance and ethnicity. Before beginning her career in anthropology, she danced professionally in classical ballet companies.

Why should anthropologists care about the arts? What are the differences between performing arts and nonperforming arts? Are Western and non-Western arts fundamentally different? Is artistic creativity different from creativity in science? What do performers and anthropologists have in common? These questions are central to an anthropology of the arts. They also help anthropologists reflect on their own discipline. Some have been addressed at length by an-thropologists—the first question, for example.

Others, like question four, have more often been examined by non-anthropologists. In fact, it has been scientists who have asked about artistic and scientific creativity. And the consensus seems to be that if we look at the creative process, rather than at the *products* of creativity, we see some amazing commonalities between the arts and the sciences.

The third question has only recently surfaced as an important issue, largely because we thought we knew the answer: that there *were* major differences between Western and non-Western arts. Early museum exhibits, with their emphasis on form, were partly to blame. When we began thinking along the process line, however, we came to the same conclusion as did the people talking about creativity in science and art: there are fundamental similarities in the process of making art and in the nature of artists.

The second and the last questions, having to do with performing arts and performers, have had to wait for a relatively new breed of anthropologist—the performer-anthropologist. As one of these (I spent twenty years in a career in classical ballet and have now spent almost the same amount of time as an anthropologist), I shall return to questions two and five.

The arts are by no means new territory for the anthropologist. But anthropologists have done more work in some areas of the arts than in others. Until recently, the visual arts captured most of the attention, simply because they are easier to document. You can collect examples of pottery, sculpture, and painting, or at least you can photograph them. You can then study them at your leisure.

Music comes next, because we have ways of recording it—both as a written score and as an audio recording.

Dance and other kinds of performance based on the human body making patterns in time and space have been the most difficult and elusive of the arts. Anthropologists talking about dance, mime, and drama have usually concentrated on the functions these art forms play in society rather than on their form. While this is understandable, it is an oddly selective approach. No anthropologist who wants to retain his or her standing in the club would dream of looking only at the functions of kinship while ignoring the form—that is, terminology, forms of address, and so forth. But kinship has long been an acknowledged mainstay of anthropology, whereas dance has not. All introductory courses talk about kinship; all field methods courses teach you how to collect genealogies and to record kin terms. Dance and other performing arts have been the poor relations in comparison. A contributing factor to their second-class status was the feeling that, while anyone can describe the form of a pot or cross-cousin marriage, to do the same for dance takes a specialist. I do not want to argue about the merits of this statement, but a reason for increased attention to both the form and the function of the performing arts must surely be that we now have anthropologists who have been or are performers. The number of performers-turned-anthropologists is growing all the time, and as a result we see more and more studies of the performing arts.

Some of us have also begun to examine the differences and similarities between the performing and nonperforming arts. I have long suspected that much of our theory in the anthropology of the arts comes from the studies done of nonperforming arts without asking whether it is applicable to performing arts.

One major difference between performing and nonperforming arts is their context. The visual arts and literature are created by individuals working in their own time and space. The performing arts exist only in performance. What happens in that arena is a unique occurrence created by the coming together of performers and audience. The context of communication changes with every performance, and performers must create their art anew each time.

In performance, the response is immediate and continuous. Performers know where an audience is throughout a performance, and certainly know at the end whether they have been judged successful by the audience. Painters, sculptors, and writers spend long, solitary days and months creating a piece, and then wait often an equally long time for a response to their work.

Out of this difference comes the issue of revision. There is no possibility for revision in the performance context. Nonperforming artists revise all throughout the process of creating their work. What is revision for them is similar to practice and preparation for the performer. However, no matter how much you practice in advance, in a performance there are still factors that you have no control over but that affect your performance: the audience, fellow performers, the condition of the performance space, your instrument. None of these factors affect the products of nonperforming artists who can, ultimately, choose *when* to display their work to the public.

Another difference concerns the nature of creativity. Performers are the medium through which audiences understand and appreciate works composed by others. This is not a mechanical act of reproduction, nor is it passive. Nor does it involve less creativity. But it is different. In the works of a great musician, Pablo Casals, it is a recreating process with no set rules.

One is not a slave to the text, which can represent only a small part of what the composer, choreographer, or writer intended, nor should one's own personality dominate. The interpretation must be a synthesis of the creators' intentions and the performers' skill, style, and ideas. Even though audiences sometimes prefer flamboyance to passion, raw emotion to distilled feeling, playing to the audience can easily lead to a cult of personality that will displace the truly skilled interpreter. It is the difference between John Wayne, who played John Wayne no matter what the role, and Sir John Gielgud, who brought out the subtle differences in each role he played.

Having established the nature of performer as interpreter, we can now begin to answer the last question: What do performers and anthropologists have in common? As you may have guessed, it is their role as interpreters. Anthropologists are the interpreters of the cultures in which they work; they translate for a world unfamiliar with those cultures their coherence, distinctiveness, excitement. They are the medium through which one culture is "performed" for another.

Performing artists are the same kind of interpreters. The musician makes Beethoven come to life for an audience. The dancer recreates the choreography of centuries past or of yesterday. Without the actor, Shakespeare is simply a text to be read in solitude. None of these forms has any existence for an audience without the interpretation of the performer.

The performer-anthropologist combines the experience and technical knowledge of the performer with the analytical skills of the scholar. That person is uniquely qualified to stand as interpreter, conveying to a larger audience by means of description, analysis, and words the phenomena that affect us so powerfully precisely because they communicate *without* description, analysis, or words.

Just as becoming a "personality" is seductive for performers, so it is for anthropologists. The performer who is a personality obscures the meaning of the original text. The anthropologist who is a personality lets that personality dominate the meaning of the culture being described. Neither is a true interpreter, and the audience in both cases is the loser.

I have posed five questions. Tackling them forces us to be more reflective about assumptions we have taken for granted, as well as about the way we do anthropology. There are hundreds of questions we can ask. We are limited only by our own imagination and daring. We must learn to be comfortable with the knowledge that there is no one right answer, just as performers understand that there is no one ideal performance. There are better and worse answers and better and worse performances. We progress by the continual performing of anthropology. Our goal is true synthesis that lies at the heart of interpretation.

World View

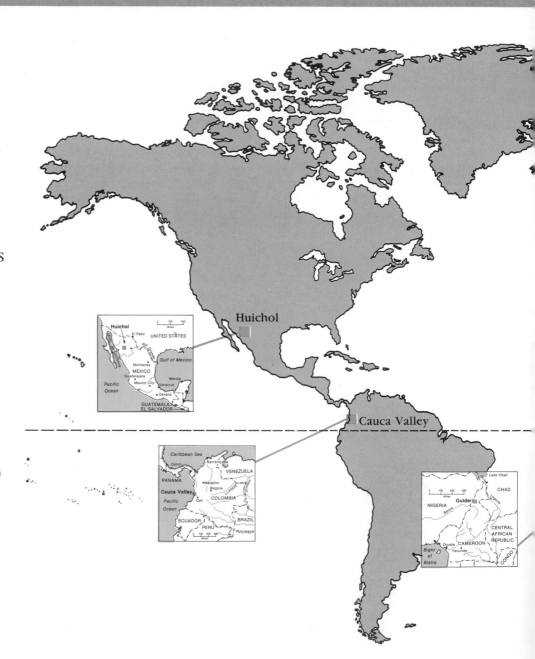

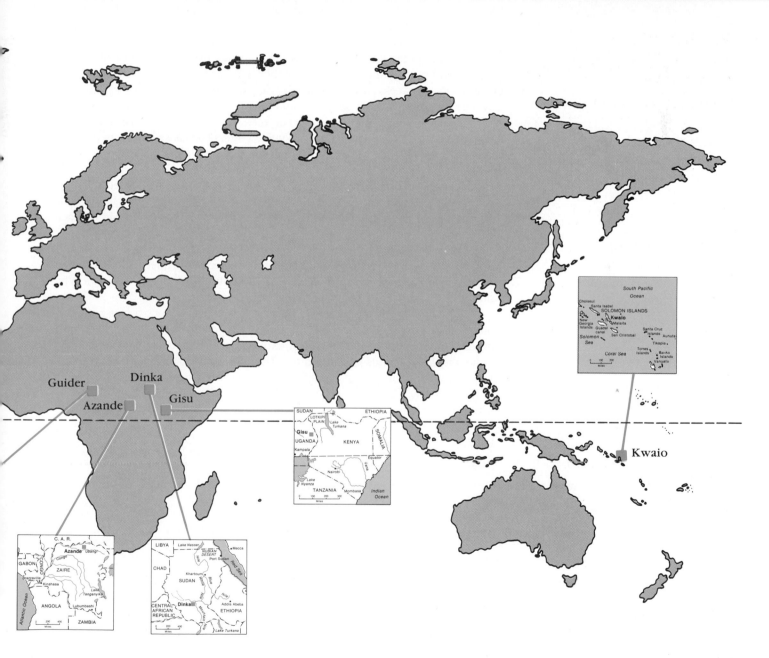

Guider

Dinka

Azande

Gisu

Kwaio

South Pacific
Ocean

Choiseul

Santa Isabel
SOLOMON ISLANDS
New
Georgia
Islands
Kwaio
Malaita
Guadal
canal
San Cristobal
Santa Cruz
Islands
Aukula
Tikopia
Solomon
Sea
Tores
Islands
Banks
Islands
Coral Sea
Vanuatu

SUDAN
ETHIOPIA
LOTKIPI
PLAIN
Lake Turkana
Gisu
UGANDA
KENYA
Kampala
Nairobi
Equator
Lake
Nyanza
TANZANIA
Mombasa
Indian
Ocean

C. A. R.
CONGO
Azande
Ubangi
GABON
Congo
ZAIRE
Brazzaville
Kinshasa
Lake
Tanganyika
ANGOLA
Lubumbashi
ZAMBIA

LIBYA
Lake Nasser
Mecca
NUBIAN
DESERT
Port Sudan
CHAD
Red Sea
Khartoum
SUDAN
White
Blue
Nile
Nile
Addis Abeba
CENTRAL
AFRICAN
REPUBLIC
Dinka
ETHIOPIA
Lake Turkana

This northern Cameroon man is believed to know powerful magic.

In 1976, The authors of this book went to Guider, in Cameroon, West Africa, so that Emily Schultz could carry out fieldwork. *(See EthnoFile 7.1: Guider.)* Soon after their arrival, they bought a bicycle. About a month later, it was stolen. The thief had been seen and was well known. Lavenda and Schultz went directly to the *gendarmerie*, where they swore out a complaint.

A month later, Lavenda was talking to Schultz's nineteen-year-old assistant, Amadou, a member of the Ndjegn ethnic group. Amadou mentioned that the Ndjegn were famous for the power of their magic. Lavenda asked him if he knew any magic. Amadou replied that he was too young but that his older brother was a powerful magician. Lavenda asked what kinds of magic his brother was best at. Amadou began to list them—one of the first was magic to return stolen property. "Why didn't you mention this when our bike was stolen?" Lavenda inquired. "Well, I talked it over with my best friend. We agreed that you white people don't believe in any of that and would laugh at us." But Lavenda wanted to know what would happen to the thief if Amadou's brother made the magic against him. "His stomach will begin to hurt," Amadou explained, "and if he doesn't return the bicycle within two weeks, his stomach will swell up until it explodes and he will die." Lavenda thought this was a good idea and said he wanted the magic made.

Amadou went home and told his brother, who agreed to cast the spell. Word quickly went around Guider that the two white visitors had caused magic to be made against the bicycle thief. The days passed, but the bicycle did not reappear. After three weeks, Lavenda asked Amadou what had happened.

"Here's the problem, M'sieu," Amadou explained. "We waited too long after the theft to cast the spell. It works better when one happens right after the other. Also, the thief is in Nigeria now. He's too far away for the magic to reach him."

Why do people believe—or not believe—in magic? Amadou was bright, suspicious of fakery, far from gullible. He had attended primary and secondary school. How could he remain convinced that his brother's magic worked? Why would many Americans be convinced that he was wrong?

Anthropologists are interested in what makes magic work because it occasionally does work: people are cursed, they sicken, and sometimes they die. How can this be? The usual anthropological explanation is that magic works when the people who believe in its power find out that it has been made against them. After all, people do often get stomachaches in northern Cameroon. Many people in Guider knew that the magic had been made, and by whom. Only a fool or a desperate person would take the chance of having his or her stomach swell up until it ex-

---

EthnoFile 7.1
GUIDER

Region: West Africa

Nation: Cameroon

Population: 18,000 (1976)

Environment: Savannah

Livelihood: Farming, commerce, civil service, cattle raising

Political organization: Traditional emirate; modern nation-state

Other: This is a small multiethnic town in the Muslim-dominated, arid north

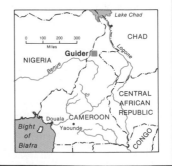

ploded. But in this case, the thief, long gone, did not know that magic had been made, and the magic's effect was neutralized by distance.

Amadou's explanation of why magic succeeds or fails is just as coherent as the traditional anthropological explanation. But each explanation is based on a different set of assumptions about what the world is like. Where do these ideas about the world come from? Why don't all people share the same ideas? This chapter suggests some answers to these questions.

From Everyday Experience to World View

In our earlier discussion of language, cognition, play, art, myth, and ritual, we looked at some of the ways human beings use culture to construct rich experiences of their everyday worlds. This chapter builds on those insights and describes how human beings use cultural creativity to make sense of the wider world on a comprehensive scale.

Anthropologists have good evidence that culture is not just a hodgepodge of unrelated elements. The directions in which cultural creativity goes may differ widely from one group to the next. But in any particular society, culture tends to be coherent, to exhibit a pattern. This means that people's everyday attempts to account for their experiences are not isolated efforts, but make use of a shared framework of assumptions about the way the world works. As everyday experiences are fitted into this framework, they come to make sense to people. The encompassing pictures of reality that result are called **world views**. Anthropologists are interested in how world views are constructed, and how people use them to make sense of their experiences in the broadest contexts. To do this, they must pay attention to the role of metaphor, metonymy, and symbol.

world views
encompassing pictures of reality created by the members of cultures

The Role of Metaphor, Metonymy, and Symbol

In Chapter 4, we argued that **metaphor** asserts the existence of a meaningful link between two expressions from different semantic domains. Metaphorical statements such as "Arnold is a turkey" create an ambiguity that can only be resolved in context. If we know Arnold is characteristically inept, ignorant, and annoying, and that turkeys are prototypically stupid and clumsy, our metaphor becomes intelligible and apt.

Why not simply say "Arnold is inept, ignorant, and annoying"? Why resort to metaphor to represent our opinion of Arnold? When we choose to use metaphoric language instead of literal language, it is usually because we sense that literal language is not equal to the task of expressing the meaning we intend. Perhaps it is not just that Arnold is inept, ignorant, and annoying. Perhaps we think he is funny looking, with a tiny head and a vast, cumbersome body. Perhaps his voice reminds us of the gobbling sound turkeys make. Perhaps his neck is loose and wobbles when he walks. There is something about the image of a turkey that encompasses more of what we think about Arnold than can ever be represented by a list of adjectives.

Put another way, our experience of Arnold is complex and difficult to pin down in literal language. We therefore select a figurative image whose features we are more familiar with and use it as a tool to help us understand what kind of person

metaphorical subject

the first part of a metaphor, which indicates the domain of experience that needs to be clarified

metaphorical predicate

the second part of a metaphor, which suggests a domain of experience that is familiar and that may help clarify the metaphorical subject

metaphorical entailments

all the attributes of a metaphorical predicate that are recognized as part of that domain of experience in a given culture

metonymy

the culturally defined relationship of the parts of a semantic domain to the domain as a whole and of the whole to its parts

Arnold is. The metaphor does not demonstrate unequivocally that Arnold *is* a turkey. It simply asserts that the link exists and invites those who know both Arnold and turkeys to decide (and perhaps to debate) the extent to which the metaphor is apt. Similarly, the metaphor "The Lord is my shepherd" links a subject we have trouble describing (the Lord) to an image (my shepherd) that is familiar and well understood. This metaphorical statement is an invitation to ponder what it means to be a shepherd, to be my shepherd, and then apply this knowledge to one's understanding of the Lord.

World views aim to encompass the widest possible understanding of the way the world works. In constructing world views, people tend to examine what they already know well for clues that might help them make sense of what puzzles them. The power of metaphor to bring insight into areas of human experience that are vague or poorly understood constitutes metaphor's chief value as a tool for constructing world views. The first part of a metaphor, the **metaphorical subject**, indicates the domain of experience that needs to be clarified (e.g., the Lord). The second part of a metaphor, the **metaphorical predicate**, suggests a domain of experience that is familiar (e.g., sheep herding) and that may help us understand what the Lord is all about.

To understand the metaphor, we have to list for ourselves every attribute of shepherds we can think of and then decide which attributes might serve as appropriate attributes of the Lord. (see figure 7.1). Those attributes might include the love a shepherd has for his sheep, or a shepherd's tireless vigilance in protecting his flock from the danger of wild animals. In addition, since the metaphor suggests that the Lord is *my* shepherd, I must think of myself as a sheep in relation to my shepherd, the Lord. This requires me to list as many attributes of sheep as I can come up with: that they are not very intelligent, for example, or that they are likely to go astray and get themselves into trouble if left on their own.

These attributes of shepherds and sheep are called **metaphorical entailments**. They suggest in detail what follows from, or is entailed by, our calling the Lord a shepherd. If we were to assert, for example, that "the Lord is my friend," an entirely different set of metaphorical entailments would follow: that my relationship with the Lord is a relationship between equals, for example, or that both of us have to make an effort if our friendship is to succeed.

Metaphors direct attention to certain aspects of experience and downplay or ignore others. As a result, different metaphors establish different referential perspectives. In so doing, metaphors assert different hypotheses, and thus have the power to create different "realities." The creation of multiple realities through metaphor generates ambiguity. Most of us avoid being overwhelmed by this ambiguity by choosing one referential perspective as paramount reality. We take this paramount reality to represent the "literal truth." The recurring patterns of experience, or schemas, found in paramount reality form domains of meaningful experience (or semantic domains). The boundaries of these domains appear so stable to us that we can take them for granted.

The relationship that links the parts of a semantic domain to one another is called **metonymy**. In the metaphor "The Lord is my shepherd," the link between the metaphorical subject shepherd and its metaphorical entailments is a link of metonymy. The word *shepherd* stands for *all* the attributes entailed by being a shepherd. At the same time, *any* of these attributes (e.g., protecting sheep from wild animals) may entail the word shepherd. Since semantic domains are culturally defined, the meaningful elements that are linked by metonymy are also culturally defined.

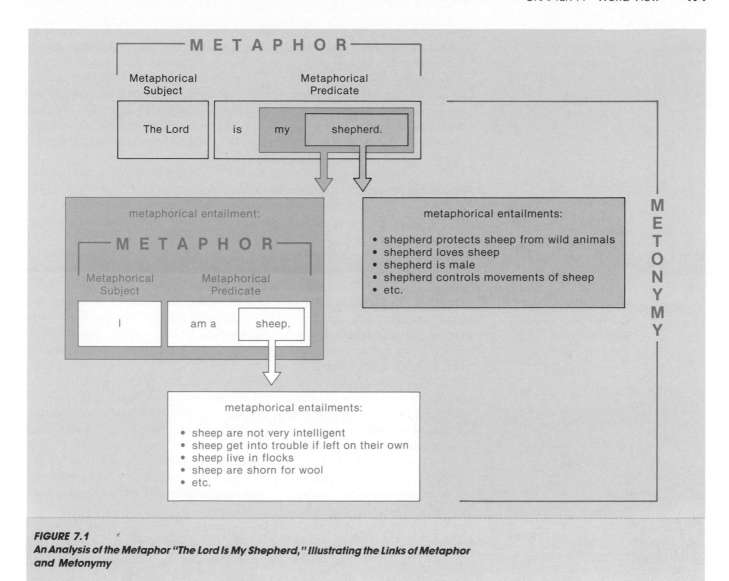

FIGURE 7.1
An Analysis of the Metaphor "The Lord Is My Shepherd," Illustrating the Links of Metaphor and Metonymy

Put another way, semantic links of metonymy are viewed as "true" or "literal" associations. By contrast, the semantic links set up by metaphor are viewed as "hypothetical" or "false." But, as noted in chapter 4, literal semantic linkages only *appear* to be true and unproblematic because they are conventionally accepted as such. Nevertheless, an apt metaphor may suit the situation it describes more fully than any literal expression. If, in addition, the metaphor illuminates other areas of our experience, we may conclude that the metaphor has enlarged our understanding. We then assimilate what we have learned into the domain of truth. In this way, metaphor is converted into metonymy. Old metaphors become new truths that we can use as metaphorical predicates of yet other shadowy domains of experience. And so the process continues.

People increase their understanding of themselves and the wider world by creating apt metaphors, which they may then convert into metonyms. Along the way, it is helpful to establish benchmarks that make it easier for us to organize this

symbols

things that stand for other things; a symbol signals the presence of an important domain of experience

knowledge. People wish to remind themselves of their significant insights and the connections between them. They devise symbols to serve this purpose. **Symbols**— be they words, images, or actions—are things that stand for other things. They signal the presence of and importance of given domains of experience. They are special cases of metonymy. Some symbols represent a whole semantic domain and invite us to consider the various elements within it. These are what Sherry Ortner (1973) calls summarizing symbols. Other symbols represent only one element of a domain and invite us to place that element in its wider semantic context. These are what Ortner calls elaborating symbols.

Summarizing symbols sum up, express, represent for the participants "in an emotionally powerful . . . way what the system means to them" (Ortner 1973:1339). To many people, for example, the American flag stands for "the American way." But the American way is a complex collection of ideas and feelings that includes such things as patriotism, democracy, hard work, free enterprise, progress, national superiority, apple pie, and motherhood. As Ortner points out, the flag focuses our attention on all these things at once. It does not encourage us to reflect on how the American way affects non-Americans, for example. And yet, the symbolic power of the flag is double-edged. For some people, Americans included, this same flag stands for imperialism, racism, opposition to the legitimate struggle of Third World peoples, and support for right-wing dictatorships. Perhaps stranger still, for many Americans who came of age during the 1960s, the flag sums up all these things at once, contradictory though they are!

Elaborating symbols are essentially analytic. They allow people to sort out and label complex and undifferentiated feelings and ideas. When this process is successful, those feelings and ideas become comprehensible and communicable, and can be translated into action. Elaborating symbols provide people with categories for thinking about the way their world is ordered. Consider the Dinka, a cattle-herding people of East Africa. *(See EthnoFile 7.2: Dinka.)* According to Godfrey Lienhardt, cattle provide the Dinka with most of the categories they use for thinking about and responding to experience. For instance, Dinka perceptions of color, light,

The American flag is a powerful summarizing symbol for citizens of the United States.

For pastoral peoples, like the Dinka and their neighbors the Nuer, cattle are elaborating symbols of paramount power.

EthnoFile 7.2
DINKA

Region: East Africa

Nation: Sudan

Population: 2,000,000

Environment: Savannah

Livelihood: Principally cattle herding, also agriculture

Political organization: Egalitarian with noble clans and chiefs

Other: The Dinka are neighbors of the Nuer (see EthnoFile 9.2), who raid them for cattle

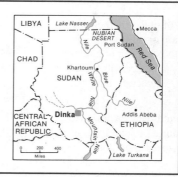

---

and shade are connected to the colors they see in cattle. They even describe the way their own society is put together by likening it to the way a bull is put together (Lienhardt 1961; Ortner 1973).

A World View in Operation

Anthropologists often say that people of different cultures live in different worlds. This itself is a metaphoric statement. It asserts that the world one lives in depends on culture, particularly on the referential perspective that one's culture embodies. Every culture contains subcultures, each of which teaches us what the world is like from a different point of view. The experience of multiple referential perspectives that we gain in our own society helps us to understand the referential perspectives of others. Our understanding is often powerfully assisted when we, or they, are able to coin an apt metaphor. Such a metaphor has the power to illuminate all at once, for them and for us, some essential features of the wider world in which we simultaneously find ourselves. When we and they together begin to explore the entailments of this metaphor, we jointly learn something about the way world views—theirs and ours—are constructed. Sometimes, as with Paul Rabinow's informant Malik, these discoveries can be surprising (see chapter 3).

We have been discussing how world views are constructed. But anthropologists and others usually encounter fully worked out world views when they come face-to-face with another way of life. The outsider discovers a rich tapestry of symbols and rituals and everyday practices linked to one another in what often appears to be a seamless web. Where does one begin to sort things out?

One anthropologist who made the attempt was E. E. Evans-Pritchard. In his classic work *Witchcraft, Oracles, and Magic among the Azande* ([1937] 1976), Evans-Pritchard shows how Azande beliefs and practices concerning witchcraft, oracles, and magic are related to one another. *(See EthnoFile 7.3: Azande.)* He describes the way Azande use witchcraft beliefs to explain what happens to them, and how they employ oracles and magic to exert a measure of control over the actions of other people. Evans-Pritchard was impressed by the intelligence, sophistication, and skepticism of his Azande informants. For this reason, he was all the more struck by the ability of these same people to hold a set of beliefs that, to a European, were superstitious at best.

Azande Witchcraft Beliefs

The Azande believe that a son inherits **witchcraft** from his father. Witchcraft is believed to take the form of a substance in the body of witches, generally located under the sternum. For the Azande, all deaths are due to witchcraft and must be avenged. **Magic** is used to avenge witchcraft deaths.

Being part of the body, witchcraft substance grows as the body grows; therefore, the older the witch, the more potent his or her witchcraft. Men and women may both be witches. Men are believed usually to practice witchcraft against other men, women against other women. The Azande believe that a "soul" of witchcraft removes the soul of a certain organ in the victim's body, usually at night, causing a

witchcraft
the performance of evil, whether intentional or self-aware or not, by human beings believed to possess a nonhuman power to do evil; in contrast to sorcery, which is learned, witchcraft is innate

magic
a set of beliefs and practices designed to control the natural or supernatural environment for specific purposes

---

EthnoFile 7.3
AZANDE

Region: Central Africa

Nation: Sudan, Zaire, Central African Republic

Population: 500,000

Environment: Sparsely wooded savannah

Livelihood: Farming, hunting, fishing; chicken raising

Political organization: Highly organized, tribal kingdoms

Other: These people were the subjects of a classic ethnography by Sir E. E. Evans-Pritchard titled *Witchcraft, Oracles, and Magic among the Azande* (1937), which inquired about the cultural patterning of belief

slow, wasting disease. Suffering this kind of disease is therefore an indication that an individual has had witchcraft directed against him or her.

Besides death, any other failure or misfortune is believed to be caused by witchcraft, unless there is a better reason. Better reasons are that the victim is incompetent, has broken a taboo, or has failed to observe a moral rule. Suppose that I am an incompetent potter and my pots break while I am firing them. I may claim that witchcraft caused them to break, but everyone will laugh at me because they all know I lack skill.

Witchcraft is an idiom the Azande use to describe and to explain all genuine misfortunes. Witchcraft is believed to be so common that the Azande are neither surprised nor awestruck when they encounter it. Quite the contrary: their usual response is anger. Witchcraft is a basic concept for the Azande, one that shapes their experience of misfortune.

The Azande are aware that there are "natural" causes for events. Consider the classic case of the collapsing granary. Azandeland is hot, and people seeking shade often sit under traditional raised granaries, which rest on logs. Termites are common in Azandeland, and sometimes they destroy the supporting logs, making a granary collapse. Occasionally, when people are sitting under the granary when it collapses, they are killed. Why does this happen? The Azande are perfectly happy to admit that the termites chewed up the wood until the supports gave way, but that to them is not answer enough. Why, after all, should that particular granary have collapsed at that particular moment? To Westerners, the only connection is coincidence in time and space. We do not provide any explanation for why these two chains of causation intersected. But the Azande do: Witchcraft caused the termites to finish chewing up the wood at just that moment, and that witchcraft must be avenged.

Witchcraft, Oracles, and Magic among the Azande ▬▬▬▬

How to expose the witch? For this task, the Azande employ *oracles*. (An oracle is a supernatural force to which people address questions, and whose responses they believe to be truthful.) Preeminent among these is the poison oracle. The poison is a strychninelike substance imported into Azandeland. The oracle "speaks" through the effect the poison has on chickens. When witchcraft is suspected, a relative of the afflicted person will take a certain number of chickens into the bush, along with a specialist in administering the oracle. This person will feed the chickens the poison and ask the oracle to identify the witch. A series of names will be presented twice to the oracle. The first time, the oracle will be asked to kill the chicken if the named person is the witch; the second time the oracle will be asked to spare the chicken. So the Azande double-check the oracle carefully; a witchcraft accusation is not made lightly.

People do not consult the oracle with a long list of names, and they do not need to. Since witchcraft is malevolent, people need only consider who might wish them or their families ill. People who have quarreled with them, who are unpleasant, who are antisocial, whose behavior is somehow out of line are the kinds of people who will ordinarily be accused. Witches are always neighbors, because neighbors are the only people who know you well enough to wish you and your family ill.

Once the oracle has identified the witch, the Azande removes the wing of the chicken and has it taken by messenger to the compound of the person who has been accused. The messenger presents the accused witch with the chicken wing and says that he has been sent concerning the illness of so-and-so's relative. "Almost invariably the witch replies courteously that he is unconscious of injuring anyone, that if it is true that he has injured the man in question he is very sorry, and that if it is he alone who is troubling him then he will surely recover, because from the bottom of his heart he wishes him health and happiness" (Evans-Pritchard 1976:42). The accused then calls for a gourd of water, takes some in his mouth, and sprays it out over the wing. He says aloud, so the messenger can hear and repeat what he says, that if he is a witch he is not aware of it and that he is not intentionally causing the sick man to be ill. He addresses the witchcraft in him, asking it to become cool, and concludes by saying that he makes this appeal from his heart, not just from his lips (ibid.).

People presented with an accusation of witchcraft are usually astounded, since no Azande thinks of himself or herself as a witch. However, the Azande do believe in witchcraft and in the oracles, and if the oracle says someone is a witch, then that person must be one. The accused witch is grateful to the family of the sick person for letting this be known. Otherwise, if the accused had been allowed to murder the victim, all the while unaware of it, he or she would surely be killed by vengeance magic. At the same time, there is a further message: the behavior of the accused is sufficiently outside the bounds of acceptable Azande behavior to have marked him or her as a potential witch. Only the names of people you suspect wish you ill are submitted to the oracle. The accused witch, then, is being told to change his or her behavior. This is the meta-communication that underlies witchcraft accusations.

Patterns of Witchcraft Accusation ▰▰▰

Compared with the image we have of sixteenth- and seventeenth-century Euro-American witchcraft—old hags dressed in black, riding on broomsticks, casting spells, causing milk to sour or people to sicken, and more—Azande witchcraft seems quite tame. We in the West have the impression that witchcraft and witch-hunting tear at the very fabric of society. Yet anthropological accounts like Evans-Pritchard's suggest that practices such as witchcraft accusation can keep societies together.

By carefully looking at the historical record of societies with witchcraft beliefs, we can see a pattern. Certain kinds of societies seem to be prone to active belief in witchcraft. These tend to be societies in which people are no longer sure about how to interact with others. Usually they find themselves having to interact closely with other people who they fear will treat them badly. As the level of insecurity rises in such societies, witchcraft accusations will also rise.

If we look at the range of witchcraft accusations worldwide, we see (following Douglas 1970:xxvi-xxvii) that they fall into two basic types. One type includes cases where the witch is an evil outsider. The other type includes cases where the witch is an internal enemy, either the member of a rival faction or a dangerous deviant. These different patterns of accusation perform different functions in a society. If the witch is an outsider, witchcraft accusation can strengthen in-group ties. If the witch is an internal enemy, accusations of witchcraft can weaken in-group ties; factions may have to regroup, communities may split, the entire social hierarchy may be reordered. If the witch is a dangerous deviant, witchcraft accusation can be seen as an attempt to control the deviant in defense of the wider values of the community. We can conclude from this that the way people understand witchcraft is based on social relations in the society where witchcraft is practiced. In each case, members of the society are asserting, metaphorically, that the supernatural realm operates the same way their society does.

Key Metaphors for Constructing World Views

Differences in world view ultimately derive from differences in experience, which people try to explain to themselves by means of metaphor. Human beings are not content to take things as they come, to refrain from asking how or why things are the way they are. World view, then, is an attempt to answer the following question: What must the world be like for my experiences to be what they are?

Over the ages, thoughtful people in all cultural traditions have suggested a variety of answers to this question. The suggestions that have become entrenched in any particular tradition are based on especially apt metaphors. The power of those metaphors to make sense of experience in a variety of circumstances and historical periods has been demonstrated repeatedly. But that power is limited. New metaphors that are appropriate for changed circumstances can provide insight when the old ways fail. They form the basis for new world views.

What makes a metaphor apt, or appropriate? A truly apt metaphor links personal experience and social experience in a convincing way. Such a linkage is possible because our personal experiences of the world are socially and culturally mediated.

Robin Horton suggests that someone who constructs a world view is "concerned above all to show order, regularity and predictability where primary theory [i.e., commonsense experience] has failed to show them. In search of his *key analogies*, therefore, he tends to look to those areas of everyday experience maximally associated with these qualities" (1982:237; emphasis added). Key analogies, or **key metaphors** that have served as the foundation of world views include societal, organic, technological, conduit, and computer metaphors.

key metaphors
metaphors that serve as the foundation of a world view

Societal Metaphors

In many societies, the model for the world is the social order. Such a **societal metaphor** is found among the Azande, for example. Horton argues that this has been the case in all traditional African societies, and that it was true of the Western world as well, until the Renaissance. "In the African setting . . . it is human action and interaction that is maximally associated with order, regularity, and predictability: hence it is from this area of experience that the key analogies are mostly drawn" (Horton 1982:237).

societal metaphor
a world-view metaphor whose model for the world is the social order

Now suppose the key metaphor in a society is "The world is (our) society." Members of this society will interpret the wider world in terms that come from their experience of society. Horton suggests that the result will be to conceive of personalized beings, such as gods or ancestor spirits, who run the wider world the same way people run human society.

World views that Western observers have called "religions" are ordinarily based on the societal metaphor. After all, the traditional hallmark of religion, from a Western perspective, is a belief in spirits or gods. Nevertheless, since societies are so different from one another, each will give rise to a rather different religion. For example, societies organized in strong groups based on kinship will usually people the wider world with the spirits of powerful ancestor figures. In contrast, societies run by vast and complex bureaucratic hierarchies are apt to picture the universe as being run by an army of hierarchically ordered spirits, perhaps topped by a chief god. We can predict that "The Lord is my shepherd" is not likely to be accepted as an apt description of cosmic reality by people living in a society that lacks class distinctions between lords and peasants and has no experience of sheep raising.

Societal metaphors are not restricted to non-Western peoples. As Horton noted, before the rise of science (which furnished the cosmos with impersonal mechanical forces), the dominant Western world views stretching back to antiquity were all based on societal metaphors. All envisioned a universe run by personalized beings (or a personalized Being) in ways that paralleled human social organization. With the growth of science in the West, our understanding of society, and our use of societal metaphors, has changed. For example, biologist Richard Lewontin and his colleagues (1984) point out that biologists studying cells used a societal metaphor almost from the very beginning. They likened cells to a factory assembling the biochemical products needed to support the body's economy. This metaphor recurs in the twentieth-century work of Francis Crick, one of the discoverers of the structure of DNA (deoxyribonucleic acid). Lewontin and colleagues suggest, "Read any introductory textbook to the new molecular biology and you will find these metaphors as a central part of the cellular description. Even the drawings of the protein synthesis sequence are often deliberately laid out in 'assembly-line' style" (1984:59).

Similarly, contemporary sociobiologists have borrowed certain concepts from modern economic thought and used them to describe the behavior of genes, or of living organisms. Thus, sociobiologists describe the nurturing behavior of parents toward their offspring as "parental investment." They talk about the cost-benefit analyses that people are supposed to make before deciding whether or not to sacrifice themselves for others, and even describe genes as "selfish." To the sociobiologist, the natural world is just the capitalist market writ large. Indeed, the anthropologist Marshall Sahlins and others have argued that from its inception modern biology took its key metaphors from the social world that was familiar to the biologists. That world, at its beginning in the late eighteenth century, was the world of early capitalism. As capitalism has changed over time, so too have the socioeconomic metaphors that biologists have chosen. The image of survival of the fittest was originally proposed in an attempt to explain how Western society worked. One wonders whether this image would ever have been viewed as an apt metaphor for the natural world in a society that did not have capitalist competition.

Organic metaphors

organic metaphors
metaphors that involve applying the image of the body to social structures and institutions

Organic metaphors apply the image of the living body to social structures and institutions. *Personification*, in which human characteristics are attributed to non-human entities, is an organic metaphor. An example of personification is the belief that rocks and trees have spirits, or that soda pop machines have a personality that is both malevolent and greedy. James Fernandez states that organic metaphors are common in the Bwiti religion of the Fang of Gabon. *(See EthnoFile 6.4: Fang.)* One, the human heart, is an apt metaphor for cult members because "(1) it is the heart which is the most alive of the bloody organs, (2) it is traditionally conceived by the Fang to be the organ of thought, and (3) in its bloodiness it is associated with the female principle. . . . Many meanings are at work in this metaphor, for that bloody organ, the heart, has a congeries of useful associations" (Fernandez 1977:112).

Anthropologist Mary Douglas (1966) has much to say about the use of organic metaphors in the construction of a society's world view. In her discussion of the world view of the ancient Hebrews, she points out that the body was understood as a metaphor for their society. As a result, threats to society were interpreted as threats to the body, and bodily rituals were prescribed to deal with them. It is difficult to say whether this is a case of a societal metaphor or an organic metaphor. Perhaps it is an example of what George Lakoff and Mark Johnson (1980) call a "bidirectional" metaphor. That is, knowledge of the body and its processes is used to illuminate society and its processes, and vice versa.

Other metaphors that could be described as organic might be cited. One that seems to be increasing in popularity in some circles in our own culture is the Web of Life. With this concept, we find life in its widest sense as an organic phenomenon: a web, with all its interconnections and natural, organic origin. Although the web referred to can be thought of as organic (e.g., a spider's web), one sometimes finds references in which the term *network* is substituted for web. The term network seems to be technological rather than organic; nets are manufactured items. There seems to be a case of overlap in entailments between the metaphors Web of Life and Network of Life that would justify the substitution of one metaphorical predicate for the other.

Technological Metaphors

Technological metaphors use objects made by human beings as metaphorical predicates. One manufactured object that has stimulated the imagination in a variety of cultures is the mirror. Western culture has certainly made use of it: the eyes are the mirror of the soul, the mind mirrors the world, and so forth.

Technological metaphors that use machines as metaphorical predicates are rampant in the world view (or world views) that have been produced in Western society since the seventeenth century. René Descartes popularized the notion that the human body was a machine, albeit one inhabited by an immortal soul. One of his near contemporaries, Julien La Mettrie, carried this analogy to its radical conclusion. In his book *L'homme machine* (Man-machine), he argued that even the concept of the soul was superfluous, because machines did not have souls.

Many thinkers have attributed the rise in machine metaphors to the growth of Western science and technology. The new and ever more complex machines that people started building following the Renaissance were tremendously powerful. They transformed the natural world in unprecedented ways, and this experience stimulated people's imaginations. The increasing complexity of machines, coupled with their builders' intimate knowledge of how they were put together, made them highly suggestive as metaphorical predicates.

The metaphoric entailments that follow from a machine metaphor are very different from those that flow from organic or societal metaphors. "Bodies are indissoluble wholes that lose their essential characteristics when they are taken into pieces. . . . Machines, on the contrary, can be disarticulated to be understood and then put back together again. Each part serves a separate and analyzable function, and the whole operates in a regular, lawlike manner that can be described by the operation of its separate parts impinging on each other" (Lewontin, Rose, and Kamin 1984:45). When we say that we are only cogs in a machine, or talk about statuses and roles as interchangeable parts, we are using machine metaphors.

technological metaphors
world-view metaphors that employ objects made by human beings as metaphorical predicates

In the Western world, the clock has become a prototype for the ingenious mechanism. Indeed, in British English, the term *clockwork* is an everyday word in people's vocabulary, used as a synonym for *mechanical*. Other products of human industry have also lent themselves to metaphor. Technology seems to be responsible for what has been called the "conduit metaphor." This metaphor is so deeply rooted in Western thought that its origin may be impossible to trace. In any case, it might be properly classed as a key metaphor in our Western world view.

George Lakoff and Mark Johnson (1980) discuss the way the conduit metaphor is used to talk about language:

The Conduit Metaphor:
Ideas (or meanings) are objects
Linguistic expressions are containers
Communication is sending

Taken together, these three metaphorical statements create the image of a communication pipeline or channel, along which message-containers filled with meaning-objects are sent back and forth. The conduit metaphor implies that words are containers that have their meanings inside them. Thus, understanding a word is simply a matter of unloading or unpacking the meaning contained within it. A failure to communicate is the result of choosing the wrong word-container to begin with (if you were the sender) or failing to empty the container properly once it arrived (if you were the receiver).

Lakoff and Johnson collected a new technological metaphor from an Iranian student of theirs, who coined it. This student had heard the expression "the solution of my problems" again and again after his arrival in the United States. He had assumed that it was a particularly apt metaphorical expression. He had imagined his problems boiling away, as in a beaker in the chemistry lab. Some of the problems would dissolve into the solution, and some of them would precipitate out as solids. But the solution was always boiling, and sooner or later these problems would dissolve, only to trigger the precipitation of other problems that had been in solution. The student was understandably disappointed when he discovered that Americans do not intend the phrase to mean what he thought it meant. Yet if we take this phrase as a metaphorical statement—the "chemical metaphor," as Lakoff and Johnson call it—a series of highly suggestive metaphorical entailments come to mind: "To live by the chemical metaphor would be to accept it as a fact that no problem ever disappears forever. . . . [It] would mean that your problems have a different kind of reality for you. A temporary solution would be an accomplishment rather than a failure. Problems would be part of the natural order" (Lakoff and Johnson 1980:144). This example illustrates not only the power of technology to suggest apt metaphors, but also how new metaphors give us new ways to interpret our experience.

Computer Metaphors

computer metaphors
a variety of technological metaphors in which the particular characteristics of computers are used as the metaphorical predicate

Computer metaphors are technological metaphors, but because of their significance in modern science, we will treat them separately. In the twentieth century, a major revolution in cognitive psychology was brought about by a shift in key technological metaphors. Psychologists rejected the steam engine metaphor taken from nineteenth-century industrial technology in favor of the computer metaphor taken from twentieth-century cybernetic technology.

Computer jargon has become popular among scientists investigating the functions of the brain, the nervous system, and even the whole human body. It seems impossible to avoid such language, given the wealth of insights into human mental functioning that the computer metaphor has made possible. Using a computer (instead of a mirror, for example) as a model for the mind can have varying consequences. Everything depends on the kind of computer you choose as the metaphoric predicate, or the aspects of computer operations you emphasize. For example, some biological determinists prefer to think of the mind as a "dedicated" computer. The functions of those machines are fully specified and wired into the hardware, allowing little flexibility.

Psychologist Richard Gregory, however, is impressed by the distinction between "hardware" and "software," between the machines themselves and the programs that run on them. In particular, he is struck by the "general-purpose" nature of sophisticated computer hardware. These complex machines can carry out widely different procedures depending on the programs fed into them. "If much of the brain is 'general-purpose' and set up for a great variety of particular functions by selected programs, much as very small changes in sentences totally change their meaning, the task of relating structure to function is extremely difficult" (Gregory 1981:180). Gregory concludes that if the mind is a computer it cannot be a dedicated one: "The most recent work in Artificial Intelligence [suggests that] procedures are more important than details of the mechanisms by which they are carried out" (1981:364). Therefore, insofar as the human brain is general-purpose, "its functional processes cannot be guessed at from its design. . . . Although we may have biological origins, these may not be much more relevant than, say, soil for flowers. . . . Soil chemistry tells us remarkably little about orchids" (Gregory 1981:566).

Were we to pursue this kind of computer metaphor, we could argue that the brain is the hardware and culture is the software. The coevolution of brain and culture could be described as the process by which an applications program hungry for random-access memory (RAM) makes demands on hardware design. Random alterations that result in new CPU (central processing unit) chips and hardware design (i.e., mutations) allow more RAM applications to be developed. At a certain point, however, the capacity of the CPU chip to access RAM is reached. An external "swap file" to handle the ever-increasing memory demands of users must be created in some sort of external storage system—on floppy or hard disks. The human cultural equivalent of this swap file would be oral tradition and later forms of symbolic inscription, such as writing.

Anthropologists have been affected by the power of computer metaphors and their highly complex entailments. Fernandez (1977) explicitly utilizes an "information-processing model" to describe the way in which a sequence of metaphors lend persuasiveness to one another as participants encounter them in the course of Bwiti ritual. He says, "This model suggests that a metaphor is not only an image, it is a plan for behavior." He goes on to argue, "The process by which metaphoric plans operate is one of looping and feedback of information flow" (Fernandez 1977:113).

Metaphor and World View as Instruments of Power

We have discussed the process that people use to build their world views. We have noted that the world views people construct vary enormously from culture to culture. But within any particular culture—insofar as boundaries can be drawn—there are also often, perhaps always, differences of opinion about the way the world truly is.

How does a particular picture of reality achieve the position of being the "official" world view for the people in a given culture? And once that position is achieved, how is it maintained? To be in the running for the official picture of reality, a world view must be able, however minimally, to make sense of some people's personal and social experiences. Sometimes minimally persuasive views of reality triumph over alternatives that seem far more plausible. At least, this is how things seem from the perspective of other members of society. So something more must be involved: power. As Lakoff and Johnson put it, "People in power get to impose their metaphors" (1980:157). People who lack power may be unable to dislodge the official world view of their society. They can, however, refuse to accept the imposition of someone else's world view. Often they are able to develop an unofficial world view based on metaphors that reflect their own condition of powerlessness. Such unofficial world views may even suggest appropriate action for transforming that condition.

How can metaphors, or the symbols that represent them, be used as instruments of power and control? First, a symbol can be used to refer to sanctified traditions when those in power seek to eliminate or impose certain forms of conduct. Thus, the memory of a dead parent, as a repository of values to be cherished, may be invoked to block some actions or to stimulate others. Holy books, like the Qur'an, may also be used in this way. For example, a legal record from Guider indicates that a son once brought suit against his father for refusing to repay him a certain amount of money. The father claimed that he had paid. Both father and son got into an increasingly heated argument in which neither would give ground. Finally, the judge in the case asked the father to take a copy of the Qur'an in his hand and swear that he was telling the truth. This he did. The son, however, refused to swear on the Qur'an, and finally admitted that he had been lying. In this case, the sanctified status of scripture, implying the power of Allah to punish liars, controlled the son's behavior.

Second, a symbol may be under the direct control of a person wishing to affect the behavior of others. Here, for example, we can think of the role of official interpreters of religious or political ideology, such as priests or kings. Their pronouncements define the bounds of permissible behavior. As Roger Keesing points out:

> *Senior men, in Melanesia as elsewhere in the tribal world, have depended heavily on control of* sacred knowledge *to maintain their control of earthly politics. By keeping in their hands relations with ancestors and other spirits, by commanding magical knowledge, senior men could maintain a control mediated by the supernatural. Such religious ideologies served too, by defining rules in terms of ancient spirits and by defining the nature of men and women in supernatural terms, to reinforce and maintain the roles of the sexes—and again to hide their nature."* (Keesing 1982:219)

Keesing's observations remind us that knowledge, like power, is not evenly distributed throughout a society. Just as some people speak or write or carve better than others, so too some people possess knowledge and control symbols to which others are denied access. Furthermore, this distribution of knowledge is not random in a society. Different *kinds* of people know different things. In some societies, what men know about their religious system is different from what women know, and what older men know may be different from what younger men know. Such discrepancies can have important consequences. Keesing suggested that men's control over women, and older men's control over younger men, are based on differential access to knowledge (ibid:14). That is, it is not just that these different kinds of people know different things. Rather, the different things they know (and don't know) enable them (or force them) to remain in the positions they hold in the society.

Religion and World View: Mind, Body, and Emotion

Many cultures assume that the universe operates according to the same principles as their society does. Those cultures tend to personify cosmic forces, and attempt to deal with them the way one attempts to deal with powerful human beings. Their societies possess what we in the West call **religion**. Anthropologists have devoted a great deal of attention to religion and have proposed many definitions for it. Clifford Geertz offered a definition that has gained currency among many anthropologists:

> *A religion is (1) a system of symbols which acts to (2) establish powerful, pervasive, and long-lasting moods and motivations in [people] by (3) formulating conceptions of a general order of existence and (4) clothing these conceptions with such an aura of factuality that (5) the moods and motivations seem uniquely realistic. (Geertz 1966:4)*

For a Western reader, one striking feature of this definition of religion is that it makes no mention of the supernatural. People in the West ordinarily assume that religion deals with the supernatural, a plane of existence that the senses cannot register but that is populated by beings or forces with powers beyond those of human beings. For Geertz, however, religion need not involve gods, spirits, or a supernatural realm. To insist that it must is to distract us from more important matters. From his perspective, world views that posit the existence of personalized supernatural beings have much in common with world views that do not. In both cases, the world view is concerned with relating people's everyday experiences of the world to a larger cosmic framework. When this is accomplished, notably in the context of ritual, people emerge with a clear idea of how they *ought* to live (Geertz 1972). Ritual makes world view plausible by creating extraordinary experiences for believers who participate in it. During ritual, the world as it is and the world as it ought to be fuse and become a single world. Participants in the ritual find themselves thinking, feeling, and acting in ways that make sense only if their world view is correct. These ritual experiences renew believers' faith. People emerge reassured that if they live their everyday lives in harmony with their world view, they will simultaneously be living in harmony with the universe.

Geertz's definition of religion fits together with our earlier discussion of world views and their underlying metaphors. That is, some metaphors personify cosmic forces, likening them to powerful human beings. This implies that we should pattern our interaction with those cosmic forces on the interaction patterns appropriate for their mortal human counterparts. It is world views of this kind that most Western observers identify as religion (see Wallace 1966).

The premise that souls, supernatural beings, and supernatural forces exist is commonly found. In fact, A.F.C. Wallace (1966:53–67) has proposed a set of the "minimal categories of religious behavior." These are, in a sense, design features of religion.

religion
according to Clifford Geertz, "a religion is (1) a system of symbols which acts to (2) establish powerful, pervasive, and long-lasting moods and motivations in [people] by (3) formulating conceptions of a general order of existence and (4) clothing these conceptions with such an aura of factuality that (5) the moods and motivations seem uniquely realistic" (1966:4)

For Wallace, religious activity involves one or more of the following:

1. *Prayer*. Every religious system in the world has a customary way of addressing the supernatural. This is frequently done by speaking or chanting out loud, holding the body in a conventional posture. Often, addressing the supernatural is done in public, at a sacred location, and with special apparatus: incense, smoke, objects.

2. *Music*. Music in some form is very often (perhaps universally) a part of religious ceremony. It may be in the form of singing, dancing, chanting, playing instruments, or reciting. While an address to the supernatural may be considered more effective in music, Wallace suggests that "musical media are preferred because of their effect upon the human performer and [his or her] audience and that sometimes . . . the participants are consciously aware that musical performance facilitates entry into a desired state of heightened suggestibility or trance in which possession and other ecstatic religious experiences can be expected to occur" (1966:34–35).

3. *Physiological exercise*. The physical manipulation of psychological states to induce an ecstatic spiritual state is found in every religious system. Wallace suggests four major kinds of manipulation: (1) drugs; (2) sensory deprivation; (3) mortification of the flesh by pain, sleeplessness, and fatigue; and (4) deprivation of food, water, or air. The experience of ecstasy, euphoria, dissociation, or hallucination seems to be a goal of religious effort, and any means that is effective in reaching it may be employed in at least some societies.

4. *Exhortation*. One human being addressing another human being on behalf of the supernatural is also found in all religious systems. Certain people are believed to have closer relationships with the supernatural than others, and they are expected to use those relationships in the spiritual interests of others. They give orders, they heal, they threaten, they comfort, they interpret.

5. *Reciting the code*. All societies have a sacred oral or written literature that asserts what is taken to be true. The code includes information about the nature of the supernatural and the universe as a whole, the religious myths, and the moral code of the religious system. At appropriate times, some or all of the code is told, recited, read, discussed, or studied.

6. *Simulation*. Ritual sometimes involves imitating things that are related to the supernatural. This may be in divination or witchcraft, but it frequently also has to do with the gods themselves. The painted or sculpted objects that are honored in some religious systems are not usually considered divine themselves. Rather, they imitate divinity, and are treated as if they were divine. In certain kinds of theatrical ritual, people sometimes impersonate the gods.

7. *Mana*. Supernatural power is sometimes believed to be transferable from an object that contains power to one that does not. The laying on of hands, in which the power of a healer enters the body of a sick person to remove or destroy an illness, is an example of the transmission of power. In Guider, some people believe that the power of the words of the Qur'an remains in the ink that has formed the letters of the words. Washing the ink

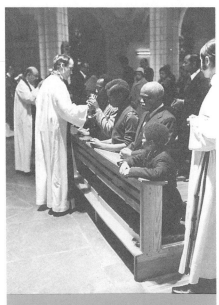

The religious design feature of *feasts* includes the Catholic Holy Communion.

The joint pilgrimage by Hindu worshippers to the Ganges River is an example of the religious design feature *congregation.*

off the board on which the words were written and drinking the ink transfers the power of the words into the body of the drinker. The principle here is that sacred things are to be touched so that power may be transferred.

8. *Taboo.* This is the opposite of mana; it is *not* touching things. It is believed that the power in some objects may injure the toucher. Many religious systems have taboo objects. Catholics may not touch the Host during communion; Jews may not touch the Torah, the scrolls of the Law. In ancient Polynesia, the chief's body could not be touched by commoners; even an accidental touch resulted in the death of the commoner. Food may also be taboo; many societies have elaborate rules concerning the foods that may or may not be eaten at different times, or by different kinds of people.

9. *Feasts.* Eating and drinking in a religious context is very common. The Catholic and Protestant Holy Communion is a sacred meal. The Passover Seder for Jews is another religious feast. For the Huichol of Mexico, the consumption of peyote is sacred. Even everyday meals may be seen to have a sacred quality if they are sanctified by an appropriate ritual.

10. *Sacrifice.* The giving of something valued by its donor to the supernatural or its agents is a feature of many religious systems. This may be an offering of money, goods, or services. It may also be the immolation of animals or, very rarely, human beings. As we saw in our discussion of Thaipusam in chapter 5, sacrifices may be made in thanks to the supernatural, in hopes of influencing it to act in a certain way, or simply to gain general religious merit.

11. *Congregation.* Religious behavior is always in part social. The people of a religious tradition sometimes come together as a group. This may take the form of processions, meetings, or convocations. The joint performance of some ritual acts is part of any religious system.

12. *Inspiration.* Not everyone in any religious system may be possessed, may undergo a dramatic conversion experience, may go into trance or other religious ecstasy. However, religious systems generally recognize that such states are the result of divine intervention in human life. "It is apparently the case that some persons in all human populations are subject to sudden, spontaneous interruptions of mood and thought. Whatever the reasons—psychodynamic or biochemical—for such alterations of mental activity, the belief in supernatural beings offers a ready and universally employed explanation. Religions differ in the extent to which they cultivate such experiences; all interpret them in religious terms" (Wallace 1966:66).

13. *Symbolism.* Certain symbols in a society's repertoire are associated with the supernatural as it is understood in the society. They may directly represent the deity or deities, or may symbolize major religious principles and beliefs. The Christian Cross is an example of the latter.

Religious Organization

The most important entailment that follows from the societal metaphor is that forces in the universe are personalized. It follows from this that people seeking to influence those forces must handle them in ways similar to the way they handle powerful human beings. Perhaps the central feature of the way we deal with human beings is by communicating with them. We can address them using language, and we expect them to respond. The same is true for personalized supernatural forces. Each design feature of religion that Wallace lists is related to human communication with personalized supernatural forces. These include not only gods, spirits, and ancestors, but also supernatural forces like witchcraft or oracles.

These forces can be addressed (in prayer), and people expect them to respond. To address these forces effectively, worshippers use all the eloquence they can muster. Religious rituals are the usual occasions in which such eloquence is required. Addressing the gods is enhanced by music and other aesthetic products and processes in which key religious symbols are highlighted. Worshippers may seek to make the supernatural forces pity them, and so sacrifices that testify to their seriousness of purpose may be offered. Physiological exercises put worshippers in the right state of awareness to approach the supernatural. Religious specialists may address the supernatural on behalf of others, since their special ritual status or skill may be more likely to engage the supernatural's sympathetic attention. These specialists may be the ones who recite the code. To encourage a favorable response, a congregation of worshippers may assume a humble body posture, touch certain objects and refrain from touching others as they engage in ritualized group simulation of actions known to please the supernaturals. The response of the supernaturals to their worshippers may be marked by communal feasts that allow worshippers to celebrate the fact that their prayers have been heeded. Alternatively, the response may be recognized by the possession of worshippers or religious specialists, or may need to be interpreted by divination, or deduced from subsequent events.

Maintaining contact with supernatural forces is thus a tremendously complex undertaking. It is not surprising, therefore, that societies have developed complex social practices to ensure that it is done properly. In other words, religion becomes institutionalized. Social positions are created for specialists who supervise or embody correct religious practice.

Anthropologists have identified two broad categories of religious specialists: shamans and priests. A **shaman** is an individual, part-time religious practitioner

shaman
an individual, part-time religious practitioner who is believed to have the power to contact supernatural forces directly, on behalf of individuals or groups; shamans are often thought able to travel to the supernatural realm to communicate with the beings or forces that dwell there; they often plead with those beings or forces to act in favor of their people, and may return with messages for them

who is believed to have the power to contact supernatural forces directly, on behalf of individuals or groups. Shamans are often thought able to travel to the supernatural realm to communicate with the beings or forces that dwell there. They often plead with those beings or forces to act in favor of their people, and may return with messages for their people. A **priest**, by contrast, is skilled in the practice of religious rituals, which he or she carries out for the benefit of the group. Priests do not necessarily have direct contact with the supernatural. Often their major role is to mediate such contact by ensuring that the required ritual activity has been properly performed.

> **priest**
> a religious practitioner skilled in the practice of religious rituals, which he or she carries out for the benefit of the group; priests do not necessarily have direct contact with the supernatural—often their major role is to mediate such contact by ensuring that the required ritual activity has been properly performed

Shamans are found even in societies where there are no other kinds of status outside kinship and gender. The !Kung, for example, recognize that some people are able to develop an internal power that enables them to travel to the world of the spirits—to enter "half death"—in order to cure those who are sick. *(See Ethno-File 9.1: !Kung.)* Priests are found in hierarchical societies. Status differences separating rulers and subjects in such societies are reflected in the unequal relationship between priest and laity.

Mind, Body, and Emotion in Religious Practice: The Huichol

Barabara Myerhoff (1974) discusses the peyote hunt of the Huichol Indians. *(See EthnoFile 7.4: Huichol.)* This ritual pilgrimage is a religious experience in which mind, body, and emotion all come together.

The Huichol are corn farmers who live in the mountains of northern Mexico. Annually, they travel to a desert about 350 miles from their homes to hunt peyote. The peyote is sacred to the Huichol, so this journey is sacred for them as well. But it also represents a journey back to *Wirikuta*, the original Huichol homeland, where the First People, both deities and ancestors, once lived. The journey is hard and dangerous, both physically and spiritually. The pilgrims seek to restore and experience anew the original state of unity that existed at the beginning of the world.

The original state of unity is symbolized by deer, maize, and peyote. The deer symbolizes the masculine, hunting past, and thus connects the Huichol with their ancestors. In Huichol thought, the deer gave them peyote and appears every year in the hunt in Wirikuta. Blood from a sacrificed deer makes the maize grow and makes it nourishing to people. The deer is more powerful than human beings but not as remote as the gods. It symbolizes independence, adventure, and freedom.

Maize is central to present-day Huichol life. It is still somewhat alien, however, since the Huichol have only recently begun to grow it. A life based on maize is

---

EthnoFile 7.4
HUICHOL

Region: Latin America

Nation: Northern Mexico

Population: 9,000

Environment: Mountains (the Sierra Madre Occidental)

Livelihood: Corn farming, deer hunting in recent past

Political organization: No formal organization; some men with influence

Other: The Huichol are known for their religious use of peyote and their colored yarn paintings

precarious and tedious: the Huichol have to stay home to watch the crops when they would rather be visiting others or hunting. Even if they are careful, the maize may not grow. Maize symbolizes the labor of the present: food, domesticity, sharing between the sexes, routine and persistent diligence. It also provides the Huichol with the language of beauty. "Maize," the Huichol say, "is our life."

Peyote, when gathered in the land of its origins, is sacred. It is used to induce private visions, which are not shared with others. It is also used ritually, in which case so little is eaten that no visions are produced. The purpose of ritual consumption seems to be to reach communion with the deities. Peyote provides an unknowable, but private, experience for the Huichol. The Huichol think of it as plant and animal at once. At the climactic moments of the peyote hunt, it is hunted like the deer. For the Huichol, peyote is a quiet gift of beauty and privacy. "Peyote is neither mundane like maize, nor exotic and exciting, like deer. It is that solitary, ahistorical, asocial, asexual, nonrational domain without which [human beings] are not complete, without which life is a lesser affair" (Myerhoff 1974:227).

In Huichol religious thought, deer, maize, and peyote fit together. Maize cannot grow without deer blood, the deer cannot be sacrificed until after the peyote hunt, the ceremony that brings the rain cannot be held without peyote, and the peyote cannot be hunted until maize has been cleaned and sanctified. The key event, then, is the peyote hunt.

In 1966, Barbara Myerhoff and Peter Furst accompanied Huichol pilgrims on the peyote hunt. Each pilgrim was given the name of a Huichol god for the duration of the pilgrimage. The pilgrims were under the guidance of a shaman. They all followed strict rules about sexual continence, and other behaviors that served to separate them from their everyday routine.

Once the pilgrims entered Wirikuta, many ways of speaking and acting were reversed. "Stand up" meant sit down; "go away" meant to come here. The van in which they traveled that year became a "burro" who would stop "if he ran out of tequila." If a man wanted to talk to someone in front of him, he would turn to the rear. The shaman who led the pilgrimage told Myerhoff that "on the peyote hunt, we change the names of things because when we cross over there, into Wirikuta, things are so sacred that all is reversed" (ibid.: 148).

In the sacred land, the pilgrims became hunters, searching for peyote. Once the first cactus was found, it was trapped by two arrows. The pilgrims then encircled it and presented their offerings. The shaman cut it out of the ground, sliced sections, and put one section in each pilgrim's mouth.

A Huichol shaman's violin and arrows, together with a basket of freshly gathered peyote.

> *The little group was sharply etched against the desert in the late afternoon sun—motionless, soundless, the once-bright colors of their costumes now muted under layers of dust—chewing, chewing the bitter plant. So Sahagún described the ancient Indians who wept in the desert over the plant they esteemed so greatly. The success of the undertaking was unquestionable and the faces changed from quiet wonder to rapture to exaltation all without words, all at the same moment. . . . Their camaraderie, the completeness of their communion with one another was self-evident. The companions were radiant. Their love for life and for one another was palpable. Though they did not speak and barely moved, no one seeing them there could call the experience anything less than collective ecstasy. (Myerhoff 1974:155–57)*

Following this moment of communitas, the pilgrims collected as much peyote as they would need for their community, and hastened to depart. The reversals and other requirements remained in effect until they reach home.

The unification of deer, maize, and peyote gives the peyote hunt its power. As Myerhoff puts it, "In the climactic moments of the rituals in Wirikuta, these symbols provide the Huichols with a formulation of the large questions dealt with by religion, the questions of ultimate meaning and purpose. In Wirikuta, a vision is attained by the operation of the deer, the maize, and the peyote; with lucidity and power, the symbols accomplish their sacred task of giving significance and order to [people's] lives" (1974:229).

Myerhoff writes that at the climax of the journey, several different unifications occur. On the societal level, the social barriers that separate the members of the group at home, and especially those that keep the shaman apart, are transcended. There are no longer distinctions between leader and led, between male and female, between old and young. For a moment, people are distinct from their social roles. At the historical level, the Huichols' past life as free, male-dominated, desert-dwelling hunters is set apart from, but also reconciled with, their present settled life in the mountains, where men and women cooperate to grow maize.

Once in Wirikuta, the relationship of the Huichol to the natural environment changes. This is the home of the ancestors, and the landscape itself is sanctified. Time itself disappears. The Huichol *become* their ancestors and their gods. There is thus no break between past and present. The Huichol come to feel that they were always a single people with a distinctive, eternal way of life.

According to Myerhoff,

This Huichol symbol complex takes up the problem of moral incoherence. By making possible the retention of the past as part of the present, it eliminates the need for dealing with the question of why the world changed, why the beauty and freedom of former times has passed away, why [people] lost touch with the gods, plants, and animals, why the Spaniards steal Huichol land, and why it is no longer possible to pursue "the perfect life—to offer to the gods and chase the deer." (1974:261)

Myerhoff suggests that the way in which the Huichol's religious system answers these problems is distinctive. Some religions explain present-day moral incoherence by asserting that following an ancient sin, an original paradise was lost. Other systems assert that there is an afterlife in which all the suffering of the world will be set right. But the Huichol refuse to let go of their past. "Their most precious religious heritage—their beginnings—is idealized and recovered. Even if only for a little while, by means of the peyote hunt, Paradise may be regained. Through the deer-maize-peyote complex, the deer and a life dedicated to hunting the deer is still a fact of present-day life rather than a fading, shabby memory, chewed over by old men at the end of the day" (ibid.: 262).

In the terms we have been using so far, the deer-maize-peyote complex and the peyote hunt represent the coming together of mind, body, and emotion. Through a holistic ritual experience that is profoundly meaningful, deeply moving, and thoroughly physical, the Huichol reexperience the correctness of their way of life.

Maintaining and Changing a World View

In the discussion of the Azande, we saw a full-fledged "traditional" world view at work. Azande beliefs and practices, as Evans-Pritchard described them, appear to form a seamless web that is capable of explaining everything and that cannot be proved false. Yet at the time Evans-Pritchard was doing his fieldwork, Azande society was undergoing some profound changes (see Gillies 1976:xxiii).

What makes a world view stable? Why is a world view rejected? These questions are related to general questions having to do with the explanation of persistence and change in human social life. Anthropologists recognize that culture change is a complex phenomenon, and they admit that they do not have all the answers.

Understanding Culture Change ▬▬▬

The first steps toward understanding culture change should involve attempts to relate any changes (or lack of them) to the experiences of people in the society under study. The kinds of experiences human beings have—of their bodies, their activities, their relationships with other people and with the natural environment—need to be accounted for. Stable, repetitive experiences reinforce the acceptability of any traditional world view that has successfully accounted for such experiences in the past. When experiences become unpredictable, and past experiences can no longer be trusted as guides for the future, traditional world views that cannot encompass these new experiences are undermined. During such periods, thinking people in any society become painfully aware that they face totally new situations. The age-old and time-tested theories that used to account successfully for experience now seem to be irrelevant (see Horton 1982:252).

Drastic changes in experience lead people to try to create new meanings that will help them cope with the changes. Sometimes these creative activities will involve elaboration of the old world view. For example, the so-called world religions have persisted many centuries and have spread over continents. One reason for this has to do with the principles upon which those world views depend. None, for example, require regular practices that are exclusively tied to a specific locality or a single individual. All are complex and supple enough to fit a wide range of human experiences in a wide range of social circumstances. Indeed, propagators of these world religions have actively adapted their organizations and their messages to meet the needs of people living in varying circumstances.

But not all world views can evolve in this way, at least not under all social conditions. Thus we have examples of societies facing drastically changed circumstances who responded by discarding the old ways and embracing the new. Sometimes the "new" comes from outsiders—Christian missionaries or Muslim traders, for example. Sometimes it arises out of the conflict between new and old and is built on both, the result being called **syncretism**. Sometimes syncretism attempts to accommodate changed circumstances, sometimes it attempts to resist them, and sometimes it is ambivalent.

The Kwaio of the Solomon Islands have redoubled their commitment to the old ways. *(See EthnoFile 7.5: Kwaio.)* Almost all their neighbors have converted to Christianity, and the nation of which they are a part is militantly Christian. Their neighbors wear clothing, work on plantations or in tourist hotels, and attend schools, and some live in cities. The Kwaio have resisted all this: "Young men carry bows and arrows; girls and women, nude except for customary ornaments, dig taro in forest gardens; valuables made of strung shell beads are exchanged at mortuary feasts; and priests sacrifice pigs to the ancestral spirits on whom prosperity and life itself depend" (Keesing 1982:1).

Why are the Kwaio different? Roger Keesing points out that while the Kwaio are aware of the alternatives and could take them up if they wished, they choose to

syncretism
a way of life of a group of people that is the result of blending their traditional way and a new way that has been brought to them by people from a different and usually more powerful culture

EthnoFile 7.5
KWAIO

Region: Oceania (Melanesia)

Nation: Solomon Islands (Malaita)

Population: 7,000 (1970s)

Environment: Tropical island

Livelihood: Horticulture and pig raising

Political organization: Some men have influence but no coercive power

Other: The Kwaio maintain their traditional way of life as a commitment to their autonomy in the face of pressures to change

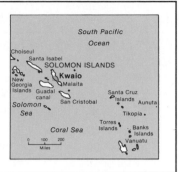

maintain their old ways. They find deep satisfaction in producing with their own hands and in family groups everything they need. They take pleasure in living surrounded by history, in a place filled with ancient landmarks. They enjoy living, gardening, and worshipping where their parents, grandparents, and great-grandparents did. They perceive the richness and value in a traditional life (ibid.: 237).

But "traditional" Kwaio life has become a life lived in a "modern" context. "In the course of anticolonial struggle, 'kastomu' (custom) and commitment to ancestral ways have become symbols of identity and autonomy" (ibid.: 240). In the eyes of the Kwaio, the many Solomon Islanders who became Christianized and acculturated lost their cultural ties and thereby their ties to the land and to their past. They have become outsiders, but in their own homeland. For the Kwaio, " 'kastomu' has become a symbol of personal and group identity. . . . Following the rules of the ancestors is a mode of political struggle, as well as a way of life" (ibid.). In other words, the Kwaio have become *reflexive*, seeing themselves and their ways in relation to the other, Christian Solomon Islanders. By maintaining their traditional ways they are consciously making a political statement. They are maintaining their traditional world view, not just because they believe it is right but also because it is *theirs*.

Revitalization

Sometimes, a group's defense of its own way of life leads to a process that anthropologists call revitalization. **Revitalization** is a conscious, deliberate, and organized attempt by some members of a society to create a more satisfying culture (Wallace 1972:75). It arises in times of crisis, most often in societies or subgroups within a society that are suffering radical transformations, usually at the hands of outsiders (e.g., colonizing powers). Sometimes revitalization takes the form of seeking a return to a golden age, when life was good, food was plentiful, and people all knew their places. When a messiah is expected to lead believers to the new golden age, this movement is often called revivalism, millenarianism, or messianism. At other times, the idea is to rid the society of all alien influences. This is called nativism. Often both nativism and revivalism appear together in a social movement that produces leaders, followers, and significant changes in social action.

A classic New World example of a revitalization movement was the Ghost Dance of 1890, among the Plains Indians of the United States. Independent Indian life on the plains ended when the buffalo were exterminated and the people were herded onto reservations by the numerically superior and better-armed Anglos. Out

revitalization
a conscious, deliberate, and organized attempt by some members of a society to create a more satisfying culture

of this final crisis emerged Wovoka, a prophet. Wovoka taught that the existing world would soon be destroyed, that a new crust would form on the earth. All whites and Indians who followed white ways would be buried at this time. But the Indians who abandoned white ways, led pure lives, and danced the Ghost Dance would be saved. As the new crust formed, the buffalo would return, as would all the ancestors of all believers. Together, all would live lives of virtue and joy.

In contrast to some revitalization movements in other parts of the world, violence against the oppressors was not part of the Ghost Dance. Violence was not necessary because the world was going to change by itself. Nevertheless, the movement frightened white settlers and the U. S. Army, who suspected an armed uprising. Those fears and suspicions led to the massacre at Wounded Knee, in which the U.S. Cavalry killed all the members of a Sioux band, principally women and children, whom they encountered off the reservation.

Inventing New Metaphors

metaphoric innovation
the invention of new metaphors to assimilate new experience into old categories

One way human beings attempt to come to terms with change is to invent new metaphors that will assimilate the new experience into old categories. Through **metaphoric innovation**, people can recast their understanding of themselves and their lives; once this is done, new action can be taken. New metaphors help people to see the world in a new way. They create a new world, and in this new world certain ways of thinking and acting become not only possible but necessary.

A metaphor has the power to create relationships among our experiences that do not exist independently of the metaphor. It defines an identifiable and coherent set of experiences. New metaphors create new referential perspectives, and make new styles of reasoning possible. The style of reasoning appropriate to the metaphor is based on the entailments that flow from the metaphor. These metaphoric entailments, not some set of abstract universal rules, define the appropriate style of reasoning.

Metaphoric innovation can proceed in more than one way. Lakoff and Johnson (1980:53) suggest three different ways:

- *Extending the "used" part of a metaphor.* Metaphors tend to be used selectively. Usually only certain entailments are highlighted in the everyday use of a metaphor. Metaphoric innovation results when these used parts of the metaphor are analyzed into smaller elements and relationships. These elements and relationships can then be used as new metaphoric predicates. For example, when mountains are personified, usually only the foot of the mountain is mentioned. An extension of this used part of the metaphor would involve mention of the arch or toes or heel of the mountain—for example, "Let's meet at the mountain's fallen arches."

- *Extending into the "unused" part of a metaphor.* Metaphoric extension would occur if, to continue the previous example, we began to speak not only of the foot of the mountain but also of the mountain's knees, legs, torso, and so on, perhaps suggesting, "This mountain has stout calves and weak knees."

- *Applying a new metaphor that is not common in ordinary discourse.* Poets specialize in this kind of thing. Metaphoric innovation about mountains might involve comparing a mountain to a wild beast, whose caves are mouths that feed on unsuspecting human beings who are foolish enough to venture inside them. This last form of innovation carries the most radical possibilities for transformation of world views.

New metaphors have the power to create a new reality. But this power may not make itself felt if the metaphoric entailments of the new metaphor do not connect with our experience. For example, it is one thing to assert that all the employees of a business firm are "one big happy family." Were this metaphor to be accepted, and were the employees to act in those terms, it would be instrumental in creating cooperation and solidarity within the firm. But metaphors must be plausible. Insisting that the firm is one big happy family may contradict the employees' everyday experiences of ruthless competition, people using other people for career advancement, hostilities between employer and employees. Employees may find a family metaphor apt, but their image would be that of a family ridden with conflict and competition—anything but happy.

The Source of New Metaphors

Where do new metaphors come from? They are the creative offerings of reflective human beings who have been grappling with new experiences, struggling to make sense of them. It is here that human creativity and agency are highlighted. To be sure, the innovator's experience is not unique to him or her. After all, the innovator's new insights would not have a social impact if they did not speak to the experiences of others in the society. Innovators do not create in a vacuum.

Similar innovations may occur to more than one individual at the same point in time. The growth of the machine metaphor in Western science, for example, is often attributed to Descartes, as though he were the first to discuss it. But in a society with proliferating technology, the aptness of the machine metaphor surely suggested itself to more than one person. Some people, however, are able to do more with a given metaphor, to seek out some of its more provocative entailments, than are others. Many people may see the aptness of a metaphor in accounting for their experience; perhaps only people of genius can discern the radical consequences that follow from the acceptance of the metaphor.

Fernandez (1977) recognizes these differences in his discussion of the Bwiti religion among the Fang of Gabon. *(See EthnoFile 6.4: Fang.)* Members of the religion all find its key metaphors apt at one level or another, or they would not participate again and again in Bwiti rituals. In fact, Fernandez suggests that Bwiti participants deliberately avoid making the entailments of key metaphors explicit. They do so because they do not want to alienate other participants whose understandings of these matters differ. Yet other members of Bwiti—the leaders, in particular—seem conscious of the range of entailments encompassed by the key metaphors they employ. The leaders of Bwiti have been and continue to be metaphoric innovators. Fernandez (1977:15) suggests that cult groups often split apart when leaders disagree over the aptness of certain metaphors and of the rituals that follow from them.

Apt new metaphors tend to be transformed into metonyms—representations of "truth." This is an open-ended process that we usually take to indicate the growth of knowledge about the world. Yet the tension of ambiguity lingers around new metaphors whose ability to represent the truth is not accepted by everyone. Fernandez (1977:113–14) gives an illustration of this process when he discusses what it means for a member of Bwiti to say "I am a Banzie." In one sense, this statement can be interpreted to mean "I am a member of Bwiti," simply indicating the speaker's "literal" claim of membership in a group. In another sense, however, "I am a Banzie" can be interpreted metaphorically. Most members of Bwiti understand *Banzie* to mean "angel" (it is an adaptation of the French *ange*). A Banzie is therefore someone who has transubstantiated and escaped corporeal afflictions. Which, then, is the true meaning of Banzie? In our view, both are.

Changing World Views: Two Examples

Let us consider two examples of change in world view, paying particular attention to the circumstances generating the experience that members of the societies in question were striving to explain.

The Fang

Caught by the French colonial presence and its Christianizing and civilizing mission, the Fang in central Africa have faced three important challenges to their world view. First, the reality of "the far away," represented by the colonizers, came to challenge the reality of "the near" and familiar. Second, the protective traditional powers of "the below" were challenged by the missionaries' message of divinity in "the above." Third, the pluralism of colonial life was a double standard in which the colonized were treated differently from the colonizers (Fernandez 1982:571).

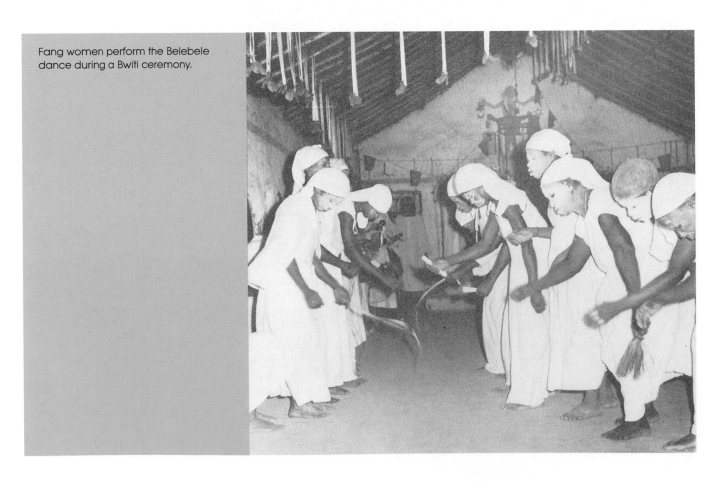

Fang women perform the Belebele dance during a Bwiti ceremony.

For many Fang, the syncretistic Bwiti religion represents a response to colonization and the pressures put on their social system. Bwiti members cope with the first challenge by using the drug *eboga* to go out to the far and convert it into the near. In the second case, the Christian god of the above and the traditional gods of the below are both incorporated into the Bwiti pantheon, establishing a creative tension. Finally, in Bwiti, ritual promotes among members the communal feeling of "one-heartedness."

Bwiti has been successful in creating a world view that allows many Fang to cope with the strains of social dislocation and exploitation (ibid.: 571). The Bwiti members have built a world in which some of the old metaphors (for example, the forest, or the body social, or the kinship system) are reanimated, and some new ones (for example, red and white uniforms, a path of birth and death, the world as a globe or a ball) are created. The old and the new are fitted together in a satisfying and syncretistic way. This world has, however, closed itself off from the wider society of the new Gabon Republic. Bwiti represents a kind of escape from the pressures of the outside world (Fernandez 1982:566).

The Cauca Valley Peasants

Michael Taussig (1980) reports a very different response to change in the tropical Cauca valley of Colombia. *(See EthnoFile 7.6: Cauca Valley Peasants.)* There, peasants who were formerly independent are being forced into working for wages on rapidly expanding sugar plantations. Although none of them has ever seen it happen, these people believe that some of their fellows enter into contracts with the devil in order to increase their production and hence their wage. Peasants working on their own land are not believed to do this. The money gained by a contract with the devil can only be used for luxury items. It may not be used to purchase capital goods like land or livestock because nothing will grow on land purchased with it, and any animals purchased will not reproduce and will die. Indeed, any sugarcane cut by a person who has such a contract will no longer sprout. In addition, many people say that a person who makes a contract with the devil will die prematurely and in pain (Taussig 1980:13).

Given these consequences, why would anyone make such a contract? Taussig suggests that we must see these devil beliefs as both a commentary on and a protest against the imposition of capitalism. Talk about the devil contract represents a peasant interpretation of capitalism, cast in an idiom drawn from peasant life and peasant understandings about labor. In other words, these people are aware of the

---

EthnoFile 7.6
CAUCA VALLEY

Region: South America

Nation: Colombia

Population: 700,000 outside the state capital, Popayán

Environment: Tropical jungle to Andean river valley

Livelihood: Plantation agriculture, coffee, cocoa, subsistence crops

Other: These people believe that some of their fellows make pacts with the devil to increase their wealth

threats that plantations pose to peasant independence. They express this awareness when they describe successful wageworkers as having made a bargain with the devil. "The religion of the oppressed can assuage that oppression and adapt people to it, but it can also provide resistance to that oppression" (ibid.: 231). By representing to the peasant proletarians of the Cauca valley, in language they understand, what capitalist agribusiness is doing to them, the metaphor of the devil contract sharpens the peasants' awareness of their plight. It may also engender resistance to that plight.

Key Terms

world views	magic	shaman
metaphorical subject	key metaphors	priest
metaphorical predicate	societal metaphor	syncretism
metaphorical entailments	organic metaphors	revitalization
metonymy	technological metaphors	metaphoric innovation
symbols	computer metaphors	
witchcraft	religion	

Chapter Summary

1. People attempting to account for their experiences make use of a shared framework of cultural assumptions about the way the world works. The encompassing pictures of reality that result are called *world views*.

2. The power of metaphor to bring insight into areas of human experience that are vague or poorly understood constitutes metaphor's chief value as a tool for constructing world views. Metaphors direct attention to certain aspects of experience and downplay or ignore others. Different metaphors assert different hypotheses and thus have the power to create different realities.

3. The distinction between *metonymy* and *metaphor* may be said to correspond to the distinction between semantic linkages viewed as literal or true and semantic linkages viewed as hypothetical or false. If metaphors fit the rest of our experience, they may be converted into metonyms.

4. As people create apt metaphors that are transformed into metonyms, they mark semantic domains by *symbols*. Symbols that sum up an entire semantic domain are summarizing symbols. Elaborating symbols are analytic and allow people to sort out complex and undifferentiated feelings and ideas.

5. Azande *witchcraft* beliefs are an example of a world view in action. For the Azande, their witchcraft beliefs provide an explanation for evil, illness, and misfortune. Witchcraft accusations also serve to indicate to the accused that his or her behavior has passed acceptable bounds.

6. Differences in world view derive from differences in experience that people try to explain by means of metaphor. Apt metaphors link up social experience and personal experience in a convincing way. People have used at least four *key metaphors* as foundations for a world view: (1) *societal metaphors*, in which the model for the world is the social order; (2) *organic metaphors*, in which the image of the body is applied to social structures and institutions; (3) *technological meta-*

phors, which employ artificial objects as the image for society (for example, "societies are machines"); and (4)*computer metaphors*, a variety of technological metaphor in which the distinction between hardware and software is highlighted.

7. Within any culture there are differences of opinion about particular images of reality: how real they are and whether they should be maintained. For example, metaphors are kept real and paramount through differentials in power. Those with power impose their metaphors, but those without power can resist this imposition by creating ther own contrasting metaphors.

8. Knowledge, like power is not evenly distributed throughout a society. Some people possess knowledge and control symbols to which others are denied access. In any society, certain kinds of people know different things, and this differential knowledge has direct effects on peoples' positions within the group.

9. When people assume that the universe operates according to the same principles as their society does, they tend to personify cosmic forces. They then base their dealings with those personified forces on the way they deal with human beings. These societies possess what we in the West call *religion*. Religion can be described in terms of design features, all of which are related to the most important attribute of personalized cosmic forces: we can address them symbolically, and we can expect them to respond. Maintaining contact with cosmic forces is very complex, and societies have complex social practices designed to ensure that this is done properly. Two important kinds of religious specialists are *shamans* and *priests*.

10. Drastic changes in peoples' experiences lead them to attempt to create new meanings to explain the changes and to cope with them. The world religions provide world views that are sufficiently complex to fit a wide range of human experiences. Sometimes, societies facing drastic change discard their old world views in favor of new ones. Sometimes a new one and the old one are creatively synthesized in a process called *syncretism*.

11. During times of crisis, there may be deliberate and organized attempts to create a new culture. Often these *revitalization* movements seek to return to a golden age, when life was better; they may be led by a prophet who proposes the new way to live.

12. People may be able to come to terms with changed experiences by inventing new metaphors to bring a new experience into line with old categories. Such *metaphoric innovation* can proceed through extensions of the used part of a metaphor, through extensions of the unused part of a metaphor, and through application of a new metaphor not common to ordinary discourse. The emergence of new metaphors highlights human creativity and agency. Innovations are rooted in their cultures and historical periods, but the insights that new metaphors provide lead to new ways of understanding the world.

Suggested Readings

Evans-Pritchard, E. E. *Witchcraft, Oracles, and Magic Among the Azande*.
    Abridged ed. Oxford: Oxford University Press, 1976. Originally published
    in 1937.
    An immensely influential and very readable anthropological classic.

Fernandez, James. *Bwiti: An Ethnography of the Religious Imagination in Africa.* Princeton: Princeton University Press, 1982.

A book that is tremendously rewarding as well as tremendously demanding. A major study of a religious movement and its associated rituals in context.

Geertz, Clifford. *Islam Observed.* Chicago: University of Chicago Press, 1968.

A brief but important statement of several issues in the anthropology of religion. This work compares two Islamic world views that turn out to be rather different from each other, those of Java and Morocco.

Geertz, Clifford. "Religion as a Cultural System." In *Anthropological Approaches to the Study of Religion*, edited by Michael Banton. London: Tavistock, 1966. Often reprinted, most notably in William Lessa and Evon Vogt, *Reader in Comparative Religion*, 4th ed. New York: Harper and Row, 1979.

An enduring classic article in anthropology. This is well worth reading, if you read nothing else from this or any other list of suggested readings.

Keesing, Roger. *Kwaio Religion: The Living and the Dead in a Solomon Island Society.* New York: Columbia University Press, 1982.

Based on twenty years of research, Keesing has provided a clear, readable, and committed discussion of what Kwaio religion is like to the Kwaio and why they continue to practice it.

Myerhoff, Barbara. *Peyote Hunt.* Ithaca: Cornell University Press, 1974.

A remarkable account of the world view and sacred journey of the Huichol Indians of Mexico, a journey in which the author participated. This work is accessible, well written, and sophisticated theoretically.

Anthropology: A Personal View

Emiko Ohnuki-Tierney (Ph.D., University of Wisconsin) is Vilas Professor of Anthropology at the University of Wisconsin, Madison. She has done fieldwork in Japan on the Ainu and has researched contemporary Japanese symbolic systems. Dr. Ohnuki-Tierney has written seven books, most recently on the historical transformation of the Japanese concept of self and on illness and healing in Japan and among the Ainu.

My entry into anthropology was quite personal. I came to the United States as a foreign student from Japan. After I began to understand English, I continued to make mistakes and did not always understand the way of life in the States. I became intrigued by the way a culture patterns individual behavior and thought processes. I have been hooked ever since, and I could not have chosen a more satisfying life and career.

Historically, one hallmark of anthropology has been the study of other cultures. It has been a quest for "the other"—a people whose way of life is quite distinct, culturally speaking, from that of the anthropologist. Anthropological studies have often turned out to be quests for the collective self, the culture of the anthropologist, through the "knowing" of the other. Initially, the conceptual distance provides a critical distance whereby the patterns of the host culture emerge clearly, although as one's study progresses the closing of the distance must take place while the "reading" of the other gains its depth.

I too started as an anthropologist studying a culture distant from my own Japanese culture. The first sixteen years of my anthropological career were spent studying the Ainu, a hunting-gathering people in northern Japan. My research focused on the symbolic dimensions of their culture—their cosmology—through the study of not only rituals but daily life as well. I examined how the Ainu classify their world—their time, space, and the beings of their universe, including humans, plants, and nonhuman animals. As my work progressed, however, I began to be intrigued by the opposite of classification—ambiguity, anomaly, and chaos—and how Ainu culture, as well as many other cultures, gives symbolic prominence to these concepts. These concepts are prominent in the Ainu understanding of illness and in their shamanistic healing ritual. I published an account of how the Ainu give order to their universe and deal with departures from order, in my *Illness and Healing among the Sakhlin Ainu* in 1981.

During the years when I was absorbed in Ainu culture, I paid little attention to my own Japanese culture. In 1979, however, I turned to Japanese culture. I had by then become acutely aware that anthropology must turn its attention to large-scale industrial societies as well. I could no longer encourage students to look for the small-scale societies that anthropologists traditionally studied. We must see how anthropological methods and theories may be applied in the study of modern nation-states. We must study societies with long historical traditions in order to understand how culture changes over time.

Contemporary Japanese culture is an ideal "field site" for exploring various theoretical concerns in contemporary anthropology. I extended my theoretical interest in order and chaos to Japanese culture and studied the understanding of health and illness held by contemporary Japanese and their health-care system. Although the domain of illness and health care in a society like Japan, where science has a long tradition, is expected to have been taken over by science, my findings suggest that the symbolic notions of purity and impurity and the basically dualist cosmology of the Japanese constitute the underlying principles behind their approach to illness and health care (*Illness and Culture in Contemporary Japan,* 1984). Thus, I was able to probe into a pressing question of our time: Do science and industrialization bring about a more-or-less homogeneous culture the world over?

With a long history of written records, Japanese culture also enables me to examine a culture through time. The study of historical transformations of a culture, or more precisely symbolic forms, meanings, and structures, has become a central concern in contemporary anthropology now that we are acutely aware that a purely synchronic (without reference to history) approach to culture has severe limitations.

My current work focuses on historical transformations of the meaning of the monkey metaphor. The monkey has been a dominant metaphor of self in that the Japanese throughout history have seen themselves in their portrayal of the monkey as if it were a mirror. However, how they saw the monkey varies from one historical period to another: its meaning has been transformed from that of a sacred mediator in early history, to a scapegoat during the Early Modern period, to a clown in contemporary Japan. Study of the monkey metaphor tells us a great deal about the conception of self in Japanese culture.

Some say that anthropology is in a crisis, but I believe that it is in a most exciting period. Recent political and epistemological questions have rocked the foundations of our discipline. Anthropology is no longer an exclusive territory for Western (admittedly a questionable blanket term) scholars. Orientalism has made us realize the partial, and often very skewed, representations of the other in Western scholarship. Native anthropologists and women are bringing in new insights to our disciplines, and, hopefully, we will see more Tocquevilles.

There have been exciting developments in theories as well. In symbolic anthropology we have been accustomed to the scientific paradigm, which emphasizes order and classification and the cognitive dimension of human behavior. But recently our study has been heavily influenced by the humanistic disciplines, which emphasize, for example, synthesizing elements in culture and the emotive dimensions of human behavior. These factors have made us reexamine the nature of fieldwork and of writing ethnography. The emphasis on practice compels us to scrutinize the interrelationship between structure and process, and between culture and individual, and a host of other dialectics we have been concerned about are receiving a new and envigorated thrust.

In addition, we are now paying serious attention to history, and this should help us understand the dynamics of culture that a synchronic study alone would not unveil. We are also meeting the challenge of extending anthropological methods and theories to nation-states. The anthropology of contemporary cultures will supply us with exciting findings and theoretical challenges, Anthropologists will be offering new insights into the workings of nation-states, and their work will gradually transform the stereotypical image of anthropology as a discipline in search only of small groups of faraway peoples.

Emiko Ohnuki-Tierney

The Initiation of Gisu Boys

The following dramatic and intriguing ethnographic example, concerning the circumcision of young men among the Gisu, illustrates many of the points we have been making in the last four chapters. Ritual in its transformative capacity, the social and cultural power of metaphor, the comprehensiveness of world views, and the Gisu's own ideas about cognition and emotion are all highlighted. For the Gisu, mind, body, and emotion come together as boys become men.

According to the anthropologist Suzette Heald (1982), the Gisu of eastern Uganda have long distinguished themselves from their neighbors because they practice circumcision and their neighbors do not. The Gisu circumcision ceremony occurs every two years and takes almost a full year to complete. The peak moment of the ritual is the circumcision itself. Known as *imbalu,* the Gisu consider it an ordeal. The initiate, still thought of as a boy, is between the ages of eighteen and twenty-five. He must stand perfectly still, showing no pain and with his stomach relaxed, while the circumcisers cut his foreskin and then strip subcutaneous flesh from around the *glans penis.*

The ritual itself really begins six months earlier, with the blowing of horns that usher in the circumcision year. From May to July, boys announce their intention to be circumcised by dressing in flamboyant and elaborate costumes and dancing. Two or three weeks before the operation is to take place, the boys who are determined to participate mark their intention to be circumcised by threshing millet that will be used to brew beer to offer to the ancestors and to guests who attend the circumcision. During this phase, the dancing becomes both more frequent and more vigorous.

Each boy must receive permission from all his close relatives to become circumcised. To show cowardice dishonors both the boy and his family and may cause destruction of the kinship group to which the boy belongs. Therefore, when he seeks approval of his decision, he is exhorted to remember that circumcision is not a game, that it depends not on the fancy costume but on the person, that he must put aside thoughts of everything else but the ordeal he faces. He is then told to show his commitment by jumping into the air. The higher and more vigorously he jumps, the more encouraged his relatives are, for these are signs of determination.

Two days before the circumcision, the boy initiates the final fermentation of the circumcision beer by pouring water over the prepared millet. He is then smeared from head to toe with millet yeast. From this point on, a series of important rituals to protect the boy from witchcraft, misfortune, and the dangers of circumcision are held. Sacrifices are offered for him, and the intensity of the ritual increases. The boy dances almost nonstop until the operation, and normal rules of conduct for him are suspended. By the day of circumcision, the boy will have achieved "a trance-like state . . . induced by exclusive preoccupation with the ordeal he faces"

EthnoFile
GISU

Region: East Africa

Nation: Uganda

Population: 500,000 (1970s)

Environment: Mountain slopes; rich volcanic soils

Livelihood: Subsistence farming, cash crop farming (coffee and cotton)

Political organization: Chiefs, headmen

Other: A dramatic circumcision ritual is performed on young men

(Heald 1982:22). To a Westerner, this is much like an athlete or actor getting so "psyched up" before a performance that nothing else seems to matter.

Two days before the operation, the boy is smeared twice by chyme from the stomachs of sacrificed goats. On the day of the operation, just before the circumcision, the boy is taken to a certain swamp. There he is blessed by the elders of the swamp, who blow beer over him. The boy then jumps into the swamp so the elders can smear black mud all over him and give him final advice before the operation. If the boy is still intent on circumcision, he now runs down the hill toward the circumcision enclosure, makes one final leap onto a spot already chosen, where protective medicines have been buried, and is cut by the circumcisers.

The final stage of the ritual is the healing. The circumciser does the first washing of the boy after the operation. This is the only period during the entire ritual when the boy is given any formal instruction on his new role as a man. The Gisu do not consider the healing of the cut to be a sure thing. It may be prolonged and painful owing to witchcraft against the boy, cursing of him by senior kinsmen, or retribution by ancestral ghosts.

Among the Gisu, circumcision is at least ostensibly a voluntary act. Boys ordinarily *want* to be circumcised. Heald points out that no attempt is made to disguise the fact that imbalu will hurt. Like the warrior of old, the boy must conquer his fear by convincing himself that he has both the physical strength and the strength of purpose to overcome an enemy. The Gisu do not rigidly distinguish between the qualities of mind or character and those of body. Thus, preparation of body and mind go together, and the signs of one are taken as indicative of the other. As the boy dances, he is seen to be strong "in his heart," which is taken to mean readiness both of body and of purpose.

But an emotional commitment is also required. This commitment is believed to derive from two sources: the boy's volition and something known to the Gisu as *lirima*, which can be translated as "violent emotion." The boy himself must decide when he is ready to be circumcised, but the boy becomes increasingly intent on being circumcised as the ritual proceeds. We could say that his volition *develops* as a result of the entire ritual.

The increase in the boy's strength comes not just from the development of volition, but also from the development of lirima. Heald tells us that the key feature of lirima is the intensity of the emotion experienced.

The nature of lirima is ambiguous. Only men have the capacity for lirima, and this makes them dangerous. A good man keeps his lirima under control. The advice given to the new man on the day after his circumcision emphasizes the ambivalent qualities of lirima, which are a basic fact of life. It is inherent in the nature of men, as the Gisu define them. "And, central to the transformational process of imbalu is that this is the first time in which the boy is expected to display the emotion. Indeed, it is induced for the first time at imbalu. Thereafter it is as much a part of his manhood as the circumcision cut itself" (ibid.:23).

Here, then, is a critical element for our understanding of the ritual: the boy is made to identify with the attitudes and emotions of adult men. Volition and lirima are key themes in the ritual because they constitute what it is to be a man. Through the process of the ritual, the boy learns to feel what it is to be a man. Enduring the operation is the final proof that the transformational process is complete. But there is more.

A key symbol of the ritual is beer. Among the Gisu, beer is essential for all rituals, but only in circumcision is a given person directly associated with making it. The association of the boy with the brewing of beer serves to synchronize two processes: the growth of the boy's determination and the fermentation of beer. Indeed, the fermentation of beer is always associated with the ancestors and indicative of lirima. The boy and the beer are thus similarly seen as imbued with ancestral power and lirima.

Yeast, chyme, and swamp mud are also understood to

be in a state of fermentation. In the smearing rites, the boy is brought into a relationship with and progressively identified with the ancestral powers and other potent things "fermenting" with lirima.

Fermentation is a major metaphor that the Gisu use to tie together certain processes that they see as being related. The smearing rites have as a psychological aim making the boy tough and fierce, but the rites themselves represent the fermentation process. Yeast initiates the process of fermentation; chyme, in the stomach of an animal, represents the process of active conversion; and swamp mud, the beer of the ancestral power of imbalu, presents fermentation as the end in itself. Lirima, the other power awakened in the boy through the ritual, is also seen as similar to fermentation; both are "volatile, strong, bitter, and potent" (ibid.:30).

The Gisu understand human fertility as fermentation. They believe that the "white blood" (semen) of a man mixes with the "red blood" (placental) of a woman to form a child. As in beer fermentation, the "bloods" inside a woman are said to "bubble up," and this volatile process may spill over into the woman's system, affecting her emotionally. Because of the connection of fermentation with lirima and the connection of lirima with the ancestral spirits, a pregnant woman is thought to have heightened emotions and to be irritable and bad tempered. Also, the ancestors are believed to be present, and the child, because of this, inherits the life force of someone in his or her kindred who has recently died.

Procreation and initiation are both understood as kinds of fermentation, as exemplifying a similar form of creative energy. As the creative power of women manifests itself in childbirth, so the creative power of men manifests itself in circumcision, and that of beer in fermentation. Thus, all these are creative processes. And the transforming effect of circumcision is real. Like pregnancy and fermentation, imbalu makes something new. It creates a man not just in the sense of role and a series of responsibilities and rites, but in terms of an existential person with different capacities and a different way of experiencing the world and the self.

Systems of Relationship

FORMS OF HUMAN SOCIETY

The Five-Element theory, which dates to the third century B.C., was one of the bases of all Chinese scientific thought. The five elements that made up the world were said to be water, fire, wood, metal, and earth. These elements were understood not as substances but as processes, differentiated from one another by the kinds of changes they underwent. Water was associated with soaking, dripping, descending. Fire was allied with heating, burning, ascending. Wood was connected with that which accepted form by submitting to cutting and carving instruments. Metal was affiliated with that which accepted form by molding when in the liquid state and had the capacity to change form by remelting and remolding. Earth was associated with the production of edible vegetation.

In Han times (about 200 B.C. to A.D. 200) the theory achieved a final form, which has been passed down through the ages. According to Colin Ronan and Joseph Needham in their Shorter Science and Civilisation in China *(1978: 142ff.) one aspect of the theory, the Mutual Conquest Order, "described the series in which each element was supposed to conquer its predecessor."*

"It was based on a logical sequence of ideas that had their basis in everyday scientific facts: for instance that Wood conquers Earth because, presumably, when in the form of a spade, it can dig up earth. Again, Metal conquers Wood since it can cut and carve it; Fire conquers Metal for it can melt or even vaporise it; Water conquers Fire because it can extinguish it; and, finally, Earth conquers Water because it can dam it and contain it—a very natural metaphor for people to whom irrigation and hydraulic engineering were so important. This order was also considered significant from the political point of view; it was put forward as an explanation for the course of history, with the implication that it would continue to apply in the future and was, therefore, useful for prediction. . . .

"The Five Elements gradually came to be associated with every conceivable category of things in the universe that it was possible to classify in fives." This included the seasons, the points of the compass, tastes, smells, numbers, kinds of musical notes, heavenly bodies, planets, weather, colors, body parts, sense organs, affective states, and human psychological functions. The fivefold scheme was used to categorize kinds of wild animals, domestic animals, and cultivated grains, as well as the periods of dynastic history, the ministries of government, and five styles of government. The styles of government included relaxed, enlightened, careful, energetic, and quiet, corresponding respectively to wood, fire, earth, metal, and water.

"As we might imagine," Needham and Ronan conclude, "these correlations met with criticism, sometimes severe, because they led to many absurdities. . . . Yet in spite of such criticisms, it seems that in the beginning these correlations were helpful to scientific thought in China. They were certainly no worse than the Greek theory of the elements that dominated European mediaeval thinking, and it was only when they became overelaborate and fanciful, too far removed from the observation of Nature, that they were positively harmful" (Ronan and Needham 1978: 156–57).

These observations are relevant to any apt metaphor or good scientific theory. The Chinese rationale for classification seems reasonable, but it is sharply at variance with our own. If the Chinese were obsessed by fives, we in the West have often been obsessed by threes. In anthropology, this has repeatedly been the case when the task has been to classify forms of human society. In this chapter we will examine some of the classifications that have been suggested, and their uses in research. Remember, it is the *usefulness* of our categories, rather than their *truthfulness*, that gives them their scientific value.

Human Imagination and the Material World

In the previous section of this book we explored the relationship of culture and human nature. We argued that culture is an aspect of human nature that is as much a source of freedom as it is a requirement for our survival. This is the paradox of the human condition. As a species, we cannot survive without inventing the tools for our survival, and yet we remain surprisingly unlimited in the specific tools we choose to invent. We have to invent some way to feed ourselves, provide ourselves with shelter, and ensure that our young are protected and taught what they in turn will need to know to survive. What we eventually come up with—what our ancestors, and the ancestors of other contemporary human communities came up with—is impressively varied.

Human imagination has tremendous power to create worlds of pure possibility, unconstrained by practical considerations in the material world. This imaginative power has produced the many and varied cultural traditions that human history reveals. But we are creatures who cannot—and do not—live in our imaginations alone, unconcerned with and untouched by our surroundings. We must cope with the material world. Failure to take adequate account of the material contexts in which we must live may mean the end of our life. No cultural invention, however subtle and seductive, can survive if it does not take account of the material aspects of human beings and the material context in which human life must be lived.

The crucial problem is the way the power of human imagination, unconstrained by material circumstances, intersects with the power of the material world, which does present constraints. The link between human imagination and the material world is an intimate one. Human imagination can suggest which aspects of the material world to pay attention to, and these suggestions become institutionalized in a cultural tradition. Once any group accepts these suggestions, it commits itself to paying attention to some parts of the material world while ignoring or downplaying other parts. As a result, it locks itself into a set of relationships with the material world that it may not be able to abandon freely. These relationships can and do exert a determinant pressure on future choices.

Culture, therefore, is *practiced* in the context of the material world. Cultural traditions take shape as a result of the dialectic between the possibilities we can imagine and the likelihood of realizing those possibilities in the material world.

What parts of the material world do human beings pay attention to, and what parts do they ignore? To answer this question, one can begin by considering the choices that human beings have made from the variety offered by the *nonhuman, "natural" environment*. This has long been the typical approach of anthropologists and others who have tried to classify human societies. We too will note the customs that human societies have developed to exploit their nonhuman surroundings in order to sustain their ways of life. But the presence of other *human* societies has also always been a constant feature of the human condition. Neighboring communities—their size and composition, how friendly they are with one another—are as much a part of any one community's *material* environment as are the amount of rainfall, the nature of the soil or the abundance of wildlife. Indeed, the size, composition, and organization of our own society affects the way we come to terms with the natural and human environment alike. This part of the text explicitly addresses the way in which the human condition is shaped by its unavoidably *social* nature.

Cross-Cultural Contacts between the West and the Rest of the World

The wider social environment cannot be forgotten as we begin to compare the many forms taken by different human societies. This is particularly the case when we consider the history of contact by anthropologists with "exotic" cultures in the non-Western world. That contact did not take place in a vacuum. If we look carefully, we see that the arrival of anthropologists was only the most recent phase of centuries-long contact by members of Western cultures and cultures of the wider world. This contact can be dated from the so-called Age of Discovery, when Western explorers like Columbus ventured beyond the boundaries of the world known to Europe and first encountered the inhabitants of Africa, America, and Asia.

These early explorers, and the traders and settlers who followed them, were not motivated to travel the distances they did and take the risks they took merely for exotic experience. They were in the pay of European monarchs whose interest in new worlds was political and economic. Historians have shown that nearly every *contact* made between the West and the outside world sooner or later turned into *conquest*. This led to the establishment of far-flung colonial empires centered in Europe. Thus, contact between Western Europe and the rest of the world neither began nor continued in neutral terms.

By the time anthropologists appeared on the scene, in the late nineteenth century, contact between their world and the world of the peoples whose lives they wanted to study had long since been established. The anthropologists and the societies from which they came were in a superior economic and political position. They were not, for the most part, paying visits to independent, autonomous, thriving cultures. They came as representatives of a conquering society to observe remnants of a population that had been conquered.

Members of the conquered societies did recall and describe their past. Most had rallied in the aftermath of conquest to reconstitute their cultures under changed circumstances. Such is the strength and resilience of human beings in adversity. But we would be naive to believe, as many early anthropologists and other observers did, that these societies and cultures were "living fossils," intact representatives of ancient ways of life, as yet untouched by history.

Anthropologist Eric Wolf (1982) discusses this tendency of Western observers to assume that people in the non-Western world are "people without history." The imperialist expansion of Europe, which coincided with the rise of industrial capitalism, was the central force leading to cross-cultural contact between the West and the rest of the world. Many of the "tribes" or "peoples" whom anthropologists later would study are relatively recent creations, forged in the field of contact between indigenous populations and Europeans. Before Europeans arrived in North America and Africa, such tribes—for example, the North American Ojibway or the African Baluba—had no separate identity and did not exist as autonomous societies. They were a *product* of the historical contact—and clash—between aggressive Europeans and local populations. In response to the European presence, these populations had to regroup and reshape their cultures.

Our survey of the forms of human society will therefore also involve an ethnography of ethnography. Anthropologists have begun to realize that no societies ever were isolated in time and space, unaffected by the world around them, and cut off from history. As a result, they have begun to consider the social and cultural circumstances of the contact between anthropologists and their informants. These circumstances have historical dimensions. For example, Schultz and Lavenda were hardly the first nonindigenous visitors to northern Cameroon. They had been preceded for more than one hundred years by German, English, and French explorers, soldiers, administrators, and missionaries. They had even been preceded, for twenty or more years, by American development experts and Peace Corps volunteers.

The experiences the Cameroonians had had with white people over the years formed the backdrop to the ethnography Schultz hoped to carry out. Like other anthropologists elsewhere in Africa, Schultz and Lavenda had to contend with previously formed and not always flattering stereotypes of Europeans. Indeed, they were initially assumed to *be* Europeans, as were a group of physicians from the People's Republic of China who arrived during their stay. From the point of view of the people of Guider, differences between Europeans, Americans, and Chinese were insignificant, compared with what they had in common. All were nonblack in appearance, spoke non-African languages, were comparatively wealthy, and were bearers of modern technology. All these strangers ran the risk that they and their activities might be viewed with suspicion.

The Cameroonian response came not out of "primitive" fears of the unknown but out of a justified memory of the activities and consequences of previous visits by Europeans. We agree with Dennis Tedlock that "there is no such thing as 'pre-contact' ethnography" (1982:161).

The Effects of Western Expansion

Background and History

To understand these changes among non-Western peoples, we must look at European history, too. Certain key commercial linkages underlay European expansion into the rest of the world. Central to the European Age of Exploration, which began in the fifteenth century, was the attempt by various European rulers to gain independent access to sources of wealth outside their own territories. The earliest explorations were undertaken by Portugal. Portugal was soon followed by Castile and Aragon, the two kingdoms that formed the core of what later would be called Spain. At the time, these kingdoms on the Iberian Peninsula were among the weakest and poorest territories in Europe. Any hopes they might have had for expansion within Europe were blocked by France to the north. Moreover, until the end of the fifteenth century, most Iberian Christian leaders were engaged in protracted warfare, both among themselves and against the Muslim overlords who had controlled the Iberian Peninsula for the previous eight hundred years.

Portugal managed to free itself from Muslim control in 1249. By the late 1300s, the kingdom was united enough to undertake attempts at expansion. Checked to the north and east by continuing conflicts between their neighbors, the Portuguese chose to move southward. Their official aim was to discover an ocean passage to the mythical Christian kingdom of Prester John, supposedly located somewhere southeast of Egypt. This was of interest to the Portuguese since gold and other riches that were coming into Europe from Africa were controlled by non-Portuguese middlemen. If the Portuguese found this kingdom, or any other kingdoms on the African continent, they would have direct access to this treasure. The Portuguese explorers never did find Prester John. During the fifteenth century, however, they "discovered" the entire Atlantic coast of Africa. Establishing trading posts as they went, they rounded the Cape of Good Hope in 1488.

In the last half of the fifteenth century, Castile and Aragon, united by the marriage of their rulers Isabella and Ferdinand, were actively involved in the "reconquest" of the remaining Muslim-ruled areas of the Iberian Peninsula. As victory neared, they too began to finance voyages of exploration. One such voyage, that of Columbus, led to the European discovery of the New World. This occurred in the same year that the Muslims were decisively expelled from Spain: 1492. By this time, the Portuguese had already explored the eastern coast of Africa and were shortly to establish direct sea trade with India. Competition between Spain and Portugal led to the Treaty of Tordesillas, in 1494, in which the pope divided the non-Christian world between them. The dividing line was intended to leave the Western Hemisphere to the Spanish and the Eastern Hemisphere to the Portuguese. Later exploration revealed that the South American coastline of what is now Brazil fell on the Portuguese side of the line. This gave Portugal a foothold in the New World, too.

The Iberians were the first to make European pressures felt in the New World, but their supremacy did not persist unchallenged. Holland, England, and France, the richer and more powerful European states, eventually turned their interests beyond Europe. In part, this was a result of their success in controlling European territory and trade relationships within it. Holland and especially England were at the forefront of the mercantile development that fueled the growth and expansion of capitalism. Although the Portuguese were the first to round the tip of Africa and make maritime contact with India, they were soon ousted by the Dutch, for whose better fleets and stronger commerce the Portuguese were no match.

The Dutch also ventured into the New World, establishing colonies in North America and vying again with the Portuguese (and other Europeans) for control of the Brazilian coast. However, the Dutch eventually withdrew from North America in favor of the English. Instead, they devoted themselves to consolidating their holdings in what is now Indonesia. The English also soon assumed control of trade with India. The French—not to be left behind—moved into North America, competing intensely with the English for access to territory and to trade goods.

Effects of Expansion in Africa and the Americas

Both in Africa and in America, the Europeans established commercial relations with the native inhabitants they encountered. The nature of those relations differed radically. In Africa, first the Portuguese and later the Dutch, British, and French found themselves confined to the coast. Often their trading posts were built on the coast or on offshore islands; for more than four hundred years they were allowed to penetrate no farther inland. Instead, they made their interests known to the local peoples living along the coast, who in turn set out to procure the trade goods sought by their European partners.

This long-lasting arrangement shows at least two important things about the Africans whom Europeans first contacted. First, their societies were resilient enough to adapt to the European presence and strong enough to keep Europeans and their commercial interests at arm's length for several centuries. In other words, the terms of trade were not dictated solely by the Europeans. Second, the European presence on the coast reshaped coastal society, stimulating the growth of hierarchical social forms in some areas where there had been none before. These changes in coastal African society had repercussions farther inland. Peacefully or by force, the new coastal kingdoms sought trade goods for their new partners from the people of the African hinterland. Only in the second half of the nineteenth century did this relationship between Europeans and Africans change.

The situation in America was quite different. The European conquest was immediate and disastrous for many native American populations. It was not merely a matter of armed force, for European-borne diseases such as measles and smallpox effectively wiped out large portions of local populations who lacked immunity. (In Africa, the situation was often just the reverse; white men succumbed to tropical maladies such as malaria to which coastal African populations had greater resistance.) In Central and South America, Spanish conquerors and then settlers arrived close on the heels of the first explorers. Thirty years after the arrival of Columbus, the two complex civilizations of the Americas, the Aztec in Mexico and the Inca in Peru, had been conquered.

Indigenous American societies disrupted by disease and conquest suffered further dislocation after Spanish colonial administration was established. The government in Spain was determined to control the exploitation of the new territories. It strove to check the attempts of colonists to set themselves up as feudal lords commanding local Indian groups as their peasants. These efforts were far from successful. Conquered Indians were put to work in mines and on plantations. Hard labor further reduced their numbers and fractured their traditional forms of social organization. By the time the worst of these abuses were finally curtailed, in the early seventeenth century, the nature of native American society in New Spain had been drastically reshaped. Throughout the more settled years of subsequent centuries, these reshaped societies affected, and were strongly affected by, the social forms and the culture of their conquerors. Indeed, it would be inaccurate to think of many postconquest Indian societies as separate societies at all. In the areas of greatest Spanish penetration and control, Indian groups were reduced to but one component in the complex hierarchy of colonial society.

The Fur Trade in North America

The nature of European penetration of North America was shaped in important ways by the early development of the fur trade. Fur trappers and traders are part of American folklore, but most white Americans are not aware of the fur trade's effect on indigenous forms of society in North America.

Background

Eric Wolf (1982: 158ff.) points out that trade in furs did not begin with discovery of the New World. For several centuries before Europe discovered America, furs had been an important source of wealth for early states in what is today the Russian part of the Soviet Union. In addition to fur collecting, fur processing became an important industry in Russia. When the Dutch first began to trade with native Americans for furs, they already had trading links to eastern Europe, and the fur they obtained in North America was later traded with Russia. The fur trade was thus an international phenomenon, and the strong stimulus that native American populations experienced to seek fur was shaped by the demand of the fur-processing industry in eastern Europe.

The most eagerly sought fur was that of the beaver, which was used to make felt for cloth and especially hats. So the hatmaking industry also contributed to the

Fur trade with Europeans transformed the lives of the native American peoples who supplied them with pelts.

search for fur in North America. This was particularly so as hats took on important social roles as symbols of superior status: rich Europeans could afford beaver hats, the poor had to be content with cloth caps.

The North American fur trade got well under way once Spain's control of the seas was broken, in the early seventeenth century. From the beginning, it was a competitive undertaking, first between the French in Quebec and the Dutch in New Amsterdam, later between the French and the English, when New Amsterdam became New York. This rivalry between France and England for control of the fur trade had repercussions on the native American populations who supplied them with pelts. Perhaps the most serious repercussion was a result of the fur traders' primary interest in beaver, rather than other fur-bearing animals. The trade flourished where there were beaver to be had. As soon as an area was trapped out, however, traders moved on to new territories where beaver might still be found.

Adaptation to Change

As a result, native American populations found their fortunes waxing as long as beaver flourished in their lands. Once the beaver were gone, their fortunes waned, often suddenly, as their European trading partners moved on too. Involvement in the fur trade significantly modified the traditional ways that native American groups made a living. As long as the beaver supply lasted, they could obtain many of the material items they needed by exchanging pelts for them at the trading post. This gave them a strong incentive to neglect or even abandon the activities that previously had supplied those items, and to devote themselves more completely to fur trapping. Over the generations, trapping itself became part of "tradition," and people came to depend on it for their livelihood, as they had formerly depending on hunting or farming.

This case clearly illustrates the point we made at the beginning of the chapter. Selective attention to one part of the natural world can lead to the formation of a way of life dependent on that part of the natural world. Once this happens, people are locked into a restricted set of choices and solutions to the problems of survival. In the fur trade, attention to the beaver led to a way of life dependent on beaver trapping and trade in beaver pelts. All was well as long as there were beaver to hunt. Once the beaver were gone, people discovered that their highly successful new adaptation had become obsolete virtually overnight. They also discovered that a return to the old ways was impossible, either because those ways had been forgotten or because the new circumstances of life made them impossible to carry out. The result often was, and can be in similar circumstances, severe social dislocation.

Regrouping and Reworking Traditions

Native American societies did not remain passive in the face of the European challenge. They regrouped. They reworked their traditional understandings of human nature and human society to minimize the negative impact of European pressures.

The Iroquois confederacy is one example of this. Wolf argues that the native American groups in the confederacy tried to create a form of society that was similar to and could counter the European trading companies with which they dealt. In forming the confederacy, however, the groups involved did not merely borrow the social organization of the European traders. They drew on traditional kinship forms and reworked these into new and broader-reaching structures that, for a time at least, functioned well to keep the Europeans at bay. The Iroquois confederacy was not an unchanging, timeless structure, predating the coming of Europeans to America. Quite the contrary; it was new. This structure was like the coastal trading kingdoms in Africa mentioned earlier. Both developed *in response to* a new state of social, political, and economic affairs initiated by European contact.

As the fur trade moved westward, competition between France and England for fur increased. This, in turn, led to rivalry between local groups for lucrative trading relationships. There were casualties. Some native American groups, such as the Huron, were wiped out. Other new groups, such as the Ojibway and Salteaux came into being. These latter tribes had only recently grown up, in response to the ravages and opportunities brought by the fur trade. Their members came from many different local groups who banded together. They settled around Green Bay, on Lake Michigan. According to Wolf, this was not their native territory, nor had they come to harvest wild rice. They came because Green Bay was an important center of the fur trade.

Here again, new groups came into being as a result of the fur trade—and were not just passively pushed by outsiders into a new social identity. The creation of this new identity must be understood as a positive effort by the group's members to rework their social forms in the face of new experiences. We can see that these new groups did develop a positive sense of who they were when we look at changes in their ritual life.

A new cult known as the Midewiwin grew up among the Ojibway and their neighbors toward the end of the seventeenth century. Replacing more localized rituals, the Midewiwin united numerous local groups. It emphasized individuals and their membership in a hierarchical association that went beyond their traditional territories and kinship groups. Wolf writes that this was an important change, since older measures of worth and value were based on status relationships in local kinship groups. Status in the association depended on wealth acquired in war or in trade, rather than on inherited status based on kinship. The cult accepted the existence of outside Europeans such as traders and missionaries, and its leaders were empowered to represent the members in dealings with them. For this reason, the Midewiwin is an example of a creative, adaptive response on the part of native Americans to cope with new and potentially threatening social experience.

The Slave and Commodities Trades ▬▬▬

The fur trade and its effects on forms of human society in North America is but one early example of the effect of Western European expansion into the non-Western world. Other later ventures included the slave trade and the trade in commodities such as cotton, which accompanied the rise of capitalist industry. These ventures not only continued to affect social life in the rest of the world; they also drew various parts of that world ever closer together into what would eventually constitute a capitalist world system.

The slave trade dominated commerce between Europeans and coastal Africans by the eighteenth century. The nature of the merchandise sought for this trade—human beings—had a devastating effect on the societies of the African hinterland whose members were captured and sold to meet European demand. The response by these societies was parallel to the North American response just reviewed. The survivors sought refuge beyond the slavers' reach, regrouping themselves into new societies with new names and reworking their collective traditions into new forms.

The slave trade did not alter the social fabric in Africa alone. Once they arrived in the New World, the slaves had to be fitted into a niche between local Indian inhabitants and European colonists. The growth of plantation economies in areas that had been used by hunters or gatherers or small-scale farmers altered the local ecology as well as local society. And the wealth produced in these economies transformed both the local gentry and the European nations who claimed sovereignty over them. As a result, Africa, America, and Europe became inextricably intertwined in one another's fate.

Toward Classifying Forms of Human Society

The preceding historical sketch is important to keep in mind as we begin a survey of the various forms human society has taken. It reminds us that the societies ethnographers began to investigate in the mid-nineteenth century had all been affected in some way by several centuries of contact and conflict with Western Europe. In many cases, they were conquered populations administered as colonial subjects of the ethnographers' own societies. This alone may have made it difficult for an ethnographer to carry out research that the colonial administration did not find relevant. Actually, studying what the researcher thought was important and gaining permission to do research could be mutually exclusive enterprises. As former colonies have become independent, these problems have not disappeared, for now the new nations' rulers have their own plans for their citizens and may be suspicious of the ethnographer's motives.

We can draw three general conclusions at this point. First, there are on this planet a variety of human societies whose natures were radically affected by their "discovery" by Europeans. As physicists learned at the beginning of the twentieth century when they sought to observe electrons, the very act of observation alters the nature of the entity being observed. When the act involved considerably more than observation, as was the case of contact between the West and the rest of the world, the changes were even more dramatic. Thus, although life in the non-Western world today is undoubtedly culturally patterned, this patterning does not necessarily represent a timeless, unchanged way of life, unaffected by history or our own presence. Extant non-Western societies have not somehow escaped the historical forces that have shaped everyone else.

Second, remnants of precontact societies survive today. These groups have not been absorbed without a trace into the society and culture of their conquerors. They have maintained a separate identity. Against high odds, they have regrouped and reshaped new identities. They have devised new social forms to deal with the effects of contact and conquest. Far from being static survivals of a timeless past, they are made up of people who are coping actively with contemporary problems and opportunities, people whose history is also our history. In some cases, these new social forms draw on very ancient traditions, which have been actively reworked to meet the demands of new experiences. In other cases, certain domains of traditional life have been less affected by outside forces. Where this is the case, a contemporary ethnographer can glimpse ways of life that were invented long ago and continue to prove their worth by being reproduced today. Sometimes, modes of living that have endured successfully for centuries are at last falling before the advance of Western technology and the rigors of the capitalist world system. But this should not be taken to mean that such modes of living are primitive, or incomplete, or lacking. These modes of living proved their adequacy by allowing human groups employing them to flourish, sometimes for millennia. The ruthless march of industrial capitalism must not blind us to these facts.

Finally, an impressive variety of forms of human society remain—in spite of the Western onslaught. Anthropologists have been able to document this variety through archaeological reconstruction, by recording the memories of old people, but also through fieldwork. Many similarities that people seem increasingly to show throughout the world turn out to be far less important than the continuing differences in world view and social organization that lie below the surface.

Making sense of the variety of forms of human society across space and through time is an ongoing task for anthropologists. One way they do this is by devising classification systems. The basic idea is to define a prototype for each form and then to sort known societies by their resemblance to these prototypes. Such exercises are useful not only when they seem successful but also when they fail. The sections that follow examine some common classifications of forms of human society. They point out both the commonalities those classifications help us to see and the differences they help to obscure.

Income from the sale of textiles enables Otavalan weavers to maintain a degree of control over their own way of life. Some have adapted designs from the Dutch artist M. C. Escher for use in their textiles because they sell well to tourists.

Evolutionary Typologies: The Nineteenth Century

A prototype reflects the features that its creator believes to be most significant. As a result, different assessments of what is significant in a set of phenomena can lead to different prototypes. In the early years of anthropology, most Westerners who compared non-Western societies with their own were struck by certain features that set apart the world of the conquering white man from the various worlds of the conquered people of color. These differences were often stated as *deficiencies* on the part of the non-Western society: lack of a state, lack of sophisticated technology, lack of organized religion, and so forth. Perhaps without realizing it, observers took Western industrial capitalist society as the prototype of all human society. Having done this, they often assumed that the alleged defects of non-Western societies were too obvious to require comment.

This approach to cultural differences was persuasive, particularly in the nineteenth century. It spoke directly to the cross-cultural experience that Western nations were having with the non-Western peoples they had colonized or with whom they traded. A colonial ruler eager to establish a smoothly working administration in New Spain, or the operator of a trading post anxious to make maximum profits in the fur trade, would be most aware of the facets of a people's life that kept him from reaching his goals.

How do you successfully collect taxes in a colony that has poor roads, lacks government officials who can read and write, and is populated by subjects who do not speak your language? How do you "pay" for beaver pelts when the "sellers" are not interested in money? Or how do you ensure a steady supply and motivate your trading partners to stay with you, rather than the competition, in the absence of strong government and strong armies? Europeans faced with such practical problems were bound to see life outside Europe in terms of a series of deficiencies, compared with what they could count on in the home country.

Observers of a more philosophical nature, too, were bound to wonder why there should be such lacks in societies outside Western Europe (or in the more provincial areas of Europe outside the capital cities). Although their research usually never took them outside their libraries, they studied the reports of travelers and missionaries, as well as history. They learned that many of the social and technological patterns they took for granted had not always existed, even in the West. They became aware of the "advances" that had occurred, and were continuing, in all areas of European social life since the Middle Ages.

It seemed clear that their ancestors too had once lacked the tools and ideas and social forms that made them powerful today. If they went back far enough, perhaps they would discover that even more distant ancestors of the Europeans had lived much as many peoples of America or Africa were living today. Writers such as Julius Caesar, who had visited ancient Europe, painted a picture of indigenous life there that resembled the contemporary customs of native Americans and Africans. As archaeology developed, particularly in the nineteenth century, researchers could supplement written records with ancient artifacts presumably made by the primitive ancestors of modern Europeans.

Unilineal Cultural Evolutionism

For many nineteenth-century thinkers, the experience of social change together with historical and archaeological evidence of past social change, was suggestive. Perhaps the ways of life of the non-Western peoples they were reading about were similar to, and even repeats of, the ways of life of European generations long past. That is, perhaps the West had already moved through periods of history in which ways of life had been the same as those of contemporary non-Western societies. According to these scholars, if non-Western societies were left to themselves and given enough time, they would make the same discoveries and change socially the same way that Western Europe had.

This way of thinking about social and cultural change has been called **unilineal cultural evolutionism**. It reached its most elaborate development in the nineteenth century, when evolutionary ideas were popular in all areas of Western thought. Unilineal cultural evolutionism was one way to explain the widespread cultural diversity that Europeans had been finding since the Age of Discovery. It proposed to account for this diversity by arguing that the different kinds of society existing in the present day were not randomly different. In fact, they represented different *stages* of societal evolution through which every human society either had passed or would pass, if it survived. Unilineal cultural evolutionists saw their own world as the summit of evolution. For them, late-nineteenth-century European capitalist industrial society was the most advanced stage of cultural evolution yet. Societies that had not already reached this level had somehow gotten stuck at a more primitive stage that the West had already successfully left behind. These more primitive societies were living relics of what was, in Europe, a dead past.

Today, anthropologists find this approach to the classification of forms of human society to be inadequate if not totally misleading in most respects. Nevertheless, it is a powerful scheme, and its continuing popularity among ordinary members of Western societies is not difficult to understand: it offers a coherent framework for classifying all the societies of the world.

Unilineal cultural evolutionism gave scholars the tools to organize different types of living societies into a sequence based on the discoveries of history and archaeology. For example, contemporary groups who made a living by gathering, hunting, and fishing were assumed to represent the way of life that had once existed universally, before farming and herding were invented. By the nineteenth century, however, it was clear that agriculture and animal husbandry had been invented only a few thousand years ago, whereas human beings had been around far longer than that. Researchers concluded that contemporary foragers had somehow gotten stuck in the earliest stage of human cultural development, while other societies had managed to move upward by domesticating plants and animals. Putting societies in this kind of order was, to a great extent, based on educated guessing. Appropriate historical texts were not always available or reliable, and archaeological dating techniques were poorly developed.

Many of the non-Western groups with which nineteenth-century Europeans and Americans were familiar did farm or herd for a living. Their societies were usually larger than those of the foragers, and technologically more complex. For example, in addition to having the technology of cultivation and the tools to go with it, farmers usually also built permanent structures and made objects, such as pottery and woven cloth, that were unknown among foragers. Their social patterns too were often more complex. They developed elaborate kinship terminologies and strong lineage organization. These peoples clearly seemed to be a rung above the foragers. But they were also very different from Europeans. In most cases they did not have writing. Their societies were not organized in anything that looked at all like a hierarchical political state. For such reasons, this group of societies, midway between the foragers and the society of Europe, were given their own category. They seemed to typify the stage through which gatherers and hunters had to pass—through which Europe's ancestral populations had already passed—before attaining modern "civilization."

In this manner the first important anthropological **typology** of human social forms emerged. It had three basic categories, corresponding to the preceding distinctions. But the labels given these categories indicated more than "objective" dif-

unilineal cultural evolutionism
a nineteenth-century theory that proposed a series of stages through which all societies must pass (or had passed) in order to reach civilization

typology
a classification in which members are related to each other in terms of family resemblance to a prototype

Lewis Henry Morgan (1818–1881)

ferences; they also carried social and moral implications. The foragers—peoples who neither farmed nor herded—were called *Savages*. Groups that had domesticated plants and animals but had not yet invented writing or the state were called *Barbarians*. *Civilization* was limited to the early states of the Mediterranean basin and the Middle East (e.g., Mesopotamia and Egypt), their successors (e.g., Greece and Rome), and certain non-Western societies boasting a similar level of achievement (e.g., India and China). However, the advances that Europe had experienced since antiquity were seen to be unique, unmatched by social changes in other civilizations, which were understood to be in decline. That decline seemed proven when representatives of Western civilization found they could conquer the rulers of such civilizations, as the English did in India.

Unilineal cultural evolution was sweeping and powerful. Yet even its proponents were aware that the simple three-part typology was too crude to capture important differences among members of one category. They also saw that their theory sometimes missed important similarities that linked members of different categories. An early American anthropologist, Lewis Henry Morgan, devoted himself to organizing these similarities and differences. His modifications of the unilineal sequence had great and far-reaching influence.

Morgan's Ethnical Periods

In his book *Ancient Society*, published in 1877, Morgan summarized the basic orientation of unilineal evolutionism: "The latest investigations respecting the early condition of the human race are tending to the conclusion that mankind commenced their career at the bottom of the scale and worked their way up from savagery to civilization through the slow accumulations of experimental knowledge" (Morgan 1877: 3). Morgan described this evolutionary career in terms of a series of stages, or *ethnical periods*, "connected with each other in a natural as well as necessary sequence of progress" (ibid.: 3). The major categories in this sequence, were Savagery, Barbarism, and Civilization. But Morgan felt the need to distinguish additional levels within Savagery and Barbarism, in order better to classify the variety of social forms known in his day. He was fully aware that some human groups might not easily fit into these categories. Hoping that future research would help resolve such ambiguities, however, he concluded that for his purposes "it will be sufficient if the principal tribes of mankind can be classified, according to the degree of their relative progress, into conditions which can be recognized as distinct" (ibid.: 9).

Table 8.1 shows the sequence of ethnical periods suggested by Morgan. Note that, almost without exception, the criteria used to separate one period from another have to do with the invention of techniques for getting food. In some cases, however, the transformation from one stage to the next was not clearly marked by changes in the "arts of subsistence." In these cases, Morgan sought other criteria, such as the invention of pottery or writing, to mark the transition. Later scholars criticized him for these inconsistencies, but he himself was aware of the difficulty. For example, in discussing his choice of the invention of pottery to divide Savagery from Barbarism, Morgan wrote:

> *The invention or practice of the art of pottery, all things considered, is probably the most effective and conclusive test that can be selected to fix a boundary line, necessarily arbitrary, between savagery and barbarism. The distinctness of the two conditions has long been recognized, but no criterion of progress out of the former into the latter has hitherto been*

Table 8.1
Morgan's Ethnical Periods

Period	Begins with
Savagery	
Lower	Origins of human race
Middle	Fishing, knowledge of use of fire
Upper	Invention of bow and arrow
Barbarism	
Lower	Invention of pottery
Middle	Domestication of animals and plants, invention of irrigation, use of adobe brick and stone
Upper	Smelting of iron ore and use of iron tools
Civilization	Invention of phonetic alphabet and use of writing

brought forward. All such tribes, then, as never attained to the art of pottery will be classed as savages, and those possessing this art but who never attained a phonetic alphabet and the use of writing will be classed as barbarians. (Ibid.:10)

This quotation highlights the standard procedure of unilineal evolutionism when faced with ambiguity in the classification of forms of human society. Morgan did not reject evolutionary classification as an invalid enterprise because there is no consistent, unambiguous cultural feature to indicate progress from one stage to another. Quite the contrary; the unilineal scheme is so convincing in making sense of cultural variation that he saw exceptions or inconsistencies as by-products of inadequate data. Surely better research in the future will eliminate them!

This hope is shared by scientists of all kinds who are committed to persuasive theories that cannot resolve every anomaly. It is, indeed, a widespread human hope. World views, like scientific theories in general, cannot explain everything we experience in a totally consistent manner. Yet we usually do not abandon them for that reason. As long as they continue to make sense of our experience, we remain willing to hope that, if only we knew more, the contradictions or inconsistencies we cannot ignore will disappear.

Social Structural Typologies: The British Emphasis

As time passed, scrupulous attention to detail and better information on more societies led anthropologists to become dissatisfied with grand generalizations about cultural diversity and cultural change. This change in perspective was the outcome of improved scholarship and better scientific reasoning, but it was also a consequence of the changes taking place in the world itself.

Origins in the Colonial Setting

As the nineteenth century turned into the twentieth, relationships between the Western and non-Western worlds changed. For one thing, the last quarter of the nineteenth century ushered in the final phase of Western colonialism. The territory of Africa and much of Asia, which until then had remained nominally independent, was divided up among European powers. About the same time, the United States assumed a similarly powerful and dominating role in its relationships with the native people of the United States and with the former colonies of Spain.

These changed political circumstances led to new experiences for representatives of the West in relation to their new subjects. Having assumed control through conquest, colonial rulers sought to establish efficient administrations that would ensure their own well-being and prosperity. Once they were in charge, the conquerors could impose their will politically or militarily; they no longer had to negotiate in order to achieve their aims in local society. Unilineal cultural evolutionism may have justified the global ambitions of Europe and made colonial rule appear inevitable and right. However, it was inadequate for meeting the practical needs of the rulers once they were in power.

Effective administration of subject peoples required accurate information about them. For example, one goal of a colonial administrator in Africa was keeping the peace among the various groups over which he ruled. To do so, he needed to know how those people were accustomed to handling disputes. Most colonies included several societies with various customs about disputes. Administrators had to be aware of the similarities and differences among their subjects in order to develop successful government policies.

At the same time, colonial officials planned to introduce certain elements of European law uniformly throughout the colony. Common examples were commercial laws permitting the buying and selling of land on the open market. They also tried to eliminate practices like witchcraft accusations or local punishment for capital crimes. Reaching these goals without totally disrupting life in the colony required firsthand understanding of local practices. The earlier "armchair anthropology" was wholly incapable of providing that understanding.

These changes in the relationships between the West and the rest of the world encouraged the development of a new kind of anthropological research. Under the colonial "peace," anthropologists found that they could carry out long-term fieldwork. Earlier, the unsettled conditions had made such work difficult. Anthropologists also found that colonial governments would support their research when persuaded that the work was scientific and could contribute to effective colonial rule. This did not mean that anthropologists who carried out fieldwork under colonial conditions supported colonialism. To the contrary, their sympathies often lay with the colonized peoples with whom they worked. For example, Sir E. E. Evans-Pritchard, who worked in central Africa for the British government in the 1920s and 1930s, saw himself as an educator of colonial administrators. He tried to convey to them a persuasive picture of the humanity and rationality of Africans. His goal was to combat the racism and oppression that seemed an inevitable consequence of colonial rule. For just these reasons, colonial officials were often wary of anthropologists and distrustful of their motives. It was all too likely that the results

Sir E. E. Evans-Pritchard (1902–1973)

of anthropological research might make colonial programs look self-serving and exploitative.

Nevertheless, anthropologists working under colonial rule provided a vast amount of detailed, accurate information about aspects of indigenous life that the colonial administration needed to understand. Sometimes, the needs of colonial rulers seem to have shaped the direction of the studies undertaken, particularly among the British. For example, perhaps the most important information to a colonial ruler was accurate data about traditional political arrangements among the conquered people. Colonial bureaucracies were thinly staffed. Colonial officers quickly learned that their task would be easier if they could rely on traditional rulers to keep the peace among their traditional subjects through traditional means. Thus developed the policy of *indirect rule*. The British colonial officials were at the top of the hierarchy. Under them, the traditional rulers (elders, chiefs, etc.) served as intermediaries with the common people.

How could anthropologists contribute to the effectiveness of indirect rule? The information they gathered about a group's traditional political structures helped them suggest the best way to adapt indirect rule to that group. Of course, the advice of anthropologists was not always heeded, for the needs of the mother country often clashed with anthropologically "appropriate" colonial policy.

The work anthropologists did in the colonial setting came to emphasize certain aspects of non-Western social organization and to ignore others. This led, in turn, to new ways of classifying human social forms. The goal of colonial governments was to have the conquered societies contribute more efficiently to the prosperity of the mother country. One way to do this was to restructure the societies they had conquered. And so we see developing, particularly among British anthropologists, a focus on the **social structure**, especially the political structure, of groups under colonial rule. That British anthropologists came to call themselves social anthropologists reflects these developments.

social structure
the enduring aspects of a society's social forms, including its political and kinship systems

In 1940, in a classic work on African political systems, Meyer Fortes and E. E. Evans-Pritchard distinguished between state and stateless societies. Within these two basic categories, they made further distinctions having to do with similarities and differences among various states or among societies that have no state. Note that this basic distinction between state and stateless societies describes many non-Western societies in terms of what they lack. In this, it is similar to unilineal evolutionary classifications. However, there is a significant difference in the social structural classification of Evans-Pritchard and Fortes: it makes no mention of "progress" from "lower" to "higher" forms of society.

Evolutionism had not been decisively refuted by this time. Nevertheless, given the new approach to society that was taking shape, it had become irrelevant. The labels Savagery, Barbarism, and Civilization had not even been officially expunged from the vocabulary of anthropology. For example, Malinowski was quite comfortable referring to the inhabitants of the Trobriand Islands, among whom he had worked, as Savages. But the emphasis on contemporary social structures was bringing rich new insights to anthropology. Questions of evolution and social change took a back seat as social anthropologists concerned themselves with figuring out the enduring traditional structures of the societies in which they worked. A detailed knowledge of social structures was supposed to allow the anthropologist to identify the social type of any particular society. These types were treated as though unchanging. They were compared for similarities and differences, and out of this comparison emerged a new set of prototypes for the classification of social forms.

The Classification of Political Structures

One typical social-structural classification of forms of human society is shown in figure 8.1. Here, the major distinction is between *centralized* political systems and *uncentralized*, or *egalitarian*, political systems. This is like the distinction that Evans-Pritchard and Fortes made between state societies and stateless societies. Only the labels have been changed, perhaps so that societies without states could be marked in a positive fashion, rather than in terms of what they lack. Still, uncentralized systems have no distinct, permanent institution exclusively concerned with public decision making. This is another way of saying that groups (and perhaps even individuals) within egalitarian systems enjoy relative autonomy and equal status and are not answerable to any higher authority.

In this scheme, egalitarian political systems can be further subdivided into two types. **Bands** are small social groupings whose members, like Morgan's Savages, neither farm nor herd, but depend on wild food sources. **Tribes** are groups that, like Morgan's Barbarians, lie between bands on the one hand and centralized political systems on the other. Tribes are larger than bands and have domesticated plants and animals, but their political organization remains egalitarian and un-

band
a term used by political anthropologists to refer to a small, egalitarian social grouping whose members neither farm nor herd, but depend on wild food resources

tribe
a term used by political anthropologists to refer to an egalitarian society larger than a band, whose members raise domesticated plants or animals

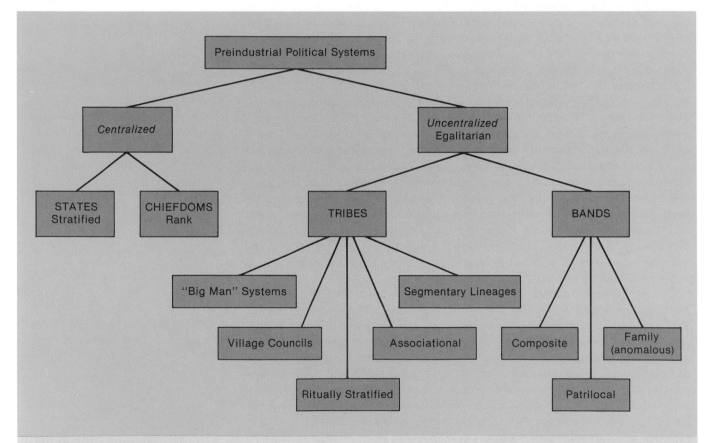

FIGURE 8.1
A Typical Classification of Forms of Human Society
Source: From *Political Anthropology* by Ted Lewellen. Copyright © 1983 Ted Lewellen. Reprinted by permission of Bergin & Garvey, Inc.

centralized. Ted Lewellen refers to three subtypes of band, including a catchall category, the *family band*, which includes "anomalous" cases that do not fit into the other two subtypes. He also identifies five subtypes of tribe, but comments that they hardly exhaust the variety of social arrangements that tribes display (Lewellen 1983:26).

Centralized political systems are different from egalitarian systems because they have a central, institutionalized focus of authority such as a chief or a king. These systems also involve hierarchy; that is, some members of centralized societies have greater prestige, power, or wealth than do other members. Centralized systems are divided into two types: chiefdoms and states. In **chiefdoms** the differences among people have to do mainly with prestige ranking. In **states**, differences in wealth and power also appear. Because some groups in a state monopolize wealth, power, and prestige, whereas other groups have highly restricted access to these values, we speak of the presence of *social stratification*.

Lewellen's typology does not attempt to make any hypotheses about evolutionary relationships. Tracing change over time is not its purpose; time has no place in such a typology. Instead, the focus is on social structural differences and similarities observed at one point in time: the here and now. This is not accidental. Remember that classifications like Lewellen's originated in response to practical needs, originally those of the colonial administrators. Colonial rulers assumed that they were "civilized" and that their colonial subjects were "primitive," and they cared little about such matters as the origin of the state. The pressing questions for them were more likely "How do *African* states work *today*?" "What do we need to know about them to make them work *for us*?"

Nevertheless, an atemporal typology can be converted into an evolutionary one with little difficulty. If you compare table 8.2 with table 8.1 (Morgan's ethnical periods), you will notice a rough correlation between bands and Savagery; between tribes and Lower and Middle Barbarism; between chiefdoms and Upper Barbarism; and between states and Civilization. However, Lewellen's classification in table 8.2 includes additional detail that was unknown in Morgan's day.

chiefdom
a term used by political anthropologists to refer to a rank society with minimal stratification

state
a term used by political anthropologists to refer to hierarchical, stratified societies in which some groups monopolize wealth, power, and prestige

Structural-Functional Theory

British social anthropologists did not spend all their intellectual energy on the practical concerns of colonial officials, but their theoretical work was still affected by those concerns. Their theories dealt increasingly with how particular social forms *functioned* from day to day in order to reproduce their traditional *structures*. Such **structural-functional theory** was perhaps most highly developed in the work of A. R. Radcliffe-Brown, whose major theoretical work was done in the 1930s and 1940s.

In this way, social anthropology began to ask why things stayed the same, rather than why they changed. Why do some social structures last for centuries (e.g., the Roman Catholic church) and others disappear quickly (e.g., the utopian communities of nineteenth-century America)? Why did some societies abandon foraging for agriculture thousands of years ago, while others were still gathering and hunting in the twentieth century? Both sets of questions are equally puzzling. However, an emphasis on social stability tends to downplay or ignore questions of change, just as an emphasis on social change tends to downplay or ignore questions of stability.

This new focus in British social anthropology, which is still with us today, has produced a succession of nonevolutionary classifications of human social forms.

structural-functional theory
a perspective, most highly developed in the 1930s and 1940s, that dealt with how particular social forms functioned from day to day in order to reproduce the traditional structure of the society

Table 8.2
Preindustrial Political Systems: An Evolutionary Typology

	Uncentralized		Centralized	
	Band	*Tribe*	*Chiefdom*	*State*
Type of Subsistence	Hunting-gathering; little or no domestication	Extensive agriculture (horticulture) and pastoralism	Extensive agriculture; intensive fishing	Intensive agriculture
Type of Leadership	Informal and situational leaders; may have a headman who acts as arbiter in group decision-making	Charismatic headman with no "power" but some authority in group decision-making	Charismatic chief with limited power based on bestowal of benefits on followers	Sovereign leader supported by an aristocratic bureaucracy
Type and Importance of Kinship	Bilateral kinship, with kin relations used differentially in changing size and composition of bands	Unilineal kinship (patrilineal or matrilineal) may form the basic structure of society	Unilineal, with some bilateral; descent groups are ranked in status	State demands suprakinship loyalties; access to power is based on ranked kin groups, either unilineal or bilateral
Major Means of Social Integration	Marriage alliances unite larger groups; bands united by kinship and family; economic interdependence based on reciprocity	Pantribal sodalities based on kinship, voluntary associations, and/or age-grades	Integration through loyalty to chief, ranked lineages, and voluntary associations	State loyalties supersede all lower-level loyalties; integration through commerce and specialization of function
Political Succession	May be hereditary headman, but actual leadership falls to those with special knowledge or abilities	No formal means of political succession	Chief's position not directly inherited, but chief must come from a high-ranking lineage	Direct hereditary succession of sovereign; increasing appointment of bureaucratic functionaries
Major Types of Economic Exchange	Reciprocity (sharing)	Reciprocity; trade may be more developed than in bands	Redistribution through chief; reciprocity at lower levels	Redistribution based on formal tribute and/or taxation; markets and trade
Social Stratification	Egalitarian	Egalitarian	Rank (individual and lineage)	Classes (minimally of rulers and ruled)
Ownership of Property	Little or no sense of personal ownership	Communal (lineage or clan) ownership of agricultural lands and cattle	Land communally owned by lineage, but strong sense of personal ownership of titles, names, privileges, ritual artifacts, etc.	Private and state ownership increases at the expense of communal ownership

Table 8.2
Preindustrial Political Systems: An Evolutionary Typology

	Uncentralized		Centralized	
	Band	*Tribe*	*Chiefdom*	*State*
Law and Legitimate Control of Force	No formal laws or punishments; right to use force is communal	No formal laws or punishments; right to use force belongs to lineage, clan, or association	May be informal laws and specified punishments for breaking taboos; chief has limited access to physical coercion	Formal laws and punishments; state holds all legitimate access to use of physical force
Religion	No religious priesthood or full-time specialists; shamanistic	Shamanistic; strong emphasis on initiation rites and other rites of passage that unite lineages	Inchoate formal priesthood, hierarchical, ancestor-based religion	Full-time priesthood provides sacral legitimization of state
Recent and Contemporary Examples	!Kung Bushmen (Africa), Pygmies (Africa), Eskimo (Canada, Alaska), and Shoshone (U.S.)	Kpelle (W. Africa), Yanomamo (Venezuela), Nuer (Sudan), and Cheyenne (U.S.)	Precolonial Hawaii, Kwakiutl (Canada), Tikopia (Polynesia), and Dagurs (Mongolia)	Ankole (Uganda), Jimma (Ethiopia), Kachari (India), and Volta (Africa)
Historic and Prehistoric Examples	Virtually all paleolithic societies	Iroquois (U.S.) and Oaxaca Valley (Mexico), 1500–1000 B.C.	Precolonial Ashanti, Benin, Dahomy (Africa), and Scottish Highlanders	Precolonial Zulu (Africa), Aztec (Mexico), Inca (Peru), and Sumeria (Iraq)

Source: From *Political Anthropology* by Ted Lewellen. Copyright © 1983 Ted Lewellen. Reprinted by permission of Bergin & Garvey, Inc.

As data on more and more varieties of social structure grow, however, these typologies seem to overflow with more and more subtypes. It is not surprising that some anthropologists have begun to question the point of it all. In this, they are like the earlier generation that questioned the point of creating increasingly elaborate and unwieldy unilineal evolutionary schemes.

Doing without Typologies: Culture Area Studies in America

Anthropologists in the United States began to voice dissatisfaction with unilineal evolutionism at about the same time their British colleagues began to do so, and for similar reasons. The most important figure in this movement was Franz Boas, the man usually referred to as the father of American anthropology. Boas and his students worked primarily among the native American populations of North America. They began to collect more and better data about those societies, especially data relating to the histories of individual groups. Change over time had not progressed through uniform stages for all those societies. For example, two societies with similar forms of social organization might have arrived at that status through different historical routes, one through a process of simplification, the other through a process of elaboration.

Boas emphasized that new forms of social life seemed to be more often *borrowed* from neighboring societies than invented. He and his followers were quick to note that if cultural borrowing, rather than independent invention, played an important role in culture change, then any unilineal evolutionary scheme was doomed. Focusing on cultural borrowing as a major source of culture change also emphasized the links between different societies that made such borrowing possible.

The view of society that developed in the United States was therefore quite different from the one taking shape in Great Britain at the same time. American anthropologists no longer saw societies as isolated representatives of universal stages, closed to outside influences, responsible on their own for progressing or failing to progress. This had been the evolutionists' view. But neither did they see societies as bounded, atemporal social types that could be classified in a social structural matrix. Instead, Boas and his followers saw social groups as fundamentally *open* to the outside world. If they changed over time, this was more the result of idiosyncratic borrowing from neighbors than of inevitable, law-governed, self-generated progress.

The whole idea of "progress" ceased to be of interest in the study of social change. Unlike the British, American anthropologists did not abandon an interest in change. Their approach to it, however, differed significantly from that of the unilineal evolutionists. They assumed that cultural change was due more to borrowing than to independent invention. If this were so, then a student of culture change should focus on patterns of cultural borrowing through time. This is exactly what Boas's followers did. The result was the development of *cultural area studies*. Anthropologists interested in this developed lists of **cultural traits**, or features, characteristic of a particular social group. They focused on only part of a society's culture, part of its heritage or customs: a particular ritual, a musical style, a way of making pots. Then then searched the ethnographic record carefully to determine how widely those cultural traits had spread into other societies. A **culture area** was defined by the limits of borrowing, or the diffusion, of a particular trait or set of traits.

This emphasis in anthropological research had consequences for typologies of social forms. If borrowing allowed societies to skip evolutionary stages entirely, then any classification of universal stages was meaningless. Furthermore, even timeless classificatory schemes, like those of the social anthropologists, were of little value. They depended on the assumption that societies were airtight entities with clear-cut social structures. But what if societies are not closed, but are perpetually open to cultural borrowing? It is then impossible to describe their structures in clear-cut terms. And indeed, the efforts of American anthropologists turned away from placing whole societies in categories and toward identifying culture traits and their regions of diffusion. Area studies aimed at classification, but at levels both above and below the level of a society itself. The end product was a list of traits and a map of cultural areas in which the traits are found. Boundaries around particular societies were ignored.

culture traits

features or parts of a cultural tradition; for example, dances or rituals

culture area

the limits of the diffusion of a particular cultural trait or set of traits

Postwar Realities

Then the world changed again. World War II was closely followed by the breakup of European colonial empires in Africa and Asia, and by the civil rights movement in the United States. Former colonies were now independent states. Their citizens rejected the traditional Western view of them as savages or barbarians. They intended to prove that they could govern their countries in a manner as "civilized" as that of Western nations.

Political realities thus created for Westerners new experiences of the non-Western "other." These experiences made the pretensions of unilineal evolutionism even less plausible. As well, the leaders of the new states set out to consolidate *national* consciousness among the supposedly structurally separate societies within their borders. This effort made the structural focus of preindependence social anthropologists seem increasingly misguided. Such efforts at nation building led some Western anthropologists to recognize that the "traditional" societies they had been studying had not, in fact, been structurally separate even under colonialism. The experience of decolonization forced anthropologists to pay direct attention to colonialism itself. They began to see it as a form of social organization that had essentially eliminated the autonomy of indigenous social groups and forcibly restructured them into subordinate positions within a larger social, political, and economic entity.

At the same time, anthropologists with roots in the non-Western world began to add their voices to those of Western anthropologists. They were and continue to be highly critical of the cultural stereotypes institutionalized by unilineal evolutionism and structural-functionalism. As a result, rankings of human social forms that seemed clear-cut and persuasive in the late nineteenth and early twentieth centuries appear blurred and questionable today. But this does not mean that typologies have disappeared altogether in contemporary cultural and social anthropology. The problem posed for the analyst by cultural diversity has not disappeared. Most anthropologists, for some purposes, still need to classify the known societies of the world in one way or another, depending on the problems they are investigating.

Studying Forms of Human Society Today

It is probably fair to say that the field of anthropology as a whole is not committed to classification as an ultimate goal. In fact, among anthropologists themselves, opinions about the importance of classifying forms of human society vary greatly. Some anthropologists, especially those interested in political and economic issues, continue to find typologies useful. Others—for example, those studying art or religion—are not much concerned with the classification of the society in which they work. More important to them are similarities that overlap cultural boundaries.

Modern anthropologists have not found universally accepted answers to the seemingly unanswerable questions of social origins, social stability, and social change. But many have come to see the similarities and differences between the West and the rest of the world in terms of "more or less" rather than "present or absent." As a result, many modern anthropologists are no longer interested in whether a society is organized on the basis of "primitive" kinship or "civilized" social class. More striking is that both kinship and class can be understood as culturally constructed idioms for organizing people and for thinking about the nature of human nature and human society.

This does not mean that the choice of a kinship idiom as opposed to a class idiom makes no difference or is without historical or cultural motivation. Many anthropologists would insist that a shift from organization by kinship to organization by class marks an important watershed in social organization. They would argue that the differences generated by this divide far outweigh any similarities that remain. Still, most anthropologists would agree that an emphasis on similarities or differences in different types of society is closely related to the *questions* anthropologists are investigating and the *theoretical assumptions* they bring with them to their research. Different schools of anthropology, not to mention different social sciences, have different professional "world views" that define for them what is worth paying attention to and what is safe to ignore. What remain are the phenomena to be classified.

Let us turn again to Lewellen's classification of social types. How meaningful is it? What does it reflect? Lewellen argues that it is designed to reflect structural, organizational similarities and differences. To defend such criteria, he employs a house metaphor:

> *Two houses built of different materials but to the same floor plan will obviously be much more alike than two houses of the same materials but very different designs (say, a town house and a ranch house). . . . In short, a house is defined in terms of its organization, not its components, and that organization will be influenced by its physical environment and the level of technology of the people who designed it. (Lewellen 1983 : 17)*

Based on the discussion of the role of structure in the social typologies of British social anthropology, you may recognize the argument Lewellen is making. Lewellen seems to be affiliated with this tradition, as he assumes that structural similarities and differences are both supremely significant and objectively obvious. Similarities and differences concerning the materials out of which the houses are made can safely be ignored. We take a contrary position. Structural similarities and differences are "obviously" supremely significant *only* if classification is approached with a previous set of assumptions concerning what is important and what is not.

"A house is defined in terms of its organization, not its components." For certain purposes, and for certain observers, this may be true. But *organization* is a subjective term. Is a house's organization manifested in its floor plan or in the way the various rooms are used regardless of floor plan? Is a bedroom "objectively" a bedroom wherever it occurs, whether in a town house or a ranch house? Is a bedroom still a bedroom, whether in town house or ranch house, when the people living in that house use it to store equipment or to cook in? Is an American living room still a living room, in any objective sense, when its primary role is to provide sleeping space for an extended family of Southeast Asian immigrants? Does that immigrant family's ideas of how living space should properly be used change when the family moves from a thatched hut to an apartment with wooden floors and plaster walls?

Structural similarities and differences that seem obvious to many political anthropologists in the British tradition lead those anthropologists to set off states and chiefdoms sharply from tribes and bands. Would these similarities and differences seem so sharp to an anthropologist interested in classifying the ways different societies make a living? As we shall see in a later chapter, anthropologists interested in making such a classification employ concepts like "subsistence strategy" or "mode of production" to order their typologies. These concepts focus on what has been called the "material life process of society." These are the strategies and technologies for organizing the production, distribution, and consumption of food, clothing, housing, tools, and other material goods. They therefore define a domain of relevance that may be quite different from that of interest to political anthropologists. Not surprisingly, they yield different typologies.

This room was built as a bedroom, was turned into a kitchen, was again used as a bedroom (while still housing cabinets and a sink), and is now a sewing room/storeroom.

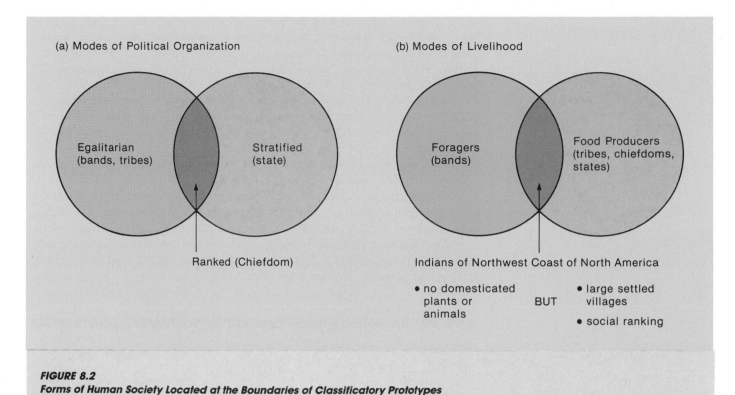

(a) Modes of Political Organization

Egalitarian
(bands, tribes)

Stratified
(state)

Ranked (Chiefdom)

(b) Modes of Livelihood

Foragers
(bands)

Food Producers
(tribes, chiefdoms,
states)

Indians of Northwest Coast of North America

- no domesticated
  plants or
  animals

BUT

- large settled
  villages
- social ranking

FIGURE 8.2
Forms of Human Society Located at the Boundaries of Classificatory Prototypes

Here is one example. It is possible to preserve the fourfold distinction among states, chiefdoms, tribes, and bands and yet to group them differently. This can be done by focusing on the subsistence strategies that each category of society typically employs. Bands depend on foraging—gathering, fishing, hunting—to meet subsistence needs. Tribes, chiefdoms, and states depend on food production—cultivation of plants, herding of animals—to meet these same needs. On this basis, bands can be set off from tribes, chiefdoms, and states. Thus, in terms of egalitarian political organization, tribes and bands may resemble one another (see figure 8.2[a]), but their subsistence strategies may divide them sharply. Tribes depend on domesticated plants and animals, and bands do not (see figure 8.2[b]). Neither set of similarities and differences is objectively more obvious than the other. Both depend on prior choice of a problem for research as well as prior assumptions, made by the researchers, concerning what is worth paying attention to and what can be safely downplayed or ignored.

The situation is even more complicated. Many social typologists are confident about separating bands from tribes, chiefdoms, and states. They do this because, in an overwhelming number of ethnographic cases, a foraging subsistence strategy is not found together with developed lineages or social ranking or settled villages. But there are troublesome exceptions to this pattern, notably among the various societies of the northwest coast of North America (see figure 8.2[b]). Such groups as the Tlingit and Kwakiutl neither farmed nor herded (they fished, hunted, and gathered), but they created complex, settled societies with developed lineages and social ranking. These features are more characteristic of tribes or chiefdoms than of bands.

Lewellen acknowledges the problems these societies pose for any political typology: "Indian societies of the Northwest Coast of North America are usually categorized as chiefdoms . . . but the fit is far from perfect. . . . Perhaps all the cultures of the Northwest Coast would seem to represent a blending of elements of both tribes and chiefdoms" (1983:33–34).

It is also possible that the existence of such societies reveals the limits of a particular typology. They might represent an authentic social form in their own right, one that the prototypes of traditional classification systems are unable to characterize unambiguously. Such societies fall *between* the categories of a classification. They can remind us that typologies are human cultural constructions, not pure reflections of objective reality.

Given this perspective, we examine in the following chapters those areas of anthropological research where the use of typologies is still important. These areas are kinship and social organization, politics, and economics. We will highlight the useful insights that result from adopting one or another typology to guide research. We will also point out the areas of social and cultural life that tend to be ignored when a particular classification is adopted.

Key Terms

unilineal cultural evolutionism	chiefdoms
typology	state societies
colonialism	structural-functional theory
social structure	culture traits
band	culture area
tribal society	

Chapter Summary

1. Cultural traditions take shape as a result of the dialectic between human imagination and the material world. Forms of human society are shaped by both the nonhuman natural environment and the human social environment (i.e. the presence of neighboring societies).

2. The imperialist expansion of Europe, which coincided with the rise of industrial capitalism, was the central force leading to cross-cultural contact between the West and the rest of the world. Many of the so-called tribes or peoples whom anthropologists later would study are relatively recent creations, forged in the field of contact between indigenous populations and Europeans.

3. An anthropological survey of the forms of human society needs to investigate the circumstances surrounding the contacts between anthropolgists and their informants. These circumstances have historical dimensions: there is no such thing as pre-contact ethnography.

4. Non-Western societies have not escaped the historical forces that have influenced everyone else. Yet remnants of precontact societies survive today, showing that conquered peoples can actively cope with contemporary problems and opportunities to reshape their own social identities. An impressive variety of forms of human society remains despite the Western onslaught.

5. Anthropologists attempting to classify societies come up with prototypes and then classify societies on the basis of their resemblance to those prototypes. Depending upon an anthropologist's analytical purposes, the same social forms can be classified in different ways.

6. The earliest important anthropological *typology* of forms of human society was that proposed by *unilineal cultural evolutionists*. They tried to explain contemporary cultural diversity by arguing that different kinds of society existing in the nineteenth century represented different stages of societal evolution. Every human society either had passed or would pass through the same stages, if it survived. Societies more primitive than Europe were viewed as living relics of the past. This typology contained three basic categories: Savagery, Barbarism, and Civilization.

7. Anthropologists doing research in a *colonial* setting in the first half of the twentieth century collected a vast amount of detailed, accurate information about aspects of indigenous life, which the colonial administration needed to understand. Their research led them to set aside questions about cultural evolution. The new focus was on *social structural* differences and similarities observed at a single point in time.

8. In American anthropology, the classification of forms of human society was ignored almost totally in the early part of the twentieth century. Following Boas, American anthropologists rejected unilineal cultural evolutionism on the grounds that societies could easily borrow cultural forms from one another, thus skipping stages. The aim of research thus became to make lists of *culture traits* and to map the *culture areas* in which they were found. Culture traits and culture areas became the focus of attention, and particular societies were of less interest.

9. Classifying forms of human society is not an ultimate goal for most anthropologists today, although some anthropologists find typologies useful. Classications differ, depending upon the problems to be solved. Thus, societies grouped together because of similarities in political organization may be separated from one another because of differences in subsistence strategies. The fuzziness of category boundaries reminds us that taxonomies are human cultural constructions, not pure reflections of objective reality.

Suggested Readings

Lewellen, Ted. *Political Anthropology*. South Hadley, Mass.: Bergin and Garvey, 1983.

    Contains much useful information about the different kinds of societies that different scholars have identified.

Wolf, Eric. *Europe and the People without History*. Berkeley: University of California Press, 1982.

    An important book on the connection of European expansion to the rest of the world. This work contains discussions of the effect that European contact had on indigenous societies.

Into the Warp and Woof of Multicultural Worlds

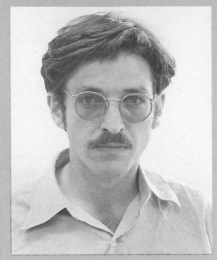

George Marcus (Ph.D., Harvard University) is Professor of Anthropology at Rice University. He has done fieldwork in Oceania (Tonga, in particular), Texas and California. He has written and edited a number of books in anthropological theory, and is the founding editor of Cultural Anthropology, *the Journal of the Society for Cultural Anthropology. He is involved in exploring the nature of anthropological writing about other cultures and the expression and construction of elite cultures in the United States.*

An enduring and powerful rationale for the research anthropologists do is that of capturing the distinctiveness and a sense of the fulness of other cultural worlds that are on the wane. Salvaging the systemic wholeness of other forms of human life, other cosmologies, on the precipice of irreversible change through contact with the West, or else demonstrating the resilience and integrity of such cultural systems even through such change, has been the primary way

ethnographers have positioned themselves in the flow of history. Anthropologists have never been naive that, from the very origins of their subject, they have undertaken their research upriver, over the mountains, or on the atoll beyond—"where they still do it"—in the larger context of lands transformed by Western colonialism. Yet, still, they have been most effective in describing cultural difference, *as if* it were whole, integral, systematic, even long after the peoples studied have been integrated into national states and market economies.

The power of global cultural homogenization in the late twentieth century challenges the conventions and rationales by which anthropology has so far produced its knowledge of other cultures. The reorganization of the world economy through technological advances in communication, production processes, and marketing has thoroughly deterritorialized culture. For example, the Tongan islanders of Polynesia that I studied in the early 1970s now constitute a diaspora of communities in locales around the Pacific rim. As many, if not more, Tongans now live permanently in Australia, New Zealand, and the United States as in the islands themselves. One might fairly ponder where both the cultural and geographical center of the Tongan people resides. Their identity is produced in many locales and through the mix of many cultural elements. And their conditions are similar to those of numerous other peoples that anthropologists have traditionally studied. It is no longer just the most powerful, large-scale, and most modern societies, such as the United States and Japan, that exist in international, transcultural science.

Among such transcultural "traditional" peoples, levels of cultural self-consciousness and alternatives increase. The authenticity of performances, rituals, or apparently deep seated norms like those of kinship cannot be merely assumed, either by locals or by visitors such as anthropologists. To some extent, media documentaries have absorbed anthropology's function of presenting vividly the lifeways of other cultures to Euro-American publics that themselves can no longer be considered as homogeneous or mainstream. And, finally, the subjects of anthropological study independently and articulately translate their own perspectives with sensitivity to the effects of different media.

Peoples who in particular have become classic anthropological subjects, such as the Samoans, Trobriand Islanders, Hopi, and Todas of India, know their status well, and have, with some ambivalence, assimilated anthropological knowledge about them as part of their sense of themselves. A recent example was the visit of a Toda woman to Houston. A trained nurse among her people as well as a cultural broker, she was on tour in the United States, giving talks about the Todas, of the sort that anthropologists might have given in past decades. By chance, she was visiting the home of a colleague just as a British documentary about the Todas appeared on the television—a documentary in which the visitor was featured prominently as the filmmaker's prime source of information. The visitor's comments as she watched the program along with my colleague did not much concern the details of Toda culture, but rather dealt with the ironies of the multiple representations of her people—by herself, by anthropologists, and by the British Broadcasting Corporation.

The lesson of this story is compelling. The penetrations of a world economy, communications, and the effects of multiple, fragmented identities on cultural authenticity, once thought restricted to advanced modernity, have increased markedly among most local and regional cultures worldwide. They have thus engendered an ethnography in reverse among many peoples who not only can assimilate the professional idioms of anthropology but can relativize them among other alternatives and ways of knowledge. This does not mean that the traditional task of anthropology to represent distinctive and systematic cultural forms of life has been fundamentally subverted by its own subjects. Rather, anthropology's traditional task is now much more complicated, requiring new sensibilities in undertaking fieldwork and different strategies for writing about it.

To find the centers of gravity by which cultural difference can be described cogently on a globe—which the ethnographic map constructed through ages of exploration, colonization, and westernization is transforming—becomes the great contemporary challenge for anthropology. For example, a renewal of interest has emerged among anthropologists in the ways different peoples conceive of the self and the person—what constitutes a self emotionally and cognitively, and what a person is capable of in social relations.

The shared cosmologies that organized daily life among many peoples have now become attenuated, fragmented, and mutually interpenetrated by a pervasive global culture of modernity. Nevertheless,

the study of how a people conceive of personal experience and orient themselves to social life *anywhere* might reveal the most distinctive and profound level at which cultures can be described. Even if, say, Tongans, Iranians, Indians, and Papuans participate in certain global institutions as workers, consumers, bureaucrats, scientists, and so on, they do so distinctively. The key to making such distinctions clear and cogent is to explain enduring assumptions about personhood, self, and experience. Certain topics, especially those that concern the body and the life cycle, become particularly important in probing these deepest and most enduring levels of cultural distinction. This is where one set of bets has been placed, so to speak, in contemporary anthropological research to find one center of gravity for cultural description. However, if it is supposed that the old ethnographic map of distinct peoples survives purely and essentially even at the site of cultural conceptions of the self and personhood, the following parable suggests this is a questionable notion.

At a recent conference at the East-West Center in Hawaii on cross-cultural ideas of the self—one of many such gatherings occurring nowadays—nine of us anthropologists sat around the table in the presence of a small but culturally diverse audience of Asians, Pacific Islanders, and Americans. During one session, the discussion turned on different concepts of mind and emotion by which experience is understood in the United States and Japan. One participant, seeking to add a different frame of comparison, addressed a man in the audience who had earlier been identified as Balinese. The anthropologist noted

that he had been told by a colleague that the Balinese don't distinguish feeling and thinking as concepts. He then asked the Balinese attending whether he or his people make such a distinction. Suddenly, we had been transported into a fieldwork situation—the anthropologist seeking general information from the native informant as representative of his culture. The Balinese was startled at being addressed. Shy, but cooperative, he answered ambiguously: certainly there were different words for mind and heart (he pointed to his head and chest), but his response was unclear as to whether he or Balinese generally merged or distinguished these terms conceptually.

The situational and cognitive reasons why this person could not reply clearly to the question are interesting to contemplate. However, the point to note here is that while the anthropologist readily saw the Balinese as an access to his culture, the Balinese had difficulty conceiving himself in the same terms. After the session, I chatted with him, finding that he was a dancer, and that he had not been in Bali for twelve years. In the meantime, he had participated in experimental dance theater in New York, as well as in Europe and Hawaii. His ideas about the relationship between feeling and thought were as much informed by his experiences as a dancer abroad as by being Balinese. Thus, what is it to study this person's self-concept? Clearly, the standard anthropological frame for so doing, which sharply distances him from us in the West, is inadequate, as the incident of "fieldwork" within our conference suggests. This person does not represent a cultural system, integral unto itself, called Bali. His experiences are complexly intercultural and global, and so were those of the other Asians in the room. And to some degree, one might surmise, so are those of the Balinese in contemporary Bali.

So, the focus on the self is indeed a useful vantage point to explore how distinctive cultural difference is constituted in the contemporary world. Yet, difference does not represent the enduring rootedness of cultures in place, but rather emerges from the combinations of personal and collective experiences of cultures subject to unprecedented mobility and fragmentation. Thus, as evoked by the apparent Balinese "person" present at our conference, cultural diversity in the late twentieth century is generated by the very possibilities engendered by forces promoting global homogenization. Furthermore, this diversity is much less known and understood than our existing ethnographic archive of territorial cultures would lead us to expect.

To see the pervasiveness of multicultural worlds and experiences among the traditional subjects of anthropology, as well as among the observing and recording anthropologists themselves, requires a different set of lenses. The consequent revision of the nineteenth- and early-twentieth-century ethnographic maps of the world by which knowledge of cultures has thus far been produced is the clear and present task of anthropology. This revision is necessary for sustaining anthropology's very traditional purpose of promoting an understanding of and respect for culturally generated variety. It is also needed to help us understand and respect anthropology's historic effects on human affairs, as they develop in the multitude of places among which anthropologists continue to explore and establish connections.

George E. Marcus

CHAPTER 9
Kinship

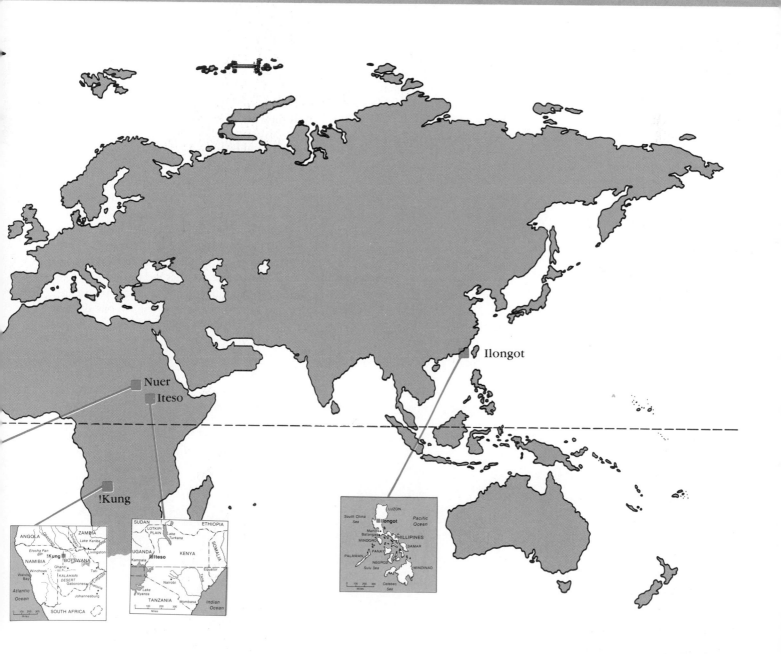

Nuer

Iteso

Ilongot

!Kung

Darcy Ribeiro is a distinguished Brazilian anthropologist, diplomat, and novelist. One of his novels, Maíra, is set among the Mairun, a fictional Amazonian Indian people. A leading character, who is a Mairun, has studied in a Catholic seminary in Rome. On his way back to the village take up his position as headman, he remembers the way social life was traditionally patterned in his village:

"But it is in the village, in its shape and its organization, where the duality of our spirit expresses itself more completely. First in the two bands: the one over there, of my brothers-in-law, and the one here of my sisters. These bands exist in space and can be seen. They are the Rising Sun and the Setting Sun, when one is looking from the Great House of Men. But they also exist inside us. Every Mairun, upon meeting another, knows at once if the Mairun is from here or there, if that Mairun can be copulated with or is tabooed, is a brother or a brother-in-law. By day or by night, wherever we are found, our tendency as Mairuns is to arrange ourselves in space in the same way that we live in the village.

"But a person from over there is not a stranger. No, a person from over there has nothing in common with this feeling of mine that here I am only a Mairun, that I am marginal, that I am lost and alone in this alien world. As to the Mairuns of all the bands and families, I am of them. And they are with me so as to form together a powerful we that protects everyone.

"It is true that I and my Jaguar people form a small, exclusive we. But we are weak, incomplete, and aware that we exist, in fact, within the oneness of the other 'wes,' all relatives. When I think of my opposite clan, the Carcaras, I see it as my complementary reciprocal. It is there, among them, that I am going to look for my woman who will bear my children. It is there, among my brothers-in-law, that I will have my closest friends. The woman and those friends will be all the more mine precisely for being of a nature different from my own. They are the ones I need so as to form together a we that is vigorous, fecund, and complete" (Ribeiro 1984:45).

This brief excerpt from *Maíra* gives us a sense of what the world looks like from inside a system organized very differently from the one with which Americans are familiar. The Mairun live in a society in which everyone belongs to one of two groups, called *moieties* (from the French *moitié*, "half"), and people belong to the half their mothers belonged to. The two halves depend on each other for their survival, carrying out the tasks of life for each other, and providing each other with

Xavante Indians in their village in the Brazilian Amazon.

spouses. Each is incomplete without the other. "The Great House of Men" is a structure in the middle of the village where the men from both groups come together, pass the time, and organize the great religious ceremonies that mark their lives. This *dual organization* that Ribeiro describes so vividly enmeshes people in a web of relatives. Each person in the web is aware of his or her responsibilities and rights; the position of each in relation to all others is made clear. Life together becomes organized.

Kinship Systems: Ways of Organizing Human Interdependence

Human life is group life. Part of our primate heritage is sociability and gregariousness. A human infant is brought into the world able only to grasp, suck, and cry. To survive, it depends on other, older human beings. Even past childhood, however, human beings need other people. Human individuals would perish without culture and human companions to sustain them.

Survival is immeasurably enhanced when groups of people are *organized*. For instance, there are many ways a group of people might go about getting food from a given environment. There is an equal variety of living arrangements and work arrangements that might be compatible with each possibility. Sooner or later, however, people must *choose* among the alternatives in order to get on with life. This does not mean that their lives are completely determined, or that creativity is illusory. It does mean that under certain circumstances, choices must be made. To live in groups in a reasonably successful fashion requires that *individual* freedom to create and act sometimes has to be constrained for the *group* to be free to create and act. While people must live in groups, the way they choose to organize themselves is open to creative variation.

Determining Group Membership and Relationships

One way of forming human social groups is to base group membership on **kinship**, that is, on relationships that are prototypically derived from the universal human experiences of mating and birth. Relationships derived from mating are called **marriage** (discussed in chapter 10), and relationships based on birth are called **descent**. Notice that while marriage is based on mating and descent is based on birth, marriage is not the same thing as mating and descent is not the same thing as birth. The human experiences of mating and birth are many–faceted. The fascinating thing about human kinship systems is that different societies have chosen to highlight some features of those experiences while downplaying or even ignoring others. As we know from our own society, mating is not the same as marriage, although a valid marriage encourages mating between the married partners. Similarly, all births do not constitute valid links of descent. Children whose parents have not been married properly are called "illegitimate." These children do not fit the cultural logic of descent, and many societies offer no positions that they can properly fill. Put another way, through kinship, people in a culture select aspects of human nature to emphasize. At the same time, kinship is part of that culture's theory of human nature.

Marriage and descent are thus selective. One society may emphasize that women bear children and base its kinship system on this fact, paying little formal

kinship
social relationships that are prototypically derived from the universal human experiences of mating and birth and are used to define social groups, locate people within those groups, and position the people and groups in relation to one another, both in space and in time

marriage
an institution that prototypically involves a man and a woman, transforms the status of the participants, carries implications about permitted sexual access, gives the children produced a position in the society, and establishes connections between the kin of the husband and the kin of the wife

descent
the cultural principle based on culturally recognized parent-child connections that defines the social categories to which people belong

attention to the role of a woman's mate in conception. Another society may trace connections through men, emphasizing the role of paternity in conception and reducing the role of the mother to that of a passive incubator for male seed. Even though they contradict one another, both understandings can be justified with reference to the human experience of mating and birth.

Consider the American kinship term *aunt*. This term seems to refer to women who occupy a unique biological position. In fact, it refers to women related to us in four different ways: father's sister, mother's sister, father's brother's wife, and mother's brother's wife. In our eyes, all those women have something in common, and we believe that they are related to us equally. "Aunt" is a *category* into which certain people perceived to be similar are placed. Prototypically, these are women one generation older than we are, who are sisters of our parents or are married to their brothers. When we refer to our mother's best friend as "Aunt," we are recognizing the strength of this system of classification.

Thus, kinship is an idiom. It is a selective interpretation of the common human experiences of mating and birth. The result is a set of coherent principles that allow people to assign one another membership in groups. These principles normally cover several significant issues. One is how to carry out the reproduction of legitimate group members (marriage). A second is where group members should live after marriage (residence rules). A third is how to establish links between generations (descent). A fourth is how to pass on positions in society (succession) or material goods (inheritance) in terms of descent. Taken together, kinship principles define social groups, locate people within those groups, and position the people and groups in relation to one another, both in space and in time.

Kinship and Gender

In this way, concepts of kinship are very much like concepts of gender. Kinship is based on, but is not reducible to, biology. It is a cultural interpretation of the culturally recognized "facts" of human reproduction. So, too, are conceptions of gender. Out of the "raw data" of male and female biology, cultures construct men and women. Cultural variations in gender categories and inequalities are thus not reducible to the biological differences between men and women. Each culture selectively pays attention to some of the biological similarities and differences between males and females, while ignoring others. The resulting gender categories are then fitted into an overall pattern of social activity, which comes to depend on their existence.

Rules governing gender and kinship aim to regulate social relations between people who are believed to be different: men and women in gender categories and (for example) mothers and aunts in kinship categories. Our folk belief, sometimes carried over into anthropological theorizing, is that these differences are "natural," part of every individual's innate makeup, regardless of the society she or he lives in. This is not the case for either kinship or gender. What it means to be a man or a woman is intimately related to cultural patterns of marriage and sexuality, matters that are usually considered to belong in the domain of kinship; these issues are explored in the next chapter. Recognizing that kinship and gender are culturally constructed in similar ways has led to important recent work in both fields (see, for example, Collier and Yanagisako 1987).

Maintaining Social Order

Because kinship is concerned with social order, it is important to anthropology. Anthropologists first began to study kinship in the mid-nineteenth century. At that time, many people wondered whether it was possible to maintain social order in a society that lacked centralized government. After all, Western history was the history of people living in states. Explorers discovered, however, that people outside the Western world somehow did manage to lead orderly lives in societies without a state. How were they able to avoid chaos and anarchy? What held their societies together? The answer, anthropologists discovered, was kinship. Kinship not only classified people, it also established the conventional ways by which different classes of people were to interact with one another. In other words, kinship, rather than written statutes, made clear for people the kinds of rights and obligations they owed one another.

Understanding Different Kinship Systems

But what strange ways of establishing these rights and obligations people had! Western explorers discovered that some non-Western people distinguished among their relatives only on the basis of age and sex. To refer to people one generation older than the speaker required only two terms: one applying to men and one applying to women. From the explorers' point of view, the people they met couldn't tell the difference between their fathers and their uncles, since they used the same kin term for both. But this was a major error on the part of the explorers. "Father" and "uncle" do not represent kinship categories that are universally recognized. The people whom the explorers met did not have "fathers" and "uncles" whom they lumped together for some reason (perhaps because they did not really know who their fathers were). Rather, people who used one term for all men older than the speaker did not understand kinship the same way the explorers did. They had one category of male relative where Europeans had two. For them, the man who was married to their mother, while known to them and personally important to them, was socially no more or less significant than that man's brothers or their mother's brothers. By referring to all these men by the same kin term, they were no more deluded than we are when we assert that our father's sister and our mother's brother's wife are equally our "aunts."

Beyond that, the categories of feeling these people associated with different kin were as real as, but different from, the emotions we associate with kin. "Just as the word *father* in English means a great deal more than lineal male ancestor of the first ascending generation, *aita* in Basque has many local connotations not reducible to *father*, as we understand the term" (Greenwood and Stini 1977:333). This takes us back to classification and the rights and obligations associated with the different classifications people employ. Because the world of kin is a world of expectations and obligations, it is fundamentally a *moral* world, and one charged with feeling. In some societies, a man's principal authority figure is his mother's brother, and his father is a figure of affection and unwavering support. "God the Father" will not mean the same thing in those societies as it will in a society in which the father has life-and-death control over his children, and mother's brothers are without significant authority.

Patterns of Descent in Kinship

An important part of kinship is descent. Descent is the cultural principle that defines social categories through culturally recognized parent-child connections. Descent groups are defined by ancestry and so have a time depth. The descent principle in-

A four-generation family gathering in the United States.

bilateral or cognatic descent
the principle that a descent group is formed by people who believe they are related to each other by connections made through their mothers and fathers equally

unilineal descent
the principle that a descent group is formed by people who believe they are related to each other by links made through either men or women

volves transmission and incorporation: the transmission of membership through parent-child links, and the incorporation of these people into groups for social action. In some societies, descent group membership controls the way in which people mobilize for social action. Note that people can acknowledge that they are linked by kinship without belonging to the same descent group. Imagine an American who is related through her father to someone who came over on the *Mayflower*. She may recognize that she is part of that descent group, and may even have joined an association of *Mayflower* descendants. But suppose her mother's parents came to the United States from Italy in 1903. They are not part of the same descent group that she belongs to through her father, but they are still her relatives.

Two major strategies are employed in establishing patterns of descent. In the first strategy, the descent group is formed by people who believe that they are related to each other by connections made through their mothers and fathers *equally*. That is, people believe themselves to be just as related to their father's side of the family as to their mother's. Anthropologists call this **bilateral** or **cognatic descent**. Two kinds of bilateral kinship groups are analyzed by anthropologists. One is made up of people who claim to be related to one another through ties to a common ancestor. This is called a bilateral descent group. The other kind of group consists of the relatives of one person or group of siblings. Anthropologists call this kind of group a bilateral kindred.

The second major strategy for establishing patterns of descent is based on the assumption that the most significant kin relationships must be traced through *either* the mother *or* the father. Anthropologists call this **unilineal descent**. Unilineal kinship groups are made up of people related to one another only through men or only through women. They are called unilineal descent groups, and are numerically the most common in the world. Unilineal descent groups that are made up of links traced through one's father are called patrilineal, and those traced through one's mother are called matrilineal.

Bilateral Kindreds

The **bilateral kindred** is the descent group that most Americans know. It is a group that forms around a particular individual. It includes all people who are linked to that individual through kin of both sexes. It includes all the people Americans conventionally call relatives. (see figure 9.1). These people form a group only because of their connection to the central person or persons, known in the terminology of kinship as *Ego*. In American society, bilateral kindreds assemble when Ego is baptized, confirmed, bar or bat mitzvahed, married, or buried. Each person within Ego's bilateral kindred has his or her own separate kindred. For example, Ego's father's sister's daughter has a kindred that includes people related to her through her father and his siblings. Ego is not related to these people. This is simultaneously the major strength and major weakness of bilateral kindreds. That is, they do not last long over time, and they have overlapping memberships. But they are widely extended and can form broad networks of people who are related in some way or another to one another.

A classic bilateral kindred is found among the !Kung San of the Kalahari Desert in southern Africa. *(See EthnoFile 9.1: !Kung.)* Anthropologist Richard Lee (1984:57ff.) points out that for the !Kung, every individual in the society can be linked to every other individual by a kinship term, either through males or through females. As a result, a person can expect to find a relative everywhere there are !Kung. The !Kung live in groups that are relatively small (ten to thirty people)

bilateral kindred
a group that consists of the relatives of one person

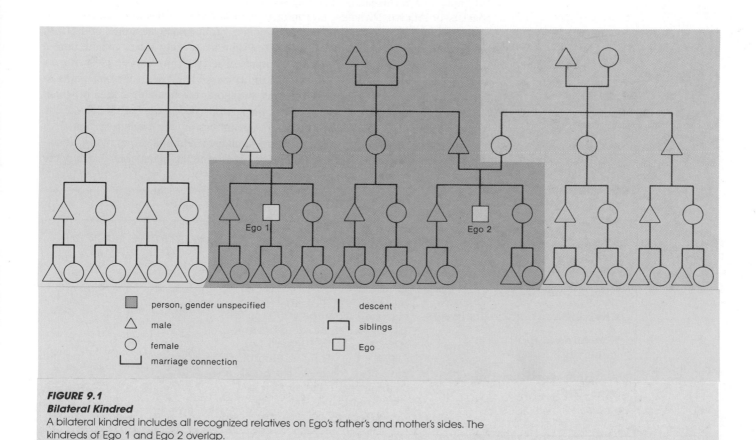

FIGURE 9.1
Bilateral Kindred
A bilateral kindred includes all recognized relatives on Ego's father's and mother's sides. The kindreds of Ego 1 and Ego 2 overlap.

Three generations of a Liberian family.

but made up of a constantly changing set of individuals. "In essence, a !Kung camp consists of relatives, friends, and in-laws who have found that they can live and work well together. Under this flexible principle, brothers may be united or divided; fathers and sons may live together or apart. Further, during his or her lifetime a !Kung may live at many waterholes with many different groups" (Lee 1984:57). A wide range of kinspeople makes this flexibility possible. When someone wants to move, he or she has kin at many different waterholes throughout the area in which the !Kung live, and can choose to activate the appropriate kin tie. For the !Kung, the bilateral kindred provides one of the many flexibilities in their kinship system.

In a society like that of the !Kung, a bilateral kindred offers many advantages. At the same time, there is ambiguity concerning the boundaries dividing the

---

EthnoFile 9.1
!KUNG

Region: Southern Africa

Nation: Botswana and Namibia

Population: 45,000

Environment: Kalahari Desert

Livelihood: Hunting and gathering

Political organization: Egalitarian bands

Other: These people, who are the best known modern hunting and gathering society, were the subjects of classic ethnographic research and films by Lorna Marshall from the 1950s to the 1970s as well as an important ethnography by Richard Lee (1983); the !Kung in Namibia have been forced by the South African government to give up their traditional way of life and live in misery on reserves

!Kung women.

social groups that make up the society. These ambiguities become problematic in at least four kinds of social circumstances. The first is where clear-cut membership in a particular social group must be determined. The second is where social action requires the formation of groups that are larger than individual families. The third is where conflicting claims to land and labor must be resolved. The fourth includes situations where people are concerned to perpetuate a particular social order over time. In societies that face these dilemmas, unilineal descent groups are usually formed.

Unilineal Descent Groups

Unilineal descent groups are found all over the world, from Australia to Africa, to Asia, to the Americas. They are all based on the principle that certain kinds of parent-child relationships are more important than others. Membership in a unilineal descent group is based on the membership of the appropriate parent in the group. In patrilineal systems, an individual belongs to a group formed through male sex links, the lineage of his or her father. In matrilineal systems, an individual belongs to a group formed by links through women, the lineage of his or her mother. *Patrilineal* and *matrilineal* do not mean that only men belong to one and women to the other. Rather, the terms refer to the principle by which membership is conferred. In patrilineal societies, women and men belong to patrilineages formed by father-child links. Similarly, in matrilineal societies, men and women belong to matrilineages formed by mother-child connections (see figures 9.2 and 9.3). In other words, membership in the group is, on the face of it, unambiguous. An individual belongs to one and only one unilineage. This is in contrast to the kindred, where an individual belongs to overlapping groups.

LINEAGES

The *lineal* in patrilineal and matrilineal refers to the nature of the social group formed. Anthropologists call these groups **lineages**, which are composed of people who believe they can specify the parent-child links that unite them. Although the abstract kinship diagrams that anthropologists draw include just a few people, lin-

lineage
the consanguineal members of a descent group who believe that they can trace their descent from known ancestors

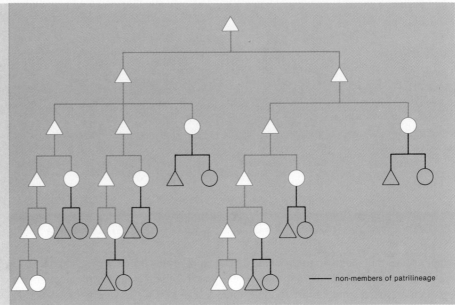

FIGURE 9.2
Patrilineal Descent
All those who trace descent through males to a common male ancestor are indicated in white.

─── non-members of patrilineage

eages in the world vary in size, ranging from twenty or thirty members to several hundred. Some Chinese lineages were composed of more than a thousand members.

Lineage Membership

The most important feature of lineages is that they are *corporate* in organization. That is, a lineage has a single legal "personality." As the Ashanti put it, a lineage is "one person" (Fortes 1953). To outsiders, all members of a lineage are equal *in law* to all others. For example, in the case of a blood feud, the death of any opposing lineage member is as good as the death of the person who started the feud. Lineages are also corporate in that they control property, specifically land. Such groups are found in societies where rights to use land are crucial and must be monitored over time.

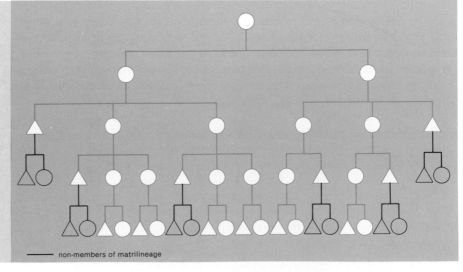

FIGURE 9.3
Matrilineal Descent
All those who trace descent through females to a common female ancestor are indicated in white.

─── non-members of matrilineage

Lineages are also the main political associations in the societies that have them. Individuals have no political or legal status in such societies except through lineage membership. They have relatives who are outside the lineage, but their own political and legal statuses come through the lineage.

Because membership in a lineage comes through a direct line from father or mother to child, lineages can endure over time and in a sense have an independent existence. As long as people can remember from whom they are descended, lineages can endure. Most lineages have a time depth of about five generations: grandparents, parents, Ego, children, and grandchildren. When members of a group believe that they can no longer accurately specify the genealogical links that connect them, but believe that they are "in some way" connected, we find the clan. **Clans** are usually made up of lineages.

clan
a descent group formed by all those who believe they have a common ancestor, even if they cannot specify the genealogical links; sometimes the ancestor is mythical

The Logic of Lineage Relationships ▬▬▬▬

The memories people have of their ancestry are not always correct. These memories are often transmitted in the form of myth or legend. Thus, it is a mistake to approach them as if they were accurate historical records. Rather, as Malinowski observed, they are better understood as mythical charters. Fortes (1953:165) quotes anthropologists Paul and Laura Bohannan, whose research was among the Tiv. *(See EthnoFile 5.5: Tiv.)* The Bohannans observed the Tiv publicly rearranging their lineage relationships to bring them into line with changed legal and political relationships. This was not an exercise in deception; quite the contrary. The Tiv assume that traditional lineage relationships determine current social arrangements, and that people do not consciously misrepresent tradition. But if current social arrangements and tradition conflict, the Tiv conclude that the tradition is faulty. Tradition must therefore be revised to bring it into line with the current situation. Genealogies and lineages may look solid and unchanging, but they are often more flexible than they appear.

Lineages endure over time in societies in which no other form of organization lasts. Hence, they provide for the "perpetual exercise of defined rights, duties, office and social tasks vested in the lineage" (Fortes 1953:165). In other words, the system of lineages becomes the foundation of social life in the society.

Patrilineages ▬▬▬▬

By far the most common form of lineage organization is the **patrilineage**. From a sample of 250 societies, anthropologist G. P. Murdock discovered that 105 (42 percent) were patrilineal, 75 were bilateral, and 52 were matrilineal.

patrilineage
a social group formed by people connected by links through men

A patrilineage consists of all the people (male and female) who believe themselves to be related to each other because they are related to a common male ancestor by links through men. The prototypical kernel of a patrilineage is the father-son pair. Women who are members of patrilineages normally leave the lineages when they marry, but they do not relinquish their interest in their own lineages. In a number of societies, they play an active role in the affairs of their own patrilineages for many years.

An assumption of hierarchy exists in patrilineal societies: men believe they are superior to women, and many women seem to agree. Despite this, there is a patrilineal puzzle at the heart of these societies. Women with little power, who are strangers to the lineage, nevertheless marry its members and produce the children who perpetuate the lineage. Ironically, the future of the patrilineage depends on people who do not belong to it! A second irony is that women must leave their own

EthnoFile 9.2
NUER

Region: East Africa

Nation: Ethiopia and Sudan

Population: 300,000

Environment: Open grassland

Livelihood: Cattle herding and
farming

Political organization:
Egalitarian tribes, no political
offices

Other: These people were subjects of a classic ethnography by
E. E. Evans-Pritchard, *The Nuer*
(1940) a study of the centrality
of cattle in their lives and the
effects of this focus on other aspects of their experience, including kinship and political
organization

lineages to reproduce the next generation of somebody else's lineage. Women in patrilineal societies are often torn between conflicting interests and loyalties (see Karp 1986). Shall they support their own children or their fathers and brothers?

A classic patrilineal system is found among the Nuer of the Sudan and Ethiopia. *(See EthnoFile 9.2: Nuer.)* According to English anthropologist E. E. Evans-Pritchard, the Nuer were divided into at least twenty clans. Evans-Pritchard defined *clan* as the largest group of people who (1) traced their descent patrilineally from a common ancestor, (2) could not marry each other, and (3) considered sexual relations within the group to be incestuous. The clan was divided, or segmented, into lineages. These lineages were themselves linked to each other by presumed ties of patrilineal descent. The most basic stage of lineage segmentation was the minimal lineage, which had a time depth of three to five generations.

The Nuer kinship system worked in the following way. Members of lineages A and B might consider themselves related because they believed that the founder of lineage A had been the older brother of the founder of lineage B. The living members of lineage A would then believe themselves to be related to the members of lineage B because the two brothers had a father in common. These two minimal lineages when together formed the *minor lineage*. Minor lineages could be connected to other minor lineages by a presumed common ancestor, forming *major lineages*. These major lineages also were believed to share a common ancestor, and they formed the *maximal lineage*. The founders of maximal lineages were believed to be the sons of the clan ancestor. In this way, all members of the clan were believed to be patrilineally related to each other.

Lineages were important to the Nuer for political purposes. Members of the same lineage in the same village were conscious of being in a social group with common ancestors and symbols, corporate rights in territory, and common interests in cattle. When a son in the lineage married, these people would help provide the bridewealth cattle.* If the son were killed, they—indeed, all members of his patrilineage, regardless of where they lived—would avenge him. When he died, they would hold the funeral ceremony for him. Nevertheless, relationships among the members of a patrilineage are not necessarily harmonious:

*Bridewealth is a payment made by the family or lineage of the husband to that of the wife to compensate them for the loss of her productive and reproductive potential. Bridewealth, along with marriage in general, is discussed in detail in the next chapter.

Among the patrilineal Nuer, a wife lives with her husband's family after marriage.

A Nuer is bound to his paternal kin from whom he derives aid, security, and status, but in return for these benefits he has many obligations and commitments. Their often indefinite character may be both evidence of, and a reason for, their force, but it also gives ample scope for disagreement. Duties and rights easily conflict. Moreover, the privileges of [patrilineal] kinship cannot be divorced from authority, discipline, and a strong sense of moral obligation, all of which are irksome to Nuer. They do not deny them, but they kick against them when their personal interests run counter to them. (Evans-Pritchard 1951:162)

Although the Nuer are patrilineal, they recognize as kin people who are not members of their lineage. In the Nuer language, the word *mar* refers to "kin": all the people to whom a person can trace a relationship of any kind. This includes people on the mother's side as well as those on the father's side. In fact, at such important ceremonial occasions as a bridewealth distribution after a woman in the lineage has been married, special attention is paid to kin on the mother's side. Certain important relatives, like the mother's brother and the mother's sister, are given cattle. A man's mother's brother is his great supporter when he is in trouble. The mother's brother is kind to him as a boy, and even in manhood the mother's brother provides a second home. If he likes his sister's son, a mother's brother will even be willing to help pay the bridewealth so that his sister's son can marry. "Nuer say of the maternal uncle that he is both father and mother, but most frequently that 'he is your mother'" (ibid.). Ultimately, for a Nuer, every other Nuer he or she meets is in some way a relative. If that person is not a relative, then he or she is believed to be a enemy.

Matrilineages

matrilineage
the social group formed by people connected by·links through women

Matrilineages are often thought to be mirror images of patrilineages, and this certainly appears to be the case. In matrilineages, descent is traced through women rather than through men. Recall that in a patrilineage, a woman's children are not in her lineage. In a matrilineage, a man's children are not in his. However, certain features of matrilineages make them more than just mirror images of patrilineages.

First, the prototypical kernel of a matrilineage is the sister-brother pair, and a matrilineage may be thought of as a group of brothers and sisters connected through links made by women. Brothers marry out and often live with the family of their wives, but they maintain an active interest in the affairs of their lineage.

Second, the most important man in a boy's life is not his father (who is not in his lineage), but his mother's brother. It is from his mother's brother that he will receive his lineage inheritance.

Third, the amount of power women exercise in matrilineages is still being hotly debated in anthropology. A matrilineage is not the same thing as a matriarchy, a society in which women rule. Brothers often retain what appears to be a controlling interest in the lineage. Some anthropologists claim that the male members of a matrilineage are supposed to run the lineage. These scholars have agreed that there is more autonomy for women in matrilineal societies than in patrilineal ones. But they have claimed that the day-to-day exercise of power is carried out by the brothers, or sometimes the husbands. Recently, however, a number of studies have questioned the validity of these generalizations. Trying to say something about matrilineal societies in general is difficult. The ethnographic evidence suggests that matrilineages must be examined on a case-by-case basis.

The Navajo are a matrilineal people. *(See EthnoFile 6.1: Navajo.)* The basic unit of Navajo social organization is the subsistence residential unit, composed of a head mother, her husband, and some of their children with their spouses and children (Witherspoon 1975:82). The leader of the unit is normally a man, usually the husband of the head mother. He directs livestock and agricultural operations and is the one who deals with the outside world: "He speaks for the unit at community meetings, negotiates with the traders and car salesmen, arranges marriages and ceremonies, talks to visiting strangers, and so on." He seems to be in charge. But it is the head mother around whom the unit is organized.

> *[The head mother] is identified with the land, the herd, and the agricultural fields. All residence rights can be traced back to her, and her opinions and wishes are always given the greatest consideration and usually prevail. In a sense, however, she delegates much of her role and prestige to the leader of the unit. If we think of the unit as a corporation, and the leader as its president, the head mother will be the chairman of the board. She usually has more sheep than the leader does. Because the power and importance of the head mother offer a deceptive appearance to the observer, many students of the Navajo have failed to see the importance of her role. But if one has lived a long time in one of these units, one soon becomes aware of who ultimately has the cards and directs the game. When there is a divorce between the leader and the head, it is always the leader who leaves and the head mother who returns, even if the land originally belonged to the mother of the leader. (Ibid.:82−83)*

Studies like these have led anthropologists to recognize that an obstacle to understanding matrilineal societies has been the Western habit of thinking hierarchically. Given any two things, Westerners want to know which is better; given any two groups of people, they want to know which is superior and which is inferior. Looking at matrilineal societies, we see groups of men and groups of women, and we "naturally" assume that either the women are in charge or the men are. But reality is more complex. Evidence from matrilineal societies reveals some domains of experience in which men and women are equal, some in which men are in control, and some in which women are in control. Observers and participants may disagree about which of these domains of experience is more or less central to Navajo life.

In an earlier section, we discussed a patrilineal puzzle. In matrilineal societies, there is a paradox sometimes called the matrilineal puzzle. This is a contradiction between the rule of residence and the rule of inheritance. The contradiction is especially clear in societies that are strongly matrilineal and that encourage residence with the wife's matrilineage. Among the Bemba of Zambia, for example, a man is a stranger in his wife's house, where he goes when he marries. A man may feel great affection for his father, but he will not be his father's heir. He will inherit from his mother's brother, who lives elsewhere. And although a father may wish to have his son inherit from him, he must give to his sister's son.

The classic case of the matrilineal puzzle was from the Trobriand Islands, and Malinowski interpreted it in the way just described. *(See EthnoFile 5.2: Trobriand Islanders.)* But recent research on the Trobriands by anthropologist Annette Weiner calls Malinowski's interpretation into question. Weiner argues that to understand matrilineal kinship in the Trobriands, one must begin by seeing the sister-brother pair as an integral unit:

> *[The sister-brother pair] makes complementary contributions both to a woman's brother's children and to a woman's own children. . . . In the former instance, a man and his sister (father and father's sister to a child) contribute their own [lineage] resources to the man's children, thus building up these children with resources that they may use, but may not subsequently pass on to their own children. . . . In the latter case, a woman and her brother (mother and mother's brother) contribute to the regeneration of [the matrilineage]—the woman through the process of conception and the man through the control and transmission of [matrilineage] property such as land and palm trees. (Weiner 1980:286–87)*

The result is that both a man and his sister "give" to the man's children, and his children return things to them later in life.

Kinship Terminologies

People everywhere use special terms to refer to people they recognize as kin. Despite the variety of kinship systems in the world, anthropologists have developed a means of classification that allows them to identify six major patterns of kinship terminology. This system is based on the ways in which people categorize their cousins. The six patterns reflect common solutions to common problems of organization faced by societies organized in terms of kinship. They provide clues concerning how the vast and undifferentiated world of potential kin may be divided up.

Kinship terminologies suggest both the external boundaries and internal divisions of the kinship groups. They also outline the structure of rights and obligations assigned to different members of the society.

Criteria for Distinctions

Kinship terminologies are built on certain widely recognized kinship criteria. From most common to least common, these criteria include the following:

- *Generation*. Kin terms distinguish relatives according to the generation to which the relatives belong. In English, the term *cousin* conventionally refers to someone of the same generation as the speaker.

- *Sex*. The sex of an individual is used to differentiate kin. In Spanish, *primo* refers to a male cousin and *prima* to a female cousin. In English, cousins are not distinguished on the basis of sex, but "uncle" and "aunt" are distinguished on the basis of both generation and sex.

- *Affinity*. A distinction is made on the basis of connection through marriage, or **affinity**. In English, when we distinguish "mother-in-law" from "mother" we use the criterion of affinity. In matrilineal societies, the mother's sister and the father's sister are distinguished from each other on the basis of affinity. The mother's sister is a direct, lineal relative, and the father's sister is an affinal relative. In English, the women are both called "aunt"; in matrilineal societies they will be called by different terms.

- *Collaterality*. A distinction is made between kin who are believed to be in a direct line and those who are "off to one side," linked to the speaker through a lineal relative. In English, the distinction of **collaterality** is exemplified by the distinction between "mother" and "aunt" and "father" and "uncle." In kinship systems where collaterality is not employed, the same term will be used for mother and mother's sister and father and father's brother.

- *Bifurcation*. The distinction of **bifurcation** is employed when kinship terms referring to the mother's side of the family are distinguished from those referring to the father's side of the family.

- *Relative age*. Relatives of the same category are distinguished on the basis of whether they are older or younger than the speaker. Among the !Kung, for example, speakers must separate "older brother" (*!ko*) from "younger brother" (*tsin*).

- *Sex of linking relative*. The criterion of sex of linking relatives is related to collaterality. It distinguishes *cross relatives* (usually cousins) from *parallel relatives* (also usually cousins). Parallel relatives are linked to each other through two brothers or two sisters. **Parallel cousins**, for example, are Ego's father's brother's children or mother's sister's children. Cross relatives are linked to each other through a brother-sister pair. Thus, **cross cousins** are Ego's mother's brother's children or father's sister's children. The sex of either Ego or the cousins does not matter. The important feature is the sex of the linking relative (see figure 9.4). If this criterion is used in kinship systems in which collaterality is important, cross cousins and parallel cousins will be called by separate kin terms.

affinity
connection through marriage

collaterality
a criterion employed in the analysis of kinship terminologies in which a distinction is made between kin who are believed to be in a direct line and those who are "off to one side"—linked to the speaker by a lineal relative; this is an important distinction in English, exemplified by the distinction between "mother" and "aunt" and "father" and "uncle"

bifurcation
a criterion employed in the analysis of kinship terminologies in which kinship terms referring to the mother's side of the family are distinguished from those referring to the father's side of the family

parallel cousins
the children of a person's parents' same-sex siblings (i.e., father's brother's children and mother's sister's children)

cross cousins
the children of a person's parents' opposite sex siblings (i.e., father's sister's children and mother's brother's children)

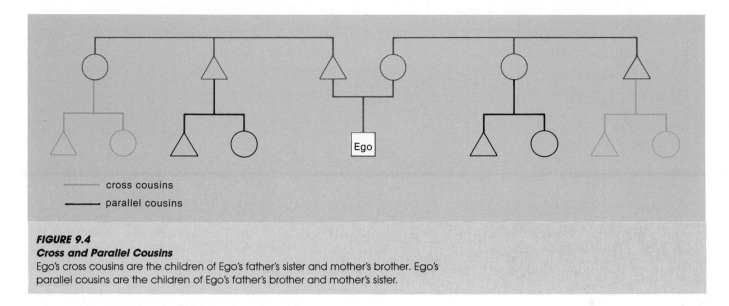

—— cross cousins
—— parallel cousins

FIGURE 9.4
Cross and Parallel Cousins
Ego's cross cousins are the children of Ego's father's sister and mother's brother. Ego's
parallel cousins are the children of Ego's father's brother and mother's sister.

Patterns of Kinship Terminology

As noted earlier, the six major patterns of kinship terminology are based on the way
cousins are classified. These patterns have been named after the societies that represent the prototypes. They are called Hawaiian, Eskimo, Iroquois, Crow, Omaha,
and Sudanese. Two of the six patterns are found in association with bilateral descent
systems; the remaining four are found in association with unilineal descent.

Bilateral Patterns:

The *Hawaiian* pattern is based on the application of the first two criteria: generation
and sex. The kin group is divided horizontally by generation, and within each generation there are only two kinship terms, one for males and one for females (see
figure 9.5). As a result, siblings and "cousins" of the same sex are called by the
same term. This terminological pattern emphasizes the equality of the father's and
mother's sides. It is found in association with residence rules that allow a newly
married couple to live with the husband's or wife's kin group. In this system, Ego
maintains a maximum degree of flexibility in choosing the descent group with
which to affiliate. Ego is also forced to look for a spouse in another kin group, since
Ego may not marry anyone in the same terminological category as a genetic parent,
a genetic sibling, or a genetic offspring.

   The terminological pattern called *Eskimo* is one of anthropology's little
jokes, since while this is the Eskimo's system, it is also the American pattern. The
Eskimo pattern reflects the symmetry of bilateral kindreds (see figure 9.6). A lineal
core—the nuclear family—is distinguished from collateral relatives, who are not
identified with the father's or the mother's side. Once past the immediate collateral
line (aunts and uncles, great-aunts and great-uncles, nephews and nieces), generation is ignored. The remaining relatives are all "cousins," sometimes distinguished
by *number* (e.g., second or third) or by *removal* (which marks generations away
from Ego*). This is the only terminological system that sets the nuclear family apart

---

*A person's "first cousin once removed" can be one generation older or younger than that person. Your
cousin Phil's daughter is your first cousin once removed, but so is your father's cousin Marlys. Marlys's
son Marvin is your second cousin.

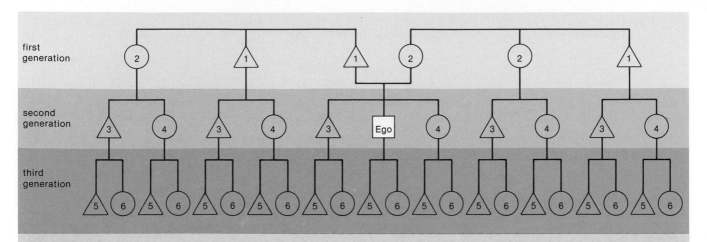

FIGURE 9.5
Hawaiian Kinship Terminology
Numbers represent kin terms. Ego uses the same kin term to refer to all those assigned the same number.

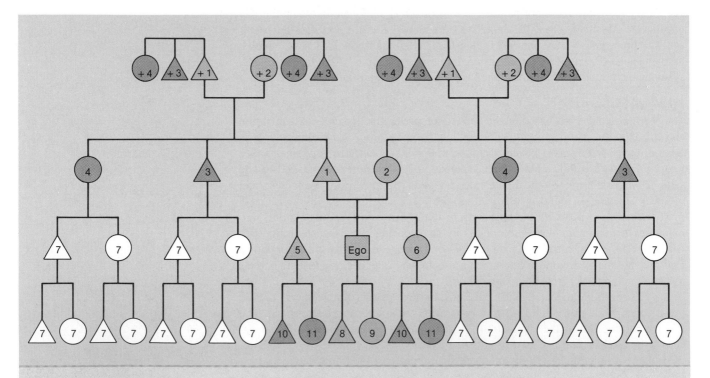

FIGURE 9.6
Eskimo Kinship Terminology
All those indicated in brown represent Ego's lineal relatives. Those in gray represent Ego's collateral relatives. Those in white are cousins. The symbol + equals grand; e.g., +1 = grandfather.

from all other kin. If the Hawaiian system is like a layer cake, made up of horizontal layers of kin, our system is like an onion, with layers of kin surrounding a core (Fox 1967:259).

Unilineal Patterns:

The *Iroquois* pattern is sometimes known as "bifurcate merging," because it merges Ego's mother's and father's parallel siblings with Ego's parents. This is so even though it is associated with unilineal, especially matrilineal, descent. The sex of the linking relatives is important in this system, since the parents' parallel siblings are grouped together with the parents, while the cross siblings are set apart. This is repeated on the level of cousins. In a bilateral system, these distinctions would be meaningless, but in a unilineal system they mirror the lines of lineage membership. If Ego is a male, he will use one term to refer to all women of his matrilineage who are one generation older than he is. Their children are all referred to by another set of terms, one for males and one for females. Similarly, in his father's matrilineage, all men in the father's generation are referred to by one term. Their children are called by the same set of terms used for the cousins on the mother's side (see figure 9.7).

The pattern called *Crow* is a matrilineal system named after the Crow Indians in the United States, but it is found in many other matrilineal societies, including the Trobriand Islands. The Crow system distinguishes the two matrilineages that are important to Ego: Ego's own, and that of Ego's father (see figure 9.8). As in the Iroquois system, the sex of the linking relative is important, and both parents and their same-sex siblings are grouped together. Their children—Ego's parallel cousins—are in the same category as Ego's siblings. The terms for cross cousins follow lineage membership, which is more important than generation. In Ego's own matrilineage, all the children of males are referred to by the same term regardless of their generation; in the Trobriand Islands, Ego's brother's daughter and mother's brother's daughter are called *latu* if Ego is male and *tabu* if Ego is female (Weiner 1979:340). Their *fathers* are in Ego's matrilineage, but *they* are not. On the side of Ego's father's matrilineage, all male members are distinguished by one term and all female members by another, regardless of generational relationship to Ego.

Weiner (1979) suggests that three kinship pairs are crucial to the operation of the Trobriand system (and perhaps other matrilineal systems). These are mother and mother's brother, father and father's sister, and father and mother. Mother and

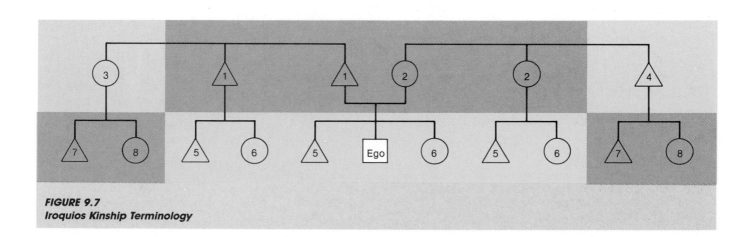

FIGURE 9.7
Iroquios Kinship Terminology

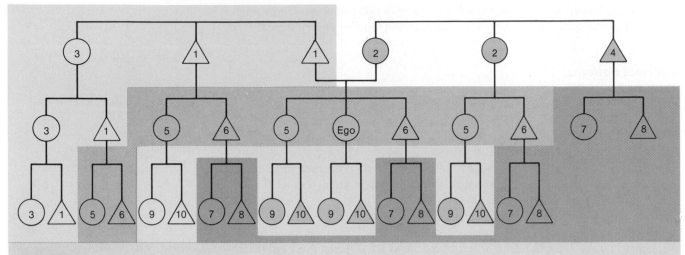

FIGURE 9.8
Crow Kinship Terminology
Members of Ego's matriline are represented in brown. Note the merging of generations and
what follows as a result: i.e., all children of 3s are 1s and 3s; all children of 2s are 5s and 6s;
all children of 5s are 9s and 10s; all children of 4s and 6s are 7s and 8s—*regardless of
generation.*

mother's brother (*ina* and *kada*) are the basis for perpetuation of the matrilineage,
but they must marry outsiders for that to happen. The "outsiders" are the father
(*tama*) and father's sister (*tabu*), who must also cross the boundaries of their matrilineage in order to keep it alive. Finally, each father and mother pair (*tama* and
ina) supply the critical element for each matrilineage: children.

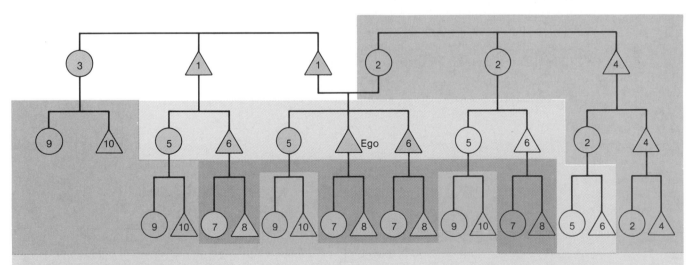

FIGURE 9.9
Omaha Kinship Terminology
Members of Ego's patriline are represented in brown. Note the merging of generations and
what follows as a result: i.e., all children of 4s are 2s and 4s; all children of 1s are 5s and 6s;
all children of 6s are 7s and 8s; all children of 3s and 5s are 9s and 10s—*regardless of
generation.*

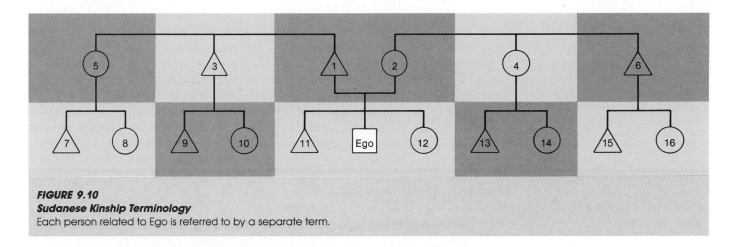

FIGURE 9.10
Sudanese Kinship Terminology
Each person related to Ego is referred to by a separate term.

The system known as *Omaha* is found among patrilineal peoples and represents the mirror image of the Crow system. All members of Ego's mother's patrilineage are distinguished only by sex, and all children of women in Ego's patrilineage are referred to by the same terms, one for males and one for females (see figure 9.9). Lineage membership again is more important than generation, a principle that is often hard for people living in bilateral kindreds to grasp.

Finally, in the *Sudanese* pattern, each related person is referred to by a separate term (see figure 9.10). This is a relatively rare terminological pattern. It is found in patrilineal societies, especially in North Africa.

Indigenous Views of Kinship

Some anthropologists have provided information about how the people they studied view kinship. For example, James Fernandez (1982:88–89) reports that the Fang use metaphors of the body to talk about lineage. *(See EthnoFile 6.4: Fang.)* A generation is called a joint. The articulation of joints in the body from chest to extended fingers corresponds to the points of articulation in the generations of the lineage. "The clan itself was represented as rising in the chest or the heart . . . and as spreading out through one or both arms to its contemporary representatives, the fingertips."

Evans-Pritchard (1940:202) notes that when drawing diagrams of related lineages on the ground, the Nuer sketch a number of lines running at angles from a common point. *(See EthnoFile 9.2: Nuer.)* The Nuer see their system as actual relations between groups of kin within local communities and not as a series of family trees. In their drawings, they place lineages together on the basis of geography, showing which lineages live near each other. For the Nuer, except for certain ritual situations, concrete spatial relations are more important than lineage theory.

Recent work by Marilyn Strathern (1987) on kinship and gender among the people of Mount Hagen, in Papua New Guinea, makes clear our earlier point about the ways in which kinship and gender ideas fit together. Hageners use gender as a metaphor for thinking about different kinds of kinship attachments (Strathern 1987:274). The *person* is essentially genderless. An adult is an autonomous, self-directed person who reveals the operation of will in his or her commitment to tasks.

But men and women vary, both in the tasks they perform and in their connection to their clans. Unlike men, women move away from their clans when they marry. However, women continue to carry their clan identity with them. This distinguishes a woman from her husband and members of his clan. As a result, clanship has a dual aspect. Women are seen as both connected and disconnected at the same time. These conceptions of kinship and gender are connected with prestige, wealth, and politics. For example, sources of male clan prestige include such items as shell valuables, pigs, and money. Because these items are detachable and come from the outside (when a daughter marries, for example), they are also thought to be "female." The significant feature of Strathern's analysis is the distinct way in which Hageners themselves use gender as a way of understanding kinship, politics, prestige, economics, and other social activity.

Kinship and Alliance through Marriage

Any society divided into subgroups must devise a way to manage intergroup relations. It must also arrange for the continuation of those relations from one generation to the next. Societies based on kinship attempt to resolve these difficulties by connecting kinship with marriage. By promoting or *prescribing* certain kinds of marriage, such societies ensure the reproduction of their own memberships. At the same time, they establish long-term alliances with other lineages.

Anthropologists find two major types of prescriptive marriage patterns in unilineal societies. One is a man's marriage with the "father's sister's daughter." The more common is a man's marriage with the "mother's brother's daughter."

direct exchange marriage
a marriage pattern in which a line that has received a wife from a certain different line in one generation provides a wife back in the next generation (sometimes called father's sister's daughter marriage)

In patrilineal societies, father's sister's daughter marriage sets up a pattern of **direct exchange marriage**. In this pattern, a line that has received a wife from another line in one generation gives a wife back in the next generation. That is, if line A receives a wife for one of its members from line B in generation I, line A will provide a wife for a member of line B in generation II. But in generation I, the men of line B cannot marry women from line A. They must find wives from somewhere else, and would marry women from line C. This pattern reverses itself in the next generation, when the obligation has been fulfilled and the original balance restored (see figure 9.11). This is called "father's sister's daughter" marriage because, from a man's point of view, that woman is the prototypical spouse. However, any woman of the appropriate line is an eligible marriage partner for him. Before the marriage occurs, the men and women of the groom's line will negotiate with the men and women of the bride's line to determine the appropriate match.

asymmetrical exchange marriage
a marriage pattern in which one line always gets wives from the same line and gives wives to a different line (sometimes called mother's brother's daughter marriage)

"Mother's brother's daughter" marriage sets up a pattern of **asymmetrical exchange marriage**. Unlike direct exchange systems, this marriage pattern does not balance out after two generations. Instead, one line *always* gets wives from the same line and gives wives to a different line. Put another way, women always marry into the line that their father's sisters married into, and men always find wives in the line their mothers came from. This pattern provides a permanent alliance among the lines involved (see figure 9.12). Here too the literal "mother's brother's daughter" is the prototypical wife for a man. However, she represents all women of the line from which the man's line gets wives. Notice that if a man in a matrilineal society actually does marry his mother's brother's daughter, he inherits doubly. He gets both what his mother's brother would give him, and what his wife's father would give her husband. This is a wise strategy for conserving an inheritance.

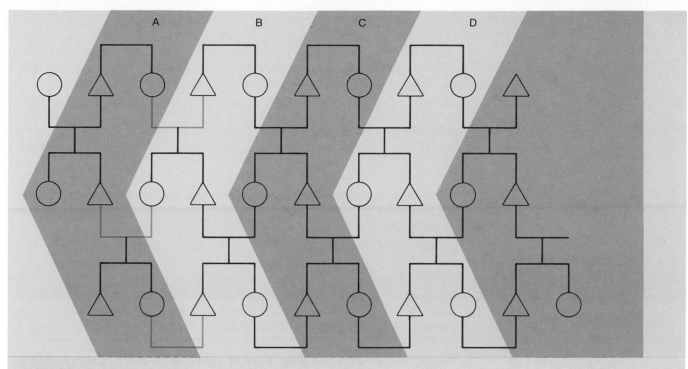

FIGURE 9.11
Father's Sister's Daughter Marriage
A, B, C, and D represent different kinship lines. From the point of view of a male Ego, his line
must give a wife to the line from which his mother came. Every male represented in this
chart has married his father's sister's daughter.

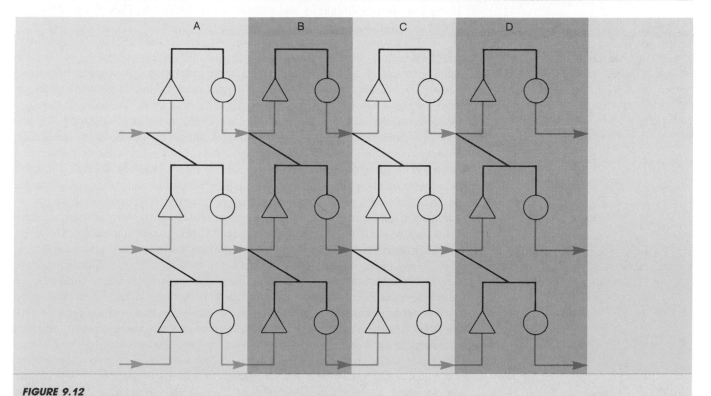

FIGURE 9.12
Mother's Brother's Daughter Marriage
A, B, C, and D represent different kinship lines. A man from B always marries a woman from
A; a man from C always marries a woman from B; and so on.

Here, then, is the final piece in the lineage puzzle. People recognize certain *classes* of kin as potential marriage partners, and their kinship terminologies reflect this. Women whom anthropologists refer to as "mother's brother's daughters" form a category of women whom a man may marry. This is also the answer to the question that inevitably arises: "What happens if Ego doesn't *have* a mother's brother's daughter?" The answer is clear: Ego may not be looking for a literal mother's brother's daughter. He and the older members of his line are looking merely for a good match in the proper category.

Negotiation over Kinship: Literal and Metaphorical Kin

So far, kinship systems have appeared to be fairly rigid sets of rules that people use to determine their relationships, and hence their rights and obligations, to one another. However, most kinship systems are flexible enough to accommodate many of the social dilemmas people must resolve in the real world.

Negotiation among the !Kung

In presenting the !Kung kinship system, Richard Lee demonstrates that "the principles of kinship constitute, not an invariant code of laws written in stone, but instead a whole series of codes, consistent enough to provide structure but open enough to be flexible." He adds: "I found the best way to look at !Kung kinship is as a game, full of ambiguity and nuance" (Lee 1984:57). *(See Ethno File 9.1: !Kung.)*

On the face of it, the !Kung have a straightforward, Eskimo terminology, which, however, alternates generations. Outside the nuclear core of the system, the same terms are used by Ego for kin of his or her generation, his or her grandparents' generation, and his or her grandchildren's generation. Likewise, the same terms are used for Ego's parent's generation and children's generation. These terms have behavioral correlates, which Lee calls "joking" and "avoidance." Anyone in Ego's own generation (except opposite-sex siblings), and in the grandparent's generation or the grandchildren's generation, is joking kin. Anyone in Ego's parent's generation or children's generation is avoidance kin, as are Ego's same-sex siblings. Relatives in a joking relationship can be relaxed and affectionate, and can speak using the familiar forms. In an avoidance relationship, however, respect and reserve are required, and the formal variety of the language must be used. Many of these relationships may be warm and friendly, if the proper respect is shown in public. However, people in an avoidance relationship may not marry one another.

Play in the !Kung system begins when a child is named. The !Kung have very few names: thirty-six for men and thirty-two for women. Every child must be named for someone: a first born son should get his father's father's name, and a first born daughter should get her father's mother's name. Second-born children are supposed to be named after the mother's father and mother. Later children are to be named after the father's brothers and sisters and the mother's brothers and sisters. The result is that up to twenty-five men may share a name, as may up to twenty-five women. It is no wonder that the !Kung invent a host of nicknames to distinguish among people who have the same name.

!Kung naming practices impinge upon the kinship system because all people with the same name claim to be related. A man older than you with your name is called *!kun!a*, "old name," which is the same term used for grandfather. A man younger than you with your name is called *!kuna*, "young name," the same term used for grandson. It does not matter how people are "really" related to others with the same name, or even if they are related at all according to the literal kinship terminology; the name relationship takes precedence.

But the complications do not end yet. By metaphorical extension, anyone with your father's name you call "father," anyone with your wife's name you call "wife," and so on. Worse, "a woman may not marry a man with her father's or brother's name, and a man may not marry a woman with his mother's or sister's name" (ibid.:68). Sometimes a man can marry a woman, but because his name is the same as her father's she can't marry him! Further, you may not marry anyone with the name of one of your avoidance kin. As a result, parents who do not want their children to marry can almost always find a kinship-related reason to block the marriage. Once again, it does not matter what the exact genealogical relationships are.

The name relationship clearly ties !Kung society closer together by making close relatives out of distant ones. At the same time, it makes nonsense of the formal kinship system. How is this dilemma resolved? The !Kung have a third component to their kinship system, the principle of *wi*, which operates as follows. Relative age is one of the few ways the !Kung have of marking distinctions. Thus, in any relationship that can be described by more than one kin relationship, the older party chooses the kin term to be used. For example, a man may get married only to discover that his wife's aunt's husband has the same name he has. What will he and his wife's aunt call each other? According to the principle of *wi*, the aunt decides because she is older. If she calls him "nephew" (rather than "husband"), he knows he should call her "aunt."

The principle of *wi* means that a person's involvement with the kinship system is continually changing over the course of his or her lifetime. For the first half of peoples' lives, they must accept the kin term's their elders choose, whether they understand why or not. After midlife, however, they begin to impose *wi* on their juniors. For the !Kung, kinship connections are open to manipulation and negotiation, rather than being rigidly imposed from the outside.

Negotiation among the Nuer

For the Nuer, people are either relatives or strangers. *(See EthnoFile 9.2: Nuer.)* How can it be that all the people a person comes in contact with are kin? In Nuer society, kinship ties are deliberately created with everyone in close physical proximity. A family that moves into a new community will, after a relatively short time, claim to be related in some way or another to the majority lineage in the community. This claim will usually be accepted by the original residents. As Evans-Pritchard writes,

> *Ultimately and potentially, everybody is kin*, or can be made to appear so if circumstances demand. *This is understandable in a society where kinship values are the only guide in interpersonal relations. When a man has constant intercourse with another it is therefore necessary that each be in some category of kinship in respect of the other so that each may have a rough-and-ready guide to the kind of behaviour expected of him and which he may expect from the other. The categories of the kinship system give him only a formal pattern of relationships, and the content of each relationship depends on genealogical distance, proximity of residence, per-*

sonal feelings, and other factors. But they enable him to systematize his social contacts, to place everybody in a definite position in relation to himself, and so to have the security of living in an ordered world. (1951:176; emphasis added)

Kinship Extended

Every Nuer clan can be segmented into smaller and smaller units until the minimal lineage, the people who live together, is reached. These units represent a way to think about political relationships using a kinship idiom. That is, the group of people known as "Nuer" believe themselves to be connected to one another by a series of assumed kinship ties. They know which segments they belong to, how those segments fit with other segments, and how they are related to people in other segments in kinship terms. Americans conceive of themselves as belonging to neighborhoods, communities, counties, districts, states, regions, and a nation. Each unit is contrasted with other such units. When we ask, "Where are you from?" we do not expect the name of a kinship group. The answer we expect is the name of a territorial unit. The American political idiom is derived from the nation-state and its territorial organization. The political idiom of the Nuer is derived from the language of kinship.

Disputes among the Nuer emerge along the lines created by lineages. Suppose a quarrel erupts between two men whose minimal lineages are in different

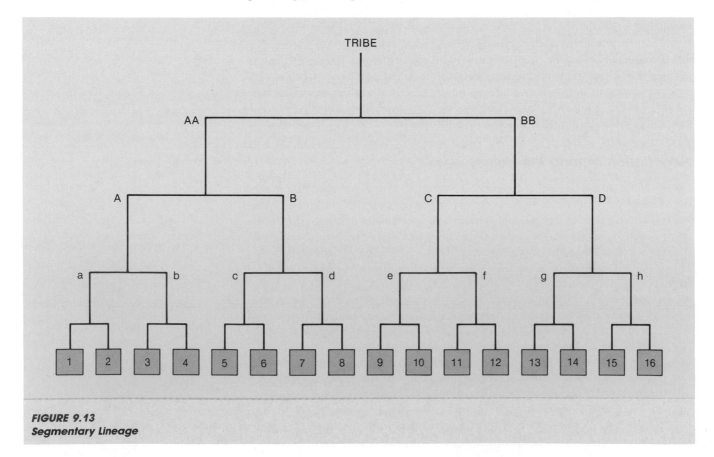

FIGURE 9.13
Segmentary Lineage

minor lineages. Each will be joined in the quarrel by men who belong to his minor lineage, even if they are not in his minimal lineage (see figure 9.13). The dispute will be resolved when the quarreling minor lineages will recognize that they are all part of the same major lineage. The process of **segmentary opposition** is expressed in kinship terms, but represents a very common process.

Compadrazgo in Latin America

One way that kinship can be extended metaphorically is found in the Latin American Roman Catholic practice of ritual coparenthood. This practice, which is also found in southern Europe, is called **compadrazgo**. The baptism of a child requires the presence of a godmother and a godfather as sponsors. By participating in this ritual, the sponsors become the ritual coparents of the child. In Latin America, godparents are expected to take an active interest in their godchildren, and to help them wherever possible. However, the more important relationship is between the godparents and the parents. They become *compadres*, "coparents," and they are expected to behave toward each other in new ways.

While the godparents are sometimes already kin, a couple usually chooses godparents whose social standing is higher than their own. Frequently, the godparents are the owners of the land the parents farm, or of the factory where they work. The connection of ritual coparenthood changes the social relationship of people who initially were unequal strangers. These people become ritual kin. Although their relationship is still unequal, it is now personalized, friendlier, more open. The parents will support the godparents when that support is needed (politically, for example) and the godparents will do favors for the parents. They even call each other *compadre* rather than, say, "Señor López" and "José."

Kinship offers an elaborate and nuanced set of categories for placing people in definite relationships with one another. As a result, it can also be an apt and all-encompassing metaphor for people to use when dealing with outsiders (such as visiting ethnographers) who have no place in the literal kinship system. This metaphoric kinship is termed *fictive kinship* by anthropologists. The possibility of turning strangers into fictive kin demonstrates how kinship is *culturally constructed*. The idiom of mating and birth can be used to organize human interdependence quite apart from any biological "facts."

segmentary opposition
a mode of hierarchical social organization in which groups beyond the most basic emerge only in opposition to other groups on the same level in the hierarchy

compadrazgo
ritual coparenthood in Latin America and Spain, established through the Roman Catholic practice of having godparents for children

Kinship and Practice

Formal kinship systems are not straitjackets. The !Kung principle of *wi* is one example of the flexibility of kinship. It shows how kinship relations can be shaped by everyday social *practice*. Kinship systems provide a more or less flexible series of opportunities for people to choose ways of dealing with others. They also provide multiple social vectors along which relations of alliance, association, mutual support, opposition, and hatred may develop.

A recent work on the Ilongot of the Philippines illustrates this point. *(See EthnoFile 9.3: Ilongot.)* Renato Rosaldo (1980) shows that Ilongot marriage and alliance decisions are not the product of a set of abstract, elegant rules. Instead, they emerge out of the social and historical context of Ilongot life. The Ilongot world is constantly changing. The nature of the relationships Ilongot have with one another,

and their feelings about those relationships, are the result of previous alliances with other kin groups. Past interactions include head-hunting raids they have participated in together or been victims of; the shared background of colonialism, first Spanish and then American; the shared experience of World War II and the Japanese army's flight into the Ilongot hills. More recently, Ilongot have had to cope with martial law in the Philippines and the penetration of soldiers into the Ilongot area; the arrival of members of other Philippines ethnic groups who have settled on the fringes of the Ilongot homeland; and the influence of New Tribes Missionaries.

All of these experiences are alive in the Ilongot mind. Rosaldo is able to show how they influence Ilongot decisions concerning feuding, head-hunting, marriage, and alliance. A dense web of affinal and consanguineal ties links members of Ilongot groups to one another. This enables people to find some form of kinship link tying them to virtually any other person in Ilongot society. The Ilongot thus face opportunities as well as potential barriers as they pursue their interests. Sometimes they get caught in the middle of conflicts because they are linked to all parties involved. At other times, their contradictory loyalties can bring peace to the feuding parties—but this is by no means guaranteed.

Rosaldo provides the example of a man named Lakay who was a member of both the Peknar and Pasigiyan groups of Ilongot. In 1924, the younger brother of a man named Pangpang beheaded a Pasigiyan woman, who was Lakay's mother's sister's daughter (but whom he called by the term *sister*). Lakay was enraged, and wanted to behead Pangpang's younger brother. Unfortunately, they were related to each other by the marriage of Lakay's maternal grandmother to a man of Pangpang's group, the Rumyads. Lakay could not resolve these conflicting loyalties. His solution was to organize a raid in which Peknars and Rumyads settled their differences by attacking a third group toward which both groups had a mutual animosity.

No kinship rules offer tried-and-true formulas for resolving such dilemmas. Resolutions are worked out in the context of the situations in which actors find themselves. As Rosaldo puts it, "In reflecting upon their own social order, the Ilongots themselves confirm that it is ever improvised anew, as they follow one another along shifting paths, at times gathering together and at times dispersing" (Rosaldo 1980:289). The result of these tensions, decisions, and improvisations is a social order that is flexible and that changes from generation to generation. Contrary to stereotype, the Ilongot do not expect children to follow in their parents' footsteps.

EthnoFile 9.4
ITESO

Region: East Africa

Nation: Kenya, Uganda border

Population: 150,000 in Kenya; 600,000 in Uganda (1970s)

Environment: High-rainfall savannah and hills

Livelihood: Agriculture, both subsistence and cash

Political organization: Chiefs, subchiefs, headmen

Other: The Iteso provide a good illustration of the patrilineal paradox: lineage members depend on outsiders (women from other lineages) to reproduce their lineage

In his work on the Iteso of Kenya, Ivan Karp discusses the options for action that a kinship system can provide (principally Karp 1978). *(See EthnoFile 9.4: Iteso.)* Karp notes that among the Iteso, affinal and consanguineal kin have very different and even contradictory rights and obligations to one another. If a person with whom an Iteso is interacting can claim both a link through marriage and a link through patrilineal descent, a space for maneuvering is created. In such cases, Iteso often prefer to emphasize the affinal tie rather than the consanguineal tie. However, they are ambivalent about the choice. Close members of a patrilineage often quarrel and may be ritually dangerous to one another, but they will—indeed, must—help one another in ritual situations and situations of conflict. By contrast, affinal relatives are amiable and helpful but cannot be counted on in times of crisis.

Karp recounts a story that the Iteso interpret as an example of the dilemma they face. A man who was widowed and had remarried moved away from his lineage and was living with his maternal kin. His daughters by his first marriage were living with their mother's brother. One daughter was bitten by a snake and died. Karp was asked to help bring the body back to her father's house for burial. The father went to all his neighbors—his maternal kin—for help in burying her, but none would help. Only at the last moment did some members of his patrilineage arrive to help with the burial. This story illustrates the drawbacks associated with living apart from one's close lineage mates. The father had left himself open to a lack of support in a crisis by cutting himself off from his lineage and choosing to live with his maternal kin. As with the Ilongot, the Iteso kinship system provides no rule to follow when attempting to resolve conflicting kinship loyalties to maternal and paternal kin. In fact, the system almost ensures the creation of overlapping loyalties that will be difficult to resolve.

Kinship: A Framework for Interpreting Life

Kinship may seem awesomely complete and utterly basic to the life of the societies just described. However, it varies in importance from society to society, and even from subgroup to subgroup within the same society. In addition, the Nuer, the !Kung, the Trobriand Islanders, and others have demonstrated that kinship categories can also be used metaphorically. To use kinship in this way is to experience one kind of thing—the division of labor, religion, political struggle, social order—in terms of another phenomenon that is better understood. Kinship is built on an interpretation of mating and birth. But our understanding of these basic human experiences is shaped by the principles of our kinship system. Kinship is "a variety of social idiom, a way of talking about and understanding, and thus of shaping, some aspects of social life" (Geertz and Geertz 1975:169). There is more to life than kinship, but kinship provides one holistic framework for interpreting life.

Key Terms

kinship	clans	cross cousins
marriage	patrilineage	direct exchange marriage
descent	matrilineages	asymmetrical exchange marriage
bilateral or cognatic descent	affinity	segmentary opposition
unilineal descent	collaterality	compadrazgo
bilateral kindred	bifurcation	
lineages	parallel cousins	

Chapter Summary

1. Human life is group life; we depend upon one another to survive. The idiom of kinship is one way in which all societies organize this interdependence. *Kinship* relations are based on, but never simply reducible to, the universal experiences of mating and birth. Kinship principles construct a coherent cultural framework by defining groups, locating people within those groups, and positioning people and groups in relation to one another in space and time.

2. The study of kinship has been of central importance in anthropology. Early anthropologists were able to show that kinship systems were able to keep society orderly in the absence of centralized governmental institutions.

3. Kinship systems are selective. *Matrilineal* societies emphasize that women bear children, and trace descent through women. *Patrilineal* societies emphasize that men impregnate women, and trace descent through men. Both of these contradictory ways of tracing descent can be justified with reference to the human experience of mating and birth.

4. *Descent* links members of different generations with one another. *Bilateral descent* results in the formation of groups called *kindreds*. *Unilineal descent* results in the formation of groups called *lineages*.

5. Unlike kindreds, *lineages* are corporate groups. Legally speaking, all members of a lineage are equal to one another. Lineages control important property, such as land, that collectively belongs to their members. Lineage members ordinarily assume that current lineage relationships within the society are faithful to tradition. If tradition contradicts the contemporary situation, it is usually assumed that knowledge of tradition is faulty and must be corrected. This is because the language of lineage is the idiom of political discussion, and lineage relationships are of current political significance.

6. Kinship terminologies apply labels to significant groups of kin by recognizing certain attributes in people, which are used to define different classes of kin. The attributes most often recognized include generation, sex, *affinity, collaterality, bifurcation,* relative age, and the sex of the linking relative.

7. Anthropologists recognize six basic terminological systems according to their patterns of referring to cousins. These systems are named after societies that represent the prototype of each pattern: Hawaiian, Eskimo, Iroquois, Crow, Omaha, and Sudanese. The first two are found in association with bilateral descent systems, and the remaining four are found in association with unilineal descent.

8. By prescribing certain kinds of marriage, lineages are able to establish long-term alliances with other lineages. Two major types of prescriptive marriage patterns in unilineal societies are (1) a man's marriage with the "father's sister's daughter" and (2) a man's marriage with the "mother's brother's daughter." Father's sister's daughter marriage sets up a pattern of *direct exchange marriage*; mother's brother's daughter marriage sets up a pattern of *asymmetrical exchange marriage*.

9. Alongside the literal kinship system defined in the terminology, there often exist relationships linking metaphorical kin. The opportunity to create metaphorical kin links with strangers adds flexibility to social relations in societies organized in terms of kinship. At the same time, the possibility of turning strangers into fictive kin demonstrates the way in which kinship is a cultural construction that employs the idiom of mating and birth to organize human interdependence quite apart from the biological facts.

Suggested Readings

Bohannan, Paul, and John Middleton. *Kinship and Social Organization.* New York: Natural History Press, 1968.

    A collection of important, classic articles from a wide range of theoretical perspectives.

Bowen, Eleanore Smith [Laura Bohannan]. *Return to Laughter.* New York: Natural History Press, Doubleday Anchor Books, 1964. Originally published in 1954.

    An anthropologist's novel, first published under a pseudonym, that gives a real sense of an alternative world, one where kinship connections are of fundamental importance.

Fox, Robin. *Kinship and Marriage.* Baltimore: Penguin, 1968.

    Although dated in some ways (much feminist scholarship has called into question some of Fox's theoretical arguments), there is still useful material in this introduction to marriage and kinship.

Graburn, Nelson. *Readings in Kinship and Social Structure.* New York: Harper and Row, 1971.

    Another collection, this one covering a wider range of topics, and with little overlap.

Weiner, Annette. "Trobriand Kinship from Another View: The Reproductive Power of Women and Men." *Man* 14(2): 328–348, 1979.

    An important article, worth the effort it may require for a beginning student.

How Useful Is Anthropology?

David Parkin (Ph.D., University of London) is Professor of Anthropology at the School of Oriental and African Studies at the University of London. He has carried out fieldwork in Uganda and Kenya, especially among the Giriama of Kenya. Dr. Parkin has written three books on the Giriama and the Luo, and has edited five other books. He is especially interested in the relationship between language and the perception of innovation and in indigenous philosophies.

At a time when the social sciences and the humanities are under attack or financial constraint in the United States and Great Britain, people are asking: Anthropology may be interesting to a few specialists, but what good is it to the nation and the world, and why should public money be spent on hiring professors to teach it? And why should young people spend their time and taxpayers' money learning an arcane subject that does not give them the skills for productive employment?

Such questions strike those who are involved with the study of anthropology as harsh and often philistine. Yet to dismiss them as pronouncement of the ignorant and not worth answering would be bigoted too. To some extent the answer an anthropologist would give would be the answer given by any scholar in the humanities. Thus, it is through art, history, literature, and philosophy that we reflect on the world. This method is normally more effective than diatribe, for these disciplines influence through their equivocation rather than through their assertions. They are the essence of debate rather than dogma. They allow for response as well as statement.

Anthropology—and I speak specifically for cultural anthropology—is in an even more equivocal position. On the one hand, it can pose as a social science. In this role it sometimes attempts to grapple with Third World problems of a developmental nature, or it may even address so-called social breakdowns in communities at home, as it continues to produce abstract theories of how society works. On the other hand, like art and the other humanities, anthropology is a discipline that reflects on the many human presentations of self that we call different cultures. Like the other humanities, anthropology does not seek to solve problems; it seeks to understand other possible ways of thinking, believing, and acting. This is unashamedly intellectual interest for its own sake. Yet because we can come to understand ourselves more by contemplating the differences found in other peoples, it is difficult to regard such activity as useless. Is it useless to discover that there is a comprehensible and even elegant logic in the apparently bizarre activities of peoples in other cultures? Such a discovery should reassure us that people everywhere strive for rationality in their own distinctive ways. Of course, all peoples are also capable of what both they and we would regard as irrational behavior, but this is one of the "imperfections" that make us human.

The knowledge that people everywhere are capable of both rational and irrational acts should reduce us all to a common recognition of our frailties and make for better communication. One telling criticism of the social sciences is their tendency, though now rare, to talk down to the people who are the subject of their study, as if the social sciences possessed the one and only solution to a problem. The humanities, because they can criticize through a kind of dialogue—between, say, artist and consumer—have managed to escape this accusation on the whole. Anthropology was justly questioned about its alleged role as handmaiden of imperialist and later neocolonial domination, yet it has also often been seen as defender of threatened minorities and of indigenous customs and traditions that those minorities want to preserve in the face of change.

Thus, just as anthropology ambivalently straddles the social sciences and humanities, so it attracts both criticism and approbation for the ways it reports on other peoples' customs. It may be true that we unwillingly distort the picture of other cultures by imposing our own Western assumptions on them, but by recognizing this perhaps inevitable problem of cultural translation, we are in a position to compare the different cultural assumptions, "theirs" and "ours," and to see the similarities between them as well as the differences. I do not, in other words, support a relativist position in anthropology. Nor do I think that anthropologists seek only universals in human thought and culture. We can assume, rather, that different cultures share some things in common and are apart in others, but that in making comparisons we discover new human potentialities or reevaluate old judgments. Because this is a constant process, it offers no promise of final conclusions. I would even say that the dichotomy of relativism and universalism has created more confusion than anything else in anthropology. No two human languages or cultures are ever so totally different that they cannot mutually communicate, and so it is absurd to relativize whole societies. Conversely, a belief in the total universality of certain human values is either too banal to be interesting (for, of course, all people have some basic wants and means of expressing them) or imposes *a priori* notions on our understanding of other cultures.

Cultural translation, like translation from one language to another, never produces a rendering that is semantically and stylistically an exact replica of the original. That much we accept. What is not often recognized, perhaps not even by the translators themselves, is that the very act of having to decide how to phrase an event, sentiment, or human character engages the translator in an act of creation. The translator does not simply re-present a picture made by an author. He or she creates a new version, and perhaps in some respects a new picture—a matter that is often of some great value.

So it is with anthropologists. But while this act of creation in reporting on "the other" may reasonably be regarded as a self-sustaining pleasure, it is also an entry into the pitfalls and traps of language use itself. One of the most interesting new fields in anthropology is the study of the relationship between language and human knowledge, both among ourselves as professional anthropologists and laypeople, and among peoples of other cultures. The study is at once both reflexive and critical.

The hidden influences at work in language use attract the most interest. For example, systems of greetings have many built-in elaborations that differentiate subtly between those who are old and young, male and female, rich and poor, and powerful and powerless. When physicians discuss a patient in his or her presence and refer to the patient in the third-person singular, they are in effect defining the patient as a passive object unable to enter into the discussion. When anthropologists present elegant accounts of "their" people that fit the demands of a convincing theory admirably, do they not also leave out the description any consideration of the informants' own fears and feelings? Or do we go too far in making such claims, and is it often the anthropologist who is indulged by the people, who give him or her the data they think is sought, either in exchange for something they want or simply because it pleases them to do so? If the latter, how did the anthropologist's account miss this critical part of the dialogue?

Anthropology is useful to the world in that it is the one discipline that aims to discover, question, and criticize human aims and actions across a spectrum of cultural possibilities. It can claim to be the bedrock on which all other forms of dialogue rest, including those of politicians, economists, and even Western analytic philosophers, each of whom draws the examples making up a grandiose schema from the particular instances of everyday life, both home and abroad, on which anthropologists report.

D. J. Parkin

291

CHAPTER 10
Marriage and the Family

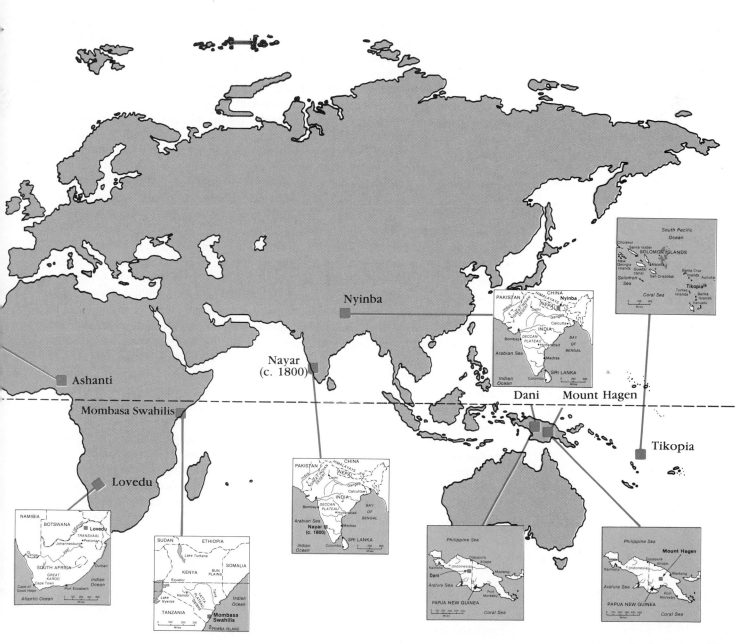

Nyinba

Nayar
(c. 1800)

Ashanti

Mombasa Swahilis

Lovedu

Dani   Mount Hagen

Tikopia

R. K. Narayan, distinguished Indian novelist (b. 1908), writes the following in his autobiography about falling in love and getting married.

"In July 1933, I had gone to Coimbatore, escorting my elder sister, and then stayed on in her house. There was no reason why I should ever hurry away from one place to another. I was a free-lance writer and I could work wherever I might be at a particular time. One day, I saw a girl drawing water from the street-tap and immediately fell in love with her. Of course, I could not talk to her. I learned later that she had not even noticed me passing and repassing in front of her while she waited to fill the brass vessels. I craved to get a clear, fixed, mental impression of her features, but I was handicapped by the time factor, as she would be available for staring at only until her vessels filled, when she would carry them off, and not come out again until the next water-filling time. I could not really stand and stare; whatever impression I had of her would be through a side-glance while passing the tap. I suffered from a continually melting vision. The only thing I was certain of was that I loved her, and I suffered the agonies of restraint imposed by the social conditions in which I lived. The tall headmaster, her father, was a friend of the family and often dropped in for a chat with the elders at home while on his way to the school, which was at a corner of our street. The headmaster, headmaster's daughter, and the school were all within geographical reach and hailing distance, but the restraint imposed by the social code created barriers. I attempted to overcome them by befriending the headmaster. He was a book-lover and interested in literary matters, and we found many common subjects for talk. We got into the habit of meeting at his school after the school-hours and discussing the world, seated comfortably on a cool granite *pyol* in front of a little shrine of Ganesha in the school compound. One memorable evening, when the stars had come out, I interrupted some talk we were having on political matters to make a bold, blunt announcement of my affection for his daughter. He was taken aback, but did not show it. In answer to my proposal, he just turned to the god in the shrine and shut his eyes in prayer. No one in our social condition could dare to proceed in the manner I had done. There were formalities to be observed, and any talk for a marriage proposal could proceed only between the elders of the families. What I had done was unheard of. But the headmaster was sporting enough not to shut me up immediately. Our families were known to each other, and the class, community, and caste requirements were all right. He just said, 'if God wills it,' and left it at that. He also said, 'Marriages are made in Heaven, and who are we to say Yes or No?' After this he explained the difficulties. His wife and womenfolk at home were to be consulted, and my parents had to approve, and so on and so forth, and then the matching of the horoscopes—this last became a great hurdle at the end. . . .

"What really mattered was not my economic outlook, but my stars. My father-in-law, himself an adept at the study of horoscopes, had consultations with one or two other experts and came to the conclusion that my horoscope and the girl's were incompatible. My horoscope had the Seventh House occupied by Mars, the Seventh House being the one that indicated nothing but disaster unless the partner's horoscope also contained the same flaw, a case in which two wrongs make one right. . . .

"In spite of all these fluctuations and hurdles, my marriage came off in a few months, celebrated with all the pomp, show, festivity, exchange of gifts, and the overcrowding, that my parents desired and expected.

"Soon after my marriage, my father became bed-ridden with a paralytic stroke, and most of my mother's time was spent at his side upstairs. The new entrant into the family, my wife Rajam, was her deputy downstairs, managing my three younger brothers, who were still at school, a cook in the kitchen, a general servant, and a gigantic black-and-white Great Dane acquired by my elder brother, who was a dog-lover. She kept an eye on the stores, replenishing the food-stuffs and guarding them from being squandered or stolen by the cook. Rajam was less than twenty, but managed the housekeeping expertly and earned my mother's praise. She got on excellently with my brothers. This was one advantage of a joint family system—one had plenty of company at home" (Narayan 1974:106–10).

Narayan had fallen in love, gotten married, and set up housekeeping with his wife. These are familiar phases in the relationship of a man and a woman, yet the details of his description seem exotic, perhaps even extraordinary. Narayan's essay makes clear how the patterns of courtship, marriage, and housekeeping in India engage people in the wider patterns of Indian life. They channel emotion and economic activity. They also link people formerly not related while binding individuals firmly to groups. One individual, Narayan, fell in love with and married another individual, Rajam. But they could never have become a married couple without knowing how to maneuver within the cultural patterns that shaped their society. Neither could they have gotten married without the active intervention of the wider social groups to which they belonged—specifically, their families.

Human life is indeed group life, and in the chapter on kinship we saw some of the ways human beings classify themselves and others. At the core of this process are a series of metaphors and metaphoric entailments drawn from the biological experiences of mating and birth. *Marriage* and *the family* are two concepts that anthropologists use to describe the way mating and birth are understood and organized in different societies.

Toward A Definition of Marriage?

Each culture has its own definition of what marriage is. Nowhere, however, is it the same thing as mating. Marriage involves a change in the social position of the people involved and affects the social position of any children they produce. While different societies highlight or downplay various features of marriage, some criteria for defining marriage are common in most societies. We will concentrate on these criteria in our own definition of marriage.

A prototypical marriage (1) involves a man and a woman, and (2) stipulates the degree of sexual access the married partners may have to each other, ranging from exclusive to preferential sexual access. It also (3) establishes the legitimacy of children born to the wife, and (4) creates relationships between the kin of the wife and the kin of the husband.

If a prototypical marriage involves a biological male and a biological female, however, what are we to make of the following cases? Each offers an alternative way of understanding the combination of features that define appropriate unions in a particular society. Although the people who are allowed to marry may vary, however, the role of legitimacy in maintaining patterns of descent over generations does not.

Nuer Woman Marriage

Among the Nuer, a woman may marry another woman and become the "father" of the children the wife bears. This practice, which appears in some other parts of

Africa as well, involves a distinction between pater and genitor: the *pater* is the legal father of a child; the *genitor* is the man who impregnated the child's mother.

The female husband must have some cattle of her own to use for bridewealth payments to the lineage of the wife. Once the bridewealth has been paid, she has taken a wife, just as a man would do. The female husband then gets a male kinsman or a friend or neighbor to impregnate the wife and to help with certain tasks around the homestead that the Nuer believe can be done only by men.

Generally, Evans-Pritchard (1951) tells us, a woman who takes a wife has been unable to have children herself, "and for this reason counts in some respects as a man." In other words, the Nuer metaphorically label such a woman as a near-man. Indeed, she plays the social role of a man. She may marry several wives if she is wealthy. She can demand damage payment if those wives engage in sexual activity without her consent. She is the pater of her wives' children. On the marriage of her daughters, she receives the portion of the bridewealth that traditionally goes to the father. Her brothers and sisters receive the portions of the bridewealth that are supposed to go to the father's side. Her children are named after her, as though she were a man, and they address her as "Father." She administers her compound and her herds as a male head of household would, and she is treated by her wives and children with the same deference that they would show to a male husband and father.

The constellation of features described here is ordinarily associated with a male head of household—a father and husband. But that is only prototypically the case. This set of roles is associated with men because usually men marry women. But the role of husband and father is independent of the sex of the person carrying out the role. For the Nuer, a social man is not necessarily a biological man. If a woman does what a man does, she is a man. The presence of the right genitalia is part of the prototype of a man, but it is not the sole defining feature. So it appears that all the features we associate with being a man or a woman are not universally accorded equal importance.

The Berdache

Among certain Indians of the North American plains, a "flamboyant masculinity" was required of men. But not all men were able or willing to conform to this ideal. Those who were interested in more peaceful activities became "men-women," or *berdache*. They dressed in women's clothing, learned women's activities, and were even able to marry men, usually as a second wife. The *berdaches'* relationships with their husbands were not necessarily sexual, although they might be. Here we find the converse of the Nuer case. Being a woman is usually associated with biological femaleness, but it is possible to become a woman by doing what women do, rather than by becoming a physiological woman.

Nuer Ghost Marriage

Another example of the split between sex and the legal characteristics of marriage is also from the Nuer, but is unusual in the world. A common feature of Nuer social life is what Evans-Pritchard calls "ghost marriage." The Nuer believe that a man who dies without male heirs leaves an unhappy and angry spirit who may trouble his living kin. The spirit is angry because a basic obligation of Nuer kinship is for a man to be remembered through and by his sons: his name must be continued in his lineage. To appease the angry spirit, a kinsman of the dead man—a brother, a brother's son—will often marry a woman "to his name." Bridewealth cattle are paid in the name of the dead man to the patrilineage of a woman. She is then married to the ghost, but resides with his living kinsman. In the marriage ceremonies and afterwards, this kinsman acts as though he were the true husband. The children of the union are referred to as though they were the kinsman's—but officially they are not. His children are considered children of the ghost husband. As the children get older, the name of their ghost father becomes increasingly important to them. The ghost father's name, not his stand-in's name, will be remembered in the history of the lineage.

In this case, biological paternity is divorced from legitimacy. But for the Nuer, legitimacy is a central attribute of marriage. The essential feature of the ghost marriage is the provision of children to the *ghost husband's* lineage. The social union between the ghost and the woman takes precedence over the sexual union between the ghost's surrogate and the woman.

Ghost marriage serves to establish a *continuation* of social patterns. It is common for a man to marry a wife to his kinsman's name before he is himself married. This makes it difficult, if not impossible, for him to marry later in his own right. His relatives tell him he is "already married." Therefore, he should allow his younger brothers to use cattle from the family herd so they can marry before he himself can contract a second, legal marriage. Even if he eventually accumulates enough cattle to afford to marry, he usually feels that those cattle should be used to pay the bridewealth for the sons he has raised for his dead kinsman. When he dies, he dies childless, since the children he raised are legally the children of the ghost. He now is an angry spirit, and someone else (in fact, one of the sons he has raised for the ghost) must marry a wife to *his* name. The pattern then continues.

Marriage as a Social Process

Marriages set up new relationships between the kin of the husband and the kin of the wife. These are called **affinal** relationships (based on affinity), and contrast with **consanguineal** (or "blood") relationships. The two issues of affinity and consanguinity are centrally associated with the definition of marriage and the formation of social groups. Mating alone does not create in-laws, nor does it set up a way of locating the offspring in space and time, as members of a particular social group. Marriage does both.

Socially, marriage has four marks. First, it transforms the status of the participants. Second, it alters the relationships among the kin of each party. Third, it makes possible the reproduction of social patterns through the production of offspring who also have certain kinds of rights and obligations (see Karp 1986). Fourth, it is always symbolically marked in some way. It may be noted by an elaborate wedding, with bridesmaids, ushers, ring bearers, trainbearers, and the like. Alternatively, the new husband and wife may simply appear seated together one morning outside her hut. Marriage is a major transition in people's lives. It represents a transformation of social position. Two individuals have become one married couple. In an important way, the third party to any wedding is the rest of the community, which must acknowledge the legitimacy of the new union.

Every society has ways of matching the right groom with the right bride. Sometimes marriages must be contracted within a particular social group. This marriage pattern is called **endogamy**. In other cases, marriage partners must be found outside a particular group. This marriage pattern is called **exogamy**. In Nuer so-

affinal
kinship connections through marriage, or affinity

consanguineal
kinship connections through direct genealogical links; from the Latin word for "blood"

endogamy
marriage within a defined social group

exogamy
marriage outside a defined social group

ciety, for example, a person must marry outside his or her lineage. Even in American society, we prefer people to marry within the bounds of certain groups. We are told to marry "our own kind," which usually means our own ethnic group, religious group, or social class. In all societies, some people are off limits as spouses or as sexual partners. This exogamous pattern is known as the *incest taboo*.

Patterns of Residence after Marriage

neolocal
a postmarital residence pattern in which married children set up an independent household at a place of their own choosing

patrilocal
a postmarital residence pattern in which married children live in the same household with, or live near, the husband's father

matrilocal
a postmarital residence pattern in which married children live in the same household with, or live near, the wife's mother

avunculocal
a postmarital residence pattern in which married children live in the same household with, or live near, the husband's mother's brother; from *avuncular*, "of uncles"

Once married, a couple must live somewhere. There are four major patterns of postmarital residence. Most familiar to Americans is **neolocal** residence, in which the new couple sets up an independent household at a place of their own choosing. Neolocal residence tends to be found in societies that are more or less atomistic in their social organization, especially those with Eskimo kinship systems.

When the married couple go to live with (or near) the husband's father's family, it is called **patrilocal** residence. This is the most common residence pattern in the world. It produces a characteristic social grouping of related men, in which a man, his brothers, and their sons, along with in-marrying wives, all live and work together. This pattern is common in both herding and farming societies. Some anthropologists have argued that this is because survival in such societies depends on activities that can best be carried out by groups of men who have worked together all their lives.

When the married couple go to live with (or near) the family in which the wife was raised, it is called **matrilocal** residence. This is usually found in association with matrilineal kinship systems. Here, the core of the social group consists of a woman, her sisters, and their daughters, together with in-marrying men. This pattern is most common among horticultural groups.

Less common, but also found in matrilineal societies, is the pattern known as **avunculocal** residence. Here, the married couple go to live with the husband's mother's brother. The most significant man in a boy's matrilineage is his mother's brother, from whom he will inherit. Avunculocal residence emphasizes this relationship.

There are other, even less common patterns of residence. In *ambilocal* residence, the couple shifts residence, living first with the family of one spouse, later with the family of the other spouse. At some point, the couple will usually have to choose which family they want to affiliate with permanently. *Duolocal* residence is found where lineage membership is so important that husbands and wives continue to live with their own lineages even after they are married. The Ashanti of Ghana observe duolocal residence. *(See EthnoFile 10.5: Ashanti.)* We will see later how this Ashanti residence pattern affects other aspects of Ashanti social and cultural life.

Single and Plural Spouses

monogamy
a marriage pattern in which a person may be married to only one spouse at a time

polygamy
a marriage pattern in which a person may be married to more than one spouse at a time

The number of spouses a person may have varies cross-culturally. Anthropologists distinguish, first of all, between forms of marriage that allow a person only one spouse (**monogamy**) and forms of marriage in which a person may have several spouses (**polygamy**). Within the category of polygamy are two subcategories: **po-**

lygyny, or multiple wives, and **polyandry**, or multiple husbands. Most societies in the world permit polygyny.

Monogamy

Monogamy is the spousal pattern characteristic of the United States and most industrialized nations, and is the only legal form of marriage in those countries. Indeed, in 1896, a condition of statehood for the territory of Utah was the abolition of polygyny, which had been practiced by Mormon settlers for nearly fifty years. There are variations in the number of times a monogamous person can be married. Traditionally in Western societies, a person could marry only once unless death intervened. Now some observers suggest that we practice "serial monogamy"; we may be married to several different people, but only one at a time.

Polygyny

Polygynous societies vary in the number of wives a man may have. Islam permits a man to have as many as four wives, but only on the condition that he can support them equally. Other polygynous societies have no limit on the number of wives a man may marry. Nevertheless, not every man can be polygynous. There is a clear demographic problem: for every man with two wives, there is one man without a wife. If men must wait until they are older to marry and women marry very young, this imbalance can be improved but not eliminated. Polygyny is also expensive, for a husband must support all his wives as well as the children born to them.

Polyandry

Polyandry is the rarest of the three marriage forms. In some polyandrous societies, a woman may marry several brothers. In others, she may marry men who are not related to each other and who all will live together in a single household. Sometimes a woman is allowed to marry several men who are not related, but she will live only with the one she most recently married. Polyandry traditionally has gotten short

polygyny
a marriage pattern in which a man may be married to more than one wife simultaneously

polyandry
a marriage pattern in which a woman may be married to more than one husband simultaneously

The wives and children of a polygynous family.

shrift in anthropology, and has sometimes been dismissed as an oddity. Recent studies of polyandrous societies, however, have challenged our traditional understanding of polyandry. At the same time, they have shed new light on the dynamics of polygyny and monogamy.

Spousal Patterns and Sexuality

Different marriage patterns offer significant variation in the way male and female sexuality are socially defined. Monogamy and polygyny are in some ways similar, since both are concerned with controlling women's sexuality while giving men freer rein. Even in monogamous societies, men (but not women) are often expected to have extramarital sexual adventures. Polyandry is worth a closer look; it differs from polygyny or monogamy in instructive ways.

Polyandry, Sexuality, and the Reproductive Capacity of Women

In an important work, Nancy Levine and Walter Sangree (1980) provide an overview of recent research on polyandry. Polyandry is found in three major regions of the world: Tibet and Nepal, South India and Sri Lanka, and northern Nigeria and northern Cameroon. The forms of polyandry in these areas are different, but all involve women with several husbands.

Fraternal Polyandry

The traditional anthropological prototype of polyandry has been found among some groups in Nepal and Tibet, where a group of brothers marry one woman. This is known as *fraternal polyandry*. One wedding is held, in which one brother, usually the oldest, serves as the groom. All brothers (including those yet to be born to the husbands' parents) are married by this wedding, which establishes public recognition of the marriage. The wife and her husbands live together, usually patrilocally. All brothers have equal sexual access to the wife, and all act as fathers to the children that are born. In some cases—notably among the Nyinba of Nepal (Levine 1988, 1980)—one of the brothers is always recognized as the genitor of each child. *(See EthnoFile 10.1: Nyinba.)* In other cases, all the brothers are considered jointly as the father, with no distinction being made as to the identity of the genitor.

EthnoFile 10.1
NYINBA

Region: Central Asia

Nation: Northwestern Nepal

Population: 1,200

Environment: Himalayan valleys

Livelihood: Agriculture, herding

Political organization: Headmen; now part of state

Other: Fraternal polyandry is practiced in this society

Contrary to the Western male stereotype, there appears to be no sexual jealousy among the men, and the brothers have a strong sense of solidarity with one another. Levine (1988) emphasizes this point for the Nyinba. If the wife proves sterile, the brothers may marry another woman in hopes that she may be fertile. As with the first wife, all brothers will have equal sexual access to the new wife and will be treated as fathers by her children. In societies that practice fraternal polyandry, marrying sisters (or *sororal polygyny*) may be preferred or permitted. In this system, a group of brothers could marry a group of sisters.

According to Levine (1988:158ff.), Nyinba polyandry is reinforced by a variety of cultural beliefs and practices. First, it has a special cultural value. Nyinba legendary ancestors are polyandrous, and they are praised for the harmony of their family life. Second, the solidarity of brothers is a central kinship ideal. Third, the corporate, landholding household, central to Nyinba life, presupposed polyandry. Fourth, the structure of Nyinba villages presupposes a limited number of households, and polyandry is highly effective in checking the proliferation of households. Finally, a household's political position and economic viability increase when its resources are concentrated.

Associated Polyandry

A second form of polyandry is known as *associated polyandry*. This refers to any system in which polyandry is a marriage strategy open to men who are not necessarily brothers (Levine and Sangree 1980). There is some evidence that associated polyandry was an acceptable marriage variant in parts of the Pacific, among some North and South American Indian groups, and among the Inuit. The best-described form of associated polyandry, however, is from Sri Lanka. *(See EthnoFile 6.8: Sinhalese.)*

Among the Sinhalese of Sri Lanka, a woman may marry two, but rarely more than two, men. Unlike fraternal polyandry, which begins as a joint venture, Sinhalese associated polyandry begins monogamously. The second husband is brought into the union later. Again unlike fraternal polyandry, the first husband is the principal husband in terms of authority. A woman and her husbands live and work together, although economic resources are held independently. All husbands are considered fathers to any children the wife bears. This system allows many individual choices. For example, two husbands and their wife may decide to take another woman into the marriage—often the sister of the wife. This means that their household becomes simultaneously polygynous and polyandrous. A term has been coined for this: *polygynandry*. Thus, depending on relative wealth and the availability of economic opportunity, a Sinhalese household may be monogamous, polyandrous, or polygynandrous.

One famous anthropological example in the study of marriage and the family is the Nayar of India as they were until the end of the seventeenth century (see, e.g., Gough 1961). *(See EthnoFile 10.2: Nayar.)* The Nayar during this period were matrilineal, and each lineage was linked to two or three other lineages of the neighborhood. These linked lineages were partners who offered help in the ceremonies of life, including the marriage rites for prepubescent girls. Every ten to twelve years, each lineage married all its immature girls to men of the linked lineages. At the ceremony, each groom tied a gold ornament around the neck of his bride, who had been chosen for him by the elders. Following this, each couple was secluded in a room in the ancestral house for three days and three nights. If the girl was old enough, sexual relations might occur. On the fourth day, the grooms left, and had no further obligations to their brides.

EthnoFile 10.2
NAYAR (c. 1800)

Region: South Asia

Nation: India (Kerala State)

Population: About 30,000 to 40,000

Environment: Flatland between mountains and coast

Livelihood: Ruling and warrior caste

Political organization: A caste in a traditional stratified kingdom; now part of the modern nation of India

Other: This is a famous example of associated polyandry

After the ceremony, a girl achieved the status of mature woman. She was permitted to establish sexual relations of a more or less enduring quality with one or more men of her own or an appropriate higher caste. These men could not be brothers, and a man could not have sexual relations with two women of the same household. The first of these relationships was marked by a brief ceremony, which might be repeated each time another of these relationships was established. Spouses lived separately, and the husband would come to visit his wife in the evening. While the relationship lasted, a husband was expected to give gifts to his wife at the three main festivals of the year. The only other obligation of a husband came at the birth of a child. One or more men of an appropriate caste had to acknowledge possible biological paternity. This was done by the husbands who had had sexual relations with the woman during the relevant time period. Their gifts were very small and economically inconsequential, but of the utmost symbolic significance. If no man would give his wife gifts, it was assumed that the woman had engaged in sexual relations with a man of lower caste or with a Muslim or Christian. She would be banished if she were lucky.

In short, the Nayar marriage system did not include many of the characteristics we take for granted in marriage. Husband and wife did not live together, women and men both had multiple spouses, no economic relationships existed between the husbands and wives as individuals, and no attempt was made to determine the biological father of the woman's children. Nevertheless, the children had a place within the society and were normal and well adjusted, and the society survived and even prospered for many generations.

As we mentioned at the beginning of the chapter, one important aspect of marriage is the creation of ties between the families of the bride and groom. In the two forms of polyandry just discussed, the potential network of ties created by marriage is sharply curtailed. This is particularly true where fraternal polyandry occurs with preferred or permitted sororal polygyny. For example, in a Tibetan household of four brothers married to one woman, the entire household is tied affinally only to the family of the wife. If these same brothers decided to take another wife—to engage in polygynandry—they may marry a sister of their first wife. In so doing, they would be giving up the possibility of establishing ties with other households in favor of fortifying the relationship already established by the first marriage. In the same way, Nayar polyandry concentrates relationships among lineages that were already associated before the marriages. Nancy Levine and Walter Sangree call this "alliance intensifying."

Secondary Marriage

The final form of polyandry is sometimes referred to as *secondary marriage*. It is found only in northern Nigeria and northern Cameroon. In secondary marriage, a woman marries one or more secondary husbands while staying married to her previously married husbands (Levine and Sangree 1980:400). The woman lives with only one husband at a time, but she retains the right to return to the first husband and to have legitimate children by him at a later date. No divorce is permitted in the societies that practice secondary marriage; all of a person's marriages are for life.

In this system, as in the other polyandrous systems we examined here, men are polygynous and women are polyandrous. A man makes a series of marriages and lives with one or more of his wives at his homestead. At the same time, women are independently pursuing their own marital careers. This system of secondary marriage is really neither polyandry nor polygyny. It is rather a combination of the two, resulting from the overlap of men seeking several wives and women seeking several husbands. Secondary marriage is the opposite of Tibetan fraternal polyandry. It is "alliance proliferative," leading to an extensive network of kinship and marriage-based ties throughout a region. It serves to unite rather than to concentrate groups.

The Distinction between Sexuality and Reproductive Capacity

Polyandry demonstrates the way in which a woman's sexuality can be distinguished from her reproductive capacity. This distinction is absent in monogamous or purely polygynous systems, in which polyandry is opposed. Those societies have a strong resistance to perceiving women's sexual and reproductive capacities as separable (except, perhaps, in prostitution). However, the separability of men's sexual and procreative attributes is usually accepted without question. "It may well be a fundamental feature of the [world view] of polyandrous peoples that they recognize such a distinction for *both* men and women" (ibid.: 388). In the better-known polyandrous groups, a woman's sexuality can be shared among an unlimited number of men, but her childbearing capacities cannot be. Indeed, among the Nyinba (Levine 1980), a woman's childbearing capacities are carefully controlled and limited to one husband at a time. But she is free to engage in sexual activity outside her marriage as long as she is not likely to get pregnant.

Inuit Marriage

The exotic popular image of Inuit marriage is one of "wife trading" and offering wives to strangers as part of "hospitality." *(See EthnoFile 10.3: Alaskan Inuit.)* Research by anthropologists has shown that neither of these images is true. Nevertheless, traditional Inuit marriage is of great interest. First, the Inuit are among the only peoples we know about who seem to have no rituals at all to celebrate marriage. Second, until the turn of the twentieth century, the Inuit practiced a form of marriage that looked much like the polygynous, polyandrous marriage discussed earlier. Ernest Burch (1975:119) notes that a major feature of traditional Inuit marriage was what he calls co–marriage. Co–marriage had nearly disappeared by 1900, although when Burch was in the field in 1970, he knew a few older Inuit who still were part of a co–marriage. Following Burch's example, our discussion is set at the end of the nineteenth century.

Traditional Inuit marriage was defined by three features. First, a couple began to live together, usually in the house of one spouse's parents. Second, the

couple engaged in sexual intercourse. Third, the couple began to refer to one another using the terms *ui* and *nuliaq*, "husband" and "wife" (Burch 1975:81). Marriage was marked by no elaborate ritual, just by the socially accepted coresidence and sexual intercourse of a couple. The couple did not even have to live together very long for the relationship to be considered established, both by them and by the other members of the community.

Burch suggests that the reason for the lack of elaboration was that marriage did not hold a very high position in the Inuit view of their own social world. It was a more or less utilitarian relationship designed to meet as effectively as possible the problems of daily existence (ibid.: 82). Apart from activities primarily oriented toward economic or sexual matters, a husband and wife rarely saw much of each other. The woman stayed in the house. The husband hunted, visited male relatives and friends, or spent time in the community social center, which was dominated by men (ibid.: 85). Put another way, Inuit kinship favored consanguinity over affinity. Relationships based on birth were privileged over relationships created through marriage. In Inuit marriage, the *ui-nuliaq* relationship was the only one in which sexual intercourse had the specific aim of producing children.

The main elaboration of the *ui-nuliaq* marriage pattern was the polygynous residential marriage. Here, one man lived with, and had sexual intercourse with, two women. This was a rare pattern, given the approximately equal number of men and women among the Inuit of northwestern Alaska, but it was an acceptable one. Terminologically, the wives were distinguished from one another, and referred to each other as co-wives.

The second and far less common elaboration on the basic marriage pattern was the polyandrous residential marriage. Here the two men referred to each other as co-husbands, and again the wife distinguished between her two husbands terminologically. Burch (1970, 1975) suggests that this form of marriage was extremely rare, in large measure because of the almost intolerable economic burdens placed on the wife. In addition to taking care of children, she had to do all the butchering, sewing, and other work involved with being married to two hunters.

The final form of institutionalized marriage, and the main form of nonresidential marriage, was the infamous "wife-exchange" pattern. This is better understood as co-marriage, or nonresidential polygynous polyandry. Here, two *ui-nuliaq* pairs become associated with each other through engaging in sexual intercourse with each other's spouse. Burch notes that intercourse had to occur only once to establish the relationship in perpetuity. Intercourse was the validating act of the union of the two couples, a union that had been agreed on by all the parties involved beforehand. The most important relationships in the co-marriage were between the co-wives, and between the co-husbands, who now established strong bonds of friendship, mutual aid, and protection (Burch 1970). This is the key to understanding co-marriage. These relationships were usually between couples living in different villages or even in different societies. Note that the Inuit, like us, did not have extensive networks of relatives spread out through their entire territory. For this reason, alternative ways of establishing trusting and close ties with other people of the same sex were vital. In fact, Burch's informants told him that co-husbands became like brothers and co-wives like sisters. The sibling relationship was of profound importance to the Inuit. Siblings were morally bound to cooperate in almost all the major activities of life. Equally interesting was the effect of co-marriage on the next generation. The children of these co-marriages were all considered brothers or sisters of one sort or another, with all the attendant obligations of siblingship. In the next generation, cousins were established, and so on, creating pockets of kinship throughout the region. Ultimately co-marriage established long-term, interregional alliances where there were none before. As one northwestern Inuit put it:

> In early days ago, Eskimo change wife in Arctic of Alaska to make big family and have lots of relatives. Suppose, here, man and wife from Kotzebue and man and wife from Point Hope. Them men they exchange wife, they agree everything among themself, and they claim their children just like one family. And when them children grow up, parents told their children they have half brother or half sister at Point Hope or Kotzebue. (Paul Green, cited in Burch 1975 : 109)

Calling co-marriage "wife swapping" or "wife exchange" distorts the practice and misses an essential point. These phrases imply that the husband initiated the practice and that the wife was traded between two men. Burch's data make it clear that husbands were exchanged as much as wives, and that wives had just as much to say about the establishment of a co-marriage as did the husbands. Indeed, wives could even take the initiative in establishing such a union.

It should be noted that although the sex act between co-spouses was the symbolic validation of the marriage, it was also enjoyed. The sexual interaction between co-spouses was believed to be considerably more elaborate and pleasurable than the conjugal relation between spouses who lived together (Burch 1975 : 117–18). The important point is what the sex act meant *in this context*, and it is clear that it meant more than sexual gratification with a new partner.

Bridewealth

Marriage is a transaction as well as a transformation. It is a flow of rights and obligations involving both sides in the union. Husband and wife gain those rights, but so too do the groups from which they come. In certain kinds of societies, these transfers are marked by the movement of young women in one direction and certain symbolically important goods in the other. Those goods are called **bridewealth**.

Bridewealth Defined

Bridewealth is most common in patrilineal societies that combine agriculture, pastoralism, and patrilocal marriage, although it is found in other types of societies as

bridewealth
certain symbolically important goods that are transferred from the family of the groom to the family of the bride on the occasion of a marriage; these are not used to "buy a wife," but as compensation to her lineage for the loss of her labor and her childbearing capacities

Woven mats are a traditional part of bridewealth payments in American Samoa.

well. When it occurs among matrilineal peoples, usually a postmarital residence rule (avunculocal, for example) takes the woman away from her matrilineage.

The goods exchanged have significant symbolic value to the people concerned. These have included shell ornaments, ivory tusks, brass gongs, bird feathers, cotton cloth, and animals. Bridewealth in animals has been best described in eastern and southern Africa, where cattle have the most profound symbolic and economic value. In these societies, a man's father, and often his entire patrilineage, will give an agreed-on number of cattle (often in installments) to the patrilineage of the man's bride. Bridewealth is usually understood as a way of compensating the bride's relatives for the loss of her labor and childbearing capacities. When the bride leaves her home, she goes to live with her husband and his lineage. She will be working and producing children for *his* people, not her own.

Bridewealth transactions create affinal relations in two directions. The obvious connection is between the relatives of the wife and those of the husband. However, the new wife's relatives will use the bridewealth they receive to establish ties with yet another kinship group, the one that provides a bride for the new wife's brother. Bridewealth therefore enables both sisters and brothers to find spouses. This connection is not lost on the people who practice it. The relationship between brothers and sisters in these societies is extremely important. In many societies in eastern and southern Africa, a woman gains power and influence over a brother because her marriage has brought the cattle that have allowed him to marry and continue their lineage. As the Southern Bantu put it, "cattle beget children" (Kuper 1982:3).

Bridewealth in Southern Africa: Linking Brothers and Sisters

Following Adam Kuper, let us consider bridewealth practices in southern Africa. As we have already noted, the fundamental bridewealth rule was that marital rights in a woman were transferred for cattle. Of particular importance was the right over the woman's childbearing. If a wife was infertile, or if she died or deserted her husband before bearing children, then either the bridewealth had to be returned or the woman's lineage had to provide another wife to the husband. The transfer of control over the woman's childbearing was permanent; her children belonged to her husband's lineage and could not be claimed by her own lineage for any reason, including divorce. If a couple divorced, the children stayed with the husband's lineage and did not follow their mother. As with the Nuer, even after the death of her husband, a widow was still expected to bear children in his name, usually by marrying his brother.

In southern Africa, when a brother uses his sister's bridewealth cattle to get himself a wife, he and his sister become known as "cattle-linked" siblings. They are bound in a special relationship with effects lasting over several generations. Among the Lovedu, for example, the brother was in his sister's debt because she had given him a wife. *(See EthnoFile 10.4: Lovedu.)* The sister had ritual power to protect her brother's new village from witches. When she came to visit, she put her things in her brother's wife's house, and her brother's wife was obligated to wait on her. She could sometimes even control whom her brother would marry.

The ethnographers of the Lovedu, E. J. and J. D. Krige, point out the following:

> *The sister even wields a certain amount of authority in the house of her brother, as was well illustrated at a gathering we attended where the man of the house was quarreling with his wife about an uninvited guest. In the midst of the uproar a voice was heard: "This is my village which I have built. I will have no unseemly behavior here." It was the sister rebuking her brother, who subsided immediately and went on with the ceremonial as if nothing had happened. (Krige and Krige 1943:75–76)*

In other places in southern Africa, a woman could help herself to the clothing and household goods of the wife of her cattle-linked brother. She could expect her younger brother's wife to wait on her and call her "female husband." But she often demanded a direct return from her brother. After all, she had obtained a wife for her brother; now he must do the same for her. In some cases, she would marry the wife herself, in woman marriage. This wife would work as her subordinate and bear children for her lineage. More often, she would claim a daughter-in-law as a wife for her son. From the son's point of view, this is marriage with the mother's brother's

---

EthnoFile 10.4
LOVEDU

Region: Southern Africa

Nation: South Africa

Population: 40,000 (1940s)

Environment: Savannah

Livelihood: Horticulture and gathering; little cattle herding

Political organization: Kingdom (queen) and aristocracy

Other: A pattern of linking siblings through the exchange of bridewealth cattle gives sisters much power over their brothers

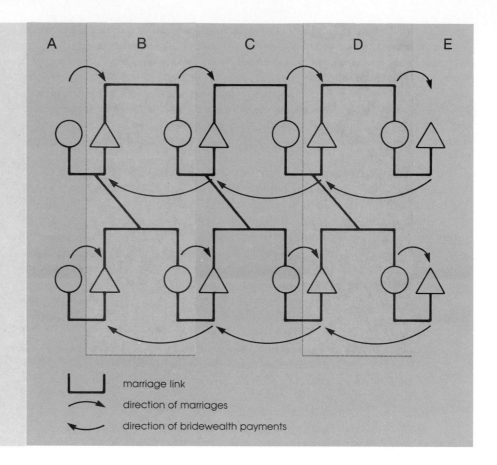

FIGURE 10.1
Marriage Alliance
Women leave their lineages to get married. Bridewealth moves from husband's lineage to wife's lineage, enabling wife's brother to pay bridewealth and get married.

⊔⊔ marriage link

⌒→ direction of marriages

←⌒ direction of bridewealth payments

daughter, a common form of preferential marriage. Notice the way bridewealth sets up ongoing ties of exchange and alliance among series of lineages. In this example, the wife's in-laws paid bridewealth to her relatives for her. Now they are paying bridewealth to her relatives again, to obtain a wife for her son (see figure 10.1).

Brothers and Sisters in Cross-Cultural Perspective

The previous examples suggest that the brother-sister relationship deserves special attention. In American society, we tend to interpret all relationships between men and women in terms of the prototypical relationship between husbands and wives. Not only is this unnecessarily limiting, but it also fails to capture the significant variations in the way people view relationships (see Sacks 1979). In some cultures, the most important relationships a man and a woman have are those with their opposite-sex siblings. This is perhaps most clear in matrilineal societies, where, for example, a man's closest ties to the next generation are with his sister's children.

Brothers and Sisters in a Matrilineal Society ▬▬▬

A classic illustration is found in the society of the Ashanti of Ghana. *(See Ethno-File 10.5: Ashanti.)* The central legal relationship in Ashanti society is the tie be-

EthnoFile 10.5
ASHANTI

Region: West Africa

Region: West Africa

Nation: Ghana

Population: 200,000

Environment: Slightly inland; partly mountainous

Livelihood: Farming, fishing, market trading (women)

Political organization: Kingdom
Other: In this matrilineal society, the brother-sister relationship is of great importance; women have great power in running the market

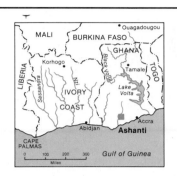

tween brother and sister. A brother has legal power over his sister's children because he is their closest male relative, and for the Ashanti legal power is vested in males (Fortes 1950). A sister has claims on her brother because she is his closest female relative and represents the only source of the continuity of his lineage. In patrilineal societies like that of the Nuer, a man is centrally concerned with his own ability to produce children. Among the Ashanti, a man is centrally concerned with his *sister's* ability to produce children. "Men find it difficult to decide which is more important to them, to have children or for their sisters to have children. But after discussion most men conclude that sad as it may be to die childless, a good citizen's first anxiety is for his lineage to survive" (ibid.: 274–75).

More than this, the Ashanti brother and sister are supposed to be close confidants:

> *Quoting their own experiences, men say that it is to his sister that a man entrusts weighty matters, never to his wife. He will discuss confidential matters, such as those that concern property, money, public office, legal suits, and even the future of his children or his matrimonial difficulties with his sister, secure in the knowledge that she will tell nobody else. He will give his valuables into her care, not his wife's. He will use her as go-between with a secret lover, knowing that she will never betray him to his wife. His sister is the appropriate person to fetch a man's bride home to him, and so a sister is the best watch-dog of a wife's fidelity. Women, again, agree that in a crisis they will side with their brothers against their husbands. There is often jealousy between a man's sister and his wife because each is thinking of what he can be made to do for her children. That is why they cannot easily live in the same house. Divorce after many years of marriage is common, and is said to be due very often to the conflict between loyalties towards spouse and towards sibling. (Fortes 1950:275)*

Because Ashanti women may be sisters and wives *simultaneously*, they often experience conflict between these two roles. We Westerners must change our frame of reference to understand this. For us, the relationship of husband and wife takes precedence over the brother-sister relationship. But for the Ashanti, the lineage comes first. In part, the closeness of Ashanti brothers and sisters is tied to the residence pattern in Ashanti settlements. People live in their matrilineages' neighborhoods, and often husbands and wives do not live together.

Within marriage, Ashanti women have much freedom. The marriage agreement grants the husband exclusive sexual rights over his wife and legal paternity over any children born. The husband also has the right to domestic and economic services. The wife is entitled to food, clothing, and housing if she needs it. She also expects sexual satisfaction, care in illness, debt coverage, and the right to approve or disapprove if her husband wishes to take another wife. For Ashanti, then, marriage grants rights in sexuality to *both* partners, and a man who wishes to take another wife must ask his first wife to share her sexual rights in him with another woman.

Brothers and Sisters in a Patrilineal Society

The relationship of brother and sister is important in patrilineal societies too, and even in some contemporary urban nation-states. Thomas Belmonte (1978:193) notes that in the slums of Naples, a brother still maintains over his sister a moral control that her husband does not have. In patrilineal societies, the strength of the relationship depends on the way the kinship group is organized. Where sisters do not move too far from home upon marriage, and where they are not incorporated into their husbands' lineages, a group of brothers and sisters may control the lineage and its economic, political, social, and religious aspects. The senior members of the lineage—males and females alike—exercise control over the junior members. While the brothers generally have more control than the sisters (in part because they are the ones who stay in place while the sisters move when they marry), sisters still have influence.

In the Mount Hagen area of the New Guinea highlands, for example, women marry into many different subtribes, usually within a two-hour walk from home. *(See EthnoFile 10.6: Mount Hagen.)* However, they retain rights to the wealth of their own lineages and to its disposal. A clan sister married outside the clan is believed to continue to be under the control of her clan ghosts. At her death, in association with them, she is able to influence the affairs of her own lineage. But over the course of time, a woman becomes more interested and involved in the affairs of her husband's clan. As this happens, it is believed that she comes increasingly under the control of her husband's clan ghosts. After her death, in addition to her influence

---

EthnoFile 10.6
MOUNT HAGEN

Region: Southeast Asia

Nation: Papua New Guinea (western highlands)

Population: 75,000 (1960s)

Environment: Forested mountain slopes; grassy plains

Livelihood: Farming, pig raising

Political organization: Some men of influence but no coercive power

Other: Over the course of a woman's life, she continues her interest in her own lineage, but becomes increasingly interested in her children's lineage; Hageners are also famous for the large distributions of property that men make in search of prestige

on her own clan as a ghostly sister, she is believed to have influence on her husband's clan as a ghostly mother (Strathern 1972:124).

Family Structure

The process by which a woman becomes gradually involved in her husband's clan or lineage can be seen among the Nuer as affinal ties gradually become kinship ties. *Ruagh* (in-law relationship) becomes *mar* (kinship) (Evans-Pritchard 1951:96). The birth of a child gives the wife kinship with her husband's relatives, and it gives the husband kinship with the wife's relatives. Over time, in many patrilineal societies, a woman begins to identify with and become more interested in the affairs of her husband's lineage. In part, this is because she has been living there for many years and comes to be more intimate with the details of her husband's lineage. But more significant is that her husband's lineage has now become her *children's* lineage. The children create a link to the lineage that is independent of her husband. This is one example of the transformations of family relationships that inevitably occur over time. The transformations people experience vary from one society to the next, according to the way families are organized.

nuclear family
a family pattern made up of two generations: parents and children

The Nuclear Family

The structure and dynamics of neolocal monogamous families are familiar to Americans. We call them nuclear families, and we believe that most Americans live in them. In fact, our families are monogamous, but not always nuclear. For anthropologists, a **nuclear family** is made up of two generations: parents and their unmarried children. Each member of a nuclear family has a series of evolving relationships with every other member: husband and wife, parents and children, children with each other. These are the principal lines along which jealousy, controversy, and affection will develop in neolocal monogamous families.

The Polygynous Family

Polygynous families are significantly different in their dynamics. Each wife has a relationship with her co-wives as individuals and as a group. Co-wives, in turn, individually and collectively, interact with the husband. These relationships change over time, as the authors of this book had occasion to learn in Guider, northern Cameroon. *(See EthnoFile 7.1: Guider.)* The nine-year-old daughter of their landlord announced one day that she was going to become Lavenda's second wife. "Madame" [Schultz], she said, "will be angry at first, because that's how first wives are when their husbands take a second wife. But after a while, she will stop being angry and will get to know me and we will become friends. That's what always happens."

The differences in internal dynamics in polygynous families are not confined to the relationships of husband and wives. An important distinction is made between children with the same mother and children with a different mother. In Guider, people ordinarily referred to all their siblings, half and full, as brothers or sisters. When they wanted to emphasize the close connection with a particular brother or sister, however, they would say that he or she was "same father, same mother." This was understood to be a relationship of special intimacy and significance. Children,

Co-wives in polygynous households frequently cooperate in daily tasks, such as food preparation.

logically, also had different kinds of relationships with their own mothers and their fathers' other wives—and with their fathers, as well.

Where there is a significant inheritance, these relationships serve as the channels for jealousy and conflict. The children of the same mother, and especially the children of different mothers, compete with one another for their father's favor. Each mother tries to protect the interests of her own children, sometimes at the expense of her co-wives' children. In polygynous societies, conflict can escalate enormously when the father is a prominent individual with a large family, significant wealth, and high social position. Isaac Schapera (quoted in Kuper 1982:51) notes that, among the members of the ruling lines in southern African societies,

> *owing to polygamy and the associated practice of ranking wives, disputes about the succession are almost inevitable. The brothers and other connections of each wife watch jealously over the interests of her sons, whose fortunes they usually do all they can to promote, if only because they themselves expect to benefit in consequence. . . . Even if the heir is definitely known and acknowledged, he is not always assured of the succession. . . . Even if the heir does become chief, he may afterwards have trouble with his brothers or uncles.*

This kind of competition is missing in traditional monogamous households. It is a distinct possibility, however, in households formed by adoption or the remarriage of parents who already have children.

Extended and Joint Families

Within any society, certain patterns of family organization are considered proper. In American nuclear families, two generations live together. In some societies, three generations—parents, married children, and grandchildren—are expected to live together in a vertical **extended family**. In still other societies, the extension is horizontal: brothers and their wives (or sisters and their husbands) live together in a **joint family**. These are ideal patterns, which not all families may be able or willing to emulate.

In their basic structures, too, individual families change over time. In a polygynous society with extended families, consider the recently married couple who set up housekeeping by themselves. They are monogamous. After a while, a child is born, and they become a monogamous nuclear family. Some time later, elderly parents come to live with them, and they become an extended family. Later the husband takes another wife, and the family becomes polygynous. Then the elderly parent dies, and the family is no longer extended. After a time, the younger brother of the husband and his wife move into the household, which becomes joint. One wife leaves, and the husband is monogamous again. His brother and his wife and children leave, the husband takes another wife, and the family is polygynous again. The eldest son marries and brings his wife to live in the household, and for the second time the household is an extended family. One wife dies, and the children all move away, and there is now a monogamous couple living in the household. Finally, with the death of the husband, there is a solitary family, made up by the widow, supported by her eldest son but living alone in the household.

In this example, each household structure is different in its dynamics. These are not several nuclear families that overlap. A joint family is fundamentally different from an extended family with regard to the relationships it engenders.

extended family
a family pattern made up of three generations—parents, married children, and grandchildren—living together

joint family
a family pattern made up of brothers and their wives or sisters and their husbands, along with the children, living together

Transformations in Families over Time

Families change over time. They have a life cycle and a life span. The same family takes on different forms and provides different opportunities for the interaction of family members at different points in its development. New households are formed and old households dissolve through divorce, remarriage, and the breakup of extended families.

Divorce and Remarriage

Most human societies make it possible for married couples to separate. In some societies, the process is long, drawn-out, and difficult, especially where bridewealth must be returned. A man who divorces a wife in such societies, or whose wife leaves him, expects some of the bridewealth back. But for the wife's family to give the bridewealth back, a whole chain of marriages might have to be broken up. Brothers of the divorced wife may have to divorce to get back enough bridewealth from their in-laws to make the return. Sometimes a new husband will pay the bridewealth return to the former husband's line, thus letting the bride's relatives off the hook.

Divorce in Guider

In other societies, divorce is easier. Marriages in Guider, for example, are easily broken up. *(See EthnoFile 7.1: Guider.)* The Fulbe of Guider prefer that a man marry his father's brother's daughter. In many cases, such marriages were contracted simply to oblige the families involved; after a few months, the couple split up. In other cases, a young girl (twelve or thirteen years old) is married to a man considerably her senior, despite any interest she may have had in men closer to her own age. Here too the marriage may not last long. In general, there is enough dissatisfaction with marriage in Guider to make household transformation through divorce quite common.

Among Muslims in Guider, divorce is controlled by men; women are not allowed legally to initiate divorces. A man who wishes to divorce his wife need only follow the simple procedure laid down in the Qur'an and sanctioned by long practice in Guider: he appears before two witnesses and pronounces the formula "I divorce you" three times. He is then divorced, and his wife must leave his household. She may take an infant with her, but any children at the toddler stage must stay with the father. If she takes an infant, it must return to its father's household by the time it is six to eight years old. A woman must wait three months after she is divorced before she can remarry, in case she was pregnant at the time of the divorce. After this time, the vast majority of women remarry.

Do women in Guider, then, have no power to escape from marriages that are unsatisfactory? Legally, perhaps not. But several conventionally recognized practices allow a woman to communicate her desire for a divorce. She can ask her husband for a divorce, and in some cases he will comply. If he does not, or if she is unwilling to confront him directly, she can neglect household duties—burn his food or stop cooking for him entirely or refuse to sleep with him. Since these are the most important services a wife provides her husband, men usually get the hint quickly.

Grounds for Divorce

Divorce in most societies is not quite so dramatic. Men usually give nagging and quarreling as their reasons for divorce, while women often claim cruelty and mis-

A Navajo woman in front of her family's summer hogan.

treatment or stinginess. Depending on the society, adultery is sometimes cause for divorce. In almost all societies, childlessness is grounds for divorce as well. For the !Kung, most divorces are initiated by women, apparently mainly because they do not like their husbands or do not want to be married (Lee 1984; Shostak 1983). *(See EthnoFile 9.1: !Kung.)* After what is often considerable debate, a couple who decide to break up will merely separate. There is no bridewealth, no legal contract to be renegotiated. Mutual consent is all that is necessary. The children go with the mother. !Kung divorces are cordial, Richard Lee (1984) tells us, at least compared with the Western norm. Ex-spouses may continue to joke with each other and even live next to each other with their new spouses.

Divorce Among the Navajo

The Navajo make divorce easy. *(See EthnoFile 6.1: Navajo.)* The wife and children remain where they are, while the husband returns to his mother's household. This is no different than what happens if a husband dies. If the wife dies, her widower is expected to remarry in the household or to leave. It is possible for Navajo to live patrilocally, but this results in a great deal more moving about at times of divorce and death. For the Navajo, matrilocal residence is less disruptive than patrilocal residence (Witherspoon 1975:75–79).

When Divorce Is Impossible

What about societies in which divorce is not recognized? There are very few such societies. In some cases (ancient Rome, for example), divorce was impossible. This followed from legal consequences of the marriage ritual. When she married, a woman was cut off from the patrilineage into which she was born and incorporated into her husband's patrilineage. Were she to leave her husband, she would have no place to go and no lineage to protect her.

Separation among the Inuit

Among the northwestern Inuit, the traditional view was that all kin relationships, including marital ones, were permanent (Burch 1970). *(See EthnoFile 10.3: Alas-*

kan Inuit.) This meant that while it was possible to deactivate a marriage by separating, a marriage could never be permanently dissolved. A couple who stopped living together and having sexual relations with each other were considered to be separated and ready for another marriage. This occurred quite often. Indeed, Burch (1970) estimates that the separation rate for the Inuit approached 100 percent; virtually everyone stopped living with a spouse at least once. Reasons for this included infidelity (which in the Inuit case meant sexual relationships outside any of the acceptable marriage patterns); failure to meet economic obligations; and favoring one child over the other parent's favorite. Not infrequently, however, the couple would get back together again. Reestablishing the residence tie served to reactivate the relationship.

The consequences of Inuit divorce were fascinating. Given the nature of Inuit separation, if each member of a separated couple remarried, the two husbands of the wife became co-husbands, the two wives of the husband became co-wives, and the children of the first and second marriages became co-siblings. The result looked almost identical to co-marriage! The only difference was that the relationship of co-spouses was not established in the case of divorce and remarriage. In effect, a "divorce" among the Inuit resulted in more, not fewer, connections.

Breaking Up Complex Households

We now turn to the formation of new households following the breakup of extended families. This process is best illustrated in joint families. In a joint family, the pressures that build up among coresident brothers or sisters often increase dramatically on the death of the father. In theory, the eldest son inherits the position of head of the household from his father, but his younger brothers may not accept his authority as readily as they did their father's. Some of the younger brothers may decide to establish their own households, and gradually the joint family splits.

This split is inevitable if all the brothers marry and have children who marry and have children. Within a very short time, there would be too many people living in one place. With so many members, the family organization could not maintain a reasonable amount of social harmony. Further, each brother whose household splits off from the joint stem usually hopes to start his own joint family as *his* sons bring their wives into the household. A new joint family emerges out of the ashes of an old one.

Something similar happens among the Nyinba, the polyandrous people of Nepal discussed earlier. *(See EthnoFile 10.1: Nyinba.)* In a family with many brothers widely separated in age, the corporation of brothers may take a second, fertile wife. At first, all brothers have equal sexual access to her, but after a time brothers will tend to form groups around each wife, with some preferring one and others preferring the second. At this point, the time is ripe for splitting the household in two. The Nyinba recognize that bringing a second fertile wife into the house sets in motion the transformation of the family into two polyandrous households, and the division of lands that the brothers have held in common. Family systems contain within them the seeds of their own transformation.

In the northern Nigerian societies where secondary marriage is practiced, there is no divorce. However, both women and men recognize that there are good reasons for leaving one marriage and contracting a new one. The practice of secondary marriage allows for burgeoning affinal links and the establishment of many households. It also makes it possible to maintain the older ties, so that a wife may always return to any of her previous husbands.

The Flexibility of Marriage

It is easy to get the impression that marriage rules compel people to do things they really do not want to do. People have to marry someone in a certain category (cross or parallel cousins, or mother's brother's daughter, for example). They have to marry into one group or out of another. Younger people seem compelled by parents and relatives to marry people they may never have seen before. Women appear to be pawns in men's "deep play" of prestige and power.

Sometimes the anthropological evidence reinforces this impression. Napoleon Chagnon's description of Yanomamo marriage is a case in point. *(See Ethno-File 10.7: Yanomamo.)* Chagnon writes: "Girls have almost no voice in the decisions reached by their elder kin in deciding whom they should marry. They are very largely pawns to be disposed of by their kinsmen, and their wishes are given very little consideration. . . . Marriage does not enhance the status of the girl, for her duties as wife require her to assume difficult and laborious tasks too menial to be executed by the men" (1983:111). If Chagnon is correct, however, this is an extreme case.

Rigidity in marriage rules are sometimes a function of the anthropologist's desire to build an airtight analytic model. Marriage rules are always subject to some negotiation. We have seen how, among the Inuit, co-marriage is negotiated by both husbands and wives. Burch (1970) notes that although the husband officially has the final authority in the family, he will never do anything of any importance without consulting his wife and taking her opinion into account.

A clear and especially revealing example is the marriage practices of the !Kung of the Kalahari Desert. *(See EthnoFile 9.1: !Kung.)* Richard Lee (1984) notes that all first marriages are set up by means of a long-term exchange of gifts between the parents of a bride and groom. As shown in chapter 9, the !Kung kinship system is as simple or as complex as people want to make it, and the game of kinship is extended to marriage. A girl may not marry a father, brother, son, uncle, or nephew, but neither may she marry a first or second cousin. She may also not

EthnoFile 10.7
YANOMAMO

Region: South America

Nation: Venezuela, Brazil

Population: 12,000

Environment: Tropical rain forest

Livelihood: Hunting, gathering, and gardening

Political organization: Headman with influence but no coercive power

Other: These subjects of a famous monograph by Napoleon Chagnon and films by Timothy Asch are known as the fierce people, an image the men cultivate; Yanomamo in northern Brazil are under threat by forces wishing to develop the resources of the area in which they live

marry a boy with her father's or brother's name, and a boy may not marry a girl with his mother's or sister's name. As well, it is not desirable to marry someone who stands in an avoidance relationship to the girl or boy.

This means that for the !Kung, about three-quarters of a person's potential spouses are off limits. In practice, parents of girls tend to be quite choosy about whom their daughter marries. If they are opposed to a particular suitor, they will come up with a kin or name prohibition to block the match. Because the parents arrange the first marriage, it appears that the girl has very little to say about it. If she protests long and hard, however, her parents may well call it off. This clear and insistent assertion of displeasure is not uncommon in the world. Even where a young woman follows the wishes of her parents for her first marriage, that first marriage may well not be her last if her dissatisfaction persists. Despite the parents' quest to find ideal spouses for their children, close to half of all first marriages among the !Kung fail. However, as in many societies, only about 10 percent of marriages that last five years or longer end in divorce (Lee 1984:79).

One promising direction for anthropological study of marriage centers on the contrast between the formal rules of marriage and the actual performance of marriage rituals. In an important article, Ivan Karp (1987) asks why Iteso women laugh at marriage ceremonies. *(See EthnoFile 9.4: Iteso.)* During his fieldwork, Karp was struck by a paradox. The marriage ritual is take very seriously by the patrilineal Iteso. It is the moment of creation for a new household, and it paves the way for the physical and social reproduction of Iteso patrilineages. But the ritual is carried out entirely by women who are *not* consanguineal members of the patrilineage! Despite the seriousness of the occasion, and although they were carrying out the ritual for the benefit of a lineage to which they did not belong, Iteso women seemed to find the ceremony enormously funny.

To explain this apparently anomalous behavior, Karp suggests that the meaning of the marriage ritual needs to be analyzed from two different referential perspectives, that of the men and that of the women. The men's perspective constitutes the official ideology of Iteso marriage. It emphasizes the way marriage brings the bride's sexuality under the control of her husband's lineage. It distinguishes between women of the mother-in-law's generation and women of the wife's own generation. It stresses the woman's role as an agent of reproduction who is equivalent, in a reproductive sense, to the bridewealth cattle.

Karp argues that the women's perspective constitutes an unofficial ideology of Iteso marriage. For the men and women of a given lineage to succeed in perpetuating that lineage, they must control women's bodies. But the bodies they must control belong to female outsiders who marry lineage men. These same female outsiders direct the two ritual events crucial to lineage reproduction: marriage and birth. And men of the lineage are not allowed to attend either of these rituals. In sum, female outsiders control the continued existence of a patrilineage whose male members are supposed to control them!

Iteso women, Karp says, can see the irony in this: they are at once controlled and controlling. In the marriage ritual itself, they comment on this paradox through their laughter. In so doing, they reveal two things to the men. First, they show that they know the men are dependent on them. Second, even as the men assert their control over women's bodies, the women's ritual actions escape the men's control. The official ideology of male control is subverted, at least momentarily, by the laughter of women. Even as they ensure that their husband's and son's lineages will continue, they are able to comment on the paradoxical relation of women to men.

Sexual Practices

Some anthropologists seem to regard marriage as an abstract formal system, having little if anything to do with human sexuality. As a result, their discussions of marriage tend to ignore the carnal aspects of marriage. But sexual intercourse is part of almost all marriages. And since in many societies marriage is the formal prerequisite for becoming sexually active (at least for females), a desire for sex is a strong motivation for getting married (Spiro 1977:212).

Ranges of Heterosexual Practices

The range of sexual practice in the world is vast. In many Oceanic societies—Tikopia, for example—it is expected that the young will have a great deal of sexual experience before marriage. *(See EthnoFile 10.8: Tikopia.)* Young men and young women begin having sexual relations at an early age, and having several lovers is considered to be a normal activity of the young. Getting married, as in many societies, is considered to be the final step (or the beginning of the final step) in becoming an adult. The distinguished British anthropologist Sir Raymond Firth notes that for the Tikopia, marriage represents a great change for both partners in this regard. The woman must abandon sexual freedom, but she replaces it with what Firth calls "a safe and legalized sexual co-habitation" (1936:434). The man is theoretically free to continue to have affairs, but in practice he will "settle down." This pattern is quite common cross-culturally.

The !Kung also begin sexual activity at an early age. As a result, the social and sexual constraints of marriage represent quite a shock at first, especially for young women. Some !Kung are strictly faithful to one another, but a significant minority take lovers. The !Kung have no double standard; both men and women are free to take lovers, and women are sometimes eloquent about the time they spend with lovers. However, discretion is necessary when taking a lover, since both husbands and wives can become very jealous and start fights. Sexual satisfaction is important to the !Kung; female orgasm is known, and women expect both husbands and lovers to satisfy them.

This attitude toward sex is not universal. Robert Murphy and Yolanda Murphy (1974) note that for the Mundurucu, a group of about 1,250 gardening and hunting people in the Brazilian Amazon, female orgasm is more accidental than ex-

EthnoFile 10.8
TIKOPIA

Region: Oceania (Polynesia)

Nation: Extreme eastern Solomon Islands

Population: 1,200 (1928)

Environment: Tropical island

Livelihood: Horticulture and pig raising

Political organization: Chiefs

Other: The Tikopia were subjects of a classic ethnography by Sir Raymond Firth, *We, The Tikopia* (1936), in which the importance of kinship in small-scale societies was set out

EthnoFile 10.9
DANI

Region: Oceania (New Guinea)

Nation: Indonesia (Irian Jaya)

Population: 100,000 (1960s)

Environment: Valley in central highlands

Livelihood: Horticulture and pig raising

Political organization: Some men have influence but no coercive power

Other: The Dani are of interest to students of marriage because of the length of their postpartum sex taboo (avoidance of sexual intercourse after the birth of a baby)

pected. Many societies require a woman's virginity at marriage, and the double standard reigns. In some Arabian societies, bloodstained sheets must be produced the morning after the consummation of a marriage to demonstrate that the bride was a virgin.

Particularly interesting in this regard is Karl Heider's research (1979) among the Dani, a people of highland New Guinea. *(See EthnoFile 10.9: Dani.)* Heider discovered that the Dani have extraordinarily little interest in sex. For five years after the birth of a child, the parents do not have sexual intercourse with each other. This practice, called a postpartum (following birth) sex taboo, is found in all cultures. In most, however, it lasts for a few weeks or months (in the United States, we say that the mother needs time to heal; other societies have other justifications). In a few cases, the postpartum sex taboo is two years long, which is considered a very long time. Five years is hard to believe. What could explain it?

Heider points out that Westerners assume the sex drive is perhaps the most powerful biological drive of all. We believe that if this drive is not satisfied directly in sexual activity, then some other outlet will be found. Heider's study of the Dani calls this assumption about human sexuality into question. The Dani are not celibate, and they certainly have sexual intercourse often enough to reproduce biologically. But they do not seem very interested in sex, and do not engage in much sexual activity (Heider 1979: 78–81).

Here again we encounter the *cultural construction of reality*; indeed, of a reality so basic that we consider it part of the biological nature of our species. Heider cannot explain why the Dani have such a low level of sexuality. He argues that it is connected with what he calls a low level of psychic energy (ibid.: 21 and passim). Nevertheless, the implications of this pattern for understanding the range of human sexual behavior are significant. The Dani, who are not abnormal physically or mentally, represent one extreme in the cultural construction of sexuality.

Homosexuality in Cross-Cultural Perspective

Some anthropologists have recently been studying homosexuality in cross-cultural perspective. They have found that the extraordinary malleability of the human species is also reflected in a wide range of attitudes toward homosexual practices. This is not an easy topic to study in the field. People learned quickly what the Euro-American attitude toward homosexuality was and said little. Through careful fieldwork, we now know something about homosexuality in a range of cultures. Among those are cultures in which institutionalized male homosexuality (particularly connected with initiation) is the preferred pattern.

Homosexuality At Initiation

Many of these societies are in one area in New Guinea, where it is believed that females are physically complete at birth, but males are incomplete. For boys to grow, it is believed, they must ingest semen through either fellatio or anal intercourse (see the collected essays in Herdt 1982). This pattern is associated with a series of beliefs among men concerning the danger of women, the need for sexual separation, and the creation of men. An extreme position here seems to be that of the Marind Anim of New Guinea. For them, heterosexual intercourse was sufficiently rare that they were unable to reproduce at a level high enough for their survival. To ensure that there would be enough people in the next generation, they captured children from neighboring societies during head-hunting raids (Van Baal 1966).

Female Homosexuality in Mombasa

A contrasting example comes from Mombasa, Kenya. *(See EthnoFile 10.10: Mombasa Swahilis.)* Anthropologist Gill Shepherd (1987:240–270) shows that both male and female homosexuality among Swahili Muslims can be understood as a rational decision, given traditional patterns of male-female interaction in Swahili society. Shepherd observes that men and women in Muslim Mombasa live in very different subcultures that are rich and satisfying for their members. Shepherd writes (1987:249) that the most enduring relationship in Swahili society is between mothers and daughters. This connection is imitated in the relationship between older married sister and younger unmarried sister. Men and women join a variety of sex-segregated groups for leisure-time activities such as dancing or religious study. Within these all-male or all-female groups, competition for social rank occurs. The relationships between brothers and sisters and mothers and sons are more distant, and the relationship of husband and wife (except in the case of young, modern, educated couples) is often not emotionally close at all (ibid.). Because the world of men and the world of women overlap so little, relationships between the sexes tend to be one-dimensional.

EthnoFile 10.10
MOMBASA
SWAHILIS

Region: East Africa

Nation: Kenya

Population: 50,000 Swahili among 350,000 total population of city (1970s)

Environment: Island in Indian Ocean, and mainland

Livelihood: Kenya's main port city

Political organization: Part of modern nation-state

Other: Mombasa has been a great port since before the British colony was established; the Swahilis are considered to be of mixed Arab and African descent

Of the some 50,000 Swahili in Mombasa, about 5,000 could be called homosexual. The number is misleading, however, since over a lifetime, both men and women shift between homosexuality and heterosexuality. Women are allowed to choose other women as sexual partners only after they have been married. Therefore, all lesbians in Mombasa are married, widowed, or divorced. Both lesbians and homosexuals are open about their behavior. They fit regularly into everyday life, and "nobody would dream of suggesting that their sexual choices had any effect on their work capabilities, reliability, or religious piety" (ibid.: 241).

Lesbian couples in Mombasa are far more likely to live together than are male homosexual couples. Since there are plenty of all-female households that are not lesbian, the term *lesbian* implies an overt sexual relationship between two women. Lesbians are distinguished by two kinds of activity. First, they engage in private, sexual relationships with other women. Second, they form clublike groups. They meet regularly in one another's houses, and choose women as their leaders. These groups form the context within which the women compete for power. Each group is composed of an inner circle of relatively wealthy older women who are friends. Their lovers, who are poorer and usually younger, make up the rest of the membership. The rule is that younger, lower-status women visit older, higher-status women. Wealthy lesbian women hold court in the afternoons, when Swahili women have the chance to go visiting (ibid.: 254). When weddings are held, wealthy lesbian women compete with each other. Each tries to outdo the others in the opulence with which she has dressed her lover for the occasion.

Women are drawn into lesbian relationships for a variety of reasons. Swahili women to whom Shepherd spoke were quite clear about the practical reasons. Women with little money or status had little chance of marrying men who could offer them financial security. A lesbian lover, however, could offer them both. In Mombasa, jewelry, shoes, new dresses, and so on are significant markers in the women's prestige system. These are the things that a wealthy lover can provide. A poor young woman in an unhappy marriage may have no way to support herself if she leaves her husband. A lesbian lover may support her. "Very occasionally a wealthy lesbian woman will help a girl who has not married but remains miserably caught within the constraints of unmarried womanhood while all her peers have moved forward. Such a girl is usually of high birth, or so well educated, that men hesitate to make offers for her since the parents refuse all suitors. Slight miscalculations may find her still unmarried in her late twenties or early thirties, and the rigidity of the division between the never married and the married, among women, is such that adult freedoms can *only* come through marriage. A lesbian woman who wants to help such a girl will find a man prepared to make a marriage of convenience and give him the money with which to go to the girl's parents and make an offer. The couple are divorced shortly after the marriage and the girl goes to live with her lesbian benefactor" (ibid.: 256–57).

The wealthy partner in a lesbian relationship is freed from the extreme constraint normally placed on high-ranking women in Muslim societies. According to Islamic law, a wealthy, high-ranking Muslim woman can only marry a man who is her equal or superior. A marriage of this kind brings a great deal of seclusion, and her wealth is administered by her husband. "Thus if she wishes to use her wealth as she likes and has a taste for power, entry into a lesbian relationship, or living alone as a divorced or widowed woman, are virtually her only options" (ibid.: 257).

Financial independence for a woman offers the chance to convert wealth to power. If she pays for the marriages of other people, or provides financial support in exchange for loyalty, a woman can create a circle of dependents. Shepherd points out that a few women, some lesbians, have achieved real political power in Mombasa in this way (ibid.).

Still, it is not necessary to be a lesbian to build a circle of dependents. Why then do some women follow this route? The answer, Shepherd tells us, is complicated. It is not entirely respectable for a woman under forty-five or fifty to be unmarried. Some women are able to maintain a good bit of autonomy by making a marriage of convenience to a man who already lives with a wife, living apart from him. Many women, however, find this arrangement both lonely and sexually unsatisfying. Living as a lesbian is less respectable than being a second, nonresident wife, but it is more respectable than not being married at all. The lesbian sexual relationship does not reduce the autonomy of the wealthy partner, "and indeed takes place in the highly positive context of the fond and supportive relationships women establish among themselves anyway" (ibid.: 258).

It should be clear from the preceding that homosexuality in Mombasa is accepted. Shepherd suggests that of the reasons this is so, perhaps the most important is in the attitude toward rank in Mombasa. Rank is built up out of wealth, the ability to claim Arab ancestry, and the degree of Muslim learning and piety. It is both ascribed and achieved. Men and women both expect to rise in rank over a lifetime. Rank determines marriage partners, as well as relations of loyalty and subservience. Although lesbian couples may violate the prototype for sexual relations, they do not violate relations of rank. Shepherd suggests that a marriage between a poor husband and a rich wife might be more shocking than a lesbian relationship between a dominant rich woman and a dependent poor one (ibid.: 262–63). It seems that rank takes precedence over gender in Mombasa: a woman strives not to be more female, but to be more Arab, a better Muslim, more important, a more dominant patron.

Sex, Marriage, and Power

How can we understand these varied sexual practices? Or what are we to make of bridewealth, the exchange of young women and men by older lineage members, marriages arranged by parents, and marriages involving young women and much older men? The practice and control of sexuality may serve as a metaphor for expressing differential power within a society. Homosexuality in the New Guinean societies we just discussed may be associated with an ideology of growth, development, and fear of women. However, it has two other results. It enables senior men to establish and symbolize their control over younger men, and it sets men apart from women. Controlling children's marriages in lineage-based societies does something similar. It maintains and perpetuates the power of older members of the lineage (male or female) over younger members. Thus, sex can be used to embody relative social position. It is an enactment, in unmistakable physical terms, of inequality and differential power. This is a central component of date rape and family violence in America today.

The physical activity that we call sexual intercourse, like so much else in human life, does not "speak for itself," nor does it have only one meaning. Sexual activity, like marriage, can be used to give concrete form to more abstract notions we have about the place of men and women in the world. The example of the !Kung is striking in this regard. In their sexual lives, !Kung men and women are essentially equal. This sexual equality is a metonym for the relations between !Kung men and women elsewhere in their society: in labor, in politics, in the family.

This reminds us that marriage never occurs in a vacuum. Complex connections link marriage to other social practices such as food production, political organization, and kinship. Plural marriage, for example, is likely to be found where many hands in the field under one person's supervision bring in more food (and power) than those hands cost in food. Similarly, plural marriage is less likely where both men and women have their hands full ensuring the survival of a spouse and children. We must not conclude from this, however, that the environmental determinists were right. Polyandry, for example, is embedded in a complex of connected cultural, social, economic, and historical factors. The natural environment is only one element among many that codetermine cultural practices. Other societies exploiting the same natural environment do not practice polyandry.

Key Terms

marriage	matrilocal	polyandry
affinal	avunculocal	bridewealth
consanguineal	monogamy	nuclear family
endogamy	polygamy	extended family
exogamy	polygyny	joint family
neolocal		
patrilocal		

Chapter Summary

1. *Marriage* is a social process that prototypically involves a man and a woman, transforms the participants, alters the relationships among the kin of each party, and establishes the potential for the reproduction of the social patterns of society through the production of offspring with certain kinds of rights and obligations.

2. Ghost marriage and woman marriage highlight several defining features of marriage and also demonstrate that the role of husband and father may be independent of the sex of the person carrying out the role.

3. There are four major patterns of postmarital residence: *neolocal, patrilocal, matrilocal,* and *avunculocal*.

4. A person may be married to only one person at a time, or to several. The former is called *monogamy* and the latter, *polygamy*. Polygamy can be further subdivided into *polygyny*, in which a man is married to two or more wives, and *polyandry*, in which a woman is married to two or more husbands.

5. The study of polyandry reveals a separation of a woman's sexuality and her reproductive capacity not found in monogamous or polygynous societies. There are three main forms of polyandry: fraternal polyandry, associated polyandry, and secondary marriage.

6. *Bridewealth* is part of a flow of rights and obligations in marriage. It consists of the payment of certain symbolically important goods by the husband's lineage to the wife's lineage. Anthropologists frequently see this as compensation for the lost productive and reproductive capacity of the woman, who will be working and producing children for her husband's lineage. A woman's bridewealth payment makes it possible for her brother to pay bridewealth to get a wife. In some societies, this produces a particularly strong relationship between brother and sister. A sister may have claims on her brother's possessions, may be able to demand a wife from him for her son, and may be the brother's closest confidante and adviser.

7. Different family structures produce different internal patterns and tensions. There are three basic family types: *nuclear*, *extended*, and *joint*. Families may change from one type to another with the passage of time and the birth, growth, and marriage of children.

8. Most human societies permit marriages to end by divorce, although it is not always easy. In most societies, childlessness is grounds for divorce. Sometimes nagging, quarreling, adultery, cruelty, and stinginess are also cited. In some societies, only men may initiate a divorce, and in a very few societies divorce is impossible.

9. Marriage rules are subject to negotiation, even when they appear rigid. This is illustrated by Iteso marriage. The Iteso depend upon women from outside to perpetuate their patrilineages, and the women express their ironic awareness of this fact through ritualized laughter at marriage.

10. Sexual practices worldwide have a vast range, from the puritanical and fearful to the casual and pleasurable. In some societies, young men and women begin having sexual relations at an early age, and marriage finally puts an end to the affairs of youth.

Suggested Readings

Bohannon, Paul, and John Middleton. *Marriage, Family, and Residence.* New York: Natural History Press, 1968.

A classic collection, with important and readable articles.

Firth, Raymond. *We, The Tikopia.* Stanford: Stanford University Press, 1984. Originally published in 1936.

An enduring classic in anthropology, set on the Pacific island of Tikopia. Firth writes engagingly and clearly about kinship and marriage.

Sacks, Karen. *Sisters and Wives.* Urbana: University of Illinois Press, 1979.

A marxian analysis of the notion of sexual equality. Includes very important data and analysis on the relations of sister and brother.

Shostak, Marjorie. *Nisa: The Life and Words of a !Kung Woman.* New York: Vintage Books, 1981.

A wonderful book. The story of a !Kung woman's life, in her own words. Shostak provides background for each chapter. There is much here on marriage, and a great deal on life.

Anthropology and the Time Factor

Marilyn Strathern (Ph.D., Cambridge University, and Fellow of the British Academy) is Professor of Social Anthropology at Manchester University. Fieldwork in the highlands of Papua New Guinea led to an interest in gender relations that is reflected in her two main books on the area. A third work deals with a different setting: rural England. Strathern insists that Papua New Guinea helps her understand England, as feminist scholarship helps her practice anthropology. She calls herself a particularist rather than a relativist.

Sometimes when one first goes to a place or meets a person, one has an immediate sense of recognition: everything learned after that simply serves to put the first impression into context. At other times, the initial encounter is so misleading one completely changes one's ideas. In either case, the passage of time affects the way the final picture is composed. Becoming familiar with a place or acquainted with a person is not only

a question of one's reactions—it also involves interaction over a duration. This is how human beings build up knowledge of themselves and their environment, and, as a human science, this is what anthropology is about.

By interaction I do not only mean the exchange of words—or blows, for that matter—with another on a one-to-one basis; I refer to any kind of situation where information received feeds into what is already known. One does this constantly, often without thinking about it. A town is not just the streets and houses that strike the eye; you draw on previous knowledge to make a guess at the amenities it has. In the case of persons you meet, a double interaction is likely to take place. People do not just offer information in themselves; they will probably actively supply information, and in turn adjust what they are supplying in their own interests of getting to know you.

It is also possible to think of "interaction" in relation to those one never meets, whom one sees from afar or just hears talked about. Each bit of information interacts with information one already has. An English person may never have met a New Guinea highlander, but from what he or she knows about non-Western societies will already have some image of what the name conjures up. There is both a negative and positive side to this. When that image reinforces general views that have nothing to do with Papua New Guinea itself, we may call it prejudicial. Here the anthropologist's job is to provide a more informed view. Yet the preexisting image may not be negative in the prejudiced sense; it may simply be the best one can do from the perspective of one's own

culture. Anthropologists call such an image ethnocentric.

Anthropologists may also point out that we cannot escape from ethnocentrism. Nor necessarily should we want to. For anthropology can go further than recognizing ethnocentrism; it can deliberately use preexisting cultural knowledge in a positive way. It does so by making the process of gaining knowledge a conscious and explicit one. Rather than just trying to hand out information, it actively encourages people to think about where they come from themselves, what values they hold, and thus what they already know—in order to make new knowledge for themselves.

This kind of interaction, between what people already know and what they will come to know, constitutes more than "reflection," though reflection is an important part of it. It is a process intrinsic to the faculty for knowledge itself: putting things in sequence, recalling and looking ahead, making patterns, creating concepts. And time is built into the process.

The time involved may be a matter of hours or of years. It may be a question of reading an ethnography about an unfamiliar people or writing a paper about everyday events from a particular perspective, or it may be a matter of living for eighteen months in a distant location or spending years developing a theory from the writings of other scholars. Students and teachers are on the same side of the line here. At whatever stage he or she is at, the anthropologist needs time for interaction to take effect.

This is true of any learning process. In the case of anthropology, the time factor itself is something about which we have to be conscious. Anthropologists collect information about the lives and values of peoples from all over the world, their cultures and artifacts, the way they organize themselves. As information, such data may well seem bizarre or pointless—rather like photographs of places or persons one is never likely to see. But that is the kind of information the anthropologist turns into knowledge. It becomes knowledge when it enlarges our perceptions of the world, extends the thoughts we already have, enables us to reach a new perspective on the familiar or discover fresh possibilities in human behavior.

That this process takes time is obvious in the case of fieldwork. Fieldworkers use their own cultural repertoire to access what they are learning about another culture. But they do not instantly know what is going to be useful. If I walk toward someone aware of greeting behavior, perhaps already sensitive to the local courtesies, I am attuned to the range of reactions I can expect. Those expectations may well make me puzzle over what actually happens, but if they were not there I could not even begin to be puzzled! Yet I might also be drawing the wrong parallel—and need other kinds of information to tell me when a greeting is or is not appropriate. Over and again, anthropologists thus use their own cultural skills to place themselves in positions from which they can elicit information. The anthropologist also has to be conscious that it cannot be done all at once: one has to live through various positions, whether one is present in person or in imagination, in order to build up an overall picture. Only then will any further piece of information extend one's understanding.

Since we are studying what is also true about ourselves—the nature of human sociality and the difference that culture makes—we study through ourselves. And however abstract our explanations and theories become, they reflect the complex patterns of thought and behavior found in all human interactions. This means that one is aware of one's own language and thus of one's own values and practices all the time. In the same way, the student reading an ethnography is aware of that work as the outcome of the investigations of a particular fieldworker, on whom he or she can build up a cultural if not a personal profile.

That process of being aware turns information into knowledge. Rather like getting to know the layout of a town or what kind of person a friend turns out to be, it needs enough time for a kind of interaction to have taken place. Whether the effect feels like a laborious attempt to grasp an idea or like a sudden flash of insight, only you can make knowledge for yourself. Someone else cannot do it for you. The position you are already in, the thoughts you already have, are extended. There are many ways of accomplishing such extensions from within our own culture. Anthropology is unique in that it not only seeks out the positions and perspectives of other cultures, it also develops theories about how that process of "having a position" itself works. In what way does a person's life make sense to that person? How consciously do we subscribe to ideologies? How is it that similar social patterns form and reform themselves in different situations? Anthropologists are as interested in the way human beings acquire information about one another as they are in

what human beings turn that information into.

Let me end with a negative. Like any enthusiast for his or her subject, anthropologists will tell you anthropology is many things—and so it is, for it extends us in innumerable ways. But there is one thing it is not: it is not instant knowledge.

Western culture invests heavily in information techniques, in the storage and retrieval of data, in relaying images in no time at all across vast spaces. Sometimes one gets the impression that since technology can take care of the storage, all one needs to know is how to call the right image up at the right time, since we shall recognize at once what it is we "see." Yet when it comes to the study of human society and culture itself, including the people that make these things, time must be built into the way we process the information. For whatever the scale—hours or years—interaction implies a duration. Without the time factor, we would lose that sense of ourselves that gives us a context for our ideas and that sense of others that comes on us freshly each time.

Marilyn Strathern

CHAPTER 11
Beyond Kinship

CHAPTER OUTLINE

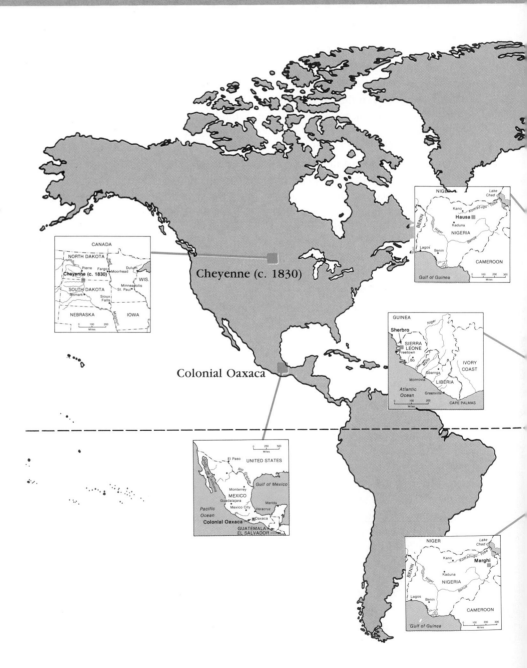

Cheyenne (c. 1830)

Colonial Oaxaca

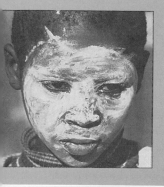

Sherbro

Hausa

Marghi

Bangwa

Boran

Nyakyusa

Gopalpur

Humorist Garrison Keillor makes the following observation about life in the mythical small town of Lake Wobegon, Minnesota:

"When the Thanatopsis Club hit its centennial in 1982 and Mrs. Hallberg wrote to the White House and asked for an essay from the President on small-town life, she got one, two paragraphs that extolled Lake Wobegon as a model of free enterprise and individualism, which was displayed in the library under glass, although the truth is that Lake Wobegon survives to the extent that it does on a form of voluntary socialism with elements of Deism, fatalism, and nepotism. Free enterprise runs on self-interest. This is socialism, and it runs on loyalty. You need a toaster, you buy it at Co-op Hardware even though you can get a deluxe model with all the toaster attachments for less money at K-Mart in St. Cloud. You buy it at Co-op because you know Otto. Glasses you will find at Clifford's which also sells shoes and ties and some gloves. . . . Though you might rather shop for glasses in a strange place where they'll encourage your vanity, though Clifford's selection of frames is clearly based on Scripture ('Take no thought for what you shall wear. . . .') and you might put a hideous piece of junk on your face and Clifford would say, 'I think you'll like those' as if you're a person who looks like you don't care what you look like—nevertheless you should think twice before you get the Calvin Klein glasses from Vanity Vision in the St. Cloud Mall. Calvin Klein isn't going to come with the Rescue Squad and he isn't going to teach your children about redemption by grace. You couldn't find Calvin Klein to save your life.

"If people were to live by comparison shopping, the town would go bust. It cannot compete with other places item by item. Nothing in town is quite as good as it appears to be somewhere else. If you live there, you have to take it as a whole. That's loyalty." (Keillor 1985:95–96)

If human beings are social by nature, then no individual can be self-sufficient and autonomous. As we have seen, patterns of kinship recognize and organize human interdependence in all societies. But even in societies where kinship considerations touch all social relationships, people are called on to deal with others who are not their kin. Every society would risk going bust if it did not provide its members with ways of establishing links with nonkin as well as kin. Such relationships must be carefully tended, however, if they are neither to wither and die nor to choke out the rest of the plants in the garden. In this chapter we shall examine some of the ways that loyalties to nonkin are created and nurtured.

Kin-Based versus Nonkin-Based societies

In non-Western societies, kinship is central to social organization. An elaborate kinship system can regulate social life and provide for orderly patterning of behavior. In the Western world, however, kinship has long been reduced to the realm of personal and family relations. Public matters have been handled by separate and specialized social structures. These include government, religion, education, or some other social institution.

For this reason, the first anthropologists were surprised to discover that a wide range of social activity in non-Western societies could be regulated solely by means of kinship. In the nineteenth century, classical scholars recognized that kinship groups had played major roles in the social organization of the ancient civilizations of Greece and Rome. It seemed as though the roots of "Western civilization" lay in societies in which the role of kinship was comparable to that found in many non-Western societies. How did contemporary Western society evolve from these beginnings? A number of early thinkers considered the transformation to be from what they considered "primitive" social organization, based on kinship, to the "modern" social organization of the nation-state.

Gemeinshaft versus Gesellschaft

The German sociologist Ferdinand Tönnies saw the contrast as one between primitive *Gemeinschaft* and civilized *Gesellschaft*. For him, Gemeinschaft involved personalized social relations based on kinship. Gesellschaft consisted of impersonal social relations based on nonkin ties. Tönnies regretted what he took to be the loss of the warm, supportive, face-to-face relations of Gemeinschaft to make way for the cold, anonymous interactions required by life in a modern state.

Societas versus Civitas

Anthropologist Lewis Henry Morgan saw the difference as a shift from *societas* to *civitas*. Societas was the face-to-face society organized wholly on the basis of kinship. Such societies lacked institutions of individual private property or the state. Civitas referred to societies that recognized private property and that governed and defended a territory by means of a non-kinship form of social organization: the state.

Status versus Contract Relationships

Sir Henry Maine, an English jurist who studied the roots of Roman law, characterized the shift as one from status to contract. In societies organized on the basis of **status**, people's relationships with one another were specified by the particular position, or status, that each held within the group. Each status carried with it a bundle of rights and duties, which modern social scientists, using a theatrical metaphor, call a **role**. Statuses (and the roles attached to them) complemented one another; holders of each status were responsible for particular tasks and could rely on other members of the status system to perform different tasks. Ideally, the multiple statuses of the society fit together like pieces of a puzzle. This ensured that all tasks needed for group survival were carried out in an orderly fashion.

> Societies organized on the basis of kinship were the prototype of status-based societies. For Maine, the crucial feature of status-based social organization was that people were not free to choose their own statuses, nor could they modify the rights and responsibilities associated with those statuses. Status-based societies contrasted in four major ways with societies organized on the basis of contract, such as modern nation-states. First, at least ideally, the parties to contractual relationships enter into them freely. Second, the contracting parties are equally free to specify the rights and obligations between them for the duration of the contract. Third, the range of possible statuses and roles is limitless, bound only by the imagination and interests of the contracting parties. Finally, once the terms of the contract are met, the parties need never have anything more to do with one another if they so choose. This would be impossible in a society based on status.

status
a particular social position in a group

role
the rights and duties associated with a status

Mechanical versus Organic Solidarity

For French social thinker Emile Durkheim, the contrast was a shift from "primitive" societies to "modern" ones. Primitive societies were held together on the

mechanical solidarity
the sense of fellow-feeling and interdependence that arises from shared language, shared modes of livelihood, and so on; characteristic of "primitive" societies, according to Emile Durkheim.

organic solidarity
the sense of fellow-feeling and interdependence that results when different groups in a society specialize in different tasks; characteristic of "modern" societies, according to Emile Durkheim.

division of labor
work specialization within a society based on membership in a given group. The most basic human divisions of labor are by sex and age

basis of **mechanical solidarity**. Modern ones were based on **organic solidarity**. In Durkheim's view, primitive societies assigned the same social tasks to everybody on the basis of kinship status. This meant that every kinship group—indeed, every family—could carry out the full range of tasks needed for survival. As a result, social solidarity, keeping kin groups together as parts of a larger whole, was problematic. Nothing bound these groups together except similarities in language, mode of livelihood, and so on. This kind of "mechanical" solidarity could easily be disrupted. Groups could split off and go their own way, without seriously affecting their ability to survive.

The "organic" solidarity of modern societies was quite different. These societies were still composed of groups, but each group specialized in a particular task needed for the survival of the larger whole. That is, organic solidarity depended on a highly developed **division of labor**. In societies with mechanical solidarity, the division of labor was limited to the division of kinship roles within each kinship group. Usually, this division was minimal, limited to task specializations based on age and sex. Each kinship group contained the full range of roles necessary to carry out subsistence activities without depending on outsiders. In societies with organic solidarity, however, the division of labor was much more elaborate. Some people specialized in food production, others in trade, others in government, others in religion. Full-time specialization meant that each group had to depend on other groups to provide it with things it could not provide for itself. Very large societies could be held together on the basis of organic solidarity. Like the separate organs of a living creature, each specialized group had to contribute its activities if society as a whole were to survive. If any one specialized group were to disappear, the society as a whole would collapse.

The Prototypical Kin-based Society

The prototypical kin-based society is small in size and characterized by face-to-face relationships of a highly personal nature. Each such group is basically autonomous and self-sufficient. Autonomy and self-sufficiency depend on the proper performance of basic survival tasks. In theory, the only way people know how to carry out these tasks is through the roles provided by the kinship system.

As long as group members continue to play their kinship roles, mechanical solidarity is possible and perhaps inevitable. It prevents the growth of large societies and the emergence of "civilizations"—which Durkheim saw as a defect. It also restricts the ability of persons to create their own statuses or control their own role obligations, which Maine saw as a defect. But mechanical solidarity can preserve a wide margin of freedom for the groups that practice it. This may be an asset if individualism and Western-style civilization are not automatically preferred. In all cases, both the burdens and the protections of fixed statuses were lost when kin-ordered society in the West vanished. The new society that replaced it was dominated by individually negotiated, short-term, impersonal contracts. The clearest prototype of such impersonal social relations is the modern bureaucracy.

Ascribed Status and Achieved Status

ascribed statuses
social positions that people hold by virtue of birth

In a kin-based society, opportunities for success in life come through the kinship system. Each status has role obligations associated with it. People can perform their role obligations well or badly, but they have no control over the statuses they hold. These are called **ascribed statuses**, reflecting their fixed nature. People are "born

Table 11.1

Some Anthropological Analyses of the Difference between Primitive and Modern Societies Common during the Late Nineteenth and Early Twentieth Centuries

Primitive	Modern	Suggested by
Gemeinschaft	Gesellschaft	Tönnies
Societas	Civitas	Morgan
Status	Contract	Maine
Mechanical solidarity	Organic solidarity	Durkheim

into" ascribed statuses, such as son or daughter, or will "grow into" others, such as wife or husband, or mother or father. But even in kin-based societies it is possible for people to attain personal distinction by their own efforts. Foragers, for example, will award the status of "good hunter" or "good gatherer" to persons who perform these activities outstandingly well. These are called **achieved statuses**. They depend not on tradition but on individual personal achievement. In kin-based societies, ascribed statuses outnumber and are more important than achieved statuses.

The shift from kin-based to modern society involves, among other things, a growth in the importance of achieved statuses. When two parties enter into a business contract, for example, they create or "achieve" new statuses, as defined by the terms of their contract. In a bureaucratically organized society, personal ties and ascribed status are excluded as the bases for opportunity and success. Rather, each bureaucratic position is an achieved status that requires a certain level of mastery. Success and opportunity depend on this mastery.

Table 11.1 summarizes the different referential perspectives adopted by early anthropologists who attempted to articulate the differences between primitive and modern societies.

achieved statuses
social position attained as a result of individual action

Metaphorical Kin Revisited

Kin-ordered societies depend on kinship to regulate the major areas of social life. But kinship relations are not the only social relations recognized and encouraged in such societies. All societies find ways to link people to other people who are not their "literal" kin. Perhaps the most widespread manner in which this is done is through the metaphorical extension of kinship status and roles to people who are not members of a given kinship group.

In Chapter 9 we discussed three instances of metaphorical kinship: the name relationship among the !Kung, extension of lineage membership among the Nuer, and Latin American Catholic ritual coparenthood, or compadrazgo. What is the status of the people linked through such arrangements? They are not literal kin, since they do not fit the prototypes of the formal kinship system. But they treat one another according to roles associated with the formal kinship system, so they are not nonkin, either. Metaphorical kin seem to be on the boundary of two categories: kin and nonkin.

Friendship

The metaphorical kin relationship makes unrelated strangers into friends. For anthropologist Robert Brain, institutions such as compadrazgo are cases of *institutionalized friendship*. Brain cites a dictionary definition of a friend as "one joined to another in intimacy and mutual benevolence independent of sexual or family love" (Brain 1976:15). He is quick to point out that the Western belief that friendship and kinship are separate phenomena often breaks down in practice. It is possible today for husbands and wives in Western societies to be "best friends." We may become friends with some of our relatives while treating other relatives the same way we treat non-relatives. Presumably people can be friends with people over and above any ties they might have with them on the basis of kinship. Thus, friendship can be defined as love that is free of bias or self-interest, as "emotional and disinterested love" (ibid.: 28).

How do societies bring strangers together in mutual benevolence? Brain says people in many non-Western societies are far less haphazard about this than are Westerners. The Bangwa of Cameroon, among whom Brain did fieldwork, seal friendships with a ritual similar to the ritual of marriage. *(See EthnoFile 11.1: Bangwa.)* But the obligations of friendship are not the same as the obligations of kinship that derive from marriage. Friendship limits the risks that follow from close relationships with consanguineal kin.

> *The Bangwa spoke of ideal friendship as one of equality and complete reciprocity, backed by moral, rather than supernatural and legal sanctions. He is my friend "because he is beautiful," "because he is good." Although there is in fact a good deal of ceremonial courtesy and gift exchange it is seen as a relationship of disinterested affection. Youths who are friends spend long hours in each other's company, holding hands when they walk together in the market. As they grow older friendships become increasingly valued—elders have little else to do but sit around with their friends, chatting about local politics, disputes over land boundaries, trouble with an obstreperous young wife. . . .*
>
> *Friendship is valued far above kinship; between kin there are niggling debts and witchcraft fears. Friendship lasts till death; kinship is brittle and involves inequalities of age and wealth and status. Friendship alone can cancel these out. A chief born on the same day as a slave*

EthnoFile 11.1
BANGWA

Region: West Africa

Nation: Cameroon

Population: 30,000 (1960s)

Environment: Broken, mountainous terrain

Livelihood: Agriculture, especially coffee growing

Political organization: Kingdoms

Other: The Bangwa practice various kinds of institutionalized friendship, as well as woman marriage

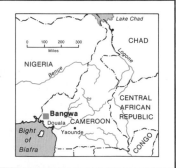

automatically becomes his "best friend" and is bound to treat him in a friendly manner, at least in some contexts. The son who succeeds to a chief's position depends on the friends he made as a child—not his kin—in the crooked corridors of palace politics. (Ibid.: 35)

Brain recognizes that certain relationships among literal kin may be viewed as prototypes of friendship in some societies. Even for the Bangwa, twins are ideal best friends, and other groups, such as the Kuma of New Guinea, see brothers-in-law as best friends. But friendship can also be seen as a nonkin link that can correct the defects and limitations of literal kinship. If this is assumed, then all social structures above and beyond the boundaries of literal kinship may be viewed as kinds of institutionalized friendship.

The Kinship in Nonkin Relationships

And yet the ambiguity remains. For the Bangwa, the closest kin—twins—are the best of friends. In general, however, kin are not trusted and friends must be sought outside the kinship group. Nonkin patterns of social relations do not follow the rules of recruitment or enforce the traditional status distinctions and role obligations that are at the heart of kinship. And yet those involved in such nonkin social relations often use a kinship idiom to refer to each other and to the expectations each has concerning the other's behavior. Ritual coparents refer to themselves as coparents, *compadres*. Members of Catholic monastic orders, who may neither marry nor bear children, nevertheless continue to refer to one another as brother, sister, father, and mother. They also take as the prototype for these interpersonal relationships the literal role obligations of family members.

Anthropologist David Schneider argues that the prototypical emotion of kinship is the feeling of "diffuse and enduring solidarity." But this definition might just as well apply to friendship, as we discussed it earlier. Perhaps diffuse and enduring solidarity is something that human beings seek to establish in their relations with other people, kin or not. The institution of kinship is one traditional means for cultivating such a sentiment. But so are the institutionalized friendships among the Bangwa. Indeed, all customary patterns of human interaction involve diffuse and enduring solidarity. This is true even for relationships characterized by respect and avoidance or by joking and license. In both cases, the individuals or groups who must avoid one another or joke with one another are people whose cooperation is essential to orderly social life. Order is preserved if people avoid confrontations with others who might disagree with them. But, if it is agreed neither party may take offense at anything that is said or done, then order can be maintained by encouraging such confrontations. "Joking relatives," in particular, are ordinarily said to be the best of friends.

In Western societies, kinship has not totally vanished, although large-scale nonkin organizations in government, religion, education, and business have taken over many functions that were once the responsibility of kinship groups. Even in these nonkin organizations, however, the idiom of kinship is often used. As we noted earlier, corporate officers sometimes like to encourage their employees to think of themselves as "one big happy family."

We now turn to some important forms of nonkin social relations. Not surprisingly, nonkin organizations in non-Western societies are often described by their members using a kinship idiom.

Nonkin Ties in Band and Tribal Societies

The kind of social relationships that we have called nonkin ties are not randomly distributed throughout the societies of the world. In general, the larger the society, the more complex the division of labor within that society. The greater the specialization in the division of labor, the more likely nonkin social patterns will be found alongside or replacing kinship organization.

The simplest and most ancient form of human social organization is found among foraging societies such as the !Kung. Foragers typically live in groups of related nuclear families called *bands*. In these societies, literal kinship relations form the basis of all social relations. The division of labor is based entirely on tasks connected to kinship roles. And yet, as we saw, the !Kung have developed a parallel system of metaphorical kinship linking people who shared the same name. This metaphorical system undermines the literal kinship system even as it borrows principles of organization from it. The !Kung case suggests that even in the small-scale society of foragers, the literal system can be bypassed in order to cultivate different forms of diffuse and enduring solidarity with strangers.

Once a society comes to depend on domesticated plants and animals for food, larger populations can be supported on less land. The cultivation of plants restricts a group's mobility, and most farmers settle in villages. Those who rely on domesticated animals may be mobile for part of the year, but their movements are dictated by the needs of their herds for pasture and water. The term *tribe* is usually used to refer to societies with these characteristics. Kinship organization remains strong in tribal societies, and unilineal kinship groups are common.

sodalities

nonkin forms of social organization that are special-purpose groupings and that may be organized on the basis of age, sex, economic role, and personal interest

The president of the Oruro (Bolivian) Devil Fraternity, a sodality organized in honor of the Virgin of Socavon, wears the costume associated with his office, crowned by the devil mask.

Sodalities

Kinship is not the only organizational principle in these societies. Nonkin forms of social organization have been created in many societies of farmers and herders. Anthropologist Elman Service (1962:113) called these nonkin structures pan-tribal sodalities. David Hunter and Phillip Whitten (1976:362) define **sodalities** as "secondary groups or associations" in which membership may be voluntary or involuntary. Sodalities are "special-purpose groupings" that may be organized on the basis of age, sex, economic role, and personal interest.

> [Sodalities] serve very different functions—among them police, military, medical, initiation, religious, and recreation. Some sodalities conduct their business in secret, others in public. Membership may be ascribed or it may be obtained via inheritance, purchase, attainment, performance or contract. Men's sodalities are more numerous and highly organized than women's and, generally, are also more secretive and seclusive in their activities. (Hunter and Whitten 1976:362)

Sodalities create diffuse and enduring solidarity among members of a large society. In part this is because they draw their personnel from a number of "primary" forms of social organization, such as lineages. They are not limited to farmers and herders, as shown by the case of Cheyenne military societies.

EthnoFile 11.2
CHEYENNE

Region: Great Plains

Nation: United States

Population: 3,500

Environment: Northern Colorado and southeastern Wyoming

Livelihood: Originally horticulture; later mounted nomadism

Political organization: Tribal council

Other: The Cheyenne now live in Montana; since 1975, they have received windfall profits from strip-mining on the reservation

The Cheyenne Military Societies

The Cheyenne Indians of the Great Plains of North America were a hunting and gathering people whose main source of meat was the buffalo. *(See EthnoFile 11.2: Cheyenne.)* They traced descent bilaterally and organized themselves into a number of kindreds. During the winter months, the Cheyenne lived in camps composed of several kindreds. During the summer months, the entire tribe camped together in order to perform important pan-tribal rituals. These included the Arrow Renewal and the Sun Dance. Tribal identity also rested in the council of forty-four peace chiefs, in whom lay supreme authority for the entire tribe.

The Cheyenne had pan-tribal sodalities whose membership cut across kindreds and bands. There were sodalities for women and men, but those for men were more numerous and their organization more complex. The most important of these were the seven military societies.

According to E. Adamson Hoebel, Cheyenne military societies "centered on the common experience of the warriors, with rituals glorifying and enhancing that experience, and with duties and services performed on behalf of the community at large" (1960:33). All seven societies were of equal status. A Cheyenne boy who was ready to go to war could join any society he chose and become a full-fledged member immediately. Membership was usually for life. Each society had four leaders, two of whom were war chiefs and two of whom were considered "the bravest men in the society." In addition, each society had ritual paraphernalia, dress, dances, and songs that distinguished it from the other societies.

The military societies were charged with maintaining order during tribal ceremonies and during the communal buffalo hunt. They were also responsible for carrying out legal decisions of the Tribal Council, such as banishment of murderers from the tribe. The Cheyenne believed that any member of the tribe who killed another member began to rot internally, and that the stench drove the buffalo away. The expulsion of murderers rid the tribe of this pollution. The system also eliminated feuds between bands and kindreds, since any retaliatory killing would only worsen the pollution and undermine the survival of the tribe as a whole.

The Cheyenne military societies were nonkin voluntary associations that cut across kinship groups. They were dedicated to glorifying and perpetuating the successes of fighting men. And yet they were not totally free of the influence of women and the idiom of kinship. A mythological female figure, Sweet Medicine, was believed to have given the Cheyenne the idea of military societies, together with their rituals. Five of the sodalities invited four virgin daughters of tribal chiefs "to participate in their ceremonies and to sit in the midst of the circle of war chiefs when they meet in common council." These young girls were similar to mascots. They represented the sodality as a whole, and its warriors would be successful in battle only as long as these young women remained chaste. "All the members of a society call their four maids by the kin term 'sister,' and they may never marry one of their own maidens" (Hoebel 1960:33–34).

Age Sets

All societies recognize in some way that people pass through stages as they grow from infancy to maturity to old age. Generational differences are marked in every kinship system. But some groups have emphasized generational distinctions to an unusual degree and used them as the basis for forming sodalities. Although distinctions in age were not marked in the Cheyenne military sodalities, the situation is different in East Africa. A number of societies there assign men from different kinship groups to sodalities defined in terms of relative age. These are called age sets.

Age-Set Systems

age sets
nonkin forms of social organization composed of people born within a specified time span (five years, for example); each age set is part of a sequence of age sets that includes all people

Age sets are composed of young men born within a specific time span (five years, for example). Each age set is "one unit in a sequence of similar units" that succeed each other in time as their members pass through youth, maturity, and old age. "Sets are part of the formal social order blessed by tradition and membership is usually ascribed, and is always obligatory" (Baxter and Almagor 1978:4). Age-set systems for women are not found in these societies. P. T. W. Baxter and Uri Almagor suggest this may be because from an early age women are involved in domestic matters and marry shortly after puberty (ibid.:11).

Age-set systems are like kinship systems in that they assign people membership in groups on the basis of generation and age. But age-set systems are built on two additional assumptions. The first is that generations of fathers and sons will succeed one another regularly. The second is that the succession will follow a uniform timetable. Unfortunately, experience belies both assumptions. The users of age-set systems must continually work to reconcile age, generation, and the passage of time. "Age systems which are based on measured units of time are unsuccessful attempts to tame time by chopping it up into manageable slices" (ibid.:5).

The East African Age-Set System

The classic study of East African age sets was by Monica Wilson (1951), who examined their role among the Nyakyusa. *(See EthnoFile 11.3: Nyakyusa.)* The Nyakyusa were patrilineal and patrilocal. Their society was divided into many independent chiefdoms. Nyakyusa age sets initially included a group of boys from about ten to fifteen years of age. When the members of this junior set were about thirty-three to thirty-five years old, an elaborate series of rituals was held to mark their "coming out." At that time, the reigning senior generation "handed the country over to them." At any point in time, there were three strata in the Nyakyusa age system: retired elders, active senior men who carried political and military responsibilities for the entire society, and immature juniors.

Members of junior East African age sets were as flashy as members of Cheyenne military societies. Each set had distinctive dress and titles and exhibited flamboyant behavior. According to Baxter and Almagor, however, it was unusual for age sets to take on political or military roles, even though they most often are

EthnoFile 11.3
NYAKYUSA

Region: Central Africa

Nation: Tanzania

Population: 160,000 (1930s)

Environment: Well-watered, fertile valley at Lake Nyasa

Livelihood: Agriculture, especially bananas and millet, and stock raising

Political organization: Small chiefdoms

Other: The Nyakyusa are famous for the age villages that young men construct

found in societies with no central authority. Baxter and Almagor argued that the colorful activities of junior sets should not distract observers from recognizing that the seniors run things. If junior sets act, they usually act as agents of seniors. Indeed, the wildness of junior sets is conventional in many societies with age systems. While this custom allows juniors to enjoy themselves, it also publicly reinforces traditional wisdom that places power and property in the hands of elders.

Fostering Solidarity with Age-Sets

Age-set systems foster a sense of diffuse and enduring solidarity among their members. This is especially so if membership in a set comes after a rigorous initiation ritual. That age-mates are supposed to be the "best of friends" is illustrated by the widespread rule that forbids age-mates to accuse one another of adultery and demand compensation. This means, in practice, that a married man cannot prevent sexual relationships that might develop between his wife and his age-mates. This leads to a relationship among age-mates similar to that of "joking kin," who are forbidden to take offense at anything they say or do to each other. Here, the refusal to recognize adultery is institutionalized. It emphasizes that nothing, especially not sexual jealousy, must come between age-mates. The rule appears most onerous for the first members of junior sets who marry. Members of senior sets will usually all have wives of their own (Baxter and Almagor 1978:17).

Nyakyusa age sets were able to cultivate an unusual degree of solidarity among their members because each set was required to live in its own village. Indeed, the Nyakyusa believed that the main purpose of age villages was to allow set members to enjoy *ukwangala*, "good company"—the company of friends and equals. Wilson writes that to attain ukwangala, "men must build not only in villages, rather than in scattered homesteads, but also with contemporaries rather than with kin, since there can be no free and easy intercourse and sharing of food and beer between fathers and sons. *Ukwangala* implies eating and drinking together frequently and cannot be fully enjoyed by people who do not live close to one another" (Wilson 1951:163).

Functions of Age-Set Systems

Age-set systems may play an important cognitive role in the societies where they are found. For example, Baxter argues that the *gada* age-set system of the Boran of Kenya provides the idiom that the Boran use to describe and debate social and political life. *(See EthnoFile 11.4: Boran.)* The complex gada system recognizes five generation sets that succeed one another over a period of forty years. Every eight

EthnoFile 11.4
BORAN

Region: East Africa

Nation: Kenya-Ethiopia border

Population: 80,000 (1970s)

Environment: Adequate range-land, also scrub and desert

Other: The Boran have a distinctive age-set system

Livelihood: Herding of cattle by preference; also sheep, goats

Political organization: Kinship-based organization, with a set of six elders who have certain responsibilities in maintaining order

years, a new generation set is formed and the oldest generation set retires. The retirement of the senior-most set is marked by an elaborate culmination ceremony called the *gaadamoji*. "The set organisation is said to be there to ensure that these ceremonies are held. From another point of view the organisation generates a set of men every eight years who, for their own ritual needs, require the opportunity, as they enter the condition of *gaadamoji*, to undergo the culmination ceremony" (Baxter 1978:160).

Other explanations for age-set systems have been offered. Monica Wilson suggests that Nyakyusa age villages played an important role in controlling sexual behavior. The Nyakyusa themselves argue that young men must live apart from their fathers to prevent incest between the son's wife and his father. The same arrangement also prevents sexual involvements between a son and his father's wives, excluding his own mother. Such involvement is a real risk, since a son traditionally inherits his father's wives when his father dies.

For Baxter, Boran discussions of gada reveal it to be a conceptual system that guides them in political and social matters. But Baxter rejects the suggestion that the gada system ever played a political role in Boran society. "Gada exists primarily . . . in the folk view as well as in mine, to ensure the well-being of the Boran and to regulate the ritual growth and development of individuals and to do so in such a way as to permit all men who survive life's full span to achieve responsible and joyful sanctity. It is this last, joyful aspect of *gada* as an institution which performs rituals that has struck intelligent non-professional observers . . . and not its political ones" (ibid.: 156).

Secret Societies in West Africa

secret society
a non-kin form of social organization, found prototypically in West Africa and responsible for initiating young men or women into social adulthood; the secrecy concerns certain knowledge that each secret society possesses but that is known only to initiated members; ordinarily, all men and women are initiated

Several neighboring societies in West Africa use **secret societies** as a way of drawing members of different kinship groups into crosscutting associations. The most famous of these are the West African Poro and Sande societies, found among the Mende, Sherbro, Kpelle, and other neighboring peoples of Sierra Leone, Ivory Coast, Liberia, and Guinea.

Membership and Initiation

Poro is a secret society for men, Sande a secret society for women. Poro is responsible for initiating young men into social manhood, Sande for initiating young women into social womanhood. These sodalities are secret in the sense that each has certain knowledge that can be revealed only to initiated members. Both sodalities are hierarchically organized. The higher a person's status within the sodality, the greater the secret knowledge revealed.

Poro and Sande are responsible for supervising and regulating the sexual, social, and political conduct of all members of the wider society. To carry out this responsibility, high-status sodality members impersonate important supernatural figures by donning masks and performing in public. One secret kept from the uninitiated is that these masked figures are not the spirits themselves.

Membership is automatic on initiation, and all men and women are ordinarily initiated. "Until he has been initiated in the society, no Mende man is considered mature enough to have sexual intercourse or to marry" (Little 1967:245). Each community has its own local Poro and Sande congregations, and a person initiated in one community is eligible to participate in the congregations of other communities. Initiates must pay a fee for initiation, and if they wish to receive advanced training and progress to higher levels within the sodality, they must pay additional fees. In any community where Poro and Sande are strong, authority in society is divided between a sodality of mature women and one of mature men. Together, they work to keep society on the correct path. Indeed, the relationship between men and women in societies with Poro and Sande tends to be highly egalitarian.

Anthropologist Beryl Bellman was initiated into a Poro chapter among the Kpelle of Liberia. *(See EthnoFile 5.6: Kpelle.)* He describes initiation as a ritual process that takes place about every sixteen to eighteen years, about once each generation (Bellman 1984). One of the Poro's forest spirits, or "devils," metaphorically captures and eats the novices—only for them later to be metaphorically reborn from the womb of the devil's "wife." Marks incised on the necks, chests, and backs of initiates represent the "devil's teeth marks." After this scarification, initiates spend a year living apart from women in a special village constructed for them in the forest. During this period, they carry out various activities under the strict supervision of senior Poro members. Female Sande initiates undergo a similar experience during their year of initiation. This normally takes place several years after the Poro initiation has been completed.

Use of the Kinship Idiom

In Kpelle society, the relationship between mother's brother (*ngala*) and sister's son (*maling*) describes the literal relationship between kin. There is also a metaphoric aspect to this connection. It is used to describe relationships between patrilineages, sections of a town, and towns themselves. "Besides the serious or formal rights and obligations between *ngala* and *maling*, other aspects of the relationship are expressed as joking behavior between kinsmen. . . . The *ngala-maling* relationship is also the basis of labor recruitment, financial assistance, and a general support network" (ibid.: 22–23). This kinship idiom is used within the Poro society to describe the relationships between certain members. For example, two important Poro officials involved in initiation are the *Zo* and the *kwelebah*. The Zo directs the ritual, and the kwelebah announces both the ritual death and the ritual rebirth of the initiates to the community at large. The Zo is said to be the ngala of the kwelebah, and the kwelebah is said to be the maling of the Zo.

The Thoma Secret Society: A Microcosm

Anthropologist Carol MacCormack (1980) studied secret societies among the Sherbro. *(See EthnoFile 11.5: Sherbro.)* In addition to Poro and Sande congregations, the Sherbro MacCormack studied had a third secret society called Thoma, which

EthnoFile 11.5
SHERBRO

Region: West Africa

Nation: Sierra Leone

Population: 15,000 (1970s)

Environment: Rainy, swampy coastal area with sandy soil

Livelihood: Shallow-water fishing and hoe cultivation of rice

Political organization: Today, chiefdoms that are part of nation-state

Other: Thoma sodality uses dramatic masks in its regular rituals

initiated both men and women. Members of one society could not be initiated into the others, and families with several children usually tried to initiate at least one child into each sodality.

MacCormack writes: "With Poro and Sande, the contrastive gender categories are split apart and the uniqueness of each gender is emphasized, but always with the final view that the complementarity of the two constitute human society, the full cultural unity. Thoma is a microcosm of the whole. Its local congregations or chapters are headed by a man and a woman, co-equal leaders who are 'husband and wife' in a ritual context but are not married in mundane life" (MacCormack 1980:97). The Sherbro are concerned with the reproduction of their society. *Reproduction* here means not just production of children, but also continuation of the division of labor between men and women. The Sherbro say that the ritual function of the Thoma sodality is to "wash the bush," that is, "to cleanse the land and the village from evil and restore its fertility and well-being" (ibid.: 98).

The purpose of Thoma initiation is to transform uninitiated, proto-social beings into initiated, fully social, adult human beings. The Thoma society had four masks representing two pairs of spirits: an animal pair and a humanoid pair. The masks, which are considered very powerful, appear when initiates are nearing the end of their ritual seclusion in the forest. They "symbolize that 'wild,' unsocialized children are being transformed into cultured adults, but will retain the fertile vigour of the animal world" (ibid.: 100). The humanoid masks represent male and female ancestral spirits who appear when the initiates are about to be reborn into their new, adult status. "Human beings must abide by ancestral rules of conduct if they are to be healthy and fertile. Indeed, they wish to be as healthy and strong as forest animals which give birth in litters. Only by becoming fully 'cultural,' vowing to live by ancestral laws, may they hope to avoid illness and barrenness" (ibid.: 116).

The Meaning of Secrecy in Secret Societies

Bellman was interested the secrecy that surrounded membership in Poro and other similar sodalities. He discovered that Poro (and Sande) initiation rituals were primarily concerned with teaching initiates how to keep a secret. Discretion—knowing when, how, and even whether to speak about various topics—is a prized virtue among the Kpelle and required of all mature members of their society. So learning how to "practice secrecy" is a central lesson of initiation. "It was always crucial for members to be certain whether they have the right to talk as well as the right to know. The two are not necessarily related. Nonmembers very often know some of the secrets of membership; yet they must maintain a description of the event comparable to that of nonmembers" (Bellman 1984:51).

Based on this interpretation of "secrecy" in secret societies, Bellman took up a central puzzle of secret societies for the outsider. What do the uninitiated actually believe about these societies? In the case of the Poro, the women speak of devils killing and eating novices as though they believe this to be literally true. Bellman and his informants believe that the women know perfectly well what is "really" happening when Poro novices are taken away into the forest. But women are not allowed to talk about what they know except in the language of ritual metaphor. In the context of the initiation ritual, participation of the "audience" of women and other noninitiates is as important as the participation of the Poro elders and the initiates themselves. In playing their appropriate ritual role, women show respect for traditional understandings concerning which members of society have the right to speak about which topics in which manner under which circumstances. "The enactment of Poro rituals serves to establish the ways in which that concealed information is communicated. . . . It offers methods for mentioning the unmentionable" (ibid.: 141).

Nonkin Ties In Stratified Societies

Forms of Stratified Societies

Sodalities are most common among societies whose social organizations are nonhierarchical; that is, where there is no central chief or king who rules over the entire group. People in those societies may gain the esteem of their fellows. Men might even have substantial support groups of wives, children, and retainers. But their status depends entirely on their own personal prowess. They cannot transform what they have achieved into permanent superiority of wealth, power, or prestige. Anthropologists refer to societies in which all members have equal access to wealth, power, and prestige as **egalitarian societies**.

Permanent hierarchies do exist. In **stratified societies**, some members of the society have privileged access to wealth, power, and prestige. This privileged access is relatively fixed, and can be inherited. Stratification may be minimal, as in societies known as **chiefdoms**, where perhaps only the office of chief is a permanently superior status. Privileges accrue to those who are closely related to the chief, while other members of the society must settle for less. As discussed in chapter 8, there is no sharp boundary between rank societies and chiefdoms. Both categories are prototypes, and the most that can reasonably be said is that a given society is ranked or stratified to a certain degree.

In some cases, stratification is pervasive and thoroughgoing. The stratified society, which can be much larger than tribes or chiefdoms, may be internally divided into a number of groups whose statuses relative to one another are carefully specified. In **caste** societies, membership in each ranked group is closed and movement of individuals from one group to another is forbidden. The prototypical caste society in anthropology has been that of India. **Class** societies also have internally ranked subgroups, but these groups are said to be open, and individuals can move upward or downward from one class to another. Modern Europe and the United States are classic examples of class societies.

egalitarian societies
societies in which all members have equal access to wealth, power, and prestige

stratified societies
societies with a permanent hierarchy in which some members have privileged access to wealth, power, and prestige

chiefdoms
minimally stratified societies in which perhaps only the office of chief is a permanently superior status

caste
a closed ranked group within a hierarchically stratified society; movement of individuals from one such group to another is forbidden

class
an open ranked group within a hierarchically stratified society; it is possible for individuals to move upward or downward from one class to another

Housing is one indicator of social class.

Criteria for Membership in Levels of Society

In stratified societies, different criteria may be used to place people in one or another stratum. Karl Marx argued, for example, that class membership in capitalist society was determined by the relationship people had to the means of production: whether they owned the tools and raw materials needed for industry. Capitalists who owned the means of production made up the ruling class. Those who worked for capitalists for wages but did not own the means of production made up the proletariat, or subject class. Other criteria can also be important in assigning membership to the various levels in a stratified society. Occupational specialization is one such criterion, and appears to be central to caste systems. **Race** and **ethnicity** involve other criteria that are of a biological or cultural nature, or both. These may complicate or contradict stratification based on other principles.

The various levels of a stratified society do not in themselves provide ties that link nonkin to one another. The key to social solidarity in stratified societies is the nature of the relationships uniting the levels. Again, in the marxian view of class, the links between capitalists and proletarians are economic; both classes must cooperate to produce goods for society as a whole. Their relationship is sealed by the transfer of money, either as wages to workers or as payment for goods. In caste societies, where the division of labor is elaborate and each caste specializes in one kind of work, castes are linked by a Durkheimian kind of organic solidarity, which is reinforced by ritual.

In many of the stratified societies studied by anthropologists, levels are linked by the institution of **clientage**. According to M. G. Smith, clientage "designates a variety of relationships, which all have inequality of status of the associated persons as a common characteristic" ([1954]1981:31). It is a relationship between individuals rather than groups. The party of superior status is the patron, and the party of inferior status is called the client. For example, clientage is characteristic of compadrazgo relationships, especially when the ritual parents are of higher social status than the biological parents. In fact, the Latin American societies in which compadrazgo flourishes are class societies, and parents often do seek their social superiors as compadres.

Stratified societies united by links of clientage between persons can be very stable. Often the stratified order is believed to be natural and not questioned. Those of low status believe their security depends on finding someone in a high-status group who can protect them. Since clientage links individuals, the clients may be unaware that they belong to a group of people who are all similarly underprivileged. In marxian terms, they lack class consciousness. In other stratified societies, underprivileged groups do have a common sense of identity. Sometimes they even have an internal organization that defends group members' interests in dealings with outsiders. This is often the case for groups whose memberships depend on race or ethnicity.

Caste Societies

The word *caste* comes from the Portuguese word *casta*, meaning "chaste." Portuguese explorers applied it to the stratification system they encountered in India in the fifteenth century. Each group in society had to remain sexually pure, or chaste: both sexual and marital links between groups were forbidden. Ever since, the stratification system of India has been taken as the prototype of caste stratification. Some scholars have even argued that caste cannot properly be said to exist outside India. If

race
a social grouping based on perceived physical differences and described in the idiom of biology

ethnicity
a set of prototypically descent-based cultural criteria that people in a group are believed to share

clientage
an institution linking individuals belonging to upper and lower levels in a stratified society

we take the Indian system as a prototype, however, we may apply the term caste to systems of social stratification that bear a family resemblance to the Indian case. One important non-Indian example, which we shall examine later in this chapter, can be found in the Sudan of West Africa.

Caste in India ■■■■■■

The Hindi word that the Portuguese translated as *casta* is *jati*. Villagers in the southern Indian town of Gopalpur defined a jati for anthropologist Alan Beals. *(See EthnoFile 11.6: Gopalpur.)* They said it was "a category of men thought to be related, to occupy a particular position within a hierarchy of jatis, to marry among themselves, and to follow particular practices and occupations" (Beals 1962:25). Beals's informants compared the relationship between jatis of different rank to the relationship between brothers. Members of low-ranking jatis respect and obey members of high-ranking jatis just as younger brothers respect and obey older brothers.

Villagers in Gopalpur were aware of at least fifty different jatis, although not all were represented in the village. Because jatis have different occupational specialties that they alone can perform, villagers are sometimes dependent on the services of outsiders. For example, there was no member of the Washerman jati in Gopalpur. As a result, a member of that jati from another village had to be employed when people in Gopalpur wanted their clothes cleaned ritually or required clean cloth for ceremonies.

Jatis are distinguished in terms of the foods they eat as well as their traditional occupations. These features have a ritual significance that affects interactions between members of different jatis. In Hindu belief, certain foods and occupations are classed as pure and others as polluting. In theory, all jatis are ranked on a scale from purest to most polluted. For example, a vegetarian diet is purest, and vegetarian castes such as Carpenters and Blacksmiths are assigned a high rank. Below the vegetarians are "clean" or "pure" meat eaters. In Gopalpur, this group of jatis included Saltmakers, Farmers, and Shepherds, who eat sheep, goats, chicken, and fish but not pork or beef. The lowest-ranking jatis are "unclean" meat eaters, who include Stoneworkers and Basketweavers (who eat pork) and Leatherworkers (who eat pork and beef). Occupations that involve slaughtering animals or touching polluted things are themselves polluting. Jatis that traditionally carry out such activities as butchering and washing dirty clothing are ranked below jatis whose traditional

---

EthnoFile 11.6
GOPALPUR

Region: South Asia

Nation: South India

Population: 540 (1960)

Environment: Center of a plain; some good farmland and pasture

Livelihood: Intensive millet farming; some cattle and sheep herding

Political organization: Caste system in modern state

Other: Gopalpur enjoys a rich and complex way of life, despite its apparent poverty

work does not involve polluting activities. Ranked highest of all are the vegetarian Brahmins, who are pure enough to approach the gods.

Hindu dietary rules deal not only with the kinds of food that may be eaten by different jatis, but also with the circumstances in which members of one jati may accept food prepared by members of another. Members of a lower-ranking jati may accept any food prepared by members of a higher-ranking jati. Members of a higher-ranking jati may accept only certain foods prepared by a lower-ranking jati. In addition, members of different jatis should not eat together.

In practice, these rules are not as confining as they appear. In Gopalpur, " 'food' refers to particular kinds of food, principally rice. 'Eating together' means eating from the same dish or sitting on the same line. . . . Members of quite different jatis may eat together if they eat out of separate bowls and if they are facing each other or turned slightly away from each other" (ibid.: 41). Members of jatis that are close in rank and neither at the top nor at the bottom of the scale often share food and eat together on a daily basis. Strict observance of the rules is saved for ceremonial occasions.

The way in which non-Hindus have been incorporated into the jati system in Gopalpur illuminates the logic of the system. For example, Muslims have long ruled the region in which Gopalpur is located, and so a salient attribute of Muslim identity has been possession of political power. In addition, Muslims do not eat pork or the meat of animals that have not been ritually slaughtered. These attributes, taken together, have led the villagers in Gopalpur to rank Muslims above the Stoneworkers and Basketweavers, who eat pork. All three groups are considered to be eaters of unclean meat.

There is no direct correlation between the status of a jati on the scale of purity and pollution and the economic status of members of that jati. Jati membership may be advantageous in some cases. Beals notes, for example, that the high status of Brahmins means that "there are a relatively large number of ways in which a poor Brahmin may become wealthy" (1962:37). Similarly, members of low-status castes may find their attempts to amass wealth curtailed by the opposition of their status superiors. In Gopalpur, a group of Farmers and Shepherds attacked a group of Stoneworkers who had purchased good rice land in the village. Those Stoneworkers were eventually forced to buy inferior land elsewhere in the village.

In general, however, regardless of caste, a person who wishes to advance economically "must be prepared to defend his gains against jealous neighbors. Anyone who buys land is limiting his neighbor's opportunities to buy land. Most people safeguard themselves by tying themselves through indebtedness to a powerful landlord who will give them support when difficulties are encountered" (Beals 1962:39).

Although the interdependence of jatis is explained in theory by their occupational specialties, the social reality is a bit different. For example, Saltmakers in Gopalpur are farmers and actually produce little salt—which can be bought in shops by those who need it. It is primarily in the context of ritual that jati interdependence is given full play. Recall that Gopalpur villagers required the services of a Washerman when they needed *ritually* clean garments or cloth; otherwise, most villagers wash their own clothing.

> *To arrange a marriage, to set up the doorway of a new house, to stage a drama, or to hold an entertainment, the householder must call on a wide range of jatis. The entertainment of even a modest number of guests requires the presence of the Singer. The Potter must provide new pots in which to cook the food; the Boin from the Farmer jati must carry the pot;*

the Shepherd must sacrifice the goat; the Crier, a Saltmaker, must invite the guests. To survive, one requires the cooperation of only a few jatis; to enjoy life and do things in the proper manner requires the cooperation of many. (Ibid.: 41)

Caste in West Africa

When anthropologists use the term *caste* to describe societies outside India, it is often because they have encountered one of two features in a society. One is endogamous occupational groupings (for example, blacksmiths) whose members are looked down on by other groups in the society. The other is an endogamous ruling elite who set themselves above those over whom they rule. Both these features are present in Indian society. The problem is that, apart from these similarities, caste systems found outside the Indian subcontinent are very different indeed.

Anthropologist James Vaughan (1970) reviewed the data on West African caste systems. The first feature of non-Hindu caste described here was common in societies of the Sahara and in the western Sudan (the band of territory between Senegal and Lake Chad, south of the Sahara and north of the coastal rain forest). Vaughan also found castes in a second culture area located in the mountain ranges that lie along the modern border between Nigeria and Cameroon. In this region, many societies had endogamous groups of "blacksmiths" whose status was distinct from that of other members of society. These people were not despised, however; if anything, they were regarded with awe or feared.

Vaughan studied such a caste of blacksmiths in a kingdom of the Marghi, whose traditional territory is in the mountains and nearby plains south of Lake Chad in present-day Nigeria. *(See EthnoFile 11.7: Marghi.)* Members of the caste, who are called *ngkyagu*, are traditional craft specialists whose major occupation is the smithing of iron. They make a variety of iron tools for ordinary Marghi, the most important of which are the hoes they use for farming. They also make weapons and iron ornaments of various kinds. They work leather, fashioning traditional items of apparel, leather-covered charms, and the sling in which infants are carried. They work wood, making beds and carving stools. They are barbers, incising traditional tribal markings on Marghi women, and responsible in some Marghi kingdoms for shaving the head of a newly installed king. They are morticians, assisting in the preparation of a body for burial, digging the grave, carrying the corpse from the compound to the grave. They are musicians, playing a distinctive drum played by no

---

EthnoFile 11.7
MARGHI

Region: West Africa

Nation: Northeastern Nigeria

Population: 100,000 to 200,000 (1960s)

Environment: Mountains and valley floor

Livelihood: Farming, selling surplus in local markets

Political organization: Kingdoms

Other: Blacksmiths make up a separate and special caste

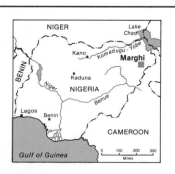

Marghi blacksmiths. The woman on the right holds a basket. The man in the left foreground is hammering a steel knife. The man in the center is making the scabbard for another knife out of crocodile skin. The man on the left (hidden by the child) is fashioning leather loin garments. Three pots in the left rear contain divining paraphernalia. Only members of the blacksmith caste may perform these tasks.

one else. Some are diviners and "doctors." Female caste members are the potters of Marghi society.

Vaughan stresses that although regular Marghi and ngkyagu both recognize that ngkyagu are different, in most ways the ngkyagu do not stand out from other Marghi. All the same, Marghi and ngkyagu do not intermarry and will not share the same food. In an interesting parallel to the Indian case described above, ngkyagu can drink beer brewed by Marghi women as long as they provide their own drinking vessel. Marghi, however, will not drink beer brewed by female ngkyagu.

When Marghi described the differences between themselves and ngkyagu, they said that caste members were "different" and "strange." In Vaughan's opinion, this has to do in large part with the fact that ngkyagu do not farm: "To be a Marghi means to be a farmer. . . . A person who does not farm cannot in the Marghi idiom be considered an altogether normal person" (Vaughan 1970:71). By contrast, ngkyagu attribute the difference between themselves and other Marghi to the division of labor and point out that both groups depend on one another. Marghi do their own smelting, but they require ngkyagu to use their skills as smiths to turn the smelted ore into implements. Thus, Marghi rely on members of the caste for their farming tools, but ngkyagu rely on Marghi for food.

Vaughan suggests that this division of labor and interdependence is not only practical but also ideological. It is part of the Marghi world view and is further revealed in the domains of politics and ritual. For example, a curious relationship links ngkyagu to Marghi kings. The most remarkable feature of this relationship is the tradition of Marghi kings taking a female member of the caste as a bride, thereby violating the rule of endogamy. Recall the role a member of the caste plays during the investiture of a new king. It is even more common for ngkyagu to bury deceased Marghi kings seated on an iron stool, surrounded by charcoal, which is the way ngkyagu themselves are buried. In addition, of all Marghi clans, only the ngkyagu clans are exempt from participating in the choice of a new Marghi king. Indeed, traditionally they had their own "king," the *ptil ngkyagu*, who decided disputes among ngkyagu without recourse to the legal advisers of the Marghi king.

All this suggests that the two categories Marghi and ngkyagu form the foundation of Marghi society. They are mutually interdependent. The ritual prohibitions that divide them, however, suggest that this interdependence carries symbolic overtones. According to Vaughan, the caste system allows the Marghi to resolve a paradox. They are a society of farmers who need to support full-time toolmaking nonfarmers in order to farm. Marghi dislike being dependent on others, yet their way of life requires them to depend on ngkyagu. The ritual prohibitions that separate ngkyagu from other Marghi also ensure that there will always be some caste specialists around to provide Marghi with the tools they cannot make themselves.

Class, Race, and Ethnicity

We now turn to the role of social class in human society, specifically as related to race and ethnicity. Recall that classes are levels in a system of social stratification whose boundaries are less rigid than those of the caste system. Unlike caste, classes are not endogamous, although members of a class often tend to choose other members of their class as spouses. Also unlike caste, the boundaries between classes are fluid enough for people to change their class membership within their lifetimes.

Social stratification is rarely a simple matter in societies as large and complex as nation-states. Social scientists mainly agree that the large-scale societies of the modern world are divided into classes. There is debate over the precise boundaries of the classes, as well as the distinctive features that indicate class membership. Position in the hierarchy depends not only on power, not only on wealth, not only on prestige, but on a mix of all three elements. As well, in a complex society, hierarchy may be complicated or contradicted by the presence of nonclass groupings based on race or ethnicity. Caste systems are faced with similar contradictions. In the example from Gopalpur, social pressure and physical violence forced the Saltmakers to buy inferior land that was more in keeping with their caste status than their economic status.

Negotiating Social Status: Mexico (1521–1812)

Anthropologist John Chance studied the role of class, race, and ethnicity in the city of Oaxaca, Mexico. *(See EthnoFile 11.8: Colonial Oaxaca.)* Oaxaca, known as Antequera during the colonial period, is a highland city founded in an area densely

---

EthnoFile 11.8
COLONIAL OAXACA

Region: Latin America

Nation: Mexico

Population: 18,000 (1792)

Environment: High mountain river basin; temperate, warm, dry

Livelihood: Administrative center, clothing and textile industries

Political organization: Colony of Spain

Other: During this period in Oaxaca's history, there were no well-defined ethnic identities attached to such terms as mestizo, mulatto, and pardo

populated by Indians who participated in Mexican high civilization. Chance's research (1978) is a bit unusual in anthropology because it is entirely historical. He examined how social stratification changed from the period of Spanish colonial conquest, in 1521, to the early years of the Mexican war of independence, in 1812. Chance used an anthropological perspective to interpret census records, wills, and other archival materials preserved in Mexico and Spain. As a result, he was able to show that changes occurred both in the *categories* used to describe social stratification and in the *meanings* attached to those categories.

The Estate System

When the Spanish arrived in Mexico in 1521, they found a number of Indian societies organized into states. The Aztecs, for example, were divided into an upper ruling stratum of nobles and a lower, commoner class. After the conquest, the stratification systems of the two societies, White and Indian, began to move toward unification. The Spanish conquerors tried to make sense of postconquest society by applying concepts based on the European system of estates. Estates were legally recognized social categories that were entitled to a voice in government. European estates prototypically included the nobility, the clergy, and the common people. In New Spain, estate membership was assigned on the basis of race. The clergy and nobility were reserved for Whites; the Indians became the common people.

There were exceptions to this system, however. Indian nobles were given special status in postconquest society and were used by the colonial administration to control their own people. Moreover, the conquistadors, who brought no Spanish women with them, soon established sexual relationships with local Indian women. In the early years, if these unions involved marriage the offspring were usually considered White, but if they were casual or clandestine the offspring were more likely to be considered Indian. Thus a population of mixed Indian and White descent was created. By 1529, African slaves had been brought to New Spain. These slaves ranked at the bottom of the colonial hierarchy, below Indians. They too began to interbreed with Indians and Whites, producing their own mixed offspring.

According to the system of estates, people of mixed race were not supposed to exist. By the mid-sixteenth century, however, their numbers and their economic importance in the colony made them impossible to ignore. As a result, the rulers of New Spain developed the *sistema de castas*, "a cognitive and legal system of ranked socioracial statuses" used to refer to all people of mixed racial heritage (Chance 1978:viii). The first castas recognized were the *mestizos* (people of mixed Spanish and Indian descent) and the *mulattoes* (people who showed evidence of African ancestry).

Whether the Spanish word *casta* should be translated "caste" or "class" or "race" or "ethnic group" is an interesting question. The original "estates" whose interbreeding produced the castas were defined in terms of race. In addition, it was understood that races should not intermarry. That is, each estate was supposed to practice endogamy, like a caste. The sixteenth-century assumption that all people of mixed race were illegitimate demonstrated this belief. Since Spaniards monopolized wealth, power, and prestige in the new colony, they could be viewed as the ruling class—with everyone else making up the subject class. Finally, members of the original colonial estates initially differed from one another not only in terms of race but also in terms of culture. So they might also be seen as constituting separate ethnic groups within colonial society.

As soon as there were enough mestizos and mulattoes to attract attention, the colonial government tried to limit their social mobility by legal means. Yet their status was ambiguous. Mestizos were ranked above mulattoes because they had no

African ancestry, but were theoretically ranked below the Whites because of their "illegitimacy." In cases where the Indian and White spouses were legally married, their children were called *españoles* (creoles). They were distinguished from *españoles europeos* (Spaniards born in Spain). In later years, the term "creole" (*criollo*) was also used to refer to people of presumably "pure" White ancestry who were born in America. Some mestizos managed to obtain elite privileges, such as the right to carry arms. Most mulattoes were classed with Blacks and could be enslaved. Yet free mulattoes could also apply for the right to carry arms, which shows that even their status was ambiguous.

During the seventeenth century, the castas were acknowledged as legitimate strata in the system of colonial stratification. A number of new castas were recognized: *castizo* (a person of mixed Spanish and mestizo descent), *mulato libre* (free mulatto), *mulato esclavo* (mulatto slave), *negro libre* (free Black), and *negro esclavo* (Black slave). Perhaps most striking is the castizo category. This seems to have been designed by the colonial elite to stem the tide of ever "whiter" mestizos who might be mistaken for genuine Spaniards. John Chance (1978:126) points out that racial mixing was primarily an urban phenomenon, and that the castas perceived themselves, and were perceived by the elite, as belonging to Hispanic rather than Indian society. It is perhaps not surprising that lighter-skinned castas became increasingly indistinguishable from middle- and lower-class creoles. In fact, census records in Oaxaca list creoles as the largest segment of the city's population throughout the entire colonial period.

Other Stratification Systems

As if the sistema de castas were not enough, colonial society recognized three additional systems of classification that cut across the castas. One distinguished groups required to pay tribute to the Spanish crown (Indians, Blacks, and mulattoes) from everyone else. The second distinguished *gente de razon* ("rational people," who practiced the Hispanic culture of the city) from *indios* (the rural, culturally alien Indian population). A third distinguished *gente decente* (respectable people) from *la plebe* (the common people). Chance (1978:127) suggests that the last distinction, which made most sense in the urban setting, represented an embryonic division into socioeconomic classes.

Mobility in the Casta System

Throughout the colonial period, the boundaries of the stratification system in Oaxaca were most rigid for those born into the Indian, Black, and peninsular Spanish groups. These were the "unmixed" categories at the bottom and top of the hierarchy. Paradoxically, those of mixed background had the most ambiguous status and had the greatest opportunity to improve it. For example, when a couple married, the priest decided the casta membership of the bride and groom. The strategy for upward mobility called for choosing a marriage partner who was light-skinned enough for the priest to decide that both spouses belonged in a high-ranking casta. Over time, such maneuvering swelled the ranks of the creoles.

The growth of the casta population coincided with the transformation of the colonial economy from one based on tribute and mining to one based on commercial capitalism. The prosperity this transformation brought to Oaxaca was greatest in the eighteenth century. That was when the city became the center of an important textile and dye-manufacturing industry. Many castas were able to accumulate wealth, which together with a light skin and urban culture made it possible for them to achieve the status of creole within their lifetimes.

Chance argues that during the late colonial period, racial status had become an achieved, rather than an ascribed, status. By that time, the increasing rate of legitimacy in all castas meant that descent lost its importance as a criterion of group membership. Creole status could be claimed by anyone who was able to show that his or her ancestors had not paid tribute. At the same time, in a dialectical fashion, people's image of what "White" people looked like had changed. As people with Indian and Black ancestry moved up the social scale, their physical appearance, or phenotype, widened the range of phenotypes considered prototypical for people of their status.

Negotiating Social Status in Other Societies

Processes similar to those Chance describes continue to take place today. In many areas of Latin America where extensive racial mixing has occurred, "racial" status is an achieved status. Benjamin Colby and Pierre van den Berghe (1969) documented the process in Guatemala in the twentieth century. Indians who left their traditional communities, learned Spanish, dressed like whites, and took a non-Indian occupation might easily pass as *ladinos* (members of the "white" population) whether they wanted to or not. Colby and van den Berghe write:

> *A factor which probably contributes to ladinoization is the ambiguity in the ethnic status of the Indian who does not belong to the local majority group. Local Indians will regard him as a stranger, and, of course, unless he speaks the local Indian language, he will be forced to use Spanish as a lingua franca. Ladinoization and "passing" of Indian "strangers" are probably more the consequences of marginality than of any conscious desire to become assimilated to the ladinos. Rejection by local Indians makes ladinoization almost inevitable. (Colby and van den Berghe 1969:172)*

Emily Schultz (1984) encountered a similar process at work in Guider, Cameroon. *(See EthnoFile 7.1: Guider.)* She found that people born outside the dominant Fulbe ethnic group could achieve Fulbe status within their lifetimes. To do this, they had be successful in three tasks. They had to adopt the Fulbe language (Fulfulde), the Fulbe religion (Islam), and the Fulbe "way of life," which was identified with urban customs and the traditional high culture of the western Sudan. Many Fulbe claimed that descent from one or another Fulbe lineage was needed in order to claim Fulbe identity. Nevertheless, they seemed willing to accept "Fulbeized Pagans" as Fulbe (for example, by giving their daughters to them as brides) because those people were committed defenders of the urban Fulbe way of life. Those who were "Fulbeizing," however, came from societies in which descent had never been an important criterion of group membership. For those people, ethnic identity depended on the language, customs, and territorial affiliation of the group to which they were currently committed. In becoming Fulbe, they had simply chosen to commit themselves to Fulfulde, Islam, and life in "Fulbe territory," the town.

The Dimensions of Group Life

In looking at the range of nonkin social ties that people invent to connect themselves to one another across kinship boundaries, we have considered some features of the larger groups into which human beings have organized themselves. As an organization or society grows in size and complexity, changes inevitably occur in economic, political, and social patterns. This is particularly striking when societies come to be based on class divisions. Many anthropologists would argue, in fact, that transition to a class-based society marks a qualitative change in the nature of social life. That is, *class organization* marks a threshold where a change in *degree* of complexity is transformed into a change in *kind* of complexity. This constitutes yet another referential perspective on the striking differences between the society of Western anthropologists and many of the societies they study. In this way, the issues that occupied the attention of such figures as Maine and Durkheim are still alive.

The next chapters examine more closely the different ways human beings have coped with power relations, economic relations, and relations with their neighbors. In particular, we shall be alert to the role played by European colonialism in shaping the forms of human society anthropologists have encountered in the modern world.

Key Terms

status	sodalities	caste
role	age sets	class
mechanical solidarity	secret society	race
organic solidarity	egalitarian societies	ethnicity
division of labor	stratified societies	clientage
ascribed statuses		
achieved statuses		

Chapter Summary

1. Early anthropologists described and explained the differences they saw between "primitive" and "modern" human societies. They thought of primitive society as organized in terms of kinship, and therefore characterized by personalized, face-to-face relationships, *ascribed statuses*, and *mechanical solidarity*. Modern society, by contrast, was characterized by impersonal relationships, *achieved statuses*, and *organic solidarity*. In modern society, kinship played a much reduced role, and most of the people with whom an individual dealt were nonkin.
2. Every society provides ways of establishing links with nonkin. One way involves the creation of metaphorical kin. Another involves the establishment of friendship. It is sometimes difficult to draw a neat line between kinship and nonkin relationships, because kinship terms may be used between "friends," or kinship roles may be the prototypes for the roles expected of friends, or both. In any case, the relationships cultivate a sentiment of diffuse and enduring solidarity between the parties involved.
3. The larger the society, the more complex its *division of labor*. The greater the specialization within that division of labor, the greater the likelihood of finding institutionalized relationships between nonkin alongside kinship relations. Such institutions are minimally developed in most band societies, but become increasingly important in tribal societies, in the form of *sodalities*.
4. Cheyenne military societies, East African age sets, and West African secret societies are all examples of pan-tribal *sodalities*. these institutions tend to be found in non-hierarchical societies. Members of the sodalities, drawn from the various kinship groups, ordinarily take on responsibility for various public func-

tions of a governmental or ritual nature. Membership in such sodalities is often a mark of adulthood, and may be connected with rituals of initiation.

5. In stratified societies, some groups have permanently privileged access to valued resources, while others have permanently restricted access. The relations between subgroups are carefully specified. Two common patterns of stratification are *caste* and *class*. Links between castes or classes may be based on such criteria as the relationship individuals have to the means of production and occupational specialization, and may be complicated by *race* or *ethnicity*. In many stratified societies, individuals from different strata are linked by *clientage*.

6. In stratified societies, particularly those in which membership in one or another stratum is based on race or ethnicity, group membership is often a matter of negotiation. Data from colonial Oaxaca show how the recognized categories of society changed over time, along with the criteria used to assign membership. These data also demonstrate that individuals could manipulate the rules to advance in status, successfully "passing" as members of groups to which they did not "literally" belong. Similar processes have been noted elsewhere in the world. They illustrate that racial, ethnic, or class prototypes are selective cultural constructions, emphasizing certain attributes of individuals while ignoring others.

Suggested Readings

Brain, Robert. *Friends and Lovers*. New York: Basic Books, 1976.
    A thorough, highly readable account of friendship taken very broadly, with excellent ethnographic examples. Brain allows himself to draw lessons for Western society from his research, with provocative results.

Keillor, Garrison. *Lake Wobegon Days*. New York: Viking, 1985.
    The best-seller, and a book about kinship and the other ties that bind in American small-town life.

Royce, Anya Peterson. *Ethnic Identity*. Bloomington, Ind.: Indiana University Press, 1982.
    An introductory level, encyclopedic treatment of the many and varied factors that go into the making of ethnic identity.

Smith, Mary F. *Baba of Karo*. New Haven: Yale University Press, 1981. Originally published in 1954.
    A remarkable document: the autobiography of a Hausa woman born in 1877. A master storyteller, Baba provides much information about the patterns of friendship, clientage, adoption, and kinship and marriage.

Anthropology 2000

Paul Rabinow (Ph.D., University of Chicago) is Professor of Anthropology at the University of California, Berkeley. He also taught at the City University of New York and at the École des Hautes Études in Paris. Dr. Rabinow's fieldwork was done in Morocco. He has edited five books and authored four more, covering both ethnography and philosophy. French social philosophy is one of his main interests.

The basic premise of modern American anthropology is that fundamental cultural differences exist and that this is a good thing. Anthropology has devoted its scientific energies to documenting and explaining this diversity. Its ethical impact is the affirmation of pluralism.

The best of American anthropology has opposed what Clifford Geertz has labeled the Enlightenment "all the world's a stage" view. This universalist stance holds that all people have basically the same underlying needs, desires, and thoughts, that we all play the same script, only in different costumes. Like Geertz I think this view is wrong. First, it is empty and shallow to say, for example, that because young men become mature males in all cultures one can equate fraternity parties with the taking of heads among the Ilongot of the Philippines. This view is also potentially dangerous. To say that all societies are competitive and to equate the display and expenditure of goods in a Kwakiutl potlatch with national competition at Europe's world fairs is nonsense. At these fairs, the West was, among other things, collecting and exhibiting the world's peoples as curiosities. The economic and political forces building behind the fairs were leading us into a century of world war. To equate this with the potlatch muddles scientific insight, covers over power relations, and violates the center of American anthropology's ethics: the respect for difference. The staging of difference as all ultimately the same is a continuation of our culture's imperial practices (everything out there is either like us or for us).

But if universalists submerge and destroy difference, the denial of commonality (solidarity) is fraught with equal scientific, political, and ethical dangers. Without a common ethical frame posited as a given, there is only difference. In the modern world at least, difference, untempered by tolerance and understanding, has led to immense horror. Modern American anthropology, from Franz Boas forward, has set itself the task of combating the xenophobias, localisms, racisms, ethnocides, and genocides that human beings have been practicing so creatively. The myth of isolated, whole, authentic, pure cultures (not to mention races, peoples, and nations) is worth rethinking.

The fates of all people are intertwined, but this does not mean they are the same. The task for anthropology in the years to come is to learn how to think about this situation to promote survival, solidarity, and diversity. The world is not becoming homogenized; new differences are everywhere. We must learn to think about all of them and to strengthen some of them.

What we share as a condition of existence, heightened today by our ability and at times eagerness to obliterate one another, is an always specific givenness of cultural and historical place, however complex and contestable it might be, and a worldwide macrodependency that goes beyond any particularity. Borrowing a term that is applied at various times (both positively and negatively) to Christians, aristocrats, merchants, Jews, and intellectuals, I call the acceptance of these twin values "cosmopolitanism." Let us define cosmopolitanism as an ethos of macrodependencies with an acute consciousness (often forced on people) of the inescapabilities and particularities of place, character, history, and fate. Although we are all cosmopolitans, humankind has done poorly with interpreting this condition. We seem to have trouble with the balancing act, preferring to reify local identities or to construct universal ones. We live in between. Cosmopolitanism rejects innate difference and emphasizes historical contingency, power relations, and worlds of meaning while refusing universals that obscure real and valuable differences between us. As French poet René Char put it, "Human history is a long succession of synonyms for the same word. To contradict this is a duty." In other words, how is it possible to think and to act within a framework of commonality with an ethic of difference?

Sisterhood in Northern Nigeria

In 1949, Mary Smith accompanied her husband, anthropologist M. G. Smith, into the field. He was to begin research on the histories and social structures of the Muslim emirates of the Hausa-speaking peoples of northern Nigeria. While he gathered information from men, she came to learn a great deal about the lives of women. One elderly woman, Baba of Karo, became a key informant, and she agreed to tell Mary Smith her life story.

Baba was born in 1877, and her youth coincided with the arrival of the British in northern Nigeria. Her early memories were therefore of life in a society that was still autonomous and had not yet undergone the homogenizing influences of colonial rule. The Muslin Hausa of northern Nigeria lived in kingdoms, or emirates, in which commerce flourished. Most ordinary citizens farmed for a living, but many also practiced a wide variety of crafts, which were produced for sale. Hausa merchants are well-known throughout West Africa for their wealth and business acumen.

The Hausa kinship system is bilateral, and residence is usually patrilocal. The principle of relative age is extremely important within the family, and the Hausa kinship terminology contains separate terms for younger and older siblings of both sexes. Men and women owe respect to older brothers and older sisters within their family, and younger siblings must heed the wishes of elder siblings even when they are grown. Fertility in women is highly valued, and so Baba's never having given birth to any children of her own might have been a tragedy. The Hausa tradition of adoption, however, made it possible for Baba to become the "fictive" mother of other women's children. The child usually offered for adoption is a mother's firstborn, with whom she develops a lifelong ritual avoidance relationship. Other children may also be offered to a co–wife or a sibling for adoption, particularly if the adoptive mother has no children of her own. Indeed, a woman with no children can demand that her brother allow her to adopt one of his. One of Baba's sisters-in-law demanded a child of Baba's husband by one of his fertile wives, and he could not refuse her request (M. F. Smith [1954] 1981 : 180).

Adoption among the Hausa functioned to make mothers of as many women as possible. The adoptive mother played the entire social role of a mother to her adopted child, which included arranging the first marriage of that child. But Hausa women were not limited to adopting children; their culture also permitted them to adopt "younger brothers" and "younger sisters." These adoptions are sealed by exchange of gifts, and periodic gift exchange and visiting keeps them alive. The adoptive younger siblings are ordinarily young men and women, not children, and may be married with families of their own. They owe respect to their adoptive elder sister, or *yayan rana*. These relationships might be interpreted as an example of fictive kinship, since kinship terminology is used by the parties involved, and because their relationship is based upon the "literal" kinship relationship

---

EthnoFile
HAUSA

Region: West Africa

Nation: Nigeria

Population: 24,000,000

Environment: Savannah and Sokoto River basin

Livelihood: Principally millet farming, also commerce and government

Political organization: Emirates with powerful rulers (emirs)

Other: One of the three major groups of Nigeria, the Hausa are famous as traders as well as farmers

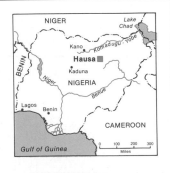

between elder sister and younger siblings. Since the parties are *not* literal brothers and sisters, however, and because the adoptive relationship is an unequal one (between elder sister and younger siblings), it might also be seen as a relationship of clientage.

When the relationship links an older woman and a younger man, it turns strangers (who theoretically might have a sexual relationship) into friends who can share secrets and discuss problems frankly, and between whom sexual relations are forbidden. In describing her relationship with her adoptive younger brother Shera, Baba said:

> I call Shera Dan-mori, the son of enjoyment, and he calls me Hanazullumi, Prevent-worry. Nothing in the world can worry him, he sees me and likes me. We enjoy things and we are satisfied, I stop him from worrying. Even now when he has a beard, if some matter needing discussion arises, he comes and we discuss it together. I go to his entrance-hut, he bows down—I am like his mother—then I sit in the entrance-hut, or we go inside the compound and we talk. If I go into the compound his wives kneel down to greet me, they call me Yayan rana or Yaya, because I am like their husband's elder sister, it is not really like a mother-in-law. (Ibid.: 195)

The relationship between an adoptive elder sister and her adopted younger sister is interesting. Although it begins with the customary gift exchange, the adoptive younger sister must adopt an attitude of ritual shyness for five months. This is explicitly likened to the behavior of a young bride: "There is shame like that between a husband and wife at a first marriage, until they become accustomed to it, then there is friendship and they share the ceremonies of life" (ibid.: 205–6). Compare the dynamics of this ritual friendship with those characterizing the relationship between a Bangwa female husband and her wife, as described by Robert Brain: "Behind the facade of etiquette imposed by their formal roles

as husband and wife, Mafwa and her spouse were great friends. The mere fact of their long intimacy and their obvious satisfaction in each other's company are evidence of a perfect alliance between two mature women who felt no need of the presence of a male husband" (Brain 1976: 58). *(See EthnoFile 11.1: Bangwa.)* Both these situations are very similar to the relationship of lesbian Swahili couples in Mombasa. *(See EthnoFile 10.10: Mombasa Swahilis.)* The only significant difference is that the Swahili women have observed the final entailment of a relationship modeled on marriage and have become lovers.

When one woman is only slightly older than her adopted sibling, their ritual friendship will be that of "elder sister" to "younger sister" or "younger brother." Old women can make themselves fictive "mothers" by taking on daughters or sons "of fortune," in addition to any children they might have adopted in the customary way. There is no shyness in this relationship. Two women who are about the same age, however, become *kawaye*, friends of equal status. Kawaye take a special interest in the firstborn children of their ritual friends who must practice avoidance. They also exchange gifts and visits with one another. Different kawaye of the same woman often quarrel with one another, just as co–wives quarrel, but this does not distress the woman who is the object of their jealousy. Baba says "Her *kawaye* are quarreling because of her, she is liked. She does not really feel cross about it. A husband, if his wives are jealous but don't fight or quarrel, is pleased because he knows he is desired" (M. F. Smith [1954] 1981: 202–3). Adopted younger brothers and sisters of the same woman are also jealous of their adoptive elder sister.

The Hausa kinship system, being bilateral, is one of the more open kinds of kinship system. Furthermore, although Hausa marry nonrelatives, they may also marry any of their cross or parallel cousins, a second index of openness. Finally, through their well-developed institutions of fictive kinship, strangers can be made friends or clients or both and linked with one another in mutually satisfying relationships for a lifetime. Similar kinds of links, in different societies, perform the same function, whether the metaphorical extension be consanguineal, or affinal, or a little of both. As we saw in Lake Wobegon, friends are customers and customers are friends. Moreover, the material link and the affective bond reinforce one another, just as gift exchanges reinforce the bond between Hausa women and their friends and fictive kin.

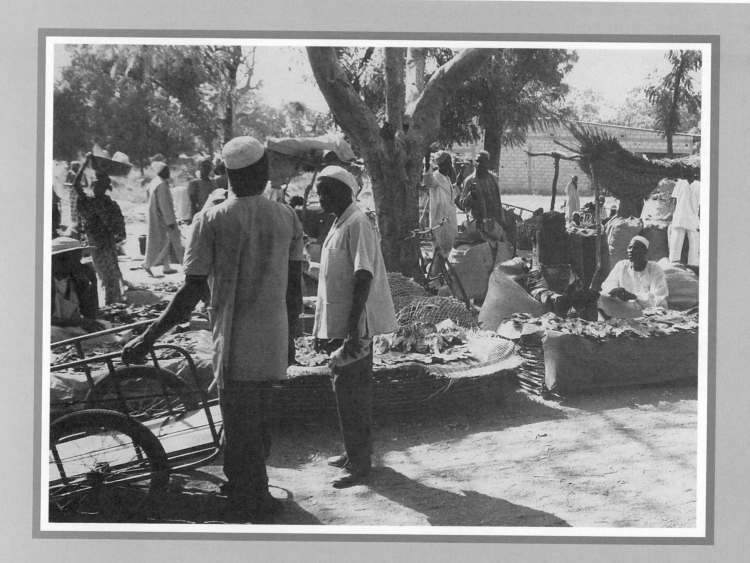

CHAPTER 12

Social Organization and Power

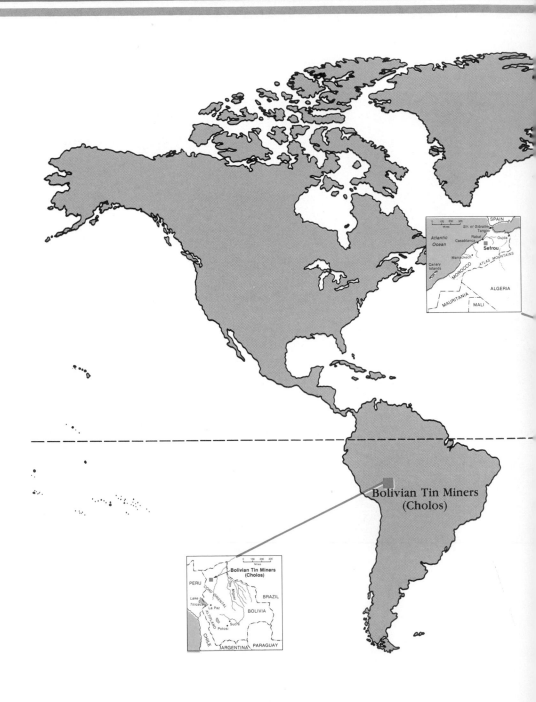

Bolivian Tin Miners
(Cholos)

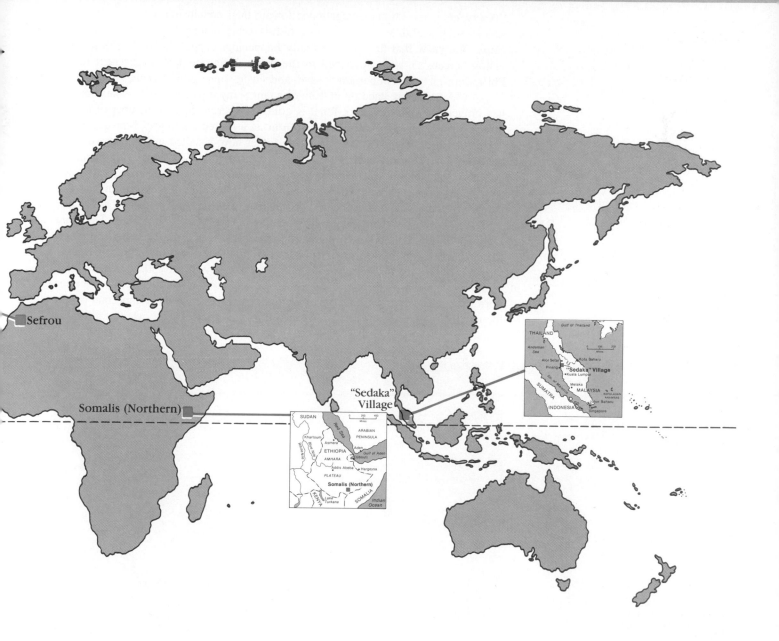

Sefrou

Somalis (Northern)

"Sedaka"
Village

361

On February 25, 1986, President Ferdinand Marcos of the Philippines went into exile, together with his family and some eighty supporters. Marcos's downfall came after a presidential election that he claimed to have won. Unfortunately for him, observers declared the election invalid because of massive and undisguised fraud and intimidation of opponents by Marcos and his supporters. The Marcos dictatorship had been backed by massive military force, much of it supplied by the United States. The American government officially viewed Marcos as a friend in the Far East and hoped, by supporting him, to protect two important U.S. military bases in the Philippines. Yet, in the end, neither American support nor repression and assassination could keep Marcos in power. The following essay appeared in The New Yorker *magazine for March 3, 1986.*

"As events in the Philippines galloped toward their conclusion, amazing scenes of successful peaceful democratic mass action—scenes that could be believed only because one knew that they were actually happening—appeared on American television screens or were described in the press. Whatever may occur next in the Philippines, it seems important to save, and savor, some of these scenes in memory:

"A woman is standing in front of a tank, praying fervently. It seems that she has prayed the tank to a stop, for it is going nowhere. She is a member of an unarmed crowd that has gone out to confront an armored column of Marines which appears to be heading toward opposition forces now installed in Defense Ministry headquarters, on the outskirts of Manila. The crowd sits in front of the armored column. As night falls, the column retreats. A young woman in the crowd says, 'We won. They went back where they came from.' But her remark seems to fall short of the full truth of what has happened. To say that 'we' have won seems to imply that 'they' have lost. But the soldiers, in deciding not to attack, 'won,' too. The front line of the battle that they won was in their minds, where common sense or humanity, or both, prevailed over their opposites. In that battle, no bullet fired from the crowd would have had any effect. But prayer may well have been the ultimate weapon. Having won their interior battle, the soldiers retreated to victory. One reporter suggested that this confrontation might prove to be the most important one in the entire struggle. If so, it was a 'battle' that was 'won' by the whole Philippine

The overthrow of the Marcos regime in the Philippines, 1986.

people, because there wasn't a battle. One man in the crowd may have expressed the deepest truth when he said, 'We are all Filipinos—there is no fight here.'

"Around the positions that have been taken over are more people, also unarmed and peaceful. The newscasters are calmly telling us that the crowd has assembled to 'protect' the soldiers, as if this were the most natural thing in the world. But, as one colonel remarks, 'this is something new,' adding, 'Soldiers are supposed to protect the civilians. In this particular case, you have civilians protecting the soldiers.' Inside, some light is shed on this surprising inversion of the usual order of things in an interview that Lieutenant General Fidel V. Ramos, a leader of the opposition forces, is giving to the NBC correspondent Marvin Kalb. Part of the interview goes as follows:

"Kalb: *Do you believe, General, that you have the tanks, the planes, to repel any kind of attack that President Marcos may feel is necessary to launch?*

"Ramos: *We do not have the military hardware to resist the attacks that we feel are forthcoming, or are being contemplated, by Mr. Marcos. However, we are utilizing people's power—*

"Kalb (*interrupting*): *What do you mean by people?*

"Ramos (*continuing*): *—that prevails over the military formations of Mr. Marcos, and so far the use of the people confronting tanks and armored columns has proved to be very successful out here.*

"Kalb (*in a 'come-off-it' tone*): *But then if the President chooses to use military force, you're a general, you know that you will have to have military force to fight back, and you're really saying you don't have it. Is that right?*

"Ramos: *We do not have as much as he has, of course. But I think that the power which is in the hands of the people to compel a decision favorable to us from Mr. Marcos is there.*

"Thus, at a key moment in the Philippine revolution, went an exchange between a reporter, who was astonished to consider the possibility that superior force might not be decisive, and a general who, after a lifetime of military service, had discovered a power greater than military force.

"The crowd has encircled an armed military unit, which sits on the grass. The scene nicely symbolizes the apparent state of the Philippine nation at that moment. An island of military force is surrounded, and, for the time being, paralyzed, by an ocean of popular resistance. Two kinds of strength confront one another: the strength of guns and the strength of the people's will—the strength of violence and the strength of peaceful action. Clearly, the guns, if they are used, can kill hundreds of the encircling civilians at any moment. And no prayers can stop the bullets once they are fired. But the bullets are not fired. Some sentiment or calculation or scruple stays the soldiers' hands, and they sit peacefully on the grass."

What motivates unarmed people to challenge the power of tanks and guns? How can such a challenge succeed? Many knowledgeable people would reject a show of "people power" as irrational. They would favor some other form of political protest that posed less of a direct risk to human life. And yet, in the Philippine case, the "irrational" won the day.

There are always choices to be made in how a society is to be organized. Who has the power to make the choices? Where does that power come from? What is power? In this chapter, we will examine how different ways of organizing society can be seen as different ways of answering these three questions.

Varieties of Social Organization

We have already described the variety of forms of human society and looked at some attempts by anthropologists to introduce order into that variety. Lewis Henry Morgan, for example, urged anthropologists to pay close attention to what he called the "arts of subsistence." He was confident that all cultural differences—in kinship patterns, marriage practices, religious beliefs, ritual—could be explained in terms of the ways different societies went about making a living. But he ran into difficulties when he observed significant differences in ways of life that were *not* connected with significant differences in ways of making a living. In Morgan's scheme, for example, both Barbarians and Civilized peoples relied on farming and herding, and in many cases their technologies were quite similar. What did separate them were differences in social organization: in who did what to produce the fruits of cultivation and animal husbandry, how it was done, and for whom. **Social organization** refers to the patterning of human interdependence in a given society through the actions and decisions of its members. This chapter focuses on social organization and the powers that human beings have to reproduce or change that organization.

social organization
the ordering of human social activity in a given society through the actions and decisions of its members

The Search for the Laws of Social Organization

Since before the birth of the social sciences, Western thinkers have sought to discover the inflexible laws of society that would allow them to explain cultural differences in a nonarbitrary way. Today, the pitfalls and excesses of certain earlier explanations are recognized. But the basic categories defined in the nineteenth century—with new labels attached—continue to be accepted as useful ways of classifying all human societies. However, differences separating societies grouped *within* any particular category are assumed to be less significant than the differences *between* such groups. This assumption is based on the idea that the differences separating categories are the result of underlying laws of social process. Disagreement exists about which social processes are involved. We discussed earlier the form these theoretical disagreements have taken. The following sections review the perspectives on the laws of social organization that anthropologists have traditionally considered.

The Historical Explanation

Morgan and other unilineal evolutionists believed that the laws of society were rooted in the dynamics of *history* and worked themselves out over time for each human group. Karl Marx was inspired by Morgan's work. He also explained variation in social organization in terms of historical laws working themselves out through the activities of human beings in the course of time. For Marx, every new form of society emerges out of its predecessor. But every form of society contains internal contradictions. As the society develops, these contradictions will become increasingly acute, finally leading to the overthrow of the social order. Modern evolutionary thinkers, whether marxian or not, continue to seek evolutionary laws whose operation would explain the appearance of similar forms of social organization in different parts of the world.

The Environmental Explanation

Other thinkers do not look to world history for the origins of lawful social process. They explain similarities and differences in social organization with reference to the *local environment* in which a particular society finds itself. These scholars view social organization as the result of *adaptation* to material, ecological conditions present in the here and now. For example, a particular environment may be seen as "requiring" only small flexible groups to exploit its meager resources. A different environment, however, might "require" large numbers of people and a complex division of labor for successful human adaptation to be possible. Here, the environment determines culture.

The Biological Explanation

The historical and environmental approaches explain similarities and differences in social organization by reference to forces outside individual human beings—either in the laws of history or in the limitations of the environment. Other approaches see the lawful processes operating deeply *within human beings*, forcing people to act in some ways, forbidding them to act in other ways. In such a view, which we call *biological determinism*, human choice is restricted, and not even the material environment can have much effect on human behavior. In the words of sociobiologist E. O. Wilson, human genetic programming has culture "on a short leash." That is, we are altruistic, aggressive, and sexual because our genes make us so, and our social organizations must adjust to the iron requirements of genetics.

The Arbitrariness of Social Organization

All these positions are the result of a positivist commitment to the basic assumption that certain objective, material similarities and differences in human societies are obviously more important than other kinds of similarities and differences. Thus, perhaps the most important and controversial contribution of anthropology to the debate about laws of social organization is the argument that social relations in any society are ultimately arbitrary. This does not mean that societies are free to do or be whatever they like. Rather, it means that there is no way to reduce the complexities of human societies to a single underlying cause.

For example, the demonstrated adaptive flexibility of human brains and bodies would be impossible if our behavior were rigidly controlled by instinct. We must invent ways of survival. But the social arrangements we come up with are bound to be arbitrary, for we could always have chosen to do otherwise. Environmental determinism is implausible because, historically speaking, no society has ever been left on its own long enough for so-called environmental pressures to exert

EthnoFile 12.1
SOMALIS
(Northern)

Region: East Africa

Nation: Somalia, Djibuti, Ethiopia, Kenya

Population: 600,000 (3,250,000 total; 2,250,000 in Somalia)

Environment: Harsh, semidesert

Livelihood: Herding of camels, sheep, goats, cattle, horses

Political organization: Lineage-based, ad hoc egalitarian councils

Other: The Somalis have no hierarchical system of political offices

their forces without outside human interference. European colonial conquest is an eloquent case in point. It demonstrates how the most delicately balanced societal adaptation to a given environment can be totally disrupted, if not destroyed, when outsiders arrive with plans of their own and the power to enforce them. Yet even if societies could be isolated from one another and left to work out their own destinies in their own environments, it is unlikely that identical societies would develop in "identical" environments. I. M. Lewis (1976:166ff.) points out, for example, that the northern Somalis and the Boran Galla live next to each other in semiarid scrubland and even herd the same animals (goats, sheep, cattle, camels). *(See EthnoFile 12.1: Somalis.)* Despite these similarities, the Somali and the Boran are quite different in social structure: the Boran engage in much less fighting and feuding than the Somali; Boran families split up to take care of the animals, the Somali do not; and lineage organization is less significant among the Boran.

The Power To Choose

So human beings do not endure environmental pressures passively, but actively work to reshape the environment to suit themselves. However, when human beings reshape the material world, they do so selectively. We choose which aspects of the material world we will depend on for our livelihood, and there is always more than one choice in any environment. Human choice is equally important in the domain of social organization. It is sometimes argued, for example, that population growth is a constant aspect of the human condition that determines forms of organization. Yet population pressure determines nothing more than the number of people that can be supported when the environment is used in a particular way. Marshall Sahlins (1976a:13) reminds us that the *response* of a particular society to this kind of pressure can be varied. People can try to get along on less, they can intensify food production by inventing new technology, they can reduce their numbers by inventing new social practices (infanticide or other forms of birth control), they can transform previously ignored elements of the environment into new resources, or part of their group can migrate elsewhere. All these choices are open to them, and none is specified by the pressure of population.

Indeed, the *manner* in which a group might choose to implement any of these options is equally undetermined by population pressure. Which members of the group will have to do with less—everyone? men? women? certain lineages? commoners? Which members will be responsible for technological innovations, or will control them once they are made? Will all women in society be required to limit the number of their offspring, or only the women of certain societal subgroups? Who will be expected to take advantage of new resources—everyone, or only some members of society? If the latter, which ones? If migration of part of the group to a new environment is the solution, who will migrate? Answers to all these questions are open. Population pressure alone cannot determine which, or how many, solutions a given society might choose.

Discussions of human choice raise the question of human responsibility. A society may be described as having collectively made a decision about how to cope, for example, with population pressure. But the potential solutions to this problem are many. How *was* the final choice made? Is compromise, as opposed to consensus, more likely in one society than in another, and if so, why? Who decides? According to what principles?

The ability to choose implies the ability to transform the situation in which one finds oneself. Thus, the ability to choose implies **power**, which may be understood broadly as "transformative capacity" (Giddens 1979:88). The prototype of power for most Americans is naked physical force, and this can be an important form of power for other peoples as well. In most societies at most times, however, power cannot be reduced to naked physical force. Power operates, and people allow it to operate, according to certain principles. Those principles are cultural creations; they are therefore arbitrary and may differ from one society to another. "It may be in the nature of agricultural production that father and son *cooperate*, but it is not in the nature of agricultural production that *father* and *son* cooperate—as opposed to mother and daughter, mother's brother and sister's son, or Don Quixote and Sancho Panza" (Sahlins 1976a: 9). Which of these ways of organizing agricultural production a society actually observes is a cultural construction. Its appropriateness is recognized for cultural reasons. It will ordinarily be enforced, or renegotiated, by the culturally appropriate deployment of social power.

power
transformative capacity

The Concept Of Social Power

The study of social power in human society is the domain of **political anthropology**. Over time, political anthropologists have investigated a broad series of different problems having to do with power and social control. Lewellen lists the following: "1) the classification of political systems, 2) the evolution of political systems, 3) the structure and functions of political systems in preindustrial societies, 4) the processes of politics in preindustrial or developing societies, 5) action, an outgrowth of the process approach with an emphasis on the manipulative strategies of individuals, 6) the modernization of formerly tribal societies and modern political institutions in industrial states" (Lewellen 1983:ix–x).

political anthropology
the study of social power in human society

The Role of the State in Western Thought

Generations of Western thinkers have been interested in the topics studied by political anthropologists. As we noted in our discussion of kinship, these thinkers began with the assumption that the state was the prototype of "civilized" social power. The absence of a state therefore had to represent anarchy and disorder—what the

English philosopher Thomas Hobbes called the "war of all against all." What prompted these thinkers to believe that disorder must reign in the absence of the state? Many Western political philosophers lived during times of social stress and social change. Old institutions were losing the loyalty of citizens but had not yet been replaced by new institutions capable of regaining that loyalty. Men like Hobbes viewed the confusion around them with alarm and were eager to find an explanation for it, as well as a solution. For many, the answer was that human beings were by nature selfish. They would war with one another to the death, destroying society in the process, unless they were forcibly prevented from doing so.

This was why the state was necessary. Its most significant role was to monopolize the use of force in order to protect the naturally weak from the naturally strong. The prototype of power—naked physical force—is the same in all cases. The assumption is that human beings will not cooperate unless they are coerced. If physical power ultimately decides all conflicts, it is better that the state control the use of such power. This is because the state presumably has the interests of everyone in mind. Thus, the state should be able to punish those who would use their own physical power to serve selfish individual interests. Most thinkers recognized that the state often perpetrated injustice or exploitation as a side effect of its monopoly of force. This was often viewed, however, as a necessary price to pay for social order.

Social Power in Societies without States

These basic Western assumptions about human nature and the role of the state have often gone unquestioned by Western observers investigating social organization and power in the non-Western world. Early anthropologists like Morgan, however, showed that kinship institutions organized social life in societies without states. A later generation of political anthropologists supplied a wealth of data on how this happened. They showed how different kinship institutions distribute power among their members. They also learned about nonkin institutions like secret societies, which, while less encompassing than the state, sometimes carried out important political roles. They were able to show again and again that societies without states were able to reach and carry out decisions affecting the entire social group, by means of orderly traditional processes.

In the absence of a state that monopolizes physical force and can punish the disobedient, why do people cooperate? Attempts to answer this question have led to a reconsideration of many traditional Western assumptions about human nature and social power. One important result has been an increasing awareness of the ambiguity of power both as a concept and as a phenomenon in everyday life.

Power as Coercion

The Role of Physical Force

The traditional Western prototype of power in human social relations is based on physical coercion. A fistfight might be seen as the typical "natural" manifestation of this prototype, perhaps as presented in the biblical story of Cain and Abel. This prototype is based on an exceedingly pessimistic, even cynical, view of human nature. It argues that, left to their own devices, all human individuals would challenge any other human beings they might encounter in order to establish power over them. In this view, human evolution took a giant leap forward when our ancestors first

An American prototype of power: "the Duke," John Wayne.

realized that sticks and stones could be used as *weapons*, not only against non-human predators, but especially against human enemies. Human history has thus been a history of the production of better and better weapons. The civilization we are so proud of has been born and sustained in violence.

Coercion in Societies without States

Some political anthropologists would subscribe, more or less, to this set of propositions about the human condition. As a result, they approach non-Western political organization in a characteristic way. They recognize that many stateless societies do not have the ability to punish those who deviate. Nevertheless, they argue that *other* institutions have a similar function. One fears not the king or the police, but the ancestors, witchcraft, or the lineage elders. Power is still viewed as physical coercion, cooperation being largely the result of fear of punishment.

This is not a persuasive portrait of life in nonstate societies, however. Evans-Pritchard argued that the Azande were not in a constant state of fear even though they lived in a stateless society and held a complex set of beliefs about witchcraft, oracles, and magic. *(See EthnoFile 7.3: Azande.)* Azande people discussed witchcraft openly. If they believed they were bewitched, they were likely to be angry rather than afraid, and so did not feel helpless. This kind of attitude was not irrational, because the threatening forces were seen as part of the fabric of the universe. Most people believed that witchcraft would not be directed against them, and in any case they had access to remedies to fight their own victimization. In such a context, the belief system and the institutionalization of power it implies seem natural and rational. For that reason, ordinary, rational people support it.

Coercion and Legitimacy

Here we encounter an ambiguity about power in human affairs. People may submit to institutionalized power because they fear punishment. But they may also submit to it because they believe that submitting is the right—perhaps the only—thing to

coercion
power based on physical force

legitimacy
power based on group consensus

do. Recognition of this problem has led political anthropologists to distinguish between power based on force, which we will call **coercion**, and power based on group consensus, which we will call **legitimacy**. The tricky thing for the analyst is deciding which motivation is operating at any one time.

After all, people can consent to submit to a system in which naked force may be used against them, if they accept the cultural principles that justify such a use of coercion. Many citizens of modern nation-states support the right of the state to monopolize deadly force, even in the nuclear age. In some cases, it is probably futile to try to separate fear of punishment from consensus in determining why most people accept the principles upon which their society depends. People may fear the loss of personal physical integrity less than they fear the collapse of a meaningful, orderly understanding of the world if principles are abandoned. They may even be willing to sacrifice themselves physically—as soldiers do in battle—if they are convinced that doing so will preserve "the world as we know it," "keep the world safe for democracy," or the like. The Hobbesian position has always had a difficult time dealing with martyrs.

The Ambiguity of Power

Violence has been part of human experience for as long as we can tell, but we cannot assume that its role is the same in all human societies. The occasional violent outburst of one member of a foraging society against another is not the same thing as the organized violence of one army against another in a conflict between modern nation-states. No one can deny that human beings can be violent with one another. But is this the whole story?

Anthropologist Richard Newbold Adams has said: "It is useful to accept the proposition that, while men have in some sense always been equal (i.e. in that each always has some independent power), they have in another sense never been equal (in that some always have more power than others)" (Adams 1979:409). Political anthropologists who think of power as coercion have traditionally emphasized the universality of human inequality. Others have taken another route, concentrating on the first part of Adams's observation. While aware of the role of the state in monopolizing physical force, they have been concerned with two additional matters. First, they have reexamined the role of power in societies without states. Second, they have reconsidered the nature of independent power available to individuals living in societies with states. The first focus involves looking at power as an independent entity. The second looks at the power of the human imagination to define the nature of social interactions and to persuade other actors to accept these definitions of the situation.

Power as an Independent Entity

Self-Interest versus Collective Obligation

exchange theory
a position that defines power as a negotiated relationship between people with different resources (land, money, strategic position in a community network, access to the supernatural)

Discussions of power as coercion tend to see political activity as a form of bargaining. Using a metaphor drawn from the marketplace, they describe political engagements as another form of haggling—not over material goods but over control. In anthropology, this approach to the study of social interaction is known as exchange theory. In **exchange theory**, political anthropologists define power as a negotiated relationship between people with different resources (land, money, strategic position in a community network, access to the supernatural).

This description of political horse-trading sounds plausible to people familiar with Western political institutions. The basic assumption is that the parties to political negotiation are *free agents*. This means that in making decisions, they are not and *should not* be duty-bound to consider the effect of their actions on anyone but themselves. No larger groups, no historical obligations, no collective beliefs can or ought to deter them from following what they perceive to be in their individual self-interest.

Social scientists have long questioned whether even members of Western societies are as "free" as they claim to be, or are urged to be, in shaping their interactions with others. But Western capitalist society has progressively broken many of the links that used to bind people to one another. In many respects, individuals in the West are freer from social obligations of all kinds than are members of most non-Western societies. Many observers see this as a sign of progress. People in America are free, so we believe, to become whatever they want to be, free of the shackles of ascribed status.

The "shackles" of kinship and community relationships, however, can be approached from a different point of view. These ascribed social ties may be seen as barriers to individual achievement. But they can also be understood as necessary protection for society's weaker members, which the stronger members are obligated for humanitarian reasons to provide. Members of societies without states often have a strong sense of collective obligation for each other's welfare. Western observers have noted that members of such societies are not free agents. For example, individuals often must consult elders or community leaders or kin before entering into contracts with outsiders. Such collective obligations are often regarded by Westerners as backward. Anthropologists would argue that they represent an alternative understanding of the human condition and of the nature of social power.

Independent Power in Stateless Societies

In the stateless societies of native North and South America, power is understood to be an entity existing in the universe independent of human beings. As such, it cannot be produced and accumulated through the interactions of human beings with one another. Strictly speaking, power does not belong to human beings at all. At most, people can hope to *gain access* to power, usually through ritual means. From this point of view, "control over resources is evidence of power, rather than the source of power" (Colson 1977:382).

If one assumes that power is part of the natural order of things yet is independent of direct human control, certain consequences seem to follow. First, it may be possible to tap some of that power if one can discover how. Societies that see power as an independent entity usually know, through tradition, of ways to tap it.

Second, societies that see power as an independent force usually embed this understanding within a larger world view in which the universe is believed to consist of a balance of different forces. Individuals may seek to manipulate those natural forces to their own ends, but they are enjoined not to tamper with the balance in doing so. The trick thus becomes tapping the power in the universe without upsetting the universal balance.

For this reason, as a third consequence, coercive means of tapping sources of power are ruled out in such societies. Violence threatens to undo the universal balance. Thus, in many native North and South American societies, gentler measures were required. One approached power through prayer and supplication. The native American vision quest (as among the Sioux) is a good example of such an approach. Through fasting and self-induced suffering, individuals engaging in that quest hoped to move the source of power to pity. The power source might then *freely bestow* on them the power they sought, in the form of a vision or a song or a set of ritual formulas. Power thus bestowed would not disrupt the balance of the universe. Attempts to intimidate the sources of power into yielding some of it up were viewed as wrong. Not only did they threaten the universal balance, but they were bound to be ineffective for that very reason.

This leads to a fourth consequence: In such a world view, violence and access to power are mutually contradictory. Physical coercion can only upset the natural balance of forces in the universe. This understanding of the role of violence has implications for its role in human affairs. If power is an independent entity that cannot be coerced, it must be approached gently, it must be supplicated. Cultures that conceive of power in this way also tend to view individual human beings as independent entities who cannot be coerced but must be supplicated. Although it may seem paradoxical from a Western point of view, individuals in such societies are viewed as independent agents, despite their manifold obligations to one another. They are not "free" in the Western sense of freedom from social ties and responsibilities. But they are free in the sense of possessing **autonomy**, that is, the right not to be forced against their will to conform to someone else's wishes.

Recognizing the autonomy of individuals affects the way members of stateless societies arrive at decisions. That is, a fifth consequence of viewing power as an independent entity is an emphasis on consensus as the appropriate means to decide issues affecting the wider group. In seeking consensus, proponents of a particular course of action must use **persuasion**, rather than coercion, to get other members of the group to support their cause. To make their case they must resort to verbal argument, not physical intimidation. As a result, the most respected members of stateless societies, those sometimes given the title "chief" by outsiders, are persuasive speakers. Indeed, as Pierre Clastres (1977) points out, such respected individuals are often referred to by other members of their society as "those who speak for us." The shamans (or *mara'akate*) of the Huichol Indians of northern Mexico serve this function. **(See EthnoFile 7.4: Huichol.)** By virtue of their ability with words, they see themselves (and are seen by their fellows) as especially well suited to negotiate for all the Huichol with outsiders, especially with representatives of the Mexican state.

The two different understandings of power reviewed here are embedded in cultural practices that presuppose different ideas of human nature and human freedom. When power is viewed exclusively as coercion, powerful individuals are those who are able to use the threat of violence to make others obey them. Such individuals are free agents because they are theoretically able to do anything their power makes possible. They are responsible only to their own desires, and this leads many of those without power to admire them. Nothing need restrain them from acting in any way at all, except the limits of their personal ability to bend others to their will.

People who see power as an entity external to themselves have a different understanding of human nature. The only power individuals possess is the power accorded to all entities in the universe. This is the power of autonomy, the right not to be forced by violence or threat of violence to do the will of others. This does not mean that people in such societies always refrain from violence in their dealings with others. It does mean that attempts to coerce are likely to be interpreted as the opposite of political wisdom. Harmony is the desired goal, in the universe as in

autonomy
the right not be forced against one's will to conform to someone else's wishes

persuasion
causing a person to do something by means of verbal arguments, not physical intimidation

For a Samoan "talking chief" from the island of Tutuila, verbal argument is the means to leadership.

social relations. It can be attained only by respecting the autonomy of others, by respecting the cosmic balance, which is threatened whenever that autonomy is infringed.

Given this world view, human beings must act in ways that preserve or restore harmony, among people and within the universe. It is assumed that human beings are all free to choose how they act. They can choose responsibly, basing their actions on traditional wisdom and experience concerning what is and is not calculated to achieve harmony. Or they can choose irresponsibly, selfishly, attempting to bend the universe and other people to their will through violence. The choice is theirs, and therefore their lives entail a clear element of risk. There is no way to prevent irresponsible choices and their destructive consequences. The best one can do is remind people, as the chief does, of their personal power to choose and their personal responsibility to choose wisely.

A classic example of this attitude toward power and leadership comes from the Pacific: the Big Man. Roger Keesing describes his Kwaio friend 'Elota as a man with influence: "When he spoke, in his hoarse voice, it was never loudly; he never shouted, never spoke in anger, never dominated conversation. Yet when he spoke people paid attention, deferred to his wisdom or laughed at his wit" (Keesing 1983:3). *(See EthnoFile 7.5: Kwaio.)* He owed part of his influence to an extraordinary memory. Keesing thinks 'Elota could recall genealogical information about some three thousand to four thousand people, as well as the details of fifty years' worth of the financial transactions that are at the heart of Kwaio feasts and marriages. In addition, "his wit and wisdom were a continuing guide towards the virtues of the past, towards thinking before rushing into action." Keesing tells us that 'Elota was "a master gamesman, in a system where prestige derives from manipulating investments and publicly giving away valuables." Finally, 'Elota also realized that the road to prominence lay in hard work devoted to producing goods that other Kwaio wanted. Those goods included taro for feasts, pigs, cane bracelets and anklets, and bark-cloth wrapping for valuables. For 'Elota, and for the Kwaio, prestige and influence come from giving away valued things. A Big Man is a master of this, especially in financing marriages and giving feasts.

Pierre Clastres (1977:35) suggests that stateless forms of social organization are strongly resistant to the emergence of hierarchy. Indeed, he argues that members of stateless societies struggle to prevent such authority from emerging. They sense that the rise of what we call state power spells the end of individual autonomy and disrupts beyond repair the harmonious balance between human beings and the forces of the wider world. Having witnessed the losses of life and liberty that accompany the rise of the state, not to mention the ecological disruption and pollution that have been a major legacy of industrial nation-states, we would find it difficult to argue that such fears are wholly unfounded.

Leaders with coercive powers: Muslim emirs from northern Cameroon.

The Power of the Imagination

We have been looking at two ways of understanding power. The first view of power is typical in societies with states. In this view, power is something that individuals, as free agents, can accumulate as a result of their attempts to coerce other people to yield to their will. From this perspective, violence is a common and effective means to increase the power of individuals and groups. The second view of power is typical in societies without states. In this view, individuals are not free agents who can accumulate power by coercive means. Power cannot be accumulated by coercive means without endangering the cosmic balance of forces. This means that power and coercion are antithetical. Nonviolent means of persuasion are the appropriate means that individuals should employ to tap independent power, both from cosmic sources and from other people. Individual human beings, while not free agents, are nevertheless autonomous beings with the right to resist having another's will imposed upon them by force.

There is yet a third way of understanding power, applicable to state societies and stateless societies alike. This approach suggests that power is defined too narrowly when it focuses on issues of physical coercion alone. To be sure, one cannot neglect the effects of physical force (or its absence) in determining the actions we may or may not undertake. But a more holistic view of power recognizes that behavior alone does not tell the whole story. We must also take into account how people *make sense of* the constraints and opportunities for action that are open to them. That is, an essential power of all human beings is the power of the human imagination to invest the world with meaning.

All people everywhere have the power to interpret their experiences, to invest their world with meanings that "objective" material and social conditions cannot dictate. This holds true regardless of the complexity of a social system, and whether or not the power of coercion has been monopolized by a central authority. This kind of power is a form of individual autonomy that may be preserved even under totalitarian dictatorship. It is notoriously difficult to erase from human consciousness, often to the frustration of political leaders, be they radical or reactionary. Hoyt Alverson argues that "a belief in one's power to invest the world with meaning (the 'will to believe') and a belief in the adequacy of one's knowledge for understanding and acting on personal experience are essential features of all human self-identity" (Alverson 1978:7). Only when human self-identity is irrevocably crushed, through extreme deprivation, is this essential human power extinguished. That may be one reason why so many contemporary political regimes have resorted to torture as a final means of violent coercion. Such regimes have a hard time persuading citizens with intact self-identities to follow them without question. They therefore try to coerce obedience by efforts that destroy human identity, when they do not destroy human life itself.

The power of the human imagination to invest the world with meaning is also the power to resist outside influences, be they material or rhetorical. This ability—not only to choose but also to reject alternative choices that others want to impose—forms the core of human self-identity. Indeed, Alverson defines self-identity as "those authentic beliefs a person holds about the *who-and-what-he-is* which resist variations in the outside forces that impel his various social actions" (ibid.: 3). This does not mean that individuals work out the meanings of their experiences in isolation. All human activities, including the growth and development of self-identity, take place in a social, cultural, and historical context. Nevertheless, each individual retains the power to interpret that context from his or her unique vantage point, in terms of his or her unique experiences.

The Power of the Weak

Cynics might argue that the power of the imagination must in the real world be restricted at most to private opinions; the mind can resist, but the body must conform. From this perspective, for example, the actions of a miner who labors underground daily for a meager wage are clear-cut and unmistakable: he works for money to buy food for his family. Yet ethnographic data suggest that this may not be the whole story. To understand why, we need to explore more fully what is involved in political domination.

In the contemporary world, the prototype of the downtrodden and exploited human being is the industrial laborer. Workers in Western countries have managed to better their lot during the twentieth century. However, their achievements have been won with considerable struggle and sacrifice, and their situation is far from secure even today. It would seem that industrial workers in the non-Western world must be far worse off. After all, their inclusion in the industrial labor force is much more recent, and most of them have not benefited from the same gains as Western workers.

Anthropologists have studied patterns of industrial employment in non-Western societies. A number of them interpret Third World industrialization as a recent consequence of Western colonial domination and exploitation. These scholars have focused on the effects industrial employment might have on preindustrial social relationships. They have wondered whether non-Western peoples respond to industrialization today the way Western people responded to industrialization in the past.

In western Europe and the United States, the Industrial Revolution of the eighteenth and nineteenth centuries brought profound social and cultural dislocation. Social scientists at that time observed those changes and tried to describe them. Emile Durkheim used the term **anomie** to refer to the pervasive sense of rootlessness and normlessness that people appeared to be experiencing. Karl Marx used the term **alienation** to describe the deep separation workers seemed to experience between their innermost sense of identity and the labor they were forced to do in order to earn enough money to live.

Were industrial workers in the Third World similarly suffering from anomie and alienation? Some argued that their condition should be far worse than that of Western workers, since the context of Third World industrialization was so much more backward. This has been called the "scars of bondage" thesis. This thesis predicts that the more complete the political domination and exploitation of a people, the more deeply they will be scarred by the experience, brutalized, dehumanized. For people suffering the twin exploitations of colonialism and industrialism, the outcome could only be the most bitter, unrelieved tragedy.

Hoyt Alverson (1978) set out to test the "scars of bondage" thesis in the field. He chose southern Africa for his research and focused on migrant workers and their experiences in the gold mines of the Republic of South Africa. His informants were Tswana living in the independent nation of Botswana, which forms part of South Africa's northern border. *(See EthnoFile 2.1: Tswana.)* Botswana is a poor country, and most of its families are supported only by the wages men receive for working in South African mines. Here was a colonized population, forced into industrial exploitation in order to survive. If the "scars of bondage" thesis were correct, the Tswana ought to be an alienated, brutalized, dehumanized lot.

Without question, the material standard of living of most of Alverson's Tswana informants was low. Without question, life in the South African mines was brutal. Without question, the difficulties families had to face when one or more of their male members was absent for months on a mining contract were considerable. And yet, for most of his informants, there was little evidence of the alienation, brutalization, and dehumanization Alverson had been expecting to find. On the contrary, his informants led lives that had coherence and meaning for them. Their experience of the mines had been integrated into their lives. Despite their "objective"

anomie
a pervasive sense of rootlessness and normlessness in a society

alienation
a term used by Marx to describe the deep separation workers seemed to experience between their innermost sense of identity and the labor they were forced to perform in order to earn enough money to live

bondage to an exploitative system, "subjectively" they remained relatively unscarred. How could this be?

Were the Tswana merely happy savages, primitives without enough intelligence to understand what had been happening to them? Were they happy because they were ignorant? Such racist explanations were not persuasive to Alverson. On the contrary, the Tswana he knew struck him as particularly thoughtful people. How, then, could they have survived their experiences so well? As it turned out, the mine experience simply did not mean to the Tswana what outside observers assumed it meant: "All phenomena, including towns and gold mines, are ambiguous and can therefore be invested with manifold meanings" (Alverson 1978:215).

In most cases, Alverson's informants suffered neither from anomie nor from alienation. Most had managed to come to terms with their experiences in a way that was meaningful for them. This was true both for those who were grateful to the mines and for those who hated the mines. Coming to terms with one's experiences involves cognitive labor. It is largely a question of finding an apt metaphor that links a person's traditional understandings with his new experiences in the mine. Different people may choose different metaphors. "One Tswana may equate the relations of bosses and workers in the mine to the relationship of parent and child. If he authentically believes this analogy, then the meaning he invests in this 'inequality' will be different from that invested in it by a Tswana who defines the relationship in terms of a set of contractual exchanges made among people bound by the same set of general rights and duties" (ibid.: 258).

The Tswana encountered brutal inequality and discrimination outside the mines as well. Here again, however, many were able successfully to draw on resources from their traditional culture in order to make sense of, and thereby transform, these experiences. For the migrant workers Alverson knew, the figure of the **Trickster** provided them with a prototype of the kind of person one had to be to survive in South Africa. The Trickster is a stock character in Tswana folklore. As his name implies, he lives by his wits, is basically amoral, and is happy to hoodwink anyone who tries to take advantage of him.

Older informants, recounting their life histories, saw themselves as Tricksters. Their greatest pride lay in the way they had managed to *get by*, despite the traps and snares all around them. According to Alverson, the strength and genius of Tswana culture is highlighted by his informants' ability to make sense of their experiences in terms of traditional Tswana narratives.

Similar observations about the power of human imagination to transform experiences by investing them with meaning have been made by June Nash (1979), who worked among tin miners in Bolivia. *(See EthnoFile 12.2: Bolivian Tin Miners.)* If anything, the "objective" conditions under which these miners labor is worse than those encountered by Tswana migrants. The labor force in Bolivian mines has been drawn from local Indian populations who, unlike the Tswana, have been effectively separated from their involvement in traditional Indian communities; they are known as Cholos. But like the Tswana of Botswana, the Cholos of Bolivia have been able creatively to combine elements of the dominant industrial culture with elements drawn from Indian traditions. This syncretistic culture creates new patterns in which elements that outsiders consider unrelated are seen by insiders as belonging together. Far from being dissonant and alienating, Cholo culture provides an intact sense of self, a lack of alienation, an ability to celebrate life because it is viewed as meaningful.

How can we explain, in the lives of Cholos or Tswana migrants, this combination of what appears to be both genuine suffering and genuine celebration? Ex-

Trickster
a traditional folktale character in many societies who lives by his wits, is basically amoral, and is happy to hoodwink anyone who tries to take advantage of him

A woman shoveling ore at the tin mines in Bolivia.

ploitation certainly leaves its mark on its victims: poor health, high infant mortality, intrafamilial abuse, shattered hopes. Yet neither Cholos nor Tswana migrants have been irrevocably brutalized by these experiences. Their powers to invest their experiences with meanings of their own devising remain intact, virtually inextinguishable despite crushing conditions of exploitation.

This is the point: "The power the Tswana will think he has will not be defined in terms of what he can get the boss to do and vice versa, but rather in terms of how freely and effectively he invests his experience with the meaning *he chooses*" (Alverson 1978:258). This power was noted by Nash for the Bolivian miners as well: "My experience living in mining communities taught me more than anything else, how a people totally involved in the most exploitative, dehumanizing form of industrialization managed to resist alienation" (Nash 1979:319–20). Like Alverson, Nash argues that the events people experience are less important than the way people *interpret* those events. Nash concludes that the ethnocentrism of Western observers has kept them from recognizing the creative, revolutionary potential embodied in syncretistic cultures like that of the Cholos.

Human beings everywhere are active creatures who *engage* the wider world as well as respond to it. A Tswana mine-labor migrant is not helpless and passive in the face of hardship and suffering: "Almost immediately he begins to cope in consciousness. . . . What began as a collision can achieve a state of coherent integration" (Alverson 1978:279). This power to cope in consciousness, to invest experience with one's own meanings, is a very real power, available to all even under the most repressive conditions of political domination.

And so we return to our original question: What does it mean to labor in the mines for a pittance? Western critics may continue to see it as dehumanizing drudgery imposed on the politically weak in a stratified society. The Tswana migrant would not necessarily deny this observation. He does not glorify the conditions in the mines, even though he knows that he needs his mine wages to buy necessities for his family. And yet he would compartmentalize his involvement in mine labor, seeing it as only one temporary aspect of his life and not a particularly meaningful one at that. As a result, the impact of the mine experience on his sense of self would be minimized, and perhaps eventually transformed into material for a personalized Trickster tale. Mine labor itself does not define the whole of the miner's existence. It is only one element in a larger picture, the Tswana world view, that migrants draw upon successfully to infuse their experiences with meaning.

The Power of Persuasion

The ability of human beings to imagine alternatives, to view experiences from more than one perspective, appears to be virtually indestructible. Perhaps for this reason, many political and social leaders seek obedient action from their followers, regardless of what those followers think about the rules they are being ordered to obey.

The power that subjects have to invest their experiences with whatever meanings they choose suggests that a ruler's power of coercion is limited. People may be unable to alter the material circumstances of coercion by thought alone. But the meaning of those material circumstances can be transformed by thoughts.

The political establishment always runs the risk that those who are dominated may create new, plausible accounts of their experiences of domination. In addition, they may be able to organize themselves socially in order to defend their accounts against attacks from the political establishment. Under such conditions, those who are dominated may become considerably more than armchair revolutionaries. They may develop the ability to go beyond their account to "make their account count" in the society at large (see Giddens 1979:83). That is, they may be able to persuade some or all of those around them that their account of social experience is better or truer than that of the current rulers. Their account "counts" if current rulers can no longer ignore it when making political choices. In some cases, making an alternative account count may even be the prelude to replacing the current rulers, as Marcos's opponents replaced him.

And so we find a fourth way of understanding power: as the ability to make certain accounts count. This view of power combines elements of the three approaches already explored. In the absence of coercive political institutions, individuals retain a significant degree of autonomous power—the power to choose their own actions and to resist imposition of choices of others. Attempts to increase this individual power are dangerous unless gentle means of persuasion are used, either on fellow group members or on independent transcendent forces.

When coercive power is monopolized by the state, the individual's power to choose and to resist the choices of others is curtailed, sometimes severely. But it is not wholly destroyed. What remains may be no more than the power of a martyr who views the sacrifice of his life as serving a higher moral purpose even though his executioners insist that his death is a just punishment for crimes he has committed. Yet a person's power may be considerably stronger than this. Individuals and groups of individuals can develop alternative accounts of their situations and mount direct or indirect challenges to the official account. Such challenges to incumbent political power are frequently too strong to ignore and too widespread to be simply obliterated by force.

When coercion no longer works, what remains is a confrontation between alternative accounts of experience. Which account eventually comes to influence major decisions and shape people's lives on a grand scale will be determined by the power of persuasion. Physical force may be one element that influences how persuasive a particular account is. This is true not just in the cynical sense that "might makes right," but also in the sense that possession of physical power may be seen as a demonstration of the ability to tap the primal forces of the universe. This is the essential political dynamic noted by Pierre Clastres (1977) for stateless societies, but this time the action may be organized within or between states. When application of physical force is recognized as a cure worse than the political ills it seeks to remove, there is no alternative but negotiation.

Negotiation ▰▰▰▰

Political activity in human society involves not just coercion by physical force or threat of force, but also **negotiation** about when such coercion may or may not be legitimate. In other words, what is considered a legitimate exercise of power must be seen to conform to political principles that are consistent with the culture's world view.

However, "political principles consistent with a culture's world view" is a highly ambiguous category. Some principles may seem to be consistent with the world view when taken individually, but when considered together contradict one another. For example, citizens of the United States would probably agree that liberty and equality are key principles defining political legitimacy in our society. However, unrestricted liberty (as exemplified by laissez-faire capitalism) can lead to the domination of the weak by the strong, which seriously undermines the principle of equality. Yet enforcing equality (as in Affirmative Action programs) is seen by some as restricting important liberties by undermining incentives for individual self-betterment. It is also possible to agree on a principle and disagree on how to put the principle in practice. Does American "equality" properly refer to equality of opportunity or to equality of outcome? Does American "liberty" protect pornographers as well as Presbyterians?

Within American society, there is a tension between the principles of liberty and equality that many would see as healthy and creative. Nevertheless, the existence of this tension reflects the difficulty we have in deciding once and for all what liberty or equality "really" means. This reflects an ongoing struggle in American society to define and redefine acceptable accounts of our shared situation in the world. Such accounts must not only be faithful to cultural principles but must also meet the practical needs of our social existence. Because different groups within a society (or different societies) may disagree about which account should prevail, negotiation among these groups is an inevitable part of ongoing social life.

Anthropologist F. G. Bailey paid close attention to the everyday workings of a non-Western political system. His research in a village in India suggested that physical coercion is normally not at issue in day-to-day politics. Rather, he saw politics as a kind of game. Like games, political systems have rules, and those rules tell who can play, which moves are legitimate and which are not, and what the reward is if one wins the game. This orientation is reflected in the title of a book Bailey wrote, *Stratagems and Spoils: A Social Anthropology of Politics* (1969). Bailey argued that much everyday political activity involved manipulating the rules of a given system in order to obtain the reward—or spoils—that success could bring.

Bailey chose what he considered an apt metaphor for interpreting the moves of political actors for whom might alone does not make right. But even people who share the most basic principles can disagree over the proper application of those principles in any particular case. In addition, people often have to interact even if they do not have the same set of rules. How can such parties engage one another in political activity? Physical coercion, from fisticuffs to armed insurrection, is one way. But violence on an everyday basis is expensive, and can backfire on the perpetrators. What occurs is more likely to be a metaphoric "fight," a war of words and covert resistance.

Political scientist James Scott carried out two years of ethnographic research among peasant rice farmers in a Malaysian village called Sedaka. *(See EthnoFile 12.3: Malaysian Peasant Farmers.)* Poor Malaysian peasants are at the bottom of a social hierarchy dominated locally by rich farmers and nationally by a powerful state apparatus. These peasants are not kept in line by some form of state-sponsored

negotiation
verbal discussions between opposed parties in which they attempt to settle their differences without recourse to physical coercion

Although everyone may agree that the introduction of mechanized rice harvesting in Malaysia hurts the poor and helps the rich, rich and poor do not agree that the benefits of the machines outweigh their costs.

EthnoFile 12.3
MALAYSIAN
PEASANT FARMERS

Region: Southeast Asia

Nation: Malaysia (village of "Sedaka"; the name is a pseudonym)

Population: 300

Environment: lush paddy land

Livelihood: Rice cultivation

Political organization: Village within a modern nation-state

Other: Social and political consequences of the Green Revolution and the introduction of mechanized agriculture have been significant in this village

terrorism. Rather, the context of their lives is shaped by what Scott calls "routine repression": "occasional arrests, warnings, diligent police work, legal restrictions, and an Internal Security Act that allows for indefinite preventive detention and proscribes much political activity" (Scott 1985:274).

Scott wanted to find out how this highly restrictive environment affected political relations between members of dominant and subordinate classes in the village. It quickly became clear to him that the poor peasants of Sedaka were not about to rise up against their oppressors. But this was not because they accepted their poverty and low status as natural and proper. For one thing, organized overt defense of their interests would have been difficult under the best of circumstances, given the conflicting loyalties generated by local economic, political, and kinship ties. For another thing, even had such organization been possible, peasants knew that overt political action in the context of routine repression would be foolhardy. And they had to feed their families. Their solution was to engage in what Scott calls "everyday forms of peasant resistance." This includes such actions as "foot dragging, dissimulation, desertion, false compliance, pilfering, feigned ignorance, slander, arson, sabotage, and so forth" (ibid.: xvi). These actions may do little to alter the peasants' situation in the short run. Scott argues, however, that in the long run they may be more effective than overt rebellion in undercutting state repression.

What we find in everyday forms of peasant resistance are indirect attempts to make an alternative account of the social situation count. Scott says, "The struggle between rich and poor in Sedaka is not merely a struggle over work, property rights, grain, and cash. It is also a struggle over the appropriation of symbols, a struggle over how the past and present shall be understood and labeled, a struggle to identify causes and assess blame" (ibid.: xvii). When peasants criticize rich landowners, or rich landowners find fault with peasants, the parties involved are not just venting emotion. According to Scott, each side is simultaneously constructing a world view. Rich and poor alike are offering "a critique of things as they are as well as a vision of things as they should be. . . . [They are writing] a kind of social text on the subject of human decency" (ibid.: 23).

Scott documents the dynamics of this struggle in his discussion of the recent introduction of mechanized rice harvesting in Sedaka. Traditionally, rice harvesting was manual labor. It regularly allowed poor peasants to earn cash and receive grain from their employers as a traditional form of charitable gift. In the late 1970s, however, combine-harvesters were introduced. Their use eliminated the rich farmers' need for hired labor, a loss that dealt poor families a severe economic blow. When rich and poor talk about the harvesters, each side offers a different account of their effect on economic life in the village. The struggle of each side to make its account count illustrates the power of persuasion in practice.

Scott tells us that both sides recognize certain obvious facts about combine-harvesters. They agree, for example, that using the machines hurts the poor and helps the rich. When each side is asked whether the benefits of the machines outweigh their costs, however, consensus evaporates. The poor offer practical reasons against the use of combine-harvesters. They claim, for example, that the heavy machines are inefficient and their operation destroys rice paddies. They also offer moral reasons against their use. They accuse the rich of being "stingy," of ignoring the traditional obligation of rich people to help the poor by providing them with work and charity. The rich deny both the practical and the moral objections of the poor. They insist that using harvesters increases their yield. They accuse poor people who complain about them of bad faith. They claim that the poor suffer because they are bad farmers, or lazy. And they attribute their own success to hard work and prudent farm management.

Rich rice farmers would never have been able to begin using combine-harvesters without the outside assistance of both the national government and the business groups who rent the machines to them at harvesttime. Poor peasants are aware of this. They do not expect the government or business organizations outside the village to help them out in times of need. That is, however, exactly what they expect from rich local farmers. After all, the rich farmers "are a part of the community and therefore *ought* not to be indifferent to the consequences of their acts for their neighbors" (ibid.: 161). The stinginess of the rich does not just bring economic loss. It also attacks the social identity of the poor, who vigorously resist being turned into nonpersons. The poor insist on being accorded the "minimal cultural decencies in this small community" (ibid.: xviii). The only weapon they control in this struggle is their ability, by word and deed, to undercut the prestige and reputation of the rich.

And so they reject the accounts rich people offer of themselves and their actions. Also, by offering an alternative account, they make it more difficult for those in power to ignore them. This strategy works in Sedaka because rich local farmers are not ready to abandon the traditional morality that used to regulate relations between rich and poor. They have not yet become so Westernized that they no longer care what other villagers think of them. A shrewd campaign of character assassination may cause at least some of the rich to hesitate before ignoring their traditional obligations. If successful, the poor may be able to persuade the rich of their right to work and charity. The improvement might be minor in strictly economic terms. But it would be major in terms of the ability of the poor to defend their claims to citizenship in the local community. In addition, the wider political arena might change in the future. Scott was convinced that many of the poor peasants he knew might well engage in open, active rebellion if routine repression disappeared.

Struggle over principles and how to apply them in real life is rife with ambiguity and potential disagreement. For this reason, debates over definitions play a central role in any human society. Clastres (1977: 128ff.) emphasizes the tremendous importance of language in stateless societies, not just as a neutral medium of communication. Especially coming from the lips of the chief, language is a source of power that shapes, identifies, and labels what is of value, what is worth paying attention to, what shall count in the world of human experience. Alverson and Scott show that this power does not disappear with the rise of the state. World views articulated in language by different social subgroups aim "not just to convince but to control; better stated, they aim to control by convincing" (Scott 1985:23). The way the Tswana and the villagers of Sedaka talked about their experiences had the potential to transform the material circumstances of their lives.

Language is not the only symbolic code that can be used to define a political position. June Nash (1979) describes the way disenfranchised Bolivian tin miners manipulated religious ritual to force their employers to pay attention to an alternative understanding of reality. *(See EthnoFile 12.2: Bolivian Tin Miners.)* Nash studied the *ch'alla*, a traditional Cholo ritual to the devil (or Tio, as he is called in Spanish). She learned that this ritual had political overtones, and that its meaning had changed significantly after the tin mines were nationalized. Before nationalization, the mines had been run privately by a white Bolivian elite and white, non-Bolivian managers who had supported the ritual and had contributed financially to it. Following nationalization, the mines were run by the Bolivian government and Bolivian managers. These people not only withdrew official support from the ritual; they tried to wipe it out altogether.

This change of policy was closely related to the social identity of the new administrators, and to their fears that their authority might be challenged on the basis of that identity. The former white Bolivian owners and their white non-Bolivian managers had a social identity clearly distinct from that of the nonwhite Cholos and Indians. They therefore felt free to encourage the practice of a nonwhite, indigenous ritual that reinforced the distinctness of the mineowners from the mineworkers. After nationalization, however, the mine owner became the Bolivian government and the mine technicians were Bolivians. Neither of these groups had unambiguous claims to white identity. They needed to find some other way to establish a social identity that was clearly distinct from Cholos and Indians, so they withdrew their support for the ch'alla ritual. The new administrators knew that they, unlike the white elite they replaced, might be suspected of sharing the miners' devotion to Tio if they lent their support to rituals honoring him. By repudiating the ch'alla, they repudiated Cholo identity as well.

This had political consequences. Before nationalization, the ch'alla ritual embodied the harmonious ties linking ruler and ruled, backed by the power of Tio. Control by the elite was uncontested, the workers accepted their place, and elite sponsorship of the ritual to Tio certified and reinforced this state of affairs. After nationalization both administrators and workers recognized that the mine administrators no longer represented an elite clearly different from and superior to the mineworkers. Threatened administrators attempted to shore up their status and authority by banning the ch'alla. Miners who continued to perform the ritual asserted an identity separate from that of the administration. At the same time by ignoring the ban on the ritual, they were challenging the authority of the national government. The meaning of the ritual changed. Performance of the ch'alla came to embody disunity between the two groups, rather than solidarity. And it enlisted the power of Tio in support of the workers against the national government.

Bargaining for Reality

Political life involves winning hearts and minds as well as—or even more than—coercing bodies. Anthropologist Lawrence Rosen worked in the Moroccan city of Sefrou. *(See EthnoFile 12.4: Sefrou.)* As he listened to his informants discussing and defining their relationships with each other, he realized that none of the tradi-

EthnoFile 12.4
SEFROU

Region: North Africa

Nation: Morocco

Population: 28,607 (1970s)

Environment: Well-watered oasis at foothills of Middle Atlas Mountains

Livelihood: Agriculture, commerce, bureaucratic service, artisanship

Political organization: Part of a modern nation-state

Other: Sefrou is a regional center in the Middle Atlas Mountains

tional concepts they used could be said to have a fixed meaning. Any definition offered by one person would be verbally challenged by another. Rosen concluded that political and social life in Sefrou could not be understood unless one accepted that, for his informants, negotiation was the norm. Rosen (1984) calls this sociopolitical negotiation **bargaining for reality**.

The reality bargained for is not an impersonal, unchangeable set of truths about the world. Like Tswana migrants, Cholo miners, and Malaysian peasants, Moroccans aim to persuade one another to accept alternative ways of understanding a particular situation. Persuasive accounts must be *coherent*. That is, they must explain events and processes central to the experience of those to whom they are addressed; they must be expressed in language that other members of society can understand; and they must hang together in a way that is not blatantly contradictory.

The power relationship between men and women in Sefrou illustrates this process. Men view women as less intelligent, less self-controlled, and more selfish than men, and they expect women to obey them. Although women often assent to the male account of this relationship, they do not accept it in all circumstances. Women have developed an alternative account that explains elements in their lives that the male account either overlooks or interprets differently.

Women in Sefrou depend on men—first their fathers and later their husbands—for material support. But marriages are fragile, and women can easily find themselves relying on brothers or sons when their husbands divorce them. As a result, security for women depends on strengthening their positions within their families. In particular, women make an active attempt to influence marriage negotiations. Any marriage automatically rearranges social relationships within the family. Women are eager to protect themselves and their daughters from oppressive demands by a husband and his kin. They view their action as sensible and compassionate, not as misplaced interference. Nor do they accept the men's view that men are superior to women intellectually and morally. Indeed, they often view men as self-centered and childish.

In effect, Moroccan men and women live side by side in different worlds. They share experiences but interpret those experiences differently. Because neither sex has much direct contact with the other during everyday life, these different interpretations of experience do not constantly come into conflict. But there are occasions—such as marriage negotiations—that bring these different sets of understanding into contention. The outcome is reality bargaining, as several different actors attempt to make their definitions of the situation prevail.

bargaining for reality
negotiation in which no assertion by one person about the meaning of social and political events is immune to challenges by others; said by Lawrence Rosen to characterize everyday verbal interaction in Morocco

Rosen (1984:40–47) describes one marriage negotiation that he encountered in Sefrou. A girl refused to marry the suitor her family chose, and her continued obstinacy had disrupted the harmony of her father's household. Rosen visited the household in the company of a respected male informant who was an old friend of the family. During their visit, the family friend and the girl's mother discussed the betrothal and the girl's refusal to consent to it.

Both parties interpreted the girl's refusal differently. The family friend described the girl's behavior as a typical case of female selfishness and immorality. What other reason could there be for her refusing to obey her father, as dutiful daughters should? He spoke harshly of her and repeatedly asserted that when her father returned they would force her to come to her senses and make the marriage. Her mother never openly contradicted the family friend's assertions. All the while, however, she quietly and insistently continued to make counterassertions of her own. She reported her daughter's reason for rejecting the match: her intended husband came from a distant city. If she married him she would have to leave her family behind and go live among strangers. It was not that she objected to an arranged marriage; rather, she did not want to marry this particular man because to do so would take her so far away from home. From a woman's perspective, the daughter's anxieties were entirely rational, given the powerlessness and isolation that a new Moroccan wife must endure in her husband's family.

As it turned out, the young girl was eventually persuaded to marry the intended spouse, but only after a year and a half of successful resistance. She only changed her mind when she became convinced that consenting to the marriage was an economically sound move, not a submission to patriarchal authority.

So women may agree with the male position in general terms and yet successfully dispute its relevance in a particular situation. Men may get women to comply with their wishes, and yet the women's reasons for doing so may have nothing to do with the reasons men offer to justify their demands. This bears a strong resemblance to the situation in South Africa, where Tswana migrants comply with the wishes of their white bosses, yet explain their compliance in terms utterly at odds with white understanding. It is also similar to the situation in Sedaka, where rich farmers and poor peasants agreed that combine-harvesters hurt the poor and helped the rich, but did not agree as to why.

When disputes are settled in this manner, experience is transformed. As Scott observes, "The key symbols animating class relations in Sedaka—generosity, stinginess, arrogance, humility, help, assistance, wealth and poverty—do not constitute a set of given rules or principles that actors simply follow. They are instead the normative raw material that is created, maintained, changed, and above all manipulated by daily human activity" (Scott 1985:309). In a similar way, Rosen refers to such central Moroccan values as intelligence, self-control, and generosity as **essentially negotiable concepts**: "There is an element of uncertainty inherent in these terms, such that their application to any situation by one person can be contested by another" (Rosen 1984:43). Bargaining for reality involves just this sort of maneuver: "What is negotiable, then, is less one's view of reality as such than its scope, its impact, and its differential importance" (ibid.: 47).

essentially negotiable concepts
cultural values evoke a wide range of meanings among those who accept them; what such a value means in any particular situation, as well as the relevance of applying that value to the situation, is never obvious but must always be negotiated

History as Prototype of and for Political Action

When individual actors within a particular cultural and situational context attempt to impose their definition of the situation on those with whom they interact, they draw on elements of a shared tradition of values and beliefs. This shared tradition, however, does not consist of values and beliefs divorced from experience and history. To some degree, people in all cultures continue to reshape—to bargain over—not merely which part of an agreed-on tradition is relevant in a particular situation, but also which version of the tradition ought to be agreed on.

The Lesson of Munich

Drawing lessons from the past is an important activity in the political life of American society. For example, some people in the United States turned one interpretation of the events surrounding the outbreak of World War II into a key metaphor for interpreting the postwar confrontation between the United States and the Soviet Union.

The prewar events seen as prototypical involve what was called "appeasement." In the 1930s, Western European democracies tried to deal with the growing threat of fascism by granting certain political and economic concessions to Adolf Hitler, hoping that those concessions would appease Hitler's apparent thirst for conquest and domination of Europe. Appeasement is supposed to have failed, since (so it appears) the more Hitler was granted, the more he wanted. The result is understood to have been the eventual outbreak of a tragic and costly war. The lesson is supposed to be that the war might have been avoided, or at least kept from becoming so devastating, if the other European powers had not attempted to appease Hitler. Had they shown firm military resolve at the outset, they might well, by threat of force, have squashed German ambition before it had a chance to develop.

This is generally called the lesson of Munich, in reference to a meeting in Munich in 1938 between Adolf Hitler and Neville Chamberlain, prime minister of Great Britain, as well as French and Italian leaders. At this meeting, Germany agreed not to declare war on Czechoslovakia, thereby drawing into war its allies France and eventually England. In exchange, Germany was to be allowed to annex a sizable chunk of Czechoslovakia, the Sudetenland.

Ever since World War II, when the United States has conflicts with the Soviet Union, some Americans point to the Munich experience as a history lesson whose meaning must not be forgotten. The often-stated aim is to avoid "another Munich." To favor diplomacy over military force is seen as a sign of weakness; after all, Chamberlain's diplomacy did not keep Hitler in check. For diplomacy to work, it is argued, one must be able to trust one's opposite numbers at the bargaining table. But power-hungry enemies of democracy cannot be trusted; they only pay attention to guns and tanks. Western leaders who deny this are contemporary Chamberlains. They are viewed as weak and naive, as Chamberlain is understood to have been. To follow their advice would be to encourage the rapacity of the enemy, as concessions are believed to have encouraged Hitler.

By the same analogy, powerful Soviet leaders are all seen as contemporary Hitlers, as ruthless and ambitious and treacherous as he is understood to have been. The diplomacy of Chamberlain is presumed to have failed to contain Hitler, and it is therefore assumed that diplomacy will be equally useless against Soviet leaders. Because they are enemies of democracy, Soviet leaders cannot be trusted. Indeed, because they understand the confrontation in terms different from our own, they are feared as malevolent creatures who are barely human. They are adherents of "godless communism" and must therefore be in league with the devil. President Ronald Reagan referred to the Soviet Union as an "evil empire." Since the citizens of Western democracies are obviously good and trustworthy human beings who believe in God, what other explanation can there be? Any society that would disagree with

Neville Chamberlain and Adolf Hitler in Munich, 1938.

ours must, by the logic of the case, be filled with bad and treacherous atheists of dubious humanity.

The Lesson of Vietnam

If some groups of Americans hope to avoid "another Munich," other groups of Americans are equally eager to avoid "another Vietnam." In the latter case, the historical prototype is based on a particular understanding of the meaning of U.S. involvement in Southeast Asian politics in the 1960s and 1970s. According to that understanding, American involvement in the Vietnam War was a prime example of the disastrous consequences of a military response to outside threat. In their view, the war in Vietnam began as an anticolonial struggle against the French. Once the French had been defeated, the struggle turned into a civil conflict between different elements of Vietnamese society. The United States refused to let the Vietnamese people settle their own local, internal differences by themselves, and began to back the South Vietnamese faction in this civil war. The U.S. government then insisted on interpreting every challenge to South Vietnam as an indirect challenge to the United States. This escalated the conflict to a far more dangerous level, and encouraged the North Vietnamese to look to the Soviet Union for support. When American soldiers were sent in to supplement the South Vietnamese army, the outcome was a shocking loss of American lives, as well as an enormous financial drain on the U.S. economy. And the side the United States backed lost anyway.

The lesson of Vietnam, therefore, is the folly of the belief that every internal conflict in every Third World nation must be understood as a miniconfrontation between Moscow and Washington that requires U.S. military intervention. As long as our allies are repressive right-wing dictators, the lesson continues, supporting them only diminishes American credibility and alienates their people from us. Furthermore, by viewing every Third World challenge to Western domination as being fomented by agents of the Soviet Union, we overlook the real grievances of such people as the Vietnamese against outside dominators and their local collaborators. Far from bringing peace to a troubled part of the world, such involvement only escalates the violence. Moreover, it is doomed to failure, as defeat in Vietnam shows.

Proponents of this interpretation of U.S. involvement in Vietnam are anxious to avoid "another Vietnam" in other parts of the world. They sometimes characterized the policies of the Reagan administration in Central America as likely to lead to "another Vietnam" in El Salvador or Nicaragua, for example (see figure 12.1). They argue that U.S. involvement in Vietnam began with financial aid, followed by the sending of military advisers, followed by the sending of troops. They then remind us of the outcome: thousands of lives lost and billions of dollars spent—for the price of defeat.

But this is not the only interpretation of "Vietnam" available. Those who backed U.S. military involvement in Southeast Asia have an answer for critics who remind them that their side did not win in Vietnam. Supporters of the war explain this defeat from a very different referential perspective. They argue that military intervention was not itself wrong. America was defeated because military leaders were not allowed to use the full range of forces available to them. The Vietnam War was a contained war that was not allowed to escalate into a more encompassing conflict. For some, this meant it was a war they were "not allowed to win." Some supporters of the war argued that if U.S. soldiers had been allowed to bomb the North Vietnamese "back to the Stone Age," we would have won handily. But officially, the Vietnam War was not termed a war, for only the U.S. Congress can declare war, and it had not done so. This led many Americans to view the situation in Vietnam as

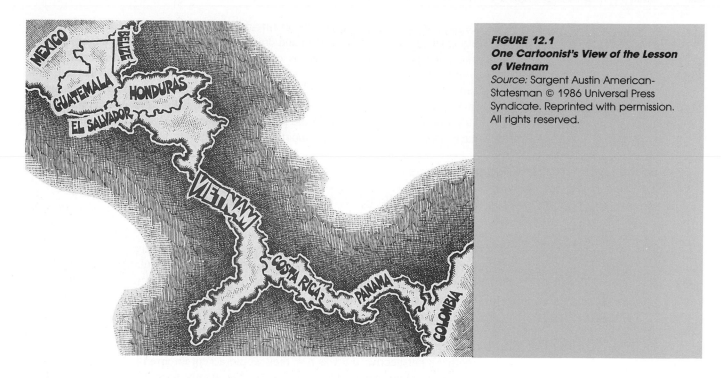

an "illegal war," fought by the president and his supporters using constitutional loopholes. Paradoxically, to be allowed to fight in Vietnam at all required the war's supporters to deny that the war was a war.

The lesson of Vietnam and the lesson of Munich each presuppose a view of reality that singles out certain elements of a historical experience as being especially meaningful. Each account is coherent. Each is articulated in language that all parties to the dispute can understand. Each hangs together in a way that is not obviously contradictory. And each acknowledges a broad range of publicly accepted facts (e.g., World War II followed Chamberlain's attempt at diplomacy; the U.S.-backed faction in Vietnam did not triumph over its enemies). But each side assigns different meanings to those facts.

What is both fascinating and troubling is that there seems to be no easy way for members of one side to persuade members of the other side that their interpretation is mistaken. As we noted in chapter 5, the resolution of cognitive disagreement is most likely when the disagreeing parties are present in the same physical context as the objects or events they disagree about. The possibility of seeing the justice of an alternative referential perspective increases when each side is free to draw the other side's attention to facts it might otherwise overlook. This sort of dialogue becomes extremely difficult when the objects or events under dispute are displaced in space or time. Developing an informed opinion about events occurring on the other side of the globe, outside one's direct experience, is as difficult as developing an informed opinion about events that took place fifty years ago.

Unfortunately, most people must base their interpretations of such matters on the partial accounts of others. Few have the opportunity to witness personally the wider context in which the reported events were embedded. We rely for such contextual information on the accounts of diplomats or journalists or ethnographers, who have spent time in the field. But we must evaluate our sources critically. We want to know who they are, what cultural assumptions about human nature, human society, and human history have shaped their referential perspective. We want to know whether they witnessed the events they are reporting, what their sources of information were, how complete and credible those sources were. Answers to such questions provide our only means of assessing the truth value of alternative accounts. They are fairly easy to obtain when they concern matters in which we ourselves are directly involved. But they are far more difficult to obtain when, as is increasingly the case, they concern other peoples in distant places with unfamiliar cultures. Perhaps at no time in the past has sound political judgment required ordinary citizens to learn so much about so many things.

Negotiating the Meaning of History

The meanings of the central symbols of any cultural tradition are essentially negotiable. That is, each symbol evokes a wide range of meanings among those who accept it. But what that symbol means in any particular situation, as well as the appropriateness of applying that symbol to the situation, is never obvious. Such matters are cultural dilemmas that people struggle creatively to resolve. In the Moroccan example, nobody denied that daughters should allow their fathers to arrange marriages for them. The issue was whether this particular daughter, in refusing to marry a particular man, was rejecting the general principle. From her and her mother's perspective she was not; they would accept an arranged marriage if it did not mean taking her far from her family. The family friend, however, insisted on interpreting her behavior as a challenge to her father's authority.

Some cultural symbols carry heavy historical freight. The political use to which such symbols are put can be far from negligible. Much depends on which events—and which version of those events—we choose to interpret using those symbols. Even if a given account of history is made coherent and persuasive, however, more must be done. People must be convinced that this particular account of past events is relevant to current events. That step is possible only if people already believe that history is patterned, that it repeats itself, that past events can be understood as metaphors for present-day events, that past actors can be equated with present actors. If all this holds, then a correct knowledge of the past confers considerable power on those who act in the present. They will be able accurately to discern the motives and predict the actions of other players in the political arena. If they are shrewd, they will be able to use this information to their own advantage.

Power lies essentially in being able to convince others that your knowledge is accurate, that your account counts. If you succeed in so convincing them, you may also persuade them that the only actions that make political sense are actions that follow from your account. Alternative accounts, and the policies that might be consistent with them, can be dismissed as irrelevant, irrational, or immoral. History, then, is an essentially negotiable activity. Political debate is often over which lessons from the past are relevant to the present.

The essential negotiability of the meaning of history is revealed in the variety of responses one gets when one asks those who lived through the period of the Vietnam War what "Vietnam" was all about. There are other examples. Suicide missions seem particularly apt historical events to be elevated into cultural prototypes. The memory of one's own people being slaughtered by the enemy, as in the case of Custer at the Little Bighorn or the Sioux at Wounded Knee, must be accounted for. Such events are not easy to cope with, morally or intellectually. If one has faith in the rightness of one's culture and the universe, they are enormously disconcerting; they are contrary to the pattern that one expects.

Even worse, perhaps, is the memory of one's own people taking their own lives rather than be slaughtered by the enemy. The horror of the events reported to have occurred in A.D. 73 at Masada, in Roman Palestine, challenges comprehension. A small community of 1,000 Jewish Zealots committed suicide rather than surrender to 15,000 Roman troops who had been besieging them. Folklorist Yael Zerubavel (1983) argues that the story of Masada has become a central metaphor for many modern Israelis, who draw contradictory messages from it. On the one hand, Masada symbolizes heroic resistance against more powerful enemies. On the other hand, the same people respond that the lesson of Masada is that such a horror must never be allowed to happen again. The story of Masada is a vivid metaphor for citizens of a tiny country whose very existence is threatened by larger neighbors, for whom death in battle is a reality faced regularly, for whom slaughter by more powerful enemies has been a commonplace of history.

Events of history like the seige of Masada are too powerful, too suggestive. They cannot be encapsulated in simple explanations. For that very reason, they threaten to destroy the sense of meaningful coherence that any cultural tradition imparts to those who live by it. At the same time, such events also require practical responses from those under stress. The presence of other societies pursuing their own interests in their own ways cannot be avoided. Political decisions must be made, and intelligent decisions depend on appropriate interpretations of the actions and motives of other groups.

In the nuclear age, political leaders are gambling for high stakes. Guns and tanks and bombs are persuasive elements in these confrontations, but using them unreservedly is self-defeating. Like the American soldiers in Vietnam who, as legend has it, destroyed villages in order to save them, the "winner" of a nuclear war would have destroyed the world in order to save it. Perhaps the paradox of such an outcome is difficult to face for many people today. For them, the prototypes of war are drawn from a nonnuclear age, when confrontations between powerful nations were never total and the spoils of victory were always more than a pile of cinders. Perhaps, more darkly, some parties to the contemporary confrontation are willing to risk total annihilation rather than give up their way of life. A taste for martyrdom has always been a difficult phenomenon for practical politicians to come to terms with.

Most political confrontations today do not, in themselves, threaten nuclear holocaust, even if some people fear that small-scale disputes, if not carefully contained, might easily escalate to such a level. In considering these localized conflicts, we confront the events of recent history. What sense can we make of them, what lessons can we draw? These events reveal evidence of political repression, torture, murder, destruction of property. Weapons have not lost their power to coerce and take life. And yet, in places like Iran and the Philippines, we also see evidence of militarily powerful regimes toppled by revolutionaries whose material weapons were few. In Poland, we see evidence of ordinary workers organizing themselves in opposition to the central government, despite reprisals and the threat of military might from the Polish state backed by the Soviet Union. Guns are powerful, but so are coherent sets of ideas professed by organized social groups.

Key Terms

social organization	autonomy	Trickster
power	persuasion	negotiation
political anthropology	anomie	bargaining for reality
coercion	alienation	essentially negotiable concepts
legitimacy	exchange theory	

Chapter Summary

1. *Social organization* refers to the patterning of human interdependence in a given society through the actions and decisions of its members. Different modes of livelihood do not by themselves shape social forms. We must also look at who takes care of crops and cattle, how it is done, and for whom it is done. This requires that we investigate the *power* that human beings have to reproduce or to change their social organization.

2. Anthropologists and others have sought laws that would explain cross-cultural similarities and differences in social organization. Evolutionists, including Marx, hoped to find those laws in the dynamics of history. Environmental determinists hoped to find them by studying how particular societies adapted to their local environments. Biological determinists looked within the human organism. All these positions assume that certain material factors determine forms of social organization. They reject the anthropological argument that social relations in any society are ultimately arbitrary, since the context of those relations can never be unambiguously defined.

3. The ability to choose implies *power*. In most societies at most times, power can never be reduced to naked physical force, although this is the Western prototype of power. Power in society operates according to principles that are cultural creations. As such, those principles are basically arbitrary and may differ from one society to another.

4. Western thinkers traditionally assumed that without a state, social life would be chaotic if not impossible. They believed that people would not cooperate unless forced to do so. Anthropologists demonstrated that stateless societies could maintain order by relying on kinship institutions. They also showed that people could cooperate without a central coercive authority.

5. People may submit to institutionalized power becasue they fear punishment, but they may also submit because they believe it is the right thing to do. In many societies, it is probably impossible to separate these two motivations. People may even be willing to give their lives to preserve a meaningful understanding of the world.

6. Those who view power as coercion see political encounters as a form of bargaining or haggling, not for material goods but for control. This perspective assumes that the parties involved are free agents who are not, and should not be, duty-bound to consider the outcome of their actions for anyone but themselves.

7. In stateless societies, social obligations restrict the opportunity of individuals to pursue their own self-interest to the detriment of the group. In those societies, power is usually seen to be an independent entity to which one may gain access by supplication, not coercion. Likewise, human individuals cannot be coerced but must be persuaded to cooperate. They are not "free" of social obligations, but they are free in that they cannot be forced to do someone else's bidding against their will.

8. In state and stateless societies alike, all human beings can be said to possess the power to invest the world with meaning. Regardless of the form of society in which they live, people can interpret their experiences in a manner that "objective" social conditions cannot dictate. This ability, not only to choose an interpretation but also to reject alternative interpretations of experience, lies at the core of human self-identity.

9. Because dominated groups retain the power to invest the world with their own meanings, rulers always face the risk that those they rule may create new persuasive accounts of their experience of being dominated, organize themselves to defend and disseminate their account, acquire a following, and unseat their rulers. Making accounts count is another way of understanding power.

10. Political activity in human society involves not just coercion but also negotiation over the legitimacy of such coercion. Much everyday political life turns on negotiation according to accepted social rules, not the threat of physical force. Politics may even be defined as a set of rules and principles for keeping social order and resolving disputes. Yet the rules and principles will always have to be interpreted before they can be applied, and group members may differ in their interpretations. When open rebellion is unrealistic, oppressed peoples may find that their defense of an alternative account of their situation is a powerful form of everyday resistance to domination.

11. Debates over definitions play a central role in political life. Disputes may be settled, but one party may have had to accept the other's interpretation of the nature of the dispute for settlement to be achieved. Interpretations are *essentially negotiable*, and people can find themselves doing the "right" thing for the "wrong" reasons. When disputes are settled in this manner, experience is transformed.

12. When people *bargain for reality*, they draw on elements of a shared culture and shared history in order to persuade others of the validity of their position. But they often must bargain over not merely which part of an agreed-on tradition is relevant, but also which version of the tradition ought to be agreed on. To find lessons in history is to use past events as metaphors for present-day events. Much political debate concerns which lessons from the past are relevant to the present.

Suggested Readings

Alverson, Hoyt. *Mind in the Heart of Darkness*. New Haven: Yale University Press, 1978.
> Difficult in places, but important and gripping. A study of how black Tswana miners in South Africa manage to maintain a sense of who they are under the most hellish circumstances.

Fogelson, Raymond, and Richard N. Adams. *The Anthropology of Power*. New York: Academic Press, 1977.
> A collection of twenty-eight ethnographic essays on power all over the world. Also contains two important essays based on the case studies.

Keesing, Roger. *'Elota's Story*. New York: Holt, Rinehart, and Winston, 1983.
> The autobiography of a Kwaio Big Man, with interpretative material by Keesing. First-rate; very readable and involving. We come to know 'Elota by the end.

Lewellen, Ted. *Political Anthropology*. South Hadley, Mass.: Bergin and Garvey, 1983.
> A basic text in political anthropology. Up-to-date survey of leading theories, scholars, problems in the field.

Walzer, Michael. *Exodus and Revolution*. New York: Basic Books, 1985.
> A fascinating, accessible study of how the story of the Exodus has been used as a prototype for political action throughout history.

Anthropology and the Colonial Legacy

Annette Weiner (Ph.D., Bryn Mawr College) is currently the David B. Kriser Professor of Anthropology at New York University. She has also taught at Franklin and Marshall College and at the University of Texas. Dr. Weiner carried out ten years of fieldwork in the Trobriand Islands, Papua New Guinea, and briefly in Western Samoa. She is the author of two books and the coeditor of another and has published many articles. Her interests include the study of gender, sexuality, and the position of women in society.

Anthropology is a relatively young scientific discipline that only became an important part of university scholarship within this century. What gave shape and force to this new field was the need to destroy the nineteenth-century myths that ranked "primitive" peoples at the lowest point along a scale of unilineal evolutionary development that culminated in civilization. These views had political underpinnings, for they coincided with colonial efforts to control the labor and resources in countries throughout Africa, Asia, the South Pacific, and Latin America, for example. These are the countries that today we call "developing" or the "Third World," countries that for the most part still carry the colonial imprint of powerless people.

Colonialism brought foreign governments, missionaries, explorers, and exploiters face-to-face with cultures whose values and beliefs were vastly different. As the harbingers of Western progress, their actions were couched in the rhetoric of doing something to and for "the natives" —giving them souls, clothes, law— whatever was necessary to lift them out of their "primitive" ways. Anthropologists were also part of the colonial scene, but what they came to "do" made them different from those who were carrying out the expectations of missions, overseas trade, and government protectorates. Anthropologists arrived in the field determined to understand the cultural realities of an unfamiliar world. The knowledge of these worlds was to serve as a warning to those in positions of colonial power by charging that villager's lives were not to be tampered with arbitrarily and that changing the lives of powerless people was insensitive and inhumane, unless one understood and took seriously the cultural meanings inherent in, for example, traditional land ownership, the technologies and rituals surrounding food cultivation, myths, magic, and gender relations.

All too often, however, the anthropologist's voice went unnoticed by those in power, for it remained a voice committed to illuminating the cultural biases under which colonialists operated. Only recently have we witnessed the final demise of colonial governments and the rise of independent countries. Economically, however, independence has not brought these countries the freedom to pursue their own course of development. In many parts of the world, Western multinational corporations, often playing a role not too dissimilar from colonial enterprises, now determine the course of that freedom, changing people's lives in a way that all too often is harmful or destructive. At the same time, we know that the world's natural resources and human productive capabilities can no longer remain isolates. Developed and developing countries are now more dependent on one another than ever before in human history. Yet this interdependency, which should give protection to indigenous peoples, is often worked out for political ends that ignore the moral issues. Racism and the practice of discrimination are difficult to destroy, as evidenced by the United States today, where we still are not completely emancipated from assumptions that relegate blacks, women, Asians, Hispanics, and other minorities to second-class status. If we cannot bridge these cultural differences intellectually within our own borders, then how can we begin to deal politically with Third World countries—those who were called "primitives" less than a century ago—in a fair, sensitive, and meaningful way?

This is the legacy of anthropology that we must never forget. Because the work of anthropology takes us to the neighborhoods, villages, and campsites—the local level—we can ourselves experience the results of how the world's economic and political systems affect those who have no voice. Yet once again our voices too are seldom heard by those who make such decisions. Anthropologists are often prevented from participating in the forums of economic and government planning. Unlike economists, political scientists, or engineers, we must stand on the periphery of such decision making, primarily because our understanding of cultural patterns and beliefs forces on others an awareness that ultimately makes such decisions more formidable.

At the beginning of the twentieth century, anthropologists spoke out strongly against those who claimed that "savage" societies represented a lower level of biological and social development. Now, as we face the next century, the anthropological approach to human nature and human societies is as vital to communicate as ever. We face a difficult, potentially dangerous, and therefore complex future. A fundamental key to our future is to make certain that the dynamic qualities of human beings in all parts of the world are recognized and that the true value of cultural complexities is not ignored. There is much important anthropology to be done.

CHAPTER 13
Making a Living

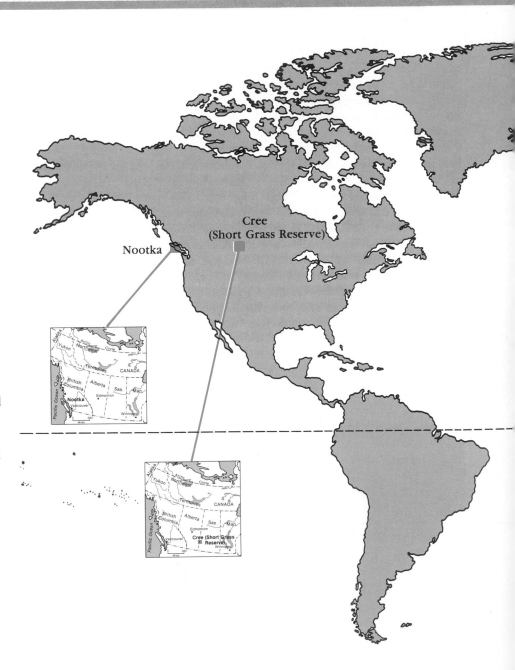

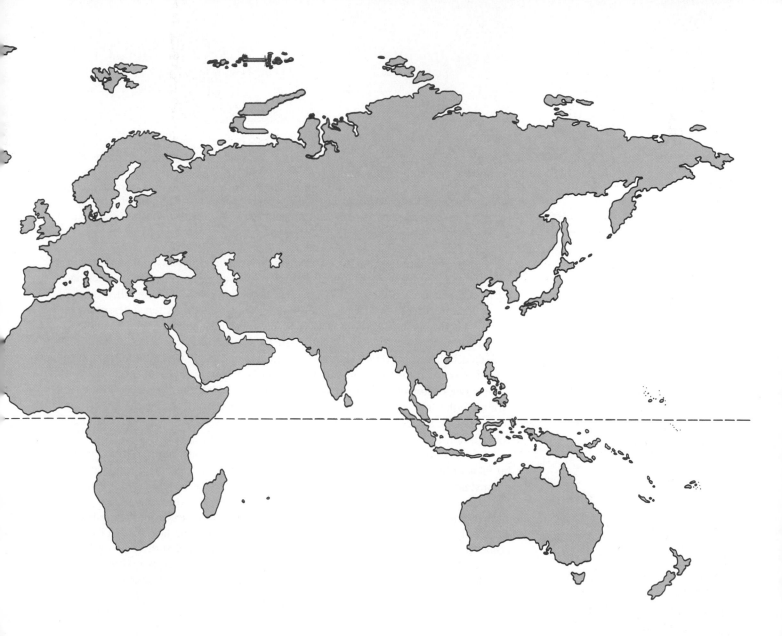

Anthropologist Richard Lee and !Kung informants gathering mongongo nuts.

The morning after ethnographer Richard Lee arrived in the Dobe !Kung area, his neighbors, including a man named N!eishi, asked him to give them a ride in his Land Rover to get some food. (See EthnoFile 9.1: !Kung.) They said there was little left in their area—mostly bitter roots and berries. They wanted to collect mongongo nuts, a staple of their diet and a great favorite. They said the mongongo grove was nearby. Lee agreed to take them.

"The travel was anything but high-speed, and our destination was anything but near. We ground along for hours in four-wheel drive at a walking pace where no truck had ever been before, swerving to avoid antbear holes and circumventing fallen trees."

By the time they stopped, Lee figured they were about ten miles north of Dobe. Lee was amazed by how fast the !Kung, both men and women, were able to gather the nuts. After two hours, they left the grove. Later, he weighed the food collected in that short time. The women had gathered loads weighing thirty to fifty pounds each, and the men had gathered fifteen to twenty-five pounds each.

Lee continues: "That worked out to about 23,000 calories for food for each woman collector, and 12,000 for each man. Each woman had gathered enough to feed a person for ten days and each man enough for five days. Not at all a bad haul for two hours' work!

"My first full day of fieldwork had already taught me to question one popular view of hunter-gatherer subsistence: that life among these people was precarious, a constant struggle for existence. My later studies were to show that the !Kung in fact enjoyed a rather good diet and that they didn't have to work very hard to get it. As we will see, even without the aid of an anthropologist's truck the !Kung had to work only 20 hours a week in subsistence. But what about the fact that N!eishi had come to me that morning saying that they were hungry and that there was no food nearby? Strictly speaking, N!eishi spoke the truth. October is one of the harder months of the year, at the end of the dry season, and the more desirable foods had been eaten out close to Dobe. What N!eishi did not say was that a little farther away food *was* available, and, if not plentiful, there was enough to see them through until the rains came. When N!eishi came to me with his proposition, he was making an intelligent use of his resources, social and otherwise. Why hike in the hot sun for a small meal, when the bearded White man might take you in his truck for ten large ones?" (Lee 1984:34–37).

It is a stereotype of Western culture that human beings who survive off nature's bounty lead lives that, in Thomas Hobbes's famous phrase, are nasty, brutish, and short. This stereotype makes it seem perfectly natural that Lewis Henry Morgan chose to call the foraging way of life "savagery." Only recently have anthropologists lived closely enough with foraging peoples to discover the inaccuracy of the Hobbesian position. Lee's !Kung informants were well nourished, with balanced diets. What is more, they were choosy about what they ate, unwilling to settle for food they disliked when Lee was there to take them to food they preferred. Such behavior is entirely familiar to us, and far from "savage." By means of culture, the !Kung are able to live rather well in what some see as a marginal environment.

Culture and Livelihood

People need one another, as well as resources from the wider world, in order to survive. Yet there is no obvious blueprint for social organization that all societies are obliged to follow. Particular societies, in particular environments, must invent ways to make use of the natural and human resources available to them. Their cultures are inventories of inventions that have been tested by time and have been shown adequate to the task. The paradox of the human condition is that while our physical survival depends on our making adequate use of the physical resources around us, our culture tells us which resources to use, and in what way. How people make their living is culturally defined.

In ordinary conversation, when we speak of making a living we usually mean doing what is necessary to obtain the material things—food, clothing, shelter—that sustain human life. Making a living thus encompasses what is generally considered *economic* activity. However, anthropologists and other social scientists have disagreed about just what the term *economy* ought to represent. The rise of the capitalist market led to the development of one view of what economy might mean: buying cheap and selling dear. That is, economy meant economizing, or "maximizing utility"—obtaining as much satisfaction as possible for the smallest possible cost. This view of economy is based on the assumption of **scarcity**. Many economists and economic anthropologists believe that people's resources (for example, money) are not, and never will be, great enough for them to obtain all the goods they want. Whether this situation is caused by the stinginess of nature, by an innate human desire for self-betterment, or simply by human greed, scarcity is assumed to be a constant of human existence. Economizing, therefore, involves setting priorities and allocating resources rationally according to those priorities.

The assumption of scarcity has not gone unchallenged. Many have argued that it is ethnocentric to assume that economic activity means "economizing" for everyone in every society. They claim that the principles central to economic activity in another society may be very different from our own. For them, the job of an economist is to describe the pattern of economic arrangements possessed by each culture. Given this perspective, in the words of Karl Polanyi, the **economy** is best understood as "the material life-process of society."

scarcity
the assumption that people's resources (for example, money) will never be great enough for them to obtain all the goods they desire; for some economic anthropologists, scarcity is assumed to be a constant of human existence

economy
for some, obtaining as much satisfaction as possible for the smallest possible cost; for others, such as Karl Polanyi, the culturally-shaped material life-processes of society

Subsistence Strategies

Human beings invent ways of using their relationships with one another and with the physical environment to make a living. *Subsistence* is the term often used to refer to the satisfaction of the most basic material survival needs of human beings, primarily those for food, clothing, and shelter. The different ways that people in different societies go about meeting these needs have been called **subsistence strategies**.

Anthropologists have devised a typology of subsistence strategies that has gained wide acceptance (see figure 13.1). As we noted in chapter 8, the basic division is between **food collectors** (those who gather, fish, or hunt for food) and **food producers** (those who depend on domesticated plants or animals or both for food). Food producers may farm exclusively or herd exclusively or do a little of both. Among those who farm, there are again distinctions. Some farmers depend primarily on human muscle power plus a few simple tools like digging sticks or hoes or machetes. They clear plots of uncultivated land, burn the brush, and plant their

subsistence strategies
the patterns of production, distribution, and consumption that members of a society employ to ensure the satisfaction of the basic material survival needs of human beings

food collectors
those who gather, fish, or hunt for food

food producers
those who depend on domesticated plants or animals or both for food

FIGURE 13.1
Subsistence Strategies

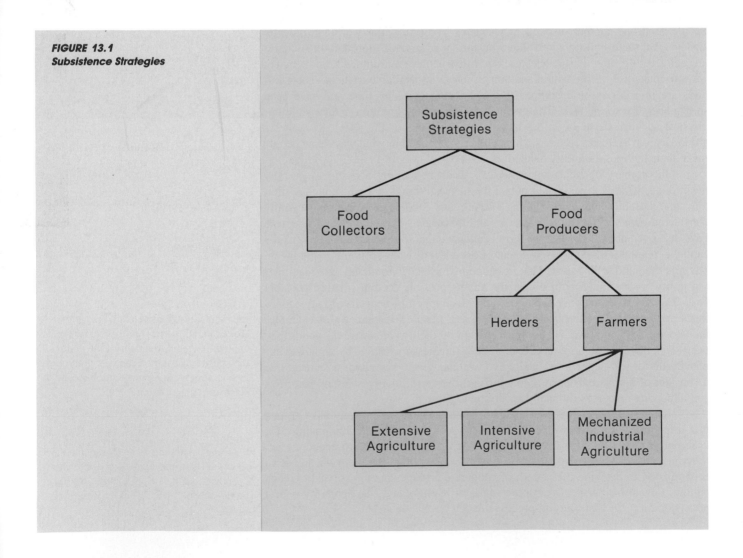

crops in the ash-enriched soil that remains. This technique exhausts the soil after two or three seasons, so the plot must then be allowed to lie fallow for several years. A new plot is cleared and the process is repeated. This form of cultivation is called **extensive agriculture**, emphasizing the extensive use of land as farm plots are moved every few years. Other farmers use plows, draft animals, irrigation, fertilizer, and the like. Their methods bring much more land under cultivation and produce significant surpluses of the crops raised. This second method of farming is known as **intensive agriculture**. Finally, if the classification is enlarged to include industrial societies as well as nonindustrial societies, we see that agriculture or animal husbandry may become *mechanized* along industrial lines. Agribusiness "factories in the field" or animal feedlots transform food production into a large-scale, highly technology–dependent industry of its own.

Many anthropologists who study human subsistence strategies see a major break separating food collecting from food producing. The first evidence of plant and animal domestication dates back to about ten thousand to twelve thousand years ago and is found in archaeological sites in several parts of the world (see figure 13.2). Once human beings took direct control over production of their food sources and stopped depending primarily on nature's bounty, many new ways of making a living became possible. For more than 90 percent of human history, our ancestors lived by food collecting. The changeover to food production accelerated population growth and social and technological innovation to an unprecedented degree.

extensive agriculture
a form of cultivation that requires moving farm plots every few years, as the soil becomes exhausted; extensive agriculture is based on the technique of clearing uncultivated land, burning the brush, and planting crops in the ash-enriched soil

intensive agriculture
a form of cultivation that employs plows, draft animals, irrigation, fertilizer, and so on to bring much land under cultivation, to use it year after year, and to produce significant surpluses

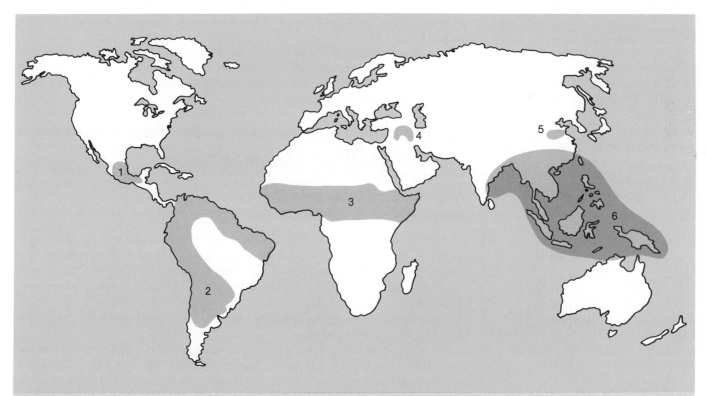

FIGURE 13.2
Areas of Early Plant and Animal Domestication
1. Meso-America, 2. South America, 3. Central Africa, 4. Southwest Asia, 5. China, and 6. Southeast Asia.

Intensive agriculture—replanting rice in Java.

production
the transformation of the raw materials of nature into a form suitable for human use

distribution
the allocation of goods and services to human groups and individuals

consumption
the use (generally the using up) of the raw materials of nature transformed for human use

neoclassical economic theory
a formal attempt to explain the workings of capitalist enterprise, with particular attention paid to distribution

Production, Distribution, and Consumption

Anthropologists have generally agreed that economic activity is usefully subdivided into three distinct phases: production, distribution, and consumption. **Production** involves transforming the raw materials of nature into products that are useful to human beings. **Distribution** involves getting those products to the people who need to use them. **Consumption** involves using up the products—for example, by eating food or wearing clothing.

When analyzing economic activity in a particular society, however, anthropologists differ in the importance they attach to each phase. For example, the distributive process known as *exchange* is central to the functioning of capitalist free enterprise. Some anthropologists have assumed that exchange is equally central to the functioning of all economies, and have tried to explain the economic life of non-Western societies in terms of exchange. Anthropologists of a marxian bent, however, have argued that exchange cannot be understood properly without first studying the nature of *production*. They point out that production shapes the context in which exchange can occur, determining which parties have how much of what kind of goods to exchange. Finally, others have suggested that neither production nor exchange patterns make any sense unless one first specifies the *consumption* priorities of the people who are producing and exchanging. Consumption priorities, they argue, are of course designed to satisfy material needs. But the recognition of needs and of appropriate ways to satisfy them is shaped by arbitrary cultural patterns.

We will examine in turn the arguments of anthropologists who have viewed either exchange, production, or consumption as most central to an explanation of economic life. We will point out the insights that each approach provides, as well as the questions it leaves unasked.

Distribution and Exchange Theory

Neoclassical Economic Theory and the Rise of Capitalism

The discipline of economics was born in the early years of the rise of capitalist industry in Western Europe. At that time, such thinkers as Adam Smith and his disciples struggled to devise theories that would explain the profound changes in economic and social life that European society had recently begun to experience. Their work has become the foundation for neoclassical economic theory in the Western world. **Neoclassical economic theory** is a formal attempt to explain the workings of capitalist enterprise.

Capitalism differed in many ways from the feudal economic system that had preceded it, but perhaps the most striking difference had to do with the way it handled **distribution**. Feudal economic relations allotted goods and services to different social groups and individuals on the basis of status. Since lords had high status and many obligations, they had a right to more. Peasants, with low status and few rights, were allowed far less. This distribution of goods was time-honored and not open to modification. The customs derived from capitalist economic relations, by contrast, were considered "free" precisely because they swept away all such traditional restrictions. As we saw in chapter 12 in our discussion of Sedaka, Malaysia, capitalism also swept away traditional protections. In any case, distribution under capitalism was negotiated between buyers and sellers in the market.

In Adam Smith's ideal market, everyone had something to sell (if only his or her willingness to work), and everyone was also a potential buyer of the goods brought to the market by others. Individual buyers and sellers met in the market to buy from and sell to each other—to engage in economic **exchange**. Ideally, because there were many buyers, many sellers, and no traditional restrictions governing who should get how much of what, prices could fluctuate depending on levels of supply and demand. Distribution would be carried out in line with the preferences of individuals. High demand by individuals for certain items would raise the price for those items, as many buyers bargained for few goods. This high demand, in turn, would entice more people to produce the goods in high demand, in order to take advantage of their higher prices. As competition between suppliers increased, however, prices would go down, as each supplier attempted to obtain a greater share of the market. Ideally, prices would stabilize as suppliers began offering desired goods at a cost sufficiently high to allow them to make a profit but sufficiently low for buyers to afford.

Market exchange of goods for other goods, or for labor, or (increasingly) for cash was an important development in Western economic history. It is not surprising, therefore, that Western economic theory was preoccupied with explaining how the market worked. Markets clearly had a new, decisive importance in capitalist society, which they had not possessed in feudal times. Western neoclassical economics is based on the assumption that market forces are the central forces determining levels of both production and consumption in society.

exchange
the process of distribution in which goods or service are transferred to one party in return for something else

A food market in India.

Formalist Studies in Economic Anthropology ▬▬▬

formalists

anthropologists who use formal neo-classical theory to explain economic activities in non-Western societies

Formal neoclassical economic theory was adopted by a number of anthropologists interested in explaining economic activities in non-Western societies. These anthropologists are known as **formalists**. Formalists recognized that in most non-Western societies there was nothing resembling a "free market." The !Kung, for example, traditionally produced food, clothing, and shelter by themselves and for themselves. They had no indigenous markets or money. Exchange took place in a ritual context and followed patterns of kinship and friendship. As in the economy of feudal Europe, distribution was hedged about with restrictions. Similar patterns were found in most of the societies anthropologists traditionally studied. Nevertheless, formalists took the Western capitalist market as their prototype of rational economic organization.

Once in the field, formalists searched for activities and institutions that might represent a metaphorical equivalent of the capitalist market—bridewealth exchanges, for example. They analyzed those transactions using the language of formal economic theory. For example, marriage negotiations were viewed as market transactions. The bride's family wished to exchange its woman for, say, cattle belonging to the groom's family. Formalists assumed that the law of supply and demand would determine how much bridewealth—or bride*price*—the groom's family would have to pay. More desirable brides—young virgins, for example—could be expected to command a higher brideprice than older, divorced women. If cattle were scarce relative to marriageable women, fewer would be demanded than if young women were scarce and cattle plentiful. The marriage market might be most volatile in societies permitting men an unlimited number of wives. Wealthy older men with lots of cattle might marry all the young women, leaving poorer young men to contend with one another over the less desirable women that remained. To talk about non-Western economic activity in this way permitted anthropologists to describe non-Western societies using terms that Western economists could understand.

Formalists do not view their undertaking as ethnocentric. In good positivist fashion, they consider formal economic theory to be scientific and therefore unaffected by culture-bound assumptions that might compromise its universal validity. In addition, formal economic theory assumes that individual actors in the capitalist market are *rational*. To suggest, therefore, that non-Western people do not make economic decisions in conformity with the principles of neoclassical theory would be the same as to call non-Western peoples *irrational*.

rational

to think and act in accord with the central principles of one's culture; in Western economic terms, to be concerned first and foremost with one's individual self-interest, as defined in terms of the market: to buy cheap, to sell dear, to realize a profit

To be **rational** in Western terms is to be concerned first and foremost with one's own individual self-interest. Individual self-interest is defined in terms of the market: to buy cheap, to sell dear, to realize a profit. People in some societies may voluntarily subordinate their individual self-interest to the social obligations of kinship or fealty. But in neoclassical economic terms, any action that benefits others at cost to oneself is, strictly speaking, irrational.

Formalists want to accept the axioms of capitalism. At the same time, they want to assert that non-Western peoples are rational. As a result, they claim that people in non-Western societies are basically closet capitalists. That is, their natural attraction to free enterprise has been stifled, or short-circuited, by traditional social institutions that drain off individual profit for the benefit of the group.

Challenges to the Formalists ▬▬▬

Some anthropologists have not been persuaded by the formalist approach. They have argued that to take self-interested, materialistic decision making in the capitalist market as the prototype of human rationality is both reductionistic and ethnocentric. These anthropologists are known as **substantivists**. Substantivists have pointed out that the capitalist market is a relatively recent cultural invention in human history. Neoclassical economic theory is an equally recent invention, designed to make sense of the capitalist market and its effects.

Substantivists are offended, on theoretical and moral grounds, by what they see as the formalist attempt to distort non-Western economic life in order to fit it into capitalist categories. They would agree, for example, that marriage transactions involving bridewealth bear a family resemblance to other kinds of exchange, including market exchange. But they assert that it is bad science, as well as morally repugnant, to reduce one to the other. It may be true, as Igor Kopytoff has recently argued, that people have often been turned into objects for sale in many societies. The most common example is slavery. But Kopytoff also points out that "the slave was unambiguously a commodity only during the relatively short period between capture and first sale and the acquisition of a new social identity; and the slave becomes less of a commodity and more of a singular individual in the process of gradual incorporation into the host society" (Kopytoff 1986:65).

Formalist analyses of bridewealth tend to reduce women to the status of things not only at the moment of marriage exchange, but permanently. Like cattle or refrigerators or new cars, women are assumed to have no voice in the transactions that concern them, whether as brides, mothers, or sisters. Passive and dumb, they are pushed here and there on the chessboard of men's ambitions.

Such analysis may make it easier for economic anthropologists and economists to compare their data, but it makes many other things far more difficult. It leads to bad science because the analyst is forced to ignore or explain away any ethnographic data that do not conform to the formal model. This means explaining away most of the cultural practices in the society in question. As we saw in chapter 10, feminist anthropologists have had to remind formalists repeatedly of the active roles women play in marriage negotiations. Formalist assumptions would not lead ethnographers to expect to find such institutions as cattle-linked siblings, for example. Formalist analysis has no interest in the role women can play as sisters in patrilineal societies. By ignoring these things, it dehumanizes women. Like the capitalist market itself, it reduces human beings to objects for sale to the highest bidder.

Substantivists suggest that capitalist market exchange is but one mode of exchange. Western capitalist societies distribute material goods in a manner that is consistent with their basic values, institutions, and assumptions about the human condition. So too non-Western, noncapitalist societies have devised alternative modes of exchange that distribute material goods in ways that are in accord with their basic values, institutions, and assumptions about the human condition. In substantivist language, patterns of economic exchange are embedded in the societies in which they are found. One cannot understand or explain patterns of exchange apart from this cultural context. Therefore, substantivists argue, while neoclassical theory may be able to account for the functioning of the economy in capitalist societies, it is not suited for analysis of noncapitalist economies.

Karl Polanyi and Modes of Exchange

Perhaps the most influential substantivist figure in anthropology has been the economist Karl Polanyi. He suggested that three **modes of exchange** could be identified historically and cross-culturally: reciprocity, redistribution, and market exchange.

substantivists
anthropologists who argue that formal neoclassical theory cannot be used to explain economic activities in non-Western societies, and who suggest that patterns of economic exchange must instead be interpreted within a society's cultural context

modes of exchange
patterns according to which distribution takes place: reciprocity, redistribution, and market exchange

The most ancient mode of exchange was *reciprocity*. Reciprocity is characteristic of egalitarian societies, like those of foraging peoples such as the !Kung. Where reciprocity operates, people exchange goods and services with one another.

Reciprocity may be generalized. That is, in **generalized reciprocity** those who exchange do so without expecting an immediate return, and they do not specify the value of the return. Everyone assumes that the exchanges will eventually balance out. This pattern of exchange usually characterizes the exchanges that occur between parents and their children. Parents do not keep a running tab on what it has cost them to raise their children and present the children with repayment schedules when they reach the age of eighteen.

Reciprocity can also be balanced. That is, in **balanced reciprocity** those who exchange do expect a return of equal value within a specified time limit. Balanced reciprocity can be seen when a brother and sister exchange gifts of equal value with one another at Christmastime. Lee (1984:98) notes that the !Kung distinguish between barter, which requires an immediate return of an equivalent, and *hxaro*, which is a kind of generalized reciprocity that encourages social obligations to be extended into the future.

Finally, reciprocity may be negative. **Negative reciprocity** is an exchange of goods and services in which at least one party attempts to get something for nothing without suffering any penalties. These attempts can range from haggling over prices to outright seizure.

Polanyi's second mode of exchange, **redistribution**, requires some form of centralized social organization. Those who occupy the central position are the recipients of economic contributions from all members of the group. It is then their responsibility to redistribute the goods they receive in a way that provides for every member of the group. In the United States, the Internal Revenue Service is probably the institution of redistribution that Americans know best. A classic anthropological case study of redistribution involves the *potlatch* of the Indians of the Northwest Coast of North America. In the highly stratified fishing and gathering society of the Nootka, for example, nobles "fought with property." *(See EthnoFile 13.1: Nootka.)* That is, each sought to outdo the others in generosity by giving away vast quantities of objects during the ceremony called the potlatch. Goods produced in one village were accumulated by the noble giving the potlatch, who redistributed those goods to other nobles attending the ceremony. When the guests returned to their own villages, they, in turn, redistributed the goods among their followers.

Market exchange, according to Polanyi, is the most recent mode of exchange, invented in capitalist society. Capitalism involves an exchange of goods

generalized reciprocity
an exchange of goods and services in which neither the time nor the values of the return are specified, although everyone assumes that the exchanges will eventually balance out.

balanced reciprocity
an exchange of goods and services in which a return of equal value is expected within a specified time limit

negative reciprocity
an exchange of goods or services in which at least one party attempts to get something for nothing without suffering any penalties

redistribution
a mode of exchange that requires the existence of some form of centralized social organization; those who occupy this central position are the recipients of economic contributions from all members of the group, and it is then their responsibility to redistribute the goods received in such a way that every group member is provided for

market exchange
according to Karl Polanyi, an exchange of goods or services (i.e., trade), calculated in terms of a multipurpose medium of exchange and standard of value (i.e., money), and carried on by means of a "supply-demand-price" mechanism (i.e., the capitalist market)

EthnoFile 13.1
NOOTKA

Region: North America

Nation: Canada (Vancouver Island)

Population: 6,000 (1970s)

Environment: Rainy, relatively warm coastal strip

Livelihood: Fishing, hunting, gathering

Political organization: Ranked individuals, chiefs

Other: The Nootka are famous for their potlatch exchange system

(*trade*), calculated in terms of a multipurpose medium of exchange and standard of value (*money*), and carried on by means of a "supply-demand-price mechanism" (*the market*). Polanyi was well aware that trade, money, and market institutions had developed independently of one another historically. He also knew that they could be found in societies outside the West. The uniqueness of capitalism was the way in which all three institutions were linked to one another in the societies of early modern Europe.

Different modes of exchange often coexist within a single society, although one mode is generally dominant. The United States, for example, is dominated by the market mode of exchange, yet redistribution and reciprocity can still be found. Within the family, parents who obtain income from the market redistribute that income, or goods obtained with that income, to their children. Generalized reciprocity also characterizes much exchange within the family: for example, parents provide their children with food and clothing without expecting any immediate return.

Social Exchange Theory

The substantivist critique of formalist economic anthropology challenged the assumption that economic activities in all human societies could be explained by the formal mechanisms of market exchange. Substantivists insisted that distribution, while important, did not take place in a cultural and historical vacuum. They stressed that economies were embedded in the cultural practices of the societies in which they were found. People could therefore be expected to exchange goods with one another according to the standards of appropriateness that their cultures taught them, whether or not this accorded with their own individual self-interest. A chief, for example, might part with all the wealth he had, even if his action brought him personal hardship, because this was the proper thing for a chief to do. In such a case, honor was preferable to individual accumulation of wealth, even though a capitalist might view that preference as irrational.

Some formalists tried to come up with a way to explain the economic behavior of people who chose honor over material wealth. The error of previous formalist analyses, they argued, was to assume that economic exchange had to do merely with material goods. But exchange operated more broadly; people could exchange not only to obtain material wealth, but also to obtain power or prestige. In this view, the generous chief was really "buying" prestige when he redistributed wealth in his society. Moreover, this prestige was a highly practical commodity to possess. It reinforced the chief's power in the community by putting the recipients of his gifts in his debt.

Thus was developed a theory of **social exchange**. The basis of this theory is the assumption that everything, even nonmaterial entities like power and prestige, can be best understood as *scarce resources*. People in all societies will compete with one another to accumulate as much of all these resources—material and non-material—as they can. In so doing, they must often exchange some of one resource (e.g., wealth) for some of another resource (e.g., prestige) in the market of life.

Social exchange theory was, among other things, a way of saving the economic "rationality" of non-Western men and women who clearly seemed to value some things above material wealth. It assumed that all people everywhere were maximizers, but that different cultures taught people to maximize different things.

With the development of social exchange theory in economic anthropology, we can see the fullest application of the marketing metaphor to social life. Social exchange theory argues that everything is for sale in all societies. All people every-

social exchange
a theory of economic behavior that assumes that power and prestige are non-material resources that are just as scarce as material wealth; that people in all societies attempt to accumulate as much of all of these resources as they can; and that in doing so, they must often exchange some of one resource for some of another resource (e.g., wealth for prestige)

where are first and foremost self-interested individuals. And such individuals always compete with one another to exchange the resources they have (in material or nonmaterial "goods") with other individuals, in hopes of reaping the greatest possible individual return.

Problems with the Emphasis on Exchange

The emphasis on exchange in economic anthropology has not been without critics. Formalists agreed that market exchange was the engine driving economic life, determining levels of production and levels of consumption. Substantivists criticized the formalist emphasis on the mechanisms of exchange in the capitalist market. They argued that more than one mode of exchange should be recognized, and insisted that modes of exchange do not operate in a vacuum but are embedded in society. Social exchange theorists seemed to be trying to counter the substantivist analysis by interpreting nonmarket modes of exchange as capitalism by other means. None of the parties appeared to be persuaded by the others' arguments, leaving the cross-cultural study of material life stymied.

Rather than choose sides in what seemed to be an increasingly sterile debate, some anthropologists decided that the problem lay in the preoccupation with exchange itself. Distribution is an important matter in the economic life of any society. But perhaps exchange is not the prime causative force that formalists, substantivists, and social exchange theorists have taken it to be. Certainly, earlier critics of neoclassical economics, such as Karl Marx, had argued that exchange could not properly be understood without a prior knowledge of production. People who met to exchange had different kinds of resources to use in bargaining with one another. Those differences in resources, Marx argued, were not shaped by the market, but rooted in the productive process itself.

Production Theory

For formalist economic anthropologists, the level of production of certain goods depends ultimately on the level of demand for those goods generated by the market. For other economic anthropologists, however, *production* is seen as the driving force behind economic activity. Production creates supplies of goods to which demand must accommodate, and it determines levels of consumption as well. Anthropologists who stress the centrality of production have borrowed their perspective on economic activity, as well as many key concepts, from the works of Karl Marx. They argue that this perspective is far more insightful than the one taken by neoclassical theorists of market exchange.

Labor

labor
the activity linking human social groups to the material world around them; from a marxian position labor is always social labor

Perhaps the most central marxian concept these anthropologists adopted is that of labor. **Labor** is the activity linking human social groups to the material world around them; human labor is therefore always social labor. Human beings must actively struggle together to transform natural substances into forms they can use. This is clearest in the case of food production. However, material production involves more than food production alone; it includes the production of clothing and shelter and tools as well. Marx emphasizes the importance of human physical labor in the material world, but he recognizes the importance of mental or cognitive labor. Human intelligence allows us to reflect on and organize productive activities. Mentally and physically, human social groups struggle together to ensure their material survival. In so struggling, they reproduce patterns of social organization, of production, and of thought.

Modes of Production

Marx saw the productive process as central to human social life, and he attempted to classify the ways different human groups carried out that process. Each way was called a **mode of production**. Anthropologist Eric Wolf has found Marx's work helpful. Wolf defines a mode of production as "a specific, historically occurring set of social relations through which labor is deployed to wrest energy from nature by means of tools, skills, organization, and knowledge" (Wolf 1982:75). Tools, skills, organization and knowledge constitute what Marx called the **means of production**. The social relations linking human beings who use a given means of production within a particular mode of production are called the **relations of production**. Those who use the mode-of-production concept in their work usually apply the term *production* to food collecting as well as to herding, farming, and industrial manufacturing.

The concept of mode of production is holistic. It highlights recurring patterns of human activity in which certain forms of social organization, production practices, and cultural knowledge codetermine one another. We might think of a mode of production as a kind of schema. Wolf notes that Marx speaks of at least eight different modes of production in his own writings, although he devoted most attention to one mode, the capitalist mode.

Wolf finds the concept of mode of production useful. But like most anthropologists inspired by Marx's work, he does not feel bound to accept Marx's conclusions as a matter of course. Wolf suggests that three modes of production have been particularly important in human history: (1) a *kin-ordered mode*, in which social labor is deployed on the basis of relations between people based on marriage and descent; (2) a *tributary mode*, "in which the primary producer, whether cultivator or herdsman, is allowed access to the means of production, while tribute is exacted from him by political or military means" (Wolf 1982:79); and (3) the *capitalist mode*. The capitalist mode has three main features: the means of production have become property owned by capitalists; workers are denied access to such ownership and must sell their labor power to the capitalists in order to survive; and labor by workers for capitalists produces surpluses of wealth (also owned by capitalists) that may be plowed back into production to increase output and generate further surpluses.

An overlap exists between this classification of modes of production and the traditional anthropological classification of subsistence strategies. The kin-ordered mode of production is found among foragers and some farmers and herders whose political organization does not involve domination by one group in the society over everyone else. The tributary mode is found among some groups of farmers or herders living in a social system that is divided into classes of rulers and subjects. Subjects produce both for themselves and for their rulers, who take a certain proportion of their subjects' product as tribute. The capitalist mode of production is the most recent to develop. Its prototype can be found in the industrial societies of North America and Western Europe beginning in the seventeenth and eighteenth centuries.

Thus, in some ways the mode-of-production concept simply recognizes the same variation in the "arts of subsistence" that Lewis Henry Morgan recognized in

mode of production
"a specific, historically occurring set of social relations through which labor is deployed to wrest energy from nature by means of tools, skills, organization, and knowledge" (Wolf 1982:75)

means of production
the tools, skills, organization, and knowledge used to extract energy from nature

relations of production
the social relations linking the people who use a given means of production within a particular mode of production

the nineteenth century. Yet the concept of mode of production also highlights certain attributes of subsistence strategies that the traditional anthropological approach tended to downplay. For example, modes of production have as much to do with forms of social and political organization as with material productive activities. That is, the kin-ordered mode of production is distinctive as much for its use of the kinship system to allocate labor to production as for the kind of production undertaken (for example, herding). In a kin-ordered mode of production, the *relations of kinship* serve as the *relations of production* that enable a particular *mode of production* to be carried out.

Mode of production and relations of production can be understood as two sides of the same coin. As aspects of human social life that influence one another and have implications for one another, they must be studied together. Anthropologists traditionally have emphasized the important links between a society's social organization (kinship groups, chiefdom, state) and the way that society meets its subsistence needs. This was originally done to demonstrate the stages of cultural *evolution*. Later, the aim was to demonstrate *functional interrelationships* between parts of an individual society regardless of its evolutionary "stage." Both approaches yielded useful information. In both cases, however, the emphasis of the analysis was on the orderly fashion in which societies either changed or stayed the same. Social harmony was understood as the natural state of affairs. Given this assumption, social stability meant that current social arrangements were appropriate and need not change. Social change was possible, but it would take place in an equally orderly fashion, in the fullness of time, according to laws of development beyond the control of individual members of society. Such approaches were therefore bound to be of limited utility for anyone who wanted to show that conflict lay behind social change, and that social stability was due to repression of that conflict. This was Marx's goal. It is shared by economic anthropologists who take a marxian perspective.

The Role of Conflict in Material Life

Many anthropologists have not been persuaded that social change is prefigured and orderly, or that social organization is by nature harmonious. They find marxian concepts useful in their work precisely because the marxian approach treats conflict as a natural part of the human condition. The concept of mode of production makes a major contribution to economic anthropology precisely because of the very different interpretation it gives to conflict, imbalance, and disharmony in social life.

Marx pointed out, for example, that the capitalist mode of production incorporates the workers and the owners in different and contradictory ways. These groups, which he called *classes*, have different interests, and what is good for one class may not be good for all classes. Capitalists own the means of production (tools, knowledge, etc.) as private property. For this reason, nonowners cannot help themselves to whatever they need to produce—say, their own food and clothing. Instead, they are forced to sell their labor power to the owner of the means of production. Their labor and the owner's resources will together produce the material goods necessary for survival. Those goods belong to the capitalist, who pays the workers wages for their labor. The workers must then use their wages to purchase the goods they need in the market. In such a situation, the desires of workers (for higher wages with which to purchase more goods) are inevitably opposed to the desires of owners (for lower wages to increase the profit they can keep for themselves or reinvest in tools and raw materials).

The interests of workers and the interests of owners in the capitalist mode of production are frequently opposed. This opposition sometimes results in strikes.

This is not to say that warfare is constant between the different classes engaged in a particular mode of production. It is to say, however, that the potential for conflict is built into the mode of production itself. The more complex and unequal the involvement of different classes in a mode of production, the more intense the struggle between them is likely to be. Such struggle may not always lead to outright rebellion for sound political reasons, as we saw in chapter 12. But we should not be surprised to find the "everyday forms of peasant resistance" that Scott discusses in his analysis of life in Sedaka. When viewed from a marxian perspective, such struggles are clearly not just "healthy competition." Marx was one of the first social analysts, and certainly one of the most eloquent, to document the high level of human suffering generated by certain modes of production, particularly the capitalist mode.

If you look again at Eric Wolf's three modes of production, you will see that the description of each one tells you more than just what a society's subsistence strategy is. It also tells you how people in that society organize themselves to carry out that subsistence strategy. And it accents the lines of cleavage along which tension and conflict may develop—or may have developed historically—between different segments of the society.

Applying Production Theory to Social and Cultural Life

Economic anthropologists who focus on production as the primal causative force in material life tend to apply the metaphor of production to other areas of social life as well. Production is seen as involving far more than short-term satisfaction of material survival needs. If a given *mode* of production is to persist over time, the *means* and *relations* of production must also be made to persist.

The relations of production of one generation are reproduced in the next generation. Here, a young Otavalan learns how to weave from his uncle. He also learns that an older weaver needs a young assistant to do the preparation.

For example, farmers produce grain and leave behind harvested fields. They exchange some grain with cattle herders for milk and meat, and they permit the herders' cattle to graze in the harvested fields in exchange for the manure (a natural fertilizer) that the cattle deposit. As a result, farmers and herders alike end up with a mix of foodstuffs to sustain human life (i.e., to reproduce the producers). In addition, each group has what it needs to renew, in the coming season, its means of production. Both groups will want to make sure that similar kinds of exchanges can be carried out by their children. That is, a way must be found to make sure that the next generation will consist of farmers and cattle herders producing the same goods, and willing to exchange those goods with one another in the same fashion. Therefore, not only the means of production itself must be perpetuated, but the relations of production as well. The result, then, is the reproduction of society from generation to generation, as means of production and relations of production are reproduced.

People also produce and reproduce *interpretations* of the productive process and their roles in that process. Marx used the term **ideology** to refer to the products of conscious reflection, such as morality, religion, or metaphysics. As used in marxian analysis, ideology refers in particular to the parts of a world view that explain and justify the relations of production to those who engage in them. For Marx, ideology was not independent of the productive process itself. On the contrary, "men, developing their material production and their material intercourse, alter, along with this their real existence, their thinking and the products of their thinking. Life is not determined by consciousness, but consciousness by life" (Marx 1932:164). As a result, marxian economic anthropologists investigate the kinds of ideas, beliefs, and values that are produced and reproduced in societies with different modes of production. As we saw in chapter 12, the class in power usually holds to an ideology that justifies their dominance. Those who are dominated may assent publicly to the ide-

ideology
products of consciousness, such as morality, religion, and metaphysics, that purport to explain to people who they are and to justify to them the kind of lives they lead

ology of the rulers, but in private they are likely to be highly critical, and to offer alternative interpretations.

Use of the production metaphor in the analysis of social and cultural life has yielded some important results in anthropology. First, it highlights certain processes and relationships that the exchange metaphor tends to downplay or ignore. For example, exchange theorists are not apt to care why the different parties to an exchange have different quantities of resources with which to bargain. Production theorists, by contrast, are interested precisely in this issue. They aim to show that access to resources is determined *before* to exchange by the relations of production, which decide who is entitled to how much of what. In particular, they reject as naive the assumption that access to valued resources is open to anyone with gumption and the spirit of enterprise. Different modes of production stack the deck in favor of some classes of people, to the detriment of other classes. This is most clear in the capitalist mode, where owners have disproportionate access to wealth, power, and prestige, and where the access of workers to these goods is sharply restricted. Thus, the classes who fare poorly do so not because of any inherent inferiority, laziness, or improvidence. They fail to get ahead because the rules of the game (i.e., of the mode of production) were set up in a way that keeps them from winning.

In the second place, a production metaphor provides an especially dynamic perspective on cultural persistence and cultural change. Production theory relates peoples' preferences for different goods to the interests and opportunities of the different classes to which they belong. People buy and sell as they do not out of idiosyncratic whimsy, but because the choices open to them are shaped by the relations of production. From this perspective, poor people do not purchase cheap goods because they have poor taste and cannot recognize quality when they see it. Rather, their deprived position within the mode of production provides them with very limited income, and they must make do with the only goods they can afford, however shoddy.

Finally, production theory focuses on *people* as much as or more than it focuses on the *goods* people produce. It views human beings as social agents involved in the construction and reconstruction of human society on all levels in every generation. Traditions persist, but only because people labor to reproduce them from one day to the next. To speak of the production (and reproduction) of goods, social relations, and ideologies highlights the contingent nature of social life, even as it suggests how traditions are carried on.

Consumption Theory

Consumption is usually understood to refer to the using up of material goods necessary for human physical survival. These goods includes food, drink, clothing, and shelter, at a minimum; they can and often do include much more. Anthropologists have taken one of three approaches to the study of consumption: the internal explanation, the external explanation, and the cultural explanation.

The Internal Explanation: Malinowski and Basic Human Needs

The *internal explanation* for human consumption patterns comes from the work of Bronislaw Malinowski. Malinowski's version of functionalist anthropology explained social practices by relating them to the basic human needs that each practice supposedly functioned to fulfill. Basic human needs might be biological or psychological, and if they went unmet, the society might not survive. In Malinowski's view, for example, all societies had economic institutions concerned with production, distribution, and consumption of material goods. This was because all people everywhere shared the basic human needs for food, clothing, shelter, tools, and so on. Malinowski proposed a list of basic human needs, which included such matters as metabolism, reproduction, bodily comforts, safety, movement, growth, and health. Every culture responds in its own way to these needs with some form of the corresponding institutions: commisariat, kinship, shelter, protection, activities, training, and hygiene (Malinowski 1944:91).

Malinowski's approach had the virtue of emphasizing the dependency of human beings on the natural world in order to survive. In addition, Malinowski was able to show that many alien customs that appeared bizarre to uninitiated Western observers were in fact "rational." He did this by explaining how those customs helped the people practicing them to satisfy their basic human needs. However, Malinowski's approach fell short of explaining why all societies did not share the same consumption patterns. After all, some people ate wild fruit and nuts and wore clothing made of animal skins, while others ate bread made from domesticated wheat and wore garments woven from the hair of domesticated sheep, and still others ate millet paste and meat from domesticated cattle and went naked. Why should these differences exist?

The External Explanation: Cultural Ecology and Ecological Determinism

A later generation of anthropologists were influenced by evolutionary and ecological studies. They provided an *external explanation* for the diversity of human consumption patterns.

The Role of Ecology

ecology
the study of the ways in which living species relate to one another and to their natural environment

niche
the portion of the natural world on which a species depends for the satisfaction of its material needs

ecozone
the particular mix of plant and animal species occupying any particular region of the earth

Ecology has to do with the ways living species relate to one another and to their natural environment. To survive in the long run, a species must find for itself some portion of the natural world on which it can depend for satisfaction of its material needs. Ecologists refer to this as the species' **niche**. Each species must share the material world with many other species. Moreover, the mix of plant and animal species occupying any particular region of the earth, or **ecozone**, varies from one part of the world to the other. A species adapts to the ecozone in which it finds itself when it is able to find a niche that allows it to sustain life. But potential *econiches* must be contructed to make use of the particular mix of resources, living and nonliving, available in the ecozone. Such resources include edible plants and animals, water, climate, and so forth.

The Cultural Ecology Approach

Cultural ecology is an anthropological attempt to apply the insights of ecology to human beings and their societies. For cultural ecologists, human consumption patterns (as well as human patterns of production and distribution) derive from features of the ecozones in which human populations live. Every human group must learn to make use of the resources available in its ecozone if it is to survive. Hence, the particular consumption patterns found in a particular society do not depend on the obvious, internal hunger drive, which is the same for all people everywhere. Rather, consumption patterns depend on the particular external resources present in the ecozone to which a society must adapt.

One anthropologist who has relied on ecological arguments to explain human consumption patterns is Marvin Harris. Among other things, Harris has been interested in explaining dietary prohibitions found in various cultures. In a well-known article published in 1965, Harris argued that the "sacred cow" of Hindu society was forbidden as food primarily because it made better ecological sense as a draft animal. In his view, the religious prohibition merely emphasized an ecologically sound consumption practice.

Harris also attempted to explain the prohibition of pork by Jews and Muslims with reference to the ecological requirements for successful animal husbandry in the Middle East. He argues that "pig farming was a threat to the integrity of the basic cultural and natural ecosystems of the Middle East" (Harris 1974:40ff.). In his view, the Middle East is too hot and dry to support pigs, which are "creatures of the forests and shaded riverbanks." Pigs thrive on grains and so compete with human beings for food; they are a poor milk source; and they are difficult to herd over long distances. Harris concedes that the taboo on pork is observed in some Muslim areas that are well watered and where pig raising might be successful. But he says this is because the taboo is used either for marking off Muslims from non-Muslims (and Jews from non-Jews) or for moral instruction among the faithful, teaching them how to avoid the temptation to indulge in a succulent treat.

These last concessions weaken Harris's ecological thesis. If it were ecologically unsound to raise pigs in the Middle East, surely no taboo would be necessary to keep people from raising them. And if the taboo is important in *some* parts of the Muslim world as a way of marking social distinctions, why might this not be the case in all parts? Harris's critics agree that pigs might suffer in a hot dry climate. They point out, however, that pigs can thrive in such a climate if they are provided with a bit of shade and some mud in which to wallow. In addition, archaeological evidence suggests that pigs were important economically and symbolically in some parts of ancient Egypt, before the rise of Islam. They were raised successfully in precisely the ecozones in which they are now prohibited. Finally, although pigs thrive on grain, they are better known in most parts of the world as "living garbage cans." They will consume even human and animal excrement, and turn it into meat. Their own feces fertilize the fields of their owners, and their grubbing for roots in those same fields breaks up the soil. For all these reasons, pigs are highly valued. Moreover, some Mayan groups in Mexico herd pigs over seventy miles regularly and successfully, with the help of dogs, a practice that was also known in ancient times in the Old World. Other Mayan groups find it difficult to raise pigs themselves, but they have not tabooed pork and will eat it when they can (Deiner and Robkin 1978:498). Clearly, dietary preferences and prohibitions cannot easily be reduced to ecological imperatives.

The work of Harris, and others like him, can be valuable when it demonstrates the rationale behind consumption patterns that seem to be irrational from a Western perspective. However, some cultural ecologists tend to assume that because some consumption patterns make good ecological sense, all cultural patterns are determined by the imperatives of ecology.

Anthropology is certainly dedicated to the proposition that human social life is patterned. Anthropologists also recognize that patterns in one domain of life tend to be consistent with patterns in other domains. In addition, anthropology has always held that a group's culture must manage to provide its members with the minimal wherewithal for physical and social survival. Were this not the case, the culture would change or the group would disappear. If Harris were claiming no more than this, his work would not be so controversial. But Harris's critics question whether the evidence is strong enough to support his much more ambitious claims, which are clearly deterministic. Many believe that it is not.

Why do people X raise peanuts and sorghum? The internal, Malinowskian explanation would be "To meet their basic human need for food." The external, ecological explanation would be "Because peanuts and sorghum are the only food crops available in their ecozone that, when cultivated, will meet their subsistence needs." Both these answers are suggestive, but they are also incomplete. To be sure, people must consume something to survive, and they will usually meet this need for food by exploiting plant and animal species locally available to them. This much seems only common sense. However, we might ask whether the local food sources that people X choose to exploit are the *only* food sources locally available to them. The data of ethnography show that no society exploits every locally available food source to meet its consumption needs. Quite the contrary, consumption "needs" are selective; in other words, they are culturally shaped.

The Cultural Patterning of Consumption ▇▇▇▇

A major shortcoming of both internal and external explanations for human consumption patterns is that they ignore or deny the possibility of choice. Malinowski and many cultural ecologists seem to assume that patterns of consumption are dictated by an iron environmental necessity that does not allow alternatives. From such a perspective, choice of diet is a luxury that non-Western, "primitive" societies cannot afford. Yet to rob non-Western peoples of choice is to dehumanize them.

Marshall Sahlins urges anthropologists to pay close attention to consumption, since consumption choices reveal what it means to be a human being. Human beings are *human*, he tells us, "precisely when they experience the world as a concept (symbolically). It is not essentially a question of priority but of the unique quality of human experience as meaningful experience. Nor is it an issue of the reality of the world; it concerns *which worldly dimension becomes pertinent*, and in what way, to a given human group" (Sahlins 1976a: 142; emphasis added).

The Original Affluent Society

Many in the Western world have long believed that foraging peoples lead the most miserable of existences. The assumption was that such people spent all their waking hours in a food quest that yielded barely enough to keep them alive. To test this assumption in the field, Richard Lee went to live among the Dobe !Kung, a foraging people of southern Africa. *(See EthnoFile 9.1: !Kung.)* As we saw at the beginning of this chapter, he accompanied his informants as they gathered and hunted, and he recorded the amounts and kinds of food they consumed.

The results of Lee's research were surprising. It turned out that the !Kung managed to provide themselves with a varied and well-balanced diet based on a *selection* from among the food sources available in their environment; the !Kung classify more than one hundred species of plants as edible, but only fourteen are primary or major (Lee 1984:40). Some 70 percent of this diet consisted of vegetable foods; 30 percent was meat. Mongongo nuts, a protein-rich food source widely available throughout the desert environment inhabited by the !Kung, alone made up more than one-quarter of the diet. Women provided about 55 percent of the diet, and men provided 45 percent, including the meat. The !Kung spent an average of 2.4 working days—or about twenty hours—per person per week in food-collecting activities. !Kung bands periodically suffered from shortages of their preferred foods

Two !Kung families go hunting and gathering.

and were forced to resort to less desired items. Most of the time, however, their diet was balanced and adequate, and consisted of foods of preference (ibid.: 51ff.).

Marshall Sahlins coined the expression "the original affluent society" to refer to the !Kung and other foragers like them. In an article published in 1973, Sahlins challenged the traditional Western assumption that the life of foragers was characterized by scarcity and near-starvation. **Affluence**, he argued, is having more than enough of whatever is required to satisfy consumption needs.

There are two ways to create affluence. One way is to *produce much*, which is the path taken by Western capitalist society. This is necessary because the underlying assumption of capitalism is constant scarcity—people will always want to consume more of everything than there is to go around. The second road to affluence is to *desire little*. This, Sahlins argues, is the option that foragers have taken. Their wants are few, but they are abundantly supplied by nature. Moreover, foragers have not suppressed their natural greed; rather, their society has simply not institutionalized greed or rewarded the greedy. As a result, foragers cannot be considered "poor," even though their material standard of living is low by Western standards. Poverty is not an absolute condition, nor is it a relationship between means and ends; it is a relationship between people. Because the consumption goals, or ends, of foragers are modest, their environment is more than able to satisfy those goals.

affluence
the condition of having more than enough of whatever is required to satisfy consumption needs

The Cultural Construction of Needs

The original affluent society of the !Kung reinforces the insight that "needs" by themselves are vague. Hunger can be satisfied by beans and rice or steak and lobster. Thirst can be quenched by water or beer or soda pop. In effect, culture defines needs and provides for their satisfaction according to its own logic. And cultural logic is reducible neither to biology nor to psychology nor to ecological pressure.

If we adopt this cultural approach to consumption, one of the first things that happens is that the distinctions between "needs" and "wants," or "necessities" and "luxuries" disappear. Mary Douglas and Baron Isherwood urge us to "put an end to the widespread and misleading distinction between goods that sustain life and health and others that service the mind and heart—spiritual goods. . . . The counterargument proposed here is that all goods carry meaning, but none by itself. . . . The meaning is in the relations between all the goods, just as music is in the relations marked out by the sounds and not in any one note" (Douglas and Isherwood 1979:72–73). For instance, a consumption item's meaning may have to do with its edibility, but this will always be a culturally appropriate edibility. Furthermore, the meaning of any individual item of food cannot be explained in isolation. That meaning only becomes clear when the item is compared with other consumption items that are also marked in terms of culturally appropriate edibility or inedibility.

The Abominations of Leviticus

Consider once again the prohibition against eating the flesh of pigs. For Jews and Muslims, pork is "inedible," culturally speaking. According to Mary Douglas (1966), this has nothing to do with ecological problems associated with pig-raising in the Middle East, nor has it anything to do with any defects in the digestive systems of Jews or Muslims. Douglas has analyzed the Jewish dietary prohibitions detailed in the Biblical Book of Leviticus. She argues that certain animals were prohibited as food because something about them violated the prototypes for edibility recognized in ancient Hebrew culture. Prototypically "clean" land animals were supposed to have four legs and cloven hooves and to chew the cud; pigs were an "abomination" because they were four-legged, cloven-hoofed beasts who did *not* chew the cud. "Clean" beasts of the air were supposed to have feathers and to fly with wings; therefore, hopping insects were "unclean" because they had six legs, neither walked nor flew, and lacked feathers. "Clean" water animals were supposed to have fins and scales; shrimp were forbidden because, although they lived in the sea, they lacked fins and scales (see table 13.1).

By itself, Douglas argues, a prohibition against eating pork is meaningless and appears to be irrational. However, when the Jewish prohibition against pork is taken together with other Jewish dietary prohibitions, and when these are compared with the foods that were permitted, the cultural pattern becomes clear. Douglas writes, "Goods assembled together in ownership make physical, visible statements about the hierarchy of values to which their chooser subscribes" (Douglas and Isherwood 1979:5). Thus, Jews who shop carefully and purchase only clean foods that meet the ritual requirements laid down by their tradition are doing more than procuring the means to satisfy their hunger. They are also making a social declaration of solidarity with Orthodox Judaism, and the care with which they adhere to the dietary laws is a measure of their commitment. Their need for food is being met, but selectively, and the selection they make carries a social message.

Dietary laws deal with food and drink, and so might still be explained in biological or ecological terms. In fact, many attempts have been made to rationalize the dietary laws in the Bible in terms of hygiene, and we have seen what Marvin Harris has to say about pork prohibition. Such rationalizations are more difficult to construct, however, when we consider the role of banana leaves in the Trobriand Islands.

Table 13.1
Jewish Dietary Prohibitions

	Class Prototype	Clean Examples	Unclean Examples	Reason Prohibited
Earth	Four-legged animals that hop, jump, or walk (i.e., cloven-hoofed, cud-chewing ungulates)	Cattle, camels, sheep, goats, frogs	Hare, hyrax	Held to be cud chewing, but not cloven hoofed
			Pig	Cloven hoofed but not cud chewing
			Weasel, mouse, crocodile, shrew, chameleon, mole	Two legs, two hands, but go about on all fours
Waters	Scaly fish that swim with fins	Carp, whitefish	Shrimp, clams	Possess neither fins nor scales, but live in water
Air	Two-legged fowl that fly with wings	Chicken		

Source: Based on Mary Douglas, *Purity and Danger* (London: Routledge & Kegan Paul, 1966), pp. 41–57.

Banana Leaves in the Trobriand Islands

Anthropologist Annette Weiner returned to Malinowski's original field site in the Trobriand Islands more than half a century after Malinowski carried out his classic research. *(See EthnoFile 5.2: Trobriand Islanders.)* To her surprise, she discovered a venerable local tradition involving accumulation and exchange of banana leaves. Malinowski had never described this tradition, even though there is evidence from photographs and writing that it was in force at the time of his fieldwork. There are probably at least two reasons why Malinowski overlooked these transactions. First, they are carried out by women (and the banana leaf bundles are known as "women's wealth"). Second, banana leaves would be an unlikely item of consumption, given Malinowski's tendency to label as "economic" only activities that satisfied biological survival needs. After all, you can't eat banana leaves. However, explaining transactions involving women's wealth turns out to be crucial for understanding Trobriand kinship obligations.

Banana leaves might be said to have a "practical" use in that women make skirts out of them. These skirts are highly valued objects, but the transactions involving women's wealth more often involve bundles of the leaves themselves. Why bother to exchange great amounts of money or other goods to obtain bundles of banana leaves? This would seem to be a classic example of irrational consumption. And yet, as Weiner demonstrates, banana bundles play exactly the role Mary Douglas has suggested that consumption goods play in society: "As an economic, political, and social force, women's wealth exists as the representation of the most fundamental relationships in the social system" (Weiner 1980:289).

Trobrianders are matrilineal, and men traditionally prepared yam gardens for their sisters. After the harvest, yams from these gardens would be distributed by a woman's brother to her husband and his male relatives. Weiner's research suggested that what Malinowski took to be the *redistribution* of yams, from a wife's kin to her husband, could be better understood as a *reciprocal exchange* of yams for women's wealth. The parties central to this exchange are a woman, her brother, and her husband. The woman is the person through whom yams are passed from her own kin to her husband, and also the person through whom women's wealth is passed from her husband to her own kin.

Transactions involving women's wealth occur when someone in the woman's kinship group dies. Surviving relatives must "buy back," metaphorically speaking, all the yams and other goods that the deceased person gave out to others during his or her lifetime. Each payment marks a social link between the deceased and the recipient, and the size of the payment marks the importance of their relationship. All the payments must be made in women's wealth.

The dead person's status, as well as the status of her or his family, depends on the size and number of the payments made, and the people who must be paid can number into the hundreds. Women of the matrilineage collect women's wealth from their husbands, and their own value is measured by the amount of women's wealth their husbands provide. Furthermore, "if a man does not work hard enough for his wife in accumulating wealth for her, then her brother will not increase his labor in the yam garden. . . . The production in yams and women's wealth is always being evaluated and calculated in terms of effort and energy expended on both sides of production. The value of a husband is read by a woman's kin as the value of his productive support in securing women's wealth for his wife" (ibid.: 282).

Weiner argues that women's wealth upholds the kinship arrangements of Trobriand society. It balances out exchange relationships between lineages linked by marriage, reinforces the pivotal role of women and matriliny, and publicly proclaims, during every funeral, the social relationships that make up the fabric of Trobriand society. The system has been stable for generations, but Weiner suggests that it could collapse if cash ever became widely substitutable for yams. Under such conditions, men might buy food and other items on the market, would no longer be dependent on yams from their wives' kin, and could therefore refuse to supply their wives' kin with women's wealth. This had not yet happened at the time of Weiner's research, but it could not be ruled out as a possible future development.

The Cultural Construction of Utility

The preceding examples have been approached from the perspective of consumption, but they have much in common with theories of social exchange, discussed earlier. Social exchange theorists argue that people exchange material goods for esteem or for power: I give you food to eat, and in return, at some later date, you will accord me honor or will support me politically. Social exchange theory argues that these trade-offs are motivated by the desire of individuals to maximize their "utility"—that is, their personal satisfaction or pleasure. But just as culture shapes needs, so it also offers standardized ways of satisfying those needs. No social exchange can occur unless the parties to that exchange are able to assess the value of the items to be exchanged. Because of the openness of culture and the ambiguity inherent in many social situations, values and exchange rates may well be bargained over. Such exchanges ultimately rest on cultural principles for assessing value and fairness.

Once consumption is defined as the use of goods and services to communicate cultural values, a new understanding of wealth and poverty is possible. We have noted Sahlins's comment that foragers with simple needs and ample means of satisfying those needs were affluent—rich, not poor. Douglas and Isherwood also refuse to use the sheer amount of material possessions as a universal measure of wealth or poverty. They write: "Many of the countries that anthropologists study are poor on such material criteria—no wall-to-wall carpets, no air conditioning—but they do not regard themselves as poor. The Nuer of the Sudan in the 1930s would not trade with the Arabs because the only things they had to sell were their herds of cattle, and the only things they could possibly want from trade were more cattle" (Douglas and Isherwood 1979:17–18). *(See EthnoFile 9.2: Nuer.)* Cattle mattered to the Nuer as much for their use as markers of social relations as for their use as food. To have few or no cattle did constitute poverty for the Nuer—as much for the lack of social relationships it indicated as for the lack of food. "To be rich means to be well integrated in a rich community. . . . To be poor is to be isolated" (ibid.: 160).

Institutionalized Sharing

Capitalism not only generates individual fortunes, it depends on them as sources of funds sufficiently great to sustain large private business enterprises. Capitalist societies have passed laws and created social institutions that reward individuals for accumulating wealth. In noncapitalist societies economic patterns are often designed to prevent individual accumulation. Rather, the goal is to spread any wealth that exists throughout the community. This pattern is called *institutionalized sharing*.

People accustomed to capitalist practices are often either incredulous or cynical when it is suggested that insitutionalized sharing can be the backbone of economic life. They assume that such widespread "generosity" can only be expected of saintly altruists, not of ordinary human beings. Yet, people in societies with institutionalized sharing are not saints who never experience greed, any more than people in capitalist societies are devils who never experience compassion. Both societies, however, make it difficult to get away publicly with practices that undercut established social arrangements.

A pattern of institutionalized sharing can be found among the Plains Cree of North America, studied by Niels Braroe (1975:143ff.). *(See EthnoFile 13.2: Cree.)* In the past, the Cree were bison hunters living in bands. Each band had a leader who provided his followers with the materials necessary for hunting. This leader was the focus of a redistributive mode of exchange, and generosity in redistribution qualified him to be band leader. Today, bison are no longer hunted, but the institutionalized sharing of consumption items such as food, clothing, beer, or cigarettes continues. For example, Braroe tells us that "it is not considered improper, as it is among Whites, to ask for someone's last cigarette; to refuse a request, however, is frowned upon" (ibid.: 145). Generosity is further reinforced in ceremonies known as "giveaway dances." The central event in those ceremonies is dancing around the room giving away such material goods as clothing to other guests. Dancers aim to give away more than they receive. Indeed, a good way to insult someone is to shower him or her with gifts in the course of such an event.

EthnoFile 13.2
CREE (Short Grass Reserve)

Region: North America

Nation: Southwestern Canada

Population: About 100

Environment: 3,040 acres of rocky soil and dense aspen brush

Livelihood: Monthly inadequate relief payments; manufacture and sale of fenceposts; casual ranch work

Political organization: Consensus of adult males announced by chief

Other: Cattle ranching is possible but there is not sufficient land to make it viable

The Cree ideal is that generosity should be spontaneous, and that contempt for material goods should be genuine. Nevertheless, Braroe's informants sometimes possessed consumption goods or money that they clearly wanted to keep for themselves. Individuals could enjoy such goods in private, but only if their existence were kept a secret. Men sometimes hid beer to avoid having to share it with others. A woman informant once asked Braroe's wife to keep a sizable amount of cash for her, so others would not know she had it and demand some. The rule seemed to be that "any visible resource may legitimately be requested by another" (ibid.: 146), and Braroe reports that direct refusals of such requests were rare.

For the Cree, institutionalized sharing following a redistributive mode ensured that consumption goods would not be hoarded, but spread out and enjoyed by all in the band. This consumption pattern clashes with that of the capitalist, who views accumulation and consumption by individuals in a positive light. Some individual Cree have earned money in the white world and have tried to save it, in order to "get ahead" (according to white standards). Those people are considered stingy by Cree standards and are resented; they cannot hope to gain a position of leadership in the band.

The Cultural Construction of the American Diet

American society is capitalist through and through. Surely it must possess an economy that is more tied to material forces than the economies of Trobriand Islanders or the Plains Cree. After all, capitalism prides itself on its hardheaded realism, its absence of sentiment, and its concern with the bottom line. Surely there is no room in a capitalist society for tastes and preferences that do not maximize efficiency and minimize waste.

Marshall Sahlins disagrees (1976a: 171ff.). He argues that the cultural pattern that shapes American dietary preferences is powerful enough to influence the world markets in foodstuffs. He further claims that Americans, like people in other societies, use dietary preferences to mark social similarities and differences.

Sahlins notes that "the exploitation of the American environment is organized by specific valuations of edibility and inedibility, themselves qualitative and in no way justifiable by biological, ecological, or economic advantage" (Sahlins 1976a: 171). Although we eat both meat and vegetables, meat is more highly valued than vegetables, and in fact is the centerpiece of the prototypical American meal.

Moreover, we do not rate all meats equally highly. Some cuts of meat that we could consume for high-quality protein we mark as inedible. Beefsteak is the prototypical American meat; it carries with it the connotation of manliness and strength. Pork is also edible, but less prestigious than beef. The meat of other domesticated animals—sheep, goats, rabbits, horses, dogs—are eaten in other parts of the world. In America, it either plays an insignificant role in the diet (e.g., the meat of sheep, goats, rabbits) or is considered unfit for human consumption (e.g., the meat of horses and dogs). Sahlins comments: "Surely it must be practicable to raise *some* horses and dogs for food in combination with pigs and cattle. There is even an enormous industry for raising horses as food for dogs. But then, America is the land of the sacred dog" (ibid.: 171).

Cattle, pigs, horses, and dogs are four important groups of domesticated animals in North America. But the meaning of any one animal cannot be understood apart from the meanings carried by the entire set. These four animal categories, Sahlins argues, can be classified as edible (cattle and pigs) or inedible (horses and dogs). Furthermore, in the edible class, beef is more preferred than pork, and in the inedible class, dogs are more strongly prohibited than horses (see figure 13.3).

A pattern begins to emerge. Sahlins suggests that the split between edible and inedible marks a split in the kind of social relationships that Americans traditionally cultivate with animals. Inedible horses and dogs are prototypical American "pets," and we usually treat them as honorary members of the human family. Edible cattle and pigs, however, are "livestock," who live apart from human beings and are not treated as members of the family. But our classification system does not stop here. Even when we consider edible animals, we differentiate between the outer muscles, or "meat," and the internal viscera, or "innards." As Sahlins points out, meat is more highly valued than innards. In fact, he suggests, one might read the entire system of classifications as "a sustained metaphor on cannibalism" (ibid.: 174). That is, Americans interpret animals' bodies as if they were human bodies. We believe that our inner selves are our "true" selves. Thus, we avoid eating the part of an animal's body that corresponds to the highly valued center of our own bodies. We also avoid eating any part of animals who live in close, quasi-human association with us.

These symbolic associations, Sahlins argues, can account for the higher value we put on steak than on, say, tongue. If price were dictated by supply, the reverse should be the case, since a cow yields more steak than tongue. As Sahlins says, "From the nutritional point of view, such a notion of 'better' and 'inferior' cuts would be difficult to defend" (ibid.: 176). But such categories are most appro-

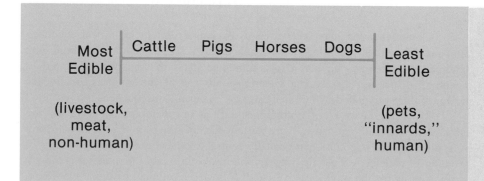

FIGURE 13.3
Edible and Inedible Domestic Animals in the United States

priate for classifying the various subgroups of American society. "Better" cuts of meat are expensive; "inferior" cuts are cheap. It follows from this that the "better" sort of people are the only ones who can afford the "better" foods. Those who must eat "inferior" foods demonstrate by so doing that they are indeed inferior. Eating organ meats is metaphorically interpreted as a form of cannibalism. According to this cultural logic, furthermore, those who eat both the innards of permitted beasts and the flesh of prohibited ones must be even more depraved.

"Proper" middle-class Americans have always been disturbed by the French practice of eating horsemeat. Emily Schultz recalls being fed a "steak" that didn't quite taste like steak when she was a guest in a French home. When she asked after the meal what sort of meat had been served, her hosts told her it was horse. They knew that Americans had certain prejudices regarding horsemeat, so they had waited until after the meal to break the truth. Similarly, many Americans were horrified to read in the newspapers that some groups of Southeast Asian refugees were said to eat dogs. This practice seemed to symbolize the "uncivilized" character of the new group of people with unfamiliar customs who were now living in their midst.

A Dialectic between the Meaningful and the Material

Production, distribution, and consumption are constant and coexisting aspects of human economic activity. Each phase can be used as a metonym representing the entire process. Entire modes of livelihood can be erected on such metonyms: witness capitalist society, a monument to the proposition that exchange is—and should be—everything. Yet each phase of economic activity shapes the others and ultimately cannot be separated from them.

Anthropologist Claude Lévi-Strauss was impressed with the way a focus on exchange helped him make sense of human cultural patterns. Lévi-Strauss saw people exchanging goods, but when he looked at kinship he saw people exchanging people, and when he looked at language he saw them exchanging signs. Yet what does it mean to "exchange signs"? Exchange seems to be rooted in hardheaded economics, so what can we make of "items" exchanged that "speak" of the values they represent?

Communication may be viewed as exchange, but metaphorical equations can be read in either direction. Thus exchange may be read as communication, with hardheaded economics having to accommodate itself to whatever is viewed as meaningful. It is not merely that material goods can be meaningful; equally, the meaningful (as stipulated by culture) can have material consequences.

Moreover, if we take "communication" as our metaphorical predicate, we can note that verbal "exchanges" are rarely problem-free in human society. Moreover, dialogue and negotiation are equally central to other "exchanges," be these of goods or of people. A dialectic between the meaningful and the material is the underlying basis for the modes of livelihood followed by human beings everywhere.

Key Terms

scarcity	exchange	market exchange
economy	neoclassical economic theory	social exchange
subsistence strategies	formalists	labor
food collectors	rational	mode of production
food producers	substantivists	means of production
extensive agriculture	modes of exchange	relations of production
intensive agriculture	generalized reciprocity	ecology
production	balanced reciprocity	niche
distribution	negative reciprocity	ecozone
consumption	redistribution	affluence

Chapter Summary

1. Survival requires that people make use of the natural resources in the wider world, and yet our culture tells us which resources to use, and in what way. Human beings have devised a variety of subsistence strategies to satisfy their material survival needs. The basic division is between food collectors and food producers. Farmers may practice extensive or intensive agriculture; in industrialized societies, food production becomes mechanized.

2. Human economic activity is usefully divided into three phases: *production, distribution,* and *consumption.* In capitalist societies, market exchange is the dominant mode of distribution, but most non-Western societies traditionally have carried out distribution without money or markets. Some economic anthropologists claim that exchange determines the nature of production and consumption. Others argue that production determines the nature of exchange and consumption. Still others are persuaded that culturally shaped consumption standards determine patterns of production and exchange. Ultimately, a holistic perspective requires that patterns of production, distribution, and consumption be viewed as codetermining one another.

3. Formal neoclassical economic theory developed in an attempt to explain how capitalism worked. Formalist economic anthropologists apply the market model to local activities in non-Western societies that bear a family resemblance to "economics" in Western societies. Their analyses involve translating the transactions of material life in the local society into the language of neoclassical theory.

4. Formalists assume that non-Western actors are as rational in their economic choices as Western actors would be. But since they define *rationality* in capitalist terms as the maximization of individual self-interest, anyone who does not maximize self-interest risks being labeled irrational. *Substantivists* pointed out that members of non-Western societies often passed up opportunities to maximize their own self-interest for the sake of honor, and they argued that it was ethnocentric to consider such action as irrational.

5. Substantivists have distinguished three major modes of exchange in human societies: *reciprocity, redistribution,* and *market exchange.* Reciprocity may be generalized, balanced, or negative. In the substantivists' view, market exchange is a recent invention of capitalist societies. All modes of exchange must be examined in the social and cultural context in which they are embedded.

6. *Social exchange theorists* responded to the substantivists by arguing that nonmaterial goods, such as honor, could be exchanged in the market for material goods, since such goods were equally scarce. Thus, members of non-Western societies who preferred honor to wealth could still be viewed as "rational," given the rules by which exchange operated in their culture.

7. Marxian economic anthropologists view *production* as more important than exchange in determining the patterns of economic life in a society. They argue that societies can be classified in terms of their *modes of production*. Each mode of production contains within it the potential for conflict between classes of people who receive differential benefits and losses from the productive process.

8. Economic anthropologists inspired by neoclassical economic theory tend to see the world as a capitalist market, applying the exchange metaphor to all social transactions. Marxian economic anthropologists similarly apply a production metaphor to aspects of society other than material production. Each metaphor highlights certain processes and relationships that the other tends to downplay or ignore.

9. The internal explanation for *consumption* patterns argues that people produce material goods to satisfy a basic human need for food, clothing, shelter, and so on. The external explanation argues that consumption patterns depend not on the hunger drive, which is the same for everyone, but on the particular external resources available within the *ecozone* to which the society in question must adapt.

10. *Ecological* arguments have value when they can demonstrate that consumption patterns that seem to be irrational from a Western perspective do make sense when placed in the ecological context of the society that follows them. Ecological arguments lose plausibility when they claim to be able to explain all cultural patterns as ecologically sound adaptations.

11. Ethnographic evidence demonstrates that both internal and external explanations for consumption patterns are inadequate because they ignore or deny openness in the selection by people of objects to meet survival needs. Culture defines our needs and provides for their satisfaction according to its own logic—a logic that is reducible neither to biology nor to psychology nor to ecological pressure. In fact, the distinction between necessities and luxuries is no longer plausible.

12. Particular consumption preferences that may seem "irrational" when considered in isolation tend to make sense when considered in the context of other consumption preferences and prohibitions in the same culture. The Jewish prohibition against pork consumption makes sense when considered together with other Jewish dietary rules. The accumulation of banana leaves in the Trobriand Islands seems bizarre until it is placed in the context of Trobriand kinship and economic arrangements. Institutionalized sharing among the Plains Cree appears wasteful and spendthrift to Whites who are committed to individual accumulation and advancement. In the context of Cree history and traditional social arrangements, however, it is a coherent pattern for evening out consumption possibilities within the group.

13. Even middle-class white Americans, who are committed to economic "rationality" and efficiency, exhibit "irrational"—that is, culturally motivated—consumption patterns in their prototypical diets.

Suggested Readings

Douglas, Mary, and Baron Isherwood. *The World of Goods: Towards an Anthropology of Comsumption*. New York: W.W. Norton, 1979.

A discussion of consumption, economic theories about consumption, and what anthropologists can contribute to the study of consumption.

Harris, Marvin. *Good to Eat*. New York: Harper and Row, 1986.
This is a recent collection of Harris' essays. This time: a materialist analysis of why people eat the things they do.

Lee, Richard. *The Dobe !Kung*. New York: Holt, Rinehart and Winston, 1984.
This highly readable ethnography contains important discussions about hunting and gathering as a way of making a living.

Sahlins, Marshall. *Stone Age Economics*. Chicago: Aldine, 1972.
A series of important, well-written essays on economic life, written from a more substantivist position. Includes "The Original Affluent Society."

Schneider, Harold. *Economic Man*. New York: Free Press, 1974.
A formalist essay on the nature of human economic life. Discusses social exchange theory.

For an Uncertain Anthropology

Don Handelman *(Ph.D., University of Manchester) is Professor of Anthropology at the Hebrew University of Jerusalem. He has conducted fieldwork in Quebec, Newfoundland, Nevada, Israel, and at the 1984 Olympic Games in Los Angeles. He has written extensively on play, ritual, work, and cosmology. Although a self-professed natural pessimist, Dr. Handelman enjoys his family, his study, and the rock-strewn fields of Jerusalem.*

Back in the 1940s—so the story goes—cultural anthropologist Ralph Linton examined Ph.D. students by twirling a globe, stopping the whirling world with an emphatic forefinger, and asking the young scholar before him to describe in detail the cultures of the peoples who inhabit that sector. Whether this is an apocryphal tale or not, it highlighted a serene confidence that the world of humankind could be known in its entirety if only one worked diligently enough at this. The anthropology that envisioned this knowable world was thought of as a holistic discipline—

"A Mirror for Man," as the title of a popular introductory textbook of the period put it. Because this mirror image encompassed a global knowledge of other peoples, it was believed that the anthropologist could master, with equal comprehension, such diverse objects as winnowing baskets and religious rites, architectural styles and economic transactions. Regardless of the tribulations involved in learning firsthand about other peoples, this anthropology of the social world was above all a certain one—certain that the progressive accumulation of knowledge should be equated with progress and ultimately with the betterment of humankind. This was a positivist vision, well adapted to industrial nation-states that were still in the throes of maximizing economic and political gains.

Especially during the past two decades, the mirror has shattered its shards reflecting the multitude of specialized parts that social and cultural anthropology have become. Today's anthropologies are the products of an exponential growth and bureaucratization of information. In other words, these numerous anthropologies, whose emergence represents the interests and needs of their practioners, have become formalized in part through the founding of professional societies and the publication of specialty journals. Increasingly, these specialist designations are self-referential—anthropologists use them to categorize their professional identities and to market their scholarly skills. Today we are anthropologists of the economic, political, urban, ecological, symbolic, religious, historical, humanistic, medical, playful, visual, applied, and other specializations.

Burdened and imbalanced by spe-cialized knowledge, anthropology has plummeted from the visionary grace of humanity's interpreter and been pinned to earth beneath the weight of human complexities and entangled in their intricacies. Nonetheless, the mirror's shards have not only retained but also clarified and strengthened their senses of certainty. The compartmentalizations of the discipline have produced specialists, and vice versa, and specialists are experts in the creation of certainty about the validity of the knowledge they are expert in. The creation of certainty reifies the phenomena of the social world. Boundaries between compartments of knowledge become more rigid as many and more ways of classifying information are produced. Certainty about the classification of knowledge generates the justification and the organization for its own continued existence and expansion. The categories themselves, of specialization, become their own rationale—rather than aids for illuminating the knowledge they purport to represent.

The earlier holism of the anthropological vision has been succeeded by the holism of each of its many parts. One sort of positivism has replaced another. In the name of their own progress, specialties are turning themselves into microcosms of the human condition, claiming to speak in its name but thereby distorting and falsifying the very humanity they are appropriating. An assumption of certainly of knowledge about others breeds contempt for them; if they can be known fully, then they lose their autonomy, becoming objects to be manipulated by specialists who lay claim to such certainty.

Specialist knowledge in scholarship is essential if anthropology is to sustain itself as a discipline, but if it is not to ossify in its bureaucratization, a different kind of anthropology also is needed—an uncertain anthropology that inserts question marks into the boundaries that classify specialities, and an anthropology that shows these to be human constructs and scholarly fictions that have value only if they can be collapsed as well as reified. Yet this is not just a matter of softening these boundaries or, in Clifford Geertz's terms, of blurring genres to enable the perspectives of other disciplines to influence our anthropologies. To often this results in the importation of ready-made paradigms and their expert wholesalers, who are too ready to colonize a neighborly market. In recent years we have witnessed this, for example, in the importation of theories of formalist economics, of varieties of Marxism, and of literary criticism.

We do not need borrowed or "new" paradigms into which we can slot ourselves. What we do need are eclectic anthropologists who neither respect boundaries of specialization nor feel obliged to carry a general vision of the mission of anthropology—eclectic anthropologists who will inject uncertainty into the reifications of our anthropologies, "scientific" and "humanistic" alike. Part gadfly, part clown, these uncertain anthropologists should set about undermining the certainty with which experts pursue specialized knowledge. Let me put it this way: As a student of uncertainty, the eclectic anthropologist recognizes that the phenomena of the social world are too complex to be grasped fully and therefore continually resist comprehension. It is our appreciation of this resistance that drives us to create ways of grappling with these phenomena. In these attempts we must fail, time and again. But these failures often are creative ones, failures that offer a better chance of adding to the appreciation of the social world, either by transcending the received wisdoms of specialties or by circumventing them. The uncertainties of eclecticism complement the uncertainties of specialization.

Let me leave you with one type of issue that an uncertain anthropology would bring to the fore. The most valuable kind of explanation is not necessarily the most complete, the neatest, or the most defendable. It is an explanation that breaks down when it is pushed to the limits of its explanatory power, thereby demonstrating instructively what it can explain—and what it cannot. But how many of us have tried to publish a paper that destroys itself? And would there be a scholarly journal prepared to publish such a work?

Don Handelman

427

CHAPTER 14
The Modern World-System

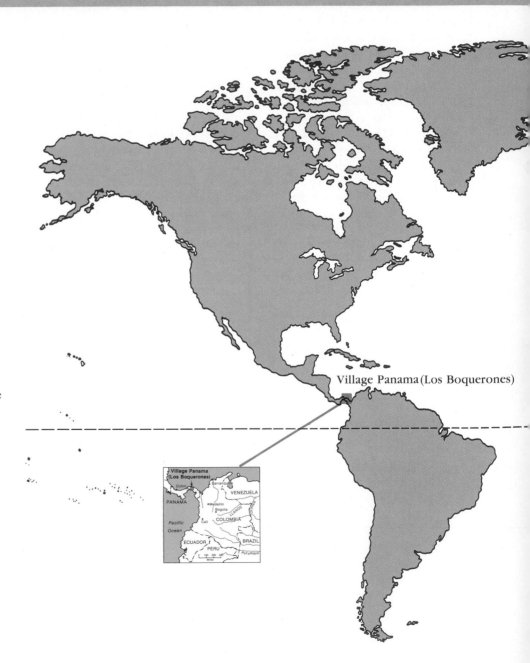

Village Panama (Los Boquerones)

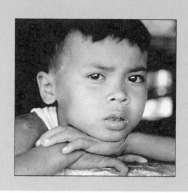

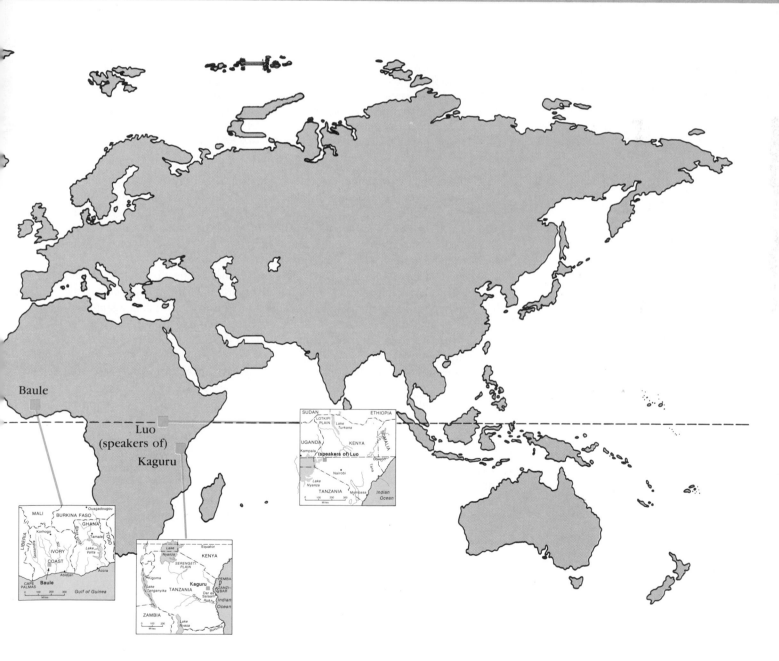

Baule

Luo
(speakers of)

Kaguru

Orlando, Claudio, and Leonardo Villas Boas were sons of a middle-class Brazilian family. As members of an expedition that explored Central Brazil in the early 1940s, they encountered numerous Indian tribes living around the headwaters of the Xingu River. Their experiences on this expedition led the three brothers to dedicate their lives to protecting Brazil's Indians from the ravages of contact with Western society. They were instrumental in persuading the government to create in 1952 the Xingu National Park, a large area in the state of Mato Grosso where Indians could live undisturbed by outsiders. Since that time, they have worked with the Brazilian National Indian Foundation (FUNAI), contacting threatened Indian groups and persuading them to move to Xingu. One such group was the Kréen-Akaróre, whose existence was menaced by a highway being built through their traditional territory.

After years of avoiding the Villas Boas brothers, and all other Brazilians, in February 1973, exhausted and sick, the Kréen-Akaróre finally gave up. They made contact with Claudio Villas Boas, who had been following them in hopes of finding them before the highway builders did. The news made headlines all over the world. As one American newspaper put it, "civilization" had finally "greeted" the Kréen-Akaróre. Shortly after this, Orlando Villas Boas gave a press conference in which he forcefully urged that a reserve be created for the Kréen-Akaróre by the Brazilian government. Anthropologist Shelton Davis tells the rest of the story.

"A month following this interview, Brazilian President Médici signed a decree for the creation of a Kréen-Akaróre reserve. Against the advice of the Villas Boas brothers, however, this decree did not include in the reserve the traditional territory of the Kréen-Akaróre tribe. Further, it made the Santarém-Cuiabá Highway one of the boundaries of the reserve. Within months, this action proved devastating for the remaining 300 members of the Kréen-Akaróre tribe.

"In January 1974, less than a year after the pacification of the Kréen-Akaróre, Brazilian newspapers cited a firsthand report on what was happening to the tribe. This report was written by Ezequias Paulo Heringer, an Indian agent commissioned to investigate conditions along the Kréen-Akaróre front. According to Heringer, the Kréen-Akaróre were dispersed along the Santarém-Cuiabá Highway, fraternizing with truck drivers, and begging for food. . . .

"Heringer told the Brazilian press that the Kréen-Akaróre had abandoned their gardens and were in a state of sickness, hunger, and despair. . . . Within a year, the population of the Kréen-Akaróre tribe had been reduced from approximately 300 to less than 135. . . .

"In October 1974, the Villas Boas brothers commissioned an airplane to transfer the Kréen-Akaróre to the Xingu National Park. At the time of this transfer, it became known that another epidemic was ravishing [*sic*] the remaining 135 members of the tribe. A Brazilian doctor aboard this airplane reported that the Kréen-Akaróre women were purposely aborting their children, rather than produce offspring who would face the new conditions of the tribe. Since this date, the Kréen-Akaróre have been living next to their traditional enemies, the Txukahamae tribe, in the northern part of the Xingu National Park" (Davis 1977:69–73).

Disease, devastation, and misery have been the all-too-common lot of native Americans who have had to deal with white society. Recently, however, remarkable things have been happening in Amazonia. In March, 1989, the Anthropology Newsletter *published a report from anthropologist Terence Turner:*

"An unprecedented attempt by Amazonian Indians to organize themselves to resist the destruction of their forest habitat and the loss of their traditional lands is currently being launched in the forests and native villages of central Brazil.

"For the past two decades, the great Amazonian forest (which includes the world's largest rain forest and one-third of the surviving forest area of the earth) has been under attack. Vast areas of virgin forest habitat are being destroyed every year by settlers, miners, ranchers and hydroelectric dam projects, encouraged by ecologically disastrous 'development' policies undertaken by the Brazilian government and supported by foreign government aid programs and lending institutions. The destruction of the forest has become a matter of urgent concern to the whole world, since it has become one of the major factors contributing to the global warming or 'greenhouse' effect and the diminution of oxygen in the atmosphere. The Amazon's native people, however, are the most directly affected, their fate inseparably linked to that of the great forest to which, over thousands of years, they have adapted themselves and their cultures. They have been widely regarded as on the way to inevitable extinction, helpless 'victims of progress' like the forest itself. That some of these primitive societies might become politically effective forces in the modern international arena of media, bureaucracies and legislatures, and even assume leading roles in the world struggle to save their land and environment, would have seemed incredible only a few years ago. Yet this is precisely what has now begun to happen. Against all odds and expectations, the native peoples of Amazonia have begun to organize and project themselves, with great courage and outspokenness, and with great political skill and effect, as a significant factor in the worldwide struggle to save their forest habitat.

"Under the leadership of the Kayapo tribe, some 28 indigenous nations of the Central Amazonian region are banding together to construct a huge intertribal village of 3000 people in the path of a proposed hydroelectric dam complex at Altamira on the Xingu River. The dams, if completed as planned, would flood more than 1600 sq kilometers of forest land—the largest manmade lake in the world. The village is conceived as the Indians' own " 'Altamira Project'—a living community, complete with families and children, in contrast to the drowned forest, dead animals and homeless people that would be created by the Altamira hydroelectric project. A small permanent population will remain at the site to oppose any dam construction. . . .

"Its builders intend this great intertribal village as a living symbol of the values of their way of life. As a total social community, celebrating agricultural rituals emphasizing the organic coexistence of society with its natural environment, it will stand in dramatic contrast to the destructiveness, to nature and human society alike, of the current exploitation of the Amazon. The integral vision of society and environment embodied by the village is also intended as a political manifesto. In the Indians' view, the environmental, human rights, and specific tribal rights aspects of the Amazonian crisis are integrally interconnected. To them this means that support organizations oriented to these various issues should work together in a common effort, rather than in mutual isolation or opposition as they have tended to do. This was the constant theme of the Kayapo leader, Paiakan, on his recent tour of Europe and North America. . . . Many environmental and other advocacy groups proved receptive to Paiakan's message.

"The Indians have realized that they must come together themselves into an effective alliance if they are to expect environmentalist, human rights and indigenous support groups from the outside world to join with one another in a common struggle to save their forest world. Their Altamira village is thus intended simulta-

The Amazonian Indian Alliance has effectively enlisted the aid of world-famous celebrities in order to defend the Brazilian rain forest. Rock star Sting appeared with Kayapo leader Raoni at a New York City press conference in 1989.

neously as a rallying point for the tribes of Amazonia and as an appeal for world support. The boldness and global vision of this project are breathtaking; nothing like such a concerted action by even a few, let alone 28 unrelated Indian societies has ever taken place in the Amazon. The Indians are trying to tell us something important; we should listen" (T. Turner 1989:21–22).

In many of the societies anthropologists have studied, people interact with one another on a local, face-to-face level. This way of life has more in common with social patterns in small American towns than it does with life in large urban, industrial cities at the cutting edge of modern Western civilization. Yet just as small-town life only appears to be cut off from the wider concerns in the larger society that affect it, so too seemingly remote non-Western peoples are hardly isolated. Indians like the Kréen-Akaróre or Kayapo, living deep in the Amazonian rain forest, would seem to be far removed from Western influences. Yet the shock waves of the Brazilian economic "miracle" reached even them, with terrible consequences.

In this chapter, we deal in a direct manner with how the Western world and the societies visited by anthropologists are interrelated. We will be looking at ourselves as much as we look at the traditional subjects of anthropological research. Through this reflexive exercise, we may learn something of the past and present relationships that link people of all societies to one another. In this way, we can establish a context for contemplating our common fate.

Source: Reproduced by permission of the American Anthropological Association from *Anthropology Newsletter* Volume 30:3, March 1989. Not for further reproduction.

The Growth of Capitalism and Western Expansion

The growth in wealth and power of western Europe coincides with the birth of the "modern" era of Western history. The pursuit of centralized monarchy at home and colonial conquest abroad had begun in the Middle Ages and flourished during the

Renaissance and the Age of Discovery. Europe could not be politically united, which meant that fledgling European states could strike out on their own without being answerable to any central authority. Individualistic adventurism, and the competition it bred among newly consolidating states, spurred on European expansion. At the same time, these dynamic Europeans were working out a new kind of society with a new kind of economy, whose development was aided by trade and conquest—namely, capitalism.

The term **capitalism** refers to at least two things. On the one hand, it is an economic system dominated by the supply-demand-price mechanism called the market. On the other hand, it describes the way of life that grew up in response to and in service to that market. This new way of life changed the face of Europe. Many changes were financed by wealth brought to Europe from other parts of the globe. Those other parts of the globe were also transformed by their contact with Europeans and the economic transactions that resulted.

One significant transformation brought about in the non-Western world as a result of contact with Western capitalism has been the growth of cities. Cities were found in many parts of the world before the arrival of Europeans, but the cities that grew up to facilitate capitalist commerce were different. Precolonial cities had been outgrowths of indigenous civilizations. By contrast, the colonial city in which capitalist transactions centered was "a conquered place" (Gilsenan 1982:197). Colonial administrators and merchants dealt with local elites in such places, and united there to defend their joint interests against those who remained in outlying areas.

City dwellers see themselves as "modern." In the context of colonialism, however, being modern has often meant nothing more than adopting the practices and world view of Western capitalism. As a result, the so-called "backward" rural peoples often turn out to be either those who have escaped capitalism's embrace or those who actively oppose it. And the colonial city, with the life it represents, can come to symbolize everything that is wrong with the colonial order. In the Middle East, for example, "in times of crisis the modern city is itself called in question, taken to symbolize forces of oppression or a non-Islamic way of life. . . . For radical and millennial groups the city is a home of unbelief, not of sober, textual Islam. The true believer should, in an image that has great historical resonance, go out from the city, leave as the Prophet Muhammad did the hypocritical and unbelieving citizens of Mecca" (ibid.: 214).

Colonial penetration reshaped conquered territories to serve the needs of

capitalism
an economic system dominated by the supply-demand-price mechanism called the market; also an entire way of life that grew up in response to, and in service to, that market

Colonial and formerly colonial cities like Caracas, Venezuela, are centers of commerce, industry, government, learning, and entertainment. These cities attract vast numbers of migrants, many of whom become squatters.

capitalist enterprise. Cities were centers of commerce, and rural areas were sources of raw materials for industry. Systems to extract raw materials set up by colonial authorities disrupted indigenous communities and created new ones. The mining towns of Bolivia or South Africa, for example, are outgrowths of this process. Labor for such enterprises was recruited, sometimes by force, from local populations. Little by little, in an effort to streamline the system of colonial exploitation, society was restructured.

The Colonial Political Economy ▮▮▮▮▮

The colonial order focused on the extraction of material wealth, and so it might be said that its reason for existence was economic. Certainly it did link together economically communities and territories that in many cases had led a fairly autonomous existence before colonization. Yet this new economic order did not spring up painlessly by itself. It was imposed by force and maintained by force. For that reason, the colonial order has been described by such anthropologists as Eric Wolf and Hoyt Alverson as a political economy. **Political economy** is a holistic term that emphasizes both the centrality of material interest and the use of power to protect and enhance that interest. Those who use the term when discussing the colonial order do so, among other reasons, to remind themselves and others not to forget history.

political economy
a holistic term that attempts to capture the centrality of material interest (economy) and the use of power (politics) to protect and enhance that interest

The colonial political economy created three kinds of links. It linked conquered communities with one another within a conquered territory. It linked different conquered territories to one another. And it linked all conquered territories with the mother country. A particularly striking example of this linkage comes from Wolf (1982:153), who describes the way silver mined in Spanish colonies in America was shipped to another Spanish colony in Asia—the Philippines—where it was then used to buy textiles from the Chinese.

More commonly, colonial enterprises drew labor from neighboring regions, as in South Africa, where blacks continue to be recruited from some distance to work in the mines. Money earned in one area is thus remitted for the economic support of families in another area. Again, these linkages did not come about spontaneously. Alverson (1978:26ff.) describes for South Africa a situation paralleled in many other colonies. The British, he argues, could not make a profit in the gold mines of the region without cheap African labor. In the late nineteenth century, however, Africans were still largely able to guarantee their own subsistence through traditional means. They were unwilling to work for wages in the mines except on a short-term basis. Profitability in mining required, therefore, that African self-sufficiency be eliminated, so that Africans would have no choice but to work for whatever wages mine owners chose to offer.

This goal was achieved in two ways. First, conquered African populations had to pay taxes, but the taxes could only be paid in cash. Second, the colonial government deliberately prevented the growth of a cash economy in African areas. Thus, the only way Africans could obtain the cash needed to pay their taxes was by working for wages in the mines. "The Tswana, along with other African populations, comprised a reserve army of potential labor—that is, labor that it was hoped would exist in inelastic supply and cost industry nothing at all when not being used. [Botswana] and the rural, native reserves in South Africa itself were, and from the capitalist viewpoint still are, social security systems that keep labor alive until such time as it is in demand by the money sector" (Alverson 1978:34–35). *(See Ethno-File 2.1: Tswana.)*

Political independence did not remove Botswana from the clutches of the South African political economy. At the time of Alverson's fieldwork, Botswana was still sending more than two workers to South Africa for every one worker it was able to supply with a job at home. And these workers were not "surplus" migrants whose home communities were eager to get rid of them. "In many ways some Tswana communities have become quasi-societies and quasi-economies, for the absence of men and women abroad has virtually destroyed institutional life and replaced it with nothing except cash" (ibid.: 62–63). What is true for Botswana has become equally true for ex-colonies elsewhere in Africa, Asia, and the New World.

The Key Metaphor of Capitalism

The capitalist political economy began in Europe, but it soon expanded to enfold a large portion of the earth into a politico-economic world system. There had been expansive empires before the rise of capitalism, but capitalist exploitation was a new kind of exploitation because it derived from a new world view. In the words of Eric Wolf, "The guiding fiction of this kind of society—one of the key tenets of its ideology—is that land, labor, and wealth are commodities, that is, goods produced not for use, but for sale" (Wolf 1969: 277). That is, the world is a market, and everything within the world has, or should have, its price.

The genius of capitalism has been the thoroughgoing way in which those committed to the marketing metaphor have been able to convert anything that exists into a commodity. They turn land into real estate and material objects into inventory. They can also attach price tags to ideas (hence the existence of copyright laws in capitalist societies) and even to human beings. The prototypical slave in Western society is considered "first and foremost a commodity. He is a chattel, totally in the possession of another person who uses him for private ends" (Kopytoff and Miers 1977: 3). Even human beings who are not slaves are nevertheless reduced to their labor power by the capitalist market and become worth whatever price the laws of supply and demand determine. In this way, human beings are also turned into objects, and labor becomes a commodity along with beans and cotton. Even when people function as buyers in the market, their actions are supposed to be governed by strict "economizing." They should buy cheap, sell dear, and not allow any personal or social considerations to divert their attention from the bottom line.

Before the rise of capitalism, land was not a commodity. Instead, it was but one element of the wider world on which human beings depended for their subsistence. Access to it was controlled and protected by the patterned social relations called relations of production. Rights to use land, or **use rights**, might be exchanged, but land ownership, or **land tenure**, was rarely in question, being regarded in most places as an inalienable possession of the social group who made use of it. Before the rise of capitalism, human beings were identified in terms of a complex web of social identities based on descent, alliance, and residence. Their status might be low, but they were usually protected from utter destitution by those of high status who were obliged to help them. Before the rise of capitalism, multipurpose money did not exist, exchanges were hedged about with social restrictions, and there was no single standard according to which anything could be assigned a value.

Capitalism changed all this. When capitalist practices were imposed on non-Western societies through colonial administration, indigenous life was forever altered. To function intelligibly within the capitalist world order, colonized peoples had also to begin to see the world as a storehouse of potential commodities. Much of recent world history can usefully be viewed as a narrative of non-Western responses to this new world view, of the practical actions it encouraged and justified. Some responses were enthusiastic, others were resentful but accommodating, still others were violent in repudiation.

use rights
rights to use but not own land for farming or grazing

land tenure
land ownership

Accounting for Social and Cultural Change ▬▬▬

Anthropology was born as a discipline during the heyday of European colonialism in the nineteenth century. Early anthropologists attempted to fit their accounts of culture change into prevailing evolutionary schemes. Taking an extremely long view, they argued that the apparent disorder and suffering that social changes seemed to have generated needed to be put into perspective. The world as a whole was moving into a new, higher level of civilization, and this movement was bound to create dislocations until it was completed. In the long run, the present social turmoil would have a positive effect in weeding out those unfit for civilization. When the social transition was completed at some unknown point in the future, stability and calm would return as those suited for a civilized life settled down to enjoy it.

Functional anthropology developed in the context of empire. Anthropologists were hired to provide specific information about particular societies under colonial rule. Colonial governments were preoccupied with day-to-day concerns of administration. From their perspective, social change involved the adjustment of conquered peoples to life under alien rule. They were interested in research that would let them rule with as little difficulty as possible.

Colonial administrations rarely denied the commercial reasons for their existence. Yet they saw their presence as simultaneously offering them an opportunity to teach their colonial subjects how to become civilized. They regretted that conquest and reintegration under colonial authority and the capitalist market had caused disruptions. But they believed those disruptions were necessary if civilization was to be achieved. As we observed in an earlier chapter, anthropologists often played an equivocal role in the colonial setting; they were valued for the expert knowledge they could provide to administrators, and at the same time they were viewed with suspicion because their expert knowledge might easily contradict or undermine administrative goals.

A number of American anthropologists also tried to clarify what their role should be in the expanding world of capitalist colonialism. In two documents, one published in 1936 and another some twenty years later, they urged that the study of change was to be impartial and scientific. The goal was to be the discovery of laws of culture change. These anthropologists had a broad understanding of culture change. They considered situations encountered under **colonialism**, where political conquest led to "cultural domination with enforced social change" (Beidelman 1982:2), but they also considered situations where contact and change occurred in the absence of political conquest. The latter cases were subject more to selection and rejection of new elements by members of autonomous groups. These anthropologists did not see themselves supporting any particular political position in advocating that culture change be approached in this way. However, they were sympathetic to the plight of colonial subjects. Melville Herskovits, in particular, was outspoken in his defense of the right of native African peoples to control their own destinies.

In the years following World War II, European colonial powers were increasingly forced to come to terms with colonial subjects who rejected the role they had been forced to play as students of civilization. The colonial order was no longer taken as given, and its ultimate benevolence was sharply called into question. This critical attitude persisted after independence was granted to most European colonies in the 1950s and 1960s. It became clear that formal political independence could not easily undo the profound social and economic entanglements linking the former colonial territories to their former mother countries. The persistence of these ties in the face of political sovereignty came to be called **neocolonialism**.

colonialism
political conquest followed by cultural domination with enforced social change

neocolonialism
The persistence of the profound social and economic entanglements linking former colonial territories to their former mother countries despite the political sovereignty of those territories

The curriculum of high schools in Cameroon is closely based on the French *lycée* curriculum.

The study of neocolonialism led to a new awareness of just how strongly the fate of colonies and the fate of mother countries had been, and continued to be, mutually interdependent. Recognition of how wide and deep this interdependence had grown led to new explanations for the "underdevelopment" that characterized the new nations in what was becoming known as the Third World.

The Roots of the Neocolonial Order

Coming to terms with the tenacious problems of neocolonialism would seem to require coming to terms with colonial domination itself. The assumption that political independence would allow Latin Americans, Africans, and Asians to become captains of their fate has turned out to be premature.

Anthropologist T. O. Beidelman says, "Colonialism is not dead in Africa if, by colonialism, we mean cultural domination with enforced social change. I refer not only to continued economic and political influence by former colonial powers but also to domination of the poor and uneducated masses by a privileged and powerful native elite fiercely determined to make change for whatever reasons" (Beidelman 1982:2). Defining colonialism in this way helps make clear why political independence in the mid-twentieth century made so little economic difference to the new nations of Africa and Asia. It also helps explain why the Latin America nations that became formally independent over a century ago have continued to languish economically. It would seem that political domination is only one option in the growth of a capitalist world system. Cultural domination with enforced social change can occur without political domination, if the people of a dominated territory decide on their own to accommodate the wishes of the outside power. But they may refuse to do so or they may lack the means to meet outside needs as fully as the outside power wishes. In either case, the outside power may decide to move in itself, making the changes it sees as necessary for its own welfare, even if local peoples object.

This certainly seems to describe the history of European colonialism in Africa. For nearly five hundred years, Europeans traded with Africans along the coast of the continent but were not allowed to penetrate inward. Coastal African societies were profoundly affected by this trade. It led to the rise of new settlements and new African leaders whose power and prestige derived directly from trade with Europeans. Before the arrival of Europeans on the Atlantic coast, the major trade routes connecting Africa to Europe had been across the Sahara to the Mediterranean Sea. European presence on the Atlantic coast served as a new magnet for commerce, substantially redirecting African trade over time. For most of this period, the commodities for which Europeans traded included human beings destined for slavery in Europe or in New World settlements. As African trading partners searched for slaves in the interior of the continent, profound reverberations were felt far inland, affecting the societies of peoples who had never seen a European.

The growth of capitalist manufacturing in the late eighteenth century altered the way European merchants viewed Africa. The lands of Africa seemed increasingly to be sources of cheap raw materials for industry and the people to be consumers of European manufactures. In the early nineteenth century, England had progressed the furthest in capitalist manufacturing. Hence, England was most interested in the "legitimate" trade in nonhuman commodities with Africa. So it was that England took a lead in abolishing the slave trade with Africa.

As the nineteenth century continued, the industrial development of France and Germany speeded up. Both countries began to compete with England in Africa and elsewhere for the same markets. As this competition heated up, it became increasingly clear that delivery of resources into European hands was too slow and fitful to suit the demands of industry. Solving such problems became a major concern to the Europeans. When European powers began to sign treaties with African leaders in the late nineteenth century, access to resources was a central topic. Once a given European power completely controlled trade within a certain region, it could both keep out competitors and make any changes in supply and transportation of raw materials that were required.

Such blatant economic motives are nakedly exploitative and would surely have been unpalatable both at home and in the colonies. But many of those who established colonies in Africa did not view their activity as naked exploitation. To be sure, they were enriching themselves and their mother country, but they saw themselves simultaneously performing a labor of civilization, carrying "the white man's burden."

Women and Colonization

Colonial administrators were generally convinced that the work of empire would benefit those they dominated—if not now, then in the future. Critics of colonialism deny that any benefits could accrue to a dominated and exploited people. Ethnographic data, however, show that colonial domination did not affect all groups in the same ways. Women are one such group. As we saw in chapter 13, Trobriand women suffered no loss of status under colonial rule. Baule women of the Ivory Coast in West Africa were less fortunate. *(See EthnoFile 14.1: Baule.)*

In precolonial Baule society, according to Mona Etienne (1980), production centered on two products: yams and cloth. Gifts of yams and cloth consolidated marriages, and both sexes worked together in the production of each. Yet the relations of production assigned men responsibility for yams, and women responsibility for cloth. Men's traditional control over yams was an outgrowth of the sexual division of labor; men cleared and prepared farm plots for planting, although the women tended the crops. Similarly, women controlled cloth because they raised the cotton and spun the thread from which it was woven, although the men did the actual weaving. Both yams and cloth were indispensable for subsistence as well as for exchange

EthnoFile 14.1
BAULE

Region: West Africa

Nation: Ivory Coast

Population: 2,760,000

Environment: Savannah

Livelihood: Farming (yams in particular) and cloth production

Political organization: In the precolonial period no state and no clear stratification

Other: In the precolonial period, cloth made by women was of great importance in many domains of life, including marriage

in various traditional social contexts. As a result, the balance of power between men and women was highly egalitarian.

Ivory Coast became a colony of France in 1893. In 1923, the French built in Baule territory a textile factory that sold factory-spun thread for cash. Baule men with cash could therefore buy their own thread, and they, not their wives, would control any cloth woven from it. French colonial administrators also encouraged Baule farmers to plant new varieties of cotton as a cash crop. Baule women had traditionally raised their cotton on fields that had been planted with yams the previous year, but these plots were now devoted to growing the new cotton. Cash-crop cotton also required new farming techniques, but for a variety of reasons those techniques were taught to Baule *men*. As a result, women's cotton production was reduced considerably. Moreover, since women had to work in their husbands' cash-crop fields in addition to working the traditional yam plots, they also had less time to spin traditional thread.

The colonial government made men responsible for paying their wives' taxes in cash, a move that seemed to justify the right of Baule men to control production of crops that could be sold for cash. Under colonial rule, cash-cropping became increasingly important. As a result, Baule women found that their traditional autonomous rights to use their husbands' land for their own production were being gradually eroded. They found that they were increasingly dependent on the arbitrary generosity of their husbands.

There is a final irony in this series of developments. Many Baule women today have become wage laborers in the textile factory in order to earn cash with which to buy their own cloth, which they can then control. They are aware of the loss of status and power they have suffered over the years, and their discontent has undermined traditional Baule marriage. "The wife-husband production relationship has become a constant source of conflict. Because the production relationship has always been the foundation of marriage, and because cloth and cash now tend to be the measure of a husband's affection and respect, the whole personal relationship is also conflict-laden. Inevitably, many women prefer to remain unmarried and all seek to acquire their own cash" (Etienne 1980:231). In this way, the traditional Baule mode of production was transformed by contact with the capitalist market. What had been egalitarian relations of production linking women and men, husbands and wives, were destroyed.

Views of the Political Economy

To explain the relationship between the West and the rest of the world, four major theoretical perspectives have been developed in anthropology. They are (1) modernization theory, (2) dependency theory, (3) world system theory, and (4) neo-marxian theory.

Modernization Theory

modernization theory
a position holding that the social change occurring in non-Western societies under colonial rule was a necessary and inevitable prelude to higher levels of social development that had been reached by the more "modern" nations; to reach "modernity," new nations must follow the path taken by the United States and the nations of Western Europe

The roots of contemporary **modernization theory** can be seen in the unilineal evolutionism of Herbert Spencer and his followers. In brief, social change in non-Western societies under colonial rule was understood as a necessary and inevitable prelude to higher levels of social development. Europe had passed through the same stages of evolution earlier in its history, and contact with Europe was now shaking these other regions out of stagnation. Colonization was thus a positive process because it taught backward peoples the skills they needed to move forward. The skills were those of capitalism, and they needed Western institutions to work properly. If conquered peoples adopted those skills and institutions, it was argued, they too would eventually become "modern" and prosperous, independent nation-states.

Spencerian evolutionism was heavily criticized in anthropology and other social sciences in the early years of the twentieth century. As late as 1960, however, we find Spencerian reasoning in the work of American economist W. W. Rostow, in his book *The Stages of Economic Growth*. This book codified the received wisdom of economics that would form the foundation of U.S. foreign aid policies in the 1960s. It thus offers in a single volume the basic tenets of modernization theory.

Rostow surveys the history of the world and decides that, economically speaking, known human societies can be sorted into five categories, each of which represents a stage of development. The first, lowest stage is that of "traditional society," which is defined in negative terms. Traditional societies are said to have productive techniques that are poorly developed, and their social institutions are viewed as stumbling blocks in the path of economic growth. Progress thus requires that these blocks be removed if prosperity and modernity are to be attained. Stages two through five chart the steps to modernity, which is defined as a stage of "high mass-consumption."

Rostow conceives of stages of economic growth as if they were stages of organic growth. He describes each new nation-state as if it were an adolescent male undergoing puberty. Young states, like young men, develop according to an inner timetable. They start out ignorant and immature, lacking the knowledge and skills to support themselves properly. In addition, they are unsure of their own identity, and so tend to get involved in fights with one another, or with more mature members of the international community. But the passage of time brings wisdom. Rostow has faith that with sound guidance from their elders, young states will eventually stand beside those elders as self-supporting, even thriving, members of the international community.

Rostow's growth metaphor makes the young state largely responsible for its own success or failure. The only role a mature or "post-mature" outside state can play is that of a wise father. That is, established states can provide the advice and the funding to get development off to a good start. After that, the rest is up to the young

Large landholdings in northern Ecuador produce crops for the world market. The farm workers are allowed small plots for their subsistence crops.

state itself. If its leaders follow the advice and take advantage of the opportunities provided, their underdeveloped economy, like an airplane leaving the ground or a college graduate with his first job, should eventually "take off" on its own into self-sustaining economic growth.

Rostow's unselfconscious paternalism and ethnocentrism are illustrated by some of the assumptions that are the basis of his approach. Perhaps the most obvious is the assumption that modernization is an automatic process operating according to eternal laws unaffected by history. The colonial past of the developing world is not seen to have played any important role in the initial modernization of the West. Equally irrelevant are any contemporary relationships that may bind underdeveloped countries to Western states. There is only one path to modernity, the path blazed by the nations of western Europe and North America and recorded in their history. Therefore, if other nations want to share in the same modern prosperity, they must make history repeat itself, and follow the same path.

Dependency Theory

Modernization theory is plausible if you accept a metaphor that equates nations with individual organisms, and that attributes organismic development largely to innate growth mechanisms beyond the reach of environmental influences. But such a view has not been acceptable to all observers. Once colonialism is considered, some argue, modernization theory appears less and less persuasive. From their perspective, the prosperity of Western nations did not depend on the development of the internal resources of those nations. Rather, it was based on the exploitation of cheap raw materials and captive markets that colonies provided. On this account, the United States differed from European colonial powers only in that the expanding American government did not have to cross oceans to find new resources. It had incorporated the lands and resources of indigenous peoples living within its own borders. In both cases, the West would never have prospered if colonial powers had not expropriated the wealth of other people to fuel their own development.

This view challenges the assumption that nations are naturally autonomous and independently responsible for their own success or failure at modernizing. If colonies and other peoples' resources are necessary for a nation to become modern, then countries without colonies, whose own resources were long ago removed by others, can never hope to become modern. The success of a few has required the failure of the many. Indeed, the "independent" capitalist nations of the world stay prosperous only as long as everyone else is dependent on them for economic direction. This understanding of development forms the basis for dependency theory.

Dependency theory argues that dependent colonies or nations must endure a situation in which the structures of their own economies are reshaped to meet demands generated outside their borders. For example, land that could be used to raise food crops for local consumption may be planted with flowers or bananas or coffee for export. In this way, local needs are pushed into the background. Dependency theorists stress that backward agricultural techniques or careless human overpopulation do not explain why people in many Third World countries cannot feed themselves. Rather, distorted national economies in Third World nations are directly produced by the international capitalist economic order.

Dependency theory argues that the development of rich capitalist nations requires the underdevelopment of colonies and less powerful trading partners. Indeed, capitalism deliberately creates "underdevelopment" in formerly prosperous areas

dependency theory
a position holding that the "independent" capitalist nations of the world stay prosperous only as long as everyone else is dependent on them for economic direction

development-of-underdevelopment
the thesis that capitalism deliberately creates "underdevelopment" in formerly prosperous areas that come under its domination

that come under its domination. This is the famous **development-of-underdevelopment** thesis of dependency theory. Dependency theorists like economist André Gunder Frank argue that the same dependency relationships that link an "underdeveloped" country to a "developed" country are found in the underdeveloped country itself. That is, the economically and politically powerful regions of an underdeveloped country dominate the less powerful areas. Local capitalist elites dominate economic transactions and keep peasants and others dependent on them, down to the level of the smallest village. Therefore, until Third World countries are able to take control of their own destinies, and to restructure their economies and societies to meet local needs, underdevelopment will persist.

World-System Theory

world-system theory
a position holding that European capitalism expanded beyond its borders in the late fifteenth and sixteenth centuries to establish an international division of labor within the framework of a world-economy that was not an empire

World-system theory is associated most closely with the work of sociologist Immanuel Wallerstein and his colleagues. In works beginning with *The Modern World-System*, published in 1974, Wallerstein set forth a global framework for understanding problems of development and underdevelopment in the modern world. Like dependency theorists, Wallerstein was concerned with the history of relationships between former colonies and their former masters. He too argued that the exploitative framework of present-day relations between those states took shape historically and was fine-tuned during the colonial era.

Wallerstein rejects the idea that modern nation-states are independent entities engaged in balanced exchange in a free market; quite the contrary. When European capitalism expanded beyond its borders, beginning in the late fifteenth and early sixteenth centuries, it incorporated other regions and peoples into a world economy based on the capitalist mode of production. Wallerstein deliberately chooses to speak of a world *economy*, rather than a world empire or other political entity. This is because a world economy "precisely encompasses within its bounds empires, city-states, and the emerging 'nation-states.' It is a 'world' system, not because it encompasses the whole world, but because it is larger than any juridically defined political unit. And it is a 'world-*economy*' because the basic linkage between the parts of the system is economic" (Wallerstein 1974:15).

Wallerstein points out that at the period in history when the European world economy took shape, it was not the only world economy in existence. Perhaps its most important competitor centered on China. But the European world economy was able to surpass the other world economies because it was based on capitalism. "The secret of capitalism was in the establishment of the division of labor within the framework of a world-economy that was *not* an empire" (ibid.: 127). Banking, finance, and highly skilled industrial production became the specialty of the Western European nations. These nations became what Wallerstein calls the **core** of the world economy. The other regions constituted the **periphery** of the world economy, supplying the core with cheap food and raw materials. The core exploited (and continues to exploit) the periphery, draining off its wealth to support highly skilled "free" labor and a high standard of living. The periphery, by contrast, practices various forms of coerced labor to produce goods to support core industries, and the standard of living for coerced workers is generally low.

core
in world system theory, the Western European nations, the United States, and Japan, which have specialized in banking, finance, and highly skilled industrial production

periphery
in world system theory, the exploited former colonies of the core, which supply the core with cheap food and raw materials

Wallerstein's model is based explicitly on a functional organismic metaphor. In fact, it was Wallerstein's search for a social system for which the metaphor seemed apt that led him to speak of a world system. Only a world system (and not the individual tribes, communities, or nation-states within it) shows the necessary integration and self-sufficiency characteristic of a living organism. Wallerstein's analysis can thus be seen as a functionalist analysis raised to a high level. He believes that the world system is the only social entity in which the relationships posited by functionalist theory actually hold.

Nevertheless, Wallerstein has been criticized for setting forth a model of the modern world in which most of the action is over. For him, the periphery has long since been transformed into a series of specialized segments of the capitalist world economy. There remain only two possibilities for future development. First, various units within the system may change roles; that is, a core state may drop to the periphery, or vice versa. Second, the system as a whole may be transformed into something else. This could come about, for instance, by a systemwide socialist revolution.

Neo-marxian Theory

The work of Karl Marx and his followers has influenced all three of the theoretical perspectives described so far. Dependency theory and world-system theory both are sympathetic to insights first stated by Marx, and both borrow heavily from marxian theory. On the other hand, modernization theory notes Marx's existence only to deny the relevance of his work to the explanation of social change in the modern world.

The anthropological perspective called **neo-marxian theory** is based on the work of a new generation of marxian scholars. Although inspired by Marx's work, they nevertheless reinterpret or reject aspects of it when necessary. Anthropologists have been especially stimulated by the work of two French neo-marxians, Louis Althusser and Etienne Balibar, whose reinterpretation of Marx offered them a new way of understanding social change in the Third World.

neo-marxian theory
an anthropological perspective based upon the work of a new generation of marxian scholars who, though inspired by the work of Karl Marx, nevertheless feel free to reinterpret or reject certain aspects of his work when necessary

Althusser and Balibar reexamined the concept of mode of production. They concluded that in the context of the Third World, economic activity did not clearly represent any one of the classic modes of production. Colonial areas, for example, were social formations in which capitalist and noncapitalist modes of production had worked out a mode of coexistence. The capitalist mode of production introduced by the colonial power had linked up with indigenous noncapitalist modes of production, modifying them but not transforming them totally. The capitalist and noncapitalist modes linked up in this fashion are described as **articulating modes of production**.

articulating modes of production
an aspect of neo-marxist thought that describes the links between capitalist and noncapitalist modes of production in the Third World

Viewing Third World countries as a series of social formations characterized by articulating modes of production leads to a different understanding of the political economy and suggests a new way of viewing social change. It contradicts the position of dependency theory and world-system theory, which hold that capitalism triumphed long ago. For Althusser and Balibar, noncapitalist modes of production are often able to hold their own against encroaching capitalism. If this is the case, then neo-marxian theory implies that engulfment by capitalism (or capitalist "modernization") is not the inevitable outcome of social change in the Third World.

Neo-marxian theory also offers a new perspective on the role of the exploited peoples in Third World countries. Some neo-marxians see those peoples as basically helpless in the face of domination by local elites who have allied themselves with well-heeled international capitalists. For other theorists, the ability of Third World peasants to hold capitalism at arm's length today suggests a more promising future. If some peasants have truly managed to resist "capture" by the capitalist mode of production, they may yet have the power and creative ability to forge for themselves a better and less exploitative mode of production in generations to come. This is what Scott saw as a possible long-term outcome of the everyday forms of peasant resistance he documented in Malaysia.

Modes of Change in the Modern World

Much of contemporary human history can be seen as attempts by people to promote the survival of meaningful social life in the face of changes in cultural practices introduced by outsiders. Two major modes of change appear to be at work in the contemporary world. The first involves the power of persuasion; the second involves the power of the gun.

The Power of Persuasion

Although many varieties of modern social change are backed by force, people attempting to introduce change often rely more on tactics of persuasion. Members of non-Western societies have had to learn to deal with two kinds of pressure to change that originated in the West. These might be called **sacred persuasion** and **secular persuasion**. The first was brought by religious missionaries and the second by secular authorities. Although the messages delivered by both means had much in common, particularly during the colonial era, they did at times clash with one another. And although their effectiveness was backed by the force of colonial conquest, sacred and secular persuasion have often led to reactions against those who first promoted it. Christian missionary activity, for example, has produced non-Western converts who have taken the Christian message offered by the West and turned it into a weapon to fight the domination of the West. Figures such as Archbishop Desmond Tutu in South Africa and liberation theologians in Latin America are only the most recent examples.

Sacred Persuasion: Missionaries in Africa

The Christian church was a powerful secular institution when young Western states pushed outward across the oceans to make their first territorial conquests. In the colonies of Spain in the New World, the church became a counterforce to be reckoned with when conquistadors attempted to set themselves up as New World feudal lords with Indians as their serfs. Missionaries of one sort or another accompanied Western expansion in the Americas, in Asia, and in Africa.

Anthropologist T. O. Beidelman (1982) examined the nature of missionary activity in Africa. He learned that all missionaries were not alike. Some mission stations were large and well funded, others were small and run on a shoestring. Catholic missionaries differed from Protestant missionaries, and the Protestants differed among themselves. In fact, there was often active antagonism between different denominations. They were competing over souls to evangelize in the same way Europeans competed for access to raw materials for industry.

On the one hand, Africans found the celibacy of Catholic priests to be a curious practice. Nevertheless, Catholic missionaries were often able to develop close ties with African converts. Priests were unencumbered by families, were well educated, were of high status, and might spend their entire careers in a single area. They tended to be more tolerant of African custom, perhaps because they expected to achieve their goals in the long run.

sacred persuasion
pressure to change brought by religious missionaries from the West, and with which members of non-Western societies must cope

secular persuasion
pressure to change brought by secular authorities from the West, and with which members of non-Western societies must cope

Missionary activity has been carried out all over the world.

Protestant missions, on the other hand, were eventually staffed by married couples or families. It was thought that those families would present positive role models for converts. Yet in many cases the presence of women and children in mission stations led to a widening of the gulf between missionaries and converts. The missionaries felt the need to protect their wives and families from too-easy contact with Africans.

Born-again Protestant missionaries believed that although genuine conversion was an inner experience, it could only be proven by outward behavior. They thus tended to demand immediate behavior changes from their converts, taking outward action as an indication of the appropriate inner state. Their prototype of the ideal Christian was based on their own Western experience, however. As a result, they often had difficulty deciding whether certain outward cultural forms, including dress, diet, music, smoking, and alcohol consumption, could be acceptable for "true" Christians.

Beidelman observes that the whole reason for existence of mission work "is the undermining of a traditional way of life."

> *In this the missionary represents the most extreme, thorough-going, and self-conscious protagonist of cultural innovation and change. . . . The missionary, at least in the past, was unashamedly ethnocentric, though he saw the struggle to impose his values as loving and altruistic. He was cruel to be kind. His ethnocentrism and proselytization represent a blend of exclusion and inclusion, domination and brotherhood, and exploitation and sacrifice. Most curious of all, he exalted Western life but loathed many of its features; he felt a parallel fascination and contempt for simpler societies. (Beidelman 1982:212)*

Beidelman focused his attention on the Church Missionary Society (CMS) missionaries who had worked among the Kaguru of Tanzania, people among whom he had carried out fieldwork. *(See EthnoFile 14.2: Kaguru.)* The CMS missionaries were born-again Anglican Protestants who first entered Kaguru territory in 1876, when life among the Kaguru was in turmoil. The Kaguru viewed the first

---

EthnoFile 14.2
KAGURU

Region: East Africa

Nation: Tanzania

Population: 100,000 (1960s)

Environment: Varied; about half plateau, some highlands and lowlands; jungle, meadow, savannah, river valley, bush

Livelihood: Agriculture (mostly maize)

Political organization: Traditionally some men with influence; now, part of a modern nation-state

Other: The Kaguru are a matrilineal society, missionized in the late nineteenth century by the Church Missionary Society

---

missionaries as "white Arabs." For more than a quarter of a century, their lands had been traversed by Arab caravans linking the East African coast and the interior of the continent. The Kaguru had reason to dislike Arabs, primarily because of their slaving activities. Nevertheless, they had developed political and economic relations with the Arabs, and they treated the new whites in the same way. From the missionary perspective, however, Arabs were evil, not only because they were slavers but also because they were Muslims. The CMS saw its role in East Africa as one of wresting control of the region not from Africans but from Arabs.

According to Beidelman, "Christian missions represent the most naive and ethnocentric, and therefore the most thorough-going, facet of colonial life. . . . Missionaries demonstrated a more radical and morally intense commitment to rule than political administrators or business men" (ibid.: 5). Although the CMS missionaries were ostensibly in Africa to save the souls of Africans, "strictly considered the missionaries were in the field to save themselves. . . . Evangelism was thus as much to build character as to convert. Failure to convert, even for decades, was seen as God's will, as a test of faith, and not as a reason either to abandon an area or to reassess methods" (ibid.: 99–100). Indeed, to some extent the missionaries seemed to expect martyrdom. Beidelman quotes from a missionary's letter home: "The resurrection of East Africa must be effected by our destruction" (ibid.: 65).

Such dedication made missionaries tirelessly devoted to changing the ways of Africans whose lives they viewed as brutal, ignorant, and miserable. Yet they were of two minds about their potential converts. They saw the Kaguru as childlike, and therefore in need of instruction and guidance. But in their supposed likeness to children, the Kaguru also appeared innocent. Beidelman remarks that it sometimes seems unclear what the missionaries' real goals were. Did they want to convert the Kaguru totally to the modern Western way of life? Or was their goal a utopian, new Christian society free of the materialism and corruption that, in their view, characterized the European society they had left behind? In any case, they had exacting standards against which Kaguru converts were to be measured.

In more than one instance, CMS missionaries found themselves at odds with secular colonial authorities. In their early years, when their areas came under German control, "the CMS, because of their alien nationality, continued to view themselves as divorced from the secular sectors of colonial life."

Dissociation from government was important to the CMS for two reasons: first, it allowed them to pursue activities unassociated with the secular

*needs which they considered inimical to spiritual life; and second, that missionaries could struggle in the wilderness unprotected and unencouraged (even thwarted) by government was a sign of divine protection.
(Ibid.: 61)*

Eventually, the CMS gained converts and established congregations. Certain practices introduced by the missionaries were embraced by the Kaguru, the most important being the religious revival. Revival "could occur only after Africans had been converted and then strayed. . . . Revival allowed a congregation to revalidate publicly certain norms which had been threatened; it also allowed readmission of persons who had been judged unfit for mission life, but whose skills were essential" (ibid.: 106–7). Revivalism was similar to traditional Kaguru witchcraft confessions. It seems likely that converts had, perhaps unwittingly, carried into their new religion practices developed in the old. Since the 1930s and 1940s, revival has become an important political mechanism among the Kaguru. "Through revival and the resultant assumption of new, superior moral status as 'saved' or 'reborn' Christians . . . local Africans could sometimes compete with local African pastors, catechists, and even European missionaries as the type of Christian most fit to judge and lead others" (ibid.: 108).

Africans and CMS missionaries often had radically opposed views of what the missionary example stood for. The missionaries saw themselves living an austere, altruistic life, with little in the way of material comforts, and they expected their converts to do with even less. Thus, they expected converts to work for the mission for less money than nonconverts, contributing the balance out of their love for God. Such practices were viewed as stingy by many Kaguru, who also thought the missionary talk about brotherhood was hypocritical, since however low missionary income was, African salaries were many times lower. "For Africans, the missionaries were failed Europeans. . . . Moreover, Africans saw the CMS as apparently not as well off as competing missions such as Roman Catholics" (ibid.: 68).

CMS missionaries supported revivalism, and yet they were wary of participating fully in revivals with Africans, lest their own admission of sin damage their prestige and authority. The CMS did not want to get involved in secular matters, such as education. Yet under the colonial regime it either provided the schools demanded by the colonial administration or lost government support. The CMS encouraged Bible study and direct inspiration by the word of God as set forth in the Bible, without the mediation of priests. But African converts who were literate were then able to read stories in the Bible about God redeeming his people from oppression. They began to identify with the oppressed and to see God as on their side. This was particularly disconcerting to the missionaries, who found themselves identified with the oppressors.

Perhaps the greatest irony revealed by Beidelman's study is that, nowadays, Kaguru who have rejected the rigorous CMS way of life are being asked by their own national government to live in much the same way. They are to work hard, deny themselves material comforts, and resist the temptation to deviate from authority. "There are new kinds of missionaries afoot in Ukaguru. Some of the sermons now preached by socialist bureaucrats may appear new, but their tactics and aims are not that different from what has passed away" (ibid.: 209).

Secular Persuasion: Modernizing the Third World ▀▀▀▀▀▀

Conquest established the fact of dominance. But to make that dominance profitable, the colonized peoples had to be molded into imperial subjects. This took persuasion. The colonial government relied in part on missionaries to win hearts and minds, but missionaries did not always see eye to eye with the colonial government. If we define colonization as cultural domination with enforced social change, then many nonmission projects were also engaged in winning hearts and minds—if not for God, then for capitalism.

Colonial authorities set about restructuring colonized territories in ways that would make those territories pay their way. To do this, they needed the active collaboration of the people. Sometimes, this collaboration was not volunteered and forced labor was employed. Yet other times, colonial authorities sought to persuade their subjects of the utility of conforming with colonial aims. For certain classes of the conquered population, conformity brought new wealth and power. They were taught—and they asked to be taught—how to do things in the Western way. Having learned, they took steps to cajole or threaten others to follow their lead.

Foreign-aid and development programs in the postcolonial period continue to follow this pattern. New states request help in industrial or agricultural development from Western nations. Implicitly or explicitly, they are offering to do things in a Western manner if the Western powers will but show them how. Locally, people may be forced to participate, but often the desire is to show the common people the advantages they personally will enjoy if they adopt new ways. Given that the secular powers are most concerned with economic development, it is often new ways of making a living that the people are urged to adopt. We can call this **secular persuasion** to the extent that peasants, for example, are not forced to plant new strains of crops at gunpoint. Of course, to the extent that all other options are beyond their reach as a result of current social, political, and economic arrangements, the element of force is never totally out of the picture.

The Demise of a Peasant Economy

For modernization theorists, the replacement of the "insufficiently developed economic techniques" of "traditional society" by the market techniques of capitalism is a sign of progress. From their perspective, therefore, the demise of a rural economy in an underdeveloped country might be cause for rejoicing. For anthropologist Stephen Gudeman (1978), however, the meaning of such transformations is highly ambiguous. Gudeman's research allowed him to watch as his self-sufficient peasant informants were transformed into a rural labor force at the bottom of the capitalist order in Panama. *(See EthnoFile 14.3: Village Panama.)*

EthnoFile 14.3
VILLAGE PANAMA
(Los Boquerones)

Region: Central America

Nation: Panama

Population: 350 (1970s)

Environment: Tropical

Livelihood: Contradictory: farming for use (rice) and sale (sugar cane)

Political organization: Part of modern state

Other: During the last twenty years there has been a transformation from subsistence rice cultivation to a total dependence upon cash-crop sugar cane production

In Gudeman's view, this economic transformation involved going from production for use (or subsistence production) to production for exchange (or commodity production). The transformation was triggered by the introduction of a cash crop, sugarcane. Traditionally, the peasants raised enough rice and other food crops to tide them over from one harvest to the next. This is the essence of subsistence production: producing what one consumes, and aiming to produce only enough of it to make it through the agricultural year. Once food needs and seed for the next season's planting have been met, the peasant need labor no more. The Panamanian peasants who were Gudeman's informants spent much of their "leisure time" involved in the celebrations of saints' days commemorated in the Roman Catholic religious calendar.

These peasants were independent producers of subsistence goods, and they all produced much the same goods. Rice was the food of choice and the centerpiece of peasant farming, and a loft full of drying rice was the symbol of the just fruits of labor. Rice farming had been practiced by generations of peasants, who passed down their knowledge to their sons. Given this culturally shaped understanding of the earth and crops and weather, the peasants then had to choose how and when and what to plant, as well as when to weed and harvest. Culture provided a rule of thumb to help them make such decisions. They would discuss the options endlessly with their neighbors, but ultimately the decisions were up to each individual peasant.

In subsistence economies, according to Gudeman, the cultural information pool does not expand. Subsistence production emphasizes not economic growth but production for *use*. The focus is on maintenance, on getting by—"to live, nothing more," as Gudeman's informants put it—in a situation of declining resources. Respectable people were people who were able to achieve this from one year to the next. Panamanian peasants pray to God for the strength to endure such repetitive work and to the saints for help in particular matters. "The Christ figure is a symbol of death and defeat more than resurrection and rebirth" (Gudeman 1978:44).

But traditional Panamanian peasants had devised only one possible way of making a living on their land. This became clear when commercial sugarcane farming was introduced in their area. The historical change from rice production for use to sugarcane production for exchange illustrates how two different modes of production can rely on different aspects of the natural environment. The choice of cash crop was in some respects decisive: sugarcane so alters the local ecology that land once planted in cane can never be used again for subsistence crops. Yet Gudeman does not make an ecological deterministic argument to explain the demise of the traditional rural economy. Instead, he points out that before sugarcane cash-cropping, before even the establishment of traditional peasant subsistence farming, there had been the conquest of Central America by the Spanish and the carving up of land by the victors. The successors of these original conquistadors continued to own all the land on which Gudeman's peasant informants were merely entitled to use rights. This prior distribution of resources meant that peasants were sharply limited in what they could do with the land they farmed under traditional circumstances. It also meant that whenever a profit-making venture involving the land was in the offing, the landowners would be the ones to control its development.

And so it was with sugarcane production. Wealthy Panamanian families owned the only two sugar mills to which farmers could sell their cane. Ironically, land reform promised to turn formerly landless peasants into small holders, but the plots they were to be allotted were too small to meet their subsistence needs. They were inexorably drawn into raising more and more sugarcane to sell for cash to buy what they needed. As this happened, the peasants' understandings of labor and time

Plantation agriculture—picking tea in Kenya.

were transformed. Cane cultivation was fitted into the "free" time, the "slack" period that had surrounded the original rice-growing season. In capitalism, time is money—but in subsistence agriculture, time is the surplus left after a person has produced enough food and seed for the next season.

The new relations of production linking mill owners, peasant landowner-producers, and landless peasant laborers were based on the traditional landlord-peasant prototype. In sugarcane production, however, owning the mill was even more important than owning land. This was because the production capacity and schedule of the mills determined the pace and level of local cane production. Gudeman writes:

> With their financial command the mills are able to loan money for all stages of crop production. Effectively, they pay for and "own" the seed, the labour invested and the product itself. At harvest time the peasant must turn over the product to liquidate these advances. Whether the final sums which [peasants] receive are to be termed profits or wages . . . is but a matter of terminology. Effectively all that the peasant as "owner" does is subcontract his labour, and this, of course, saves the mills a certain amount of administrative cost. (Ibid.: 139)

Production for exchange cannot be justified according to the system of values that peasants use to make sense of production for use: "Cane has 'utility' only when the peasant rids himself of it, the reverse of that which he does with rice" (ibid.: 121). What is required is a new frame of reference, new understandings about the meaning and end of labor. As soon as peasants become dependent on the sale of their sugarcane for their livelihood, they become dependent on the capitalist market, which had previously ignored them. The consequences are enormous, according to Gudeman: "This minimal shift in productive techniques actually represents and leads to a total economic transformation, for the peasants change their worldly conditions, from being independent, self-sufficient producers to becoming petty capitalists and day labourers" (ibid.: 122). Moreover, "as the peasant plants sugarcane, subsistence no longer refers to producing for consumption, it becomes only the standard of living. And this standard, which previously was defined in relation to others in the countryside and controlled by the individual labourer, now is defined in relation to other strata in Panamanian society and controlled by market prices in relation to the wage in sugarcane. . . . In this fashion a peasantry may become 'impoverished' by moving into capitalism. The 'underdevelopment' of a rural area may develop from the advent of capitalism itself" (ibid.: 140).

When Gudeman returned to the field in the mid-1970s, about a decade after his original study, he discovered that all the land was now owned by the government and devoted to raising sugarcane. In addition, the government had started its own mill. The shift from private enterprise to government ownership, plus a high world sugar price, had totally transformed the village economy. Gudeman calls it a transition from capitalism to state socialism. The government-owned mill controlled all aspects of sugarcane production. Since all available land had been planted with sugarcane, villagers could no longer depend on the countryside to support them. They now depended on the government.

As a result of these changes, Gudeman argues, the villagers can no longer be called peasants, because they lack the peasants' self-sufficiency. Their livelihood now depends entirely on the market in sugarcane. For every hectare of his land planted in sugarcane, a man receives seventy dollars at harvesttime from the mill, "regardless of land quality and actual yield" (ibid.: 158). In addition, most men work at the mill; the labor is easier, wages are much higher owing to high world sugar prices, and there are more amenities, market goods, and health and pension benefits. Yet these improvements are fragile. They have been obtained at the price of a loss of self-sufficiency and seem sustainable only as long as sugar prices remain high. When sugar prices drop, as they must, these former peasants will have little to fall back on.

Peasant Defenses against the Challenge of Capitalism

If the situation of Panamanian peasants is prototypical, then Gudeman's picture of "development" in the periphery of the world system paints a dismal future for peasants everywhere in the Third World. His informants are an example of a peasantry that has been totally "captured" by the capitalist mode of production. But some neo-marxian anthropologists question whether that fate is inevitable. Gudeman himself notes that one factor in the demise of peasant production for use in the village was the lack of institutionalized social relationships linking peasant families with one another. His informants thus lacked an established organizational framework on which they might have relied to defend their interests.

Strong suprafamilial social structures still flourish, however, in other societies of the periphery. It appears, for example, that indigenous kinship structures may sometimes be strong enough to allow peasants to defend their mode of production in the face of capitalist challenge. This seems to be the case among the Luo speakers of western Kenya, whose mode of livelihood was studied by anthropologist Steven Johnson (1988). *(See EthnoFile 14.4: Luo.)* In western Kenya, as in the interior of Panama, land is a crucial force of production both for subsistence and for exchange. All land is now privately owned, but peasants in need of land for production have a choice as to how to go about obtaining access to it. They can purchase it or rent it, or they can approach landowners who are members of their clan and ask that they be granted a plot for cultivation. This last system of land allocation does

EthnoFile 14.4
LUO (Speakers of)

Region: East Africa

Nation: Western Kenya

Population: 3,250,000

Environment: High plateau near Lake Victoria

Livelihood: Agriculture (maize, beans, sorghum)

Political organization: Traditionally some men with influence; now elected subchiefs and chiefs, part of modern state

Other: The Luo were formerly a cattle-herding people

not treat land as a commodity, and use rights to land are distributed on the basis of traditional generalized reciprocity. Access to other forces of production are equally available in the same two ways. For example, ox-plow teams, seed, and even labor may be purchased on the market for cash, or else one may gain access to them without charge from neighbors or relatives.

Johnson argues that among his informants in western Kenya, "the importance of kinship obligations and generalized reciprocity suggest an association with a noncapitalist mode of production" (1988:15). He describes his research area as a social formation characterized by two articulating modes of production, one capitalist and one noncapitalist. "The point of articulation between capitalist and noncapitalist modes of production is the peasant household where decisions are made regarding which set of social relationships is to be activated at particular points in the production process" (ibid.). Kinship institutions are strong, and peasants remain committed to their kin as well as to ideas of prestige and autonomy that are apt in a kin-ordered mode of production. These sociocultural facts, together with the fact that peasants still exercise some control over the forces of production, have allowed them to prevent the demise of their rural economy despite the penetration of western Kenya by the capitalist mode of production.

The Power of the Gun

As with everything else in social life, the plausibility of theories about the destiny of Third World peoples depends on which aspects of their experiences are focused on. A deterministic view holds that capitalism was bound to triumph, whether for good or for ill. But such a view is challenged by the last example, in which capitalism's advance seems to have stalled indefinitely. Even more challenging are cases in which the victims of cultural domination with forced social change resist the dominators and reject the social changes being forced on them. Specifically, these were indigenous peoples who not only cut political ties to colonial or neocolonial rulers, but also attempted to cut economic ties to the entire capitalist world system. Such dramatic actions often involved the use of military force and might reasonably be called, as Eric Wolf (1969) calls them, *peasant wars of the twentieth century.*

Wolf examined six cases of peasant revolution in the twentieth century: Mexico, Russia, China, Vietnam, Algeria, and Cuba. To understand these revolutions, he argues, requires looking at the historical developments leading up to them. In all six cases, those developments can be traced to the "world-wide spread and diffusion of a particular cultural system, that of North Atlantic capitalism," which was "profoundly alien to many of the areas which it engulfed in its spread" (Wolf 1969:276).

The prototypical situation in these cases is colonialism, understood as cultural domination with forced social change. The dominating cultural system in colonialism was capitalism. As a result, forced social change involved getting local peoples to accept the key capitalist metaphor: that land, people, and things can all be treated as objects made for sale on the market. Most peasants who tried to live by this capitalist metaphor were ill equipped to withstand the risks and losses it entailed. Some peasants, however, were not only threatened by capitalism but had sufficient resources to try to resist it, by force if necessary. These were "middle peasants" who owned some land, or peasants living in regions on the fringe of control by landlords. They acted not with the intention of ushering in a new order, but with the goal of making the world they knew safe for peasants like themselves. Once successful, however, their revolutionary actions made it impossible to return to the way of life they originally set out to defend.

The revolutions examined by Wolf all were waged by armed bands of peasants, but they probably would not have succeeded had not other indigenously organized social groups been fighting with them. Sometimes peasants fought alongside a "paramilitary party organized around a certain vision of what the new society is to be" (ibid.: 296), such as the Bolsheviks in Russia. The Russian revolution was widely viewed as the first successful overthrow of capitalism. It thus became the earliest prototype for revolutionaries seeking to oust capitalists elsewhere. This was the case, for example, in the Chinese and Vietnamese revolutions: "A common Marxist ideology—and especially the Leninist concept of the revolutionary leadership, leading the masses in the interest of the masses—furnished a ready-made idiom in which to cast their own experience of fusion between rebel soldiery and revolutionary leadership" (ibid.: 297). But revolutionary leaders soon discovered that the Russian example could not be slavishly imitated. Thus, in China, for example, Mao concluded that peasants, rather than industrial workers, constituted the oppressed class in whose interest war would be waged.

Peasant revolutionaries were also able to draw on other traditional group structures and use them to organize their armed resistance. The idiom of socialism meshed nicely with communal idioms characteristic of traditional village organization in China and Vietnam, for example. What was revolutionary, however, was taking what had been a village idiom and applying it to relations linking villages with one another and with the army. Indeed, a large part of the subversive power of revolution comes from the way it allows new metaphors to enter social life through armed struggle. That is, it is not enough simply to declare that all people are brothers and sisters. Nor is it enough to preach that peasants, soldiers, workers, and intellectuals are equals. The experience that makes these metaphorical assertions plausible occurs for revolutionaries as they make their revolution. Wolf states, for example, that by the time they achieved victory in 1949, the citizen-soldiers of the Chinese revolution had lived through a variety of practical experiences that had turned ideological claims into reality:

> *The experience of war in the hinterland had taken them far from cities and industrial areas; it had taught them the advantages of dispersal, of a wide distribution of basic skills rather than a dense concentration of advanced skills. The citizen-soldiers of the guerrilla army had, in fact, lived lives in which the roles of peasant, worker, soldier, and intellectual intermingled to the point of fusion. . . . In China the relation of the peasant to the citizen-army was immediate and concrete. (Ibid.: 300)*

Wolf's study of these six peasant revolutions only reinforces the view that people in Third World societies who resist capitalism, with or without violence, have legitimate grievances. The anthropological assumption that Third World peasants are human beings, fully capable of recognizing when they are being taken advantage of, would lead us to expect no less. Yet from colonial times to the present day, those in power, whose ways are being rejected, have often experienced great difficulty accepting that this can be the case. Ethnocentrism and anxiety about their own interests lead them to assume that because they are dominant, those they dominate must be lesser human beings. Lesser beings should be content with a lesser life, and should not complain about their lot, which is suitable for them. If they do complain, the only explanation can be that someone from the outside is stirring them up. Underestimating the humanity of the world's disinherited classes, while it may be comforting to those in power, can be tragically misleading.

Many of the case materials in this chapter demonstrate the human ability to cope creatively with changed life circumstances. They remind us that human beings are not passive in the face of the new, that they actively and resiliently respond to the challenges life brings them. Yet the example of the Kréen-Akaróre and others like them reminds us that successful adaptation is never assured. Modes of livelihood that may benefit some human groups can overwhelm and destroy others. Western capitalism has created a world system of powerful interlocking interests that resists easy control. A critical self-awareness of our common humanity, together with concerted practical action to lessen exploitation, may be all that can prevent the modern world system from destroying us all.

Key Terms

capitalism	modernization theory	neo-marxian theory
political economy	dependency theory	articulating modes of
use rights	development-of-underdevelopment	production
land tenure	world-system theory	sacred persuasion
colonialism	core	secular persuasion
neocolonialism	periphery	

Chapter Summary

1. Modern Western history has been characterized by the rise of *capitalism*, both as a particular kind of economic system and as a way of life that developed in response to, and in service to, the economic system. The achievements of European capitalism were in many cases financed by wealth brought to Europe from other parts of the globe. As a result, other parts of the globe were also transformed.
2. The arrival of capitalism outside the West was often accompanied by the growth of new, commercially oriented cities, which became the focus of intense culture change. Western influence was usually greatest in such cities, and since the West was seen as "modern," city life came to be seen as modern life. Depending upon how this Western "modernity" affected them, people could view cities positively or negatively—or even both ways at once.
3. The capitalist penetration of non-Western societies was frequently followed by the political conquest of such societies, which were then reshaped to streamline the system of economic exploitation. Indigenous peoples were radically transformed, as they lost their autonomy and were reintegrated as component groups within a larger new society.

4. The *colonial* order may be viewed as a *political economy*; although its primary reason for existing rested on the material interest of the colonizers, that interest was defended and enhanced by means of political and military power. Colonial empires drew together vast and previously unconnected areas of the world, economically and politically.

5. Although colonies were politically controlled by the colonizers, political independence did not free former colonies from deeply entangling economic ties with their former masters. These entanglements have, in some cases, persisted for over a hundred years, and have been called *neocolonialism*.

6. The key metaphor of capitalism is that everything in the world is a commodity. Put another way, the world is a market and everything within the world—including land, human beings, and material objects—can be bought and sold. Such a view was unknown in noncapitalist societies, but Western colonialism changed things. To function intelligibly within the capitalist world order, colonized peoples had also to begin to see the world as a storehouse of potential commodities.

7. Western colonialism triggered a series of profound changes throughout the world. During its heyday in the late nineteenth century, early social scientists began to offer theories designed to explain these changes. Today, there are four major theoretical positions that anthropologists have used to explain culture change in the non-Western world. These are *modernization theory, dependency theory, world system theory*, and *neo-marxian theory*.

8. Although many varieties of modern social change are backed by force, people attempting to introduce change often rely more on tactics of persuasion. Missionaries accompanied Western colonizers wherever they went and attempted to persuade conquered peoples of the superiority of Western religious world views. Secular authorities likewise attempted to persuade conquered peoples of the superiority of capitalist economic and political institutions. Many colonized groups embraced these world views and institutions, often with unforeseen consequences.

9. Many anthropologists assumed that capitalist takeover of traditional societies either had long since occurred or inevitably would occur at some point in the future. Nevertheless, some societies seem successfully to have resisted capitalist takeover, either by maintaining noncapitalist modes of production alongside the capitalist mode, or by using military force to eject the capitalists from their midst.

Suggested Readings

Bodley, John. *Tribal Peoples and Development Issues*. Palo Alto, Calif.: Mayfield Publishing Company, 1988.
> An excellent collection of articles, some recent, some dating back into the nineteenth century, that provide examples of the effect of the modern world system on tribal peoples.

——. *Victims of Progress*. 2d ed. Palo Alto, Calif.: Mayfield Publishing Company, 1988.
> A very accessible, but very depressing, documentation of the destruction of tribal peoples throughout the world, all in the name of progress.

Davis, Shelton. *Victims of the Miracle: Development and the Indians of Brazil*. New York: Cambridge University Press, 1977.
> A devastating examination of the effect of the "Brazilian Miracle" on the Indians of Brazil. Excellent documentation, profoundly disturbing.

Gudeman, Stephen. *The Demise of a Rural Economy*. London: Routledge and Kegan Paul, 1978.

A case study in the transformations of production brought about by the imposition of cash-cropping in rural Panama.

Wallerstein, Immanuel. *The Modern World-System*. New York: Academic Press, 1974.

A difficult but tremendously influential work that started the world-system approach to understanding and explaining patterns of social change in recent Western history.

Wolf, Eric. *Peasant Wars of the Twentieth Century*. New York: Harper and Row, 1969.

An important, readable study of the commonalities of this century's major wars of revolution.

The Skills and Work of The Anthropologist

Stephen Gudeman (Ph.D., Cambridge University) is a Professor of Anthropology at the University of Minnesota. He has undertaken fieldwork in the lowlands of Panama and the highlands of Colombia. Author of numerous works on Latin American social life, he has also published two books on Panama and a cross-cultural work on metaphors and models of economic practices. Recently he has been investigating the past and present relations between the house and corporation in the rural regions of Colombia and the economies of Europe.

According to the accepted wisdom, poets should be especially facile with language and stretch our vision with freshly cut images. Historians, with their knowledge of past events, offer a wise and sweeping view of human change and continuities. Physical scientists, who have analytical yet creative minds, bring us discoveries and insights about the natural world.

What about anthropologists? Have we any finely honed talents and gifts for the world? In my view, anthropology is the most demanding of all the disciplines, but the skills of the anthropologist and the rewards receive little publicity.

The well-known image, repeated in popular films and the *National Geographic,* is partially true. Anthropologists do not have to be fearless explorers, but it is challenging to live in the humid rain forest, on the hot savannah, or on giddy slopes ten thousand feet above sea level. Undertaking field research requires physical stamina and wry if not perverse pleasure at having to make sudden changes in one's diet and life-style. Fieldwork is hard.

But the struggle against adversity soon loses its glitter, and I have found that the anthropologist's romance is more subtle and internal. My excitement comes not from uncovering a stone or lost city, for these are only lifeless residues, but in discovering the patterns that other humans have made in and of their lives. People leave their traces in history, and they inscribe their imaginative faculties in their world. The anthropologist often has the special privilege of discovering a different pattern of life—a marriage form, a religious belief, a way of securing the necessaries of life. Eventually, we may find that some of these patterns are repeated time and again, but because they are human products, their discovery is more fundamental than in the natural sciences. One hot and muggy summer in Panama, I was thrilled to realize that relations among parents, godparents, and godchildren in Latin America (the *compadrazgo*) is a kind of mirror reversal of the ties found between nuclear family members. Two decades later, when I heard Colombian country people talk like European economists of several centuries past, I feverishly set off on a five-year voyage through historical texts —and the Andes of Colombia.

Because anthropology is the study of human life, the anthropologist needs to know a little something about everything—from psychology to legal history to ecology. Our field equipment is primitive, for we rely mainly on the eye, the ear, and the tongue. Because ethnographers carry few tools to the field and the tools they have can hardly capture the totality of the situation, the background and talents of the researcher strongly determine what is "seen" and how it is understood. But the field experience itself has a special impact, too. I studied economic practices in Panama because I was trained to do so, but the field research forced me to alter all the notions I had been taught. Most of them were useless! Anthropologists try to open themselves up to every facet of their field situation and to allow its richness to envelop them. In this, the tasks of the anthropologist are very unlike those of the normal laboratory scientist: the anthropologist can have no predefined hypothesis and testing procedures. The best equipment an ethnographer can possess is a "good ear" and patience to let the "data talk."

This is not all. In the field, anthropologists carry out intense and internal conversations with themselves. Every observation, whether clearly seen or dimly realized, must be brought to consciousness, shuffled about, and questioned. Only by recognizing and acknowledging their own incomprehension can anthropologists generate new questions and lines of inquiry. In the solitude of the field, the anthropologist must try to understand the limits of her or his knowledge, have the courage to live with uncertainty, and retain the ambition to seize on openings to insight.

But field studies constitute only a part of the total research process. Once home, the field notes have to be read and reread, put aside, and then rearranged. The anthropologist is a pattern seeker, believing that within the data human designs are to be found. The task is like solving a puzzle, except that there is no fixed solution and the puzzle's pieces keep changing their shapes! With work and insight, however, a picture—an understanding or an explanation—begins to emerge.

Eventually, the results of all these efforts are conveyed to others, and so anthropologists also need to have expository skills and persuasive powers, for they have to convince others of their picture and of their viewpoint about how cultures and social lives are put together.

The skills needed to be an anthropologist are as limitless as the cultures we study. Could any discipline be as challenging or rewarding? In this lies the fascination and allure of anthropology.

Stephen Gudeman

Islam in the Modern World

Ever since a group of so-called Islamic fundamentalists seized the U.S. Embassy in Tehran in 1979, Americans have been both fascinated and repelled by the glimpse they had of the beliefs and practices of Islam. Militant Muslims whose political aims are cast in the language of religion, and who do not fear violent confrontation with their enemies, have been stereotyped as religious fanatics with a thirst for blood. Anthropologist Michael Gilsenan, who has spent more than twenty years studying life in the Middle East, takes issue with such popular stereotypes.

Gilsenan recognizes that contemporary political struggles in the Muslim world have involved physical violence. But this violence can be understood as only one element in a far more fundamental struggle over the definition of what it means to be a Muslim. Muslims must come to terms with a modern world in which their traditional societies have been ravaged by colonial and neocolonial exploitation by the West. Their goal is to rebuild an authentic Islamic way of life, free of Western domination and exploitation and yet responsive to the problems and needs of life in the twentieth century.

Islam provides its adherents with a number of conceptual tools with which to make sense of the world and to formulate action in the world. Of these, Gilsenan emphasizes the centrality of three such elements: the Book (i.e., the Qur'an, containing the word of God as revealed through the lips of Muhammad and later written down); the Family (i.e.,

Iranian women demonstrate against the United States, 1979.

the Prophet Muhammad, his family, and their living descendants); and the Tradition (i.e., "that which we have always done and believed and from which we have derived our social forms" [Gilsenan 1982:15]).

Muslims do not always agree on what role each of these elements should play in everyday life. For example, what role should be accorded the descendants of the Prophet and his family? Are they entitled to an elevated status because of their close relationship (both physical and mystical) to the Prophet? Or because the Prophet emphasized that he was but a human being and that all reverence should be accorded God, should his descendants have no rights beyond those of ordinary Muslims?

The position one defends on this point is of far more than academic significance. The major division in the Muslim community—that between Sunni and Shi'ite sects—is based on a disagreement dating back to the early years of Islam. That disagreement was over how to choose leaders for the Muslim community after the death of Muhammad. This was an important matter, since the proper way to choose a successor was not set out in the Qur'an or anywhere else. The Sunni tradition originated among those who argued that the proper successor was someone who most closely represented the piety and practice of the Prophet, whether he was kin to the Prophet or not. The Shi'ite tradition originated among those who argued that kinship to the Prophet *did* matter and that successors to Muhammad should be chosen from among his relatives. When the prophet's grandson, Hussein, was killed at the Battle of Kerbela in A.D. 680, those responsible for his death assumed leadership of the Muslim community. They founded the Umayyid dynasty, whose legitimacy rested on presumed faithfulness to the spirit and practice of Islam, rather than on descent from the Prophet's family.

Yet this Sunni victory, brought on by force of arms, did not eliminate the Shi'ite cause. The Shi'ites were able to turn Hussein and his father, Ali, who was also murdered, into martyrs whose symbolic power continues to infuse their movement with energy. Sunni Muslims have been challenged and

repudiated by successors to the first Shi'ites. Indeed, after a few decades, they overthrew the Umayyid caliphate and replaced it with their own Abbasid dynasty. Physical opposition alone could not wipe them out; in fact, it seems only to have stimulated the growth of their cause. Consequently, over time, the Shi'ites have been able to develop a complex theology concerning the legitimate leadership of the community by one of the Prophet's descendants or, barring that, by his legitimate representatives.

Muslims face the same kind of dilemma that Americans face when they must decide not only the meaning of liberty and equality, but also which should take precedence over the other when the two conflict. Different factions in the Muslim world can be distinguished by their accounts of the meaning of the Book, the Family, and the Tradition—and how these should be related to one another in times of uncertainty. Part of the difficulty involves relating traditional principles to the current historical context. Muslims struggling to define "true Islam" are no less free of this difficulty than modern Americans attempting to define "the American way of life."

For example, one frequently quoted traditional saying of the Prophet is "My community will not agree on error." But who are the "community"—legal scholars? a ruling elite? all faithful Muslims? And how is "agreement" to be established—by edict? by voting, in a manner analogous to what occurs in Western democracies? Or is voting, because its modern form was a Western invention, to be ruled out as un-Islamic? And who decides?

Gilsenan uses the example of Turkey to illustrate the political repercussions of such divided opinion. For centuries, Turkey was the center of the Muslim Ottoman Empire. The ruling elite's support of the opinions of traditional Islamic legal scholars, the 'ulema, certified the country's Islamic character. In exchange for this enormous social power, the 'ulema were content to leave matters of state in the hands of a nonscholarly elite. The outcome of the alliance between ruling elite and the 'ulema was an official Turkish version of Islam that identified the authentic faith with the version propounded by the 'ulema.

This arrangement troubled some Turks who, in the early twentieth century, had gained experience of Western ideas and practices. They wanted to "modernize" their country along Western lines and believed that to do so, Islam too would have to be "modernized." Eventually, under the leadership of Kemal Ataturk, the modernizers were able to overthrow the Ottoman state and replace it with a new form of government from which religion was explicitly excluded. The modern Turkish government would observe strict separation of "mosque" and "state." This meant that the 'ulema lost their traditional authority among the rulers, together with their elite status.

These transformations of Turkish society have often been termed *secularization,* the elimination of religion or religious considerations from political affairs. But, although the ruling elite may have been secularized by the changes, this does not imply that the rest of society was also secularized. Indeed, Gilsenan argues, quite the opposite was the case. The entrenchment of the new Westernized elite under Ataturk meant not just that the traditional religious scholars had been demoted. It meant also that the restructuring of Turkish society along Western capitalist lines had been officially sanctioned, a state of affairs that threatened the poorer classes with permanent dislocation and deprivation. The stage was set for an alliance between both outcast groups, and, Gilsenan claims, this is exactly what happened.

Once the 'ulema had been repudiated by the ruling elite, they were, in Gilsenan's words, "allowed to become popular." Both the 'ulema and the urban and rural lower classes felt betrayed by the new Turkish government. They articulated this sense of betrayal in the one idiom they shared: the language of Islam. The hardship of the lower classes and the demotion of the religious scholars were taken as evidence that the new rulers were not practicing true Islam. Where Islam is truly observed, they seemed to be saying, the sufferings of the poor are eased, not intensified, and the opinions of learned scholars are respected and heeded. The new rulers, on their part, viewed both the lower classes and the 'ulema as vestiges of backwardness whose ignorance of the modern world made them obstacles to Turkish national progress. They were equally convinced that their version of Islam—" 'properly' organized, responsible to the state, limited in its functions to carefully defined spheres, and concerned with a sober, 'rationalist' reading of scripture" (Gilsenen 1982:43)—was wholly authentic and appropriate to the modern world. The resulting political opposition within the Turkish state persists into the present day.

Similar conflicts rend other Islamic societies. In all cases, each party to the dispute "has strong definitions of true religion" and each can be observed "using the same signs and codes but seeing events in quite different ways" (ibid.: 11). All parties turn to Tradition for clues to help them make sense of their current experiences, but they make use of Tradition in different ways. Gilsenan argues that Tradition "is a term that is in fact highly variable and shifting in content."

> *In the name of tradition many traditions are born and come into opposition with others. It becomes a language, a weapon against internal and external enemies, a refuge, an evasion, or part of the entitlement to domination and authority over others. One of the single most important elements in what is often called Islamic fundamentalism is precisely this struggle over the definition of what is the tradition. This means not only a religious interpretation but a whole form of life. (Ibid.: 15)*

Alaskan Inuit (Eskimo)

Utkuhikhalingmiut (Utku Eskimos)

Cree
(Short Grass Reserve)

Nootka

Cheyenne
(c. 1830)

Minnesota

Navajo

Huichol

Sefrou

Cairo

Sidi Lahcen Lyussi

Colonial Oaxaca

Village Panama (Los Boquerones)

Yucatecan Maya

Wolof   Hausa   Guider

Dinka

Kuranko

Cauca Valley

Yanomamo

Sherbro

Baule

Marghi

Nuer

Otavalo

Kpelle

Tiv

Ashanti

Mbuti

Brazil

Igbo

Kaguru

Samoa

Bangwa

Nyakyusa

Fang

Bolivian Tin Miners
(Cholos)

Azande

Lovedu

Tswana

(speakers of) Luo

!Kung

Iteso

Giriama

Mombasa Swahilis

Gisu

Boran

Somalis (Northern)

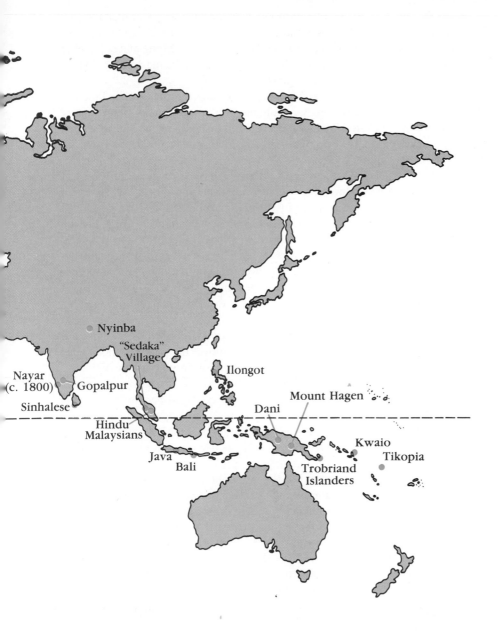

Nyinba

"Sedaka"
Village

Nayar
(c. 1800)　Gopalpur

Sinhalese

Ilongot

Mount Hagen

Dani

Hindu
Malaysians

Java

Bali

Kwaio

Tikopia

Trobriand
Islanders

Sir E. B. Tylor (1832–1917).

Many students say that they have found anthropology interesting—very interesting in fact—and that they have learned a great deal about ethnocentrism, about other cultures, and about themselves. But they frequently go on and ask what use it is. What can they *do* with it? What is the *point* of it if they don't go on to university teaching? An appropriate response usually comes in three parts.

Anthropology beyond the University

The students' first concern is practical: Do anthropologists do anything other than teach at universities? The answer is yes.

Sir E. B. Tylor, a founder of anthropology in the early 1870s, called the new field "a reformer's science." The commitment to changing things did not last, however. Anthropology soon came to be concerned more with describing and explaining the world rather than changing it. Even so, there were always some anthropologists who believed that their discipline had a practical side.

Margaret Mead saw anthropology's practical side throughout her long career. Following her first fieldwork in Samoa in the 1920s, she began to speak out on issues of concern in the United States. She suggested that adolescence in the United States did no have to be as stormy as it was. Perhaps we could learn from the Samoans about the nature of adolescence.

In the 1930s and 1940s, several anthropologists played important roles in attempts to reform the U.S. Bureau of Indian Affairs. During World War II, Mead and other anthropologists were actively involved in the war effort. They developed strategies for boosting morale at home. As the war ended, they helped draw up terms that would allow the Japanese to surrender with as little turmoil as possible.

After World War II, most anthropologists left government work and went back to their universities, becoming more concerned with the details of anthropological theory than with any practical impact they might have had. During this period, the discipline grew at a phenomenal rate, but the growth of the practical aspects and applications of anthropology lagged.

Anthropology was strongly affected by the events of the 1960s. The general distrust of authority was tied to an increasing concern over the uses to which social science data were being put. These concerns increased during the war in Vietnam. For many anthropologists, as for professionals in many other disciplines, the times seemed to demand social action. Coupled with what Erve Chambers (1985:9) calls four major events, *applied anthropology* became increasingly popular and important.

The first of these events was a gradual maturation of the discipline. This led to a broader range of concerns, including those associated with regional, national, and even international systems.

The second event was that the peoples with whom anthropologists have traditionally worked have become more sophisticated and aware as they have become part of the world system. As a result, they are increasingly pointing to the power imbalance between themselves and the anthropologists. As noted in chapter 3, anthropologists leave the cultures they study; local people cannot. In addition, while anthropologists have taken much from the societies they have studied, they have not always given much in return. Some anthropologists have felt that the knowledge they have gained and the careers they have established as a result require greater return than a mention in a footnote. In some places, anthropologists have been

Applied anthropologists work in a variety of settings. Here, gerontologist Dena Shenk interviews an informant while carrying out a research project for a local social service agency on the status of the rural elderly.

called on to remedy this imbalance by demonstrating how their work will directly benefit the local community.

The third event was that anthropologists have become more likely to undertake work in the United States. This trend is in part a result of the difficulty of obtaining grants to support fieldwork outside the United States. (Anthropologists, like other scholars, find that they must sometimes make decisions based on factors that are outside the discipline. Sociopolitical, historical, or economic issues may sometimes prove as important as anthropological theory.) The trend toward working in the United States also stems from a concern about the problems of our own society and what an anthropological perspective can bring to their solution.

The fourth event was that over the past fifteen years there have been more and more new Ph.D. anthropologists and fewer and fewer academic jobs. As a result, students and professors have had to realize that "the profession must either shrink or prepare its students for a greater variety of employment possibilities" (Chambers 1985:10).

In answer to this need, applied anthropology programs have appeared and grown all over the United States during the last decade. This new direction in the field finds anthropologists today in all sorts of areas. Some are psychotherapists, employing the insights of anthropologist Gregory Bateson and others on family systems and family therapy. Others are cross-cultural social workers. Still others have become actively involved in international development, often working for or on contract with the U.S. Agency for International Development (AID). Their work includes projects dealing with such issues as appropriate technology, fuelwood shortages, agricultural credit, new lands development, feasibility studies for dams and other projects, bilingual education, livestock improvement and range management, and the like (for more examples, see Partridge 1984).

Other anthropologists are in medical anthropology, a new and rapidly growing field. Some are involved in gerontology, designing programs for the elderly and doing research on aging in different cultures. Others work in public or community health, medical education, nursing, or hospital planning. Another important area of work is in medical care delivery to distinct ethnic groups. This is related to applied anthropological work in international health, which includes demographics, epidemiology, planning and development of health programs, family planning, environmental health, and the like. Some anthropologists have gone into public policy and planning as interpreters, mediators, civil servants, or urban planners.

We will look at two cases in greater detail.

Sorghum and Millet in Honduras and the Sudan

Applied anthropologists carry out much work in international development, often in agricultural programs. The U.S. Agency for International Development is the principal instrument of U.S. foreign development assistance. One new direction taken by AID in the mid-1970s was to create multidisciplinary research programs to improve food crops in developing countries. An early research program dealt with sorghum and millet, which are important grains in some of the poorest countries in the world. This was the International Sorghum/Millet Research Project (INTSORMIL). Selected American universities investigated in one of six areas: plant breeding, agronomy, plant pathology, plant physiology, food chemistry, and socioeconomic studies.

Anthropologists from the University of Kentucky were selected for the socioeconomic study. They used ethnographic field research techniques to gain firsthand knowledge of the socioeconomic constraints on the production, distribution, and consumption of sorghum and millet among limited-resource agricultural producers in the western Sudan and in Honduras. They intended to make their findings available to INTSORMIL as well as to scientists and government officials in the host countries. They believed sharing such knowledge could lead to more effective research and development. This task also required ethnographic research and anthropological skill.

The principal investigators from the University of Kentucky were Edward Reeves, Billie DeWalt, and Katherine DeWalt. The approach they took was a holistic and comparative one, called Farming Systems Research (FSR). This approach attempts to determine the techniques used by farmers with limited resources to cope with the social, economic, and ecological conditions under which they live. What makes FSR holistic is that it examines how the different crops and livestock raised are integrated and managed as a system. It also relates farm productivity to household consumption and off-farm sources of family income (Reeves, DeWalt, and DeWalt 1987:74). This is very different from the traditional methods of agricultural research, which grow and test one crop at a time in an experiment station. The scientists at INTSORMIL are generally acknowledged among the best sorghum and millet researchers in the world, but their expertise comes from traditional agricultural research methods. They have spent little time working on the problems of limited-resource farmers in Third World countries.

The anthropologists saw their job as facilitating "a constant dialog between the farmer, who can tell what works best given the circumstances, and agricultural scientists, who produce potentially useful new solutions to old problems" (ibid.: 74–75). However, this was easier said than done in the sorghum/millet project. The referential perspectives of farmers and scientists were very different from one another. The anthropologists found themselves having to learn the languages and the conceptual systems of both the farmers and the agricultural scientists in order for the two groups to be able to communicate with each other.

The FSR anthropologists had the following research goals:

1. To find those things that were holding back the increased production of sorghum and millet. By doing this, they could identify areas that needed attention from the agricultural researchers.

2. To discover which aspects of new technology the farmers thought might benefit them the most.

3. To suggest how new crop "varieties and/or technologies might most easily and beneficially be introduced into communities and regions."

4. "To suggest the long-term implications that changing production, distribution, and consumption patterns might have on these communities" (Ibid.: 74).

The anthropologists began research in June 1981 in western Sudan and in southern Honduras. They were in the field for fourteen months of participant-observation and in-depth interviewing, as well as survey interviewing of limited-resource farmers, merchants, and middlemen. They discovered that the most significant constraints the farmers faced were uncertain rainfall, low soil fertility, and inadequate labor and financial resources (ibid.: 80). Equally important were the social and cultural systems within which the farmers were embedded. Farmers based their farming decisions on their understanding of who they were and what farming meant in their own cultures.

As a result of the FSR group's research, it became increasingly clear that "real progress in addressing the needs of small farmers in the Third World called for promising innovations to be tested at village sites and on farmers' fields under conditions that closely approximated those which the farmers experience" (ibid.: 77). Convincing the scientists and bureaucrats of this required the anthropologists to become advocates for the limited-resource farmers. Bill DeWalt and Edward Reeves

Economic development in Third World countries often proceeds unevenly. Applied anthropologists are concerned to promote policies that do not neglect the people with the fewest resources.

ended up negotiating INTSORMIL's contracts with the Honduran and Sudanese governments, and were successful at representing the farmers. They had to learn enough about the bureaucracies and the agricultural scientists so they could put the farmers' interests in terms the others could understand.

As a result of the applied anthropologists' work, INTSORMIL scientists learned to understand how small farmers in two countries made agricultural decisions. They also learned that not all limited-resource farmers are alike. The poorest third of the Sudanese farmers, for example, have to decide during the cropping season whether to weed their own gardens or weed someone else's for a wage. If they choose the former, they realize a long-term gain but they and their families go hungry. The latter choice enables them to buy food in the short run, but lowers their own harvests later. The decisions farmers make, and the needs they have, are context sensitive.

Together with INTSORMIL, the Honduran and Sudanese governments have increased funding for projects aimed at limited-resource farmers. Staff have been assigned to work with INTSORMIL, new programs have begun, and the research results of the anthropologists are guiding the breeding of sorghum.

Reeves, DeWalt, and DeWalt warn that it is too early to demonstrate gains in sorghum or millet production and use in either country. "Nevertheless, INTSORMIL scientists are clearly coming to accept the farming systems research goals and the value of anthropological fieldwork. The FSR Group has argued that on-site research is both desirable and necessary for the problems of farmers to be correctly identified and that eventually on-farm testing of new plant varieties and technologies will be essential to ensure that farmers are going to accept them" (ibid.: 79).

The INTSORMIL staff was so impressed by the work of the applied anthropologists that it has begun funding long-term research directed at relieving the constraints that limited-resource farmers face. For example, rather than trying to develop and then introduce hybrids, INTSORMIL research is now aimed at modifying the existing varieties of sorghum. The goal is better-yielding local varieties that can be grown together with other crops.

In summary, Reeves, DeWalt, and DeWalt point out that without the anthropological research, fewer development funds would have been allocated to research in Sudan and Honduras. More important, without the anthropological research, the nature of the development aid would have been different.

Lead Poisoning among Mexican American Children

In the summer of 1981, a Mexican American child was treated for lead poisoning in the emergency room of a Los Angeles hospital. When the child's stomach was pumped, a bright orange powder was found. It was lead tetroxide, more than 90 percent elemental lead. Lead in that form is not found in the three most common sources of lead poisoning in children in the United States: eating lead-based paint chips, living and playing near a smelter where even the dust has a high lead content, and eating off pottery with an improperly treated lead glaze. Under questioning by health professionals, the mother revealed that her child had been given a folk remedy in powdered form—*azarcon*. Azarcon was used to treat an illness called *empacho*, part of the Mexican American set of culturally recognized diseases. Empacho is believed to be a combination of indigestion and constipation.

As a result of this case, a public health alert was sent out nationally to clinics and physicians. The alert turned up another case of lead poisoning from azarcon in Greeley, Colorado. A culturally sensitive nurse had read about the Los Angeles case, and asked if the mother was treating the child for empacho. She was. Additional questioning in Los Angeles and Greely turned up what appeared to be widespread knowledge of azarcon in both Mexican American communities. The US Public Health Service decided that an anthropological study of azarcon would be useful.

The Public Health Service in Dallas called Dr. Robert Trotter, who had done research on Mexican American folk medicine. Trotter had never heard of azarcon. Although he checked in all the herb shops where folk medicines are sold in four towns, and talked with folk healers, he did not find it in south Texas. Trotter was relieved that the problem seemed to be confined to the western United States.

A short time later, Trotter received a packet of information from the Los Angeles County Health Department, which had discovered that there were several different names for the same preparation. He went back to the herb shops with the new names. When he asked for *greta*, he was sold a heavy yellow powder that turned out to be lead oxide with an elemental lead content of approximately 90 percent. The shop owners said it was used to treat empacho. Here was confirmation that two related lead-based remedies were being used to treat empacho. Trotter discovered that a wholesale distributor in Texas was selling greta to over 120 herb shops.

Trotter was asked to work in a health education project designed to reduce the use of these lead-based remedies. Because of the nature of the problem, he had six different clients with somewhat different needs and responsibilities. The first client was the Public Health Service office in Dallas, which sponsored the first study he did.

The second client was the task force that had been formed to create and implement a health education project in Colorado and California. Task force members wanted to reduce the risk of people using azarcon. In doing so, however, they did not want to attack or denigrate the folk medical system that promoted the use of azarcon. They knew that attacks on folk beliefs would produce strong resistance to the entire health campaign and make people ignore the message, no matter how important it was. The task force hoped Trotter's ethnographic data on Mexican American folk medicine could be used to help design a health awareness campaign that would encourage a switch to nonpoisonous remedies.

The goal of the task force became product substitution—to convince people to switch from greta or azarcon to another remedy for empacho that was already part of the folk medical system but was harmless. This strategy was based on an old advertising technique: It is easier to get people to switch from one product to another when both products perform the same function; it is difficult or impossible to get people to stop using a product they think they need, regardless of its known danger, unless an acceptable alternative is provided. As Trotter points out, it is easy to get a smoker to switch from Camel filters to Winstons, but very hard to get that person to stop smoking altogether (Trotter 1987:148).

Trotter's third client was the Food and Drug Administration (FDA). The FDA decided it needed basic ethnographic information on the use of greta. The staff wanted to know who used it, what it was used for, how it was used, and where it could be purchased. The FDA had never considered that lead oxide could be a food additive or a drug, and it needed verifiable data that the compound was being used in this way. As a result of Trotter's research, the FDA concluded that greta was a food additive. It issued a Class I recall to ban the sale of greta as a remedy.

Client number four was the Texas regional office of the Department of Health and Human Services. It needed assistance in creating and carrying out a survey along the United States–Mexico border to discover what people knew about greta and azarcon and how many people used them. Trotter's survey indicated that as many as 10 percent of the Mexican American households along the border had at one time used greta or azarcon. The survey also turned up several other potentially toxic compounds that were in use.

Trotter's fifth client was the Hidalgo County Health Care Corporation, a local migrant clinic. It needed a survey that would compare the level of greta and azarcon usage in the local population in general with the level of usage among the people who came to the clinic. Trotter found that there was no significant difference between the two groups in terms of knowledge about and use of the two preparations. The clinic population was more likely to treat folk illnesses with folk medicines than was the population at large.

The sixth client was the Migrant Health Service. It needed to know whether it was necessary to design a nationwide lead project. Based on the research that Trotter and others did, it became clear that such a major project was not necessary. Rather, health projects were targeted, and health professionals notified, in the areas of high greta and azarcon use only.

Because Trotter had several clients, his work led to a variety of outcomes. The health education project resulted in considerable media exposure on the dangers of greta and azarcon. Public Service Announcements were broadcast on Spanish-language radio stations, special television programs aired in Los Angeles county, and information packets were sent to migrant clinics. Trotter commissioned Mexican American students at Pan American University to design a culturally appropriate poster warning of the dangers of greta and azarcon. The poster uses the culturally powerful symbol of *La Muerte* (a skeleton) to warn of the dangers. It has been placed in over five thousand clinics and other public access sites (ibid.: 152).

The various health education measures may be judged successful by the fact that two years after the project began, both greta and azarcon were hard to find in the United States. In addition, the various surveys Trotter carried out led to better screening procedures for lead poisoning. Information on traditional medications are now routinely gathered when lead poisoning is suspected, and several other potentially toxic compounds have been discovered. Health professionals were able to learn about the current use of traditional medications in their areas, and about the specific health education needs of their clients.

"Perhaps the most important overall result of the project was an increased awareness of the utility of anthropology in solving culturally related health care problems in at least one segment of the medical care delivery system. . . . Our discovery of the use of greta and azarcon and the subsequent discoveries that similar remedies are causing lead poisoning in Hmong, Saudi Arabian, and Chinese communities have finally demonstrated a clear link between anthropological research and the dominant biophysical side of modern medicine. Anthropological knowledge, research methods, and theoretical orientations are finally being used to solve epidemiological problems overlooked by the established disciplines" (ibid.: 154).

Trotter brought to the project the skills of the anthropologist. His principal focus was on culture. He took a holistic, comparative approach. He was willing to innovate, to look for explanations in areas that investigators from other disciplines had not thought to look.

Anthropology and Policy

In all this work—and there is much more—the same anthropological perspective illustrated throughout this book has been employed. Applied anthropologists do their work using holism, comparison, relativism, and a concern for particular cases.

Yet anthropologists have been hesitant to make the detailed kinds of policy recommendations that other professional disciplines make. This may be because anthropologists are particularly aware of the problems in applied work, the problems in trying to make people, or systems, change. Anthropologists have been trained to analyze social and cultural systems, but when they are asked how to change them, they begin to ask questions. The questions they ask are based on an awareness of the enormous complexity of human life, when it is viewed from ground level. Anthropologists have developed a keen awareness that not everyone in the world makes the same basic assumptions about the world that planners and officials make. They are aware that sometimes the technical experts providing help in other cultures know less than the people they are advising, or are giving advice that is culturally inappropriate. They realize that no change benefits everyone equally, that some gain as others lose. Anthropologists are also well aware that even if they get involved in planning a program, implementation depends on external factors over which they have no control: cash flow problems to the AID office, fear over a congressman's response, political issues, elections, budget reductions, lack of interest, and so on.

Anthropologists believe they have much to contribute in helping build a better world. Yet they are also highly sensitive to the kinds of issues that are involved when dealing with the complex, human systems which we have been discussing throughout this text. Applied anthropologists are well aware of the ambiguities of the human experience.

Uncertainty and Awareness

The second part of our conclusion is the second part of our answer to students, and it is personal.

Studying cultural anthropology brings students into contact with different ways of life. It makes them aware of just how arbitrary their own understanding of the world is. In addition, if they are from Western countries who were responsible for colonialism and its consequences, it makes them painfully aware of just how much their own tradition has to answer for in the modern world.

Knowing and experiencing cultural variety gives rise, perhaps inevitably, to doubt. We come to doubt the ultimate validity of the central truths of our own cultural tradition, which have been ratified and sanctified by the generations who preceded us. We doubt because a familiarity with alternative ways of living makes the ultimate meaning of any action, of any object, a highly ambiguous matter. Ambiguity is part and parcel of the human condition. Human beings have coped with ambiguity from time immemorial by means of culture, which places objects and actions in contexts and thereby makes their meanings plain. This doubt can lead to anxiety, but it can also be liberating.

Freedom and Constraint

The third part of our response is, for want of a better word, humanistic.

All human beings, ourselves included, live in culturally shaped worlds, enmeshed in webs of interpretation and meaning that they themselves have spun. It has been the particular task of anthropology and its practitioners to go out into the world to bear witness to and record the vast creative diversity in world-making that has been the history of our species. In our lifetimes, we will witness the end of many of those ways of life—and if we are not careful, of all ways of life. This loss is tragic, for as these worlds disappear, so too does something special about humanity: variety, creativity, and awareness of alternatives.

Our survival as a species, and our viability as individuals, depends on the possibility of choice, of perceiving and being able to act on alternatives in the various situations we encounter during our lives. If, as a colleague has suggested, human life is a mine field, then the more paths we can see and imagine through that mine field, the more likely we are to make it through—or at least to have an interesting time trying. As alternatives are destroyed, wantonly smashed, or thoughtlessly crushed, our own human possibilities are reduced. A small group of men and women have for the last century labored in corners of the world, both remote and nearby, to write the record of human accomplishment and bring it back and teach it to others.

Surely our greatest human accomplishment is the creation of the sometimes austerely beautiful worlds in which we all live. Anthropologists have rarely given in to the romantic notion that these other worlds are all good, all life enhancing, all fine or beautiful. They are not. Ambiguity and ambivalence are, as we have seen, hallmarks of the human experience. There are no guarantees that human cultures will be compassionate rather than cruel, or that people will agree they are one or the other. There are not even any guarantees that our species will survive. But all anthropologists have believed that these are *human* worlds that have given those who have lived in them the ability to make sense out of their experiences and to derive meaning for their lives, that we are a species at once bound by our culture and free to change it.

This is a perilous and fearsome freedom, a difficult freedom to grasp and to wield. Nevertheless, the freedom is there, and in this dialectic of freedom and constraint lies our future. It is up to us to create it.

Adams, Richard Newbold
1977 "Power in Human Societies: A Synthesis." In *The Anthropology of Power: Ethnographic Studies from Asia, Oceania, and the New World,* ed. R. Fogelson and R. N. Adams, pp. 387–410. New York: Academic Press.
1979 *Energy and Structure: A Theory of Social Power.* Austin: University of Texas Press.
Akmajian, Adrian, Richard Demers, and Robert Harnish
1984 *Linguistics.* 2d ed. Cambridge: MIT Press.
Alland, Alexander
1977 *The Artistic Animal.* New York: Doubleday Anchor Books.
Althusser, Louis, and Etienne Balibar
1971 *Reading* Capital. London: New Left Books.
Alverson, Hoyt
1978 *Mind in the Heart of Darkness.* New Haven, Conn.: Yale University Press.
Arens, W.
1981 "Professional Football: An American Symbol and Ritual." In *The American Dimension,* ed. Susan P. Montague and W. Arens, pp. 1–9. Sherman Oaks, Calif.: Alfred.
Avery, Laurence, and James Peacock
1980 "Drama: Aristotle in Indonesia." In *Not Work Alone,* ed. J. Cherfas and R. Lewin, pp. 181–98. Beverly Hills, Calif.: Sage Publications.
Bailey, F. G.
1969 *Stratagems and Spoils: A Social Anthropology of Politics.* New York: Shocken Books.
Barnes, Barry, and David Bloor
1982 "Relativism, Rationalism and the Sociology of Knowledge." In *Rationality and Relativism,* ed. Martin Hollis and Steven Lukes, pp. 21–47. Cambridge: MIT Press.
Basham, Richard
1978 *Urban Anthropology.* Palo Alto, Calif.: Mayfield.
Bateson, Gregory
1972 *Steps to an Ecology of Mind.* New York: Ballantine Books.
Baxter, P.T.W.
1978 "Boran Age-Sets and Generation-Sets: *Gada,* a Puzzle or a Maze?" In *Age, Generation and Time,* ed. P.T.W. Baxter and Uri Almagor, pp. 151–82. New York: St. Martin's Press.
Baxter, P.T.W., and Uri Almagor
1978 Introduction to *Age, Generation and Time,* ed. P.T.W. Baxter and Uri Almagor, pp. 1–36. New York: St. Martin's Press.
Beals, Alan
1962 *Gopalpur, a South Indian Village.* New York: Holt, Rinehart and Winston.
Beidelman, T. O.
1982 *Colonial Evangelism.* Bloomington: Indiana University Press.

Bellman, Beryl
1984 *The Language of Secrecy.* New Brunswick, N.J.: Rutgers University Press.
Belmonte, Thomas
1978 *The Broken Fountain.* New York: Columbia University Press.
Berlin, Brent
1978 "Ethnobiological Classification." In *Cognition and Categorization,* ed. E. Rosch and B. Lloyd, pp. 9–26. Hillsdale, N.J.: Lawrence Erlbaum Associates.
Blanchard, Kendall
1974 "Basketball and the Culture Change Process: The Rimrock Navajo Case." *Council on Anthropology and Education Quarterly* 5(4):8–13.
1981 *The Mississippi Choctaw at Play: The Serious Side of Leisure.* Urbana: University of Illinois Press.
Blanchard, Kendall, and Alyce Cheska
1985 *The Anthropology of Sport.* South Hadley, Mass.: Bergin and Garvey.
Brain, Robert
1976 *Friends and Lovers.* New York: Basic Books.
Braroe, Niels
1975 *Indian and White.* Stanford, Calif.: Stanford University Press.
Briggs, Jean
1980 "Kapluna Daughter: Adopted by the Eskimo." In *Conformity and Conflict.* 4th ed., J. Spradley and O. McCurdy, pp. 44–62. Boston: Little, Brown. Originally published in 1970.
Burch, Ernest S., Jr.
1970 "Marriage and Divorce among the North Alaska Eskimos.: In *Divorce and After,* ed. Paul Bohannan, pp. 152–81. Garden City, N.Y.: Doubleday.
1975 *Eskimo Kinsmen: Changing Family Relationships in North West Alaska.* American Ethnological Society Monograph 59. St. Paul: West.
Chagnon, Napoleon
1983 *Yanomamo: The Fierce People.* 3d ed. New York: Holt, Rinehart and Winston.
Chambers, Erve
1985 *Applied Anthropology: A Practical Guide.* New York: Prentice-Hall.
Chance, John K.
1978 *Race and Class in Colonial Oaxaca.* Stanford, Calif.: Stanford University Press.
Chomsky, Noam
1957 *Syntactic Structures.* The Hague: Mouton.
1965 *Aspects of the Theory of Syntax.* Cambridge: MIT Press.

Clastres, Pierre
 1977 *Society against the State*. Trans. Robert Hurley. New York: Urizen Books.
Colby, Benjamin, and Pierre van den Berghe
 1969 *Ixil Country*. Berkeley: University of California Press.
Cole, Michael, and Sylvia Scribner
 1974 *Culture and Thought: A Psychological Introduction*. New York: Wiley.
Collier, Jane, and Sylvia Yanagisako, ed.
 1987 *Gender and Kinship: Essays toward a Unified Analysis*. Stanford, Calif.: Stanford University Press.
Colson, Elizabeth
 1977 "Power at Large: Meditation on 'The Symposium on Power.'" In *The Anthropology of Power: Ethnographic Studies from Asia, Oceania, and the New World*, ed. R. Fogelson and R. N. Adams, pp. 375–86. New York: Academic Press.
Crick, Malcolm
 1976 *Explorations in Language and Meaning: Towards a Semantic Anthropology*. New York: Wiley.
Csikszentmihalyi, Mihalyi
 1981 "Some Paradoxes in the Definition of Play." In *Play and Context*, ed. Alyce Cheska, pp. 14–25. West Point, N.Y.: Leisure Press.
Dallmayr, F., and Thomas A. McCarthy
 1977 "Introduction to 'The Positivist Reception.'" In *Understanding and Social Inquiry*, ed. F. Dallmayr and T. McCarthy, pp. 77–78. South Bend, Ind.: University of Notre Dame Press.
Davis Shelton
 1977 *Victims of the Miracle: Development and the Indians of Brazil*. Cambridge: Cambridge University Press.
Diener, Paul, and Eugene E. Robkin
 1978 "Ecology, Evolution, and the Search for Cultural Origins: The Question of Islamic Pig Prohibition." *Current Anthropology* 19(3):493–540.
Douglas, Mary
 1966 *Purity and Danger*. London: Routledge and Kegan Paul.
 1970 *Natural Symbols*. New York: Pantheon.
Douglas, Mary, and Baron Isherwood
 1979 *The World of Goods: Towards an Anthropology of Consumption*. New York: Norton.
Dumont, Jean Paul
 1978 *The Headman and I: Ambiguity and Ambivalence in the Fieldwork Experience*. Austin: University of Texas Press.
Edelsky, Carole
 1977 "Acquisition of Communicative Competence: Learning What It Means to Talk Like a Lady." In *Child Discourse*, ed. S. Ervin-Tripp and C. Mitchell-Kernan, pp. 225–44. New York: Academic Press.
Elliot, Alison
 1981 *Child Language*. Cambridge: Cambridge University Press.
Etienne, Mona
 1980 "Women and Men, Cloth and Colonization: The Transformation of Production-Distribution Relations among the Baule (Ivory Coast)." In *Women and Colonization: Anthropological Perspectives*, ed. Mona Etienne and Eleanor Leacock, pp. 270–93. New York: Praeger.
Evans-Pritchard, E. E.
 1940 *The Nuer*. Oxford: Oxford University Press.
 1951 *Kinship and Marriage among the Nuer*. Oxford: Oxford University Press.
 1963 *Social Anthropology and Other Essays*. New York: Free Press.
 1976 *Witchcraft, Oracles, and Magic among the Azande*. Abridged edition. Oxford: Oxford University Press. Originally published in 1937.
Fagen, Robert
 1981 *Animal Play Behavior*. New York: Oxford University Press.
Fernandez, James W.
 1971 "Principles of Opposition and Vitality in Fang Aesthetics." In *Art and Aesthetics in Primitive Societies*, ed. Carol Jopling, pp. 356–73. New York: Dutton. Originally published in 1966.
 1977 "The Performance of Ritual Metaphors." In *The Social Use of Metaphors*, ed. J. O. Sapir and J. C. Crocker. Philadelphia: University of Pennsylvania Press.
 1980 "Edification by Puzzlement." In *Explorations in African Systems of Thought*, ed. Ivan Karp and Charles Bird, pp. 44–69. Bloomington: Indiana University Press.
 1982 *Bwiti: An Ethnography of the Religious Imagination in Africa*. Princeton, N.J.: Princeton University Press.
Firth, Raymond
 1936 *We, the Tikopia*. London: George Allen and Unwin.
Fortes, Meyer
 1950 "Kinship and Marriage among the Ashanti." In *African Systems of Kinship and Marriage*, ed. A. R. Radcliffe-Brown and Daryll Forde. Oxford: Oxford University Press.
 1953 "The Structure of Unilineal Descent Groups." *American Anthropologist* 55:25–39.
Fortes, Meyer, and E. E. Evans-Pritchard, ed.
 1940 *African Political Systems*. Oxford: Oxford University Press.
Fox, Robin
 1967 *Kinship and Marriage*. Harmondsworth, England: Penguin.
Gardner, Howard
 1982 *Art, Mind, and Brain: A Cognitive Approach to Creativity*. New York: Basic Books.
Geertz, Clifford
 1966 "Religion as a Cultural System." In *Anthropological Approaches to the Study of Religion*, ed. M. Banton. London: Tavistock.
 1972 "Deep Play: Notes on the Balinese Cockfight." *Daedalus* 101:1–37.
 1973 *The Interpretation of Cultures*. New York: Basic Books.
Geertz, Hildred, and Clifford Geertz
 1975 *Kinship in Bali*. Chicago: University of Chicago Press.
Giddens, Anthony
 1979 *Central Problems in Social Theory*. Berkeley: University of California Press.

1978 "Positivism and Its Critics." In *A History of Sociological Analysis,* ed. T. Bottomore and R. Nisbet, pp. 237–86. New York: Basic Books.

Gillies, Eva
1976 Introduction to *Witchcraft, Oracles, and Magic among the Azande,* by Evans-Pritchard. Oxford: Oxford University Press.

Gilligan, Carol
1982 *In a Different Voice.* Cambridge: Harvard University Press.

Gilsenan, Michael
1982 *Recognizing Islam: Religion and Society in the Modern Arab World.* New York: Pantheon.

Gough, Katherine
1961 "Nayar: Central Kerala." In *Matrilineal Societies,* ed. David Schneider and Katherine Gough, pp. 298–384. Berkeley: University of California Press.

Gould, Stephen Jay
1983 *Hen's Teeth and Horse's Toes.* New York: Norton.

Greenwood, Davydd, and William Stini
1977 *Nature, Culture, and Human History.* New York: Harper and Row.

Gregory, Richard
1981 *Mind in Science: A History of Explanations in Psychology and Physics.* New York: Cambridge University Press.
1983 "Visual Perception and Illusions: Dialogue with Richard Gregory." In *States of Mind,* by Jonathan Miller, pp. 42–64. New York: Pantheon.

Gudeman, Stephen
1978 *The Demise of a Rural Economy.* London: Routledge and Kegan Paul.

Gumperz, John
1982 *Discourse Strategies.* Cambridge: Cambridge University Press.

Handelman, Don
1977 "Play and Ritual: Complementary Frames of Meta-Communication." In *It's a Funny Thing, Humour,* ed. A. J. Chapman and H. Foot, pp. 185–92. London: Pergamon.
1983 "Presenting, Representing, and Modelling the World: Toward the Study of Public Events and Media Events." Photocopied working paper.

Hanna, Judith Lynne
1979 *To Dance Is Human.* Austin: University of Texas Press.

Harris, Marvin
1965 "The Myth of the Sacred Cow." In *Man, Culture, and Animals,* ed. A. Leeds and A. P. Vayda, pp. 217–28. Washington, D.C.: American Association for the Advancement of Science.
1974 *Cows, Pigs, Wars and Witches.* New York: Vintage Books.

Heald, Suzette
1982 "The Making of Men: The Relevance of Vernacular Psychology to the Interpretation of a Gisu Ritual." *Africa* 52(1): 15–35.

Heider, Karl
1979 *Grand Valley Dani.* New York: Holt, Rinehart and Winston.

Herdt, Gilbert, ed.
1982 *Rituals of Manhood: Male Initiation in Papua New Guinea.* Berkeley: University of California Press.

Herskovits, Melville
1973 *Cultural Relativism.* Ed. Frances Herskovits. New York: Vintage Books.

Hockett, Charles, and Robert Ascher
1964 "The Human Revolution." *Current Anthropology* 5: 135–47.

Hoebel, E. Adamson
1960 *The Cheyennes.* New York: Holt, Rinehart and Winston.

Hoijer, Harry
1953 "The Relation of Language to Culture." In *Anthropology Today,* ed. A. L. Kroeber, pp. 554–73. Chicago: University of Chicago Press.

Holm, John
1988 *Pidgins and Creoles.* Vol. 1, *Theory and Structure.* Cambridge: Cambridge University Press.

Horton, Robin
1982 "Tradition and Modernity Revisited." In *Rationality and Relativism,* ed. M. Hollis and Steven Lukes, pp. 201–60. Cambridge: MIT Press.

Hudson, R. A.
1980 *Sociolinguistics.* Cambridge: Cambridge University Press.

Hunter, David, and Phillip Whitten, ed.
1976 *Encyclopedia of Anthropology.* New York: Harper and Row.

Hymes, Dell
1972 "On Communicative Competence." In *Sociolinguistics: Selected Readings,* ed. J. B. Pride and J. Holmes, pp. 269–93. Baltimore: Penguin Books.

Jackson, Michael
1982 *Allegories of the Wilderness.* Bloomington: Indiana University Press.

Johnson, Steven L.
1988 "Ideological Dimensions of Peasant Persistence in Western Kenya." In *New Perspectives on Social Class and Political Action in the Periphery,* ed. R. Curtain, N. W. Keith, and N. E. Keith. Westport, Conn.; Greenwood Press.

Kapferer, Bruce
1983 *A Celebration of Demons.* Bloomington: Indiana University Press.

Karp, Ivan
1978 *Fields of Change among the Iteso of Kenya.* London: Routledge and Kegan Paul.
1981 "Good Marx for the Anthropologist: Structure and Anti-Structure in 'Duck Soup.'" In *The American Dimension,* ed. W. Arens and Susan Montague, pp. 37–50. Sherman Oaks, Calif.: Alfred.
1987 "Laughter at Marriage: Subversion in Performance." In *The Transformation of African Marriage,* ed. David Parkin. London: International African Institute.

Karp, Ivan, and Martha B. Kendall
1982 "Reflexivity in Field Work." In *Explanation in Social Science,* ed. P. Secord. Los Angeles: Sage.

Karp, Ivan, and Kent Maynard
    1983 "Reading *The Nuer*." *Current Anthropology* 24(4).
Keesing, Roger
    1982 *Kwaio Religion*. New York: Colulmbia University Press.
    1873 *'Elota's Story*. New York: Holt, Rinehart and Winston.
Keillor, Garrison
    1985 *Lake Wobegon Days*. New York: Viking Press.
Kiel, Charles
    1979 *Tiv Song*. Chicago: University of Chicago Press.
Kopytoff, Igor
    1986 "The Cultural Biography of Things: Commoditization as
        Process." In *The Social Life of Things*, ed. Arjun Appadurai,
        pp. 64–91. Cambridge: Cambridge University Press.
Kopytoff, Igor, and Suzanne Miers
    1977 "Introduction: African 'Slavery' as an Institution of Mar-
        ginality." In *Slavery in Africa,* ed. Suzanne Miers and Igor
        Kopytoff, pp. 3–84. Madison: University of Wisconsin
        Press.
Krige, E. J., and J. D. Krige
    1943 *Realm of a Rain Queen*. London: Oxford University Press.
Kuhn, Thomas
    1979 "Metaphor in Science." In *Metaphor and Thought,* ed.
        Andrew Ortony, pp. 409–19. Cambridge: Cambridge Uni-
        versity Press.
Kuper, Adam
    1982 *Wives for Cattle: Bridewealth and Marriage in Southern
        Africa*. London: Routledge and Kegan Paul.
Labov, William
    1972 *Language in the Inner City: Studies in the Black English
        Vernacular*. Philadelphia: University of Pennsylvania Press.
Lakoff, George, and Mark Johnson
    1980 *Metaphors We Live By*. Berkeley: University of California
        Press.
Lave, Jean
    1988 *Cognition in Practice*. Cambridge: Cambridge University
        Press.
Lavenda, Robert H.
    1983 "Family and Corporation: Two Styles of Celebration in Cen-
        tral Minnesota." In *The Celebration of Society: Perspectives
        on Contemporary Cultural Performance,* ed. Frank Manning.
        Bowling Green, Ohio: Bowling Green University Popular
        Press.
    1984 "Festivals annd Uncertainty." Revision of paper presented
        at Annual Meetings of the American Anthropological Asso-
        ciation, Chicago.
Lavenda, Robert H., et al.
    1984 "Festivals and the Organization of Meaning: An Introduc-
        tion to Community Festivals in Minnesota." In *The Masks of
        Play,* ed. D. Kelley-Byrne and B. Sutton-Smith. West Point,
        N.Y.: Leisure Press.
Lee, Richard
    1984 *The Dobe !Kung*. New York: Holt, Rinehart and Winston.
Lever, Janet
    1983 *Soccer Madness*. Chicago: University of Chicago Press.

Levine, Nancy
    1980 "Nyinba Polyandry and the Allocation of Paternity." *Jour-
        nal of Comparative Family Studies* 11(3):283–88.
    1988 *The Dynamics of Polyandry: Kinship, Domesticity, and
        Population on the Tibetan Border*. Chicago: University of
        Chicago Press.
Levine, Nancy, and Walter Sangree
    1980 "Women with Many Husbands." *Journal of Comparative
        Family Studies* 11(3) (Special Issue).
Lévi-Strauss, Claude
    1962 *L'anthropologie structurale*. Paris: Plon. Translated under
        the title *Structural Anthropology*. New York: Doubleday An-
        chor Books, 1967.
    1955 *Tristes Tropiques*. Paris: Plon. Translated by John and Dor-
        een Weightman under the title *Tristes Tropiques*. New York:
        Atheneum 1974.
Lewellen, Ted
    1983 *Political Anthropology*. South Hadley, Mass.: Bergin and
        Garvey.
Lewis, I. M.
    1976 *Social Anthropology in Perspective*. Harmondsworth, En-
        gland: Penguin.
Lewontin, Richard
    1982 *Human Diversity*. New York: Scientific American Library.
Lewontin, Richard, Steven Rose, and Leon J. Kamin
    1984 *Not in Our Genes*. New York: Pantheon.
Lienhardt, Godfrey
    1961 *Divinity and Experience: The Religion of the Dinka*. Ox-
        ford: Oxford University Press.
Little, Kenneth
    1967 *The Mende of Sierra Leone*. London: Routledge and Kegan
        Paul.
Lyons, John
    1969 *Theoretical Linguistics*. Cambridge: Cambridge University
        Press.
    1981 *Language and Linguistics*. Cambridge: Cambridge Univer-
        sity Press.
MacCormack, Carol P.
    1980 "Nature, Culture, and Gender: A Critique." In *Nature,
        Culture and Gender,* ed. Carol MacCormack and Marilyn
        Strathern, pp. 1–24. Cambridge: Cambridge University
        Press.
Malinowski, Bronislaw
    1929 *The Sexual Life of Savages*. New York: Harcourt, Brace
        and World.
    1944 *A Scientific Theory of Culture and Other Essays*. New
        York: Oxford University Press.
    1948 *Magic, Science, and Religion, and Other Essays*. New
        York: Doubleday Anchor Books.
Mandler, George
    1975 *Mind and Emotion*. New York: Wiley.
    1983 "The Nature of Emotion: Dialogue with George Mandler."
        In *States of Mind,* by Jonathan Miller, pp. 136–52. New
        York: Pantheon.
Marx, Karl
    1932 *The German Ideology*. Selections reprinted in *Karl Marx:*

Selected Writings, ed. David McLellan. Oxford: Oxford University Press, 1977.

Morgan, Lewis Henry
1877 *Ancient Society.* Reprint. Cleveland: Meridian Books, World Publishing Company, 1963.

Murphy, Robert
1986 *Social and Cultural Anthropology: An Overture.* 2d ed. New York: Prentice-Hall.

Murphy, Robert, and Yolanda Murphy
1974 *Women of the Forest.* New York: Columbia University Press.

Myerhoff, Barbara
1974 *Peyote Hunt.* Ithaca, N.Y.: Cornell University Press.

Myerhoff, Barbara, and Jay Ruby
1982 Introduction to *A Crack in the Mirror: Reflexive Perspectives in Anthropology,* ed. Jay Ruby. Philadelphia: University of Pennsylvania Press.

Narayan, R. K.
1974 *My Days.* New York: Viking Press.

Nash, June
1979 *We Eat the Mines and the Mines Eat Us.* New York: Columbia University Press.

Norbeck, Edward
1974 *Religion in Human Life.* New York: Holt, Rinehart and Winston.

Ochs, Elinor
1986 Introduction to *Language Socialization across Cultures,* ed. Bambi Schieffelin and Elinor Ochs, pp. 1–13. Cambridge: Cambridge University Press.

Ortner, Sherry
1973 "On Key Symbols." *American Anthropologist* 75(5): 1338–46.

Ortony, Andrew
1979 "Metaphor: A Multidimensional Problem." In *Metaphor and Thought,* ed. Andrew Ortony, pp. 1–18. Cambridge: Cambridge University Press.

Parkin, David
1984 "Mind, Body, and Emotion among the Giriama." Paper presented in *Humanity as Creator* lecture series, St. Cloud State University.

Partridge, William L., ed.
1984 *Training Manual in Development Anthropology.* Special Publication of the American Anthropological Association and the Society for Applied Anthropology, no. 17. Washington, D.C.: American Anthropological Association.

Peacock, James
1968 *Rites of Modernization.* Chicago: University of Chicago Press.

Platt, Martha
1986 "Social Norms and Lexical Acquisition: A Study of Deictic Verbs in Samoan Child Language." In *Language Socialization across Cultures,* ed. Bambi Schieffelin and Elinor Ochs, pp. 127–52. Cambridge: Cambridge University Press.

Rabinow, Paul
1977 *Reflections on Fieldwork in Morocco.* Berkeley: University of California Press.

Reeves, Edward, Billie DeWalt, and Kathleen DeWalt
1987 "The International Sorghum/Millet Research Project." In *Anthropological Praxis,* ed. Robert Wolfe and Shirley Fiske, pp. 72–83. Boulder, Colo.: Westview Press.

Ribeiro, Darcy
1984 *Maíra.* Trans. E. H. Goodland and Thomas Colchie. New York: Vintage Books, Adventura. Translation of *Maíra,* Rio de Janeiro: Editora Civilizaçao Brasileira, 1978.

Ronan, Colin A., and Joseph Needham
1978 *The Shorter Science and Civilisation in China.* An abridgement of Joseph Needham's original text, vol. 1. Cambridge: Cambridge University Press.

Rosaldo, Renato
1980 *Ilongot Headhunting, 1883–1974: A Study in Society and History.* Stanford, Calif.: Stanford University Press.

Rosen, Lawrence
1984 *Bargaining for Reality: The Constructions of Social Relations in a Muslim Community.* Chicago: University of Chicago Press.

Rostow, W. W.
1971 *Stages of Economic Growth.* 2d ed. New York: Cambridge University Press.

Sacks, Karen
1979 *Sisters and Wives.* Urbana: University of Illinois Press.

Sahlins, Marshall
1972 *Stone Age Economics.* Chicago: Aldine.
1976a *Culture and Practical Reason.* Chicago: University of Chicago Press.
1976b *The Use and Abuse of Biology.* Ann Arbor: University of Michigan Press.

Sapir, Edward
1966 *Culture, Language, and Personality.* ed. David Mandelbaum. Berkeley: University of California Press.

Sapir, J. David
1977 "The Anatomy of Metaphor." In *The Social Use of Metaphors,* ed. J. D. Sapir and J. C. Crocker. Philadelphia: University of Pennsylvania Press.

Schultz, Emily
1984 "From Pagan to *Pullo:* Ethnic Identity Change in Northern Cameroon." *Africa* 54(1): 46–64.
1990 *Dialogue at the Margins: Whorf, Bakhtin, and Linguistic Relativity.* In press, Madison: University of Wisconsin Press.

Schwartzman, Helen
1978 *Transformations The Anthropology of Children's Play.* New York: Plenum.

Scott, James
1985 *Weapons of the Weak.* New Haven: Yale University Press.

Service, Elman
1962 *Primitive Social Organization.* New York: Random House.

Shepherd, Gill
1987 "Rank, Gender, and Homosexuality: Mombasa as a Key to Understanding Sexual Options." In *The Cultural Construction of Sexuality,* ed. Pat Caplan, pp. 240–70. London: Tavistock.

Shostak, Marjorie
  1983 *Nisa: The Life and Words of a !Kung Woman.* New York: Vintage Books.
Silverstein, Michael
  1976 "Shifters, Linguistic Categories, and Cultural Description." In *Meaning in Anthropology,* ed. Keith Basso and Henry Selby, pp. 11–55. Albuquerque: University of New Mexico Press.
  1985 "The Functional Stratification of Language and Ontogenesis." In *Culture, Communication, and Cognition: Vygotskian Perspectives,* ed. James Wertsch, pp. 205–35. Cambridge: Cambridge University Press.
Smith, M. G.
  1981 Introduction to *Baba of Karo,* by Mary F. Smith. Reprint. New Haven: Yale University Press. Originally published in 1954.
Smith, Mary F.
  1981 *Baba of Karo.* Reprint. New Haven: Yale University Press. Originally published in 1954.
Smith, Wilfred Cantwell
  1982 *Towards a World Theology.* Philadelphia: Westminster.
Spiro, Melford
  1977 *Kinship and Marriage in Burma: A Cultural and Psychodynamic Account.* Berkeley: University of California Press.
Spooner, Brian
  1986 "Weavers and Dealers: The Authenticity of an Oriental Carpet." In *The Social Life of Things,* ed. Arjun Appadurai, pp. 195–235. Cambridge: Cambridge University Press.
Strathern, Marilyn
  1972 *Women in Between.* London: Seminar Press.
  1987 "Producing Difference: Connections and Disconnections in Two New Guinea Highland Kinship Systems." In *Gender and Kinship: Essays toward a Unified Analysis,* eds. Jane Collier and Sylvia Yanagisako, pp. 271–300. Stanford, Calif.: Stanford University Press.
Sutton-Smith, Brian
  1980 "The Playground as a Zoo." *Newsletter of the Association for the Anthropological Study of Play* 7(1):4–8.
  1984 "Recreation as Folly's Parody." *Newsletter of the Association for the Anthropological Study of Play* 10(4):4–13, 22.
"Talk of the Town." *The New Yorker* (March 3) 1986.
Taussig, Michael
  1980 *The Devil and Commodity Fetishism in Latin America.* Chapel Hill: University of North Carolina Press.
Tedlock, Dennis
  1982 "Anthropological Hermeneutics and the Problem of Alphabetic Literacy." In *A Crack in the Mirror: Reflexive Perspectives in Anthropology,* ed. Jay Ruby, pp. 149–61. Philadelphia: University of Pennsylvania Press.
Trotter, Robert
  1987 "A Case of Lead Poisoning from Folk Remedies in Mexican American Communities." In *Anthropological Praxis,* ed. Robert Wolfe and Shirley Fiske, pp. 146–59. Boulder, Colo.: Westview Press.

Turnbull, Colin
  1961 *The Forest People.* New York: Simon and Shuster.
Turner, Terence
  1989 "Amazonian Indians Fight to Save Their Forest." *Anthropology Newsletter* 30(3):21–22.
Turner, Victor
  1969 *The Ritual Process.* Chicago: Aldine.
Valentine, Bettylou
  1978 *Hustling and Other Hard Work.* New York: Free Press.
Valentine, Charles
  1978 Introduction to *Hustling and Other Hard Work,* by Bettylou Valentine, pp. 1–10. New York: Free Press.
Van Baal, J.
  1966 *Dema: Description and Analysis of Culture.* The Hague: Martinus Nijhoff.
Vaughan, James
  1970 "Caste Systems in the Western Sudan." In *Social Stratification in Africa,* ed. Arthur Tuden and Leonard Plotnicov, pp. 59–92. New York: Free Press.
  1973 "Ngkyagu as Artists in Marghi Society." In *The Traditional Artist in African Societies,* ed. Warren L. d'Azevedo, pp. 162–93. Bloomington: Indiana University Press.
Voloshinov, V. N.
  1986 *Marxism and the Philosophy of Language.* Trans. Ladislav Matejka and I. R. Titunik. Cambridge: Harvard University Press. Originally published in 1929.
  1987 "Discourse in Life and Discourse in Art." In *Freudianism,* Trans. I. R. Titunik and E. Bruss, pp. 93–116. Bloomington: Indiana University Press. Originally published in 1926.
Vygotsky, L. S.
  1962 *Thought and Language.* Cambridge: MIT Press
  1978 *Mind in Society: The Development of Higher Psychological Processes.* Cambridge: Harvard University Press.
Wallace, A.F.C.
  1966 *Religion: An Anthropological View.* New York: Random House.
  1972 *The Death and Rebirth of the Seneca.* New York: Vintage Books.
Wallerstein, Immanuel
  1974 *The Modern World System.* New York: Academic Press.
Weiner, Annette
  1976 *Women of Value, Men of Renown.* Austin: University of Texas Press.
  1979 "Trobriand Kinship from Another View: The Reproductive Power of Women and Men." *Man* n.s. 14(2):328–48.
  1980 "Stability in Banana Leaves: Colonization and Women in Kiriwina, Trobriand Islands." In *Women and Colonization: Anthropological Perspectives,* ed. Mona Etienne and Eleanor Leacock, pp. 270–93. New York: Praeger.
  1988 *The Trobrianders of Papua New Guinea.* New York: Holt, Rinehart and Winston.
Wertsch, James V.
  1985 *Vygotsky and the Social Formation of Mind.* Cambridge: Harvard University Press.

Whorf, Benjamin
    1956 *Language, Thought, and Reality.* Ed. John B. Carroll. Cambridge: MIT Press.
Wilson, Monica
    1951 *Good Company.* Oxford: Oxford University Press.
Witherspoon, Gary
    1975 *Navajo Kinship and Marriage.* Chicago: University of Chicago Press.
Wolf, Eric
    1969 *Peasant Wars of the Twentieth Century.* New York: Harper and Row.
    1982 *Europe and the People without History.* Berkeley: University of California Press.

Yanagisako, Sylvia, and Jane Collier
    1987 "Toward a Unified Analysis of Gender and Kinship." In *Gender and Kinship: Essays toward a Unified Analysis,* ed. Jane Collier and Sylvia Yanagisako, pp. 14–50. Stanford, Calif.: Stanford University Press.
Zerubavel, Yael
    1983 "The Concept of Heroism in Modern Israel: Masada and Bar Kochba." Lecture in the Series "Humanity as Creator: The Creation of Meaning." St. Cloud State University, December 8, 1983.

498